THE OFFICIAL®
PRICE GUIDE TO
HOCKEY
CARDS

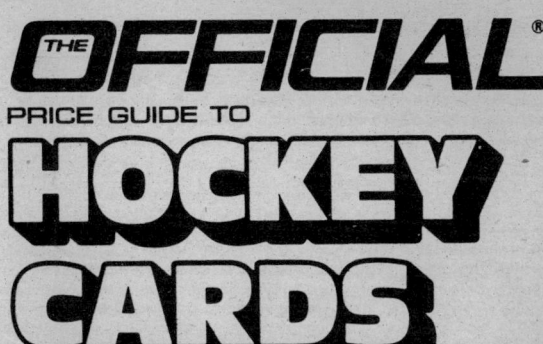

W9-AFY-057

BY
DR. JAMES BECKETT

FIRST EDITION

HOUSE OF COLLECTIBLES • NEW YORK

Important Notice. All of the information, including valuations, in this book has been compiled from the most reliable sources, and every effort has been made to eliminate errors and questionable data. Nevertheless, the possibility of error, in a work of such immense scope, always exists. The publisher will not be held responsible for losses which may occur in the purchase, sale, or other transaction of items because of information contained herein. Readers who feel they have discovered errors are invited to *write* and inform us, so they may be corrected in subsequent editions. Those seeking further information on the topics covered in this book are advised to refer to the complete line of *Official Price Guides* published by the House of Collectibles.

© 1991 by James Beckett III

This is a registered trademark of Random House, Inc.

All rights reserved under International and Pan-American Copyright Conventions.

Published by:
House of Collectibles
201 East 50th Street
New York, New York 10022

Distributed by Ballantine Books, a division of Random House, Inc., New York, and simultaneously in Canada by Random House of Canada Limited, Toronto.

Manufactured in the United States of America

ISBN: 0-876-37866-1

First Edition: October 1991

10 9 8 7 6 5 4 3 2 1

TABLE OF CONTENTS

Introduction 1
How to Collect 4
   Obtaining Cards 6
   Preserving Your Cards 6
   Collecting/Investing 12
Nomenclature 14
Glossary/Legend 18
History of Hockey Cards 34
Business of Sports Card Collecting 38
   Determining Value 38
   Regional Variation 40
   Set Prices 42
   Scarce Series 44
   Grading Your Cards 44
   Condition Guide 54
   Selling Your Cards 58
Interesting Notes 62
Advertising 64
Recommended Reading 66
Prices in This Guide 74
   Bowman (1990–1991) 77
   O-Pee-Chee (1968–1991) 83
   Parkhurst (1951–1964) 294
   Pro Set (1990–1991) 324
   Score (1990–1991) 346
   Topps (1954–1991) 359
   Upper Deck (1990–1991) 511

PREFACE

Isn't it great? Finally, we have a book just for hockey card collectors. We're always hearing about the tremendous growth in interest in baseball cards, but hockey cards are popular as well. In fact, interest in hockey cards is currently at an all-time high. Hockey cards are becoming increasingly visible at card shows and card stores from San Diego to Saskatchewan.

The reason for the emergence of these cards, in particular, is due in large part to the continuing and increasing popularity of the sports themselves. This increased popularity has made the stars and superstars of hockey and basketball well known to millions of fans who have watched them during the winter and spring and read about them year round. Wayne Gretzky is at least as popular as Don Mattingly and has been more dominant within his sport. Finally, the comparatively high cost of premium baseball cards has turned many card collectors to other sports card collecting as a more affordable means of pursuing the sports collectibles hobby. Nevertheless, as you can see from this price guide, hockey cards are valuable—and they are perceived by their collectors as being a good value for their hobby dollar.

Many of the features contained in the other *Beckett Price Guides* have been incorporated into this volume since condition grading, nomenclature, and many other aspects of collecting are common to the card hobby in general. We hope you find the book both interesting and useful in your collecting pursuits.

Hockey cards are also typically produced in smaller sets, making it easier for collectors to complete them. Most sets concentrate on each team's "name"players; therefore there are fewer commons. Obviously, purchasers will get more superstars per pack, making these cards even more attractive to collectors.

The *Beckett Guide* has been successful where other attempts have failed because it is complete, current, and valid. This price guide contains not just one, but three prices by condition for all the sports cards listed. These account for almost all the cards in existence. The prices were added to the card lists just prior to printing and reflect not the author's opinions or desires but the going retail prices for each card, based on the marketplace (sports memorabilia conventions and shows, hobby papers, current mail order catalogs, local club meetings, auction results, and other firsthand reportings of actually realized prices).

PRÉFACE

Est-ce que ce n'est pas magnifique? Nous avons enfin un livre tout spécialement pour les collectionneurs de cartes de hockey. Nous entendons constamment parler de l'accroissement prodigieux d'intérêt pour les cartes de base-ball, mais les cartes de hockey sont tout aussi populaires. En fait, l'intérêt pour les cartes de hockey est actuellement à un niveau constamment élevé. Les cartes de hockey se font voir de plus en plus aux expositions de cartes et dans les magasins spécialisés depuis San Diego jusqu'à Saskatchewan.

La raison particulière de l'apparition de ces cartes est due en grande partie à la popularité continuelle et croissante des sports eux-mêmes. Cet accroissement de popularité a fait bien connaître les vedettes et super-vedettes du hockey et du basket-ball à des millions d'admirateurs qui les ont regardés pendant l'hiver et le printemps et ont lu à leur propos toute l'année. Wayne Gretzky est au moins aussi populaire que Don Mattingly et a dominé davantage dans sa spécialité. Finalement, le coût élevé, comparativement, des cartes-primes de base-ball a fait que de nombreux collectionneurs se sont tournés vers des cartes d'autres activités sportives comme un moyen plus abordable de continuer leur passe-temps de collectionneurs d'objets en rapport avec les sports. Quoiqu'il en soit, comme vous pouvez le constater avec ce guide des prix, les cartes de hockey ont de la valeur—et elles sont considérées par leurs collectionneurs comme une bonne valeur par rapport à l'argent consacré à ce passe-temps.

Beaucoup des différents aspects contenus dans les autres guides Beckett ont été incorporés dans ce volume puisque le classement en fonction de l'état, la nomenclature, et de nombreuses autres caractéristiques d'une collection sont communes au fait de collectionner les cartes en général. Nous espérons que vous trouverez ce livre à la fois intéressant et utile dans la poursuite de vos collections.

Les cartes de hockey sont aussi produites en plus petites séries d'une manière typique, ce qui les rend plus faciles à compléter pour leurs collectionneurs. La plupart des séries se concentrent sur chaque nom d'équipe de joueurs; en conséquence il y en a peu de communes. Visiblement, les acheteurs auront davantage de super-vedettes par paquet, faisant ces cartes encore plus attrayantes pour les collectionneurs.

Le guide Beckett a réussi là où d'autres essais ont échoué parce qu'il

What is the BEST price guide available (on the market) today? Of course card sellers will prefer the price guide with the highest prices as the best—while card buyers will naturally prefer the one with the lowest prices. Accuracy, however, is the true test. Use the price guide used by more collectors and dealers than all the others combined. Look for the Beckett name. I won't put my name on anything I won't stake my reputation on. Not the lowest and not the highest—but the most accurate, with integrity.

To facilitate your use of this book, read the complete introductory section in the pages following before going to the pricing pages. Every collectible field has its own terminology; we've tried to capture most of these terms and definitions in our glossary. Please read carefully the section on grading and the condition of your cards as you will not be able to determine which price column is appropriate for a given card without first knowing its condition.

Welcome to the world of collecting cards.

Sincerely, Dr. James Beckett

est complet, d'actualité, et valable. Ce guide des prix ne contient pas seulement un, mais trois prix en fonction de leur condition, pour toutes les cartes inventoriées. Ces règles s'appliquent à pratiquement toutes les cartes existantes. Les prix ont été ajoutés aux listes de cartes immédiatement avant de passer à l'imprimerie, et reflètent, non pas les opinions de l'auteur, mais les prix de vente courants au détail pour chaque carte, en fonction des divers marchés (conventions et spectacles sportifs, journaux spécialisés, catalogues de vente par correspondance, réunions de clubs locaux, résultats de ventes aux enchères, et autres renseignements de première main de prix réellement pratiqués).

Quel est le MEILLEUR guide des prix disponible (sur le marché) actuellement ? Evidemment les marchands de cartes détermineront le guide avec les prix les plus élevés comme étant le meilleur—tandis que les acheteurs préféreront celui avec les prix les plus bas. L'exactitude cependant, est le véritable critère. Utilisez le guide des prix choisi par la plupart des collectionneurs et des revendeurs plutôt que tous les autres guides réunis. Cherchez le nom Beckett. Je ne voudrais mettre mon nom sur quoi que ce soit qui puisse entacher ma réputation. Non pas le plus bas ou le plus élevé—mais le plus équitable, avec intégrité.

Pour vous faciliter l'usage du livre, lisez complètement l'introduction qui suit avant d'aller aux pages contenant les prix. Chaque secteur d'objets de collections possède sa propre terminologie; nous avons essayé d'accaparer la plupart de ces termes et définitions dans notre glossaire. Lisez s'il vous plaît avec attention la partie relative au classement et à l'état de vos cartes faute de quoi il ne vous sera pas possible de déterminer quelle colonne de prix est appropriée pour une carte donnée sans d'abord connaître son état.

Bienvenue dans le monde de collection des cartes.

Sincèrement, Dr. James Beckett

ACKNOWLEDGMENTS

This edition is dedicated to the memory of Dennis W. Eckes, Mr. Sport Americana, who passed away tragically and unexpectedly earlier this year. Denny and I started all this back in 1978 as we began working on our first price guide book. He will be missed by all who knew him. For those who didn't know him, you should know that he left a wonderful legacy of a thriving hobby that he was instrumental in helping build. Denny's vision is still being realized. We hope to carry on with the same high ideals Denny always exemplified.

This edition of the price guide contains several new sets and, of course, completely revised prices on all the cards listed. A great deal of hard work went into this volume, and it could not have been done without a considerable amount of help from many people. Our thanks are extended to each and every one of you.

The success of the *Beckett Price Guides* has always been the result of a team effort. This hockey card price guide is our best yet, thanks to our numerous contributors and full-time staff members. As the hobby continues to grow, we have grown right along by adding a Technical Services group. Those who didn't handle the technical details or assist in pricing for this edition of the annual hockey guide contributed by picking up the slack for those who did.

The Technical Services group includes Manager Jay Johnson, Senior Analyst B.A. Murry, and Price Guide Analysts Theo Chen (all sports), Mike Hersh (hockey), Dan Hitt (football), Mary Huston (minor leagues), Rich Klein (all sports), and Grant Sandground (baseball/basketball). Technical Services staffers Wendy Bird, Jana Threatt and Scott Layton capably assisted their efforts. The price gathering and analytical talents of this fine group of hobbyists has helped make our Beckett team stronger, while making this guide and its companion *Beckett Hockey Monthly* even more widely recognized as the hobby's most reliable and relied upon sources of pricing information.

It is very difficult to be "accurate"—one can only do one's best. Our particular job is especially difficult, since we're shooting at moving targets as prices fluctuate all the time. Combining the efforts of many full-time pricing experts has definitely proven

AVANT-PROPOS

Cette édition est dédiée à la mémoire de Dennis W. Eckes, Monsieur Sport-Amérique, décédé tragiquement et inopinément en ce début d'année. Denny et moi-même avions commencé tout cela ensemble en 1978 avec notre premier guide des prix. Il va manquer à tous ceux qui l'ont connu. Quant à ceux qui ne l'ont pas connu, sachez qu'il a laissé un magnifique héritage concernant un passe- temps florissant qu'il a contribué à édifier. Les vues de Denny continuent d'être réalisées. Nous espérons continuer avec le même idéal élevé que Denny a constamment démontré.

Cette édition du guide des prix comprend plusieurs nouvelles séries et, évidemment, des prix totalement revus concernant toutes les cartes inventoriées. Ce volume contient un gros effort de travail difficile, et il n'aurait pas pu être réalisé sans la participation considérable de la part de nombreuses personnes. Nos remerciements s'adressent à tous et à chacun de vous.

Le succès des guides de prix Beckett a toujours été le résultat d'un effort d'équipe. Ce guide des prix pour les cartes de hockey est de tous le meilleur, grâce à nos nombreux collaborateurs et aux membres de notre équipe plein-temps. De la même façon que ce passe-temps continue a grandir, nous avons grandi parallèlement en créant un groupe de services techniques. Ceux qui n'avaient pas à s'occuper des détails techniques ou à apporter leur contribution dans l'établissement des prix pour cette édition du guide annuel concernant le hockey, ont aidé en compensant des lacunes de la part de ceux dont c'était le travail.

Le groupe des services techniques comprend le directeur Jay Johnson, l'analyste principal B.A. Murry, et les analystes pour le guide des prix Théo Chen (pour tous les sports), Mike Hersh (pour le hockey), Dan Hitt (le foot-ball), Mary Huston (les ligues d'ordre secondaire), Rich Klein (tous les sports), et Grant Sandground (base-ball/basket-ball). Les membres des services techniques Wendy Bird, Jana Threatt et Scott Layton les ont assisté avec compétence. La perception des valeurs et les talents analytiques de cette équipe accomplie de spécialistes en la matière, ont contribué à l'établissement d'une équipe Beckett plus énergique, tout en faisant de ce guide et de son compagnon, le guide mensuel Beckett sur le hockey, des sources d'informations de prix encore davantage reconnues comme les plus dignes de confiance et auxquelles on peut se fier.

Il est très difficile d'être "précis"... On ne peut faire que de son

better than relying upon the labors of just one person, and I thank all of them for working together to provide you, our readers, the most accurate prices possible.

Those who have worked closely with us on this and many other books, have again proven themselves invaluable in every aspect of producing this book: Ab D Cards (Dale Wesolewski), Mike Aronstein, *Baseball Hobby News* (Frank and Vivian Barning), Chris Benjamin, Sy Berger (Topps Chewing Gum), Bill Bossert (Mid-Atlantic Coin Exchange), Cartomania (Joseph E. Filion), Cartophilium (Andrew Pywowarczuk), Collection de Sport AZ (Roald Villanueve), Mike Cramer (Pacific Trading Cards), Bill and Diane Dodge, Gervise Ford, Steve Freedman, Larry and Jeff Fritsch, John Furniss, Gary Gagen (Let's Collect), Tony Galovich, Jim Galusha, Dick Gilkeson, Mike and Howard Gordon, George Grauer, John Greenwald, Wayne Grove, Bill Haber, Bill Henderson, Jerry Hersh, Gary Hlady, Richard Hohman, Alan Kaye (*Sports Card News*), Alex Klenman, Lesnik Public Relations (Timm Boyle and Bob Ibach), Lew Lipset, Jim Macie, Paul Marchant, Dick Millerd, Michael Moretto, Brian Morris, Jean-Guy Pichette, Jack Pollard, Tom Reid, Gavin Riley, Alan Rosen (Mr. Mint), John Rumierz, San Diego Sport Collectibles (Bill Goepner and Nacho Arredondo), Kevin Savage (Sports Gallery), Angelo Savelli, Mike Schechter (MSA), Richard Sherman, John Spalding, Phil and Joan Spector, Nigel Spill (Oldies and Goodies), Sports Collectors Store (Pat Quinn and Don Steinbach), Frank Steele, Murvin Sterling, Paul S. Taylor, Lee Temanson, Shirl Volk, Bill Wesslund, Kit Young, Robert Zanze, and Bill Zimpleman.

Many other individuals have provided price input, illustrative material, checklist verifications, errata, and/or background information. At the risk of inadvertently overlooking or omitting these many contributors, we should like to personally thank Jerry Adamic, Mike Abar, Rick Ambrozic, Dennis Anderson, Russell Armine, Neil Armstrong (World Series Cards), Lindell Austin, B & M's Card Shop, Jay Baldwin (Riding The Pine Sportscards), Baseball Card Baron, Charles Beckert, Bryan Behling, Charles Belzil, Jacob Benor, Beulah Sports (Jeff Blatt), Brian L. Bigelow, Tom Blade, Michel Bolduc, Dan Bruner, Eric Burgoyne, Calling All Cards, Giuseppe Capobianco, Danny Cariseo, Chris Carlson, Greg Caskey, Charles Champion, Dwight Chapin, Steve Chiaramonte, Adrian Ciani, Andrew Clair, James E. Clark, Shane Cohen (Grand

mieux. Notre minutieux travail est particulièrement difficile du fait que nous sommes en prise avec des objectifs mouvants en fonction de la variation constante des valeurs. La combinaison des efforts de nombreux experts à plein-temps en matière d'évaluations, s'est définitivement avérée meilleure que de se fier aux conclusions d'une seule personne, et je les ai tous remerciés d'avoir bien voulu travailler ensemble pour vous fournir, à vous nos lecteurs, les prix les plus précis possibles.

Ceux qui ont étroitement travaillé avec nous sur ce livre et sur de nombreux autres, se sont une nouvelle fois avérés inestimables dans tous les domaines de sa production: Ab D Cards (Dale Wesolewski), Mike Aronstein, *Baseball Hobby News* (Frank and Vivian Barning), Chris Benjamin, Sy Berger (Topps Chewing Gum), Bill Bossert (Mid-Atlantic Coin Exchange), Cartomania (Joseph E. Filion), Cartophilium (Andrew Pywowarczuk), Collection de Sport AZ (Roald Villanueve), Mike Cramer (Pacific Trading Cards), Bill and Diane Dodge, Gervise Ford, Steve Freedman, Larry and Jeff Fritsch, John Furniss, Gary Gagen (Let's Collect), Tony Galovich, Jim Galusha, Dick Gilkeson, Mike and Howard Gordon, George Grauer, John Greenwald, Wayne Grove, Bill Haber, Bill Henderson, Jerry Hersh, Gary Hlady, Richard Hohman, Alan Kaye (*Sports Card News*), Alex Klenman, Lesnik Public Relations (Timm Boyle and Bob Ibach), Lew Lipset, Jim Macie, Paul Marchant, Dick Millerd, Michael Moretto, Brian Morris, Jean-Guy Pichette, Jack Pollard, Tom Reid, Gavin Riley, Alan Rosen (Mr. Mint), John Rumierz, San Diego Sport Collectibles (Bill Goepner and Nacho Arredondo), Kevin Savage (Sports Gallery), Angelo Savelli, Mike Schechter (MSA), Richard Sherman, John Spalding, Phil and Joan Spector, Nigel Spill (Oldies and Goodies), Sports Collectors Store (Pat Quinn and Don Steinbach), Frank Steele, Murvin Sterling, Paul S. Taylor, Lee Temanson, Shirl Volk, Bill Wesslund, Kit Young, Robert Zanze, and Bill Zimpleman.

Beaucoup d'autres individus ont procuré une collaboration de prix, du matériel d'illustration, des vérifications de listes, des corrections d'erreurs, et/ou de l'information de recherche. Au risque d'oublier ou de négliger par inadvertance ces nombreux collaborateurs, nous voudrions personnellement remercier Jerry Adamic, Mike Abar, Rick Ambrozic, Dennis Anderson, Russell Armine, Neil Armstrong (World Series Cards), Lindell Austin, B & M's Card Shop, Jay Baldwin (Riding The Pine Sportscards), Baseball Card Baron, Charles Beckert, Bryan Behling, Charles Belzil, Jacob Benor, Beulah Sports (Jeff Blatt), Brian L. Bigelow, Tom Blade, Michel Bolduc, Dan Bruner, Eric Burgoyne, Calling All Cards, Giuseppe Capobianco, Danny Cariseo, Chris Carlson, Greg Caskey, Charles Champion, Dwight Chapin, Steve Chiaramonte, Adrian Ciani, Andrew Clair, James E. Clark, Shane Cohen

Slam), Barry Colla, Collector's Dreams, Matt Collett, Jon Combs, The Comic Den, Joe Conte, Ryan Cope, Douglas Coss, Dan Cox, Michael J. Cox, Taylor Crane, Chip Crawford, Wil Curtis, Dee's Baseball Cards, Dave Deveney, Mario DiPastena, Marc Dixon (International Sports Investibles), Chad Drew, John Driemeyer, Charles Dugre, Bill Dzuima, Rebecca Eaton, Kerry Edwards, D. Ellis, Kim English, Michael Esposito, Morrie Estrada, Doak Ewing, Marc Fertik, Joseph E. Filion (Cartomania), Donald Foglietta Jr., Frank Fox, Gary Freels, Henry Furton, Justin Gargiulo, Michael R. Gionet, Gary Goertzen, Jeff Goldstein, Lewie Graner, Erik Gravel, Pierre-Luc Gravel, Hall's Nostalgia, Daniel Hannah, Daniel Hansen, Tim Hanson, Sean Hartman, Shawn Hayes, Greg Hendricks, Guy Henggeler, Clay Hill, D. Howery Jr., Robert Jansing, Larry Jelsch, Victor Kalustian, Jay and Mary Kasper, Rick Keplinger, Scott Knorr, Tim Krauss, Robert A. Kuhlman, Thomas Kunnecke, Robert Kwonrans, Martin Lader, Peter Lazarerski, Roger LeBlanc, Scott LeLievre, Irv Lerner, Howie Levy of Blue Chip, Bob Liddle, Nicholas LoCasto, Louie Lugo, Glenn Lukas, Andy Markowski, John Massey, Raymond May (Sports Connection), Michael McDonald (*The Sports Page*), Branson H. McKay, Thomas McMurray, Jim Melnyk, Blake Meyer, Steve Meyer, Ben Miller, Jason Douglas Mills, Joe Morano, Kevin Mudrak, Robert Muller, Tom Murley, Todd Nelkin, David Newman, Duncan O'Brien, Robert Ochsner, John O'Hara, Joe Orban Jr., Lee Owen, Andrew Pak, Clay Pasternack, W. Patterson, Joseph Pezzillo, James Polkowski, Rick Przybyla, Andy Rachfalski, Chad Raeside, Red River Coins & Cards, Oliver Reinholt, Ralph Reitsma, Owen Ricker, Shane Rieberger, Gary Robbins, Michael Rogers, Jed Roll,. Charles Rooke, Kris L. Row, Clint Rudloff, Alan Ryan (Champion Sports Cards), Terry Sack, Joe Sak, Mike Salisbury, Jean Sauriol, James Schopi, Kasey Seymour, Allan Sharpe, Andy Silverman, Slapshot Sports Collectibles, Michael Spoor, Sports Kard Korner, Allen Stengel, Cary Stephenson, Dan Stickney, Dave Sularz, Karyn Summers, Eric Tao, Terry & Sons, Chuck Thomas, Kevin Thorburn, Patrick Timlin, Eric Tissue, Joe Tomasik, Steven W. Vadasz, Michel Vaillancourt, John Vanden Beek, Robert Vandergraaf, Variete Sports Verville Enr., Sean Wachsman, David Weiner, Andrew B. Weisenfeld (Rocky Mtn. Trading Card Co.), Frank Wenzel, Bob Wilke (The Shoe Box), K.J. (Kelly) Wionzek (Coty Collectibles), Orest Wowkodaw, Paul Zakrzewski, and David Zwally.

(Grand Slam), Barry Colla, Collector's Dreams, Matt Collett, Jon Combs, The Comic Den, Joe Conte, Ryan Cope, Douglas Coss, Dan Cox, Michael J. Cox, Taylor Crane, Chip Crawford, Wil Curtis, Dee's Baseball Cards, Dave Deveney, Mario DiPastena, Marc Dixon (International Sports Investibles), Chad Drew, John Driemeyer, Charles Dugre, Bill Dzuima, Rebecca Eaton, Kerry Edwards, D. Ellis, Kim English, Michael Esposito, Morrie Estrada, Doak Ewing, Marc Fertik, Joseph E. Filion (Cartomania), Donald Foglietta Jr., Frank Fox, Gary Freels, Henry Furton, Justin Gargiulo, Michael R. Gionet, Gary Goertzen, Jeff Goldstein, Lewie Graner, Erik Gravel, Pierre-Luc Gravel, Hall's Nostalgia, Daniel Hannah, Daniel Hansen, Tim Hanson, Sean Hartman, Shawn Hayes, Greg Hendricks, Guy Henggeler, Clay Hill, D. Howery Jr., Robert Jansing, Larry Jelsch, Victor Kalustian, Jay and Mary Kasper, Rick Keplinger, Scott Knorr, Tim Krauss, Robert A. Kuhlman, Thomas Kunnecke, Robert Kwonrans, Martin Lader, Peter Lazarerski, Roger LeBlanc, Scott LeLievre, Irv Lerner, Howie Levy of Blue Chip, Bob Liddle, Nicholas LoCasto, Louie Lugo, Glenn Lukas, Andy Markowski, John Massey, Raymond May (Sports Connection), Michael McDonald (*The Sports Page*), Branson H. McKay, Thomas McMurray, Jim Melnyk, Blake Meyer, Steve Meyer, Ben Miller, Jason Douglas Mills, Joe Morano, Kevin Mudrak, Robert Muller, Tom Murley, Todd Nelkin, David Newman, Duncan O'Brien, Robert Ochsner, John O'Hara, Joe Orban Jr., Lee Owen, Andrew Pak, Clay Pasternack W. Patterson, Joseph Pezzillo, James Polkowski, Rick Przybyla, Andy Rachfalski, Chad Raeside, Red River Coins & Cards, Oliver Reinholt, Ralph Reitsma, Owen Ricker, Shane Rieberger, Gary Robbins, Michael Rogers, Jed Roll, Charels Rooke, Kris L. Row, Clint Rudloff, Alan Ryan (Champion Sports Cards), Terry Sack, Joe Sak, Mike Salisbury, Jean Sauriol, James Schopi, Kasey Seymour, Allan Sharpe, Andy Silverman, Slapshot Sports Collectibles, Michael Spoor, Sports Kard Korner, Allen Stengel, Cary Stephenson, Dan Stickney, Dave Sularz, Karyn Summers, Eric Tao, Terry & Sons, Chuck Thomas, Kevin Thorburn, Patrick Timlin, Eric Tissue, Joe Tomasik, Steven W. Vadasz, Michel Vaillancourt, John Vanden Beek, Robert Vandergraaf, Variete Sports Verville Enr., Sean Wachsman, David Weiner, Andrew B. Weisenfeld (Rockey Mtn. Trading Card Co.), Frank Wenzel, Bob Wilke (The Shoe Box), K.J. (Kelly), Wionzek (Coty Collectibles), Orest Wowkodaw, Paul Zakrzewski, and David Zwally.

Chaque année nous sollicitons activement toute contribution en faveur de la nouvelle édition, et nous sommes particulièrement reconnaissants pour l'aide (importante ou modeste) apportée à la mise en place de ce volume. Alors que nous recevons de nombreuses demandes de renseignements, des appréciations, et des questions relatives aux éléments de ce livre . . . et, en

Every year we make active solicitations for input to that year's edition, and we are particularly appreciative of help (large and small) provided for this volume. While we receive many inquiries, comments, and questions regarding material within this book—and, in fact, each and every one is read and digested—time constraints prevent us from personally replying. We hope that the letters will continue and that, even though no reply is received, you will feel that you are making significant contributions to the hobby through your interest and comments.

In the years since this guide debuted, Beckett Publications has grown beyond any rational expectation. A great many talented and hard working individuals have been instrumental in this growth and success. Our whole team is to be congratulated for what we together have accomplished.

Our Beckett Publications team is led by Vice Presidents Joe Galindo and Fred Reed, Associate Publisher Claire Backus, and Director of Marketing Jeff Amano. Providing able assistance are:

Editorial: Pepper Hastings, Susan K. Elliott, Rudy J. Klancnik, Theo Chen, Jeff Cohen, Randy Cummings, E.J. Hradek, Matt Keifer, Mike Payne, Gary Santaniello, Louis Marroquin, Steve Wilson, Catherine Button Colbert, George Watson. *Advertising:* Frances Knight, Rebecca Reed. Administration—Lori Lindsey, Teri McGahey, Angela Hogans. *Production:* Reed Poole, Theresa Anderson, Omar Mediano, Sara Jenks, Kaki Matheson, Lisa O'Neill, Valerie Wegener, Robert Yearby, Airey Baringer, Barbara Barry, Maria L. Gonzalez-Davis, Renata Campos, Carmen Hand. *Design:* Lynne Chinn, Therese Bellar, Wendy Tripp. *Computer Services:* Rich Olivieri, Kirk McKinney.

Dealer Services: Cindy Struble, Louise Bird, Cathryn Black, Kim Ford, Anita Gonzalez, Gayle Jeffcoat, Fran Keng, Sheryl McCain, Mike Moss, LaQuita Norton, Linda Rainwater, Carol Slawson, Lisa Spaight, Jim Tereschu. *Dealer Operations:* Tom Collins, Lisa Borden, Gena Andrews, Nancy Bassi, Deana Chapman, Belinda Cross, Louise Ebaugh, Jeany Finch, Julie Grove, Ronda Pearson, Maggie Seward.

Marketing: Beth Harwell, Jeff Greer, Joanna K. Guajardo, Karen Penhollow, Ruth Price, Mark Stokes. *Beckett Sports Products:* Chris Calandro, Amy Kirk, Patrick Richard, Kim Whitesell. *Company Services:* Mary Campana, Leslie Brown, Joanna Hayden, Marion Jarrell, Lynn Nelson, Sabrina Polley, Christiann Thomas. *Information Services:*

fait, toutes sont individuellement lues et examinées, les contraintes de temps nous empêchent d'y répondre personnellement. Nous espérons que les lettres continueront d'arriver et que, même en l'absence de réponse, vous vous rendrez compte que vous apportez une contribution d'importance à ce passe-temps grâce à l'intérêt que vous y portez et à vos observations.

Au fil des années depuis les origines de ce guide, les Editions Beckett ont pris une extension au-delà de toute attente raisonnable. De nombreuses personnes de talent et travaillant ferme ont contribué à cet accroissement et à la réussite. Notre équipe au complet mérite d'être félicitée pour ce que nous avons accompli ensemble.

Notre équipe des Editions Beckett est dirigée par les vice-présidents Joe Galingo et Fred Reed, l'éditeur associé Claire Backus, et le directeur des ventes Jeff Amano. Procurant leur habile concours, nous trouvons :

A la rédaction: Pepper Hastings, Susan K. Elliott, Rudy J. Klancnik, Theo Chen, Jeff Cohen, Randy Cummings, E.J. Hradek, Matt Keifer, Mike Payne, Gary Santaniello, Louis Marroquin, Steve Wilson, Catherine Button Colbert, George Watson. *A la publicité*: Frances Knight, Rebecca Reed. *A la gestion*: Lori Lindsey, Teri McGahey, Angela Hogans. *A la production*: Reed Poole, Theresa Anderson, Omar Mediano, Sara Jenks, Kaki Matheson, Lisa O'Neill, Valerie Wegener, Robert Yearby, Airey Baringer, Barbara Barry, Maria L. Gonzalez-Davis, Renata Campos, Carmen Hand. *Au dessin*: Lynne Chinn, Therese Bellar, Wendy Tripp. *Aux ordinateurs*: Rich Olivieri, Kirk McKinney.

Au service des dépositaires: Cindy Struble, Louise Bird, Cathryn Black, Kim Ford, Anita Gonzalez, Gayle Jeffcoat, Fran Keng, Sheryl McCain, Mike Moss, LaQuita Norton, Linda Rainwater, Carol Slawson, Lisa Spaight, Jim Tereschu. *Aux opérations pour dépositaires*: Tom Collins, Lisa Borden, Gena Andrews, Nancy Bassi, Deana Chapman, Belinda Cross, Louise Ebhaugh, Jeany Finch, Julie Grove, Ronda Pearson, Maggie Seward.

Aux ventes: Beth Harwell, Jeff Greer, Joanna K. Guajardo, Karen Penhollow, Ruth Price, Mark Stokes. *Aux produits de sport Beckett*: Chris Calandro, Amy Kirk, Patrick Richard, Kim Whitesell. *Aux services de la société*: Mary Campana, Leslie Brown, Joanna Hayden, Marion Jarrell, Lynn Nelson, Sabrina Polley, Christiann Thomas. *Au service des informations*: Sammy Cantrell, Mark Harwell. *A la circulation*: Debra S. Kingsburry, Suzee Payton, Barbara Hinkle, Jenny Harwell, Lori Harmeyer.

Sammy Cantrell, Mark Harwell. *Circulation:* Debra S. Kingsbury, Suzee Payton, Barbara Hinkle, Jenny Harwell, Lori Harmeyer. *Fulfillment Services:* Monte King, Fernando Albieri, Roy Bond, Billy Culbert, Patrick Cunningham, Andrew Drago, Danny Evans, Bruce Felps, George Field, Sara Field, Gean Paul Figari, Mark Goeglein, Marcio Guimaraes, Charles Hodges, Rex Hudson, Don James, Chris Longeway, Robson Magno, Glen Morante, Mila Morante, Daniel Moscoso, Daniel Moscoso Jr., Abraham Pacheco, Guillermo Pacheco, Roberto Ramirez, Gabriel Santos, Steve Slawson, Mark Whitesell.

In addition, our consultants James and Sandi Beane and Dan Swanson performed several major system programming jobs for us again this year to help us accomplish our work faster and more accurately. The whole Beckett Publications team has my thanks for jobs well done. Thank you, everyone.

I also would like to thank my family, especially my wife, Patti, and daughters, Christina, Rebecca, and Melissa, for putting up with me again.

Aux services d'exécution: Monte King, Fernando Albieri, Roy Bond, Billy Culbert, Patrick Cunningham, Andrew Drago, Danny Evans, Bruce Felps, George Field, Sara Field, Gean Paul Figari, Mark Goeglein, Marcio Guimaraes, Charles Hodges, Rex Hudson, Don James, Chris Longeway, Robson Magno, Glen Morante, Mila Morante, Daniel Moscoso, Daniel Moscoso Jr., Abraham Pacheco, Guillermo Pacheco, Roberto Ramirez, Gabriel Santos, Steve Slawson, Mark Whitesell].

De plus, nos conseillers James et Sandi Beane, ainsi que Dan Swanson, ont effectué différents travaux de programmation d'un système important, afin de nous aider à nouveau cette année à l'accomplissement d'un travail plus rapide et plus effectif. J'adresse mes remerciements à l'ensemble de l'équipe des Editions Beckett pour un travail bien fait. Merci à chacun de vous.

J'aimerais aussi remercier ma famille, en particulier ma femme Patti, et mes filles Christina, Rébecca et Mélissa pour leur soutien cette fois encore.

ERRATA

There are thousands of names, more than 100,000 prices, and untold other words in this book. There are going to be a few typographical errors, a few misspellings, and possibly, a number or two out of place. If you catch a blooper, drop me a note directly or in care of the publisher, and we will fix it in the next year's edition.

ERRATA

Il existe des milliers de mons, plus de 100.000 prix, et d'autres mots non révélés dans ce livre. Il y aura forcément quelques erreurs typographiques, quelques fautes d'ortographe, et sans doute, un chiffre ou deux qui ne seront pas à l'attention de l'éditeur, et nous effectuerons la correction dans l'édition de l'année prochaine.

INTRODUCTION

Welcome to the exciting world of sports card collecting, America's fastest growing avocation. You have made a good choice in buying this book, since it will open up to you the entire panorama of this field in the simplest, most concise way.

Hundreds of thousands of different sports cards have been issued during the past century. And the number of total cards put out by all manufacturers last year has been estimated in the billions with a retail value of several hundred million dollars. Sales of older (non-current year) cards by dealers may account for an even greater amount. With all that collectible cardboard available in the marketplace, it should be no surprise that several million sports fans like you collect sports cards today, and that number is growing each year.

The growth of *Beckett Baseball Card Monthly, Beckett Basketball Monthly, Beckett Football Card Monthly, Beckett Hockey Monthly* and *Beckett Focus on Future Stars* is another indication of this rising crescendo of popularity for sports cards. Founded less than six years ago by Dr. James Beckett, the publisher of this price guide, *BBCM* has reached the pinnacle of the sports card hobby with approximately two million readers anxiously awaiting each enjoyable and informative issue. The other four magazines have met similar success, with hundreds of thousands of readers devoted to each.

So collecting sports cards—while still pursued as a hobby with youthful exuberance by kids in your neighborhood—has also taken on the trappings of an industry, with thousands of full- and part-time card dealers, as well as vendors of supplies, clubs, and conventions. Each year since 1980, in fact, thousands of hobbyists have assembled for a National Sports Collectors Convention, at which hundreds of dealers have displayed their wares, seminars have been conducted, autographs penned by sports notables, and millions of cards changed hands. These colossal affairs have been staged in Los Angeles, Detroit, St. Louis, Chicago, New York, Anaheim, Arlington (TX), San Francisco, Atlantic City, Arlington again, Anaheim again and next year in Atlanta. So sports card collecting really *is* national in scope!

This increasing interest has been reflected in card values. As more collectors compete for available supplies, card prices (especially for premium-grade cards) rise. A national publication indicated a "very strong advance" in sports card prices during the past decade, and a quick

INTRODUCTION

Bienvenue dans le monde passionnant des collections de cartes sportives, la distraction qui grandit le plus vite en Amérique. Vous avez effectué un bon choix en achetant ce livre, car il va ouvrir pour vous le panorama complet de cette activité de la plus simple et plus succincte manière.

Des centaines de milliers de différentes cartes sportives ont été émises pendant le siècle dernier. Et le nombre total des cartes mises en circulation par tous les fabricants l'année dernière a été estimé en milliards avec une valeur au détail évaluée à plusieurs centaines de millions de dollars. Les ventes de cartes plus anciennes (pas celles de l'année en cours) par les revendeurs doivent vraisemblablement se chiffrer à un montant plus important encore. Compte tenu de l'éventail à collectionner disponible sur le marché, il ne serait pas étonnant que plusieurs millions d'admirateurs sportifs tels que vous collectionnent des cartes sportives aujourd'hui, et que le nombre s'en accroisse chaque année.

La croissance des revues mensuelles Beckett sur les cartes de base-ball, le basket-ball, les cartes de foot-ball, le hockey, la concentration sur les vedettes futures, est une autre indication du crescendo croissant de popularité des cartes sportives. Fondé depuis moins de six ans par le Dr. James Beckett, l'éditeur de ce guide des prix, *BBCM (Beckett Baseball Card Monthly)*, le mensuel sur les cartes de base-ball, a atteint le pinacle du passe-temps concernant les cartes sportives avec environ deux millions de lecteurs attendant anxieusement chaque agréable et instructif numéro. Les quatre autres magazines ont atteint un succès équivalent, avec les centaines de milliers de lecteurs qui leur sont dévoués.

Aussi, collectionner les cartes sportives—bien que toujours perçu comme un passe-temps avec une exubérance pleine de jeunesse par les gamins de votre voisinage—a également attrapé l'industrie par les harnais, avec des milliers de revendeurs à plein temps et à temps partiel, aussi bien que les vendeurs d'accessoires en tous genres, les clubs et conventions. En fait, chaque année depuis 1980, des milliers d'amateurs se sont réunis au cours d'une convention nationale des collectionneurs sportifs au cours de laquelle des centaines de revendeurs ont exposé leurs articles, des groupes de travail ont été organisés, des autographes ont été accordés par des Notables sportifs, et des millions de cartes ont changé de mains. Ces événements colossaux ont eu lieu à Los Angelès,

perusal of the prices in this book compared to the figures in earlier editions of this price guide will confirm this. Which brings us back to the book you have in your hands. It is the best guide available to the exciting world of your favorite sport's cards. Read it and use it. May your enjoyment and your card collection increase in the coming months and years.

Détroit, Saint Louis, Chicago, New York, Anaheim, Arlington (Texas), San Francisco, Atlantic City, Arlington à nouveau, Anaheim encore une fois, et l'année prochaine à Atlanta. Désormais collectionner les cartes sportives est réellement d'une portée nationale!

Cet intérêt croissant s'est reporté sur la valeur des cartes. En même temps que des collectionneurs rivalisent pour les éléments disponibles, les prix des cartes ont augmenté (en particulier pour les cartes en parfait état). Une publication nationale a indiqué une "avancée très prononcée" concernant les prix des cartes sportives durant la dernière décennie, et un examen rapide des prix dans ce livre comparé aux indications des éditions antérieures de ce guide des prix le confirmera. Ceci nous ramène au livre que vous avez entre les mains. Il s'agit du meilleur guide mis à la disposition du monde passionnant de vos cartes sportives favorites. Lisez-le et servez-vous-en. Puissent votre satisfaction et votre collection de cartes s'accroître durant les mois et années à venir.

HOW TO COLLECT

Each collection is personal and reflects the individuality of its owner. There are no set rules on how to collect cards. Since card collecting is a hobby or leisure pastime, what you collect, how much you collect, and how much time and money you spend collecting are entirely up to you. The funds you have available for collecting and your own personal taste should determine how you collect. Information and ideas presented here are intended to help you get maximum enjoyment from this hobby.

It is impossible to collect every card ever produced. Therefore, beginners as well as intermediate and advanced collectors usually specialize in some way. One of the reasons why this hobby is so popular is that individual collectors can define and tailor their collecting methods to match their own tastes. To give you some ideas of the various approaches to collecting, we will list some of the more popular areas of specialization.

Many collectors specialize in the cards of a specific sport or sports that they personally follow. Many collect complete sets from particular years. For example, their goal may be to assemble complete sets from all the years since their birth or since they became avid sports fans. Or they may try to collect a card for every player during that specified period of time.

Many others wish to acquire only cards of certain players. Usually such players are the superstars of their respective sports, but occasionally collectors will specialize in all the cards of players who attended certain colleges or who came from certain towns. Some collectors are only interested in the first cards or Rookie Cards of particular players.

Another fun way to collect cards (for team sports) is by team. Most fans have a favorite team or two, and it is natural for that loyalty to be translated into a desire for cards of the players on particular teams.

COMMENT COLLECTIONNER

Chaque collection est personnelle et reflète l'individualité de son propriétaire. Il n'existe pas de règles établies afin de savoir comment collectionner les cartes. Puisque collectionner des cartes est un passe-temps et un loisir, ce que vous collectionnez et comment, combien de temps et d'argent vous y consacrez, sont à votre entière discrétion. Les fonds que vous mettez à la disposition de votre collection et votre personnelle appréciation devraient déterminer votre façon de procéder. Les informations et idées présentées ici ont l'intention de vous aider à profiter au maximum de ce passe-temps.

Il est impossible de collectionner toutes les cartes qui sont diffusées. En conséquence, les débutants tout aussi bien que les collectionneurs moyens ou avancés se spécialisent habituellement d'une certaine façon. L'une des raisons pour lesquelles ce passe-temps est tellement populaire est que les collectionneurs individuels peuvent définir et façonner leurs méthodes de collection afin de satisfaire leurs goûts propres. Afin de vous donner quelques idées relatives aux diverses approches d'une collection, nous allons établir une liste de quelques-uns des secteurs de spécialisation les plus populaires.

Beaucoup de collectionneurs se spécialisent dans les cartes touchant un sport spécifique qu'ils suivent personnellement. Beaucoup collectionnent des séries complètes d'années particulières. Par exemple, leur but peut être de rassembler les séries complètes de toutes les années depuis leur naissance ou depuis qu'ils sont devenus des admirateurs sportifs passionnés. Ou encore ils peuvent essayer de collectionner une carte pour chaque joueur durant une période de temps spécifique.

Beaucoup d'autres souhaitent acquérir les cartes concernant seulement certains joueurs. Habituellement ces joueurs sont les super-vedettes de leurs sports respectifs, mais occasionnellement des collectionneurs se spécialiseront dans toutes les cartes de joueurs qui ont étudié dans certaines universités ou qui sont originaires de certaines villes. Quelques collectionneurs sont seulement intéressés par les premières cartes dites "Rookie Cards" de joueurs bien particuliers.

Une autre façon amusante de collectionner les cartes (pour les sports d'équipes) est de le faire par équipe. La plupart des admirateurs ont une équipe favorite ou deux, et il est normal que cette admiration se reporte sur le désir de posséder les cartes des joueurs des équipes en question.

Obtaining Cards

Several avenues are open to sports card collectors. Cards can be purchased in the traditional way at the local candy, grocery, or drug stores, with bubble gum or other freebies included. In recent years, it has also become possible to purchase complete sets of the various sports cards through mail-order advertisers found in traditional sports media publications, such as *The Sporting News, Sport, Hockey Digest, The Hockey News, Street & Smith* yearbooks, and others. These sets are also advertised in the ever-increasing number of card collecting periodicals. Many collectors will begin by subscribing to at least one of the hobby publications, which can provide solid, up-to-date information.

Most serious card collectors obtain old (and new) cards from one or more of several main sources: (1) trading with or buying from other collectors or dealers; (2) responding to sale or auction ads in hobby publications; and/or (3) attending sports collectibles shows or conventions. We advise that you try all three methods since each has its own distinct advantages: (1) trading is a great way to make new friends; (2) hobby periodicals help you keep up with what's going on in the hobby (including when and where the conventions are happening); and (3) shows provide the opportunity to view thousands or even millions of collectibles under one roof, and you also have the chance to meet many other collectors who may have interests similar to yours.

Preserving Your Cards

Cards are fragile. They must be handled properly in order to retain their value. Careless handling can easily result in creased or bent cards. It is, however, not recommended that tweezers or tongs be used to pick up your cards, since such utensils could mar or indent card surfaces and thus reduce those cards' conditions and values. In general, your cards should be handled as little as possible. This is easier to say than to do. Among the storage formats available are

L'obtention des cartes

Différentes avenues sont ouvertes aux collectionneurs de cartes sportives. Les cartes peuvent être achetées de façon traditionnelle dans les boutiques de bonbons, les épiceries ou les pharmacies, boules de gomme et autres primes comprises. Durant les dernières années, il est également devenu possible d'acheter des jeux de cartes de sports variés à la suite d'annonces de vente par correspondance publiées dans les revues sportives telles que *The Sporting News*, *Street & Smith Yearbooks* et bien d'autres. Ces jeux sont également mis en publicité dans des périodiques de collections de cartes dont le nombre est en pleine croissance. Beaucoup de collectionneurs commenceront par s'abonner à l'une au moins de ces publications spécialisées dans les passe-temps, lesquelles peuvent procurer des informations solides et actualisées.

La plupart des sérieux collectionneurs de cartes obtiennent les cartes anciennes (et nouvelles) d'une ou plusieurs sources principales: (1) échange ou achat avec d'autres collectionneurs ou revendeurs ; (2) réponse à des annonces de ventes ou ventes aux enchères dans des revues sur les passe-temps ; et/ou (3) assistance aux expositions ou conventions d'objets sportifs de collections. Nous vous conseillons d'essayer ces trois méthodes car chacune d'elles possède ses propres avantages: (1) l'échange est une façon agréable de se faire de nouveaux amis ; (2) les périodiques sur les passe-temps vous aident à vous tenir au courant de l'actualité concernant votre passe-temps (en ce compris où et quand ont lieu les conventions) ; et (3) les expositions procurent l'occasion de voir des milliers ou même des millions d'objets de collections sous le même toit, et vous avez aussi la chance de rencontrer de nombreux autres collectionneurs pouvant avoir des intérêts similaires aux vôtres.

Conserver vos cartes

Les cartes sont fragiles. Elles doivent être manipulées proprement de façon à conserver leur valeur. Une manipulation sans précaution peut facilement aboutir à des cartes fripées ou pliées. Il n'est toutefois pas

individual card holders, custom boxes, storage trays, and display sheets. Card holders are good for displaying prize cards. Boxes allow you to store hundreds of cards while taking up very little room. Storing cards in display pages in a three-ring album allows you to view your collection at any time without the need to touch the cards themselves. For large collections, collectors generally use a combination of the above methods: perhaps individual storage for cards of a certain value, display sheets for those of a lesser value, and finally storage boxes for complete sets, commons, or minor stars.

Individual card holders come in many forms, from card sleeves to hard plastic shields. Sleeves are like miniature plastic bags that should hold your card(s) firmly, but *not* tightly. They offer protection against accidental spillage but not against more serious physical damage. Sleeves made from polypropylene or polyethylene are the cheapest, most common—and the safest for long-term storage. Sleeves made from Mylar (a form of polyester) are clearer, stiffer, just as safe, but less common and much more expensive. More solid individual card storage is available in various materials such as hard acrylic, lucite, or even Plexiglas. These card protectors are good for display and offer protection against almost every physical harm imaginable. However, they are relatively expensive and the materials used have not been around long enough to ensure long-term safety. The best way to store valuable individual cards is to insert them into polypropylene, polyethylene, or Mylar sleeves and then into a card protector of your choice.

Since modern cards are issued in sets of several hundred cards, it is obviously not feasible to store each card in an individual holder. For years now there have been cardboard boxes made specifically for the storage of sports cards. They are made to hold various quantities of cards. Look for boxes with completely flat bottoms because those with flaps protruding can cause serious damage to cards. Because the cardboard used to make all card storage boxes is acidic to some degree, some precautions should be taken to minimize possible chemical damage to your cards. When storing sets in boxes, you should consider first putting the "key" cards in the set into "safe" sleeves within the box. This allows you to find them more easily, anyway. Finally, it should be noted that acid-free cardboard boxes are available, but not yet in sizes made to fit sports cards, and at prices that are several times more expensive than regular boxes.

Display sheets are an inexpensive, flexible, and popular way to store and show off sports cards. When purchasing sheets for your

recommandé d'utiliser des petites pinces ou des pincettes pour prendre les cartes, car de tels ustensiles peuvent gâter ou ébrécher la surface des cartes et, par conséquent, amoindrir la qualité de ces cartes et diminuer leur valeur. En général, vos cartes devraient être aussi peu manipulées que possible. C'est plus facile à dire qu'à faire. Parmi les méthodes de classement disponibles on trouve des porte-cartes individuels, des boîtes sur mesure, des classeurs, et des feuillets d'exposition. Les porte-cartes sont bien pour exposer des cartes représentant un prix, une récompense.

Les boîtes vous permettent de ranger des centaines de cartes dans un espace très réduit. Disposer les cartes dans un classeur, genre trois anneaux, vous permet de regarder votre collection n'importe quand sans avoir à toucher les cartes elles-mêmes. Pour des collections importantes, les collectionneurs se servent généralement d'une combinaison des méthodes ci-dessus: peut-être un classement individuel pour les cartes d'une certaine valeur, des porte-cartes pour celles d'une valeur moindre, et enfin des boîtes pour les jeux complets, ordinaires ou représentant des vedettes moins importantes.

Les porte-cartes individuels se présentent sous diverses formes, de la chemise de carton à l'écran protecteur en plastique rigide. Les chemises se présentent comme de petits sacs en plastique devant maintenir vos cartes fermement mais sans les serrer. Elles protègent des déversements accidentels mais non des accidents sérieux. Les écrans faits de polypropylène ou de polyéthylène sont les moins chers, les plus répandus—et les plus sûrs pour un classement à longue échéance. Les écrans faits de mylar (une sorte de polyester) sont plus clairs, plus durs, tout aussi sûrs, mais moins répandus et beaucoup plus chers. Des rangements individuels plus robustes sont disponibles en diverses matières comme de l'acrylique dur, le lucite ou même le Plexiglas. Ces genres de protecteurs sont parfaits pour exposer les cartes et offrent une protection contre pratiquement tout danger imaginable. Toutefois ils sont relativement chers et les matériaux utilisés ne sont pas connus depuis si longtemps que l'on puisse être certain d'une protection à long terme. Le meilleur moyen de ranger individuellement les cartes est de les insérer dans des feuilles de polypropylène, de polyéthylène ou de Mylar puis de les ramasser dans le classeur de votre choix.

Etant donné que les cartes modernes sont éditées par jeux de plusieurs centaines à la fois, il n'est évidemment pas pensable de les ranger dans des porte-cartes individuels. Depuis des années il existe des boîtes qui sont spécialement faites pour y ramasser les cartes sportives. Elles sont conçues pour recevoir des quantités variées de cartes. Recherchez les boîtes avec un fond absolument plat parce que celles qui

cards, be sure you find the pocket size that fits the cards snugly. Don't put your 1964-65 Topps hockey cards in a sheet designed to fit 1965-66 Topps hockey cards. Most hobby and collectibles shops and virtually all collectors' conventions will have these pages available in quantity for various sizes, or you can purchase them directly from the advertisers in this book. If you intend to store your cards for a long time, try to buy sheets made of polypropylene or polyethylene as opposed to polyvinyl chloride (PVC). The oils (technically known as plasticizers) used to make PVC flexible may permeate your cards and damage them after a long period of time. One good way to identify PVC sheets is by smell. PVC sheets will usually smell like vinyl, while sheets made of polypropylene or polyethylene should not have any odor at all. Unfortunately, card sheets made of polypropylene and polyethylene are generally flimsier and less transparent than PVC pages.

Damp, sunny, and/or hot conditions—no, this is not a weather forecast—are three elements to avoid in extremes if you are interested in preserving your collection. Too high (or more seldomly, too low) humidity can cause gradual deterioration of a card. Direct, bright sun (or fluorescent light) will eventually bleach out the color of a card. Extreme heat accelerates the decomposition of cards. On the other hand, many cards have lasted more than 50 years without much scientific intervention. So be cautious, even if the above factors typically present a problem only in extremes. It never hurts to be prudent.

possèdent des rabats en saillie peuvent sérieusement abîmer les cartes. Le carton utilisé pour la fabrication de toutes ces boites étant acide à un certain point, quelques précautions devraient être prises pour minimiser des dégâts d'ordre chimique à vos cartes. Lorsque vous mettez des jeux de cartes en boites, vous devriez penser à mettre les cartes importantes de chaque jeu à l'intérieur d'une chemise protectrice dans ces mêmes boites. Vous les retrouveriez d'ailleurs ainsi plus facilement. Enfin, il est à noter que des cartons sans acide sont disponibles, malheureusement pas dans les tailles s'accordant avec les cartes sportives, et à des prix représentant plusieurs fois le prix des boites normales.

Les feuillets de présentation sont un économique, souple et populaire moyen de classer et de montrer vos cartes. En achetant ces feuillets, faites attention de prendre une taille qui s'accorde commodément avec les cartes. Ne mettez pas vos cartes de hockey Topps 1964-65 dans un feuillet fait pour recevoir les cartes hockey Topps 1965-66. La plupart des magasins de passe-temps et de collections et virtuellement toutes les conventions de collectionneurs auront ces feuillets disponibles en quantités pour diverses tailles, ou vous pouvez les commander directement à ceux qui font de la publicité dans ce livre. Si vous avez l'intention de ramasser vos cartes pour longtemps, tâchez de vous procurer des feuillets en polypropylène ou polyéthylène plutôt qu'en chlorure vinylique (polyvinyl chloride = PVC). Les huiles (techniquement connues comme plasticides) utilisées pour assouplir le PVC peuvent causer quelqu'endommagement à vos cartes après un certain laps de temps. Une bonne façon d'identifier les feuillets en PVC est l'odeur. Les feuilles de PVC sentent d'habitude le vinyl, alors que celles en polypropylène ou en polyéthylène ne devraient avoir aucune odeur. Malheureusement, les feuillets pour cartes, en polypropylène et polyéthylène sont généralement moins robustes et moins transparents que ceux en PVC.

Humidité, ensoleillement, et/ou hautes températures—non, il ne s'agit pas de prévisions météorologiques—sont trois éléments à éviter au plus haut point si vous avez l'intention de protéger votre collection. Trop d'humidité (ou plus rarement, pas assez) peut causer une dégradation graduelle d'une carte. L'ensoleillement direct, éclatant (ou une lumière fluorescente) peut éventuellement décolorer une carte. Une chaleur extrême accélère la décomposition des cartes. D'un autre côté, de nombreuses cartes ont passé le cap des 50 ans sans grande intervention scientifique. Donc faites attention, même si les facteurs présentés ci-dessus ne sont typiquement que des extrêmes, il ne nuit jamais d'être prudent.

Collecting/Investing

Collecting individual players and collecting complete sets are both popular vehicles for investment and speculation. Most investors and speculators stock up on complete sets or on quantities of players they think have good investment potential. There is obviously no guarantee in this book, or anywhere else for that matter, that cards will outperform the stock market or other investment alternatives in the future. After all, sports cards do not pay quarterly dividends. And selling cards at the "going rate" is more difficult than selling stocks; instead of calling a broker and getting instant results, a card seller may have to contact several potential buyers to get the best price. Nevertheless, investors have noticed a favorable trend in the past performance of sports collectibles, and certain cards and sets have outperformed just about any other investment in recent years.

Some of the obvious questions are: Which cards? When to buy? When to sell? The best initial investment you can make is in your own education. The more you know about your collection and the hobby, the more informed the decisions you will be able to make. We're not selling investment tips. We're selling information about the current values of sports cards. It's up to you to use that information to your best advantage.

Collectionner/Investir

Faire collection de joueurs individuels et collectionner des jeux complets sont tous deux des moyens populaires d'investissement et de spéculation. La plupart des investisseurs et des spéculateurs conservent les cartes en jeux complets ou en quantités de joueurs qu'ils estiment être potentiellement un bon investissement. Il n'y a évidemment aucune garantie dans ce livre, ou nulle part ailleurs à ce propos, que les cartes dépasseront un jour la bourse ou d'autres solutions d'investissements. Après tout, les cartes sportives ne paient pas de dividendes trimestriels. Et de vendre des cartes "au prix courant" est plus difficile que de vendre des actions; au lieu d'appeler un courtier en bourse et d'obtenir des résultats immédiats, le vendeur d'une carte peut avoir à contacter plusieurs acheteurs possibles afin d'obtenir le meilleur prix. Quoiqu'il en soit, les investisseurs ont remarqué une tendance favorable lors des dernières transactions d'objets de collections concernant les sports, et certaines cartes et des jeux ont dépassé pratiquement tous les autres investissements au cours des années récentes.

Quelques-unes des questions qui sont évidentes sont: quelles cartes? Quand acheter ? Quand les vendre ? Le meilleur investissement de base que vous puissiez faire dépend de vos propres connaissances. Plus vous en saurez sur votre collection et ce passe-temps, plus les décisions que vous serez capable de prendre seront valables. Nous ne sommes pas ici pour vous vendre des conseils en matière d'investissements. Nous vendons de l'information au sujet de la valeur actuelle des cartes sportives. C'est à vous d'utiliser cette information au mieux de vos intérêts.

NOMENCLATURE

Each hobby has its own language to describe its area of interest. The nomenclature traditionally used for trading cards is derived from the *American Card Catalog* (frequently referenced as *ACC*), published in 1960 by Nostalgia Press. That catalog, written by Jefferson Burdick (who is called the "Father of Card Collecting" for his pioneering work), uses letter and number designations for each separate set of cards.

The letter used in the *ACC* designation refers to the generic type of card. While both sport and non-sport issues are classified in the *ACC*, we shall confine ourselves to the sport issues. The following list defines the letters and their meanings as used by the *American Card Catalog*.

E - Early Candy and Gum
F - Food Inserts
H - Advertising
M - Periodicals
N - 19th-Century U.S. Tobacco
PC - Postcards
R - Recent Candy and Gum Cards, 1930 to Present
T - 20th-Century U.S. Tobacco
UO - Gas and Oil Inserts
V - Canadian Candy
W - Exhibits, Strip Cards, Team Cards

Following the letter prefix and an optional hyphen are one-, two-, or three-digit numbers, 1–999. These typically represent the company or entity issuing the cards. In several cases, the *ACC* number is extended by an additional hyphen and another one- or two-digit numerical suffix. For example, the 1933-34 Canadian Gum hockey card issue carries an *ACC* designation of V252. The "V" indicates a Canadian candy. The "252" is the *ACC* designation for Canadian Gum.

Like other traditional methods of identification, this system provides order to the process of cataloging cards; however, most serious collectors learn the *ACC* designation of the popular sets by repetition and familiarity, rather than by attempting to "figure out" what they might or should be.

From 1951 forward, collectors and dealers commonly refer to all sets

NOMENCLATURE

Chaque passe-temps possède son propre langage pour décrire sa zône d'intérêt. La nomenclature traditionnellement utilisée pour le commerce des cartes provient du catalogue de la carte américaine, *American Card Catalog*, (souvent appelé *ACC*) publié en 1960 par la maison de presse Nostalgia. Ce catalogue, écrit par Jefferson Burdick (appelé le "père de la collection des cartes" pour son travail d'innovateur), se sert d'appellations par une lettre et un chiffre pour chaque jeu séparé de cartes.

La lettre utilisée dans le *ACC* s'applique au type générique de carte. Alors que les émissions de cartes sportives et non-sportives sont toutes deux identifiées dans le *ACC*, nous nous concentrerons sur les cartes sportives. La liste suivante identifie les lettres et leur signification dans l'utilisation qui en est faite par le *ACC*.

E - "Early Candy and Gum" (nouveaux bonbons et gomme)
F - "Food Inserts" (en complément avec de la nourriture)
H - "Advertising" (publicité)
M - "Periodicals" (périodiques)
N - "19th-Century U.S. Tobacco" (tabac américain du 19ème siècle)
PC - "Postcard" (carte postale)
R - "Recent Candy and Gum Cards, 1930 to Present" (cartes des bonbons et gomme récents, de 1930 à nos jours)
T - "20th-Century U.S. Tobacco" (tabac américain du 20ème siècle)
UO - "Gas and Oil Inserts" (en complément avec de l'essence et de l'huile)
V - "Canadian Candy" (bonbon canadien)
W - "Exhibits, Strip Cards, Team Cards" (expositions, cartes en bandes, cartes d'équipes)

A la suite de la lettre préfixe et d'un trait d'union optionnel il y a des nombres de un, deux, ou trois chiffres, 1–999. Ceux-ci représentent typiquement la compagnie ou l'entité émettant les cartes. Dans plusieurs cas, le nombre *ACC* est suivi d'un trait d'union complémentaire et d'un autre suffixe composé d'un ou deux chiffres. Par exemple, la carte de hockey émise par la gomme canadienne "Canadian Gum" en 1933–34 porte la référence *ACC*: V252. Le "V" indique qu'il s'agit d'un bonbon canadien. Le nombre "252" est la désignation *ACC* pour "Canadien Gum."

by their year, maker, type of issue, and any other distinguishing characteristic. For example, such a characteristic could be an unusual issue or one of several regular issues put out by a specific maker in a single year. Regional issues are usually referred to by year, maker, and sometimes by title or theme of the set.

De même que les autres méthodes traditionnelles d'identification, le système procure une règle quant à la façon de cataloguer les cartes; toutefois, la plupart des collectionneurs sérieux apprennent la désignation *ACC* des séries populaires plutôt par répétition et familiarité que par une tentative de se représenter ce que cela pourrait ou devrait être.

Dorénavant depuis 1951, les collectionneurs et les revendeurs se réfèrent ordinairement aux jeux de cartes d'après leur année, leur émetteur, et toute autre caractéristique distinctive. Par exemple, une telle caractéristique pourrait être une émission inhabituelle, ou l'une de plusieurs émissions régulières lancée par un fabriquant précis au cours d'une seule année. Des émissions régionales ont souvent pour références leur année, leur émetteur, et quelquefois le titre ou le sujet du jeu.

GLOSSARY/LEGEND

Our glossary defines terms frequently used in the card collecting hobby. Many of these terms are also common to other types of sports memorabilia collecting. Some terms may have several meanings, depending on use and context.

ACTION SCENES CARD. A special type of card showing an action photo of a player or players with a description.

ADAMS. Trophy awarded to NHL's coach of the year.

AHL. American Hockey League.

ALL-STAR CARD. A card portraying an All-Star player of the previous year that says "All Star" on its face. Sometimes denoted as AS in the price listings.

ALPH. Alphabetical.

ANN. Announcer.

ART. All-Rookie Team.

ATG. All Time Great card.

BRICK. A group of cards, usually 50 or more having common characteristics, that is intended to be bought, sold, or traded as a unit.

BYNG. Lady Byng trophy, award for NHL's most gentlemanly player.

CALDER. Trophy awarded to NHL's rookie of the year.

CHECKLIST. A list of the cards contained in a particular set. The list is always in numerical order if the cards are numbered. Some unnumbered sets are artificially numbered in alphabetical order, or by team and alphabetically within the team for convenience.

CHECKLIST CARD. A card that lists in order the cards and players in the set or series. Older checklist cards in Mint condition that have not been checked off are very desirable.

CL. Abbreviation for Checklist.

GLOSSAIRE/LÉGENDE

Notre glossaire définit des termes fréquemment utilisés dans le passe-temps concernant la collection des cartes. Beaucoup de ces termes sont aussi communs à d'autres genres de collections dans le monde du sport. Quelques termes peuvent avoir différentes significations, en fonction de leur usage ou du contexte.

ACTION SCENES CARD. Carte de scènes d'action: un type spécial de carte montrant une photo d'un ou plusieurs joueurs en action accompagnée d'une explication.

ADAMS. Trophée accordé à l'entraineur NHL de l'année (NHL: "National Hockey League": ligue nationale de hockey).

AHL. "American Hockey League": ligue américaine de hockey.

ALL-STAR CARD. Une carte représentant un joueur "All-Star" de l'année passée: la vedette toutes catégories, et précisant "All-Star" côté face. Parfois il est seulement précisé AS sur les listes de prix.

ALPH. Alphabétique.

ART. L'équipe "All-Rookie Team."

ATG. Une carte "All Time Great."

BRICK. Un groupe de cartes, ou paquet, habituellement de 50 ou plus ayant des caractéristiques communes, qu'il y a tendance à acheter, à vendre ou à échanger en temps qu'unité.

BYNG. Le trophée Madame Byng, récompense remise au joueur NHL le plus honorable.

CALDER. Trophée remis au débutant NHL de l'année.

CHECKLIST. Une liste de cartes contenues dans une série précise. La liste est toujours en ordre numérique si les cartes sont numérotées. Quelques séries non numérotées sont artificiellement classées par ordre alphabétique, ou par équipes et en ordre alphabétique à l'intérieur de chaque équipe pour raison de commodité.

CHECKLIST CARD. Une carte qui inventorie dans l'ordre les cartes et les joueurs d'un jeu ou de séries. Ces types de cartes, anciennes et en parfaite condition, si elles n'ont pas été soustraites, sont particulièrement désirables.

CLANCY. NHL Trophy awarded for humanitarian contributions.

CO. Abbreviation for Coach.

COIN. A small disc of metal or plastic portraying a player in its center.

COLLECTOR. A person who engages in the hobby of collecting cards primarily for his own enjoyment, with any profit motive being secondary.

COLLECTOR ISSUE. A set produced for the sake of the card itself with no product or service sponsor. It derives its name from the fact that most of these sets are produced for sale directly to the hobby market.

COMBINATION CARD. A single card depicting two or more players (but not a team card).

COMMON CARD. The typical card of any set; it has no premium value accruing from subject matter, numerical scarcity, popular demand, or anomaly.

CONVENTION. A large gathering of dealers and collectors at a single location for the purpose of buying, selling, and sometimes trading sports memorabilia items. Conventions are open to the public and sometimes also feature autograph guests, door prizes, films, contests, etc.

CONVENTION ISSUE. A set produced in conjunction with a sports collectibles convention to commemorate or promote the show.

COR. Correct or corrected card.

COUNTERFEIT. An unauthorized reproduction of a card. Sometimes only very close inspection reveals the difference between a real and a fake card.

COUPON. See Tab.

CREASE. A wrinkle on the card, usually caused by bending the card. Creases are a common defect from careless handling.

DEALER. A person who engages in buying, selling, and trading sports collectibles or supplies. A dealer may also be a collector, but as a dealer, he anticipates a profit.

CL. Abbréviation pour "Checklist."

CLANCY. Trophée NHL attribué pour contributions humanitaires.

CO. Abbréviation pour "Coach": entraîneur.

COIN. Un petit disque de métal ou de plastique représentant un joueur en son centre.

COLLECTOR. Un collectionneur: une personne dont le passe-temps de collectionner les cartes n'est tout d'abord que pour sa propre satisfaction, la recherche d'un gain ne venant qu'en second plan.

COLLECTOR ISSUE. Un jeu émis pour l'art de la carte en soi, sans support d'aucun produit ou service. L'origine de l'appellation vient du fait que la plupart de ces jeux sont produits pour être commercialisés directement.

COMBINATION CARD. Une carte décrivant à elle seule deux ou plusieurs joueurs (mais n'étant pas une carte d'équipe).

COMMON CARD. La carte typique de n'importe quelle série ; elle ne possède pas de valeur spéciale en fonction de la matière du sujet, d'une rareté numérique, d'une demande populaire, ou d'une anomalie.

CONVENTION. Une réunion importante de revendeurs et de collectionneurs dans un lieu unique dans le but d'acheter, de vendre et parfois d'échanger des objets en rapport avec les sports. Ces assemblées sont ouvertes au public et ont quelquefois au programme des invités accordant des autographes, des remises de prix, des films, des concours, etc...

CONVENTION ISSUE. Une série produite en rapport avec une convention traitant de collections d'objets en rapport avec les sports, afin de commémorer ou de promouvoir l'exposition.

COR. Une carte correcte ou corrigée.

COUNTERFEIT. Une reproduction non autorisée d'une carte. Quelquefois seulement une vérification très attentive révèle la différence entre une carte authentique et une imitation.

COUPON. Voir le mot TAB.

CREASE. Un faux pli sur la carte, habituellement la conséquence d'une courbure de la carte. Ces faux plis sont un défaut provenant d'une manipulation sans ménagement.

DEALER. Une personne qui s'occupe d'acheter, vendre et échanger

DECKLE EDGE. Jagged edge found on a special 1970–71 set.

DIE-CUT. A card with part of its stock partially cut, allowing one or more parts to be folded or removed. After removal or appropriate folding, the remaining part of the card can frequently be made to stand up.

DIR. Director of Player Personnel.

DISC. A circular-shaped card.

DISPLAY CARD. A sheet, usually containing three to nine cards, that is printed and used by the manufacturer to advertise and/or display the packages containing his products and cards. The backs of display cards are blank or contain advertisements.

DP. Double Print (a card that was printed in double the quantity compared to the other cards in the same series).

ERR. Error card (see also COR).

ERROR CARD. A card with erroneous information, spelling, or depiction on either side of the card. Most errors are never corrected by the producing card company.

EXHIBIT. The generic name given to thick stock, postcard-size cards with single-color obverse pictures. The name is derived from the Exhibit Supply Co. of Chicago, the principal manufacturer of this type of card. These are also known as Arcade cards, since they were found in many arcades.

FULL SHEET. A complete sheet of cards that has not been cut up into individual cards by the manufacturer. Also called an uncut sheet.

GAME CARD. Scarce special insert cards issued in 1962–63 Parkhurst.

GM. General Manager.

GOALIE CARD. Cards of goalies, even average ones, command slight premiums.

HALL OF FAMER. (HOFer) A card that portrays a player who has been inducted into the Hall of Fame.

HART. Hart Trophy, awarded to the NHL's most valuable player.

des accessoires et objets de collections se rapportant aux sports. Ce revendeur peut aussi être un collectionneur, mais en tant que revendeur il envisage de gagner de l'argent.

DECKLE EDGE. Bordure dentelée trouvée sur une série particulière de 1970-71.

DIE-CUT. Une carte dont le sujet est partiellement coupé, permettant ainsi d'en plier ou supprimer une ou plusieurs parties. Après suppression ou pliage approprié, la partie restante de la carte peut souvent être faite pour tenir debout.

DISC. Une carte en forme de cercle.

DISPLAY CARD. Une feuille, contenant habituellement de trois à neuf cartes, imprimée et utilisée par le fabricant pour faire de la publicité et/ou faire voir les emballages contenant ses produits et cartes. Le dos de ces feuilles est blanc ou contient des publicités.

DP. "Double Print" (une carte imprimée au double de la quantité des autres cartes des mêmes séries).

ERR. Carte erronée (voir également COR).

ERROR CARD. Une carte avec une information, une orthographe, ou une description inexactes d'un côté ou de l'autre. La majorité des erreurs n'est jamais corrigée par la compagnie émettrice.

EXHIBIT. Nom générique donné à des cartes d'un matériel épais, de la taille des cartes postales, avec des images d'une seule couleur sur une face. Le nom vient de la société "Exhibit Supply Co." de Chicago, le fabricant principal de cette sorte de cartes. Elles sont également connues sous le terme "Arcade" parce qu'elles étaient trouvées sous beaucoup d'arcades marchandes.

FULL SHEET. Une feuille complète de cartes qui n'a pas été coupée par le fabricant pour séparer les cartes. On l'appelle aussi une feuille entière ou brute.

GAME CARD. Rare cartes pour un complément spécial émises par Parkhurst en 1962-63.

GOALIE CARD. Cartes de gardiens de buts, même moyens, inspirant des primes modestes.

HALL OF FAMER. (HOFer) une carte représentant un joueur qui est entré au "Hall of Fame" (gallerie de la renommée).

HART. Le trophée Hart, accordé au meilleur joueur de la ligue

HIGH NUMBER. The cards in the last series of numbers in a year in which such higher-numbered cards were printed or distributed in significantly lesser amounts than the lower-numbered cards. The high-number designation refers to a scarcity of the high-numbered cards. Not all years have high numbers in terms of this definition.

HL. Highlight card.

HOF. Acronym for Hall of Fame.

HOLOGRAM. Inserts produced by Upper Deck.

HOR. Horizontal pose on card as opposed to the standard vertical orientation found on most cards.

IHL. International Hockey League.

IN ACTION CARD. A special type of card depicting a player in an action photo. Denoted in the price guide as "IA."

INSERT. A card of a different type, e.g., a poster, or any other sports collectible contained and sold in the same package along with a card or cards of a major set.

ISSUE. Synonymous with set, but usually used in conjunction with a manufacturer, e.g., a Topps issue.

JENNINGS. Trophy awarded to team with most outstanding goaltending.

LAYERING. The separation or peeling of one or more layers of the card stock, usually at the corner of the card.

LEGITIMATE ISSUE. A set produced to promote or boost sales of a product or service, e.g., bubble gum, cereal, cigarettes, etc. Most collector issues are not legitimate issues in this sense.

LID. A circular-shaped card (possibly with tab) that forms the top of the container for the product being promoted.

LL. League Leader card.

MAJOR SET. A set produced by a national manufacturer of cards containing a large number of cards. Usually 100 or more different cards comprise a major set.

MASTERSON. Trophy awarded for perseverance, sportsmanship, and dedication.

nationale de hockey.

HIGH NUMBER. Les cartes d'une année situées dans les dernières séries de chiffres imprimées ou distribuées en nombre d'une manière significative moins important que les cartes avec des chiffres moins élevés. Cette désignation ("High Number") réflète la rareté des cartes avec un haut numérotage. Cette catégorie ainsi définie n'existe pas pour toutes les années.

HL. Carte "Highlight."

HOF. Initiales de "Hall of Fame."

HOLOGRAM. Cartes de complément produites par Upper Deck.

HOR. Aspect horizontal de la carte, par opposition à l'orientation traditionnelle verticale de la majeure partie des cartes.

IHL. "International Hockey League": ligue internationale de hockey.

IN ACTION CARD. Un type spécial de carte montrant un joueur en action. Ce type de carte est identifié dans le guide des prix comme "IA."

INSERT. Une carte d'un modèle différent, par exemple une affiche, ou tout autre objet à collectionner et en relation avec les sports, contenue dans le même paquet en tant que complément et vendue avec une carte ou des cartes d'une série importante.

ISSUE. Synonyme de "set": jeu, mais habituellement utilisé en rapport avec un fabricant, comme "Topps issue" (jeu émis par Topps).

JENNINGS. Trophée accordé à l'équipe ayant marqué le plus de buts.

LAYERIING. Séparation ou intercalaire d'une ou plusieurs couches de l'approvisionnement de cartes, normalement au coin d'une carte.

LEGITIMATE ISSUE. Un jeu produit pour promouvoir ou lancer les ventes d'un produit ou d'un service, comme la gomme à bulles, des céréales, des cigarettes etc... Beaucoup de jeux de collectionneurs ne sont pas réellement des jeux dans le sens du terme.

LID. Une carte en forme de cercle (vraisemblablement avec une patte) qui constitue le dessus du récipient contenant le produit en promotion.

LL. "League leader card": carte du chef de ligue.

MAJOR SET. Un jeu produit par un fabricant national de cartes, contenant un grand nombre de cartes. Habituellement 100 cartes différentes ou plus composent un "Major Set."

MASTERSON. Trophée accordé pour persévérance, sportivité, et dévouement.

MEM. Memorial card.

MEMORIAL CUP. Award given to the overall champions of the Junior Leagues.

MG. Manager card.

MINI. A small card or stamp (for example, the 1988-89 O-Pee-Chee mini set).

MVP. Abbreviation for Most Valuable Player.

NHL. National Hockey League.

NNO. No number on card.

NORRIS. Trophy awarded to NHL's outstanding defenseman.

NOTCHING. The grooving of a card, usually caused by fingernails, rubber bands, or bumping card edges against other objects, which reduce the condition and value of the card.

NYI. New York Islanders.

NYR. New York Rangers.

OBVERSE. The front, face, or pictured side of the card.

OHL. Ontario Hockey League.

OPC. O-Pee-Chee.

P1. First Printing.

P2. Second Printing.

P3. Third Printing.

PANEL. An extended card that is composed of two or more individual cards. Often the panel forms the back part of the container for the product being promoted.

PLASTIC SHEET. A clear, plastic page that is punched for insertion into a binder (with standard three-ring spacing) containing pockets for displaying cards. Many different styles of sheets exist with pockets of varying sizes to hold the many differing card formats.

PR. President or Public Relations.

PREMIUM. A card, sometimes on photographic stock, that is purchased or obtained in conjunction with/or redemption for another card or product. The premium is not packaged in the

MEM. Carte commémorative.

MEMORIAL CUP. Récompense remise à l'ensemble des champions des ligues cadettes ou junior.

MG. "Manager card": carte du directeur.

MINI. Une petite carte ou un timbre (par exemple, le mini-jeu O-Pee-Chee 1988-89).

MVP. Abbréviation pour "Most Valuable Player": le joueur le plus précieux.

NHL. "National Hockey League": ligue nationale de hockey.

NNO. Pas de numéro sur la carte.

NORRIS. Trophée accordé au meilleur homme de défense NHL.

NOTCHING. Des rainures sur une carte, généralement provoquées par les ongles, des élastiques, ou des coups occasionnés aux tranches des cartes par d'autres objets, et qui réduisent l'état et la valeur de la carte.

NYI. L'équipe "New York Islanders."

NYR. L'équipe "New York Rangers."

OBVERSE. Le dessus, côté face, ou le côté imagé de la carte.

OHL. "Ontario Hockey League": ligue de hockey de Ontario.

OPC. O-Pee-Chee.

P1. Première édition.

P2. Seconde édition.

P3. Troisième édition.

PANEL. Une carte agrandie, composée de deux ou plusieurs cartes individuelles. Souvent ce panneau constitue le dos d'une boîte d'un produit en promotion.

PLASTIC SHEET. Une feuille de plastique transparent, poinçonnée afin de s'insérer dans un classeur (convenant au classeur normal à trois anneaux) avec des cases pour disposer les cartes. De nombreux styles différents de ces feuilles existent avec des cases de tailles variées afin de convenir à des formats différents de cartes.

PREMIUM. Une carte, parfois sur papier photo, qui est achetée ou obtenue en relation avec/ou contre la remise d'une autre carte ou d'un

same unit as the primary item.

PROMO CARD. A sample card produced by a manufacturer to preview the next year's set and usually distributed to a select group of collectors and dealers and/or given away at a major card show. Also called PROTOTYPE.

QMJHL. Quebec Major Junior Hockey League.

RARE. A card or series of cards of very limited availability. Unfortunately, "rare" is a subjective term sometimes used indiscriminately. Rare cards are harder to obtain than scarce cards.

RB. Record Breaker card.

REGIONAL. A card issued and distributed only in a limited geographical area of the country. The producer is not a major, national producer of trading cards.

REVERSE. The back or narrative side of the card.

ROOKIE CARD. A player's first appearance on a regular issue card from one of the major card companies. Each company has only one regular issue set, and that is the traditional set that is widely available. Until the recent growth of the hockey card market, which saw several manufacturers begin producing NHL cards, each player had only one Rookie Card (RC). A Rookie Card cannot be a Record Breaker, All-Star, Action Scenes, trophy winner or other "special" card.

ROSS. Art Ross trophy, awarded to NHL's points scoring leader.

ROY. Acronym for Rookie of the Year.

SA. Super Action (1981-82 O-Pee-Chee and Topps).

SCARCE. A card or series of cards of limited availability. This subjective term is sometimes used indiscriminately to promote or hype value. Scarce cards are not as difficult to obtain as rare cards.

SELKE. Trophy awarded to NHL's best defensive forward.

SEMI-HIGH. A card from the next to last series of a sequentially issued set. It has more value than an average card and generally less value than a high number. A card is not called a semi-high unless the next to last series in which it exists has an

autre produit. Cette carte-prime n'est pas emballée avec le paquet principal.

PROMO CARD. Une carte produite à titre de spécimen par un fabricant pour annoncer le jeu de l'année suivante, et habituellement distribuée à un groupe choisi de collectionneurs et de revendeurs et/ou distribuée à l'occasion d'une importante exhibition de cartes. On l'appelle également un PROTOTYPE.

QMJHL. "Quebec Major Junior Hockey League."

RARE. Une carte ou des séries de cartes d'une très faible disponibilité. Malheureusement, le mot "rare" est un terme parfois utilisé à tort et à travers, les cartes rares sont plus difficiles à trouver que les cartes à édition limitée.

RB. "Record Breaker card": carte d'un batteur de record.

REGIONAL. Une carte émise et distribuée seulement dans un secteur géographique limité du pays. Le producteur n'est pas un producteur important, national, de cartes trouvées dans le commerce.

REVERSE. Le dos ou le côté descriptif de la carte.

ROOKIE CARD. La première apparition d'un joueur sur une édition normale d'une des principales compagnies produisant des cartes. Chaque compagnie n'émet qu'une édition normale, et c'est la série traditionnellement largement disponible. Jusqu'au développement important du marché des cartes de hockey, qui a vu plusieurs fabricants commencer la production de cartes NHL, chaque joueur n'avait seulement qu'une carte de débutant ou "Rookie Card" (RC). Une carte de débutant ne peut pas être une carte de batteur de record (Record Breaker), ou de vedette toutes catégories (All-Star), de scènes d'actions (Action scenes), d'un gagneur de trophée ou autre carte "spéciale."

ROSS. Le trophée Art Ross, accordé au joueur NHL ayant marqué le plus de points.

ROY. Initiales pour "Rookie of the Year," ou le débutant de l'année.

SA. Super Action (0-Pee-Chee et Topps de 1981-82).

SCARCE. Une carte ou une série de cartes d'une disponibilité limitée. Ce terme est quelquefois utilisé à tort et à travers pour pousser ou exagérer la valeur. Les cartes à tirage limité ne sont pas aussi difficiles à trouver que les cartes dites "rares."

SELKE. Trophée accordé au meilleur défense-avant NHL.

SEMI-HIGH. Une carte des prochaines aux dernières séries

additional premium attached to it.

SERIES. The entire set of cards issued by a particular producer in a particular year, e.g., the 1971-72 Topps series. Also, within a particular set, series can refer to a group of (consecutively numbered) cards printed at the same time, e.g., the last series of the 1972-73 O-Pee-Chee issue (numbers 290 through 341) encompasses the WHA subset.

SET. One each of the entire run of cards of the same type produced by a particular manufacturer during a single year. In other words, if you have a complete set of 1975-76 Topps hockey cards, then you have every card from number 1 up to and including number 330; i.e., all the different cards that were produced.

SMYTHE. Conn Smythe Trophy, awarded to most outstanding player in the NHL playoffs.

SP. Single or Short Print (a card which was printed in lesser quantity compared to the other cards in the same series; see also DP and TP).

SPECIAL CARD. A card that portrays something other than a single player or team; for example, a card that portrays the previous year's statistical leaders or the results from the previous year's post-season action.

STAMP. Adhesive-backed papers depicting a player. The stamp may be individual or in a sheet of many stamps. Moisture must be applied to the adhesive in order for the stamp to be attached to another surface.

STANLEY CUP. Trophy awarded to NHL championship team.

STAR CARD. A card that portrays a player of some repute, usually determined by his ability, but sometimes referring to sheer popularity.

STICKER. A card with a removable layer that can be affixed to (stuck onto) another surface.

STOCK. The cardboard or paper on which the card is printed.

SUPER ACTION. Card type similar to In Action. Abbreviated in the price guide as SA.

SUPERSTAR CARD. A card that portrays a superstar,

d'ensemble de cartes continuellement en production. Elle a davantage de valeur que la moyenne et en général moins de valeur qu'un haut chiffre. Une carte n'est pas appelée un "Semi-High" à moins que la prochaine jusqu'aux dernières émissions dans laquelle elle se trouve ait une prime additionnelle qui lui soit attachée.

SERIES. La production totale de cartes émises par un producteur particulier au cours d'une année déterminée, par exemple les séries Topps 1971-72. Egalement, à l'intérieur d'un paquet particulier, les séries peuvent s'appliquer à un groupe de cartes (dont les nombres se suivent) imprimées en même temps, par exemple les dernières séries O-Pee-Chee 1972-73 (numéros 290 à 341) renferment la sous-collection de l'association mondiale de hockey.

SET. Chaque tirage complet de cartes de la même espèce produit par un fabricant donné au cours d'une seule année. Autrement dit, si vous possédez un "set" ou jeu complet des cartes de hockey Topps de 1975-76, vous avez alors toutes les cartes depuis le numéro 1 jusqu'au numéro 330 inclus ; en d'autres termes: toutes les différentes cartes qui ont été émises.

SMYTHE. Le trophée Conn Smythe, accordé au meilleur joueur des finales NHL.

SP. Impression unique ou limitée (une carte qui a été imprimée en quantité moindre par comparaison aux autres cartes des mêmes séries ; voir aussi DP et TP).

SPECIAL CARD. Une carte qui représente autre chose qu'un seul joueur ou une équipe ; par exemple, une carte qui représente les meilleurs joueurs d'après les statistiques de l'année précédente, ou les résultats de l'arrière saison précédente.

STAMP. Timbre de papier, avec colle au dos, représentant un joueur. Ce timbre peut être individuel ou en feuilles. Il faut humidifier la partie enduite de colle pour appliquer ce timbre sur une autre surface.

STANLEY CUP. Trophée accordé à l'équipe NHL championne.

STAR CARD. Une carte qui représente un joueur d'une certaine réputation, ordinairement en fonction de son talent, mais aussi parfois purement à cause de sa popularité.

STICKER. Une carte avec une pellicule amovible et qui peut être appliquée sur une autre surface (autocollant).

STOCK. Le matériel, carton ou papier, sur lequel la carte est imprimée.

e.g., a Hall of Fame member or a player whose current performance will eventually warrant Hall of Fame consideration.

TAB. A card portion set off from the rest of the card, usually with perforations, that may be removed without damaging the central character or event depicted by the card.

TEAM CARD. A card that depicts an entire team.

TEST SET. A set, usually containing a small number of cards, issued by a national card producer and distributed in a limited section or sections of the country. Presumably, the purpose of a test set is to measure market appeal for a particular type of card.

THER. Athletic therapists.

TL. Team Leader card.

TR. Trade or Traded or Trainer.

TRIMMED. A card cut down from its original size. Trimmed cards are undesirable to most collectors, and are therefore much less valuable than otherwise identical untrimmed cards.

UER. Uncorrected error.

VARIATION. One of two or more cards from the same series with the same number (or player with identical pose if the series is unnumbered) differing from one another in some aspect, from the printing, stock or other feature of the card. This is usually caused when the manufacturer of the cards notices an error in one (or more) of the cards, makes the changes, and then resumes the print run. In this case there will be two versions or variations of the same card. Sometimes one of the variations is relatively scarce.

VERT. Vertical pose on card.

VEZINA. Trophy awarded to NHL's outstanding goaltender.

VP. Vice president.

WHA. World Hockey Association.

WHL. Western Hockey League.

SUPER ACTION. Sorte de carte similaire à celle représentant une action (IN ACTION). Abrégé ainsi dans le guide des prix: SA.

SUPERSTAR CARD. Une carte représentant une super-vedette, par exemple un membre du Hall of Fame, ou un joueur dont les performances devraient le faire entrer au Hall of Fame.

TAB. Une portion de la carte séparée du reste de la carte, d'habitude avec des perforations, et qui peut être enlevée sans abîmer le caractère principal ou l'évènement décrit par la carte.

TEAM CARD. Une carte montrant une équipe au complet.

TEST SET. Un ensemble contenant habituellement un petit nombre de cartes, émis par un fabricant national de cartes dans une partie limitée ou quelques parties du pays. Probablement, le but de cette expérience est d'évaluer le marché pour un modèle particulier de carte.

TL. "Team Leader card": carte de chef d'équipe.

TR. Échange ou échangé.

TRIMMED. Une carte diminuée de taille par rapport à sa taille d'origine. Ces cartes sont sans intérêt pour la plupart des collectionneurs, et par conséquent ont moins de valeur que les mêmes cartes dans leur taille normale.

UER. Erreur non corrigée.

VARIATION. Une, deux ou davantage de cartes des mêmes séries portant le même numéro (ou un joueur dans la même pose si les séries ne sont pas numérotées) différant les unes des autres d'une certaine façon, soit l'imprimerie, soit le matériel employé ou une autre caractéristique de la carte. Ceci arrive en général quand le fabricant relève une erreur sur une carte (ou plusieurs) et effectue des rectifications, puis continue à les imprimer. En ce cas, il y aura deux versions ou variations de la même carte. Parfois, l'une des variations est à tirage relativement limité.

VERT. Pose verticale de la carte.

VEZINA. Trophée accordé au meilleur gardien de but NHL.

VP. Vice président.

WHA. "World Hockey Association": association mondiale de hockey.

WHL. "Western Hockey League": ligue de hockey de l'ouest.

HISTORY OF HOCKEY CARDS

Hockey cards have been produced for much longer periods than football or basketball cards—a fact no doubt influenced by hockey's predominance in Canada as their national pastime. Cigarette companies issued hockey cards from 1910 to 1913. While three distinct cigarette card sets have been identified, the manufacturers of these sets have not been determined. During the 1920s, four candy hockey sets and one cigarette hockey set were issued; none were in color. It was not until the 1930s that the Canadian gum companies started issuing card premiums with their chewing gum. World Wide Gum Company and the familiar O-Pee-Chee were among these early Canadian hockey issuers. Bee Hive photos made their first appearance during the 1930s also. This Canadian chewing gum card awakening parallels Goudey and National Chicle emerging as gum card issuers in the United States.

The recent history of hockey cards begins with the post-World War II Parkhurst issues of the 1950s and early 1960s. Parkhurst issued hockey card sets from 1951 through 1964, except for the 1956-57 season. Topps started issuing hockey cards in 1954. Then after a two-year hiatus, it issued cards regularly from the 1957-58 season to the present with the exception of a break for the 1982-83 and 1983-84 seasons. During the 1950s, Topps typically issued cards of players from American teams while Parkhurst issued cards with players from the two Canadian teams existing at the time, Montreal and Toronto. From the 1960-61 season until its demise after the 1963-64 season, Parkhurst issued cards of the two Canadian teams plus Detroit, while Topps issued cards of the remaining three American teams. Beginning with the 1964-65 season, Topps issued players from all teams in the NHL.

Topps attempted to produce a 66-card set aimed strictly for the American market, with no French on the cards, in 1966-67. This test issue, now quite scarce, is very similar to the regular 1966-67 Topps set and includes a Bobby Orr card.

O-Pee-Chee reentered the hockey card market in 1968, and has issued sets from the 1968–69 season to the present. O-Pee-Chee sets are larger in size compared to Topps sets, perhaps a reflection of the relative popularity of hockey in Canada as compared to the United States. O-Pee-Chee also issued separate card sets containing World Hockey Association players for a four-year period between the 1974–75 and 1977–78 seasons. During recent years, beginning with the 1974-75

L'HISTOIRE DES CARTES DE HOCKEY

Les cartes de hockey sont en production depuis beaucoup plus longtemps que les cartes de foot-ball ou de basket-ball—un fait qui a sans aucun doute été influencé par la prédominance du Hockey au Canada en temps que passe-temps national. Les marques de cigarettes ont émis des cartes de hockey depuis 1910 jusqu'en 1913. Alors que trois jeux de cartes distincts de marques de cigarettes ont pu être identifiés, les fabricants de ces jeux n'ont pas pu être définis. Au cours des années 20, quatre jeux de hockey ont été produits par des marques de bonbons, et un jeu par une marque de cigarettes; pas un seul en couleur. Ce n'est pas avant les années 30 que les marques canadiennes de gommes ont commencé à émettre des cartes distribuées en primes avec leur chewing-gum. "World Wide Gum Company" et la familière société "O-Pee-Chee" font partie de ces émetteurs canadiens du début. Les photographies "Bee Hive" ont fait leur première apparition pendant les années 30 également. Cette carte canadienne de chewing-gum a parallèlement éveillé l'attention des compagnies "Goudey" et "National Chicle" en tant qu'initiateurs de producteurs de cartes aux Etats-Unis.

L'histoire récente des cartes de hockey commence avec les émissions de Parkhurst après la deuxième guerre mondiale au cours des années 50 et au début des années 60. Parkhurst a émis des jeux de cartes de hockey de 1951 à 1964, sauf pour la saison 1956-57. Topps a commencé à faire des cartes de hockey en 1954. Puis, après deux années de relâche, Topps a émis régulièrement des cartes depuis la saison 1957-58 jusqu'à maintenant à l'exception d'un arrêt concernant les saisons 1982-83 et 1983-84. Au cours des années 50, Topps a produit de façon typique des cartes de joueurs des équipes américaines alors que Parkhurst a émis des cartes de joueurs des deux équipes canadiennes existantes à l'époque, Montréal et Toronto. De la saison 1960-61 jusqu'à sa fin après la saison 1963-64, Parkhurst a produit des cartes des deux équipes canadiennes et de l'équipe de Détroit, tandis que Topps produisait les cartes des trois équipes américaines subsistantes. A partir de la saison 1964-65, Topps a fait des cartes des joueurs de toutes les équipes du NHL.

En 1966-67, Topps a essayé de faire un jeu des cartes-66 consacré exclusivement au marché américain, sans un mot en français sur les cartes. Cette édition d'essai, pas spécialement à tirage limité, est très ressemblante au jeu normal Topps 1966- 67 et comprend une carte de

season, the Topps cards have been nearly identical to the O-Pee-Chee cards (the OPC's have white backs, the Topps gray).

In 1990–91, the NHL card market saw five new major sets: Bowman, O-Pee-Chee Premier, Pro Set, Score, and Upper Deck. Most represented significant improvements over the quality of previous sets, and all enjoyed moderate to superb levels of success. Needless to say, this reflects the growing interest in hockey cards. Score and Upper Deck issued Canadian and French sets, respectively, which drew attention from collectors due to their perceived relative scarcity. Score's debut sets were partially fueled by the inclusion of ultratalented prospect Eric Lindros. Upper Deck matched Score by including a Canadian National Junior Championship subset (featuring Lindros, Pat Falloon, and Scott Neidermayer, who were the top three picks, respectively, in the 1991 NHL draft) in its "high number" set.

Bobby Orr.

O-Pee-Chee revient au marché de la carte de hockey en 1968, et a émis des jeux de la saison 1968-69 jusqu'à maintenant. Les jeux de O-Pee-Chee sont d'une taille plus importante que ceux de Topps, sans doute une conséquence de la popularité relative du hockey au Canada par rapport aux Etats-Unis. O-Pee-Chee a également produit des jeux de cartes distincts concernant les joueurs de l'association mondiale de hockey durant une période de quatre années entre 1974-75 et 1977-78. Au cours des années récentes, à partir de la saison 1974-75, les cartes Topps ont été pratiquement identiques aux cartes O-Pee-Chee (les cartes OPC ont un dos blanc, et les cartes Topps un dos gris).

En 1990-91, le marché des cartes NHL a vu l'arrivée de cinq nouveaux jeux principaux: "Bowman," "O-Pee-Chee Premier," "Pro Set," "Score" et "Upper Deck." La plupart présentent des améliorations substantielles par rapport à la qualité des jeux précédents, et tous ont goûté un succés soit modéré soit magnifique. Il n'est pas besoin de dire que cela reflète un intérêt croissant concernant les cartes de hockey. Score et Upper Deck ont sorti des jeux canadiens et français, respectivement, qui ont attiré l'attention des collectionneurs à cause d'un tirage relativement limité. Les premiers jeux de Score ont été partiellement alimentés par l'inclusion de l'espoir plein de talent Eric Lindros. Upper Deck a maintenu le niveau avec Score en incluant un sous-jeu, dans les chiffres élevés ("high number") pour le championnat canadien "Canadian National Junior Championship" (représentant Lindros, Pat Falloon et Scott Neidermayer, les trois meilleurs choix, respectivement, du tirage NHL 1991).

BUSINESS OF SPORTS CARD COLLECTING

Determining Value

Why are some cards more valuable than others? Obviously, the economic law of supply and demand is applicable to sports card collecting just as it is to any other field where a commodity is bought, sold, or traded.

Supply (the number of cards available on the market) is less than the total number of cards originally produced since attrition diminishes that original quantity. Each year a percentage of cards is thrown away, destroyed, or otherwise lost to collectors. This percentage is much smaller today than it was in the past because more and more people have become increasingly aware of the value of sports cards. For those who collect only Mint condition cards, the supply of older cards can be quite small indeed. Until recently, collectors were not so conscious of the need to preserve the condition of their cards. For this reason, it is difficult to know exactly how many 1957-58 Topps hockey cards are currently available—Mint or otherwise. It is generally accepted that there are fewer 1957-58 Topps available than 1967-68, 1977-78, or 1987-88 Topps hockey cards. If demand were equal for each of these sets, the law of supply and demand would increase the price for the least available sets. But demand is based on many factors and changes constantly, making price correlation an inexact science.

The total number of cards produced for any given issue can only be approximated, as compared to other collectibles such as coins and stamps. The reason is simple: card manufacturers are predominantly private companies which are not required to reveal such internal information, while governments are required to release figures regarding currency and postage stamp production.

The demand for any given card is influenced by many factors. These include: (1) the age of the card; (2) the number of cards printed; (3) the

COMMENT COLLECTIONNER
LES CARTES SPORTIVES

L'évaluation

Pourquoi certaines cartes ont-elles plus de valeur que d'autres? Visiblement, la loi économique de l'offre et de la demande est applicable à la collection des cartes sportives comme à n'importe quel autre domaine où une marchandise est achetée, vendue ou échangée.

Le volume disponible (le nombre de cartes sur le marché) est inférieur au nombre total de cartes originellement produites du fait d'un phénomène d'attrition. Chaque année un pourcentage de cartes est jeté, détruit, ou de toute façon perdu pour les collectionneurs. Ce pourcentage est beaucoup moins important aujourd'hui qu'il ne l'était dans le passé parce que de plus en plus de gens ont pris davantage conscience de la valeur des cartes sportives. Pour ceux qui ne collectionnent que les cartes en état absolument parfait, le volume de cartes plus anciennes peut évidemment devenir assez réduit. Jusqu'à une période récente, les collectionneurs n'avaient pas autant conscience de la nécessité de préserver l'état de leurs cartes. Pour cette raison, il est difficile de savoir exactement combien de cartes de hockey Topps 1957-58 sont actuellement disponibles—qu'elles soient en parfait état ou non. Il est généralement accepté qu'il y a moins de cartes de hockey Topps disponibles pour 1957-58 que pour 1967-68, 1977-78 ou 1987-88. S'il y avait la même demande pour chacun de ces jeux, la loi de l'offre et de la demande augmenterait le prix des jeux les moins disponibles. Mais la demande est basée sur de nombreux facteurs et change constamment, faisant de la corrélation du prix une science inexacte.

Le nombre total de cartes produites pour chaque émission donnée ne peut qu'être approximatif, par comparaison à d'autres objets de collections comme les pièces de monnaie et les timbres.

La raison en est simple: les fabricants de cartes sont en majorité des sociétés privées qui n'ont pas l'obligation de révéler semblable information, alors que les gouvernements ont l'obligation de publier le volume de leurs productions de pièces et de timbres.

player(s) portrayed on the card; (4) the attractiveness and popularity of the set; and perhaps most importantly, (5) the physical condition of the card.

In general, (1) the older the card, (2) the fewer the number of the cards printed, (3) the more famous and/or successful the player, (4) the more attractive and popular the set, or (5) the better the condition of the card, the higher the value of the card will be. There are exceptions to all but one of these factors: the condition of the card. Given two cards similar in all respects except condition, the one in the best condition will *always* be valued higher.

While there are certain guidelines that help to establish the value of a card, the numerous exceptions and peculiarities make any simple, direct mathematical formula to determine card values impossible.

One certainty in the sports card hobby is the high demand for Rookie Cards, specifically for RCs of superstar players. A Rookie Card is defined as the first card from a major set of a particular player.

Regional Variation

Two types of regional price variations exist. The first is the general variation on all cards bought and sold in one geographical area as compared to another. Card prices are slightly higher on the East and West coasts, and slightly lower in the middle of the country. Although prices may vary from the East to the West, or from the Southwest to the Midwest, the prices listed in this guide are nonetheless presented as a consensus of all sections of this large and diverse country. Canadian prices, reflecting the exchange rate, generally are 10 percent higher than the prices in this guide.

Still, prices for a particular player's cards are usually higher in his home team's area than in other regions. This represents the second type of regional price variation in which local players are favored over those from distant areas. For example, a Bobby Hull card is valued higher in Chicago than in Boston because Hull played in Chicago; therefore, the demand there for Hull cards is higher than it is in Boston. On the other hand, a Bobby Orr card is priced higher in Boston than in Chicago for similar reasons. Sometimes even common player cards command a premium from hometown collectors. Hockey, in fact, probably has the

La demande concernant toute carte en particulier est influencée par de nombreux facteurs. Cela comprend: (1) l'âge de la carte ; (2) le nombre de cartes imprimées ; (3) le ou les joueurs représentés sur la carte ; (4) l'attraction ou la popularité exercées par ce jeu de cartes ; et peut-être le plus important, (5) la condition physique de la carte.

Généralement, (1) plus la carte est ancienne, (2) moins il en a été imprimé, (3) le plus célèbre et/ou le plus couvert de succès se trouve le joueur, (4) le plus attractif et populaire est le jeu, ou (5) le meilleur état dans lequel se trouve la carte, le plus élevé sera le prix de la carte. Il existe des exceptions pour tous les facteurs sauf l'un d'eux: l'état dans lequel se trouve la carte. Prenez deux cartes similaires en tout sauf leur état, celle en meilleur état vaudra toujours davantage.

Alors qu'il existe certaines directives qui aident à définir la valeur d'une carte, de nombreuses exceptions et particularités font qu'il est impossible d'établir une formule mathématique simple pour établir la valeur des cartes.

Une chose certaine dans le passe-temps des cartes sportives est la demande élevée pour les cartes de débutants, les "Rookie Cards," spécialement pour les "RC" des super-vedettes. Une "Rookie Card" est définie en tant que la première carte d'un jeu important concernant un joueur précis.

Variation régionale

Il existe deux genres de variations régionales pour le prix. La première est une variation concernant toutes les cartes achetées et vendues à l'intérieur d'une zone géographique par rapport à une autre. Les prix des cartes sont légèrement plus élevés sur les côtes est et ouest, et légèrement plus faibles à l'intérieur du pays. Bien que les prix puissent varier de l'est àl'ouest, ou du sud-ouest au centre occidental, les prix établis dans ce guide sont néanmoins le reflet unanime de toutes les régions de ce grand et varié pays. Les prix canadiens, en conséquence du taux du change, sont généralement 10 pour cent plus élevés que les prix indiqués dans ce guide.

D'autre part, les prix des cartes d'un joueur spécifique sont habituellement plus élevés dans la région berceau de son équipe que

strongest regional premiums of all the major sports. Hockey also is a very seasonal market, with much more activity during the season.

Set Prices

A somewhat paradoxical situation often exists in the price of a complete set versus the combined cost of the individual cards in the set. In most cases, the sum of the prices for the individual cards is higher than the cost for the complete set. This is especially prevalent for cards issued during the past few years. The reasons for this apparent anomaly stem from the habits of collectors and from the inventory costs of dealers. Today, each card in a set is normally produced in the same quantity as all others in its set. However, many collectors pick up only cards of stars, superstars, and players from particular teams. As a result, the dealer is left with a shortage of certain player cards and an abundance of others. He therefore incurs an expense in simply "carrying" these less desirable cards in stock. On the other hand, if he sells a complete set, he gets rid of a large number of cards at one time. For this reason, he is usually willing to receive less money for a complete set. By doing this, he recovers all of his costs and also earns some profit.

The disparity between the price of the complete set and that for the sum of the individual cards has also been influenced by the fact that the major manufacturers are now pre-collating card sets. Since "pulling" individual cards from the sets of all three manufacturers involves a specific amount of labor (and cost), the "singles" or star card market is not affected significantly by pre-collation. This price disparity is becoming less prevalent among older and scarcer sets, where set prices are now much closer to the sum of the individual card prices. Note that values for O-Pee-Chee cards generally are higher than for the corresponding Topps cards due to scarcity.

Set prices also do not include rare card varieties, unless specifically stated. Of course, the prices for sets do include one example of each type for the given set, but it is assumed to be the least expensive variety.

dans les autres régions. C'est là le second type de variation régionale du prix par laquelle les joueurs locaux sont favorisés au détriment de ceux des régions éloignées. Par exemple, une carte de Bobby Hull vaut plus cher à Chicago qu'à Boston parce que Hull joue à Chicago ; il s'ensuit que la demande pour les cartes de Hull est plus importante à Chicago qu'à Boston. D'un autre côté, une carte de Bobby Orr est parfois plus chère à Boston qu'à Chicago pour les mêmes raisons. Quelquefois, même les cartes d'un joueur ordinaire inspirent une prime de la part des collectionneurs de sa ville. Le hockey, en fait, possède sans doute les primes régionales les plus importantes parmi les sports principaux. Le hockey est aussi un marché très saisonnier, avec une activité beaucoup plus importante durant la saison.

Prix des jeux

Une situation en quelque sorte paradoxale survient souvent dans le prix d'un jeu complet en fonction de la valeur combinée des cartes individuelles de ce jeu. Dans la plupart des cas, le total des prix des cartes prises individuellement est plus élevé que le prix du jeu complet. Ceci prévaut particulièrement en ce qui concerne les cartes émises depuis peu d'années. Les raisons de cette apparente anomalie proviennent des habitudes des collectionneurs et du coût des inventaires des revendeurs. Aujourd'hui, chaque carte d'un jeu est en principe produite dans la même quantité que toutes les autres cartes de ce jeu. Cependant, beaucoup de collectionneurs prélèvent seulement les cartes des vedettes, des super-vedettes, et des joueurs de certaines équipes. Il en résulte que le revendeur se retrouve avec un manque de cartes concernant certains joueurs et une abondance d'autres cartes. Il subit donc un coût à simplement "conserver" dans son inventaire ces cartes moins recherchées.

D'un autre côté, s'il vend un jeu complet, il se défait d'un grand nombre de cartes à la fois. Pour cette raison, il accepte de se faire généralement payer moins cher pour un jeu complet. En agissant ainsi, il couvre toutes ses dépenses et en même temps fait un bénéfice.

La différence entre le prix d'un jeu complet et le total des prix individuels des cartes a également été influencée par le fait que les principaux fabricants pré-collationnent désormais les jeux de cartes. Etant donné

Scarce Series

Scarce series occur because certain O-Pee-Chee and Topps sets were made available to the public each year in more than one series of finite numbers of cards, as opposed to all cards of the set being available for purchase at one time. At some point during the season, interest in the current-year cards usually waned. Consequently, the manufacturers produced smaller numbers of these later series cards. Specific series information, if any, is included above the price lists for each set.

Grading Your Cards

Each hobby has its own grading terminology—stamps, coins, comic books, beer cans, right down the line. Collectors of sports cards are no exception. The one invariable criterion for determining the value of a card is its condition: the better the condition of the card, the more valuable it is. However, condition grading is very subjective. Individual card dealers and collectors differ in the strictness of their grading, but the stated condition of a card should be determined without regard to whether it is being bought or sold.

The physical defects which lower the condition of a card are usually quite apparent, but each individual places his own estimation (negative value in this case) on these defects. We present the condition guide for use in determining values listed in this price guide in the hopes that excess subjectivity can be minimized.

The defects listed in the condition guide below are those either created at the time of printing, such as uneven borders—or those defects that occur to a card under normal handling—corner sharpness, gloss, edge wear, light creases—and finally, environmental conditions, such as browning. Other defects to

que de "soustraire" des cartes individuelles des jeux des trois fabricants implique une quantité spécifique de travail (et d'argent), le marché des cartes individuelles ("singles") de vedettes n'est pas affecté de façon significative par cette pré-collation. Cette différence de prix devient moins dominante parmi les jeux plus anciens ou à plus faible tirage, pour lesquels les prix par jeux sont maintenant beaucoup plus proches du total des prix des cartes individuelles. Notez que les valeurs des cartes 0-Pee-Chee sont en général plus élevées que celles des cartes correspondantes Topps, à cause d'un tirage plus limité.

De plus les prix des jeux ne comprennent pas de variétés de cartes rares, à moins que ce ne soit spécifiquement précisé. Evidemment, les prix des jeux incluent un exemplaire de chaque espèce pour le jeu en question, mais on suppose qu'il s'agit de la variété la moins chère.

Séries à faible tirage

Il existe des séries à faible tirage du fait que O-Pee-Chee et Topps ont rendu certains jeux disponibles au public chaque année dans plus d'une série de nombres définis de cartes, par opposition à toutes les cartes d'un jeu pouvant être achetées d'un coup. A un certain point au cours de la saison, l'intérêt pour les cartes de l'année s'est affaibli. En conséquence, les fabricants ont produit un plus petit nombre de ces cartes de dernières séries. Des renseignements sur des séries particulières, s'il en existe, sont compris au-dessus des listes de prix pour chaque jeu.

La notation de vos cartes

Chaque passe-temps possède sa propre terminologie de notation—les timbres, les pièces, les bandes dessinées, les boites de bière au premier chef. Les collectionneurs de cartes sportives n'échappent pas à cette règle. Un critère invariable pour évaluer une carte est son état: plus la carte est en bon état, plus sa valeur est élevée. Toutefois, la notation de l'état d'une carte est très subjective. Les revendeurs de cartes individuelles et les collectionneurs diffèrent quant à la rigidité de leur notation, mais l'état défini de la carte devrait être établi sans considérer s'il s'agit d'un achat ou d'une vente.

Les défauts physiques qui diminuent l'état d'une carte sont

cards are caused by human carelessness and in all cases should be noted separately and in addition to the condition grade. Among the more common alterations are tape, tape stains, heavy creases, rubber band marks, water damage, smoke damage, trimming, paste, tears, writing, pin or tack holes, any back damage, and missing parts (tabs, tops, coupons, backgrounds).

Centering

It is important to define in words and pictures what is meant by certain frequently used hobby terms relating to grading cards. The following pictures portray various stages of centering. Centering can range from well-centered to slightly off-centered to off-centered to badly off-centered to miscut.

Slightly Off-Centered: A slightly off-center card is one which upon close inspection is found to have one border bigger than the opposite border. This degree is only offensive to a purist.

Off-Centered: An off-center card has one border which is more than twice as wide as the opposite border.

Badly Off-Centered: A badly off-center card has virtually no border on one side of the card.

Miscut: A miscut card actually shows part of the adjacent card in its larger border and consequently a corresponding amount of the primary card is cut off.

Corner Wear

Degrees of corner wear generate several common terms used to facilitate accurate grading. The wear on card corners can be expressed as fuzzy corners, corner wear or slightly rounded corners, rounded corners, or badly rounded corners.

Fuzzy Corners: Fuzzy corners still come to a right angle (to a point) but the point has begun to fray slightly.

d'habitude relativement apparents, mais chacun fait sa propre estimation (en valeur négative dans ce cas) de ces défauts. Nous présentons un guide de l'état des cartes, à utiliser pour déterminer les valeurs inventoriées dans ce guide des prix, avec l'espoir de minimiser une subjectivité excessive.

Les défauts cités dans ce guide de l'état des cartes ci-après, sont ceux provenant soit d'une faute d'imprimerie, comme des bordures inégales—soit de la conséquence normale de manipulations—brillance d'un coin, lustre, usure du bord, plis légers—et finalement des conditions d'environnement comme l'assombrissement brunâtre. D'autres défauts sont causés par le manque d'attention et, en tout état de cause, devraient être notés séparément en plus de la notation de l'état de la carte. Parmi les changements les plus courants subis par les cartes, on trouve la bande adhésive, les taches de bande adhésive, les plis accusés, les marques d'élastiques, les dommages par l'eau, les dommages par la fumée, les rognures, la colle, les déchirures, de l'écriture, des trous d'épingles ou de punaises, toutes sortes de dommages au dos, et des parties manquantes (pattes, le haut, coupons, arrière-plan).

Centrage

Il est important de définir en mots et schémas la signification de certains termes fréquemment utilisés et relatifs à ce passe-temps, pour ce qui est de la notation des cartes. Les schémas représentés ici montrent différentes phases de centrage. Le centrage peut varier de bien centré, à légèrement décentré, à décentré, à largement décentré, jusqu'à mal coupé.

Légèrement décentré: Une carte légèrement décentrée est une carte qui, lors d'une inspection sérieuse, révèle une marge plus importante d'un côté que du côté opposé. Ce stage est désagréable seulement pour un puriste.

Décentré: Une carte décentrée possède une marge plus de deux fois plus large que la marge opposée.

Largement décentré: Une carte largement décentrée pratiquement ne possède aucune marge d'un côté.

Mal coupé: Une carte mal coupée montre positivement une partie de

CENTERING

Slightly Off-Centered

Off-Centered

Badly Off-Centered

Miscut

Corner Wear or Slightly Rounded Corners: The slight fraying of the corners has increased to where there is no longer a point to the corner. Nevertheless, the corner is still reasonably sharp. There may be evidence of some slight loss of color in the corner also.

Rounded Corners: The corner is definitely no longer sharp but is not badly rounded.

Badly Rounded Corners: The corner is rounded to an objectionable degree. Excessive wear and rough handling are evident.

Creases

The third, and perhaps most frequent, common defect is the crease. Unfortunately, the degree of creasing in a card is very difficult to show in a drawing or picture. On giving the specific condition of an expensive card for sale, the seller should note any creases additionally. Creases can be categorized as to severity according to the following scale.

Light Crease: A light crease is a crease which is barely noticeable on close inspection. In fact, when cards are in plastic sheets or holders, a light crease may not be visible until the card is removed from the sheet or holder. A light crease on the front is much more serious than a light crease on the card's back only.

Medium Crease: A medium crease is noticeable when held and studied at arm's length by the naked eye, but does not overly detract from the appearance of the card. It is an obvious crease, but not one that breaks the picture surface of the card.

Heavy Crease: A heavy crease is one which has torn or broken through the card's picture surface, e.g., puts a tear in the photo surface.

Alterations

Deceptive Trimming: Deceptive trimming occurs when someone alters the card in order (1) to shave off edge wear, (2) to improve the sharpness of the corners, or (3) to improve centering.

la carte adjacente du côté de sa marge la plus large et, par voie de conséquence, il lui manque la même portion sur le côté opposé.

Usure des coins

Des degrés d'usure des coins engendrent plusieurs termes communément utilisés pour faciliter une notation correcte. L'usure des coins de cartes peut se définir par des coins duveteux, coins usés ou coins légèrement arrondis, coins ronds, ou coins profondément arrondis.

Coins duveteux: Les coins duveteux possèdent toujours un angle correct (jusqu'à un certain point) mais commencent à s'effilocher légèrement.

Coins usés ou légèrement arrondis: L'effilochure légère des coins s'est augmentée au point que le coin n'est plus anguleux.
Il n'en reste pas moins que le coin montre toujours un angle raisonnable. Il peut y avoir une évidence d'une légère perte de couleur également dans les coins.

Coin rond: Le coin n'est définitivement plus anguleux mais n'est pas encore profondément arrondi.

Coin profondément arrondi: Le coin est rond à un point incontestable. Une usure excessive et une manipulation brutale sont évidentes.

Plis

Le troisième, et sans doute le plus fréquent défaut commun, est le pli. Malheureusement, l'ampleur du pli d'une carte est très difficile à montrer sur un dessin ou une photographie. En décrivant l'état spécifique d'une coûteuse carte à vendre, le vendeur devrait en outre préciser s'il y a des plis. Les plis peuvent être classés en importance selon l'échelle suivante.

Léger pli: Un léger pli est un pli qui est à peine détectable au cours d'une inspection. En fait, quand les cartes sont dans des feuillets ou présentoirs en plastique, un léger pli peut bien ne pas être visible jusqu'à ce que la carte soit retirée de ce feuillet ou ce présentoir. Un léger pli côté face est beaucoup plus sérieux qu'un léger pli au dos de la carte seulement.

Pli moyen: Un pli moyen est détectable quand la carte est tenue et

Obviously, the trimmer's objective is to falsely increase the perceived value of the card to an unsuspecting buyer. The shrinkage is usually only evident if the trimmed card is compared to an adjacent full-sized card or if the trimmed card is itself measured.

Obvious Trimming: This type of trimming is noticeable—and unfortunate. It is usually performed by non-collectors who give no thought to the present or future value of their cards.

Deceptively Retouched Borders: This occurs when the borders (especially on those cards with dark borders) are touched up on the edges and corners with a magic marker of the matching color in order to make the card appear to be Mint.

Categorization of Defects

A *"Micro Defect"* would be fuzzy corners, slight off-centering, printer's lines, printer's spots, slightly out of focus, or slight loss of original gloss. An NrMT card may have one micro defect. An EX-MT card may have two or more micro defects.

A *"Minor Defect"* would be corner wear or slight rounding, off-centering, light crease on back, wax or gum stains on reverse, loss of original gloss, writing or tape marks on back, or rubber band marks. An Excellent card may have minor defects.

A *"Major Defect"* would be rounded corner(s), badly off-centering, crease(s), deceptive trimming, deceptively retouched borders, pin hole, staple hole, incidental writing or tape marks on front, warping, water stains, or sun fading. A VG card may have one major defect. A Good card may have two or more major defects.

A *"Catastrophic Defect"* is the worst kind of defect and would include such defects as badly rounded corner(s), miscutting, heavy crease(s), obvious trimming, punch hole, tack hole, tear(s), corner missing or clipped, destructive writing on front. A Fair card may have one catastrophic defect. A Poor card has two or more catastrophic defects.

examinée à longueur de bras à l'oeil nu, mais ne détruit pas exagérément l'apparence de la carte. C'est un pli sans aucun doute, mais qui n'affecte pas la surface de l'image représentée par la carte.

Pli prononcé: Un pli prononcé a déchiré ou brisé la surface de l'image, par exemple une cassure sur la surface d'une photo.

Altérations

Rognure trompeuse: il y a rognure trompeuse quand une personne retouche la carte dans le but de (1) de faire disparaître l'usure des bords, (2) d'améliorer la brillance des coins, ou (3) d'améliorer le centrage. Assurément, l'objectif du trompeur est d'apporter une plus value falsifiée à la carte au regard d'un acheteur sans soupçons. La diminution de la taille de la carte ne devient généralement évidente que lorsque la carte rognée est comparée à une carte de taille complète, ou en mesurant la carte rognée.

Rognure évidente: Ce type de rognure est détectable—et malheureux. Elle est généralement effectuée par des non-collectionneurs qui n'accordent aucune attention à la valeur actuelle ou future de leurs cartes.

Marges trompeusement retouchées: Ceci arrive quand les marges (particulièrement pour les cartes avec des marges sombres) sont retouchées sur leurs bords et les coins avec un marqueur magique de même couleur afin de faire croire à une carte en parfait état.

Classification des défauts

Un défaut minuscule ou "micro" serait d'avoir des coins duveteux, une image légèrement décentrée, des lignes d'imprimerie, des taches d'imprimerie, un léger flou, ou une perte légère du brillant d'origine. Une carte NrMT (voir ci-dessous) peut avoir un minuscule défaut. Une carte EX-MT (voir ci-dessous) peut avoir deux ou plusieurs défauts minuscules.

Un défaut mineur serait d'avoir un coin usé ou légèrement arrondi, un décentrage, un léger pli au dos, des taches de cire ou de gomme sur l'envers, une perte du brillant original, de l'écriture ou des marques de bande adhésive au dos, ou des marques d'élastiques. Une carte excellente peut avoir des défauts mineurs.

Un défaut majeur serait d'avoir un ou plusieurs coins ronds, un sérieux décentrage, un ou des plis, des rognures détectables, des marges trompeusement retouchées, un trou d'épingle, un trou d'agrafe, une

Condition Guide

MINT (M or MT): A card with no defects. The card has sharp corners, even borders, original gloss or shine on the surface, sharp focus of the picture, smooth edges, no signs of wear, and white borders. A Mint card (that is, a card that is worth a "Mint" price) does NOT have printers' lines or other printing defects or other serious quality control problems that should have been discovered by the producing card company before distribution. Note also that there is no allowance made for the age of the card.

NEAR MINT (NrMT): A card with a micro defect. Any of the following would be sufficient to lower the grade of a card from Mint to the Near Mint category: layering at some of the corners (fuzzy corners), a very small amount of the original gloss lost, very minor wear on the edges, slightly off-center borders, slight wear visible only on close inspection, slight off-whiteness of the borders.

EXCELLENT-MINT (EX-MT): A card with micro defects, but no minor defects. Two or three of the following would be sufficient to lower the grade of a card from Mint to the Excellent-Mint category: layering at some of the corners (fuzzy corners), a very small amount of the original gloss lost, minor wear on the edges, slightly off-center borders, slight wear visible only on close inspection, slight off-whiteness of the borders.

EXCELLENT (EX or E): A card with minor defects. Any of the following would be sufficient to lower the grade of a card from Mint to the Excellent category: slight rounding at some of the corners, a small amount of the original gloss lost, minor wear on the edges, off-center borders, wear visible only on close inspection; off-whiteness of the borders.

VERY GOOD (VG): A card that has been handled but not abused: Some rounding at all corners, slight layering or scuffing at one or two corners, slight notching on edges, gloss lost from the surface but not scuffed, borders might be somewhat uneven but some white is visible on all borders, noticeable yellowing or browning of borders, pictures may be slightly off focus.

GOOD (G): A well-handled card, rounding and some layering at the corners, scuffing at the corners and minor scuffing on the face, borders noticeably uneven and browning, loss of gloss on

trace d'écriture fortuite ou des traces de bande adhésive sur le devant, un gauchissement, des taches d'eau, ou d'être passé par le soleil. Une carte VG (voir ci-dessous) peut avoir un défaut majeur. Une bonne carte peut avoir deux ou plusieurs défauts majeurs.

Un défaut catastrophique: c'est la pire espèce de la catégorie et cela pourrait être un ou des coins profondément arrondis, un mauvais coupage, un ou des plis profonds, rognure évidente, un trou à l'emporte-pièce, un trou de punaise, déchirure(s), un coin manquant ou coupé, trace d'écriture fatale côté face. Une carte passable peut avoir un défaut catastrophique. Une carte mauvaise a deux ou plusieurs défauts catastrophiques.

Guide de l'état des cartes

MINT (M ou MT). Une carte sans défauts, parfaite. La carte a des coins anguleux, des marges égales, le brillant d'origine ou satiné en surface, une netteté de l'image, des bords lisses, aucun signe d'usure, et des bordures blanches. Une carte parfaite (c'est à dire une carte méritant un prix indiscutable) n'a AUCUNE marque d'imprimerie, lignes ou autres, ou ne montre aucun problème relevant d'un contrôle de qualité sérieuse, et qui aurait été dû être découvert par la compagnie productrice avant distribution. Notez également qu'il n'y a aucune indulgence du fait de l'ancienneté de la carte.

NEAR MINT (NrMT). Une carte avec un minuscule défaut: presque parfaite. N'importe lequel des défauts ci-après serait suffisant pour ramener la notation de la carte de "parfaite" à "presque parfaite": épaisseur à quelques-uns des coins (coins duveteux), une très légère perte du brillant d'origine, usure minime sur les bords, marges légèrement décentrées, usure légère seulement visible lors d'une inspection approfondie, légère perte de blancheur des bordures.

EXCELLENT-MINT (EX-MT). Une carte en excellent-proche-de-parfait état, avec des défauts minuscules mais pas de défauts mineurs. Deux ou trois des défauts suivants seraient suffisants pour ramener l'état de la carte de "parfait" à "excellent-proche- de-parfait": épaisseur à quelques-uns des coins (coins duveteux), perte légère du brillant d'origine, usure mineure des bords, marges légèrement décentrées, usure légère seulement visible lors d'une inspection approfondie, légère perte

the face, notching on the edges.

FAIR (F): Round and layering corners, brown and dirty borders, frayed edges, noticeable scuffing on the face, white not visible on one or more borders, cloudy focus.

POOR (P): An abused card: The lowest grade of card, frequently some major physical alteration has been performed on the card, collectible only as a filler until a better-condition replacement can be obtained.

Categories between these major condition grades are frequently used, such as Very Good to Excellent (VG-E), Fair to Good (F-G), etc. Such grades indicate a card with all qualities at least in the lower of the two categories, but with several qualities in the higher of the two categories. In the case of EX-MT, it essentially refers to a card which is halfway between Excellent and Mint.

Unopened Mint cards and factory-collated sets are considered Mint in their unknown (and presumed perfect) state. However, once opened or broken out, each of these cards is graded (and valued) in its own right by taking into account any quality control defects (such as off-centering, printer's lines, machine creases, or gum stains) that may be present in spite of the fact that the card has never been handled outside of the factory.

Cards before 1980 which are priced in the price guide in a top condition of NrMT, are obviously worth an additional premium when offered in strict Mint condition. This additional premium increases relative to the age and scarcity of the card. For example, Mint cards from the late '70s may bring only a 10% premium for Mint (above NrMT), whereas high-demand cards from pre-World War II vintage sets can be sold for as much as double the NrMT price when offered in strict Mint condition.

Note that 1952-53 Parkhurst cards often were damaged when collectors inserted them into the albums designed for the cards. The 1952-53 album in particular was poorly designed—cards almost had to be bent to be inserted—so high-quality examples can command significant additional value.

de blancheur des bordures.

EXCELLENT (EX ou E). Une excellente carte avec des défauts mineurs. N'importe lequel des défauts suivants serait suffisant pour ramener la carte de l'état de "parfait" à "excellent": arrondissement léger de quelques-uns des coins, perte légère du brillant d'origine, usure minime des bords, marges décentrées, usure visible seulement lors d'une inspection approfondie, perte de blancheur des bordures.

VERY GOOD (VG). Très bon état, une carte qui a été manipulée mais sans exagération: quelqu'arrondissement de tous les coins, légère épaisseur ou érafflure d'un ou deux coins, légères ébréchures sur les bords, brillant perdu en surface mais pas d'égratinures, les marges peuvent être en quelque sorte inégales mais du blanc est visible sur les bordures, détectable jaunissement ou brunissement des bordures, images légèrement floues.

GOOD (G). Bon état, une carte convenablement tenue, avec un peu d'arrondissement ou d'épaississement aux angles, érafflures aux coins et quelqu'égratignure mineure en surface, bordures inégales et brunies, perte du brillant sur la face, entailles sur les bords.

FAIR (F). Passable ; coins ronds et égratignés, bordures brunes et sales, bords effilochés, détectables érafflures sur le côté face, blanc disparu sur une ou plusieurs bordures, netteté douteuse.

POOR (P). Une carte mauvaise et dont il n'a pas été pris soin: l'état le plus mauvais pour une carte. Il est fréquent que quelqu'altération physique importante ait été infligée à la carte. A ne collectionner seulement que pour combler un vide en attendant de trouver une carte de remplacement en meilleur état.

Des catégories entre ces principales descriptions d'état des cartes sont souvent utilisées, telles que "de très bon à excellent" (VG-E), "de passable à bon" (F-G) etc... De semblables notations indiquent une carte avec toutes les qualités, tout au moins en fonction de la plus basse de deux catégories, mais avec plusieurs qualités dans la catégorie la plus élevée des deux. Dans le cas de "excellent-proche-de-parfait" (EX-MT), il est essentiellement donné référence à une carte à mi chemin entre excellente et parfaite.

Les jeux non ouverts et collationnés par le fabricant sont considérés parfaits dans leur état non connu (et supposé parfait). Cependant, une fois le paquet ouvert et les cartes séparées, chaque carte est individuellement notée (et évaluée) en tenant compte de tous les défauts de contrôle de qualité (comme un mauvais centrage, des lignes

Selling Your Cards

Just about every collector sells cards or will sell cards eventually. Someday you may be interested in selling your duplicates or maybe even your whole collection. You may sell to other collectors, friends, or dealers. You may even sell cards you purchased from a certain dealer back to that same dealer. In any event, it helps to know some of the mechanics of the typical transaction between buyer and seller.

Dealers will buy cards in order to resell them to other collectors who are interested in the cards. Dealers will always pay a higher percentage for items which (in their opinion) can be resold quickly, and a much lower percentage for those items which are perceived as having low demand and hence are slow moving. In either case, dealers must buy at a price that allows for the expense of doing business and a fair margin for profit.

If you have cards for sale, the best advice we can give is that you get several offers for your cards and take the best offer, all things considered. Note, the "best" offer may not always be the one for the highest amount. And remember, if a dealer really wants your cards, he won't let you get away without making his best competitive offer. Another alternative is to take your cards to a nearby convention and either auction them off in the show auction or offer them for sale to some of the dealers present.

Many people think nothing of going into a department store and paying $15 for an item of clothing for which the store paid $5. But, if you were selling your $15 card to a dealer and he offered you only $5 for it, you might think his mark-up unreasonable. To complete the analogy: most retail stores (and card dealers) that pay $10 for $15 items eventually go out of business. An exception to this is when the dealer knows that a willing buyer for the merchandise you are attempting to sell is only a phone call away. Then an offer of up to 75% of the book value will still allow him to make a reasonable profit due to the short time he will need to hold the merchandise.

d'imprimerie, des faux plis mécaniques, des taches de gomme) qui peuvent être détectés en dépit du fait que la carte n'ait jamais été manipulée en dehors de la fabrique.

Les cartes antérieures à 1980 évaluées dans le guide des prix, en état presque parfait ou NrMT, méritent certainement une prime complémentaire lorsqu'elles sont présentées comme étant en état absolument parfait. Cette prime complémentaire prend de la valeur selon l'ancienneté et la disponibilité de la carte. Par exemple, les cartes parfaites de la fin des années 70 peuvent fournir une prime de seulement 10% pour MT (mieux que NrMT) alors que des cartes en forte demande, des jeux antérieurs à la seconde guerre mondiale, peuvent se vendre pour pratiquement le double de la cote NrMT lorsqu'elles sont offertes strictement en parfaite condition (MT).

Notez que les cartes Parkhurst 1952-53 ont souvent été endommagées lorsque leurs collectionneurs les ont rangées dans des classeurs étudiés pour les cartes. L'album 1952-53 en particulier était mal fait—les cartes devaient presque être pliées pour y être classées—des exemples d'une telle ampleur peuvent occasionner une valeur additionnelle significative.

La vente de vos cartes

Pratiquement tous les collectionneurs vendent ou vendront éventuellement des cartes. Un jour, vous pouvez avoir envie de vendre vos doubles ou peut-être même votre entière collection. Vous pouvez vendre à d'autres collectionneurs, à des amis ou des revendeurs. Vous pouvez même revendre des cartes achetées d'un certain revendeur, à ce même revendeur. Dans tous les cas, il est utile de connaître certains des mécanismes d'une transaction typique entre acheteur et vendeur.

Les revendeurs achèteront des cartes dans le but de les revendre à d'autres collectionneurs de cartes. Les revendeurs paieront toujours un pourcentage plus élevé pour des objets qui (à leur avis) peuvent se revendre rapidement, et un pourcentage nettement plus faible pour des objets réputés comme peu recherchés et donc ne se revendant que lentement. Dans l'un et l'autre cas, les revendeurs doivent acheter à un prix qui couvre leurs dépenses et leur permettent de faire un passable bénéfice.

Si vous avez des cartes à vendre, le meilleur conseil que nous puissions vous donner est de prendre plusieurs offres pour vos cartes et

Nevertheless, most cards and collections will bring offers in the range of 25% to 50% of retail price. Material from the past five to ten years or so is very plentiful. Don't be surprised if your best offer is only 20% of the book value for cards from these recent years.

n'accepter que la meilleure, toutes choses considérées. Notez que la "meilleure" offre n'est pas forcément celle du montant le plus élevé. Et souvenez-vous, si un revendeur désire absolument vos cartes, il ne vous lâchera pas avant de vous avoir fait son offre la plus concurrentielle. Une autre formule est d'emporter vos cartes à une convention proche et soit les vendre aux enchères durant l'exposition soit les proposer à quelques uns des revendeurs présents.

Beaucoup de gens ne trouvent rien à redire au fait de se rendre dans un grand magasin et de payer $15.00 pour une pièce de vêtement que le magasin aura acheté $5.00. Par contre, si vous vouliez vendre votre carte de $15.00 à un revendeur qui ne vous en offrirait que $5.00, vous pourriez penser que sa marge n'est pas raisonnable. Afin de compléter l'analogie: la plupart des boutiques de détail (et les revendeurs de cartes) qui paient $10.00 des objets valant $15.00 font éventuellement faillite. Il peut y avoir une exception à cela quand le revendeur sait que pour la marchandise que vous essayez de lui vendre, il connaît un acheteur à qui il n'a qu'un coup de fil à donner. Alors un offre jusqu'à 75% de l'évaluation indiquée dans le livre lui permettra encore de faire un bénéfice raisonnable dû au fait qu'il ne conservera la marchandise que pendant un court laps de temps.

Quoiqu'il en soit, la plupart des cartes et des collections apporteront des offres de l'ordre de 25% à 50% du prix de détail. La marchandise des cinq à dix dernières années environ existe en grande quantité. Ne soyez pas surpris si votre meilleure offre n'est que de 20% de la valeur portée au livre pour ce qui est des cartes de ces récentes années.

INTERESTING NOTES

The numerically first card of an issue is the single card most likely to experience excessive wear. Consequently, you will typically find the price on card #1 (in Mint condition) much higher than might otherwise be the case. Similarly, but to a lesser extent (because normally the less important, reverse side of the card is the one exposed), the numerically last card in an issue is also prone to abnormal wear. This extra wear and tear occurs because the first and last cards are exposed to the elements (human element included) more than any other cards. They are generally end cards in any "brick" formations, rubber bandings, stackings on wet surfaces, and like situations.

Sports cards have no intrinsic value. The value of a card, like the value of other collectibles, can only be determined by you and your enjoyment in viewing and possessing these cardboard swatches.

Remember, the buyer ultimately determines the price of each sports card. You are the determining price factor because you have the ability to say "no" to the price of any card by not exchanging your hard-earned money for a given card. When the cost of a trading card exceeds the enjoyment you will receive from it, your answer *should* be "no." We assess and report the prices. *You* set them!

We are always interested in receiving the price input of collectors and dealers from around the country. We happily credit major contributors. We welcome your opinions, since your contributions assist us in ensuring a better guide each year. If you would like to join our survey list for the next editions of this book and others authored by Dr. Beckett, please send your name and address to Dr. James Beckett, 4887 Alpha Road, Suite 200, Dallas, Texas 75244.

NOTES D'INTÉRET

La première carte d'une édition, dans l'ordre numérique, est la seule carte devant en principe endurer une usure anormale. En conséquence, vous devriez trouver le prix sur la carte N°1 (en condition parfaite) beaucoup plus élevé qu'il ne devrait l'être autrement. De la même façon, mais à un niveau moindre (parce que l'envers de la carte, le côté normalement le moins important, est celui qui est exposé) la dernière carte d'une édition, dans l'ordre numérique, est aussi sujette à une usure anormale. Cette usure et ces éraflures supplémentaires se produisent parce que les premières et dernières cartes sont plus exposées aux éléments (élément humain compris) que les autres cartes. Il y a généralement des cartes de protection dessus et dessous chaque paquet, supportant les élastiques, le rangement sur des surfaces humides et autres situations du même genre.

Les cartes sportives n'ont pas de valeur intrinsèque. La valeur d'une carte, comme la valeur de tout objet de collection, ne peut être déterminée que par vous-même et le plaisir que vous avez à regarder et posséder ces échantillons de carton.

Souvenez-vous, l'acheteur est celui qui détermine le prix de chaque carte sportive en dernier ressort. Vous êtes le facteur déterminant parce que vous avez la possibilité de dire "non" pour le prix de n'importe quelle carte en refusant d'échanger votre argent dûrement gagné pour une carte donnée. Lorsque le prix d'une carte trouvée dans le commerce dépasse le plaisir que vous en recevrez, votre réponse devrait être "non." Nous évaluons et indiquons des prix. Vous les fixez !

Nous sommes toujours intéressés à écouter la notion d'un prix de la part de collectionneurs ou de revendeurs à travers l'ensemble du pays. Par bonheur, nous avons foi dans ceux qui veulent le plus souvent apporter leur contribution. Vos avis sont les bienvenus, d'autant plus que votre contribution nous aide à assurer une meilleure édition de notre guide chaque année. Si vous désirez faire partie de notre liste d'experts pour les éditions à venir de ce livre ainsi que d'autres écrits par le Dr. Beckett, veuillez envoyer votre nom et adresse à: Dr. James Beckett, 4887 Alpha Road, Suite 200, Dallas, Texas 75244.

ADVERTISING

Within this guide you will find advertisements for sports memorabilia material, mail order, and retail sports collectibles establishments. All advertisements were accepted in good faith based on the reputation of the advertiser; however, neither the author, the publisher, the distributors, nor the other advertisers in the price guide accept any responsibility for any particular advertiser not complying with the terms of his or her ad.

Readers should also be aware that prices in advertisements are subject to change over the annual period before a new edition of this volume is issued each fall. When replying to an advertisement late in the sporting year following the fall release of this volume, the reader should take this into account, and contact the dealer by phone or in writing for up-to-date price quotes and availability. Should you come into contact with any of the advertisers in this guide as a result of their advertisement herein, please mention to them this source as your contact.

PUBLICITÉ

Vous trouverez de la publicité dans ce livre pour le matériel en relation avec les sports, la vente par correspondance, et les établissements de vente au détail d'objets de collection en rapport avec les sports. Toutes les publicités ont été acceptées de bonne foi, basées sur la réputation de leur initiateur ; toutefois ni l'auteur, ni l'éditeur, ni les distributeurs, ou les autres personnes faisant de la publicité dans le guide des prix n'acceptent quelque responsabilité que ce soit à l'égard d'un personne faisant de la publicité et qui ne se conformerait pas aux termes de ladite publicité.

Les lecteurs devraient être également conscients que les prix contenus dans les publicités peuvent changer au-delà de la période annuelle et avant la sortie de l'édition suivante survenant chaque automne. Répondant à une publicité, tard au cours de l'année sportive, à la suite de la mise en circulation de ce volume, le lecteur devrait tenir compte de cela et prendre contact avec le revendeur par téléphone ou par courrier pour une actualisation des prix et de la disponibilité. Si vous contactez des personnes faisant de la publicité dans ce guide, voudriez-vous s'il vous plaît leur faire savoir que ce guide est à l'origine de votre prise de contact.

RECOMMENDED READING

With the increase in popularity of the hobby in recent years, there has been a corresponding increase in available literature. Below is a list of the books and periodicals that receive our highest recommendation and that we hope will further your knowledge and enjoyment of our great hobby.

The Sport Americana Baseball Card Price Guide by Dr. James Beckett (Thirteenth Edition, $14.95, released 1991, published by Edgewater Book Company)—the most informative, up-to-date, and reliable price guide/checklist on its subject matter ever compiled. No serious hobbyist should be without it.

The Official Price Guide to Baseball Cards by Dr. James Beckett (Eleventh Edition, $5.95, released 1991, published by House of Collectibles)—this work is an abridgment of the *Sport Americana Price Guide* immediately above, published in a convenient and economical pocket-size format and provides Dr. Beckett's pricing of the major baseball sets since 1948.

The Sport Americana Football Card Price Guide by Dr. James Beckett (Eighth Edition, $14.95, released 1991, published by Edgewater Book Company)—the most comprehensive price guide/checklist ever issued on football cards. No serious football card hobbyist should be without it.

The Official Price Guide to Football Cards by Dr. James Beckett (Eleventh Edition, $5.95, released 1991, published by House of Collectibles)—an abridgment of the *Sport Americana Price Guide* listed above in a convenient and economical pocket-size format, providing Dr. Beckett's pricing of the major football sets since 1948.

The Sport Americana Hockey Card Price Guide by Dr. James Beckett (First Edition, $12.95, released 1991, published by Edgewater Book Company)—the most informative, up-to-date, and reliable price guide/checklist on its subject matter ever compiled. No serious hobbyist should be without it.

The Official Price Guide to Hockey Cards by Dr. James Beckett (First Edition, $5.95, released 1991, published by House of Collectibles)—this

LECTURES RECOMMANDÉES

Avec l'accroissement de popularité de ce passe-temps au cours des années récentes, il s'est avéré un accroissement identique de littérature disponible sur le sujet. A suivre, il y a une liste de livres et de périodiques que nous recommandons chaudement et qui, espérons-le, augmenteront votre savoir et votre plaisir pour ce qui est de ce magnifique passe-temps.

The Sport Americana Baseball Card Price Guide par le Dr. James Beckett (treizième édition, $14.95, publiée en 1991, éditée par Edgewater Book Company)—le guide des prix/inventaire le plus éducatif, actualisé, et digne de confiance en la matière, qui ait jamais été composé.

The Official Price Guide to Baseball Cards par le Dr. James Backett (onzième édition, $5.95, publiée en 1991, éditée par House of Collectibles)—ce travail est un abrégé du *Sport Americana Price Guide* précédemment décrit, édité dans un format de poche pratique et économique, et qui indique les prix, par le Dr. Beckett, des principaux jeux de base-ball depuis 1948.

The Sport Americana Football Card Price Guide par le Dr. James Beckett (huitième édition, $14.95, publiée en 1991, éditée par Edgewater Book Company)—le guide des prix/inventaire le plus compréhensif jamais publié sur les cartes de foot-ball. Il n'y a pas un sérieux amateur de cartes de foot-ball qui puisse s'en passer.

The Official Price Guide to Football Cards par le Dr. James Beckett (onzième édition, $5.95, publiée en 1991, éditée par House of Collectibles)—un abrégé du *Sport Americana Price Guide* précédemment décrit, édité dans un format de poche pratique et économique indiquant les prix, par le Dr. Beckett, des principaux jeux de foot-ball depuis 1948.

The Sport Americana Hockey Card Price Guide par le Dr. James Beckett (première édition, $12.95, publiée en 1991, éditée par Edgewater Book Company)—le guide des prix/inventaire le plus éducatif, actualisé et digne de confiance sur ce sujet jamais composé. Il n'y a pas un sérieux amateur de cartes de hockey qui puisse s'en passer.

The Official Price Guide to Hockey Cards par le Dr. James Beckett

work is an abridgment of the *Sport Americana Price Guide* immediately above, published in a convenient and economical pocket-size format, and provides Dr. Beckett's pricing of the major hockey sets since 1951.

The Sport Americana Basketball Card Price Guide by Dr. James Beckett (First Edition, $12.95, released 1991, published by Edgewater Book Company)—the most informative, up-to-date, and reliable price guide/checklist on its subject matter ever compiled. No serious hobbyist should be without it.

The Official Price Guide to Basketball Cards by Dr. James Beckett (First Edition, $5.95, released 1991, published by House of Collectibles)—this work is an abridgment of the *Sport Americana Price Guide* immediately above, published in a convenient and economical pocket-size format and provides Dr. Beckett's pricing of the major basketball sets since 1948.

The Sport Americana Price Guide to Baseball Collectibles by Dr. James Beckett (Second Edition, $12.95, released 1988, published by Edgewater Book Company)—the complete guide and checklist with up-to-date values for box cards, coins, decals, R-cards, bread labels, exhibits, discs, lids, fabric, pins, Canadian cards, stamps, stickers, and miscellaneous Topps issues.

The Sport Americana Alphabetical Baseball Card Checklist by Dr. James Beckett (Fourth Edition, $12.95, released 1990, published by Edgewater Book Company)—an alphabetical listing, by the last name of the player portrayed on the card, of virtually all major and minor league baseball cards produced through the 1990 major sets.

The Sport Americana Price Guide to the Non-Sports Cards, 1930–1960, by Christopher Benjamin and Dennis W. Eckes ($14.95, released 1991, published by Edgewater Book Company)—the definitive guide to virtually all popular non-sports American tobacco and bubble gum cards issued between 1930 and 1960. In addition to cards, illustrations and prices for wrappers are also included.

The Sport Americana Price Guide to the Non-Sports Cards by Christopher Benjamin and Dennis W. Eckes (Third Edition, Part Two, $12.95, released 1988, co-published by Den's Collectors Den and

(première édition, \$5.95, publiée en 1991, éditée par House of Collectibles)—ce travail est un abrégé du *Sport Americana Price Guide* précédemment décrit, édité dans un format de poche pratique et économique et indiquant les prix, par le Dr. Beckett, des principaux jeux de hockey depuis 1951.

The Sport Americana Basketball Card Price Guide par le Dr. James Beckett (première édition, \$12.95, publiée en 1991, éditée par Edgewater Book Company)—le guide des prix/inventaire le plus éducatif, actualisé, et digne de confiance sur ce sujet jamais publié. Il n'y a pas d'amateur sérieux qui puisse s'en passer.

The Official Price Guide to Basketball Cards par le Dr. James Beckett (première édition, \$5.95, publiée en 1991, éditée par House of Collectibles)—ce travail est un abrégé du *Sport Americana Price Guide* précédemment décrit, édité dans un format de poche pratique et économique et indiquant les prix, par le Dr. Beckett, des principaux jeux de basket-ball depuis 1948.

The Sport Americana Price Guide to Baseball Collectibles par le Dr. James Beckett (seconde édition, \$12.95, publiée en 1988, éditée par Edgewater Book Company)—le guide/inventaire complet avec les valeurs actualisées des boîtes pour cartes, des pièces, des décalques, des cartes "R," des étiquettes à pain, des expositions, disques, couvercles, écussons, insignes, cartes canadiennes, timbres, auto-collants, et autres objets fabriqués par Topps.

The Sport Americana Alphabetical Baseball Card Checklist par le Dr. James Beckett (quatrième édition, \$12.95, publiée en 1990, éditée par Edgewater Book Company)—un inventaire alphabétique, d'après le nom de famille du joueur montré sur la carte, de pratiquement toutes les cartes des ligues majeures et minimes produites jusqu'aux jeux importants de 1990.

The Sport Americana Price Guide to the Non-Sports Cards, 1930–1960, par Christopher Benjamin et Dennis W. Eckes (\$14.95, publié en 1991, édité par Edgewater Book Company)—le guide déterminant de virtuellement toutes les cartes populaires non-sportives de tabac américain et bubble-gum émises entre 1930 et 1960. En plus de ces cartes, des illustrations et des prix d'emballages sont aussi inclus.

Edgewater Book Company)—the definitive guide to all popular non-sports American tobacco and bubble gum cards. In addition to cards, illustrations and prices for wrappers are also included. Part Two covers non-sports cards from 1961 to 1987.

The Sport Americana Baseball Address List by Jack Smalling and Dennis W. Eckes (Sixth Edition, $12.95, released 1990, published by Edgewater Book Company)—the definitive guide for autograph hunters, giving addresses and deceased information for virtually all major league baseball players, managers, and even umpires, past and present.

The Sport Americana Baseball Card Team Checklist by Jeff Fritsch and Dennis W. Eckes (Fifth Edition, $12.95, released 1990, co-published by Den's Collectors Den and Edgewater Book Company)—includes all Topps, Bowman, Fleer, Play Ball, Goudey, Upper Deck, and Donruss cards, with the players portrayed on the cards listed with the teams for whom they played. The book is invaluable to the collector who specializes in an individual team because it is the most complete baseball card team checklist available.

The Sport Americana Team Football and Basketball Card Checklist by Jane Fritsch, Jeff Fritsch, and Dennis W. Eckes (First Edition, $10.95, released 1990, published by Edgewater Book Company)—the book is invaluable to the collector who specializes in an individual team because it is the most complete football and basketball card team checklist available.

Beckett Baseball Card Monthly, published and edited by Dr. James Beckett—contains the most extensive and accepted monthly price guide, collectible glossy superstar covers, colorful feature articles, "Who's Hot and Who's Not" section, convention calendar, tips for beginners, "Readers Write" letters to and responses from the editor, information on errors and varieties, autograph collecting tips, and profiles of the sport's hottest stars. Published every month, BBCM is the hobby's largest paid circulation periodical.

Beckett Football Card Monthly, Beckett Basketball Monthly, Beckett Hockey Monthly, and *Beckett Focus on Future Stars* were

The Sport Americana Price Guide to the Non-Sports Cards par Christopher Benjamin et Dennis W. Eckes (troisième édition, deuxième partie, $12.95, publiée en 1988, publiée par Den's Collectors Den et par Edgewater Book Company)—le guide déterminant de toutes les cartes non-sportives de tabac américain et bubble-gum. En plus des cartes, des illustrations et des prix d'emballages sont inclus. La deuxième partie couvre les cartes non-sportives de 1961 à 1987.

The Sport Americana Baseball Address List par Jack Smalling et Dennis W. Eckes (sixième édition, $12.95, publiée en 1990, éditée par Edgewater Book Company)—le guide déterminant des chasseurs d'autographes, donnant les adresses et informations défuntes de virtuellement tous les joueurs, directeurs, et même des arbitres, passés et présents, de ligues majeures de base-ball.

The Sport Americana Baseball Card Team Checklist par Jeff Fritsch et Dennis W. Eckes (cinquième édition, $12.95, publiée en 1990, éditée par Den's Collector's Den et Edgewater Book Company)—comprend toutes les cartes Topps, Bowman, Fleer, Play Ball, Goudey, Upper Deck et Donruss, avec le portrait des joueurs sur les cartes inventoriées et les équipes pour lesquelles ils ont joué. Le livre est inestimable pour le collectionneur qui se spécialise dans une équipe unique parce qu'il contient l'inventaire disponible le plus complet des cartes de base-ball.

The Sport Americana Team Football and Basketball Card Checklist par Jane Fritsch, Jeff Fritsch, et Dennis W. Eckes (première édition, $10.95, publiée en 1990, éditée par Edgewater Book Company)—le livre est inestimable pour le collectionneur qui se spécialise dans une équipe unique parce qu'il contient l'inventaire disponible le plus complet des cartes de foot-ball et de basket-ball.

Beckett Baseball Card Monthly, édité et rédigé par le Dr. James Beckett—il s'agit du guide des prix mensuel le plus étendu et accepté, avec, en couverture, images brillantes et à collectionner des super-vedettes, articles d'un caractère coloré, "qui est en vue et qui ne l'est pas," calendrier des conventions, conseils pour débutants, "les lecteurs écrivent": lettres à l'éditeur et ses réponses, information sur les erreurs et variations, conseils pour collectionner les autographes, profils des vedettes de sports les plus en vue. Publié chaque mois, BBCM est le périodique de passe-temps le plus divulgué.

built on the success of *BBCM*. These other publications contain many of the same features as *BBCM* and contain the most relied upon price guides to their respective segments of the sports card hobby.

Beckett Football Card Monthly, *Beckett Basketball Monthly*, *Beckett Hockey Monthly*, et *Beckett Focus on Future Stars* ont été conçus sur le succès de *BBCM*. Ces autres publications comportent la plupart des mêmes caractéristiques que *BBCM* et contiennent les guides de prix les plus dignes de confiance dans leurs secteurs respectifs pour ce qui touche le passe-temps des cartes sportives.

PRICES IN THIS GUIDE

Prices found in this guide reflect current retail rates just prior to the printing of this book. They do *not* reflect the FOR SALE prices of the author, the publisher, the distributors, the advertisers, or any card dealers associated with this guide. No one is obligated in any way to buy, sell, or trade his or her cards based on these prices. The price listings were compiled by the author from actual buy/sell transactions at sports conventions, buy/sell advertisements in the hobby papers, for sale prices from dealer catalogs and price lists, and discussions with leading hobbyists in the United States and Canada. All prices are in U.S. dollars.

PRIX INDIQUÉS DANS LE GUIDE

Les prix trouvés dans ce guide sont le reflet actuel des prix de détail précédant immédiatement la mise de ce livre à l'imprimerie. Ils ne sont pas le reflet du prix "A VENDRE" par l'auteur, l'éditeur, les distributeurs, les personnes faisant de la publicité, ou tous revendeurs de cartes en rapport avec ce guide. Absolument personne n'est obligé, en aucune manière, d'acheter, vendre, ou échanger sa ou ses cartes en se basant sur ces prix. Les listes de prix ont été établies par l'auteur à partir de transactions réelles ventes/achats aux conventions sportives, ventes/achats mis en publicité dans les journaux de passe-temps, prix de ventes indiqués dans des catalogues de revendeurs et listes de prix, et des discussions avec ceux qui sont en tête de file de ce passe-temps aux Etats-Unis et au Canada. Tous les prix sont indiqués en dollars Etats-Unis.

1990-91 Bowman

The 1990-91 Bowman hockey set contains 264 cards measuring the standard size (2½" by 3½"). The fronts feature action color photos with variegated borders in green, yellow, and red. The team name and player's name appear in black lettering below the picture. The backs are tinted blue with black lettering on gray card stock, and provide biographical information and career statistics. The cards are numbered on the back and are arranged alphabetically according to team name as follows: Chicago Blackhawks (1-13), St. Louis Blues (14-26), Boston Bruins (27-40), Montreal Canadiens (41-53), Vancouver Canucks (54-65), Washington Capitals (66-78), New Jersey Devils (79-90), Calgary Flames (91-103), Philadelphia Flyers (104-114), New York Islanders (115-127), Winnipeg Jets (128-139), Los Angeles Kings (140-152), Toronto Maple Leafs (153-164), Quebec Nordiques (165-175), Minnesota North Stars (176-188), Edmonton Oilers (189-201), Pittsburgh Penguins (202-213), New York Rangers (214-226), Detroit Red Wings (227-238), Buffalo Sabres (239-250), and Hartford Whalers (251-262). Topps also produced a high-gloss Tiffany version of this Bowman set that was only available to hobby dealers in complete set cases; supposedly only 3000 Tiffany sets were produced. The Tiffany versions are valued at five times the values listed below.

Le jeu Bowman 1990-91 contient 264 cartes de format standard (2¹/₂" x 3¹/₂"). La face représente une photo d'action en couleurs entourée d'un bord bigarré vert, jaune et rouge. Le nom de l'équipe et du joueur apparaissent en lettres noires sous la photo. Le dos est d'une teinte bleuâtre, avec des lettres noires imprimées sur une pâte de papier grise, et fournit des données biographiques et des statistiques de carrière. Topps a également produit une version Tiffany très luisante du jeu Bowman, uniquement distribuée aux négociants en boîtes de jeux complets. Il semblerait que seulement 3000 de ces jeux aient été produits. Les versions Tiffany sont estimées à quatre fois les valeurs indiquées ci-dessous.

			MINT	EXC	G-VG
	COMPLETE SET (264)		15.00	7.50	1.50
	COMMON PLAYER (1-264)		.03	.01	.00
☐	1	Jeremy Roenick	1.75	.60	.12
☐	2	Doug Wilson	.10	.05	.01
☐	3	Greg Millen	.06	.03	.00
☐	4	Steve Thomas	.06	.03	.00
☐	5	Steve Larmer	.10	.05	.01
☐	6	Denis Savard	.15	.07	.01
☐	7	Ed Belfour	3.00	1.50	.30
☐	8	Dirk Graham	.03	.01	.00
☐	9	Adam Creighton	.08	.04	.01
☐	10	Keith Brown	.03	.01	.00
☐	11	Jacques Cloutier	.12	.06	.01
☐	12	Al Secord UER	.06	.03	.00
		(Photo actually Duane Sutter)			
☐	13	Troy Murray	.06	.03	.00
☐	14	Kelly Chase	.08	.04	.01
☐	15	Dave Lowry	.10	.05	.01
☐	16	Adam Oates	.20	.10	.02
☐	17	Sergio Momesso	.15	.07	.01
☐	18	Paul MacLean	.06	.03	.00
☐	19	Peter Zezel	.06	.03	.00
☐	20	Vincent Riendeau	.25	.12	.02
☐	21	Dave Thomlinson	.12	.06	.01
☐	22	Paul Cavallini	.08	.04	.01
☐	23	Rod Brind'Amour	.40	.20	.04
☐	24	Brett Hull	1.25	.60	.12
☐	25	Jeff Brown	.06	.03	.00
☐	26	Dominic Lavoie	.08	.04	.01
☐	27	Andy Brickley	.03	.01	.00
☐	28	Bob Sweeney	.03	.01	.00
☐	29	Cam Neely	.30	.15	.03
☐	30	Bob Carpenter	.06	.03	.00
☐	31	Ray Bourque	.30	.15	.03
☐	32	Rejean Lemelin	.06	.03	.00
☐	33	Craig Janney	.30	.15	.03
☐	34	Bob Beers	.10	.05	.01
☐	35	Andy Moog	.12	.06	.01
☐	36	Dave Poulin	.06	.03	.00
☐	37	Brian Propp	.08	.04	.01
☐	38	John Byce	.08	.04	.01
☐	39	John Carter	.10	.05	.01
☐	40	Dave Christian	.06	.03	.00
☐	41	Shayne Corson	.12	.06	.01
☐	42	Chris Chelios	.10	.05	.01
☐	43	Mike McPhee	.06	.03	.00
☐	44	Guy Carbonneau	.06	.03	.00
☐	45	Stephane Richer	.12	.06	.01
☐	46	Petr Svoboda UER	.08	.04	.01
		(Photo actually Chris Chelios)			
☐	47	Russ Courtnall	.06	.03	.00
☐	48	Sylvain Lefebvre	.12	.06	.01
☐	49	Brian Skrudland	.06	.03	.00

			MINT	EXC	G-VG
☐	50	Patrick Roy	.20	.10	.02
☐	51	Bobby Smith	.08	.04	.01
☐	52	Mathieu Schneider	.20	.10	.02
☐	53	Stephan Lebeau	.40	.20	.04
☐	54	Petri Skriko	.03	.01	.00
☐	55	Jim Sandlak	.03	.01	.00
☐	56	Doug Lidster	.03	.01	.00
☐	57	Kirk McLean	.08	.04	.01
☐	58	Brian Bradley	.03	.01	.00
☐	59	Greg Adams	.06	.03	.00
		Vancouver Canucks			
☐	60	Paul Reinhart	.06	.03	.00
☐	61	Trevor Linden	.25	.12	.02
☐	62	Adrien Plavsic	.08	.04	.01
☐	63	Igor Larionov	.15	.07	.01
☐	64	Steve Bozek	.03	.01	.00
☐	65	Dan Quinn	.06	.03	.00
☐	66	Mike Liut	.08	.04	.01
☐	67	Nick Kypreos	.08	.04	.01
☐	68	Michael Pivonka	.10	.05	.01
☐	69	Dino Ciccarelli	.08	.04	.01
☐	70	Kevin Hatcher	.08	.04	.01
☐	71	Dale Hunter	.03	.01	.00
☐	72	Don Beaupre	.06	.03	.00
☐	73	Geoff Courtnall	.10	.05	.01
☐	74	Rob Murray	.10	.05	.01
☐	75	Calle Johansson	.03	.01	.00
☐	76	Kelly Miller	.06	.03	.00
☐	77	Mike Ridley	.06	.03	.00
☐	78	Allan May	.10	.05	.01
☐	79	Bob Brooke	.03	.01	.00
☐	80	Viacheslav Fetisov	.20	.10	.02
☐	81	Sylvain Turgeon	.03	.01	.00
☐	82	Kirk Muller	.08	.04	.01
☐	83	John MacLean	.08	.04	.01
☐	84	Jon Morris	.10	.05	.01
☐	85	Brendan Shanahan	.08	.04	.01
☐	86	Peter Stastny	.15	.07	.01
☐	87	Bruce Driver	.06	.03	.00
☐	88	Neil Brady	.10	.05	.01
☐	89	Patrik Sundstrom	.06	.03	.00
☐	90	Eric Weinrich	.25	.12	.02
☐	91	Joe Nieuwendyk	.30	.15	.03
☐	92	Sergei Makarov	.40	.20	.04
☐	93	Al MacInnis	.15	.07	.01
☐	94	Mike Vernon	.12	.06	.01
☐	95	Gary Roberts	.06	.03	.00
☐	96	Doug Gilmour	.06	.03	.00
☐	97	Joe Mullen	.08	.04	.01
☐	98	Rick Wamsley	.06	.03	.00
☐	99	Joel Otto	.03	.01	.00
☐	100	Paul Ranheim	.20	.10	.02
☐	101	Gary Suter	.10	.05	.01

		MINT	EXC	G-VG
☐ 102	Theo Fleury	.75	.35	.07
☐ 103	Sergei Priakin	.12	.06	.01
☐ 104	Tony Horacek	.12	.06	.01
☐ 105	Ron Hextall	.12	.06	.01
☐ 106	Gord Murphy	.10	.05	.01
☐ 107	Pelle Eklund	.06	.03	.00
☐ 108	Rick Tocchet	.15	.07	.01
☐ 109	Murray Craven	.06	.03	.00
☐ 110	Doug Sulliman	.03	.01	.00
☐ 111	Kjell Samuelsson	.03	.01	.00
☐ 112	Ilkka Sinisalo	.03	.01	.00
☐ 113	Keith Acton	.03	.01	.00
☐ 114	Mike Bullard	.03	.01	.00
☐ 115	Doug Crossman	.03	.01	.00
☐ 116	Tom Fitzgerald	.08	.04	.01
☐ 117	Don Maloney	.06	.03	.00
☐ 118	Alan Kerr	.03	.01	.00
☐ 119	Mark Fitzpatrick	.08	.04	.01
☐ 120	Hubie McDonough	.08	.04	.01
☐ 121	Randy Wood	.03	.01	.00
☐ 122	Jeff Norton	.03	.01	.00
☐ 123	Pat LaFontaine	.20	.10	.02
☐ 124	Patrick Flatley	.03	.01	.00
☐ 125	Joe Reekie	.08	.04	.01
☐ 126	Brent Sutter	.06	.03	.00
☐ 127	David Volek	.06	.03	.00
☐ 128	Shawn Cronin	.08	.04	.01
☐ 129	Dale Hawerchuk	.12	.06	.01
☐ 130	Brent Ashton	.03	.01	.00
☐ 131	Bob Essensa	.25	.12	.02
☐ 132	Dave Ellett	.03	.01	.00
☐ 133	Thomas Steen	.06	.03	.00
☐ 134	Doug Smail	.06	.03	.00
☐ 135	Fredrik Olausson	.03	.01	.00
☐ 136	Dave McLwain	.03	.01	.00
	(Card says shoots right, should say left)			
☐ 137	Pat Elynuik	.10	.05	.01
☐ 138	Teppo Numminen	.10	.05	.01
☐ 139	Paul Fenton	.03	.01	.00
☐ 140	Tony Granato	.15	.07	.01
☐ 141	Tomas Sandstrom	.10	.05	.01
☐ 142	Rob Blake	.50	.25	.05
☐ 143	Wayne Gretzky	1.25	.60	.12
☐ 144	Kelly Hrudey	.08	.04	.01
☐ 145	Mike Krushelnyski	.06	.03	.00
☐ 146	Steve Duchesne	.06	.03	.00
☐ 147	Steve Kasper	.06	.03	.00
☐ 148	John Tonelli	.06	.03	.00
☐ 149	Dave Taylor	.08	.04	.01
☐ 150	Larry Robinson	.10	.05	.01
☐ 151	Todd Elik	.15	.07	.01
☐ 152	Luc Robitaille	.20	.10	.02
☐ 153	Al Iafrate	.06	.03	.00

		MINT	EXC	G-VG
☐ 154	Allan Bester	.06	.03	.00
☐ 155	Gary Leeman	.06	.03	.00
☐ 156	Mark Osborne	.03	.01	.00
☐ 157	Tom Fergus	.03	.01	.00
☐ 158	Brad Marsh	.03	.01	.00
☐ 159	Wendel Clark	.06	.03	.00
☐ 160	Daniel Marois	.10	.05	.01
☐ 161	Ed Olcyk	.08	.04	.01
☐ 162	Rob Ramage	.06	.03	.00
☐ 163	Vincent Damphousse	.10	.05	.01
☐ 164	Lou Franceschetti	.10	.05	.01
☐ 165	Paul Gillis	.03	.01	.00
☐ 166	Craig Wolanin	.10	.05	.01
☐ 167	Mark Fortier	.08	.04	.01
☐ 168	Tony McKegney	.03	.01	.00
☐ 169	Joe Sakic	.75	.35	.07
☐ 170	Michael Petit	.03	.01	.00
☐ 171	Scott Gordon	.10	.05	.01
☐ 172	Tony Hrkac	.03	.01	.00
☐ 173	Bryan Fogarty	.25	.12	.02
☐ 174	Mike Hough	.08	.04	.01
☐ 175	Claude Loiselle	.10	.05	.01
☐ 176	Ulf Dahlen	.06	.03	.00
☐ 177	Larry Murphy	.06	.03	.00
☐ 178	Neal Broten	.06	.03	.00
☐ 179	Don Barber	.08	.04	.01
☐ 180	Shawn Chambers	.06	.03	.00
☐ 181	Clark Donatelli UER	.08	.04	.01
	(Born 11/22/67, should be 11/22/65; '77-78 U.S. Olympic team)			
☐ 182	Brian Bellows	.12	.06	.01
☐ 183	Jon Casey	.15	.07	.01
☐ 184	Neil Wilkinson	.10	.05	.01
☐ 185	Aaron Broten	.03	.01	.00
☐ 186	Dave Gagner	.12	.06	.01
☐ 187	Basil McRae	.10	.05	.01
☐ 188	Mike Modano	1.00	.50	.10
☐ 189	Grant Fuhr	.15	.07	.01
☐ 190	Martin Gelinas	.30	.15	.03
☐ 191	Jari Kurri	.20	.10	.02
☐ 192	Geoff Smith	.10	.05	.01
☐ 193	Craig MacTavish	.06	.03	.00
☐ 194	Esa Tikkanen	.12	.06	.01
☐ 195	Glenn Anderson	.08	.04	.01
☐ 196	Joe Murphy	.25	.12	.02
☐ 197	Petr Klima	.10	.05	.01
☐ 198	Kevin Lowe	.06	.03	.00
☐ 199	Mark Messier	.30	.15	.03
☐ 200	Steve Smith	.10	.05	.01
☐ 201	Craig Simpson	.10	.05	.01
☐ 202	Rob Brown	.15	.07	.01
☐ 203	Wendell Young	.15	.07	.01

		MINT	EXC	G-VG
☐ 204	Mario Lemeiux	1.00	.50	.10
☐ 205	Phil Bourque	.03	.01	.00
☐ 206	Mark Recchi	1.50	.75	.15
☐ 207	Zarley Zalapski	.08	.04	.01
☐ 208	Kevin Stevens	1.00	.50	.10
☐ 209	Tom Barrasso	.08	.04	.01
☐ 210	John Cullen	.30	.15	.03
☐ 211	Paul Coffey	.25	.12	.02
☐ 212	Bob Errey	.03	.01	.00
☐ 213	Tony Tanti	.06	.03	.00
☐ 214	Carey Wilson	.03	.01	.00
☐ 215A	Brian Leetch ERR	1.00	.50	.10
☐ 215B	Brian Leetch COR	.50	.25	.05
☐ 216	Daren Turcotte	.75	.35	.07
☐ 217	Brian Mullen	.06	.03	.00
☐ 218	Mike Richter	.45	.22	.04
☐ 219	Troy Mallette	.10	.05	.01
☐ 220	Mike Gartner	.10	.05	.01
☐ 221	Bernie Nichols	.12	.06	.01
☐ 222	John Vanbiesbrouck	.10	.05	.01
☐ 223	John Ogrodnick	.06	.03	.00
☐ 224	Paul Broten	.08	.04	.01
☐ 225	James Patrick	.03	.01	.00
☐ 226	Mark Janssens	.08	.04	.01
☐ 227	Randy McKay	.10	.05	.01
☐ 228	Marc Habscheid	.03	.01	.00
☐ 229	Jimmy Carson	.12	.06	.01
☐ 230	Yves Racine	.12	.06	.01
☐ 231	Dave Barr	.03	.01	.00
☐ 232	Shawn Burr	.03	.01	.00
☐ 233	Steve Yzerman	.35	.17	.03
☐ 234	Steve Chiasson	.06	.03	.00
☐ 235	Daniel Shank	.12	.06	.01
☐ 236	John Chabot	.03	.01	.00
☐ 237	Gerard Gallant	.10	.05	.01
☐ 238	Bernie Federko	.06	.03	.00
☐ 239	Phil Housley	.08	.04	.01
☐ 240	Alexander Mogilny	.50	.25	.05
☐ 241	Pierre Turgeon	.25	.12	.02
☐ 242	Daren Puppa	.12	.06	.01
☐ 243	Scott Arniel	.03	.01	.00
☐ 244	Christian Ruuttu	.03	.01	.00
☐ 245	Doug Bodger	.03	.01	.00
☐ 246	Dave Andreychuk	.06	.03	.00
☐ 247	Mike Foligno	.03	.01	.00
☐ 248	Dean Kennedy	.10	.05	.01
☐ 249	Dave Snuggerud	.12	.06	.01
☐ 250	Rick Vaive	.06	.03	.00
☐ 251	Todd Krygier	.12	.06	.01
☐ 252	Adam Burt	.10	.05	.01
☐ 253	Scott Young	.10	.05	.01
☐ 254	Ron Francis	.12	.06	.01
☐ 255	Peter Sidorkiewicz	.08	.04	.01

			MINT	EXC	G-VG
☐	256	Dave Babych	.06	.03	.00
☐	257	Pat Verbeek	.08	.04	.01
☐	258	Ray Ferraro	.03	.01	.00
☐	259	Chris Goverdaris	.12	.06	.01
☐	260	Brad Shaw	.12	.06	.01
☐	261	Kevin Dineen	.06	.03	.00
☐	262	Dean Evason	.03	.01	.00
☐	263	Checklist 1-132	.06	.01	.00
☐	264	Checklist 133-264	.06	.01	.00

1968-69 O-Pee-Chee

The 1968-69 O-Pee-Chee set contains 216 color cards. The cards measure the standard 2½" by 3½". The horizontally oriented fronts feature the player in the foreground with a washed-out hockey scene in the background. The backs, in both French and English, are printed in red and black ink. The card number, 1967-68 records, a short biography, and a cartoon-illustrated fact about the player are included on the back. The cards were printed in Canada and were issued by O-Pee-Chee, even though the Topps Gum copyright is found on the reverse. The O-Pee-Chee set features many different poses from the corresponding Topps poses of the same player. Card number 193 can be found either numbered or unnumbered. The key rookie in this set is Bernie Parent.

Le jeu O-Pee-Chee 1968-69 contient 216 cartes en couleurs de format standard, 2½" x 3½". La face, orientée horizontalement, représente le joueur à l'avant-plan, avec une scène de hockey en flou à l'arrière-plan. Le dos est imprimé en français et en anglais en encre rouge et noire. Il comprend le numéro de la carte, les statistiques pour 1967-68, une biographie concise, et un fait notable concernant le joueur, illustré d'une caricature. Bien que le droit d'auteur de Topps Gum apparaît au dos, les cartes ont été imprimées au Canada et sont émises par O-Pee-Chee. Le jeu O-Pee-Chee

représente de nombreuses poses qui diffèrent des poses Topps correspondantes du même joueur. La carte numéro 193 se trouve avec ou sans numéro. Bernie Parent est le débutant le plus important de ce jeu.

			NRMT	VG-E	GOOD
		COMPLETE SET (216)	1200.00	600.00	125.00
		COMMON PLAYER (1-216)	2.00	1.00	.20
☐	1	Doug Harvey	15.00	5.00	1.00
☐	2	Bobby Orr	180.00	90.00	18.00
☐	3	Don Awrey UER	2.00	1.00	.20
		(Photo actually Skip Krake)			
☐	4	Ted Green	2.50	1.25	.25
☐	5	Johnny Bucyk	8.00	4.00	.80
☐	6	Derek Sanderson	3.00	1.50	.30
☐	7	Phil Esposito	50.00	25.00	5.00
☐	8	Ken Hodge	3.00	1.50	.30
☐	9	John McKenzie	2.00	1.00	.20
☐	10	Fred Stanfield	2.00	1.00	.20
☐	11	Tom Williams	2.00	1.00	.20
☐	12	Denis DeJordy	2.50	1.25	.25
☐	13	Doug Jarrett	2.00	1.00	.20
☐	14	Gilles Marotte	2.50	1.25	.25
☐	15	Pat Stapleton	2.50	1.25	.25
☐	16	Bobby Hull	65.00	32.50	6.50
☐	17	Chico Maki	2.00	1.00	.20
☐	18	Pit Martin	2.00	1.00	.20
☐	19	Doug Mohns	2.50	1.25	.25
☐	20	John Ferguson	2.50	1.25	.25
☐	21	Jim Pappin	2.00	1.00	.20
☐	22	Ken Wharram	2.00	1.00	.20
☐	23	Roger Crozier	2.50	1.25	.25
☐	24	Bob Baun	2.00	1.00	.20
☐	25	Gary Bergman	2.00	1.00	.20
☐	26	Kent Douglas	2.00	1.00	.20
☐	27	Ron Harris	2.00	1.00	.20
☐	28	Alex Delvecchio	8.00	4.00	.80
☐	29	Gordie Howe	70.00	35.00	7.00
☐	30	Bruce MacGregor	2.00	1.00	.20
☐	31	Frank Mahovlich	15.00	7.50	1.50
☐	32	Dean Prentice	3.00	1.50	.30
☐	33	Pete Stemkowski	2.00	1.00	.20
☐	34	Terry Sawchuk	22.00	11.00	2.20
☐	35	Larry Cahan	2.00	1.00	.20
☐	36	Real Lemieux	2.00	1.00	.20
☐	37	Bill White	4.00	2.00	.40
☐	38	Gord Labossiere	2.00	1.00	.20
☐	39	Ted Irvine	2.00	1.00	.20
☐	40	Eddie Joyal	2.00	1.00	.20
☐	41	Dale Rolfe	2.00	1.00	.20
☐	42	Lowell MacDonald	2.50	1.25	.25
☐	43	Skip Krake UER	2.00	1.00	.20
		(Photo actually Don Awrey)			

			NRMT	VG-E	GOOD
☐	44	Terry Gray	2.00	1.00	.20
☐	45	Cesare Maniago	2.50	1.25	.25
☐	46	Mike McMahon	2.00	1.00	.20
☐	47	Wayne Hillman	2.00	1.00	.20
☐	48	Larry Hillman	2.00	1.00	.20
☐	49	Bob Woytowich	2.00	1.00	.20
☐	50	Wayne Connelly	2.00	1.00	.20
☐	51	Claude Larose	2.00	1.00	.20
☐	52	Danny Grant	2.50	1.25	.25
☐	53	Andre Boudrias	2.00	1.00	.20
☐	54	Ray Cullen	2.00	1.00	.20
☐	55	Parker MacDonald	2.00	1.00	.20
☐	56	Gump Worsley	8.00	4.00	.80
☐	57	Terry Harper	2.50	1.25	.25
☐	58	Jacques Laperriere	4.50	2.25	.45
☐	59	J.C. Tremblay	2.50	1.25	.25
☐	60	Ralph Backstrom	2.00	1.00	.20
☐	61	Checklist 2	40.00	4.00	.80
☐	62	Yvan Cournoyer	8.00	4.00	.80
☐	63	Jacques Lemaire	8.00	4.00	.80
☐	64	Mickey Redmond	4.00	2.00	.40
☐	65	Bobby Rousseau	2.00	1.00	.20
☐	66	Gilles Tremblay	2.00	1.00	.20
☐	67	Ed Giacomin	7.00	3.50	.70
☐	68	Arnie Brown	2.00	1.00	.20
☐	69	Harry Howell	4.50	2.25	.45
☐	70	Alan Hamilton	2.00	1.00	.20
☐	71	Rod Seiling	2.00	1.00	.20
☐	72	Rod Gilbert	7.00	3.50	.70
☐	73	Phil Goyette	2.00	1.00	.20
☐	74	Larry Jeffrey	2.00	1.00	.20
☐	75	Don Marshall	2.00	1.00	.20
☐	76	Bob Nevin	2.00	1.00	.20
☐	77	Jean Ratelle	7.00	3.50	.70
☐	78	Charlie Hodge	2.50	1.25	.25
☐	79	Bert Marshall	2.00	1.00	.20
☐	80	Billy Harris	2.00	1.00	.20
☐	81	Carol Vadnais	2.00	1.00	.20
☐	82	Howie Young	2.00	1.00	.20
☐	83	John Brenneman	2.00	1.00	.20
☐	84	Gerry Ehman	2.00	1.00	.20
☐	85	Ted Hampson	2.00	1.00	.20
☐	86	Bill Hicke	2.00	1.00	.20
☐	87	Gary Jarrett	2.00	1.00	.20
☐	88	Doug Roberts	2.00	1.00	.20
☐	89	Bernie Parent	85.00	42.50	8.50
☐	90	Joe Watson	2.00	1.00	.20
☐	91	Ed Van Impe	2.00	1.00	.20
☐	92	Larry Zeidel	2.00	1.00	.20
☐	93	John Miszuk	2.00	1.00	.20
☐	94	Gary Dornhoefer	2.50	1.25	.25
☐	95	Leon Rochefort	2.00	1.00	.20
☐	96	Brit Selby	2.00	1.00	.20

		NRMT	VG-E	GOOD
☐ 97	Forbes Kennedy	2.00	1.00	.20
☐ 98	Ed Hoekstra	2.00	1.00	.20
☐ 99	Garry Peters	2.00	1.00	.20
☐ 100	Les Binkley	4.00	2.00	.40
☐ 101	Leo Boivin	4.50	2.25	.45
☐ 102	Earl Ingarfield	2.00	1.00	.20
☐ 103	Lou Angotti	2.00	1.00	.20
☐ 104	Andy Bathgate	5.00	2.50	.50
☐ 105	Wally Boyer	2.00	1.00	.20
☐ 106	Ken Schinkel	2.00	1.00	.20
☐ 107	Ab McDonald	2.00	1.00	.20
☐ 108	Charlie Burns	2.00	1.00	.20
☐ 109	Val Fonteyne	2.00	1.00	.20
☐ 110	Noel Price	2.00	1.00	.20
☐ 111	Glenn Hall	8.00	4.00	.80
☐ 112	Bob Plager	3.50	1.75	.35
☐ 113	Jim Roberts	2.00	1.00	.20
☐ 114	Red Berenson	2.50	1.25	.25
☐ 115	Larry Keenan	2.00	1.00	.20
☐ 116	Camille Henry	2.00	1.00	.20
☐ 117	Gary Sabourin	2.00	1.00	.20
☐ 118	Ron Schock	2.00	1.00	.20
☐ 119	Gary Veneruzzo	2.00	1.00	.20
☐ 120	Gerry Melnyk	2.00	1.00	.20
☐ 121	Checklist Card	40.00	4.00	.80
☐ 122	Johnny Bower	6.50	3.25	.65
☐ 123	Tim Horton	7.00	3.50	.70
☐ 124	Pierre Pilote	4.50	2.25	.45
☐ 125	Marcel Pronovost	4.50	2.25	.45
☐ 126	Ron Ellis	2.00	1.00	.20
☐ 127	Paul Henderson	2.50	1.25	.25
☐ 128	Al Arbour	3.50	1.75	.35
☐ 129	Bob Pulford	4.50	2.25	.45
☐ 130	Floyd Smith	2.00	1.00	.20
☐ 131	Norm Ullman	6.00	3.00	.60
☐ 132	Mike Walton	2.50	1.25	.25
☐ 133	Ed Johnston	3.00	1.50	.30
☐ 134	Glen Sather	3.00	1.50	.30
☐ 135	Ed Westfall	2.50	1.25	.25
☐ 136	Dallas Smith	2.50	1.25	.25
☐ 137	Eddie Shack	2.50	1.25	.25
☐ 138	Gary Doak	2.50	1.25	.25
☐ 139	Ron Murphy	2.00	1.00	.20
☐ 140	Gerry Cheevers	9.00	4.50	.90
☐ 141	Bob Falkenberg	2.00	1.00	.20
☐ 142	Garry Unger	9.00	4.50	.90
☐ 143	Peter Mahovlich	3.00	1.50	.30
☐ 144	Roy Edwards	2.00	1.00	.20
☐ 145	Gary Bauman	2.00	1.00	.20
☐ 146	Bob McCord	2.00	1.00	.20
☐ 147	Elmer Vasko	2.00	1.00	.20
☐ 148	Bill Goldsworthy	3.50	1.75	.35
☐ 149	Jean Paul Parise	2.50	1.25	.25

		NRMT	VG-E	GOOD
☐ 150	Dave Dryden	2.50	1.25	.25
☐ 151	Howie Young	2.00	1.00	.20
☐ 152	Matt Ravlich	2.00	1.00	.20
☐ 153	Dennis Hull	3.00	1.50	.30
☐ 154	Eric Nesterenko	2.50	1.25	.25
☐ 155	Stan Mikita	15.00	7.50	1.50
☐ 156	Bob Wall	2.00	1.00	.20
☐ 157	Dave Amadio	2.00	1.00	.20
☐ 158	Howie Hughes	2.00	1.00	.20
☐ 159	Bill Flett	2.00	1.00	.20
☐ 160	Doug Robinson	2.00	1.00	.20
☐ 161	Dick Duff	2.00	1.00	.20
☐ 162	Ted Harris	2.00	1.00	.20
☐ 163	Claude Provost	2.00	1.00	.20
☐ 164	Rogatien Vachon	8.00	4.00	.80
☐ 165	Henri Richard	7.50	3.75	.75
☐ 166	Jean Beliveau	14.00	7.00	1.40
☐ 167	Reg Fleming	2.00	1.00	.20
☐ 168	Ron Stewart	2.00	1.00	.20
☐ 169	Dave Balon	2.00	1.00	.20
☐ 170	Orland Kurtenbach	2.50	1.25	.25
☐ 171	Vic Hadfield	2.50	1.25	.25
☐ 172	Jim Neilson	2.50	1.25	.25
☐ 173	Bryan Watson	2.00	1.00	.20
☐ 174	George Swarbrick	2.50	1.25	.25
☐ 175	Joe Szura	2.50	1.25	.25
☐ 176	Gary Smith	3.00	1.50	.30
☐ 177	Barclay Plager UER	3.50	1.75	.35
	(Photo actually Bob Plager)			
☐ 178	Tim Ecclestone	2.00	1.00	.20
☐ 179	Jean Guy Talbot	2.00	1.00	.20
☐ 180	Ab McDonald	2.00	1.00	.20
☐ 181	Jacques Plante	20.00	10.00	2.00
☐ 182	Bill McCreary	3.50	1.75	.35
☐ 183	Allan Stanley	4.50	2.25	.45
☐ 184	Andre Lacroix	3.50	1.75	.35
☐ 185	Jean Guy Gendron	2.00	1.00	.20
☐ 186	Jim Johnson	2.00	1.00	.20
☐ 187	Simon Nolet	2.00	1.00	.20
☐ 188	Joe Daley	3.50	1.75	.35
☐ 189	John Arbour	2.00	1.00	.20
☐ 190	Billy Dea	2.00	1.00	.20
☐ 191	Bob Dillabough	2.00	1.00	.20
☐ 192	Bob Woytowich	2.00	1.00	.20
☐ 193A	Keith McCreary ERR	6.00	3.00	.60
	(No number)			
☐ 193B	Keith McCreary COR	3.00	1.50	.30
☐ 194	Murray Oliver	2.00	1.00	.20
☐ 195	Larry Mickey	2.00	1.00	.20
☐ 196	Bill Sutherland	2.00	1.00	.20
☐ 197	Bruce Gamble	2.00	1.00	.20
☐ 198	Dave Keon	6.00	3.00	.60
☐ 199	Gump Worsley AS1	5.00	2.50	.50

		NRMT	VG-E	GOOD
☐ 200	**Bobby Orr AS1**	75.00	37.50	7.50
☐ 201	**Tim Horton AS1**	5.50	2.75	.55
☐ 202	**Stan Mikita AS1**	10.00	5.00	1.00
☐ 203	**Gordie Howe AS1**	45.00	22.50	4.50
☐ 204	**Bobby Hull AS1**	40.00	20.00	4.00
☐ 205	**Ed Giacomin AS2**	4.50	2.25	.45
☐ 206	**J.C. Tremblay AS2**	2.50	1.25	.25
☐ 207	**Jim Neilson AS2**	2.50	1.25	.25
☐ 208	**Phil Esposito AS2**	25.00	12.50	2.50
☐ 209	**Rod Gilbert AS2**	5.50	2.75	.55
☐ 210	**Johnny Bucyk AS2**	5.50	2.75	.55
☐ 211	**Stan Mikita** .... Hart Trophy Ross Trophy Lady Byng Trophy	16.00	8.00	1.60
☐ 212	**Worsley/Vachon** .... Vezina Trophy	6.00	3.00	.60
☐ 213	**Derek Sanderson** .... Calder Trophy	2.50	1.25	.25
☐ 214	**Bobby Orr** .... Norris Trophy	75.00	37.50	7.50
☐ 215	**Glenn Hall** .... Conn Smythe Trophy	6.00	3.00	.60
☐ 216	**Claude Provost** .... Masterson Trophy	6.00	1.50	.30

1969-70 O-Pee-Chee

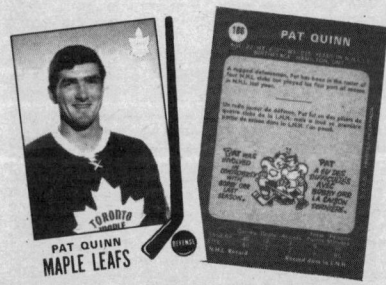

The 1969-70 O-Pee-Chee set contains 231 color cards. The cards measure the standard 2½" by 3½". The backs, in both French and English, contain the card number, 1968-69 and lifetime NHL records, a short biography, and a cartoon-

illustrated fact about the player. The cards were printed in Canada, and the Topps Gum Company copyright appears on the reverse. Many player poses in this set are different from the corresponding player poses of the Topps set of this year. Card 193, Gordie Howe, "Mr. Hockey," apparently exists with or without the number. Those players in this set who were also included in the insert of stamps have a place on the card back for placing that player's stamp; this is not recommended. The key rookie cards in this set are Tony Esposito and Serge Savard.

Le jeu O-Pee-Chee 1969-70 contient 231 cartes en couleurs de format standard, 2¹/₂" x 3¹/₂". Le dos, imprimée en français et en anglais, comprend le numéro de carte, les statistiques pour 1968-69 et pour la carrière NHL du joueur, une biographie concise, et un fait notable concernant le joueur, illustré d'une caricature. Les cartes ont été imprimées au Canada, et le droit d'auteur de la société Topps Gum apparaît au dos. Plusieurs poses des joueurs de ce jeu diffèrent des poses correspondantes du jeu Topps de cette année. La carte numéro 193, représentant Gordie Howe, ou "Monsieur Hockey", existe apparemment avec ou sans numéro. Les cartes des joueurs dont le nom fut inclus dans le supplément de timbres, ont un endroit au dos de la carte pour y placer le timbre; ceci n'est pas recommandé. Les cartes des débutants importants représentent Tony Esposito et Serge Savard.

			NRMT	VG-E	GOOD
		COMPLETE SET (231)	900.00	450.00	90.00
		COMMON PLAYER (1-231)	1.50	.75	.15
☐	1	Gump Worsley	15.00	5.00	1.00
☐	2	Ted Harris	1.50	.75	.15
☐	3	Jacques Laperriere	3.50	1.75	.35
☐	4	Serge Savard	33.00	15.00	3.00
☐	5	J.C. Tremblay	2.00	1.00	.20
☐	6	Yvan Cournoyer	6.50	3.25	.65
☐	7	John Ferguson	2.00	1.00	.20
☐	8	Jacques Lemaire	5.00	2.50	.50
☐	9	Bobby Rousseau	1.50	.75	.15
☐	10	Jean Beliveau	12.00	6.00	1.20
☐	11	Dick Duff	1.50	.75	.15
☐	12	Glenn Hall	7.00	3.50	.70
☐	13	Bob Plager	2.00	1.00	.20
☐	14	Ron Anderson	1.50	.75	.15
☐	15	Jean Guy Talbot	1.50	.75	.15
☐	16	Andre Boudrias	1.50	.75	.15
☐	17	Camille Henry	1.50	.75	.15
☐	18	Ab McDonald	1.50	.75	.15
☐	19	Gary Sabourin	1.50	.75	.15
☐	20	Red Berenson	2.00	1.00	.20
☐	21	Phil Goyette	1.50	.75	.15
☐	22	Gerry Cheevers	6.50	3.25	.65
☐	23	Ted Green	2.00	1.00	.20
☐	24	Bobby Orr	100.00	50.00	10.00
☐	25	Dallas Smith	2.00	1.00	.20
☐	26	Johnny Bucyk	7.00	3.50	.70
☐	27	Ken Hodge	2.50	1.25	.25
☐	28	John McKenzie	1.50	.75	.15

			NRMT	VG-E	GOOD
☐	29	Ed Westfall	2.50	1.25	.25
☐	30	Phil Esposito	30.00	15.00	3.00
☐	31	Checklist 2	27.00	2.50	.50
☐	32	Fred Stanfield	1.50	.75	.15
☐	33	Ed Giacomin	5.50	2.75	.55
☐	34	Arnie Brown	1.50	.75	.15
☐	35	Jim Neilson	1.50	.75	.15
☐	36	Rod Seiling	1.50	.75	.15
☐	37	Rod Gilbert	6.00	3.00	.60
☐	38	Vic Hadfield	2.00	1.00	.20
☐	39	Don Marshall	1.50	.75	.15
☐	40	Bob Nevin	1.50	.75	.15
☐	41	Ron Stewart	1.50	.75	.15
☐	42	Jean Ratelle	6.00	3.00	.60
☐	43	Walt Tkaczuk	6.50	3.25	.65
☐	44	Bruce Gamble	1.50	.75	.15
☐	45	Jim Dorey	1.50	.75	.15
☐	46	Ron Ellis	1.50	.75	.15
☐	47	Paul Henderson	2.00	1.00	.20
☐	48	Brit Selby	1.50	.75	.15
☐	49	Floyd Smith	1.50	.75	.15
☐	50	Mike Walton	2.00	1.00	.20
☐	51	Dave Keon	4.50	2.25	.45
☐	52	Murray Oliver	1.50	.75	.15
☐	53	Bob Pulford	3.25	1.60	.32
☐	54	Norm Ullman	4.50	2.25	.45
☐	55	Roger Crozier	2.00	1.00	.20
☐	56	Roy Edwards	1.50	.75	.15
☐	57	Bob Baun	1.50	.75	.15
☐	58	Gary Bergman	1.50	.75	.15
☐	59	Carl Brewer	1.50	.75	.15
☐	60	Wayne Connelly	1.50	.75	.15
☐	61	Gordie Howe	60.00	30.00	6.00
☐	62	Frank Mahovlich	11.00	5.50	1.10
☐	63	Bruce MacGregor	1.50	.75	.15
☐	64	Ron Harris	1.50	.75	.15
☐	65	Pete Stemkowski	1.50	.75	.15
☐	66	Denis DeJordy	2.00	1.00	.20
☐	67	Doug Jarrett	1.50	.75	.15
☐	68	Gilles Marotte	2.00	1.00	.20
☐	69	Pat Stapleton	2.00	1.00	.20
☐	70	Bobby Hull	40.00	20.00	4.00
☐	71	Dennis Hull	2.50	1.25	.25
☐	72	Doug Mohns	1.50	.75	.15
☐	73	Howie Menard	1.50	.75	.15
☐	74	Ken Wharram	1.50	.75	.15
☐	75	Pit Martin	1.50	.75	.15
☐	76	Stan Mikita	12.50	6.25	1.25
☐	77	Charlie Hodge	2.00	1.00	.20
☐	78	Gary Smith	1.50	.75	.15
☐	79	Harry Howell	3.50	1.75	.35
☐	80	Bert Marshall	1.50	.75	.15
☐	81	Doug Roberts	1.50	.75	.15

		NRMT	VG-E	GOOD
☐ 82	Carol Vadnais	1.50	.75	.15
☐ 83	Gerry Ehman	1.50	.75	.15
☐ 84	Brian Perry	1.50	.75	.15
☐ 85	Gary Jarrett	1.50	.75	.15
☐ 86	Ted Hampson	1.50	.75	.15
☐ 87	Earl Ingarfield	1.50	.75	.15
☐ 88	Doug Favell	3.00	1.50	.30
☐ 89	Bernie Parent	16.00	8.00	1.60
☐ 90	Larry Hillman	1.50	.75	.15
☐ 91	Wayne Hillman	1.50	.75	.15
☐ 92	Ed Van Impe	1.50	.75	.15
☐ 93	Joe Watson	1.50	.75	.15
☐ 94	Gary Dornhoefer	2.00	1.00	.20
☐ 95	Reg Fleming	1.50	.75	.15
☐ 96	Ralph McSweyn	1.50	.75	.15
☐ 97	Jim Johnson	1.50	.75	.15
☐ 98	Andre Lacroix	1.50	.75	.15
☐ 99	Gerry Desjardins	3.00	1.50	.30
☐ 100	Dale Rolfe	1.50	.75	.15
☐ 101	Bill White	1.50	.75	.15
☐ 102	Bill Flett	1.50	.75	.15
☐ 103	Ted Irvine	1.50	.75	.15
☐ 104	Ross Lonsberry	1.50	.75	.15
☐ 105	Leon Rochefort	1.50	.75	.15
☐ 106	Bryan Campbell	1.50	.75	.15
☐ 107	Dennis Hextall	3.00	1.50	.30
☐ 108	Eddie Joyal	1.50	.75	.15
☐ 109	Gord Labossiere	1.50	.75	.15
☐ 110	Les Binkley	2.00	1.00	.20
☐ 111	Tracy Pratt	1.50	.75	.15
☐ 112	Bryan Watson	1.50	.75	.15
☐ 113	Bob Blackburn	1.50	.75	.15
☐ 114	Keith McCreary	1.50	.75	.15
☐ 115	Dean Prentice	2.50	1.25	.25
☐ 116	Glen Sather	3.00	1.50	.30
☐ 117	Ken Schinkel	1.50	.75	.15
☐ 118	Wally Boyer	1.50	.75	.15
☐ 119	Val Fonteyne	1.50	.75	.15
☐ 120	Ron Schock	1.50	.75	.15
☐ 121	Cesare Maniago	2.00	1.00	.20
☐ 122	Leo Boivin	3.25	1.60	.32
☐ 123	Bob McCord	1.50	.75	.15
☐ 124	John Miszuk	1.50	.75	.15
☐ 125	Danny Grant	1.50	.75	.15
☐ 126	Bill Collins	1.50	.75	.15
☐ 127	Jean Paul Parise	1.50	.75	.15
☐ 128	Tom Williams	1.50	.75	.15
☐ 129	Charlie Burns	1.50	.75	.15
☐ 130	Ray Cullen	1.50	.75	.15
☐ 131	Danny O'Shea	1.50	.75	.15
☐ 132	Checklist 1	27.00	2.50	.50
☐ 133	Jim Pappin	1.50	.75	.15
☐ 134	Lou Angotti	1.50	.75	.15

		NRMT	VG-E	GOOD
☐ 135	Terry Cafery	1.50	.75	.15
☐ 136	Eric Nesterenko	2.00	1.00	.20
☐ 137	Chico Maki	1.50	.75	.15
☐ 138	Tony Esposito	90.00	45.00	9.00
☐ 139	Eddie Shack	2.00	1.00	.20
☐ 140	Bob Wall	1.50	.75	.15
☐ 141	Skip Krake	1.50	.75	.15
☐ 142	Howie Hughes	1.50	.75	.15
☐ 143	Jimmy Peters	1.50	.75	.15
☐ 144	Brent Hughes	1.50	.75	.15
☐ 145	Bill Hicke	1.50	.75	.15
☐ 146	Norm Ferguson	1.50	.75	.15
☐ 147	Dick Mattiussi	1.50	.75	.15
☐ 148	Mike Laughton	1.50	.75	.15
☐ 149	Gene Ubriaco	3.00	1.50	.30
☐ 150	Bob Dillabough	1.50	.75	.15
☐ 151	Bob Woytowich	1.50	.75	.15
☐ 152	Joe Daley	2.00	1.00	.20
☐ 153	Duane Rupp	1.50	.75	.15
☐ 154	Bryan Hextall	3.00	1.50	.30
☐ 155	Jean Pronovost	5.00	2.50	.50
☐ 156	Jim Morrison	1.50	.75	.15
☐ 157	Alex Delvecchio	6.50	3.25	.65
☐ 158	Poul Popiel	1.50	.75	.15
☐ 159	Garry Unger	2.50	1.25	.25
☐ 160	Garry Monahan	1.50	.75	.15
☐ 161	Matt Ravlich	1.50	.75	.15
☐ 162	Nick Libett	1.50	.75	.15
☐ 163	Henri Richard	6.00	3.00	.60
☐ 164	Terry Harper	2.00	1.00	.20
☐ 165	Rogatien Vachon	5.00	2.50	.50
☐ 166	Ralph Backstrom	1.50	.75	.15
☐ 167	Claude Provost	1.50	.75	.15
☐ 168	Gilles Tremblay	1.50	.75	.15
☐ 169	Jean Guy Gendron	1.50	.75	.15
☐ 170	Earl Heiskala	1.50	.75	.15
☐ 171	Garry Peters	1.50	.75	.15
☐ 172	Bill Sutherland	1.50	.75	.15
☐ 173	Dick Cherry	1.50	.75	.15
☐ 174	Jim Roberts	1.50	.75	.15
☐ 175	Noel Picard	1.50	.75	.15
☐ 176	Barclay Plager	2.00	1.00	.20
☐ 177	Frank St.Marseille	1.50	.75	.15
☐ 178	Al Arbour	3.00	1.50	.30
☐ 179	Tim Ecclestone	1.50	.75	.15
☐ 180	Jacques Plante	14.00	7.00	1.40
☐ 181	Bill McCreary	1.50	.75	.15
☐ 182	Tim Horton	5.00	2.50	.50
☐ 183	Rick Ley	4.00	2.00	.40
☐ 184	Wayne Carleton	1.50	.75	.15
☐ 185	Marv Edwards	1.50	.75	.15
☐ 186	Pat Quinn	5.00	2.50	.50
☐ 187	Johnny Bower	5.50	2.75	.55

		NRMT	VG-E	GOOD
☐ 188	Orland Kurtenbach	2.00	1.00	.20
☐ 189	Terry Sawchuk	20.00	10.00	2.00
☐ 190	Real Lemieux	1.50	.75	.15
☐ 191	Dave Balon	1.50	.75	.15
☐ 192	Alan Hamilton	1.50	.75	.15
☐ 193A	Gordie Howe ERR "Mr. Hockey" (No number)	150.00	75.00	15.00
☐ 193B	Gordie Howe COR "Mr. Hockey"	75.00	37.50	7.50
☐ 194	Claude Larose	1.50	.75	.15
☐ 195	Bill Goldsworthy	1.50	.75	.15
☐ 196	Bob Barlow	1.50	.75	.15
☐ 197	Ken Broderick	1.50	.75	.15
☐ 198	Lou Nanne	3.00	1.50	.30
☐ 199	Tom Polonic	1.50	.75	.15
☐ 200	Ed Johnston	2.50	1.25	.25
☐ 201	Derek Sanderson	2.00	1.00	.20
☐ 202	Gary Doak	1.50	.75	.15
☐ 203	Don Awrey	1.50	.75	.15
☐ 204	Ron Murphy	1.50	.75	.15
☐ 205A	Phil Esposito Art Ross Trophy Hart Trophy (214 on back and no number on front)	25.00	12.50	2.50
☐ 205B	Phil Esposito Art Ross Trophy Hart Trophy (214 on back and 205 on front)	20.00	10.00	2.00
☐ 206	Alex Delvecchio Lady Byng Trophy	4.00	2.00	.40
☐ 207	Vezina Trophy Winners: Jacques Plante and Glenn Hall	11.00	5.50	1.10
☐ 208	Danny Grant Calder Trophy	2.00	1.00	.20
☐ 209	Bobby Orr Norris Trophy	45.00	22.50	4.50
☐ 210	Serge Savard Conn Smythe Trophy	5.00	2.50	.50
☐ 211	Glenn Hall AS	4.00	2.00	.40
☐ 212	Bobby Orr AS	45.00	22.50	4.50
☐ 213	Tim Horton AS	3.50	1.75	.35
☐ 214	Phil Esposito AS	20.00	10.00	2.00
☐ 215	Gordie Howe AS	40.00	20.00	4.00
☐ 216	Bobby Hull AS	25.00	12.50	2.50
☐ 217	Ed Giacomin AS	3.75	1.85	.37
☐ 218	Ted Green AS	2.00	1.00	.20
☐ 219	Ted Harris AS	2.00	1.00	.20
☐ 220	Jean Beliveau AS	8.00	4.00	.80
☐ 221	Yvan Cournoyer AS	5.00	2.50	.50

		NRMT	VG-E	GOOD
☐ 222	Frank Mahovlich AS	8.00	4.00	.80
☐ 223	Art Ross Trophy	3.50	1.75	.35
☐ 224	Hart Trophy	3.50	1.75	.35
☐ 225	Lady Byng Trophy	3.50	1.75	.35
☐ 226	Vezina Trophy	3.50	1.75	.35
☐ 227	Calder Trophy	3.50	1.75	.35
☐ 228	James Norris Trophy	3.50	1.75	.35
☐ 229	Conn Smythe Trophy	3.50	1.75	.35
☐ 230	Prince of Wales Trophy	3.50	1.75	.35
☐ 231	The Stanley Cup	15.00	5.00	1.00

1970-71 O-Pee-Chee

DARRYL SITTLER   CENTER
TORONTO MAPLE LEAFS

The 1970-71 O-Pee-Chee set contains 264 color cards. The cards measure the standard, 2½" by 3½". The backs, in both French and English, feature the card number, a short biography, the player's NHL record, and the O-Pee-Chee copyright. The cards were printed in Canada, and many player poses are different from the Topps set of this year. Card 231 is a special memorial to Terry Sawchuk, who passed away earlier in the year. The key rookie cards in this set are Bobby Clarke, Brad Park, Gilbert Perreault, and Darryl Sittler.

Le jeu O-Pee-Chee de 1970-71 contient 264 cartes en couleurs de format standard, 2½" x 3½". Le dos, imprimé en français et en anglais, comprend le numéro de carte, une biographie concise, la fiche NHL du joueur, et le droit d'auteur O-Pee-Chee. Les cartes ont été imprimées au Canada, et plusieurs poses des joueurs diffèrent de celles du jeu Topps de cette année. La carte numéro 231 commémore Terry Sawchuk, décédé en début d'année. Les cartes des débutants importants représentent Bobby Clarke, Brad Park, Gilbert Perreault, et Darryl Sittler.

			NRMT	VG-E	GOOD
		COMPLETE SET (264)	800.00	400.00	80.00
		COMMON PLAYER (1-264)	1.35	.65	.13
☐	1	Gerry Cheevers	16.00	5.00	1.00
☐	2	Johnny Bucyk	6.00	3.00	.60
☐	3	Bobby Orr	75.00	37.50	7.50
☐	4	Don Awrey	1.35	.65	.13
☐	5	Fred Stanfield	1.35	.65	.13
☐	6	John McKenzie	1.35	.65	.13
☐	7	Wayne Cashman	10.00	5.00	1.00
☐	8	Ken Hodge	2.00	1.00	.20
☐	9	Wayne Carleton	1.35	.65	.13
☐	10	Garnet Bailey	1.35	.65	.13
☐	11	Phil Esposito	21.00	10.50	2.10
☐	12	Lou Angotti	1.35	.65	.13
☐	13	Jim Pappin	1.35	.65	.13
☐	14	Dennis Hull	2.00	1.00	.20
☐	15	Bobby Hull	30.00	15.00	3.00
☐	16	Doug Mohns	1.35	.65	.13
☐	17	Pat Stapleton	1.75	.85	.17
☐	18	Pit Martin	1.35	.65	.13
☐	19	Eric Nesterenko	1.75	.85	.17
☐	20	Stan Mikita	12.00	6.00	1.20
☐	21	Roy Edwards	1.35	.65	.13
☐	22	Frank Mahovlich	10.00	5.00	1.00
☐	23	Ron Harris	1.35	.65	.13
☐	24	Checklist 1	25.00	2.50	.50
☐	25	Pete Stemkowski	1.35	.65	.13
☐	26	Garry Unger	2.50	1.25	.25
☐	27	Bruce MacGregor	1.35	.65	.13
☐	28	Larry Jeffrey	1.35	.65	.13
☐	29	Gordie Howe	45.00	22.50	4.50
☐	30	Billy Dea	1.35	.65	.13
☐	31	Denis DeJordy	1.75	.85	.17
☐	32	Matt Ravlich	1.35	.65	.13
☐	33	Dave Amadio	1.35	.65	.13
☐	34	Gilles Marotte	1.75	.85	.17
☐	35	Eddie Shack	1.75	.85	.17
☐	36	Bob Pulford	2.75	1.35	.27
☐	37	Ross Lonsberry	1.35	.65	.13
☐	38	Gord Labossiere	1.35	.65	.13
☐	39	Eddie Joyal	1.35	.65	.13
☐	40	Gump Worsley	6.50	3.25	.65
☐	41	Bob McCord	1.35	.65	.13
☐	42	Leo Boivin	3.00	1.50	.30
☐	43	Tom Reid	1.35	.65	.13
☐	44	Charlie Burns	1.35	.65	.13
☐	45	Bob Barlow	1.35	.65	.13
☐	46	Bill Goldsworthy	1.75	.85	.17
☐	47	Danny Grant	1.35	.65	.13
☐	48	Norm Beaudin	1.35	.65	.13
☐	49	Rogatien Vachon	4.00	2.00	.40
☐	50	Yvan Cournoyer	5.00	2.50	.50

			NRMT	VG-E	GOOD
☐	51	Serge Savard	4.00	2.00	.40
☐	52	Jacques Laperriere	3.00	1.50	.30
☐	53	Terry Harper	1.75	.85	.17
☐	54	Ralph Backstrom	1.35	.65	.13
☐	55	Jean Beliveau	10.00	5.00	1.00
☐	56	Claude Larose	1.35	.65	.13
☐	57	Jacques Lemaire	4.50	2.25	.45
☐	58	Peter Mahovlich	1.75	.85	.17
☐	59	Tim Horton	4.50	2.25	.45
☐	60	Bob Nevin	1.35	.65	.13
☐	61	Dave Balon	1.35	.65	.13
☐	62	Vic Hadfield	1.75	.85	.17
☐	63	Rod Gilbert	5.00	2.50	.50
☐	64	Ron Stewart	1.35	.65	.13
☐	65	Ted Irvine	1.35	.65	.13
☐	66	Arnie Brown	1.35	.65	.13
☐	67	Brad Park	45.00	22.50	4.50
☐	68	Ed Giacomin	4.25	2.10	.42
☐	69	Gary Smith	1.35	.65	.13
☐	70	Carol Vadnais	1.35	.65	.13
☐	71	Doug Roberts	1.35	.65	.13
☐	72	Harry Howell	3.00	1.50	.30
☐	73	Joe Szura	1.35	.65	.13
☐	74	Mike Laughton	1.35	.65	.13
☐	75	Gary Jarrett	1.35	.65	.13
☐	76	Bill Hicke	1.35	.65	.13
☐	77	Paul Andrea	1.35	.65	.13
☐	78	Bernie Parent	12.00	6.00	1.20
☐	79	Joe Watson	1.35	.65	.13
☐	80	Ed Van Impe	1.35	.65	.13
☐	81	Larry Hillman	1.35	.65	.13
☐	82	George Swarbrick	1.35	.65	.13
☐	83	Bill Sutherland	1.35	.65	.13
☐	84	Andre Lacroix	1.35	.65	.13
☐	85	Gary Dornhoefer	1.75	.85	.17
☐	86	Jean Guy Gendron	1.35	.65	.13
☐	87	Al Smith	1.35	.65	.13
☐	88	Bob Woytowich	1.35	.65	.13
☐	89	Duane Rupp	1.35	.65	.13
☐	90	Jim Morrison	1.35	.65	.13
☐	91	Ron Schock	1.35	.65	.13
☐	92	Ken Schinkel	1.35	.65	.13
☐	93	Keith McCreary	1.35	.65	.13
☐	94	Bryan Hextall	1.35	.65	.13
☐	95	Wayne Hicks	1.35	.65	.13
☐	96	Gary Sabourin	1.35	.65	.13
☐	97	Ernie Wakely	1.35	.65	.13
☐	98	Bob Wall	1.35	.65	.13
☐	99	Barclay Plager	1.75	.85	.17
☐	100	Jean Guy Talbot	1.35	.65	.13
☐	101	Gary Veneruzzo	1.36	.65	.13
☐	102	Tim Ecclestone	1.35	.65	.13
☐	103	Red Berenson	1.75	.85	.17

		NRMT	VG-E	GOOD
☐ 104	Larry Keenan	1.35	.65	.13
☐ 105	Bruce Gamble	1.35	.65	.13
☐ 106	Jim Dorey	1.35	.65	.13
☐ 107	Mike Pelyk	1.35	.65	.13
☐ 108	Rick Ley	1.75	.85	.17
☐ 109	Mike Walton	1.75	.85	.17
☐ 110	Norm Ullman	4.00	2.00	.40
☐ 111A	Brit Selby	3.50	1.75	.35
	(No mention of trade)			
☐ 111B	Brit Selby	1.75	.85	.17
	(Trade noted)			
☐ 112	Garry Monahan	1.35	.65	.13
☐ 113	George Armstrong	3.00	1.50	.30
☐ 114	Gary Doak	1.35	.65	.13
☐ 115	Darryl Sly	1.35	.65	.13
☐ 116	Wayne Maki	1.35	.65	.13
☐ 117	Orland Kurtenbach	1.75	.85	.17
☐ 118	Murray Hall	1.35	.65	.13
☐ 119	Marc Reaume	1.35	.65	.13
☐ 120	Pat Quinn	1.75	.85	.17
☐ 121	Andre Boudrias	1.35	.65	.13
☐ 122	Poul Popiel	1.35	.65	.13
☐ 123	Paul Terbenche	1.35	.65	.13
☐ 124	Howie Menard	1.35	.65	.13
☐ 125	Gerry Meehan	3.50	1.75	.35
☐ 126	Skip Krake	1.35	.65	.13
☐ 127	Phil Goyette	1.35	.65	.13
☐ 128	Reg Fleming	1.35	.65	.13
☐ 129	Don Marshall	1.35	.65	.13
☐ 130	Bill Inglis	1.35	.65	.13
☐ 131	Gilbert Perreault	65.00	32.50	6.50
☐ 132	Checklist 2	25.00	2.50	.50
☐ 133	Ed Johnston	2.00	1.00	.20
☐ 134	Ted Green	1.75	.85	.17
☐ 135	Rick Smith	1.35	.65	.13
☐ 136	Derek Sanderson	2.00	1.00	.20
☐ 137	Dallas Smith	1.75	.85	.17
☐ 138	Don Marcotte	2.50	1.25	.25
☐ 139	Ed Westfall	2.00	1.00	.20
☐ 140	Floyd Smith	1.35	.65	.13
☐ 141	Randy Wyrozub	1.35	.65	.13
☐ 142	Cliff Schmautz	2.00	1.00	.20
☐ 143	Mike McMahon	1.35	.65	.13
☐ 144	Jim Watson	1.35	.65	.13
☐ 145	Roger Crozier	1.75	.85	.17
☐ 146	Tracy Pratt	1.35	.65	.13
☐ 147	Cliff Koroll	1.35	.65	.13
☐ 148	Gerry Pinder	2.50	1.25	.25
☐ 149	Chico Maki	1.35	.65	.13
☐ 150	Doug Jarrett	1.35	.65	.13
☐ 151	Keith Magnuson	2.50	1.25	.25
☐ 152	Gerry Desjardins	1.75	.85	.17
☐ 153	Tony Esposito	20.00	10.00	2.00

		NRMT	VG-E	GOOD
□ 154	Gary Bergman	1.35	.65	.13
□ 155	Tom Webster	5.00	2.50	.50
□ 156	Dale Rolfe	1.35	.65	.13
□ 157	Alex Delvecchio	5.50	2.75	.55
□ 158	Nick Libett	1.35	.65	.13
□ 159	Wayne Connelly	1.35	.65	.13
□ 160	Mike Byers	1.35	.65	.13
□ 161	Bill Flett	1.35	.65	.13
□ 162	Larry Mickey	1.35	.65	.13
□ 163	Noel Price	1.35	.65	.13
□ 164	Larry Cahan	1.35	.65	.13
□ 165	Jack Norris	1.35	.65	.13
□ 166	Ted Harris	1.35	.65	.13
□ 167	Murray Oliver	1.35	.65	.13
□ 168	Jean Paul Parise	1.35	.65	.13
□ 169	Tom Williams	1.35	.65	.13
□ 170	Bobby Rousseau	1.35	.65	.13
□ 171	Jude Drouin	1.35	.65	.13
□ 172	Walt McKechnie	2.00	1.00	.20
□ 173	Cesare Maniago	1.75	.85	.17
□ 174	Rejean Houle	2.00	1.00	.20
□ 175A	Mickey Redmond	3.50	1.75	.35
	(No mention of trade)			
□ 175B	Mickey Redmond	1.75	.85	.17
	(Trade noted)			
□ 176	Henri Richard	5.50	2.75	.55
□ 177	Guy Lapointe	7.50	3.75	.75
□ 178	J.C. Tremblay	1.75	.85	.17
□ 179	Marc Tardif	3.00	1.50	.30
□ 180	Walt Tkaczuk	1.75	.85	.17
□ 181	Jean Ratelle	4.25	2.10	.42
□ 182	Pete Stemkowski	1.35	.65	.13
□ 183	Gilles Villemure	1.75	.85	.17
□ 184	Rod Seiling	1.35	.65	.13
□ 185	Jim Neilson	1.35	.65	.13
□ 186	Dennis Hextall	1.75	.85	.17
□ 187	Gerry Ehman	1.35	.65	.13
□ 188	Bert Marshall	1.35	.65	.13
□ 189	Gary Croteau	1.35	.65	.13
□ 190	Ted Hampson	1.35	.65	.13
□ 191	Earl Ingarfield	1.35	.65	.13
□ 192	Dick Mattiussi	1.35	.65	.13
□ 193	Earl Heiskala	1.35	.65	.13
□ 194	Simon Nolet	1.35	.65	.13
□ 195	Bobby Clarke	100.00	50.00	10.00
□ 196	Garry Peters	1.35	.65	.13
□ 197	Lew Morrison	1.35	.65	.13
□ 198	Wayne Hillman	1.35	.65	.13
□ 199	Doug Favell	1.75	.85	.17
□ 200	Les Binkley	1.75	.85	.17
□ 201	Dean Prentice	2.00	1.00	.20
□ 202	Jean Pronovost	2.00	1.00	.20
□ 203	Wally Boyer	1.35	.65	.13

		NRMT	VG-E	GOOD
☐ 204	Bryan Watson	1.35	.65	.13
☐ 205	Glen Sather	3.00	1.50	.30
☐ 206	Lowell MacDonald	1.75	.85	.17
☐ 207	Andy Bathgate	3.00	1.50	.30
☐ 208	Val Fonteyne	1.35	.65	.13
☐ 209	Jim Dorentz	1.35	.65	.13
☐ 210	Glenn Hall	6.00	3.00	.60
☐ 211	Bob Plager	1.75	.85	.17
☐ 212	Noel Picard	1.35	.65	.13
☐ 213	Jim Roberts	1.35	.65	.13
☐ 214	Frank St.Marseille	1.35	.65	.13
☐ 215	Ab McDonald	1.35	.65	.13
☐ 216	Brian Glennie	1.35	.65	.13
☐ 217	Paul Henderson	1.75	.85	.17
☐ 218	Darryl Sittler	45.00	22.50	4.50
☐ 219	Dave Keon	3.50	1.75	.35
☐ 220	Jim Harrison	1.35	.65	.13
☐ 221	Ron Ellis	1.35	.65	.13
☐ 222	Jacques Plante	12.00	6.00	1.20
☐ 223	Bob Baun	1.35	.65	.13
☐ 224	George Gardner	1.35	.65	.13
☐ 225	Dale Tallon	2.50	1.25	.25
☐ 226	Rosaire Paiement	1.35	.65	.13
☐ 227	Mike Corrigan	1.35	.65	.13
☐ 228	Ray Cullen	1.35	.65	.13
☐ 229	Charlie Hodge	1.75	.85	.17
☐ 230	Len Lunde	1.35	.65	.13
☐ 231	Terry Sawchuk Memorial	25.00	12.50	2.50
☐ 232	Boston Bruins Team Stanley Cup Champs	6.00	3.00	.60
☐ 233	Esposito line: Cashman/Hodge	10.00	5.00	1.00
☐ 234	Tony Esposito AS1	7.50	3.75	.75
☐ 235	Bobby Hull AS1	20.00	10.00	2.00
☐ 236	Bobby Orr AS1	35.00	17.50	3.50
☐ 237	Phil Esposito AS1	14.00	7.00	1.40
☐ 238	Gordie Howe AS1	30.00	15.00	3.00
☐ 239	Brad Park AS1	7.00	3.50	.70
☐ 240	Stan Mikita AS2	7.00	3.50	.70
☐ 241	John McKenzie AS2	1.75	.85	.17
☐ 242	Frank Mahovlich AS2	7.00	3.50	.70
☐ 243	Carl Brewer AS2	1.75	.85	.17
☐ 244	Ed Giacomin AS2	3.00	1.50	.30
☐ 245	Jacques Laperriere AS2	2.50	1.25	.25
☐ 246	Bobby Orr Hart Trophy	35.00	17.50	3.50
☐ 247	Tony Esposito Calder Trophy	7.50	3.75	.75
☐ 248A	Bobby Orr Norris Trophy (No mention of Howe as NHL all-time leading scorer)	35.00	17.50	3.50

		NRMT	VG-E	GOOD
☐ 248B	**Bobby Orr** Norris Trophy (Mentions Howe as NHL all-time leading scorer)	35.00	17.50	3.50
☐ 249	**Bobby Orr** Art Ross Trophy	35.00	17.50	3.50
☐ 250	**Tony Esposito** Vezina Trophy	7.50	3.75	.75
☐ 251	**Phil Goyette** Lady Byng Trophy	1.75	.85	.17
☐ 252	**Bobby Orr** Conn Smythe Trophy	35.00	17.50	3.50
☐ 253	**Pit (Bill) Martin** Masterson Trophy	1.75	.85	.17
☐ 254	**The Stanley Cup**	3.00	1.50	.30
☐ 255	**Prince of Wales Trophy**	2.50	1.25	.25
☐ 256	**Conn Smythe Trophy**	2.50	1.25	.25
☐ 257	**James Norris Trophy**	2.50	1.25	.25
☐ 258	**Calder Trophy**	2.50	1.25	.25
☐ 259	**Vezina Trophy**	2.50	1.25	.25
☐ 260	**Lady Byng Trophy**	2.50	1.25	.25
☐ 261	**Hart Trophy**	2.50	1.25	.25
☐ 262	**Art Ross Trophy**	2.50	1.25	.25
☐ 263	**Clarence S. Campbell Bowl**	2.50	1.25	.25
☐ 264	**John Ferguson**	3.50	1.00	.20

1971-72 O-Pee-Chee

The 1971-72 O-Pee-Chee set contains 264 color cards featuring the players in large ovals on the fronts. The cards in the set measure 2½" by 3½". The backs, in both French and English, feature the card number, a short biography, the player's NHL career record, and a cartoon-illustrated fact about the player. The O.P.C. copyright appears on the backs of these cards which were printed in Canada. Cards 262 and 263 are special cards honoring "retiring" superstars Gordie Howe (sic) and Jean Beliveau. The key rookies in this set are Marcel Dionne, Ken Dryden, and Guy Lafleur.

Le jeu O-Pee-Chee 1971-72 contient 264 cartes en couleurs, dont la face représente un joueur entouré d'un grand ovale. Les cartes de ce jeu mesurent 2½" x 3½". Le dos, imprimé en français et en anglais, comprend le numéro de carte, une biographie concise, la fiche NHL du joueur, et un fait notable concernant le joueur, illustré d'une caricature. Le droit d'auteur O.P.C. apparaît au dos de ces cartes imprimées au Canada. Les cartes 262 et 263 honorent les superstars Gordie Howe et Jean Beliveau, qui "terminent leur carrière" (sic). Les débutants importants de ce jeu sont Marcel Dionne, Ken Dryden, et Guy Lafleur.

			NRMT	VG-E	GOOD
	COMPLETE SET (264)		800.00	400.00	80.00
	COMMON PLAYER (1-132)		1.00	.50	.10
	COMMON PLAYER (133-264)		1.00	.50	.10
☐	1	Poul Popiel	2.00	.75	.15
☐	2	Pierre Bouchard	1.25	.60	.12
☐	3	Don Awrey	1.00	.50	.10
☐	4	Paul Curtis	1.00	.50	.10
☐	5	Guy Trottier	1.00	.50	.10
☐	6	Paul Shmyr	1.00	.50	.10
☐	7	Fred Stanfield	1.00	.50	.10

			NRMT	VG-E	GOOD
☐	8	Mike Robitaille	1.00	.50	.10
☐	9	Vic Hadfield	1.25	.60	.12
☐	10	Jim Harrison	1.00	.50	.10
☐	11	Bill White	1.25	.60	.12
☐	12	Andre Boudrias	1.00	.50	.10
☐	13	Gary Sabourin	1.00	.50	.10
☐	14	Arnie Brown	1.00	.50	.10
☐	15	Yvan Cournoyer	4.00	2.00	.40
☐	16	Bryan Hextall	1.00	.50	.10
☐	17	Gary Croteau	1.00	.50	.10
☐	18	Gilles Villemure	1.25	.60	.12
☐	19	Serge Bernier	1.00	.50	.10
☐	20	Phil Esposito	15.00	7.50	1.50
☐	21	Tom Reid	1.00	.50	.10
☐	22	Doug Barrie	1.00	.50	.10
☐	23	Eddie Joyal	1.00	.50	.10
☐	24	Dunc Wilson	1.50	.75	.15
☐	25	Pat Stapleton	1.25	.60	.12
☐	26	Garry Unger	1.50	.75	.15
☐	27	Al Smith	1.00	.50	.10
☐	28	Bob Woytowich	1.00	.50	.10
☐	29	Marc Tardif	1.25	.60	.12
☐	30	Norm Ullman	3.50	1.75	.35
☐	31	Tom Williams	1.00	.50	.10
☐	32	Ted Harris	1.00	.50	.10
☐	33	Andre Lacroix	1.00	.50	.10
☐	34	Mike Byers	1.00	.50	.10
☐	35	Johnny Bucyk	4.50	2.25	.45
☐	36	Roger Crozier	1.25	.60	.12
☐	37	Alex Delvecchio	4.50	2.25	.45
☐	38	Frank St.Marseille	1.00	.50	.10
☐	39	Pit Martin	1.00	.50	.10
☐	40	Brad Park	8.00	4.00	.80
☐	41	Greg Polis	1.00	.50	.10
☐	42	Orland Kurtenbach	1.00	.50	.10
☐	43	Jim McKenny	1.00	.50	.10
☐	44	Bob Nevin	1.00	.50	.10
☐	45	Ken Dryden	125.00	60.00	12.50
☐	46	Carol Vadnais	1.00	.50	.10
☐	47	Bill Flett	1.00	.50	.10
☐	48	Jim Johnson	1.00	.50	.10
☐	49	Allan Hamilton	1.00	.50	.10
☐	50	Bobby Hull	25.00	12.50	2.50
☐	51	Chris Bordeleau	1.75	.85	.17
☐	52	Tim Ecclestone	1.00	.50	.10
☐	53	Rod Seiling	1.00	.50	.10
☐	54	Gerry Cheevers	5.00	2.50	.50
☐	55	Bill Goldsworthy	1.25	.60	.12
☐	56	Ron Schock	1.00	.50	.10
☐	57	Jim Dorey	1.00	.50	.10
☐	58	Wayne Maki	1.00	.50	.10
☐	59	Terry Harper	1.00	.50	.10
☐	60	Gilbert Perreault	20.00	10.00	2.00

			NRMT	VG-E	GOOD
☐	61	Ernie Hicke	1.00	.50	.10
☐	62	Wayne Hillman	1.00	.50	.10
☐	63	Denis DeJordy	1.25	.60	.12
☐	64	Ken Schinkel	1.00	.50	.10
☐	65	Derek Sanderson	1.25	.60	.12
☐	66	Barclay Plager	1.25	.60	.12
☐	67	Paul Henderson	1.25	.60	.12
☐	68	Jude Drouin	1.00	.50	.10
☐	69	Keith Magnuson	1.25	.60	.12
☐	70	Ron Harris	1.00	.50	.10
☐	71	Jacques Lemaire	3.50	1.75	.35
☐	72	Doug Favell	1.25	.60	.12
☐	73	Bert Marshall	1.00	.50	.10
☐	74	Ted Irvine	1.00	.50	.10
☐	75	Walt Tkaczuk	1.25	.60	.12
☐	76	Bob Berry	1.50	.75	.15
☐	77	Syl Apps	1.00	.50	.10
☐	78	Tom Webster	2.50	1.25	.25
☐	79	Danny Grant	1.00	.50	.10
☐	80	Dave Keon	3.50	1.75	.35
☐	81	Ernie Wakely	1.00	.50	.10
☐	82	John McKenzie	1.00	.50	.10
☐	83	Ron Stackhouse	1.00	.50	.10
☐	84	Peter Mahovlich	1.25	.60	.12
☐	85	Dennis Hull	1.50	.75	.15
☐	86	Juha Widing	1.00	.50	.10
☐	87	Gary Doak	1.00	.50	.10
☐	88	Phil Goyette	1.00	.50	.10
☐	89	Lew Morrison	1.00	.50	.10
☐	90	Ab Demarco	1.00	.50	.10
☐	91	Red Berenson	1.25	.60	.12
☐	92	Mike Pelyk	1.00	.50	.10
☐	93	Gary Jarrett	1.00	.50	.10
☐	94	Bob Pulford	2.50	1.25	.25
☐	95	Dan Johnson	1.00	.50	.10
☐	96	Eddie Shack	1.50	.75	.15
☐	97	Jean Ratelle	4.00	2.00	.40
☐	98	Jim Pappin	1.00	.50	.10
☐	99	Roy Edwards	1.00	.50	.10
☐	100	Bobby Orr	55.00	27.50	5.50
☐	101	Ted Hampson	1.00	.50	.10
☐	102	Mickey Redmond	1.50	.75	.15
☐	103	Bob Plager	1.25	.60	.12
☐	104	Barry Ashbee	1.00	.50	.10
☐	105	Frank Mahovlich	8.00	4.00	.80
☐	106	Dick Redmond	1.00	.50	.10
☐	107	Tracy Pratt	1.00	.50	.10
☐	108	Ralph Backstrom	1.00	.50	.10
☐	109	Murray Hall	1.00	.50	.10
☐	110	Tony Esposito	12.00	6.00	1.20
☐	111	Checklist Card	18.00	1.50	.30
☐	112	Jim Neilson	1.00	.50	.10
☐	113	Ron Ellis	1.00	.50	.10

		NRMT	VG-E	GOOD
☐ 114	Bobby Clarke	40.00	20.00	4.00
☐ 115	Ken Hodge	1.50	.75	.15
☐ 116	Jim Roberts	1.00	.50	.10
☐ 117	Cesare Maniago	1.25	.60	.12
☐ 118	Jean Pronovost	1.50	.75	.15
☐ 119	Gary Bergman	1.00	.50	.10
☐ 120	Henri Richard	4.00	2.00	.40
☐ 121	Ross Lonsberry	1.00	.50	.10
☐ 122	Pat Quinn	1.25	.60	.12
☐ 123	Rod Gilbert	4.00	2.00	.40
☐ 124	Walt McKechnie	1.00	.50	.10
☐ 125	Stan Mikita	10.00	5.00	1.00
☐ 126	Ed Van Impe	1.00	.50	.10
☐ 127	Terry Crisp	2.25	1.10	.22
☐ 128	Fred Barrett	1.00	.50	.10
☐ 129	Wayne Cashman	1.25	.60	.12
☐ 130	J.C. Tremblay	1.25	.60	.12
☐ 131	Bernie Parent	6.50	3.25	.65
☐ 132	Bryan Watson	1.00	.50	.10
☐ 133	Marcel Dionne	125.00	60.00	12.50
☐ 134	Ab McDonald	1.00	.50	.10
☐ 135	Leon Rochefort	1.00	.50	.10
☐ 136	Serge Lajeunesse	1.00	.50	.10
☐ 137	Joe Daley	1.25	.60	.12
☐ 138	Brian Conacher	1.00	.50	.10
☐ 139	Bill Collins	1.00	.50	.10
☐ 140	Nick Libett	1.00	.50	.10
☐ 141	Bill Sutherland	1.00	.50	.10
☐ 142	Bill Hicke	1.00	.50	.10
☐ 143	Serge Savard	3.00	1.50	.30
☐ 144	Jacques Laperriere	2.50	1.25	.25
☐ 145	Guy Lapointe	2.50	1.25	.25
☐ 146	Claude Larose UER	1.00	.50	.10
	(Misspelled La Rose on both sides)			
☐ 147	Rejean Houle	1.00	.50	.10
☐ 148	Guy Lafleur UER	125.00	60.00	12.50
	(Misspelled La Fleur on both sides)			
☐ 149	Dale Hoganson	1.00	.50	.10
☐ 150	Al McDonough	1.00	.50	.10
☐ 151	Gilles Marotte	1.25	.60	.12
☐ 152	Butch Goring	6.00	3.00	.60
☐ 153	Harry Howell	2.50	1.25	.25
☐ 154	Real Lemieux	1.00	.50	.10
☐ 155	Gary Edwards	1.00	.50	.10
☐ 156	Rogatien Vachon	3.25	1.60	.32
☐ 157	Mike Corrigan	1.00	.50	.10
☐ 158	Floyd Smith	1.00	.50	.10
☐ 159	Dave Dryden	1.25	.60	.12
☐ 160	Gerry Meehan	1.25	.60	.12
☐ 161	Richard Martin	6.00	3.00	.60
☐ 162	Steve Atkinson	1.00	.50	.10
☐ 163	Hon Anderson	1.00	.50	.10
☐ 164	Dick Duff	1.00	.50	.10

		NRMT	VG-E	GOOD
☐ 165	Jim Watson	1.00	.50	.10
☐ 166	Don Luce	1.00	.50	.10
☐ 167	Larry Mickey	1.00	.50	.10
☐ 168	Larry Hillman	1.00	.50	.10
☐ 169	Ed Westfall	1.25	.60	.12
☐ 170	Dallas Smith	1.25	.60	.12
☐ 171	Mike Walton	1.25	.60	.12
☐ 172	Ed Johnston	1.50	.75	.15
☐ 173	Ted Green	1.25	.60	.12
☐ 174	Rick Smith	1.00	.50	.10
☐ 175	Reggie Leach	5.00	2.50	.50
☐ 176	Don Marcotte	1.00	.50	.10
☐ 177	Bobby Sheehan	1.00	.50	.10
☐ 178	Wayne Carleton	1.00	.50	.10
☐ 179	Norm Ferguson	1.00	.50	.10
☐ 180	Don O'Donoghue	1.00	.50	.10
☐ 181	Gary Kurt	1.00	.50	.10
☐ 182	Joey Johnston	1.00	.50	.10
☐ 183	Stan Gilbertson	1.00	.50	.10
☐ 184	Craig Patrick	2.50	1.25	.25
☐ 185	Gerry Pinder	1.00	.50	.10
☐ 186	Tim Horton	3.75	1.85	.37
☐ 187	Darryl Edestrand	1.00	.50	.10
☐ 188	Keith McCreary	1.00	.50	.10
☐ 189	Val Fonteyne	1.00	.50	.10
☐ 190	Sheldon Kannegiesser	1.00	.50	.10
☐ 191	Nick Harbaruk	1.00	.50	.10
☐ 192	Les Binkley	1.25	.60	.12
☐ 193	Darryl Sittler	8.00	4.00	.80
☐ 194	Rick Ley	1.25	.60	.12
☐ 195	Jacques Plante	10.00	5.00	1.00
☐ 196	Bob Baun	1.00	.50	.10
☐ 197	Brian Glennie	1.00	.50	.10
☐ 198	Brian Spencer	1.00	.50	.10
☐ 199	Don Marshall	1.00	.50	.10
☐ 200	Denis Dupere	1.00	.50	.10
☐ 201	Bruce Gamble	1.00	.50	.10
☐ 202	Gary Dornhoefer	1.25	.60	.12
☐ 203	Bob Kelly	1.00	.50	.10
☐ 204	Jean Guy Gendron	1.00	.50	.10
☐ 205	Brent Hughes	1.00	.50	.10
☐ 206	Simon Nolet	1.00	.50	.10
☐ 207	Rick MacLeish	7.50	3.75	.75
☐ 208	Doug Jarrett	1.00	.50	.10
☐ 209	Cliff Koroll	1.00	.50	.10
☐ 210	Chico Maki	1.00	.50	.10
☐ 211	Danny O'Shea	1.00	.50	.10
☐ 212	Lou Angotti	1.00	.50	.10
☐ 213	Eric Nesterenko	1.25	.60	.12
☐ 214	Bryan Campbell	1.00	.50	.10
☐ 215	Bill Fairbairn	1.00	.50	.10
☐ 216	Bruce MacGregor	1.00	.50	.10
☐ 217	Pete Stemkowski	1.00	.50	.10

			NRMT	VG-E	GOOD
☐ 218	Bobby Rousseau		1.00	.50	.10
☐ 219	Dale Rolfe		1.00	.50	.10
☐ 220	Ed Giacomin		3.25	1.60	.32
☐ 221	Glen Sather		2.50	1.25	.25
☐ 222	Carl Brewer		1.00	.50	.10
☐ 223	George Morrison		1.00	.50	.10
☐ 224	Noel Picard		1.00	.50	.10
☐ 225	Peter McDuffe		1.00	.50	.10
☐ 226	Brit Selby		1.00	.50	.10
☐ 227	Jim Lorentz		1.00	.50	.10
☐ 228	Phil Roberto		1.00	.50	.10
☐ 229	Dave Balon		1.00	.50	.10
☐ 230	Barry Wilkins		1.00	.50	.10
☐ 231	Dennis Kearns		1.00	.50	.10
☐ 232	Jocelyn Guevremont		1.25	.60	.12
☐ 233	Rosaire Paiement		1.00	.50	.10
☐ 234	Dale Tallon		1.25	.60	.12
☐ 235	George Gardner		1.00	.50	.10
☐ 236	Ron Stewart		1.00	.50	.10
☐ 237	Wayne Connelly		1.00	.50	.10
☐ 238	Charlie Burns		1.00	.50	.10
☐ 239	Murray Oliver		1.00	.50	.10
☐ 240	Lou Nanne		1.25	.60	.12
☐ 241	Gump Worsley		6.00	3.00	.60
☐ 242	Doug Mohns		1.00	.50	.10
☐ 243	Jean Paul Parise		1.00	.50	.10
☐ 244	Dennis Hextall		1.25	.60	.12
☐ 245	Bobby Orr		30.00	15.00	3.00
	Hart Trophy				
	Norris Trophy				
☐ 246	Gilbert Perreault		6.00	3.00	.60
	Calder Trophy				
☐ 247	Phil Esposito		8.00	4.00	.80
	Ross Trophy				
☐ 248	Ed Giacomin and		2.00	1.00	.20
	Gilles Villemure				
	Vezina Trophy				
☐ 249	Johnny Bucyk		2.50	1.25	.25
	Lady Byng Trophy				
☐ 250	Ed Giacomin AS1		2.25	1.10	.22
☐ 251	Bobby Orr AS1		27.00	13.50	2.70
☐ 252	J.C. Tremblay AS1		1.25	.60	.12
☐ 253	Phil Esposito AS1 UER		8.00	4.00	.80
	(Back reads Phil.,				
	shouldn't be a				
	period after Phil)				
☐ 254	Ken Hodge AS1		1.25	.60	.12
☐ 255	Johnny Bucyk AS1		2.50	1.25	.25
☐ 256	Jacques Plante AS2 UER		7.00	3.50	.70
	(63 shutouts, should				
	be 77 shutouts)				
☐ 257	Brad Park AS2		2.50	1.25	.25
☐ 258	Pat Stapleton AS2		1.25	.60	.12

		NRMT	VG-E	GOOD
☐ 259	Dave Keon AS2	2.00	1.00	.20
☐ 260	Yvan Cournoyer AS2	2.50	1.25	.25
☐ 261	Bobby Hull AS2	12.00	6.00	1.20
☐ 262	Gordie Howe	50.00	25.00	5.00
	(Retirement Special)			
☐ 263	Jean Beliveau	15.00	7.50	1.50
	(Retirement Special)			
☐ 264	Checklist Card	18.00	1.50	.30

1972-73 O-Pee-Chee

The 1972-73 O-Pee-Chee set features 341 cards with the name of the player portrayed's team on the border of the obverse. Cards in the set measure 2¹/₂" by 3¹/₂". The backs, in both French and English, feature the card number, a year-by-year record of the player's career, a short biography, and a cartoon-illustrated fact about the player. The cards were printed in Canada. The card stock can be found in white or gray. There are a number of In Action (IA) cards of popular players distributed throughout the set. Card number 208 was never issued. The last series, which was printed in lesser quantities, features players from the newly formed WHA. There are 22 double-printed cards in the first series (1-110), but the identity of these 22 is not known at this time except that Johnny Bucyk and Frank Mahovlich are DP's. There are no key rookie cards in this set.

Le jeu O-Pee-Chee 1972-73 contient 341 cartes, indiquant, le long du bord de la face, le nom de l'équipe du joueur représenté. Les cartes mesurent 2¹/₂" x 3¹/₂". Le dos, imprimé en français et en anglais, comprend le numéro de carte, les statistiques par année de carrière du joueur, une biographie concise, et un fait notable concernant le joueur, illustré d'une caricature. Les cartes ont été imprimées au Canada. La pâte à papier se trouve en blanc ou en gris. Le jeu comprend plusieurs cartes "In Action" (IA) pour des joueurs populaires. La carte numéro 208 n'a jamais été émise. La dernière

série, imprimée en plus petite quantité, représente les joueurs de la WHA, nouvellement formée. Ce jeu ne contient pas de cartes de débutants importants.

			NRMT	VG-E	GOOD
		COMPLETE SET (341)	800.00	400.00	80.00
		COMMON PLAYER (1-110)	.60	.30	.06
		COMMON PLAYER (111-209)	.80	.40	.08
		COMMON PLAYER (210-289)	1.75	.85	.17
		COMMON PLAYER (290-341)	3.00	1.50	.30
☐	1	Johnny Bucyk DP	6.50	2.00	.40
☐	2	Rene Robert	2.50	1.25	.25
☐	3	Gary Croteau	.60	.30	.06
☐	4	Pat Stapleton	1.00	.50	.10
☐	5	Ron Harris	.60	.30	.06
☐	6	Checklist 1	10.00	.75	.15
☐	7	Playoff Game 1	1.00	.50	.10
☐	8	Marcel Dionne	35.00	17.50	3.50
☐	9	Bob Berry	1.00	.50	.10
☐	10	Lou Nanne	1.00	.50	.10
☐	11	Marc Tardif	1.00	.50	.10
☐	12	Jean Ratelle	3.50	1.75	.35
☐	13	Craig Cameron	.60	.30	.06
☐	14	Bobby Clarke...	14.00	7.00	1.40
☐	15	Jim Rutherford	1.50	.75	.15
☐	16	Andre Dupont	1.50	.75	.15
☐	17	Mike Pelyk	.60	.30	.06
☐	18	Dunc Wilson	.60	.30	.06
☐	19	Checklist 2	10.00	.75	.15
		(See also card 190)			
☐	20	Playoff Game 2	1.00	.50	.10
		Bruins 2,			
		Rangers 1			
☐	21	Dallas Smith	1.00	.50	.10
☐	22	Gerry Meehan	1.00	.50	.10
☐	23	Rick Smith UER	.60	.30	.06
		(Wrong total games,			
		should be 262, not 265)			
☐	24	Pit Martin	1.00	.50	.10
☐	25	Keith McCreary	.60	.30	.06
☐	26	Alex Delvecchio	4.00	2.00	.40
☐	27	Gilles Marotte	1.00	.50	.10
☐	28	Gump Worsley	4.50	2.25	.45
☐	29	Yvan Cournoyer	3.50	1.75	.35
☐	30	Playoff Game 3	1.00	.50	.10
		Rangers 5,			
		Bruins 2			
☐	31	Vic Hadfield	1.00	.50	.10
☐	32	Tom Miller	.60	.30	.06
☐	33	Ed Van Impe	.60	.30	.06
☐	34	Greg Polis	.60	.30	.06
☐	35	Barclay Plager	1.00	.50	.10

			NRMT	VG-E	GOOD
☐	36	Ron Ellis	.60	.30	.06
☐	37	Jocelyn Guevremont	.60	.30	.06
☐	38	Playoff Game 4	1.00	.50	.10
		Bruins 3,			
		Rangers 2			
☐	39	Carol Vadnais	.60	.30	.06
☐	40	Steve Atkinson	.60	.30	.06
☐	41	Ivan Boldirev	2.00	1.00	.20
☐	42	Jim Pappin	.60	.30	.06
☐	43	Phil Myre	2.00	1.00	.20
☐	44	Yvan Cournoyer IA	2.50	1.25	.25
☐	45	Nick Libett	.60	.30	.06
☐	46	Juha Widing	.60	.30	.06
☐	47	Jude Drouin	.60	.30	.06
☐	48A	Jean Ratelle IA ERR	5.00	2.50	.50
		(Defense on front)			
☐	48B	Jean Ratelle IA COR	2.50	1.25	.25
		(Center on front)			
☐	49	Ken Hodge	1.25	.60	.12
☐	50	Roger Crozier	1.00	.50	.10
☐	51	Reggie Leach	1.50	.75	.15
☐	52	Dennis Hull	1.25	.60	.12
☐	53	Larry Hale	.60	.30	.06
☐	54	Playoff Game 5	1.00	.50	.10
		Rangers 3,			
		Bruins 2			
☐	55	Tim Ecclestone	.60	.30	.06
☐	56	Butch Goring	1.50	.75	.15
☐	57	Danny Grant	.60	.30	.06
☐	58	Bobby Orr IA	18.00	9.00	1.80
☐	59	Guy Lafleur	35.00	17.50	3.50
☐	60	Jim Neilson	.60	.30	.06
☐	61	Brian Spencer	.60	.30	.06
☐	62	Joe Watson	.60	.30	.06
☐	63	Playoff Game 6	1.00	.50	.10
		Bruins 3,			
		Rangers 0			
☐	64	Jean Pronovost	1.00	.50	.10
☐	65	Frank St. Marseille	.60	.30	.06
☐	66	Bob Baun	.60	.30	.06
☐	67	Poul Popiel	.60	.30	.06
☐	68	Wayne Cashman	1.00	.50	.10
☐	69	Tracy Pratt	.60	.30	.06
☐	70	Stan Gilbertson	.60	.30	.06
☐	71	Keith Magnuson	1.00	.50	.10
☐	72	Ernie Hicke	.60	.30	.06
☐	73	Gary Doak	.60	.30	.06
☐	74	Mike Corrigan	.60	.30	.06
☐	75	Doug Mohns	.60	.30	.06
☐	76	Phil Esposito IA	6.00	3.00	.60
☐	77	Jacques Lemaire	3.00	1.50	.30
☐	78	Pete Stemkowski	.60	.30	.06
☐	79	Bill Mikkelson	.60	.30	.06

		NRMT	VG-E	GOOD
☐ 80	Rick Foley	.60	.30	.06
☐ 81	Ron Schock	.60	.30	.06
☐ 82	Phil Roberto	.60	.30	.06
☐ 83	Jim McKenny	.60	.30	.06
☐ 84	Wayne Maki	.60	.30	.06
☐ 85A	Brad Park IA ERR	5.00	2.50	.50
	(Center on front)			
☐ 85B	Brad Park IA COR	2.50	1.25	.25
	(Defense on front)			
☐ 86	Guy Lapointe	1.50	.75	.15
☐ 87	Bill Fairbairn	.60	.30	.06
☐ 88	Terry Crisp	1.25	.60	.12
☐ 89	Doug Favell	1.00	.50	.10
☐ 90	Bryan Watson	.60	.30	.06
☐ 91	Gary Sabourin	.60	.30	.06
☐ 92	Jacques Plante	8.00	4.00	.80
☐ 93	Andre Boudrias	.60	.30	.06
☐ 94	Mike Walton	1.00	.50	.10
☐ 95	Don Luce	.60	.30	.06
☐ 96	Joey Johnston	.60	.30	.06
☐ 97	Doug Jarrett	.60	.30	.06
☐ 98	Bill MacMillan	.60	.30	.06
☐ 99	Mickey Redmond	1.00	.50	.10
☐ 100	Rogatien Vachon UER	3.00	1.50	.30
	(Misspelled Ragatien on card back)			
☐ 101	Barry Gibbs	.60	.30	.06
☐ 102	Frank Mahovlich DP	6.50	3.25	.65
☐ 103	Bruce MacGregor	.60	.30	.06
☐ 104	Ed Westfall	1.00	.50	.10
☐ 105	Rick MacLeish	2.25	1.10	.22
☐ 106	Nick Harbaruk	.60	.30	.06
☐ 107	Jack Egers	.60	.30	.06
☐ 108	Dave Keon	3.00	1.50	.30
☐ 109	Barry Wilkins	.60	.30	.06
☐ 110	Walt Tkaczuk	1.00	.50	.10
☐ 111	Phil Esposito	12.00	6.00	1.20
☐ 112	Gilles Meloche	1.75	.85	.17
☐ 113	Gary Edwards	.80	.40	.08
☐ 114	Brad Park	4.50	2.25	.45
☐ 115	Syl Apps	.80	.40	.08
☐ 116	Jim Lorentz	.80	.40	.08
☐ 117	Gary Smith	.80	.40	.08
☐ 118	Ted Harris	.80	.40	.08
☐ 119	Gerry Desjardins	1.25	.60	.12
☐ 120	Garry Unger	1.25	.60	.12
☐ 121	Dale Tallon	.80	.40	.08
☐ 122	Bill Plager	1.00	.50	.10
☐ 123	Red Berenson	1.00	.50	.10
☐ 124	Peter Mahovlich	1.00	.50	.10
☐ 125	Simon Nolet	.80	.40	.08
☐ 126	Paul Henderson	1.00	.50	.10
☐ 127	Hart Trophy Winners	1.50	.75	.15

		NRMT	VG-E	GOOD
☐ 128	Frank Mahovlich IA	4.00	2.00	.40
☐ 129	Bobby Orr	45.00	22.50	4.50
☐ 130	Bert Marshall	.80	.40	.08
☐ 131	Ralph Backstrom	.80	.40	.08
☐ 132	Gilles Villemure	1.25	.60	.12
☐ 133	Dave Burrows	.80	.40	.08
☐ 134	Calder Trophy Winners	1.50	.75	.15
☐ 135	Dallas Smith IA	1.00	.50	.10
☐ 136	Gilbert Perreault	7.50	3.75	.75
☐ 137	Tony Esposito	6.50	3.25	.65
☐ 138	Cesare Maniago	1.00	.50	.10
☐ 139	Gerry Hart	1.50	.75	.15
☐ 140	Jacques Caron	.80	.40	.08
☐ 141	Orland Kurtenbach	.80	.40	.08
☐ 142	Norris Trophy Winners	1.50	.75	.15
☐ 143	Lew Morrison	.80	.40	.08
☐ 144	Arnie Brown	.80	.40	.08
☐ 145	Ken Dryden	35.00	17.50	3.50
☐ 146	Gary Dornhoefer	1.00	.50	.10
☐ 147	Norm Ullman	3.00	1.50	.30
☐ 148	Art Ross Trophy Winners	1.50	.75	.15
☐ 149	Orland Kurtenbach IA	.80	.40	.08
☐ 150	Fred Stanfield	.80	.40	.08
☐ 151	Dick Redmond	.80	.40	.08
☐ 152	Serge Bernier	.80	.40	.08
☐ 153	Rod Gilbert	3.75	1.85	.37
☐ 154	Duane Rupp	.80	.40	.08
☐ 155	Vezina Trophy Winners	1.50	.75	.15
☐ 156	Stan Mikita IA	4.50	2.25	.45
☐ 157	Richard Martin	1.50	.75	.15
☐ 158	Bill White	1.00	.50	.10
☐ 159	Bill Goldsworthy	1.00	.50	.10
☐ 160	Jack Lynch	.80	.40	.08
☐ 161	Bob Plager	1.00	.50	.10
☐ 162	Dave Balon (Misspelled Ballon on card back)	.80	.40	.08
☐ 163	Noel Price	.80	.40	.08
☐ 164	Gary Bergman	.80	.40	.08
☐ 165	Pierre Bouchard	.80	.40	.08
☐ 166	Ross Lonsberry	.80	.40	.08
☐ 167	Denis Dupere	.80	.40	.08
☐ 168	Byng Trophy Winners	1.50	.75	.15
☐ 169	Ken Hodge	1.25	.60	.12
☐ 170	Don Awrey	.80	.40	.08
☐ 171	Marshall Johnston	.80	.40	.08
☐ 172	Terry Harper	.80	.40	.08
☐ 173	Ed Giacomin	2.75	1.35	.27
☐ 174	Bryan Hextall	.80	.40	.08
☐ 175	Conn Smythe Trophy Winners	1.50	.75	.15
☐ 176	Larry Hillman	.80	.40	.08

		NRMT	VG-E	GOOD
☐ 177	Stan Mikita	7.50	3.75	.75
☐ 178	Charlie Burns	.80	.40	.08
☐ 179	Brian Marchinko	.80	.40	.08
☐ 180	Noel Picard	.80	.40	.08
☐ 181	Bobby Schmautz	1.50	.75	.15
☐ 182	Rick Martin IA UER	2.00	1.00	.20
	(Photo actually			
	Gilbert Perreault)			
☐ 183	Pat Quinn	1.25	.60	.12
☐ 184	Denis DeJordy UER	1.25	.60	.12
	(Back says plays for			
	Flames, should be Red Wings)			
☐ 185	Serge Savard	3.00	1.50	.30
☐ 186	Eddie Shack	1.25	.60	.12
☐ 187	Bill Flett	.80	.40	.08
☐ 188	Darryl Sittler	5.00	2.50	.50
☐ 189	Gump Worsley IA	3.50	1.75	.35
☐ 190	Checklist 2	15.00	1.25	.25
	(See also card 19)			
☐ 191	Garnet Bailey	.80	.40	.08
☐ 192	Walt McKechnie	.80	.40	.08
☐ 193	Harry Howell	2.00	1.00	.20
☐ 194	Rod Seiling	.80	.40	.08
☐ 195	Darryl Edestrand	.80	.40	.08
☐ 196	Tony Esposito IA	4.00	2.00	.40
☐ 197	Tim Horton	3.00	1.50	.30
☐ 198	Chico Maki	.80	.40	.08
☐ 199	Jean Paul Parise	.80	.40	.08
☐ 200	Germain Gagnon	.80	.40	.08
☐ 201	Danny O'Shea	.80	.40	.08
☐ 202	Richard Lemieux	.80	.40	.08
☐ 203	Dan Bouchard	1.75	.85	.17
☐ 204	Leon Rochefort	.80	.40	.08
☐ 205	Jacques Laperriere	2.00	1.00	.20
☐ 206	Barry Ashbee	.80	.40	.08
☐ 207	Garry Monahan	.80	.40	.08
☐ 208	Never Issued	0.00	.00	.00
☐ 209	Dave Keon IA	2.00	1.00	.20
☐ 210	Rejean Houle	1.75	.85	.17
☐ 211	Dave Hudson	1.75	.85	.17
☐ 212	Ted Irvine	1.75	.85	.17
☐ 213	Don Saleski	2.50	1.25	.25
☐ 214	Lowell MacDonald	2.25	1.10	.22
☐ 215	Mike Murphy	1.75	.85	.17
☐ 216	Brian Glennie	1.75	.85	.17
☐ 217	Bobby Lalonde	1.75	.85	.17
☐ 218	Bob Leiter	1.75	.85	.17
☐ 219	Don Marcotte	1.75	.85	.17
☐ 220	Jim Schoenfeld	4.00	2.00	.40
☐ 221	Craig Patrick	2.25	1.10	.22
☐ 222	Cliff Koroll	1.75	.85	.17
☐ 223	Guy Charron	1.75	.85	.17
☐ 224	Jim Peters	1.75	.85	.17

		NRMT	VG-E	GOOD
☐ 225	**Dennis Hextall**	2.25	1.10	.22
☐ 226	**Tony Esposito AS1**	5.00	2.50	.50
☐ 227	**Orr/Park AS1**	20.00	10.00	2.00
☐ 228	**Bobby Hull AS1**	12.50	6.25	1.25
☐ 229	**Rod Gilbert AS1**	3.50	1.75	.35
☐ 230	**Phil Esposito AS1**	10.00	5.00	1.00
	(Brother Tony pictured in background)			
☐ 231	**Claude Larose UER**	1.75	.85	.17
	(Misspelled La Rose on both sides)			
☐ 232	**Jim Mair**	1.75	.85	.17
☐ 233	**Bobby Rousseau**	1.75	.85	.17
☐ 234	**Brent Hughes**	1.75	.85	.17
☐ 235	**Al McDonough**	1.75	.85	.17
☐ 236	**Chris Evans**	1.75	.85	.17
☐ 237	**Pierre Jarry**	1.75	.85	.17
☐ 238	**Don Tannahill**	1.75	.85	.17
☐ 239	**Rey Comeau**	1.75	.85	.17
☐ 240	**Gregg Sheppard UER**	1.75	.85	.17
	(Misspelled Shepherd on card front)			
☐ 241	**Dave Dryden**	2.25	1.10	.22
☐ 242	**Ted McAneeley**	1.75	.85	.17
☐ 243	**Lou Angotti**	1.75	.85	.17
☐ 244	**Len Fontaine**	1.75	.85	.17
☐ 245	**Bill Lesuk**	1.75	.85	.17
☐ 246	**Fred Harvey**	1.75	.85	.17
☐ 247	**Ken Dryden AS2**	16.00	8.00	1.60
☐ 248	**Bill White AS2**	2.25	1.10	.22
☐ 249	**Pat Stapleton AS2**	2.25	1.10	.22
☐ 250	**Ratelle/Cournoyer/**	3.50	1.75	.35
	Hadfield AS2			
☐ 251	**Henri Richard**	4.00	2.00	.40
☐ 252	**Bryan Lefley**	1.75	.85	.17
☐ 253	**Stanley Cup Trophy**	3.00	1.50	.30
☐ 254	**Steve Vickers**	2.50	1.25	.25
☐ 255	**Wayne Hillman**	1.75	.85	.17
☐ 256	**Ken Schinkel UER**	1.75	.85	.17
	(Misspelled Shinkel on card front)			
☐ 257	**Kevin O'Shea**	1.75	.85	.17
☐ 258	**Ron Low**	3.00	1.50	.30
☐ 259	**Don Lever**	1.75	.85	.17
☐ 260	**Randy Manery**	1.75	.85	.17
☐ 261	**Ed Johnston**	2.25	1.10	.22
☐ 262	**Craig Ramsay**	1.75	.85	.17
☐ 263	**Pete Laframboise**	1.75	.85	.17
☐ 264	**Dan Maloney**	2.25	1.10	.22
☐ 265	**Bill Collins**	1.75	.85	.17
☐ 266	**Paul Curtis**	1.75	.85	.17
☐ 267	**Bob Nevin**	1.75	.85	.17

		NRMT	VG-E	GOOD
☐ 268	**Penalty Min. Leaders**	2.25	1.10	.22
	Bryan Watson			
	Keith Magnuson			
	Gary Dornhoefer			
☐ 269	**Jim Roberts**	1.75	.85	.17
☐ 270	**Brian Lavender**	1.75	.85	.17
☐ 271	**Dale Rolfe**	1.75	.85	.17
☐ 272	**Goals Leaders**	5.00	2.50	.50
	Phil Esposito			
	Vic Hadfield			
	Bobby Hull			
☐ 273	**Michel Belhumeur**	2.50	1.25	.25
☐ 274	**Eddie Shack**	2.50	1.25	.25
☐ 275	**Wayne Stephenson UER**	3.50	1.75	.35
	(Back has Forward stats			
	instead of Goalie stats)			
☐ 276	**Stanley Cup Winner**	3.00	1.50	.30
	Boston Bruins Team			
☐ 277	**Rick Kehoe**	3.50	1.75	.35
☐ 278	**Gerry O'Flaherty**	1.75	.85	.17
☐ 279	**Jacques Richard**	1.75	.85	.17
☐ 280	**Scoring Leaders**	20.00	10.00	2.00
	Phil Esposito			
	Bobby Orr			
	Jean Ratelle			
☐ 281	**Nick Beverley**	2.50	1.25	.25
☐ 282	**Larry Carriere**	2.50	1.25	.25
☐ 283	**Assists Leaders**	20.00	10.00	2.00
	Bobby Orr			
	Phil Esposito			
	Jean Ratelle			
☐ 284	**Rick Smith IA**	1.75	.85	.17
☐ 285	**Jerry Korab**	2.50	1.25	.25
☐ 286	**Goals Against**	3.50	1.75	.35
	Average Leaders			
	Tony Esposito			
	Gilles Villemure			
	Gump Worsley			
☐ 287	**Ron Stackhouse**	1.75	.85	.17
☐ 288	**Barry Long**	2.50	1.25	.25
☐ 289	**Dean Prentice**	2.50	1.25	.25
☐ 290	**Norm Beaudin**	3.00	1.50	.30
☐ 291	**Mike Amodeo**	3.00	1.50	.30
☐ 292	**Jim Harrison**	3.00	1.50	.30
☐ 293	**J.C. Tremblay**	4.00	2.00	.40
☐ 294	**Murray Hall**	3.00	1.50	.30
☐ 295	**Bart Crashley**	3.00	1.50	.30
☐ 296	**Wayne Connelly**	3.00	1.50	.30
☐ 297	**Bobby Sheehan**	3.00	1.50	.30
☐ 298	**Ron Anderson**	3.00	1.50	.30
☐ 299	**Chris Bordeleau**	3.00	1.50	.30
☐ 300	**Les Binkley**	4.00	2.00	.40
☐ 301	**Ron Walters**	3.00	1.50	.30

		NRMT	VG-E	GOOD
☐ 302	Jean Guy Gendron	3.00	1.50	.30
☐ 303	Gord Labossiere	3.00	1.50	.30
☐ 304	Gerry Odrowski	3.00	1.50	.30
☐ 305	Mike McMahon	3.00	1.50	.30
☐ 306	Gary Kurt	3.00	1.50	.30
☐ 307	Larry Cahan	3.00	1.50	.30
☐ 308	Wally Boyer	3.00	1.50	.30
☐ 309	Bob Charlebois	3.00	1.50	.30
☐ 310	Bob Falkenberg	3.00	1.50	.30
☐ 311	Jean Payette	3.00	1.50	.30
☐ 312	Ted Taylor	3.00	1.50	.30
☐ 313	Joe Szura	3.00	1.50	.30
☐ 314	George Morrison	3.00	1.50	.30
☐ 315	Wayne Rivers	3.00	1.50	.30
☐ 316	Reg Fleming	3.00	1.50	.30
☐ 317	Larry Hornung	3.00	1.50	.30
☐ 318	Ron Climie	3.00	1.50	.30
☐ 319	Val Fonteyne	3.00	1.50	.30
☐ 320	Michel Archambault	3.00	1.50	.30
☐ 321	Ab McDonald	3.00	1.50	.30
☐ 322	Bob Leduc	3.00	1.50	.30
☐ 323	Bob Wall	3.00	1.50	.30
☐ 324	Alain Caron	3.00	1.50	.30
☐ 325	Bob Woytowich	3.00	1.50	.30
☐ 326	Guy Trottier	3.00	1.50	.30
☐ 327	Bill Hicke	3.00	1.50	.30
☐ 328	Guy Dufour	3.00	1.50	.30
☐ 329	Wayne Rutledge	3.00	1.50	.30
☐ 330	Gary Veneruzzo	3.00	1.50	.30
☐ 331	Fred Speck	3.00	1.50	.30
☐ 332	Ron Ward	3.00	1.50	.30
☐ 333	Rosaire Paiement	3.00	1.50	.30
☐ 334A	Checklist 3	25.00	2.00	.40
	(Numbers 335-341 listed as More WHA Stars)			
☐ 334B	Checklist 3	25.00	2.00	.40
	(Numbers 335-341 listed correctly)			
☐ 335	Michel Parizeau	3.00	1.50	.30
☐ 336	Bobby Hull	40.00	20.00	4.00
☐ 337	Wayne Carleton	3.00	1.50	.30
☐ 338	John McKenzie	3.00	1.50	.30
☐ 339	Jim Dorey	3.00	1.50	.30
☐ 340	Gerry Cheevers	15.00	7.50	1.50
☐ 341	Gerry Pinder	6.00	1.75	.35

1973-74 O-Pee-Chee

VIC HADFIELD   left wing

The 1973-74 O-Pee-Chee NHL set features 264 NHL players in color. Cards are 2½" by 3½". The border color on the obverse has been changed from the Topps set of this same year. All the first series O-Pee-Chee cards have a red border whereas the second series cards have a green border. The backs, in both French and English, contain 1972-73 records, the card number, a short biography, and a cartoon-illustrated fact about the player. Team cards (92-107) give team and player records on the back. The cards were printed in Canada. The key rookie cards in this set are Bill Barber, Larry Robinson, and Billy Smith.

Le jeu NHL O-Pee-Chee 1973-74 représente 264 joueurs NHL en couleurs. Les cartes mesurent 2½" x 3½". La couleur bordant la face des cartes diffère de celle du jeu Topps de la même année. Toutes les cartes O-Pee-Chee de première série ont un bord rouge, alors que les cartes de deuxième série ont un bord vert. Le dos, imprimé en français et en anglais, comprend les statistiques pour 1972-73, le numéro de carte, une biographie concise, et un fait notable concernant le joueur, illustré d'une caricature. Les cartes d'équipe (92-107) indiquent, au dos, les statistiques pour l'équipe et les joueurs. Les cartes ont été imprimées au Canada. Les débutants importants représentés dans ce jeu sont Bill Barber, Larry Robinson et Billy Smith.

			NRMT	VG-E	GOOD
	COMPLETE SET (264)		325.00	160.00	32.00
	COMMON PLAYER (1-264)		.55	.27	.05
☐	1	Alex Delvecchio	5.00	1.50	.30
☐	2	Gilles Meloche	.85	.40	.08
☐	3	Phil Roberto	.55	.27	.05
☐	4	Orland Kurtenbach	.55	.27	.05
☐	5	Gilles Marotte	.85	.40	.08
☐	6	Stan Mikita	6.00	3.00	.60

		NRMT	VG-E	GOOD
☐ 7	Paul Henderson	.85	.40	.08
☐ 8	Gregg Sheppard	.55	.27	.05
☐ 9	Rod Seiling	.55	.27	.05
☐ 10	Red Berenson	.85	.40	.08
☐ 11	Jean Pronovost	.85	.40	.08
☐ 12	Dick Redmond	.55	.27	.05
☐ 13	Keith McCreary	.55	.27	.05
☐ 14	Bryan Watson	.55	.27	.05
☐ 15	Garry Unger	.85	.40	.08
☐ 16	Neil Komadoski	.55	.27	.05
☐ 17	Marcel Dionne	13.50	6.00	1.00
☐ 18	Ernie Hicke	.55	.27	.05
☐ 19	Andre Boudrias	.55	.27	.05
☐ 20	Bill Flett	.55	.27	.05
☐ 21	Marshall Johnston	.55	.27	.05
☐ 22	Gerry Meehan	.85	.40	.08
☐ 23	Ed Johnston	1.00	.50	.10
☐ 24	Serge Savard	2.00	1.00	.20
☐ 25	Walt Tkaczuk	.85	.40	.08
☐ 26	Ken Hodge	1.00	.50	.10
☐ 27	Norm Ullman	2.00	1.00	.20
☐ 28	Cliff Koroll	.55	.27	.05
☐ 29	Rey Comeau	.55	.27	.05
☐ 30	Bobby Orr	27.00	13.50	2.70
☐ 31	Wayne Stephenson	.85	.40	.08
☐ 32	Dan Maloney	.85	.40	.08
☐ 33	Henry Boucha	.55	.27	.05
☐ 34	Gerry Hart	.55	.27	.05
☐ 35	Bobby Schmautz	.55	.27	.05
☐ 36	Ross Lonsberry	.55	.27	.05
☐ 37	Ted McAneeley	.55	.27	.05
☐ 38	Don Luce	.55	.27	.05
☐ 39	Jim McKenny	.55	.27	.05
☐ 40	Jacques Laperriere	1.75	.85	.17
☐ 41	Bill Fairbairn	.55	.27	.05
☐ 42	Craig Cameron	.55	.27	.05
☐ 43	Bryan Hextall	.55	.27	.05
☐ 44	Chuck Lefley	.55	.27	.05
☐ 45	Dan Bouchard	.85	.40	.08
☐ 46	Jean Paul Parise	.55	.27	.05
☐ 47	Barclay Plager	.85	.40	.08
☐ 48	Mike Corrigan	.55	.27	.05
☐ 49	Nick Libett	.55	.27	.05
☐ 50	Bobby Clarke	9.00	4.50	.90
☐ 51	Bert Marshall	.55	.27	.05
☐ 52	Craig Patrick	.85	.40	.08
☐ 53	Richard Lemieux	.55	.27	.05
☐ 54	Tracy Pratt	.55	.27	.05
☐ 55	Ron Ellis	.55	.27	.05
☐ 56	Jacques Lemaire	2.00	1.00	.20
☐ 57	Steve Vickers	.55	.27	.05
☐ 58	Carol Vadnais	.55	.27	.05
☐ 59	Jim Rutherford	.85	.40	.08

			NRMT	VG-E	GOOD
☐	60	Rick Kehoe	.85	.40	.08
☐	61	Pat Quinn	.85	.40	.08
☐	62	Bill Goldsworthy	.85	.40	.08
☐	63	Dave Dryden	.85	.40	.08
☐	64	Rogatien Vachon	2.00	1.00	.20
☐	65	Gary Bergman	.55	.27	.05
☐	66	Bernie Parent	4.00	2.00	.40
☐	67	Ed Westfall	.85	.40	.08
☐	68	Ivan Boldirev	.85	.40	.08
☐	69	Don Tannahill	.55	.27	.05
☐	70	Gilbert Perreault	5.50	2.75	.55
☐	71	Mike Pelyk	.55	.27	.05
☐	72	Guy Lafleur	13.50	6.00	1.00
☐	73	Pit Martin	.55	.27	.05
☐	74	Gilles Gilbert	2.00	1.00	.20
☐	75	Jim Lorentz	.55	.27	.05
☐	76	Syl Apps	.55	.27	.05
☐	77	Phil Myre	.85	.40	.08
☐	78	Bill White	.85	.40	.08
☐	79	Jack Egers	.55	.27	.05
☐	80	Terry Harper	.55	.27	.05
☐	81	Bill Barber	25.00	12.50	2.50
☐	82	Roy Edwards	.55	.27	.05
☐	83	Brian Spencer	.55	.27	.05
☐	84	Reggie Leach	1.00	.50	.10
☐	85	Wayne Cashman	.85	.40	.08
☐	86	Jim Schoenfeld	1.00	.50	.10
☐	87	Henri Richard	3.50	1.75	.35
☐	88	Dennis O'Brien	.55	.27	.05
☐	89	Al McDonough	.55	.27	.05
☐	90	Tony Esposito	5.00	2.50	.50
☐	91	Joe Watson	.55	.27	.05
☐	92	Flames Team	1.25	.60	.12
☐	93	Bruins Team	1.25	.60	.12
☐	94	Sabres Team	1.25	.60	.12
☐	95	Golden Seals Team	1.25	.60	.12
☐	96	Blackhawks Team	1.25	.60	.12
☐	97	Red Wings Team	1.25	.60	.12
☐	98	Kings Team	1.25	.60	.12
☐	99	North Stars Team	1.25	.60	.12
☐	100	Canadiens Team	1.25	.60	.12
☐	101	Islanders Team	1.25	.60	.12
☐	102	Rangers Team	1.25	.60	.12
☐	103	Flyers Team	1.25	.60	.12
☐	104	Penguins Team	1.25	.60	.12
☐	105	Blues Team	1.25	.60	.12
☐	106	Maple Leafs Team	1.25	.60	.12
☐	107	Canucks Team	1.25	.60	.12
☐	108	Vic Hadfield	.85	.40	.08
☐	109	Tom Reid	.55	.27	.05
☐	110	Hilliard Graves	.55	.27	.05
☐	111	Don Lever	.55	.27	.05
☐	112	Jim Pappin	.55	.27	.05

			NRMT	VG-E	GOOD
☐ 113	Andre Dupont		.55	.27	.05
☐ 114	Guy Lapointe		1.25	.60	.12
☐ 115	Dennis Hextall		.85	.40	.08
☐ 116	Checklist 1		10.00	.75	.15
☐ 117	Bob Leiter		.55	.27	.05
☐ 118	Ab Demarco		.55	.27	.05
☐ 119	Gilles Villemure		.85	.40	.08
☐ 120	Phil Esposito		10.00	5.00	1.00
☐ 121	Mike Robitaille		.55	.27	.05
☐ 122	Real Lemieux		.55	.27	.05
☐ 123	Jim Neilson		.55	.27	.05
☐ 124	Steve Durbano		.85	.40	.08
☐ 125	Jude Drouin		.55	.27	.05
☐ 126	Gary Smith		.55	.27	.05
☐ 127	Cesare Maniago		.85	.40	.08
☐ 128	Lowell MacDonald		.85	.40	.08
☐ 129	Checklist 2		10.00	.75	.15
☐ 130	Billy Harris		.55	.27	.05
☐ 131	Randy Manery		.55	.27	.05
☐ 132	Darryl Sittler		4.00	2.00	.40
☐ 133	Goals Leaders		3.00	1.50	.30
	Phil Esposito				
	Rick MacLeish				
☐ 134	Assists Leaders		4.00	2.00	.40
	Phil Esposito				
	Bobby Clarke				
☐ 135	Scoring Leaders		4.00	2.00	.40
	Phil Esposito				
	Bobby Clarke				
☐ 136	Goals Against		3.50	1.75	.35
	Average Leaders				
	Ken Dryden				
	Tony Esposito				
☐ 137	Penalty Min. Leaders		.85	.40	.08
	Jim Schoenfeld				
	Dave Schultz				
☐ 138	Power Play Goal		3.00	1.50	.30
	Leaders				
	Phil Esposito				
	Rick MacLeish				
☐ 139	Rene Robert		.85	.40	.08
☐ 140	Dave Burrows		.55	.27	.05
☐ 141	Jean Ratelle		2.50	1.25	.25
☐ 142	Billy Smith		27.00	13.50	2.70
☐ 143	Jocelyn Guevremont		.55	.27	.05
☐ 144	Tim Ecclestone		.55	.27	.05
☐ 145	Frank Mahovlich		6.00	3.00	.60
☐ 146	Rick MacLeish		2.00	1.00	.20
☐ 147	Johnny Bucyk		3.00	1.50	.30
☐ 148	Bob Plager		.85	.40	.08
☐ 149	Curt Bennett		.55	.27	.05
☐ 150	Dave Keon		2.50	1.25	.25
☐ 151	Keith Magnuson		.85	.40	.08

			NRMT	VG-E	GOOD
☐	152	Walt McKechnie	.55	.27	.05
☐	153	Roger Crozier	.85	.40	.08
☐	154	Ted Harris	.55	.27	.05
☐	155	Butch Goring	1.25	.60	.12
☐	156	Rod Gilbert	2.50	1.25	.25
☐	157	Yvan Cournoyer	3.00	1.50	.30
☐	158	Doug Favell	.85	.40	.08
☐	159	Juha Widing	.55	.27	.05
☐	160	Ed Giacomin	2.25	1.10	.22
☐	161	Germain Gagnon	.55	.27	.05
☐	162	Dennis Kearns	.55	.27	.05
☐	163	Bill Collins	.55	.27	.05
☐	164	Peter Mahovlich	.85	.40	.08
☐	165	Brad Park	3.00	1.50	.30
☐	166	Dave Schultz	3.00	1.50	.30
☐	167	Dallas Smith	.85	.40	.08
☐	168	Gary Sabourin	.55	.27	.05
☐	169	Jacques Richard	.55	.27	.05
☐	170	Brian Glennie	.55	.27	.05
☐	171	Dennis Hull	1.00	.50	.10
☐	172	Joey Johnston	.55	.27	.05
☐	173	Richard Martin	1.25	.60	.12
☐	174	Barry Gibbs	.55	.27	.05
☐	175	Bob Berry	.85	.40	.08
☐	176	Greg Polis	.55	.27	.05
☐	177	Dale Rolfe	.55	.27	.05
☐	178	Gerry Desjardins	.85	.40	.08
☐	179	Bobby Lalonde	.55	.27	.05
☐	180	Mickey Redmond	.85	.40	.08
☐	181	Jim Roberts	.55	.27	.05
☐	182	Gary Dornhoefer	.85	.40	.08
☐	183	Derek Sanderson	1.00	.50	.10
☐	184	Brent Hughes	.55	.27	.05
☐	185	Larry Romanchych	.55	.27	.05
☐	186	Pierre Jarry	.55	.27	.05
☐	187	Doug Jarrett	.55	.27	.05
☐	188	Bob Stewart	.55	.27	.05
☐	189	Tim Horton	2.50	1.25	.25
☐	190	Fred Harvey	.55	.27	.05
☐	191	Series A Canadiens 4, Sabres 2	1.25	.60	.12
☐	192	Series B Flyers 4, North Stars 2	1.25	.60	.12
☐	193	Series C Blackhawks 4, Blues 1	1.25	.60	.12
☐	194	Series D Rangers 4 Bruins	1.25	.60	.12

			NRMT	VG-E	GOOD
☐	195	Series E .... Canadiens 4, Flyers 1	1.25	.60	.12
☐	196	Series F .... Blackhawks 4, Rangers 1	1.25	.60	.12
☐	197	Series G .... Canadiens 4, Blackhawks 2	1.25	.60	.12
☐	198	Stanley Cup Champs .... Montreal Canadiens	1.75	.85	.17
☐	199	Gary Edwards	.85	.40	.08
☐	200	Ron Schock	.55	.27	.05
☐	201	Bruce MacGregor............................	.55	.27	.05
☐	202	Bob Nystrom	3.00	1.50	.30
☐	203	Jerry Korab	.55	.27	.05
☐	204	Thommie Bergman	1.00	.50	.10
☐	205	Bill Lesuk	.55	.27	.05
☐	206	Ed Van Impe	.55	.27	.05
☐	207	Doug Roberts	.55	.27	.05
☐	208	Chris Evans	.55	.27	.05
☐	209	Lynn Powis.....................................	.55	.27	.05
☐	210	Denis Dupere	.55	.27	.05
☐	211	Dale Tallon	.55	.27	.05
☐	212	Stan Gilbertson	.55	.27	.05
☐	213	Craig Ramsay	.55	.27	.05
☐	214	Danny Grant	.55	.27	.05
☐	215	Doug Volmar	.55	.27	.05
☐	216	Darryl Edestrand	.55	.27	.05
☐	217	Pete Stemkowski	.55	.27	.05
☐	218	Lorne Henning	.55	.27	.05
☐	219	Bryan McShefrey	.55	.27	.05
☐	220	Guy Charron	.55	.27	.05
☐	221	Wayne Thomas	1.25	.60	.12
☐	222	Simon Nolet	.55	.27	.05
☐	223	Fred O'Donnell	.55	.27	.05
☐	224	Lou Angotti	.55	.27	.05
☐	225	Arnie Brown	.55	.27	.05
☐	226	Garry Monahan	.55	.27	.05
☐	227	Chico Maki	.55	.27	.05
☐	228	Gary Croteau	.55	.27	.05
☐	229	Paul Terbenche..............................	.55	.27	.05
☐	230	Gump Worsley	4.00	2.00	.40
☐	231	Jim Peters	.55	.27	.05
☐	232	Jack Lynch	.55	.27	.05
☐	233	Bobby Rousseau	.55	.27	.05
☐	234	Dave Hudson	.55	.27	.05
☐	235	Gregg Boddy	.55	.27	.05
☐	236	Ron Stackhouse	.55	.27	.05
☐	237	Larry Robinson	45.00	22.50	4.50
☐	238	Bobby Taylor	.55	.27	.05
☐	239	Nick Beverley	.55	.27	.05
☐	240	Don Awrey	.55	.27	.05

			NRMT	VG-E	GOOD
☐ 241	Doug Mohns		.55	.27	.05
☐ 242	Eddie Shack		1.00	.50	.10
☐ 243	Phil Russell		.55	.27	.05
☐ 244	Pete Laframboise		.55	.27	.05
☐ 245	Steve Atkinson		.55	.27	.05
☐ 246	Lou Nanne		.55	.27	.05
☐ 247	Yvon Labre		.55	.27	.05
☐ 248	Ted Irvine		.55	.27	.05
☐ 249	Tom Miller		.55	.27	.05
☐ 250	Gerry O'Flaherty		.55	.27	.05
☐ 251	Larry Johnston		.55	.27	.05
☐ 252	Michel Plasse		1.00	.50	.10
☐ 253	Bob Kelly		.55	.27	.05
☐ 254	Terry O'Reilly		3.50	1.75	.35
☐ 255	Pierre Plante		.85	.40	.08
☐ 256	Noel Price		.55	.27	.05
☐ 257	Dunc Wilson		.55	.27	.05
☐ 258	J.P. Bordeleau		.55	.27	.05
☐ 259	Terry Murray		2.00	1.00	.20
☐ 260	Larry Carriere		.55	.27	.05
☐ 261	Pierre Bouchard		.55	.27	.05
☐ 262	Frank St.Marseille		.55	.27	.05
☐ 263	Checklist 2		10.00	.75	.15
☐ 264	Fred Barrett		.85	.40	.08

1974-75 O-Pee-Chee NHL

The 1974-75 O-Pee-Chee NHL set contains 396 color cards; the first 264 cards feature identical fronts to those of the Topps set of this year. The backs, in both French and English, feature the card number, the player's NHL record, a short

biography, and a cartoon-illustrated fact about the player. The first six cards in the set (1-6) feature the statistical league leaders of the previous season. Cards are 2'/₂" by 3'/₂". The cards were printed in Canada. The key rookies in this set are Lanny McDonald and Denis Potvin.

Le jeu NHL O-Pee-Chee 1974-75 contient 396 cartes en couleurs; la face des 264 premières cartes est identique àcelle du jeu Topps de cette année. Le dos, imprimé en français et en anglais, comprend le numéro de carte, la fiche NHL du joueur, une biographie concise, et un fait notable concernant le joueur, illustré d'une caricature. Les six premières cartes du jeu (1-6) représentent les champions statistiques de la saison précédente. Les cartes mesurent 2'/₂" x 3'/₂", et ont été imprimées au Canada. Les débutants importants de ce jeu sont Larry McDonald et Denis Potvin.

			NRMT	VG-E	GOOD
		COMPLETE SET (396)	300.00	150.00	30.00
		COMMON PLAYER (1-396)	.40	.20	.04
☐	1	**Goal Leaders**	4.00	.00	.00
		Phil Esposito			
		Bill Goldsworthy			
☐	2	**Assists Leaders**	5.00	2.50	.50
		Bobby Orr			
		Dennis Hextall			
☐	3	**Scoring Leaders**	4.00	2.00	.40
		Phil Esposito			
		Bobby Clarke			
☐	4	**Goals Against Leaders**	1.00	.50	.10
		Doug Favell			
		Bernie Parent			
☐	5	**Penalty Min. Leaders**	.60	.30	.06
		Bryan Watson			
		Dave Schultz			
☐	6	**Power Play Goal**	.60	.30	.06
		Leaders			
		Mickey Redmond			
		Rick MacLeish			
☐	7	**Gary Bromley**	.40	.20	.04
☐	8	**Bill Barber**	4.00	2.00	.40
☐	9	**Emile Francis CO**	.75	.35	.07
☐	10	**Gilles Gilbert**	.60	.30	.06
☐	11	**John Davidson**	1.25	.60	.12
☐	12	**Ron Ellis**	.40	.20	.04
☐	13	**Syl Apps**	.40	.20	.04
☐	14	**Flames Leaders**	.60	.30	.06
		Jacques Richard			
		Tom Lysiak			
		Tom Lysiak			
		Keith McCreary			
☐	15	**Dan Bouchard**	.60	.30	.06
☐	16	**Ivan Boldirev**	.60	.30	.06
☐	17	**Gary Coalter**	.40	.20	.04
☐	18	**Bob Berry**	.60	.30	.06

			NRMT	VG-E	GOOD
☐	19	Red Berenson	.60	.30	.06
☐	20	Stan Mikita	5.00	2.50	.50
☐	21	Fred Shero CO	1.50	.75	.15
☐	22	Gary Smith	.40	.20	.04
☐	23	Bill Mikkelson	.40	.20	.04
☐	24	Jacques Lemaire UER	2.00	1.00	.20
		(Pictured in Sabres sweater)			
☐	25	Gilbert Perreault	3.50	1.75	.35
☐	26	Cesare Maniago	.60	.30	.06
☐	27	Bobby Schmautz	.40	.20	.04
☐	28	Bruins Leaders	9.00	4.50	.90
		Phil Esposito			
		Bobby Orr			
		Phil Esposito			
		Johnny Bucyk			
☐	29	Steve Vickers	.40	.20	.04
☐	30	Lowell MacDonald	.60	.30	.06
		(Home: Thornburn,			
		should be Thorburn)			
☐	31	Fred Stanfield	.40	.20	.04
☐	32	Ed Westfall	.60	.30	.06
☐	33	Curt Bennett	.40	.20	.04
☐	34	Bep Guidolin CO	.40	.20	.04
☐	35	Cliff Koroll	.40	.20	.04
☐	36	Gary Croteau	.40	.20	.04
☐	37	Mike Corrigan	.40	.20	.04
☐	38	Henry Boucha	.40	.20	.04
☐	39	Ron Low	.60	.30	.06
☐	40	Darryl Sittler	2.00	1.00	.20
☐	41	Tracy Pratt	.40	.20	.04
☐	42	Sabres Leaders	.60	.30	.06
		Richard Martin			
		Rene Robert			
		Richard Martin			
		Richard Martin			
☐	43	Larry Carriere	.40	.20	.04
☐	44	Gary Dornhoefer	.60	.30	.06
☐	45	Denis Herron	1.25	.60	.12
☐	46	Doug Favell	.60	.30	.06
☐	47	Dave Gardner	.40	.20	.04
☐	48	Morris Mott	.40	.20	.04
☐	49	Marc Boileau CO	.40	.20	.04
☐	50	Brad Park	2.00	1.00	.20
☐	51	Bob Leiter	.40	.20	.04
☐	52	Tom Reid	.40	.20	.04
☐	53	Serge Savard	1.75	.85	.17
☐	54	Checklist 1-132 UER	7.50	.50	.10
		(73 Brent Hughes, should			
		be 73 Butch Deadmarsh)			
☐	55	Terry Harper	.40	.20	.04

			NRMT	VG-E	GOOD
☐	56	Golden Seals	.60	.30	.06
		Leaders			
		Joey Johnston			
		Joey Johnston			
		Joey Johnston			
		Walt McKechnie			
☐	57	Guy Charron	.40	.20	.04
☐	58	Pit Martin	.40	.20	.04
☐	59	Chris Evans	.40	.20	.04
☐	60	Bernie Parent	3.50	1.75	.35
☐	61	Jim Lorentz	.40	.20	.04
☐	62	Dave Kryskow	.40	.20	.04
☐	63	Lou Angotti CO	.40	.20	.04
☐	64	Bill Flett	.40	.20	.04
☐	65	Vic Hadfield	.60	.30	.06
☐	66	Wayne Merrick	.40	.20	.04
☐	67	Andre Dupont	.40	.20	.04
☐	68	Tom Lysiak	1.00	.50	.10
☐	69	Blackhawks Leaders	1.00	.50	.10
		Jim Pappin			
		Stan Mikita			
		J.P. Bordeleau			
☐	70	Guy Lapointe	1.00	.50	.10
☐	71	Gerry O'Flaherty	.40	.20	.04
☐	72	Marcel Dionne	11.00	5.50	1.10
☐	73	Butch Deadmarsh	.40	.20	.04
☐	74	Butch Goring	.75	.35	.07
☐	75	Keith Magnuson	.60	.30	.06
☐	76	Red Kelly CO	1.50	.75	.15
☐	77	Pete Stemkowski	.40	.20	.04
☐	78	Jim Roberts	.40	.20	.04
		Montreal Canadiens			
☐	79	Don Luce	.40	.20	.04
☐	80	Don Awrey	.40	.20	.04
☐	81	Rick Kehoe	.60	.30	.06
☐	82	Billy Smith	4.50	2.25	.45
☐	83	Jean Paul Parise	.40	.20	.04
☐	84	Red Wings Leaders	1.50	.75	.15
		Mickey Redmond			
		Marcel Dionne			
		Marcel Dionne			
		Bill Hogaboam			
☐	85	Ed Van Impe	.40	.20	.04
☐	86	Randy Manery	.40	.20	.04
☐	87	Barclay Plager	.60	.30	.06
☐	88	Inge Hammarstrom	.40	.20	.04
☐	89	Ab Demarco	.40	.20	.04
☐	90	Bill White	.60	.30	.06
☐	91	Al Arbour CO	1.50	.75	.15
☐	92	Bob Stewart	.40	.20	.04
☐	93	Jack Egers	.40	.20	.04
☐	94	Don Lever	.40	.20	.04
☐	95	Reggie Leach	.75	.35	.07

			NRMT	VG-E	GOOD
☐	96	Dennis O'Brien	.40	.20	.04
☐	97	Peter Mahovlich	.60	.30	.06
☐	98	Kings Leaders	.60	.30	.06
		Butch Goring			
		Frank St. Marseille			
		Butch Goring			
		Don Kozak			
☐	99	Gerry Meehan	.75	.35	.07
☐	100	Bobby Orr	24.00	12.00	2.40
☐	101	Jean Potvin	1.00	.50	.10
☐	102	Rod Seiling	.40	.20	.04
☐	103	Keith McCreary	.40	.20	.04
☐	104	Phil Maloney CO	.40	.20	.04
☐	105	Denis Dupere	.40	.20	.04
☐	106	Steve Durbano	.40	.20	.04
☐	107	Bob Plager UER	.60	.30	.06
		(Photo actually			
		Barclay Plager)			
☐	108	Chris Oddleifson	.40	.20	.04
☐	109	Jim Neilson	.40	.20	.04
☐	110	Jean Pronovost	.60	.30	.06
☐	111	Don Kozak	.40	.20	.04
☐	112	North Stars Leaders	.60	.30	.06
		Bill Goldsworthy			
		Dennis Hextall			
		Dennis Hextall			
		Danny Grant			
☐	113	Jim Pappin	.40	.20	.04
☐	114	Richard Lemieux	.40	.20	.04
☐	115	Dennis Hextall	.60	.30	.06
☐	116	Bill Hogaboam	.40	.20	.04
☐	117	Canucks Leaders	.60	.30	.06
		Dennis Ververgaert			
		Bobby Schmautz			
		Andre Boudrias			
		Andre Boudrias			
		Don Tannahill			
☐	118	Jimmy Anderson CO	.40	.20	.04
☐	119	Walt Tkaczuk	.60	.30	.06
☐	120	Mickey Redmond	.60	.30	.06
☐	121	Jim Schoenfeld	.75	.35	.07
☐	122	Jocelyn Guevremont	.40	.20	.04
☐	123	Bob Nystrom	1.00	.50	.10
☐	124	Canadiens Leaders	2.50	1.25	.25
		Yvan Cournoyer			
		Frank Mahovlich			
		Frank Mahovlich			
		Claude Larose			
☐	125	Lew Morrison	.40	.20	.04
☐	126	Terry Murray	1.00	.50	.10
☐	127	Richard Martin AS	.60	.30	.06
☐	128	Ken Hodge AS	.60	.30	.06
☐	129	Phil Esposito AS	5.00	2.50	.50

		NRMT	VG-E	GOOD
☐ 130	Bobby Orr AS	14.00	7.00	1.40
☐ 131	Brad Park AS	1.25	.60	.12
☐ 132	Gilles Gilbert AS	.60	.30	.06
☐ 133	Lowell MacDonald AS	.60	.30	.06
☐ 134	Bill Goldsworthy AS	.60	.30	.06
☐ 135	Bobby Clarke AS	4.00	2.00	.40
☐ 136	Bill White AS	.60	.30	.06
☐ 137	Dave Burrows AS	.60	.30	.06
☐ 138	Bernie Parent AS	2.00	1.00	.20
☐ 139	Jacques Richard	.40	.20	.04
☐ 140	Yvan Cournoyer	2.50	1.25	.25
☐ 141	Rangers Leaders	2.00	1.00	.20
	Rod Gilbert			
	Brad Park			
	Brad Park			
	Rod Gilbert			
☐ 142	Rene Robert	.60	.30	.06
☐ 143	J. Bob Kelly	.40	.20	.04
☐ 144	Ross Lonsberry	.40	.20	.04
☐ 145	Jean Ratelle	2.00	1.00	.20
☐ 146	Dallas Smith	.60	.30	.06
☐ 147	Boom Boom Geoffrion CO	1.50	.75	.15
☐ 148	Ted McAneeley	.40	.20	.04
☐ 149	Pierre Plante	.40	.20	.04
☐ 150	Dennis Hull	.75	.35	.07
☐ 151	Dave Keon	1.75	.85	.17
☐ 152	Dave Dunn	.40	.20	.04
☐ 153	Michel Belhumeur	.60	.30	.06
☐ 154	Flyers Leaders	2.00	1.00	.20
	Bobby Clarke			
	Bobby Clarke			
	Bobby Clarke			
	Dave Schultz			
☐ 155	Ken Dryden	12.50	6.25	1.25
☐ 156	John Wright	.40	.20	.04
☐ 157	Larry Romanchych	.40	.20	.04
☐ 158	Ralph Stewart	.40	.20	.04
☐ 159	Mike Robitaille	.40	.20	.04
☐ 160	Ed Giacomin	2.00	1.00	.20
☐ 161	Don Cherry CO	4.00	2.00	.40
☐ 162	Checklist 133-264	7.50	.50	.10
☐ 163	Rick MacLeish	1.25	.60	.12
☐ 164	Greg Polis	.40	.20	.04
☐ 165	Carol Vadnais	.40	.20	.04
☐ 166	Pete Laframboise	.40	.20	.04
☐ 167	Ron Schock	.40	.20	.04
☐ 168	Lanny McDonald	35.00	17.50	3.50
☐ 169	Scouts Emblem	.75	.35	.07
	Draft Selections on back			
☐ 170	Tony Esposito	4.00	2.00	.40
☐ 171	Pierre Jarry	.40	.20	.04
☐ 172	Dan Maloney	.60	.30	.06
☐ 173	Peter McDuffe	.40	.20	.04

		NRMT	VG-E	GOOD
☐ 174	Danny Grant	.40	.20	.04
☐ 175	John Stewart	.40	.20	.04
☐ 176	Floyd Smith CO	.40	.20	.04
☐ 177	Bert Marshall	.40	.20	.04
☐ 178	Chuck Lefley UER	.40	.20	.04
	(Photo actually Pierre Bouchard)			
☐ 179	Gilles Villemure	.60	.30	.06
☐ 180	Borje Salming	7.50	3.75	.75
☐ 181	Doug Mohns	.40	.20	.04
☐ 182	Barry Wilkins	.40	.20	.04
☐ 183	Penguins Leaders	.60	.30	.06
	Lowell MacDonald			
	Syl Apps			
	Syl Apps			
	Lowell MacDonald			
☐ 184	Gregg Sheppard	.40	.20	.04
☐ 185	Joey Johnston	.40	.20	.04
☐ 186	Dick Redmond	.40	.20	.04
☐ 187	Simon Nolet	.40	.20	.04
☐ 188	Ron Stackhouse	.40	.20	.04
☐ 189	Marshall Johnston	.40	.20	.04
☐ 190	Rick Martin	.75	.35	.07
☐ 191	Andre Boudrias	.40	.20	.04
☐ 192	Steve Atkinson	.40	.20	.04
☐ 193	Nick Libett	.40	.20	.04
☐ 194	Bob Murdoch	.60	.30	.06
	Los Angeles Kings			
☐ 195	Denis Potvin	50.00	25.00	5.00
☐ 196	Dave Schultz	.60	.30	.06
☐ 197	Blues Leaders	.60	.30	.06
	Garry Unger			
	Garry Unger			
	Garry Unger			
	Pierre Plante			
☐ 198	Jim McKenny	.40	.20	.04
☐ 199	Gerry Hart	.40	.20	.04
☐ 200	Phil Esposito	7.50	3.75	.75
☐ 201	Rod Gilbert	2.00	1.00	.20
☐ 202	Jacques Laperriere	1.50	.75	.15
☐ 203	Barry Gibbs	.40	.20	.04
☐ 204	Billy Reay CO	.40	.20	.04
☐ 205	Gilles Meloche	.60	.30	.06
☐ 206	Wayne Cashman	.60	.30	.06
☐ 207	Dennis Ververgaert	.40	.20	.04
☐ 208	Phil Roberto	.40	.20	.04
☐ 209	Quarter Finals	.75	.35	.07
	Flyers sweep Flames			
☐ 210	Quarter Finals	.75	.35	.07
	Rangers over			
	Canadiens			
☐ 211	Quarter Finals	.75	.35	.07
	Bruins sweep			
	Maple Leafs			

		NRMT	VG-E	GOOD
☐ 212	**Quarter Finals**	.75	.35	.07
	Blackhawks over L.A. Kings			
☐ 213	**Semi-Finals**	.75	.35	.07
	Flyers over Rangers			
☐ 214	**Semi-Finals**	.75	.35	.07
	Bruins over Blackhawks			
☐ 215	**'73-'74 Finals**	.75	.35	.07
	Flyers over Bruins			
☐ 216	**Cup Champions**	1.00	.50	.10
	Philadelphia Flyers			
☐ 217	**Joe Watson**	.40	.20	.04
☐ 218	**Wayne Stephenson**	.60	.30	.06
☐ 219	**Maple Leaf Leaders**	1.00	.50	.10
	Darryl Sittler			
	Norm Ullman			
	Darryl Sittler			
	Paul Henderson			
	Denis Dupere			
☐ 220	**Bill Goldsworthy**	.60	.30	.06
☐ 221	**Don Marcotte**	.40	.20	.04
☐ 222	**Alex Delvecchio CO**	1.50	.75	.15
☐ 223	**Stan Gilbertson**	.40	.20	.04
☐ 224	**Mike Murphy**	.40	.20	.04
☐ 225	**Jim Rutherford**	.60	.30	.06
☐ 226	**Phil Russell**	.40	.20	.04
☐ 227	**Lynn Powis**	.40	.20	.04
☐ 228	**Billy Harris**	.40	.20	.04
☐ 229	**Bob Pulford CO**	1.25	.60	.12
	L.A. Kings Coach			
☐ 230	**Ken Hodge**	.75	.35	.07
☐ 231	**Bill Fairbairn**	.40	.20	.04
☐ 232	**Guy Lafleur**	12.00	6.00	1.20
☐ 233	**Islanders Leaders UER**	1.50	.75	.15
	Bill Harris			
	Ralph Stewart			
	Denis Potvin			
	Denis Potvin			
	Ralph Stewart			
	(Steward on front)			
☐ 234	**Fred Barrett**	.40	.20	.04
☐ 235	**Rogatien Vachon**	1.50	.75	.15
☐ 236	**Norm Ullman**	1.75	.85	.17
☐ 237	**Garry Unger**	.90	.45	.09
☐ 238	**Jack Gordon CO**	.40	.20	.04
☐ 239	**Johnny Bucyk**	2.00	1.00	.20
☐ 240	**Bob Dailey**	.40	.20	.04
☐ 241	**Dave Burrows**	.60	.30	.06
☐ 242	**Len Frig**	.40	.20	.04
☐ 243	**Masterson Trophy**	1.75	.85	.17
	Henri Richard			

		NRMT	VG-E	GOOD
☐ 244	**Hart Trophy** Phil Esposito	4.50	2.25	.45
☐ 245	**Byng Trophy** Johnny Bucyk	1.50	.75	.15
☐ 246	**Ross Trophy** Phil Esposito	4.50	2.25	.45
☐ 247	**Prince of Wales Trophy** Boston Bruins	.75	.35	.07
☐ 248	**Norris Trophy** Bobby Orr	14.00	7.00	1.40
☐ 249	**Vezina Trophy** Bernie Parent	1.75	.85	.17
☐ 250	**Stanley Cup** Philadelphia Flyers	1.00	.50	.10
☐ 251	**Smythe Trophy** Bernie Parent	1.75	.85	.17
☐ 252	**Calder Trophy** Denis Potvin	9.00	4.50	.90
☐ 253	**Campbell Trophy** Philadelphia Flyers	.75	.35	.07
☐ 254	**Pierre Bouchard**	.40	.20	.04
☐ 255	**Jude Drouin**	.40	.20	.04
☐ 256	**Capitals Emblem** (Draft Selections on back)	.75	.35	.07
☐ 257	**Michel Plasse**	.60	.30	.06
☐ 258	**Juha Widing**	.40	.20	.04
☐ 259	**Bryan Watson**	.40	.20	.04
☐ 260	**Bobby Clarke**	7.50	3.75	.75
☐ 261	**Scotty Bowman CO**	2.00	1.00	.20
☐ 262	**Craig Patrick**	.60	.30	.06
☐ 263	**Craig Cameron**	.40	.20	.04
☐ 264	**Ted Irvine**	.40	.20	.04
☐ 265	**Ed Johnston**	.75	.35	.07
☐ 266	**Dave Forbes**	.40	.20	.04
☐ 267	**Detroit Red Wings** Team Card (checklist back)	1.00	.50	.10
☐ 268	**Rick Dudley**	1.50	.75	.15
☐ 269	**Darcy Rota**	.40	.20	.04
☐ 270	**Phil Myre**	.60	.30	.06
☐ 271	**Larry Brown**	.40	.20	.04
☐ 272	**Bob Neely**	.40	.20	.04
☐ 273	**Jerry Byers**	.40	.20	.04
☐ 274	**Pittsburgh Penguins** Team Card (checklist back)	1.00	.50	.10
☐ 275	**Glenn Goldup**	.60	.30	.06
☐ 276	**Ron Harris**	.40	.20	.04
☐ 277	**Joe Lundrigan**	.40	.20	.04
☐ 278	**Mike Christie**	.40	.20	.04
☐ 279	**Doug Rombough**	.40	.20	.04
☐ 280	**Larry Robinson**	10.00	5.00	1.00

		NRMT	VG-E	GOOD
☐ 281	St. Louis Blues	1.00	.50	.10
	Team Card			
	(checklist back)			
☐ 282	John Marks	.40	.20	.04
☐ 283	Don Saleski	.40	.20	.04
☐ 284	Rick Wilson	.40	.20	.04
☐ 285	Andre Savard	.40	.20	.04
☐ 286	Pat Quinn	.60	.30	.06
☐ 287	Los Angeles Kings	1.00	.50	.10
	Team Card			
	(checklist back)			
☐ 288	Norm Gratton	.40	.20	.04
☐ 289	Ian Turnbull	1.00	.50	.10
☐ 290	Derek Sanderson	.75	.35	.07
☐ 291	Murray Oliver	.40	.20	.04
☐ 292	Wilf Paiement UER	1.00	.50	.10
	(Misspelled Paiemont			
	on card front)			
☐ 293	Nelson Debenedet	.40	.20	.04
☐ 294	Greg Joly	.40	.20	.04
☐ 295	Terry O'Reilly	1.00	.50	.10
☐ 296	Rey Comeau	.40	.20	.04
☐ 297	Michel Larocque	1.00	.50	.10
☐ 298	Floyd Thomson	.40	.20	.04
☐ 299	Jean Guy Lagace	.40	.20	.04
☐ 300	Philadelphia Flyers	1.00	.50	.10
	Team Card			
	(checklist back)			
☐ 301	Al MacAdam	1.00	.50	.10
☐ 302	George Ferguson	.40	.20	.04
☐ 303	Jim Watson	.40	.20	.04
☐ 304	Rick Middleton	10.00	5.00	1.00
☐ 305	Craig Ramsay	.40	.20	.04
☐ 306	Hilliard Graves	.40	.20	.04
☐ 307	New York Islanders	1.00	.50	.10
	Team Card			
	(checklist back)			
☐ 308	Blake Dunlop	.40	.20	.04
☐ 309	J.P. Bordeleau	.40	.20	.04
☐ 310	Brian Glennie	.40	.20	.04
☐ 311	Checklist 265-396 UER	7.50	.50	.10
	(373 Gilies Marotte,			
	should be Gilles)			
☐ 312	Doug Roberts	.40	.20	.04
☐ 313	Darryl Edestrand	.40	.20	.04
☐ 314	Ron Anderson	.40	.20	.04
☐ 315	Chicago Blackhawks	1.00	.50	.10
	Team Card			
	(checklist back)			
☐ 316	Steve Shutt	10.00	5.00	1.00
☐ 317	Doug Horbul	.40	.20	.04
☐ 318	Billy Lochead	.40	.20	.04
☐ 319	Fred Harvey	.40	.20	.04

		NRMT	VG-E	GOOD
☐ 320	Gene Carr	.40	.20	.04
☐ 321	Henri Richard	2.00	1.00	.20
☐ 322	Vancouver Canucks	1.00	.50	.10
	Team Card			
	(checklist back)			
☐ 323	Tim Ecclestone	.40	.20	.04
☐ 324	Dave Lewis	.40	.20	.04
☐ 325	Lou Nanne	.40	.20	.04
☐ 326	Bobby Rousseau	.40	.20	.04
☐ 327	Dunc Wilson	.40	.20	.04
☐ 328	Brian Spencer	.40	.20	.04
☐ 329	Rick Hampton	.40	.20	.04
☐ 330	Montreal Canadiens	1.00	.50	.10
	Team Card UER			
	(checklist back;			
	275 Glen Holdup,			
	should be Goldup)			
☐ 331	Jack Lynch	.40	.20	.04
☐ 332	Garnet Bailey	.40	.20	.04
☐ 333	Al Sims	.40	.20	.04
☐ 334	Orest Kindrachuk	.60	.30	.06
☐ 335	Dave Hudson	.40	.20	.04
☐ 336	Bob Murray	.40	.20	.04
☐ 337	Buffalo Sabres	1.00	.50	.10
	Team Card			
	(checklist back)			
☐ 338	Sheldon Kannegiesser	.40	.20	.04
☐ 339	Bill MacMillan	.40	.20	.04
☐ 340	Paulin Bordeleau	.40	.20	.04
☐ 341	Dale Rolfe	.40	.20	.04
☐ 342	Yvon Lambert	.60	.30	.06
☐ 343	Bob Paradise	.40	.20	.04
☐ 344	Germain Gagnon	.40	.20	.04
☐ 345	Yvon Labre	.40	.20	.04
☐ 346	Chris Ahrens	.40	.20	.04
☐ 347	Danny Grant	.40	.20	.04
☐ 348	Blaine Stoughton	1.25	.60	.12
☐ 349	Gregg Boddy	.40	.20	.04
☐ 350	Boston Bruins	1.00	.50	.10
	Team Card			
	(checklist back)			
☐ 351	Doug Jarrett	.40	.20	.04
☐ 352	Terry Crisp	.75	.35	.07
☐ 353	Glenn Resch	10.00	5.00	1.00
☐ 354	Jerry Korab	.40	.20	.04
☐ 355	Stan Weir	.40	.20	.04
☐ 356	Noel Price	.40	.20	.04
☐ 357	Bill Clement	1.50	.75	.15
☐ 358	Neil Komadoski	.40	.20	.04
☐ 359	Murray Wilson	.40	.20	.04
☐ 360	Dale Tallon UER	.40	.20	.04
	(Misspelled Talon			
	on card front)			

		NRMT	VG-E	GOOD
☐ 361	Gary Doak	.40	.20	.04
☐ 362	Randy Rota	.40	.20	.04
☐ 363	Minnesota North Stars	1.00	.50	.10
	Team Card			
	(checklist back)			
☐ 364	Bill Collins	.40	.20	.04
☐ 365	Thommie Bergman UER	.40	.20	.04
	(Misspelled Tommie			
	on card front)			
☐ 366	Dennis Kearns	.40	.20	.04
☐ 367	Lorne Henning	.40	.20	.04
☐ 368	Gary Sabourin	.40	.20	.04
☐ 369	Mike Bloom	.40	.20	.04
☐ 370	New York Rangers	1.00	.50	.10
	Team Card			
	(checklist back)			
☐ 371	Gary Simmons	1.00	.50	.10
☐ 372	Dwight Bialowas	.40	.20	.04
☐ 373	Gilles Marotte	.60	.30	.06
☐ 374	Frank St.Marseille	.40	.20	.04
☐ 375	Garry Howatt	.75	.35	.07
☐ 376	Ross Brooks	.40	.20	.04
☐ 377	Atlanta Flames	1.00	.50	.10
	Team Card			
	(checklist back)			
☐ 378	Bob Nevin	.60	.30	.06
☐ 379	Lyle Moffat	.40	.20	.04
☐ 380	Bob Kelly	.40	.20	.04
☐ 381	John Gould	.40	.20	.04
☐ 382	Dave Fortier	.40	.20	.04
☐ 383	Jean Hamel	.40	.20	.04
☐ 384	Bert Wilson	.40	.20	.04
☐ 385	Chuck Arnason	.40	.20	.04
☐ 386	Bruce Cowick	.40	.20	.04
☐ 387	Ernie Hicke	.40	.20	.04
☐ 388	Bob Gainey	12.00	6.00	1.20
☐ 389	Vic Venasky	.40	.20	.04
☐ 390	Toronto Maple Leafs	1.00	.50	.10
	Team Card			
	(checklist back)			
☐ 391	Eric Vail	1.00	.50	.10
☐ 392	Bobby Lalonde	.40	.20	.04
☐ 393	Jerry Butler	.40	.20	.04
☐ 394	Tom Williams	.40	.20	.04
☐ 395	Chico Maki	.40	.20	.04
☐ 396	Tom Bladon	1.25	.60	.12

1974-75 O-Pee-Chee WHA

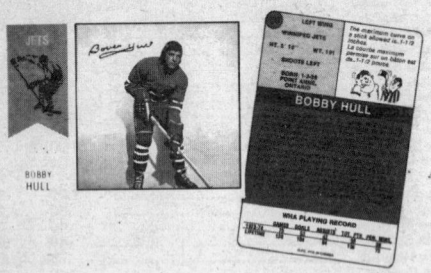

The 1974-75 O-Pee-Chee WHA set consists of 66 color cards of WHA players. Cards are 2½" by 3½". The backs, in both French and English, feature the card number, a short biography, the player's WHA record, and a cartoon-illustrated hockey fact or referee's signal. The cards were printed in Canada. The only notable rookie cards in this set are Anders Hedberg and Ulf Nilsson, although some collectors and dealers consider the Howe Family card to be the rookie for Mark and Marty.

Le jeu WHA O-Pee-Chee 1974-75 contient 66 cartes en couleurs de joueurs de la WHA. Les cartes mesurent 2½" x 3½". Le dos, imprimé en français et en anglais, comprend le numéro de carte, une biographie concise, la fiche WHA du joueur, et un exploit de hockey ou un signal d'arbitre, illustré d'une caricature. Les cartes ont été imprimées au Canada. Les seules débutants notables de ce jeu sont Anders Hedberg et Ulf Nilsson, quoique certains collectionneurs et négociants considèrent Mark et Marty, sur la carte de la famille Howe, comme débutants prometteurs.

			NRMT	VG-E	GOOD
		COMPLETE SET (66)	125.00	60.00	12.50
		COMMON PLAYER (1-66)	.80	.40	.08
☐	1	The Howes	60.00	12.00	2.50
		Gordie Howe			
		Mark Howe			
		Marty Howe			
☐	2	Bruce MacGregor	.80	.40	.08
☐	3	Wayne Dillon	.80	.40	.08
☐	4	Ulf Nilsson	3.50	1.75	.35
☐	5	Serge Bernier	1.00	.50	.10
☐	6	Bryan Campbell	.80	.40	.08
☐	7	Rosaire Paiement	.80	.40	.08
☐	8	Tom Webster	1.75	.85	.17

			NRMT	VG-E	GOOD
☐	9	Gerry Pinder	1.00	.50	.10
☐	10	Mike Walton	1.25	.60	.12
☐	11	Norm Beaudin	.80	.40	.08
☐	12	Bob Whitlock	.80	.40	.08
☐	13	Wayne Rivers	.80	.40	.08
☐	14	Gerry Odrowski	.80	.40	.08
☐	15	Ron Climie	.80	.40	.08
☐	16	Tom Simpson	.80	.40	.08
☐	17	Anders Hedberg	3.50	1.75	.35
☐	18	J.C. Tremblay	1.50	.75	.15
☐	19	Mike Pelyk	.80	.40	.08
☐	20	Dave Dryden	1.25	.60	.12
☐	21	Ron Ward	.80	.40	.08
☐	22	Larry Lund	.80	.40	.08
☐	23	Ron Buchanan	.80	.40	.08
☐	24	Pat Hickey	1.75	.85	.17
☐	25	Danny Lawson	.80	.40	.08
☐	26	Bob Guindon	.80	.40	.08
☐	27	Gene Peacosh	.80	.40	.08
☐	28	Fran Huck	.80	.40	.08
☐	29	Al Hamilton	.80	.40	.08
☐	30	Gerry Cheevers	6.00	3.00	.60
☐	31	Heikki Riihiranta	.80	.40	.08
☐	32	Don Burgess	.80	.40	.08
☐	33	John French	.80	.40	.08
☐	34	Jim Wiste	.80	.40	.08
☐	35	Pat Stapleton	1.25	.60	.12
☐	36	J.P. Leblanc	.80	.40	.08
☐	37	Mike Antonovich	.80	.40	.08
☐	38	Joe Daley	1.00	.50	.10
☐	39	Ross Perkins	.80	.40	.08
☐	40	Frank Mahovlich	7.50	3.75	.75
☐	41	Rejean Houle	1.00	.50	.10
☐	42	Ron Chipperfield	.80	.40	.08
☐	43	Marc Tardif	1.25	.60	.12
☐	44	Murray Keogan	.80	.40	.08
☐	45	Wayne Carleton	.80	.40	.08
☐	46	Andre Gaudette	.80	.40	.08
☐	47	Ralph Backstrom	1.00	.50	.10
☐	48	Don McLeod	.80	.40	.08
☐	49	Vaclav Nedomansky	1.75	.85	.17
☐	50	Bobby Hull	22.00	11.00	2.20
☐	51	Rusty Patenaude	.80	.40	.08
☐	52	Michel Parizeau	.80	.40	.08
☐	53	Checklist	6.00	.50	.10
☐	54	Wayne Connelly	1.00	.50	.10
☐	55	Gary Veneruzzo	.80	.40	.08
☐	56	Dennis Sobchuk	.80	.40	.08
☐	57	Paul Henderson	1.25	.60	.12
☐	58	Andy Brown	.80	.40	.08
☐	59	Poul Popiel	.80	.40	.08
☐	60	Andre Lacroix	1.00	.50	.10
☐	61	Gary Jarrett	.80	.40	.08

			NRMT	VG-E	GOOD
☐	62	Claude St. Sauveur	.80	.40	.08
☐	63	Real Cloutier	1.25	.60	.12
☐	64	Jacques Plante	9.00	4.50	.90
☐	65	Gilles Gratton	1.25	.60	.12
☐	66	Lars-Erik Sjoberg..................................	1.50	.75	.15

1975-76 O-Pee-Chee NHL

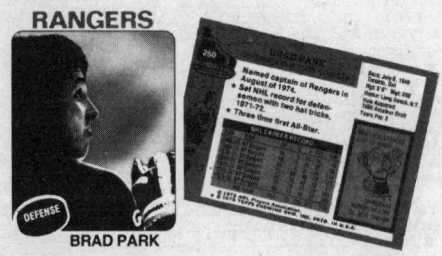

The 1975-76 O-Pee-Chee NHL set consists of 396 color cards of NHL players. The first 330 cards have identical fronts (except perhaps for a short traded line) as the Topps set of this year. Cards are 2¹/₂" by 3¹/₂". Number 395 was not issued; however, the O-Pee-Chee set contains two numbers 267 (both are checklist cards). Cards 26, 27, 200, 236, 243, 260, and 359 come with or without a traded line. Team cards (81-98) have a team checklist (of that team's players in the set) on the back. The backs, in both French and English, contain the card number, NHL records, a short biography, and a cartoon-illustrated NHL fact or referee's signal. The cards were printed in Canada. 75-6 OPC NHL: The key rookies in this set are Clark Gillies, Pierre Larouche, and Harold Snepsts.

Le jeu NHL O-Pee-Chee 1975-76 contient 396 cartes en couleurs de joueurs NHL. Les 330 premières cartes ont une face identique à celle du jeu Topps de cette année (avec l'exception possible d'une petite liste d'échanges). Les cartes mesurent 2¹/₂" x 3¹/₂". Le numéro 395 n'a pas été émis; le jeu O-Pee-Chee contient, cependant, deux numéros 267 (les deux cartes étant des cartes de contrôle). Les cartes 26, 27, 200, 236, 243, 260, et 359 sont disponibles avec ou sans liste d'échange. Les cartes d'équipe (81-98) ont, au dos, une liste de contrôle d'équipe (des joueurs de l'équipe de ce jeu). Le dos, imprimé en français et en anglais, comprend le numéro de carte, les statistiques NHL, une biographie concise, et un exploit NHL ou un signal d'arbitre, illustré d'une caricature. Les cartes ont été imprimées au Canada. OPC NHL 75-6; les débutants importants de ce jeu sont Clark Gillies, Pierre Larouche et Harold Snepsts.

			NRMT	VG-E	GOOD
		COMPLETE SET (396)	250.00	125.00	25.00
		COMMON PLAYER (1-396)	.30	.15	.03
☐	1	**Stanley Cup Finals**	2.50	.50	.10
		Philadelphia 4, Buffalo 2			
☐	2	**Semi-Finals**	.75	.35	.07
		Philadelphia 4, N.Y. Islanders 3			
☐	3	**Semi-Finals**	.75	.35	.07
		Buffalo 4, Montreal			
☐	4	**Quarter Finals**	.75	.35	.07
		N.Y. Islanders 4, Pittsburgh 2			
☐	5	**Quarter Finals**	.75	.35	.07
		Montreal 4, Vancouver 1			
☐	6	**Quarter Finals**	.75	.35	.07
		Buffalo 4, Chicago 1			
☐	7	**Quarter Finals**	.75	.35	.07
		Philadelphia 4, Toronto 0			
☐	8	**Curt Bennett**	.30	.15	.03
☐	9	**Johnny Bucyk**	1.50	.75	.15
☐	10	**Gilbert Perreault**	3.00	1.50	.30
☐	11	**Darryl Edestrand**	.30	.15	.03
☐	12	**Ivan Boldirev**	.30	.15	.03
☐	13	**Nick Libett**	.30	.15	.03
☐	14	**Jim McElmury**	.30	.15	.03
☐	15	**Frank St.Marseille**	.30	.15	.03
☐	16	**Blake Dunlop**	.30	.15	.03
☐	17	**Yvon Lambert**	.30	.15	.03
☐	18	**Gerry Hart**	.30	.15	.03
☐	19	**Steve Vickers**	.30	.15	.03
☐	20	**Rick MacLeish**	.75	.35	.07
☐	21	**Bob Paradise**	.30	.15	.03
☐	22	**Red Berenson**	.50	.25	.05
☐	23	**Lanny McDonald**	4.00	2.00	.40
☐	24	**Mike Robitaille**	.30	.15	.03
☐	25	**Ron Low**	.50	.25	.05
☐	26A	**Bryan Hextall**	.50	.25	.05
		(No mention of trade)			
☐	26A	**Bryan Hextall**	.50	.25	.05
		(Trade noted)			
☐	27A	**Carol Vadnais**	.30	.15	.03
		(No mention of trade)			
☐	27B	**Carol Vadnais**	.30	.15	.03
		(Trade noted)			
☐	28	**Jim Lorentz**	.30	.15	.03
☐	29	**Gary Simmons**	.50	.25	.05
☐	30	**Stan Mikita**	4.00	2.00	.40
☐	31	**Bryan Watson**	.30	.15	.03

			NRMT	VG-E	GOOD
☐	32	Guy Charron	.30	.15	.03
☐	33	Bob Murdoch	.30	.15	.03
		Los Angeles Kings			
☐	34	Norm Gratton	.30	.15	.03
☐	35	Ken Dryden	10.00	5.00	1.00
☐	36	Jean Potvin	.30	.15	.03
☐	37	Rick Middleton	2.00	1.00	.20
☐	38	Ed Van Impe	.30	.15	.03
☐	39	Rick Kehoe	.50	.25	.05
☐	40	Garry Unger	.60	.30	.06
☐	41	Ian Turnbull	.30	.15	.03
☐	42	Dennis Ververgaert	.30	.15	.03
☐	43	Mike Marson	.30	.15	.03
☐	44	Randy Manery	.30	.15	.03
☐	45	Gilles Gilbert	.50	.25	.05
☐	46	Rene Robert	.50	.25	.05
☐	47	Bob Stewart	.30	.15	.03
☐	48	Pit Martin	.30	.15	.03
☐	49	Danny Grant	.30	.15	.03
☐	50	Peter Mahovlich	.50	.25	.05
☐	51	Dennis Patterson	.30	.15	.03
☐	52	Mike Murphy	.30	.15	.03
☐	53	Dennis O'Brien	.30	.15	.03
☐	54	Garry Howatt	.30	.15	.03
☐	55	Ed Giacomin	2.00	1.00	.20
☐	56	Andre Dupont	.30	.15	.03
☐	57	Chuck Arnason	.30	.15	.03
☐	58	Bob Gassoff	.30	.15	.03
☐	59	Ron Ellis	.30	.15	.03
☐	60	Andre Boudrias	.30	.15	.03
☐	61	Yvon Labre	.30	.15	.03
☐	62	Hilliard Graves	.30	.15	.03
☐	63	Wayne Cashman	.50	.25	.05
☐	64	Danny Gare	1.00	.50	.10
☐	65	Rick Hampton	.30	.15	.03
☐	66	Darcy Rota	.30	.15	.03
☐	67	Bill Hogaboam	.30	.15	.03
☐	68	Denis Herron	.50	.25	.05
☐	69	Sheldon Kannegiesser	.30	.15	.03
☐	70	Yvan Cournoyer	2.00	1.00	.20
☐	71	Ernie Hicke	.30	.15	.03
☐	72	Bert Marshall	.30	.15	.03
☐	73	Derek Sanderson	.50	.25	.05
☐	74	Tom Bladon	.30	.15	.03
☐	75	Ron Schock	.30	.15	.03
☐	76	Larry Sacharuk	.30	.15	.03
☐	77	George Ferguson	.30	.15	.03
☐	78	Ab Demarco	.30	.15	.03
☐	79	Tom Williams	.30	.15	.03
☐	80	Phil Roberto	.30	.15	.03
☐	81	Bruins Team	1.00	.50	.10
		(checklist back)			

			NRMT	VG-E	GOOD
☐	82	Seals Team (checklist back)	1.00	.50	.10
☐	83	Sabres Team (checklist back)	1.00	.50	.10
☐	84	Blackhawks Team (checklist back)	1.00	.50	.10
☐	85	Flames Team (checklist back)	1.00	.50	.10
☐	86	Kings Team (checklist back)	1.00	.50	.10
☐	87	Red Wings Team (checklist back)	1.00	.50	.10
☐	88	Scouts Team (checklist back)	1.00	.50	.10
☐	89	North Stars Team (checklist back)	1.00	.50	.10
☐	90	Canadiens Team (checklist back)	1.00	.50	.10
☐	91	Maple Leafs Team (checklist back)	1.00	.50	.10
☐	92	Islanders Team (checklist back)	1.00	.50	.10
☐	93	Penguins Team (checklist back)	1.00	.50	.10
☐	94	Rangers Team (checklist back)	1.00	.50	.10
☐	95	Flyers Team (checklist back)	1.00	.50	.10
☐	96	Blues Team (checklist back)	1.00	.50	.10
☐	97	Canucks Team (checklist back)	1.00	.50	.10
☐	98	Capitals Team (checklist back)	1.00	.50	.10
☐	99	Checklist 1-110	5.00	.35	.07
☐	100	Bobby Orr	20.00	10.00	2.00
☐	101	Germain Gagnon	.30	.15	.03
☐	102	Phil Russell	.30	.15	.03
☐	103	Billy Lochead	.30	.15	.03
☐	104	Robin Burns	.30	.15	.03
☐	105	Gary Edwards	.30	.15	.03
☐	106	Dwight Bialowas	.30	.15	.03
☐	107	Doug Risebrough UER (Photo actually Bob Gainey)	2.00	1.00	.20
☐	108	Dave Lewis	.30	.15	.03
☐	109	Bill Fairbairn	.30	.15	.03
☐	110	Ross Lonsberry	.30	.15	.03
☐	111	Ron Stackhouse	.30	.15	.03
☐	112	Claude Larose	.30	.15	.03
☐	113	Don Luce	.30	.15	.03
☐	114	Errol Thompson	.30	.15	.03
☐	115	Gary Smith	.30	.15	.03

			NRMT	VG-E	GOOD
☐	116	Jack Lynch	.30	.15	.03
☐	117	Jacques Richard	.30	.15	.03
☐	118	Dallas Smith	.30	.15	.03
☐	119	Dave Gardner	.30	.15	.03
☐	120	Mickey Redmond	.50	.25	.05
☐	121	John Marks	.30	.15	.03
☐	122	Dave Hudson	.30	.15	.03
☐	123	Bob Nevin	.50	.25	.05
☐	124	Fred Barrett	.30	.15	.03
☐	125	Gerry Desjardins	.60	.30	.06
☐	126	Guy Lafleur UER	10.00	5.00	1.00
		(Shown as Defenseman on card front)			
☐	127	Jean Paul Parise	.30	.15	.03
☐	128	Walt Tkaczuk	.50	.25	.05
☐	129	Gary Dornhoefer	.50	.25	.05
☐	130	Syl Apps	.30	.15	.03
☐	131	Bob Plager	.50	.25	.05
☐	132	Stan Weir	.30	.15	.03
☐	133	Tracy Pratt	.30	.15	.03
☐	134	Jack Egers	.30	.15	.03
☐	135	Eric Vail	.50	.25	.05
☐	136	Al Sims	.30	.15	.03
☐	137	Larry Patey	.30	.15	.03
☐	138	Jim Schoenfeld	.60	.30	.06
☐	139	Cliff Koroll	.30	.15	.03
☐	140	Marcel Dionne	9.00	4.50	.90
☐	141	Jean Guy Lagace	.30	.15	.03
☐	142	Juha Widing	.30	.15	.03
☐	143	Lou Nanne	.30	.15	.03
☐	144	Serge Savard	1.50	.75	.15
☐	145	Glenn Resch	1.75	.85	.17
☐	146	Ron Greschner	2.00	1.00	.20
☐	147	Dave Schultz	.50	.25	.05
☐	148	Barry Wilkins	.30	.15	.03
☐	149	Floyd Thomson	.30	.15	.03
☐	150	Darryl Sittler	1.50	.75	.15
☐	151	Paulin Bordeleau	.30	.15	.03
☐	152	Ron Lalonde	.30	.15	.03
☐	153	Larry Romanchych	.30	.15	.03
☐	154	Larry Carriere	.30	.15	.03
☐	155	Andre Savard	.30	.15	.03
☐	156	Dave Hrechkosy	.30	.15	.03
☐	157	Bill White	.50	.25	.05
☐	158	Dave Kryshow	.30	.15	.03
☐	159	Denis Dupere	.30	.15	.03
☐	160	Rogatien Vachon	1.25	.60	.12
☐	161	Doug Rombough	.30	.15	.03
☐	162	Murray Wilson	.30	.15	.03
☐	163	Bob Bourne	1.50	.75	.15
☐	164	Gilles Marotte	.50	.25	.05
☐	165	Vic Hadfield	.50	.25	.05
☐	166	Reggie Leach	.60	.30	.06

		NRMT	VG-E	GOOD
☐ 167	Jerry Butler	.30	.15	.03
☐ 168	Inge Hammarstrom	.30	.15	.03
☐ 169	Chris Oddleifson	.30	.15	.03
☐ 170	Greg Joly	.30	.15	.03
☐ 171	Checklist 111-220	5.00	.35	.07
☐ 172	Pat Quinn	.50	.25	.05
☐ 173	Dave Forbes	.30	.15	.03
☐ 174	Len Frig	.30	.15	.03
☐ 175	Rick Martin	.60	.30	.06
☐ 176	Keith Magnuson	.50	.25	.05
☐ 177	Dan Maloney	.50	.25	.05
☐ 178	Craig Patrick	.50	.25	.05
☐ 179	Tom Williams	.30	.15	.03
☐ 180	Bill Goldsworthy	.50	.25	.05
☐ 181	Steve Shutt	2.00	1.00	.20
☐ 182	Ralph Stewart	.30	.15	.03
☐ 183	John Davidson	.50	.25	.05
☐ 184	Bob Kelly	.30	.15	.03
☐ 185	Ed Johnston	.50	.25	.05
☐ 186	Dave Burrows	.50	.25	.05
☐ 187	Dave Dunn	.30	.15	.03
☐ 188	Dennis Kearns	.30	.15	.03
☐ 189	Bill Clement	.60	.30	.06
☐ 190	Gilles Meloche	.50	.25	.05
☐ 191	Bob Leiter	.30	.15	.03
☐ 192	Jerry Korab	.30	.15	.03
☐ 193	Joey Johnston	.30	.15	.03
☐ 194	Walt McKechnie	.30	.15	.03
☐ 195	Wilf Paiement	.60	.30	.06
☐ 196	Bob Berry	.50	.25	.05
☐ 197	Dean Talafous	.30	.15	.03
☐ 198	Guy Lapointe	.75	.35	.07
☐ 199	Clark Gillies	3.00	1.50	.30
☐ 200A	Phil Esposito	6.50	3.25	.65
	(No mention of trade)			
☐ 200B	Phil Esposito	6.50	3.25	.65
	(Trade noted)			
☐ 201	Greg Polis	.30	.15	.03
☐ 202	Jim Watson	.30	.15	.03
☐ 203	Gord McRae	.30	.15	.03
☐ 204	Lowell MacDonald	.50	.25	.05
☐ 205	Barclay Plager	.50	.25	.05
☐ 206	Don Lever	.30	.15	.03
☐ 207	Bill Mikkelson	.30	.15	.03
☐ 208	Goals Leaders	2.50	1.25	.25
	Phil Esposito			
	Guy Lafleur			
	Rick Martin			
☐ 209	Assists Leaders	3.50	1.75	.35
	Bobby Clarke			
	Bobby Orr			
	Pete Mahovlich			

		NRMT	VG-E	GOOD
☐ 210	**Scoring Leaders**	7.50	3.75	.75
	Bobby Orr			
	Phil Esposito			
	Marcel Dionne			
☐ 211	**Penalty Min. Leaders**	.50	.25	.05
	Dave Schultz			
	Andre Dupont			
	Phil Russell			
☐ 212	**Power Play**	1.00	.50	.10
	Goal Leaders			
	Phil Esposito			
	Rick Martin			
	Danny Grant			
☐ 213	**Goals Against**	3.50	1.75	.35
	Average Leaders			
	Bernie Parent			
	Rogatien Vachon			
	Ken Dryden			
☐ 214	**Barry Gibbs**	.30	.15	.03
☐ 215	**Ken Hodge**	.60	.30	.06
☐ 216	**Jocelyn Guevremont**	.30	.15	.03
☐ 217	**Warren Williams**	.30	.15	.03
☐ 218	**Dick Redmond**	.30	.15	.03
☐ 219	**Jim Rutherford**	.50	.25	.05
☐ 220	**Simon Nolet**	.30	.15	.03
☐ 221	**Butch Goring**	.50	.25	.05
☐ 222	**Glen Sather**	.75	.35	.07
☐ 223	**Mario Tremblay UER**	1.25	.60	.12
	(Photo not him)			
☐ 224	**Jude Drouin**	.30	.15	.03
☐ 225	**Rod Gilbert**	2.00	1.00	.20
☐ 226	**Bill Barber**	2.00	1.00	.20
☐ 227	**Gary Inness**	.30	.15	.03
☐ 228	**Wayne Merrick**	.30	.15	.03
☐ 229	**Rod Seiling**	.30	.15	.03
☐ 230	**Tom Lysiak**	.50	.25	.05
☐ 231	**Bob Dailey**	.30	.15	.03
☐ 232	**Michel Belhumeur**	.50	.25	.05
☐ 233	**Bill Hajt**	.30	.15	.03
☐ 234	**Jim Pappin**	.30	.15	.03
☐ 235	**Gregg Sheppard**	.30	.15	.03
☐ 236A	**Gary Bergman**	.30	.15	.03
	(No mention of trade)			
☐ 236B	**Gary Bergman**	.30	.15	.03
	(Trade noted)			
☐ 237	**Randy Rota**	.30	.15	.03
☐ 238	**Neil Komadoski**	.30	.15	.03
☐ 239	**Craig Cameron**	.30	.15	.03
☐ 240	**Tony Esposito**	3.00	1.50	.30
☐ 241	**Larry Robinson**	5.00	2.50	.50
☐ 242	**Billy Harris**	.30	.15	.03
☐ 243A	**Jean Ratelle**	2.00	1.00	.20
	(No mention of trade)			

		NRMT	VG-E	GOOD
☐ 243B	Jean Ratelle	2.00	1.00	.20
	(Trade noted)			
☐ 244	Ted Irvine UER	.30	.15	.03
	(Photo actually Ted Harris)			
☐ 245	Bob Kelly	.30	.15	.03
☐ 246	Bobby Lalonde	.30	.15	.03
☐ 247	Ron Jones	.30	.15	.03
☐ 248	Rey Comeau	.30	.15	.03
☐ 249	Michel Plasse	.50	.25	.05
☐ 250	Bobby Clarke	6.00	3.00	.60
☐ 251	Bobby Schmautz	.30	.15	.03
☐ 252	Peter McNab	.60	.30	.06
☐ 253	Al MacAdam	.50	.25	.05
☐ 254	Dennis Hull	.60	.30	.06
☐ 255	Terry Harper	.30	.15	.03
☐ 256	Peter McDuffe	.30	.15	.03
☐ 257	Jean Hamel	.30	.15	.03
☐ 258	Jacques Lemaire	1.75	.85	.17
☐ 259	Bob Nystrom	.50	.25	.05
☐ 260A	Brad Park	1.50	.75	.15
	(No mention of trade)			
☐ 260B	Brad Park	1.50	.75	.15
	(Trade noted)			
☐ 261	Cesare Maniago	.50	.25	.05
☐ 262	Don Saleski	.30	.15	.03
☐ 263	J. Bob Kelly	.30	.15	.03
☐ 264	Bob Hess	.30	.15	.03
☐ 265	Blaine Stoughton	.50	.25	.05
☐ 266	John Gould	.30	.15	.03
☐ 267A	Checklist 221-330	7.50	.50	.10
	(See number 395)			
☐ 267B	Checklist 331-396	7.50	.50	.10
☐ 268	Dan Bouchard	.50	.25	.05
☐ 269	Don Marcotte	.30	.15	.03
☐ 270	Jim Neilson	.30	.15	.03
☐ 271	Craig Ramsay	.30	.15	.03
☐ 272	Grant Mulvey	1.00	.50	.10
☐ 273	Larry Giroux	.30	.15	.03
☐ 274	Real Lemieux	.30	.15	.03
☐ 275	Denis Potvin	12.50	6.25	1.25
☐ 276	Don Kozak	.30	.15	.03
☐ 277	Tom Reid	.30	.15	.03
☐ 278	Bob Gainey	2.50	1.25	.25
☐ 279	Nick Beverley	.30	.15	.03
☐ 280	Jean Pronovost	.50	.25	.05
☐ 281	Joe Watson	.30	.15	.03
☐ 282	Chuck Lefley	.30	.15	.03
☐ 283	Borje Salming	-1.50	.75	.15
☐ 284	Garnet Bailey	.30	.15	.03
☐ 285	Gregg Boddy	.30	.15	.03
☐ 286	Bobby Clarke AS1	3.00	1.50	.30
☐ 287	Denis Potvin AS1	3.50	1.75	.35
☐ 288	Bobby Orr AS1	12.00	6.00	1.20

		NRMT	VG-E	GOOD
☐ 289	Rick Martin AS1	.50	.25	.05
☐ 290	Guy Lafleur AS1	4.50	2.25	.45
☐ 291	Bernie Parent AS1	1.75	.85	.17
☐ 292	Phil Esposito AS2	3.00	1.50	.30
☐ 293	Guy Lapointe AS2	.60	.30	.06
☐ 294	Borje Salming AS2	.60	.30	.06
☐ 295	Steve Vickers AS2	.50	.25	.05
☐ 296	Rene Robert AS2	.50	.25	.05
☐ 297	Rogatien Vachon AS2	.75	.35	.07
☐ 298	Buster Harvey	.30	.15	.03
☐ 299	Gary Sabourin	.30	.15	.03
☐ 300	Bernie Parent	2.50	1.25	.25
☐ 301	Terry O'Reilly	.75	.35	.07
☐ 302	Ed Westfall	.50	.25	.05
☐ 303	Pete Stemkowski	.30	.15	.03
☐ 304	Pierre Bouchard	.50	.25	.05
☐ 305	Pierre Larouche	3.50	1.75	.35
☐ 306	Lee Fogolin	.30	.15	.03
☐ 307	Gerry O'Flaherty	.30	.15	.03
☐ 308	Phil Myre	.50	.25	.05
☐ 309	Pierre Plante	.30	.15	.03
☐ 310	Dennis Hextall	.50	.25	.05
☐ 311	Jim McKenny	.30	.15	.03
☐ 312	Vic Venasky	.30	.15	.03
☐ 313	Flames Leaders	.50	.25	.05
	Eric Vail			
	Tom Lysiak			
	Tom Lysiak			
	Tom Lysiak			
☐ 314	Bruins Leaders	6.50	3.25	.65
	Phil Esposito			
	Bobby Orr			
	Phil Esposito			
	Johnny Bucyk			
☐ 315	Sabres Leaders	.50	.25	.05
	Rick Martin			
	Rene Robert			
	Rene Robert			
	Rick Martin			
☐ 316	Seals Leaders	.50	.25	.05
	Dave Hrechkosy			
	Larry Patey			
	Stan Weir			
	Stan Weir			
	Larry Patey			
	Dave Hrechkosy			
☐ 317	Blackhawks Leaders	1.50	.75	.15
	Stan Mikita			
	Jim Pappin			
	Stan Mikita			
	Stan Mikita			
	Stan Mikita			

	NRMT	VG-E	GOOD
☐ 318 **Red Wings Leaders**	1.00	.50	.10
Danny Grant			
Marcel Dionne			
Marcel Dionne			
Danny Grant			
☐ 319 **Scouts Leaders**..........................	.50	.25	.05
Simon Nolet			
Wilf Paiement			
Simon Nolet			
Guy Charron			
Simon Nolet			
☐ 320 **Kings Leaders**	.50	.25	.05
Bob Nevin			
Bob Nevin			
Bob Nevin			
Bob Nevin			
Juha Widing			
Bob Berry			
☐ 321 **North Stars Leaders**	.50	.25	.05
Bill Goldsworthy			
Dennis Hextall			
Dennis Hextall			
Bill Goldsworthy			
☐ 322 **Canadiens Leaders**	1.50	.75	.15
Guy Lafleur			
Pete Mahovlich			
Guy Lafleur			
Guy Lafleur			
☐ 323 **Islanders Leaders**......................	1.00	.50	.10
Bob Nystrom			
Denis Potvin			
Denis Potvin			
Clark Gillies			
☐ 324 **Rangers Leaders**	1.00	.50	.10
Steve Vickers			
Steve Vickers			
Rod Gilbert			
Rod Gilbert			
Jean Ratelle			
☐ 325 **Flyers Leaders**	1.00	.50	.10
Reggie Leach			
Bobby Clarke			
Bobby Clarke			
Reggie Leach			
☐ 326 **Penguins Leaders**	.50	.25	.05
Jean Pronovost			
Ron Schock			
Ron Schock			
Jean Pronovost			

		NRMT	VG-E	GOOD
☐ 327	**Blues Leaders**	.50	.25	.05
	Garry Unger			
	Garry Unger			
	Garry Unger			
	Garry Unger			
	Larry Sacharuk			
☐ 328	**Maple Leafs Leaders**	1.25	.60	.12
	Darryl Sittler			
	Darryl Sittler			
	Darryl Sittler			
	Darryl Sittler			
☐ 329	**Canucks Leaders**	.50	.25	.05
	Don Lever			
	Don Lever			
	Andre Boudrias			
	Andre Boudrias			
☐ 330	**Capitals Leaders**	.50	.25	.05
	Tommy Williams			
	Garnet Bailey			
	Tommy Williams			
	Garnet Bailey			
	Tommy Williams			
☐ 331	**Noel Price**	.30	.15	.03
☐ 332	**Fred Stanfield**	.30	.15	.03
☐ 333	**Doug Jarrett**	.30	.15	.03
☐ 334	**Gary Coalter**	.30	.15	.03
☐ 335	**Murray Oliver**	.30	.15	.03
☐ 336	**Dave Fortier**	.30	.15	.03
☐ 337	**Terry Crisp UER**	.60	.30	.06
	(Photo actually Don Saleski)			
☐ 338	**Bert Wilson**	.30	.15	.03
☐ 339	**John Grisdale**	.30	.15	.03
☐ 340	**Ken Broderick**	.30	.15	.03
☐ 341	**Frank Spring**	.30	.15	.03
☐ 342	**Mike Korney**	.30	.15	.03
☐ 343	**Gene Carr**	.30	.15	.03
☐ 344	**Don Awrey**	.30	.15	.03
☐ 345	**Pat Hickey**	.50	.25	.05
☐ 346	**Colin Campbell**	.30	.15	.03
☐ 347	**Wayne Thomas**	.50	.25	.05
☐ 348	**Bob Gryp**	.30	.15	.03
☐ 349	**Bill Flett**	.30	.15	.03
☐ 350	**Roger Crozier**	.50	.25	.05
☐ 351	**Dale Tallon**	.30	.15	.03
☐ 352	**Larry Johnston**	.30	.15	.03
☐ 353	**John Flesch**	.30	.15	.03
☐ 354	**Lorne Henning**	.30	.15	.03
☐ 355	**Wayne Stephenson**	.50	.25	.05
☐ 356	**Rick Wilson**	.30	.15	.03
☐ 357	**Garry Monahan**	.30	.15	.03
☐ 358	**Gary Doak**	.30	.15	.03
☐ 359A	**Pierre Jarry**	.30	.15	.03
	(No mention of trade)			

		NRMT	VG-E	GOOD
☐ 359B	Pierre Jarry	.30	.15	.03
	(Trade noted)			
☐ 360	George Pesut	.30	.15	.03
☐ 361	Mike Corrigan	.30	.15	.03
☐ 362	Michel Larocque	.50	.25	.05
☐ 363	Wayne Dillon	.30	.15	.03
☐ 364	Pete Laframboise	.30	.15	.03
☐ 365	Brian Glennie	.30	.15	.03
☐ 366	Mike Christie	.30	.15	.03
☐ 367	Jean Lemieux	.30	.15	.03
☐ 368	Gary Bromley	.50	.25	.05
☐ 369	J.P. Bordeleau	.30	.15	.03
☐ 370	Ed Gilbert	.30	.15	.03
☐ 371	Chris Ahrens	.30	.15	.03
☐ 372	Billy Smith	3.00	1.50	.30
☐ 373	Larry Goodenough	.30	.15	.03
☐ 374	Leon Rochefort	.30	.15	.03
☐ 375	Doug Gibson	.30	.15	.03
☐ 376	Mike Bloom	.30	.15	.03
☐ 377	Larry Brown	.30	.15	.03
☐ 378	Jim Roberts	.30	.15	.03
	Montreal Canadiens			
☐ 379	Gilles Villemure	.50	.25	.05
☐ 380	Dennis Owchar	.30	.15	.03
☐ 381	Doug Favell	.50	.25	.05
☐ 382	Stan Gilbertson UER	.30	.15	.03
	(Photo actually Denis Dupere)			
☐ 383	Ed Kea	.30	.15	.03
☐ 384	Brian Spencer	.30	.15	.03
☐ 385	Mike Veisor	.50	.25	.05
☐ 386	Bob Murray	.30	.15	.03
☐ 387	Andre St.Laurent	.30	.15	.03
☐ 388	Rick Chartraw	.60	.30	.06
☐ 389	Orest Kindrachuk	.30	.15	.03
☐ 390	Dave Hutchinson	.30	.15	.03
☐ 391	Glenn Goldup	.30	.15	.03
☐ 392	Jerry Holland	.30	.15	.03
☐ 393	Peter Sturgeon	.30	.15	.03
☐ 394	Alain Daigle	.30	.15	.03
☐ 395	Never Issued	0.00	.00	.00
	(Checklist 330-396, numbered as 267 and listed as 267B)			
☐ 396	Harold Snepsts	4.00	1.00	.20

1975-76 O-Pee-Chee WHA

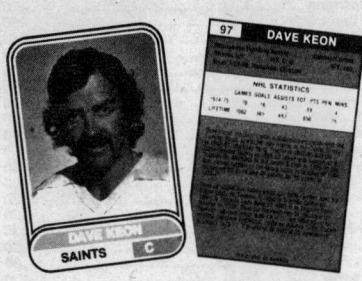

The 1975-76 O-Pee-Chee WHA set consists of 132 color cards featuring WHA players. Cards are 2½" by 3½". The backs, in both French and English, feature the card number, WHA statistics, and a short biography of the player. The cards were printed in Canada. The key rookies in this set are Richard Brodeur, Robbie Ftorek, and Mark Howe.

Le jeu WHA O-Pee-Chee 1975-76 contient 132 cartes en couleurs, représentant des joueurs WHA. Les cartes mesurent 2½" x 3½". Le dos, imprimé en français et en anglais, comprend le numéro de carte, les statistiques WHA, et une biographie concise du joueur. Les cartes ont été imprimées au Canada. Les débutants importants de ce jeu sont Richard Brodeur, Robbie Ftorek et Mark Howe.

			NRMT	VG-E	GOOD
	COMPLETE SET (132)		275.00	135.00	27.00
	COMMON PLAYER (1-132)		1.25	.60	.12
☐	1	Bobby Hull	36.00	10.00	2.00
☐	2	Dale Hoganson	1.25	.60	.12
☐	3	Serge Aubry	1.25	.60	.12
☐	4	Ron Chipperfield	1.25	.60	.12
☐	5	Paul Shmyr	1.50	.75	.15
☐	6	Perry Miller	1.25	.60	.12
☐	7	Mark Howe	12.00	6.00	1.20
☐	8	Mike Rogers	3.00	1.50	.30
☐	9	Bryon Baltimore	1.25	.60	.12
☐	10	Andre Lacroix	2.00	1.00	.20
☐	11	Nick Harbaruk	1.25	.60	.12
☐	12	John Garrett	2.50	1.25	.25
☐	13	Lou Nistico	1.25	.60	.12
☐	14	Rick Ley	2.00	1.00	.20

			NRMT	VG-E	GOOD
☐	15	Veli Pekka Ketola	1.25	.60	.12
☐	16	Real Cloutier	1.50	.75	.15
☐	17	Pierre Guite	1.25	.60	.12
☐	18	Duane Rupp	1.25	.60	.12
☐	19	Robbie Ftorek	4.00	2.00	.40
☐	20	Gerry Cheevers	5.50	2.75	.55
☐	21	John Schella	1.25	.60	.12
☐	22	Bruce MacGregor	1.25	.60	.12
☐	23	Ralph Backstrom	1.50	.75	.15
☐	24	Gene Peacosh	1.25	.60	.12
☐	25	Pierre Roy	1.25	.60	.12
☐	26	Mike Walton	2.00	1.00	.20
☐	27	Vaclav Nedomansky	1.50	.75	.15
☐	28	Christer Abrahamsson	1.50	.75	.15
☐	29	Thommie Bergman	1.50	.75	.15
☐	30	Marc Tardif	2.00	1.00	.20
☐	31	Bryan Campbell	1.25	.60	.12
☐	32	Don McLeod	1.50	.75	.15
☐	33	Al McDonough	1.25	.60	.12
☐	34	Jacques Plante	10.00	5.00	1.00
☐	35	Andre Hinse	1.25	.60	.12
☐	36	Eddie Joyal	1.25	.60	.12
☐	37	Ken Baird	1.25	.60	.12
☐	38	Wayne Rivers	1.25	.60	.12
☐	39	Ron Buchanan	1.25	.60	.12
☐	40	Anders Hedberg	2.00	1.00	.20
☐	41	Rick Smith	1.25	.60	.12
☐	42	Paul Henderson	2.00	1.00	.20
☐	43	Wayne Carleton	1.50	.75	.15
☐	44	Richard Brodeur	4.00	2.00	.40
☐	45	John Hughes	1.25	.60	.12
☐	46	Larry Israelson	1.25	.60	.12
☐	47	Jim Harrison	1.25	.60	.12
☐	48	Cam Connor	1.50	.75	.15
☐	49	Al Hamilton	1.25	.60	.12
☐	50	Ron Grahame	2.00	1.00	.20
☐	51	Frank Rochon	1.25	.60	.12
☐	52	Ron Climie	1.25	.60	.12
☐	53	Murray Heatley	1.25	.60	.12
☐	54	John Arbour	1.25	.60	.12
☐	55	Jim Shaw	1.25	.60	.12
☐	56	Larry Pleau	2.50	1.25	.25
☐	57	Ted Green	2.50	1.25	.25
☐	58	Rick Dudley	2.00	1.00	.20
☐	59	Butch Deadmarsh	1.25	.60	.12
☐	60	Serge Bernier	1.50	.75	.15
☐	61	Ron Grahame AS	1.50	.75	.15
☐	62	J.C. Tremblay AS	2.00	1.00	.20
☐	63	Kevin Morrison AS	1.50	.75	.15
☐	64	Andre Lacroix AS	1.50	.75	.15
☐	65	Bobby Hull AS	12.50	6.25	1.25
☐	66	Gordie Howe AS	22.00	11.00	2.20
☐	67	Gerry Cheevers AS	3.00	1.50	.30

			NRMT	VG-E	GOOD
☐	68	Poul Popiel AS	1.50	.75	.15
☐	69	Barry Long AS	1.50	.75	.15
☐	70	Serge Bernier AS	1.50	.75	.15
☐	71	Marc Tardif AS	2.00	1.00	.20
☐	72	Anders Hedberg AS	2.00	1.00	.20
☐	73	Ron Ward	1.25	.60	.12
☐	74	Michel Cormier	1.25	.60	.12
☐	75	Marty Howe	3.00	1.50	.30
☐	76	Rusty Patenaude	1.25	.60	.12
☐	77	John McKenzie	1.50	.75	.15
☐	78	Mark Napier	2.50	1.25	.25
☐	79	Henry Boucha	1.25	.60	.12
☐	80	Kevin Morrison	1.25	.60	.12
☐	81	Tom Simpson	1.25	.60	.12
☐	82	Brad Selwood	1.25	.60	.12
☐	83	Ulf Nilsson	2.00	1.00	.20
☐	84	Rejean Houle	1.50	.75	.15
☐	85	Normand Lapointe UER	1.50	.75	.15
		(Misspelled Lapoint on card back)			
☐	86	Danny Lawson	1.25	.60	.12
☐	87	Gary Jarrett	1.25	.60	.12
☐	88	Al McLeod	1.25	.60	.12
☐	89	Gord Labossiere	1.25	.60	.12
☐	90	Barry Long	1.50	.75	.15
☐	91	Rick Morris	1.25	.60	.12
☐	92	Norm Ferguson	1.25	.60	.12
☐	93	Bob Whitlock	1.25	.60	.12
☐	94	Jim Dorey	1.25	.60	.12
☐	95	Tom Webster	2.50	1.25	.25
☐	96	Gordie Gallant	1.25	.60	.12
☐	97	Dave Keon	3.50	1.75	.35
☐	98	Ron Plumb	1.50	.75	.15
☐	99	Rick Jodzio	1.25	.60	.12
☐	100	Gordie Howe	40.00	20.00	4.00
☐	101	Joe Daley	1.50	.75	.15
☐	102	Wayne Muloin	1.25	.60	.12
☐	103	Gavin Kirk	1.25	.60	.12
☐	104	Dave Dryden	2.00	1.00	.20
☐	105	Bob Liddington	1.25	.60	.12
☐	106	Rosaire Paiement	1.25	.60	.12
☐	107	John Sheridan	1.25	.60	.12
☐	108	Nick Fotiu	1.50	.75	.15
☐	109	Lars-Erik Sjoberg	1.50	.75	.15
☐	110	Frank Mahovlich	5.00	2.50	.50
☐	111	Mike Antonovich	1.25	.60	.12
☐	112	Paul Terbenche	1.25	.60	.12
☐	113	Rich Leduc	1.25	.60	.12
☐	114	Jack Norris	1.25	.60	.12
☐	115	Dennis Sobchuk	1.25	.60	.12
☐	116	Chris Bordeleau	1.50	.75	.15
☐	117	Doug Barrie	1.25	.60	.12
☐	118	Hugh Harris	1.25	.60	.12
☐	119	Cam Newton	1.25	.60	.12

		NRMT	VG-E	GOOD
☐ 120	Poul Popiel	1.50	.75	.15
☐ 121	Fran Huck	1.25	.60	.12
☐ 122	Tony Featherstone	1.25	.60	.12
☐ 123	Bob Woytowich	1.25	.60	.12
☐ 124	Claude St. Sauveur	1.25	.60	.12
☐ 125	Heikki Riihiranta	1.50	.75	.15
☐ 126	Gary Kurt	1.50	.75	.15
☐ 127	Thommy Abrahamsson	1.50	.75	.15
☐ 128	Danny Gruen	1.25	.60	.12
☐ 129	Jacques Locas	1.25	.60	.12
☐ 130	J.C. Tremblay	2.00	1.00	.20
☐ 131	Checklist Card	10.00	1.00	.20
☐ 132	Ernie Wakely	2.50	.75	.15

1976-77 O-Pee-Chee NHL

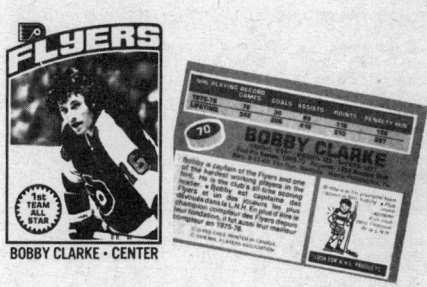

BOBBY CLARKE • CENTER

The 1976-77 O-Pee-Chee NHL set consists of 396 color cards featuring NHL players. Card numbers 1 to 264 have nearly identical fronts to the Topps set of this year. There are a few exceptions where cards that feature California players in the 1976-77 Topps hockey set have been updated in this set to show them with Cleveland. Cards are 2½" by 3½". Several Record Breaker (RB) cards feature achievements from the previous season. Team cards (132-149) have a team checklist on the back. The backs, in both French and English, contain the card number, the player's NHL record, a short biography, and a cartoon-illustrated fact about the player. The cards, printed in Canada, contain both the O-Pee-Chee and the NHL Players Association copyright. The key rookie card in this set is Bryan Trottier.

Le jeu NHL O-Pee-Chee 1976-77 contient 396 cartes en couleurs, représentant des joueurs NHL. La face des cartes 1-264 est pratiquement identique à celle du jeu Topps de cette année. Quelques cartes qui, dans le jeu Topps de 1976-77, représentaient des

joueurs californiens, ont, cependant, été mises à jour dans le jeu O.P.C. pour placer ces joueurs avec Cleveland. Les cartes mesurent 2¹/₂" x 3¹/₂". Plusieurs cartes Record Breaker (RB) indiquent les exploits de la saison précédente. Les cartes d'équipe (132-149) contiennent, au dos, une liste de contrôle d'équipe. Le dos, imprimé en français et en anglais, comprend le numéro de carte, la fiche NHL du joueur, une biographie concise, et un fait notable concernant le joueur, illustré d'une caricature. Les cartes, imprimées au Canada, comportent les droits d'auteur d'O-Pee-Chee et de l'Association des Joueurs NHL. Le débutant prometteur de ce jeu est Bryan Trottier.

			NRMT	VG-E	GOOD
		COMPLETE SET (396)	150.00	75.00	15.00
		COMMON PLAYER (1-396)	.20	.10	.02
☐	1	**Goals Leaders**	1.50	.40	.08
		Reggie Leach			
		Guy Lafleur			
		Pierre Larouche			
☐	2	**Assists Leaders**	2.00	1.00	.20
		Bobby Clarke			
		Peter Mahovlich			
		Guy Lafleur			
		Gilbert Perrault			
		Jean Ratelle			
☐	3	**Scoring Leaders**	2.00	1.00	.20
		Guy Lafleur			
		Bobby Clarke			
		Gilbert Perreault			
☐	4	**Penalty Min. Leaders**	.35	.17	.03
		Steve Durbano			
		Bryan Watson			
		Dave Schultz			
☐	5	**Power Play Goals Leaders**	2.00	1.00	.20
		Phil Esposito			
		Guy Lafleur			
		Rick Martin			
		Pierre Larouche			
		Denis Potvin			
☐	6	**Goals Against Average Leaders**	1.00	.50	.10
		Ken Dryden			
		Glenn Resch			
		Michel Larocque			
☐	7	**Gary Doak**	.20	.10	.02
☐	8	**Jacques Richard**	.20	.10	.02
☐	9	**Wayne Dillon**	.20	.10	.02
☐	10	**Bernie Parent**	2.50	1.25	.25
☐	11	**Ed Westfall**	.35	.17	.03
☐	12	**Dick Redmond**	.20	.10	.02
☐	13	**Bryan Hextall**	.20	.10	.02
☐	14	**Jean Pronovost**	.35	.17	.03
☐	15	**Peter Mahovlich**	.35	.17	.03
☐	16	**Danny Grant**	.20	.10	.02

			NRMT	VG-E	GOOD
☐	17	Phil Myre	.35	.17	.03
☐	18	Wayne Merrick	.20	.10	.02
☐	19	Steve Durbano	.20	.10	.02
☐	20	Derek Sanderson	.35	.17	.03
☐	21	Mike Murphy	.20	.10	.02
☐	22	Borje Salming	.75	.35	.07
☐	23	Mike Walton	.35	.17	.03
☐	24	Randy Manery	.20	.10	.02
☐	25	Ken Hodge	.50	.25	.05
☐	26	Mel Bridgman	.60	.30	.06
☐	27	Jerry Korab	.20	.10	.02
☐	28	Gilles Gratton	.35	.17	.03
☐	29	Andre St. Laurent	.20	.10	.02
☐	30	Yvan Cournoyer	1.75	.85	.17
☐	31	Phil Russell	.20	.10	.02
☐	32	Dennis Hextall	.35	.17	.03
☐	33	Lowell MacDonald	.35	.17	.03
☐	34	Dennis O'Brien	.20	.10	.02
☐	35	Gerry Meehan	.35	.17	.03
☐	36	Gilles Meloche	.35	.17	.03
☐	37	Wilf Paiement	.35	.17	.03
☐	38	Bob MacMillan	.35	.17	.03
☐	39	Ian Turnbull	.20	.10	.02
☐	40	Rogatien Vachon	1.25	.60	.12
☐	41	Nick Beverley	.20	.10	.02
☐	42	Rene Robert	.35	.17	.03
☐	43	Andre Savard	.20	.10	.02
☐	44	Bob Gainey	1.25	.60	.12
☐	45	Joe Watson	.20	.10	.02
☐	46	Billy Smith	1.25	.60	.12
☐	47	Darcy Rota	.20	.10	.02
☐	48	Rick Lapointe	.50	.25	.05
☐	49	Pierre Jarry	.20	.10	.02
☐	50	Syl Apps	.20	.10	.02
☐	51	Eric Vail	.35	.17	.03
☐	52	Greg Joly	.20	.10	.02
☐	53	Don Lever	.20	.10	.02
☐	54	Bob Murdoch	.20	.10	.02
		Seals Right Wing			
☐	55	Denis Herron	.35	.17	.03
☐	56	Mike Bloom	.20	.10	.02
☐	57	Bill Fairbairn	.20	.10	.02
☐	58	Fred Stanfield	.20	.10	.02
☐	59	Steve Shutt	1.25	.60	.12
☐	60	Brad Park	1.50	.75	.15
☐	61	Gilles Villemure	.35	.17	.03
☐	62	Bert Marshall	.20	.10	.02
☐	63	Chuck Lefley	.20	.10	.02
☐	64	Simon Nolet	.20	.10	.02
☐	65	Reggie Leach RB	.35	.17	.03
		Most Goals, Playoffs			
☐	66	Darryl Sittler RB	1.00	.50	.10
		Most Points, Game			

			NRMT	VG-E	GOOD
☐	67	Bryan Trottier RB	4.50	2.25	.45
		Most Points, Season, Rookie			
☐	68	Garry Unger RB	.35	.17	.03
		Most Consecutive Games, Lifetime			
☐	69	Ron Low	.35	.17	.03
☐	70	Bobby Clarke	3.00	1.50	.30
☐	71	Michel Bergeron	1.00	.50	.10
☐	72	Ron Stackhouse	.20	.10	.02
☐	73	Bill Hogaboam	.20	.10	.02
☐	74	Bob Murdoch	.20	.10	.02
		Kings Defenseman			
☐	75	Steve Vickers	.20	.10	.02
☐	76	Pit Martin	.20	.10	.02
☐	77	Gerry Hart	.20	.10	.02
☐	78	Craig Ramsay	.20	.10	.02
☐	79	Michel Larocque	.35	.17	.03
☐	80	Jean Ratelle	1.75	.85	.17
☐	81	Don Saleski	.20	.10	.02
☐	82	Bill Clement	.35	.17	.03
☐	83	Dave Burrows	.35	.17	.03
☐	84	Wayne Thomas	.35	.17	.03
☐	85	John Gould	.20	.10	.02
☐	86	Dennis Maruk	2.00	1.00	.20
☐	87	Ernie Hicke	.20	.10	.02
☐	88	Jim Rutherford	.35	.17	.03
☐	89	Dale Tallon	.20	.10	.02
☐	90	Rod Gilbert	1.75	.85	.17
☐	91	Marcel Dionne	7.50	3.75	.75
☐	92	Chuck Arnason	.20	.10	.02
☐	93	Jean Potvin	.20	.10	.02
☐	94	Don Luce	.20	.10	.02
☐	95	Johnny Bucyk	1.75	.85	.17
☐	96	Larry Goodenough	.20	.10	.02
☐	97	Mario Tremblay	.35	.17	.03
☐	98	Nelson Pyatt	.20	.10	.02
☐	99	Brian Glennie	.20	.10	.02
☐	100	Tony Esposito	2.50	1.25	.25
☐	101	Dan Maloney	.35	.17	.03
☐	102	Dunc Wilson	.20	.10	.02
☐	103	Dean Talafous	.20	.10	.02
☐	104	Ed Staniowski	.50	.25	.05
☐	105	Dallas Smith	.20	.10	.02
☐	106	Jude Drouin	.20	.10	.02
☐	107	Pat Hickey	.20	.10	.02
☐	108	Jocelyn Guevremont	.20	.10	.02
☐	109	Doug Risebrough	.35	.17	.03
☐	110	Reggie Leach	.50	.25	.05
☐	111	Dan Bouchard	.35	.17	.03
☐	112	Chris Oddleifson	.20	.10	.02
☐	113	Rick Hampton	.20	.10	.02
☐	114	John Marks	.20	.10	.02

		NRMT	VG-E	GOOD
☐ 115	Bryan Trottier	50.00	25.00	5.00
☐ 116	Checklist 1-132	3.50	.25	.05
☐ 117	Greg Polis	.20	.10	.02
☐ 118	Peter McNab	.20	.10	.02
☐ 119	Jim Roberts	.20	.10	.02
	Montreal Canadiens			
☐ 120	Gerry Cheevers	2.00	1.00	.20
☐ 121	Rick MacLeish	.50	.25	.05
☐ 122	Billy Lochead	.20	.10	.02
☐ 123	Tom Reid	.20	.10	.02
☐ 124	Rick Kehoe	.35	.17	.03
☐ 125	Keith Magnuson	.35	.17	.03
☐ 126	Clark Gillies	.60	.30	.06
☐ 127	Rick Middleton	1.25	.60	.12
☐ 128	Bill Hajt	.20	.10	.02
☐ 129	Jacques Lemaire	1.50	.75	.15
☐ 130	Terry O'Reilly	.60	.30	.06
☐ 131	Andre Dupont	.20	.10	.02
☐ 132	Flames Team (checklist back)	.75	.35	.07
☐ 133	Bruins Team (checklist back)	.75	.35	.07
☐ 134	Sabres Team (checklist back)	.75	.35	.07
☐ 135	Seals Team (checklist back)	.75	.35	.07
☐ 136	Blackhawks Team (checklist back)	.75	.35	.07
☐ 137	Red Wings Team (checklist back)	.75	.35	.07
☐ 138	Scouts Team (checklist back)	.75	.35	.07
☐ 139	Kings Team (checklist back)	.75	.35	.07
☐ 140	North Stars Team (checklist back)	.75	.35	.07
☐ 141	Canadiens Team (checklist back)	.75	.35	.07
☐ 142	Islanders Team (checklist back)	.75	.35	.07
☐ 143	Rangers Team (checklist back)	.75	.35	.07
☐ 144	Flyers Team (checklist back)	.75	.35	.07
☐ 145	Penguins Team (checklist back)	.75	.35	.07
☐ 146	Blues Team (checklist back)	.75	.35	.07
☐ 147	Maple Leafs Team (checklist back)	.75	.35	.07
☐ 148	Canucks Team (checklist back)	.75	.35	.07
☐ 149	Capitals Team (checklist back)	.75	.35	.07

		NRMT	VG-E	GOOD
☐ 150	Dave Schultz	.35	.17	.03
☐ 151	Larry Robinson	2.50	1.25	.25
☐ 152	Al Smith	.20	.10	.02
☐ 153	Bob Nystrom	.35	.17	.03
☐ 154	Ron Greschner	.50	.25	.05
☐ 155	Gregg Sheppard	.20	.10	.02
☐ 156	Alain Daigle	.20	.10	.02
☐ 157	Ed Van Impe	.20	.10	.02
☐ 158	Tim Young	.20	.10	.02
☐ 159	Bryan Lefley	.20	.10	.02
☐ 160	Ed Giacomin	1.25	.60	.12
☐ 161	Yvon Labre	.20	.10	.02
☐ 162	Jim Lorentz	.20	.10	.02
☐ 163	Guy Lafleur	8.00	4.00	.80
☐ 164	Tom Bladon	.20	.10	.02
☐ 165	Wayne Cashman	.35	.17	.03
☐ 166	Pete Stemkowski	.20	.10	.02
☐ 167	Grant Mulvey	.35	.17	.03
☐ 168	Yves Belanger	.35	.17	.03
☐ 169	Bill Goldsworthy	.35	.17	.03
☐ 170	Denis Potvin	5.00	2.50	.50
☐ 171	Nick Libett	.20	.10	.02
☐ 172	Michel Plasse	.35	.17	.03
☐ 173	Lou Nanne	.20	.10	.02
☐ 174	Tom Lysiak	.35	.17	.03
☐ 175	Dennis Ververgaert	.20	.10	.02
☐ 176	Gary Simmons	.35	.17	.03
☐ 177	Pierre Bouchard	.35	.17	.03
☐ 178	Bill Barber	1.25	.60	.12
☐ 179	Darryl Edestrand	.20	.10	.02
☐ 180	Gilbert Perreault	2.00	1.00	.20
☐ 181	Dave Maloney	.60	.30	.06
☐ 182	Jean Paul Parise	.20	.10	.02
☐ 183	Jim Harrison	.20	.10	.02
☐ 184	Pete Lopresti	.20	.10	.02
☐ 185	Don Kozak	.20	.10	.02
☐ 186	Guy Charron	.20	.10	.02
☐ 187	Stan Gilbertson	.20	.10	.02
☐ 188	Bill Nyrop	.50	.25	.05
☐ 189	Bobby Schmautz	.20	.10	.02
☐ 190	Wayne Stephenson	.35	.17	.03
☐ 191	Brian Spencer	.20	.10	.02
☐ 192	Gilles Marotte	.35	.17	.03
☐ 193	Lorne Henning	.20	.10	.02
☐ 194	Bob Neely	.20	.10	.02
☐ 195	Dennis Hull	.50	.25	.05
☐ 196	Walt McKechnie	.20	.10	.02
☐ 197	Curt Ridley	.20	.10	.02
☐ 198	Dwight Bialowas	.20	.10	.02
☐ 199	Pierre Larouche	.75	.35	.07
☐ 200	Ken Dryden	8.00	4.00	.80
☐ 201	Ross Lonsberry	.20	.10	.02
☐ 202	Curt Bennett	.20	.10	.02

		NRMT	VG-E	GOOD
☐ 203	**Hartland Monahan**	.20	.10	.02
☐ 204	**John Davidson**	.35	.17	.03
☐ 205	**Serge Savard**	1.00	.50	.10
☐ 206	**Garry Howatt**	.20	.10	.02
☐ 207	**Darryl Sittler**	1.25	.60	.12
☐ 208	**J.P. Bordeleau**	.20	.10	.02
☐ 209	**Henry Boucha**	.20	.10	.02
☐ 210	**Rick Martin**	.50	.25	.05
☐ 211	**Vic Venasky**	.20	.10	.02
☐ 212	**Buster Harvey**	.20	.10	.02
☐ 213	**Bobby Orr**	18.00	9.00	1.80
☐ 214	**French Connection**	1.00	.50	.10
	Rick Martin			
	Gilbert Perreault			
	Rene Robert			
☐ 215	**LCB Line**	1.50	.75	.15
	Bill Barber			
	Bobby Clarke			
	Reggie Leach			
☐ 216	**Long Island Lightning**	1.50	.75	.15
	Clark Gillies			
	Bryan Trottier			
	Billy Harris			
☐ 217	**Checking Line**	.60	.30	.06
	Bob Gainey			
	Doug Jarvis			
	Jim Roberts			
☐ 218	**Bicentennial Line**	.50	.25	.05
	Lowell MacDonald			
	Syl Apps			
	Jean Pronovost			
☐ 219	**Bob Kelly**	.20	.10	.02
☐ 220	**Walt Tkaczuk**	.35	.17	.03
☐ 221	**Dave Lewis**	.20	.10	.02
☐ 222	**Danny Gare**	.35	.17	.03
☐ 223	**Guy Lapointe**	.60	.30	.06
☐ 224	**Hank Nowak**	.20	.10	.02
☐ 225	**Stan Mikita**	3.50	1.75	.35
☐ 226	**Vic Hadfield**	.35	.17	.03
☐ 227	**Bernie Wolfe**	.20	.10	.02
☐ 228	**Bryan Watson**	.20	.10	.02
☐ 229	**Ralph Stewart**	.20	.10	.02
☐ 230	**Gerry Desjardins**	.35	.17	.03
☐ 231	**John Bednarski**	.20	.10	.02
☐ 232	**Yvon Lambert**	.20	.10	.02
☐ 233	**Orest Kindrachuk**	.20	.10	.02
☐ 234	**Don Marcotte**	.20	.10	.02
☐ 235	**Bill White**	.35	.17	.03
☐ 236	**Red Berenson**	.35	.17	.03
☐ 237	**Al MacAdam**	.35	.17	.03
☐ 238	**Rick Blight**	.20	.10	.02
☐ 239	**Butch Goring**	.35	.17	.03
☐ 240	**Cesare Maniago**	.35	.17	.03

		NRMT	VG-E	GOOD
☐ 241	Jim Schoenfeld	.35	.17	.03
☐ 242	Cliff Koroll	.20	.10	.02
☐ 243	Scott Garland	.20	.10	.02
☐ 244	Rick Chartraw	.20	.10	.02
☐ 245	Phil Esposito	5.00	2.50	.50
☐ 246	Dave Forbes	.20	.10	.02
☐ 247	Joe Watson	.20	.10	.02
☐ 248	Ron Schock	.20	.10	.02
☐ 249	Fred Barrett	.20	.10	.02
☐ 250	Glenn Resch	1.25	.60	.12
☐ 251	Ivan Boldirev	.20	.10	.02
☐ 252	Billy Harris	.20	.10	.02
☐ 253	Lee Fogolin	.20	.10	.02
☐ 254	Murray Wilson	.20	.10	.02
☐ 255	Gilles Gilbert	.35	.17	.03
☐ 256	Gary Dornhoefer	.35	.17	.03
☐ 257	Carol Vadnais	.20	.10	.02
☐ 258	Checklist 133-264	3.50	.25	.05
☐ 259	Errol Thompson	.20	.10	.02
☐ 260	Garry Unger	.50	.25	.05
☐ 261	J. Bob Kelly	.20	.10	.02
☐ 262	Terry Harper	.20	.10	.02
☐ 263	Blake Dunlop	.20	.10	.02
☐ 264	Stanley Cup Champs	.75	.35	.07
	Montreal Canadiens			
☐ 265	Richard Mulhern	.20	.10	.02
☐ 266	Gary Sabourin	.20	.10	.02
☐ 267	Bill McKenzie	.20	.10	.02
☐ 268	Mike Corrigan	.20	.10	.02
☐ 269	Rick Smith	.20	.10	.02
☐ 270	Stan Weir	.20	.10	.02
☐ 271	Ron Sedlbauer	.20	.10	.02
☐ 272	Jean Lemieux	.20	.10	.02
☐ 273	Hilliard Graves	.20	.10	.02
☐ 274	Dave Gardner	.20	.10	.02
☐ 275	Tracy Pratt	.20	.10	.02
☐ 276	Frank St. Marseille	.20	.10	.02
☐ 277	Bob Hess	.20	.10	.02
☐ 278	Bobby Lalonde	.20	.10	.02
☐ 279	Tony White	.20	.10	.02
☐ 280	Rod Seiling	.20	.10	.02
☐ 281	Larry Romanchych	.20	.10	.02
☐ 282	Ralph Klassen	.20	.10	.02
☐ 283	Gary Croteau	.20	.10	.02
☐ 284	Neil Komadoski	.20	.10	.02
☐ 285	Ed Johnston	.35	.17	.03
☐ 286	George Ferguson	.20	.10	.02
☐ 287	Gerry O'Flaherty	.20	.10	.02
☐ 288	Jack Lynch	.20	.10	.02
☐ 289	Pat Quinn	.35	.17	.03
☐ 290	Gene Carr	.20	.10	.02
☐ 291	Bob Stewart	.20	.10	.02
☐ 292	Doug Favell	.35	.17	.03

		NRMT	VG-E	GOOD
☐ 293	Rick Wilson	.20	.10	.02
☐ 294	Jack Valiquette	.20	.10	.02
☐ 295	Garry Monahan	.20	.10	.02
☐ 296	Michel Belhumeur	.35	.17	.03
☐ 297	Larry Carriere	.20	.10	.02
☐ 298	Fred Ahern	.20	.10	.02
☐ 299	Dave Hudson	.20	.10	.02
☐ 300	Bob Berry	.35	.17	.03
☐ 301	Bob Gassoff	.20	.10	.02
☐ 302	Jim McKenny	.20	.10	.02
☐ 303	Gord Smith	.20	.10	.02
☐ 304	Garnet Bailey	.20	.10	.02
☐ 305	Bruce Affleck	.20	.10	.02
☐ 306	Doug Halward	.20	.10	.02
☐ 307	Lew Morrison	.20	.10	.02
☐ 308	Bob Sauve	1.00	.50	.10
☐ 309	Bob Murray	.20	.10	.02
☐ 310	Claude Larose	.20	.10	.02
☐ 311	Don Awrey	.20	.10	.02
☐ 312	Bill MacMillan	.35	.17	.03
☐ 313	Doug Jarvis	1.50	.75	.15
☐ 314	Dennis Owchar	.20	.10	.02
☐ 315	Jerry Holland	.20	.10	.02
☐ 316	Guy Chouinard	.60	.30	.06
☐ 317	Gary Smith	.20	.10	.02
☐ 318	Pat Price	.20	.10	.02
☐ 319	Tom Williams	.20	.10	.02
☐ 320	Larry Patey	.20	.10	.02
☐ 321	Claire Alexander	.20	.10	.02
☐ 322	Larry Bolonchuk	.20	.10	.02
☐ 323	Bob Sirois	.20	.10	.02
☐ 324	Joe Zanussi	.20	.10	.02
☐ 325	Joey Johnston	.20	.10	.02
☐ 326	J.P. Leblanc	.20	.10	.02
☐ 327	Craig Cameron	.20	.10	.02
☐ 328	Dave Fortier	.20	.10	.02
☐ 329	Ed Gilbert	.20	.10	.02
☐ 330	John Van Boxmeer	.20	.10	.02
☐ 331	Gary Inness	.20	.10	.02
☐ 332	Bill Flett	.20	.10	.02
☐ 333	Mike Christie	.20	.10	.02
☐ 334	Denis Dupere	.20	.10	.02
☐ 335	Sheldon Kannegiesser	.20	.10	.02
☐ 336	Jerry Butler	.20	.10	.02
☐ 337	Gord McRae	.20	.10	.02
☐ 338	Dennis Kearns	.20	.10	.02
☐ 339	Ron Lalonde	.20	.10	.02
☐ 340	Jean Hamel	.20	.10	.02
☐ 341	Barry Gibbs	.20	.10	.02
☐ 342	Mike Pelyk	.20	.10	.02
☐ 343	Rey Comeau	.20	.10	.02
☐ 344	Jim Neilson	.20	.10	.02
☐ 345	Phil Roberto	.20	.10	.02

			NRMT	VG-E	GOOD
☐ 346	Dave Hutchinson		.20	.10	.02
☐ 347	Ted Irvine		.20	.10	.02
☐ 348	Lanny McDonald		2.25	1.10	.22
☐ 349	Jim Moxey		.20	.10	.02
☐ 350	Bob Dailey		.20	.10	.02
☐ 351	Tim Ecclestone		.20	.10	.02
☐ 352	Len Frig		.20	.10	.02
☐ 353	Randy Rota		.20	.10	.02
☐ 354	Juha Widing		.20	.10	.02
☐ 355	Larry Brown		.20	.10	.02
☐ 356	Floyd Thomson		.20	.10	.02
☐ 357	Richard Nantais		.20	.10	.02
☐ 358	Inge Hammarstrom		.20	.10	.02
☐ 359	Mike Robitaille		.20	.10	.02
☐ 360	Rejean Houle		.20	.10	.02
☐ 361	Ed Kea		.20	.10	.02
☐ 362	Bob Girard		.20	.10	.02
☐ 363	Bob Murray		.20	.10	.02
☐ 364	Dave Hrechkosy		.20	.10	.02
☐ 365	Gary Edwards		.35	.17	.03
☐ 366	Harold Snepsts		.35	.17	.03
☐ 367	Pat Boutette		.50	.25	.05
☐ 368	Bob Paradise		.20	.10	.02
☐ 369	Bob Plager		.35	.17	.03
☐ 370	Tim Jacobs		.20	.10	.02
☐ 371	Pierre Plante		.20	.10	.02
☐ 372	Colin Campbell		.20	.10	.02
☐ 373	Dave Williams		.90	.45	.09
☐ 374	Ab Demarco		.20	.10	.02
☐ 375	Mike Lampman		.20	.10	.02
☐ 376	Mark Heaslip		.20	.10	.02
☐ 377	Checklist Card		3.50	.25	.05
☐ 378	Bert Wilson		.20	.10	.02
☐ 379	Flames Leaders		.35	.17	.03
	Curt Bennett				
	Tom Lysiak				
	Pat Quinn				
	Claude St. Sauveur				
☐ 380	Sabres Leaders		.50	.25	.05
	Danny Gare				
	Gilbert Perreault				
	Danny Gare				
	Rick Martin				
☐ 381	Bruins Leaders		1.00	.50	.10
	Johnny Bucyk				
	Jean Ratelle				
	Jean Ratelle				
	Terry O'Reilly				
	Jean Ratelle				

		NRMT	VG-E	GOOD
☐ 382	**Blackhawks Leaders**	.35	.17	.03
	Pit Martin			
	Dale Tallon			
	Phil Russell			
	Cliff Koroll			
☐ 383	**Seals Leaders**	.35	.17	.03
	Wayne Merrick			
	Al MacAdam			
	Rick Hampton			
	Mike Christie			
	Bob Murdoch			
☐ 384	**Scouts Leaders**..............................	.35	.17	.03
	Guy Charron			
	Guy Charron			
	Steve Durbano			
	Guy Charron			
☐ 385	**Red Wings Leaders**	.35	.17	.03
	Michel Bergeron			
	Walt McKechnie			
	Bryan Watson			
	Michel Bergeron			
☐ 386	**Kings Leaders**	.75	.35	.07
	Marcel Dionne			
	Marcel Dionne			
	Dave Hutchison			
	Mike Corrigan			
☐ 387	**North Stars Leaders**	.35	.17	.03
	Bill Hogaboam			
	Tim Young			
	Dennis O'Brien			
	Bill Hogaboam			
☐ 388	**Canadiens Leaders**	1.25	.60	.12
	Guy Lafleur			
	Pete Mahovlich			
	Doug Risebrough			
	Guy Lafleur			
☐ 389	**Islanders Leaders**.........................	.75	.35	.07
	Clark Gillies			
	Denis Potvin			
	Garry Howatt			
	Denis Potvin			
☐ 390	**Rangers Leaders**	1.25	.60	.12
	Rod Gilbert			
	Steve Vickers			
	Carol Vadnais			
	Phil Esposito			
☐ 391	**Flyers Leaders**	1.25	.60	.12
	Reggie Leach			
	Bobby Clarke			
	Dave Schultz			
	Bill Barber			

		NRMT	VG-E	GOOD
☐ 392	**Penguins Leaders**	.35	.17	.03
	Pierre Larouche			
	Syl Apps			
	Ron Schock			
	Pierre Larouche			
☐ 393	**Blues Leaders**	.35	.17	.03
	Chuck Lefley			
	Garry Unger			
	Bob Gassoff			
	Garry Unger			
☐ 394	**Maple Leafs Leaders**	.50	.25	.05
	Errol Thompson			
	Darryl Sittler			
	Dave Williams			
	Errol Thompson			
☐ 395	**Canucks Leaders**	.35	.17	.03
	Dennis Ververgaert			
	Chris Oddleifson			
	Dennis Kearns			
	Harold Snepsts			
	Dennis Ververgaert			
☐ 396	**Capitals Leaders**	.50	.25	.05
	Nelson Pyatt			
	Gerry Meehan			
	Yvon Labre			
	Tony White			

1976-77 O-Pee-Chee WHA

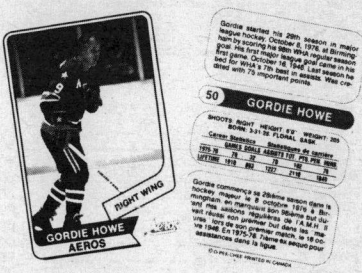

The 1976-77 O-Pee-Chee WHA set consists of 132 color cards featuring WHA players. Cards are 2¹/₂" by 3¹/₂". The backs, in both French and English, feature the card number, a short biography of the player, and career statistics. The cards were printed in Canada. Cards 1-6 feature the league leaders from the previous season in various statistical categories. There are no key rookie cards in this set.

Le jeu WHA O-Pee-Chee 1976-77 contient 132 cartes en couleurs, représentant des joueurs WHA. Les cartes mesurent 2¹/₂" x 3¹/₂". Le dos, imprimé en français et en anglais, comprend le numéro de carte, une biographie concise du joueur, et les statistiques de sa carrière. Les cartes ont été imprimées au Canada. Les cartes 1-6 représentent les champions de la saison précédente dans des catégories statistiques variées. Il n'y a pas de cartes de débutants importants dans ce jeu.

			NRMT	VG-E	GOOD
		COMPLETE SET (132)	100.00	50.00	10.00
		COMMON PLAYER (1-132)	.35	.17	.03
☐	1	**Goals Leaders** .... Marc Tardif Real Cloutier Vaclav Nedomansky	1.25	.35	.07
☐	2	**Assists Leaders** .... J.C. Tremblay Marc Tardif Ulf Nilsson	.60	.30	.06
☐	3	**Scoring Leaders** .... Marc Tardif Bobby Hull Real Cloutier Ulf Nilsson	2.50	1.25	.25

			NRMT	VG-E	GOOD
☐	4	**Penalties Leaders**	.50	.25	.05
		Curt Brackenbury			
		Gord Gallant			
☐	5	**Points Leaders**	2.50	1.25	.25
		Marc Tardif			
		Bobby Hull			
		Ulf Nilsson			
☐	6	**Goals Against**	.50	.25	.05
		Average Leaders			
		Michel Dion			
		Joe Daley			
		Wayne Rutledge			
☐	7	**Barry Long**	.50	.25	.05
☐	8	**Danny Lawson**	.50	.25	.05
☐	9	**Ulf Nilsson**	.90	.45	.09
☐	10	**Kevin Morrison**	.30	.15	.03
☐	11	**Gerry Pinder**	.50	.25	.05
☐	12	**Richard Brodeur**	.90	.45	.09
☐	13	**Robbie Ftorek**	1.00	.50	.10
☐	14	**Tom Webster**	1.00	.50	.10
☐	15	**Marty Howe**	.75	.35	.07
☐	16	**Bryan Campbell**	.30	.15	.03
☐	17	**Rick Dudley**	.75	.35	.07
☐	18	**Jim Turkiewicz**	.30	.15	.03
☐	19	**Rusty Patenaude**	.30	.15	.03
☐	20	**Joe Daley**	.60	.30	.06
☐	21	**Gary Veneruzzo**	.30	.15	.03
☐	22	**Chris Evans**	.30	.15	.03
☐	23	**Mike Antonovich**	.30	.15	.03
☐	24	**Jim Dorey**	.30	.15	.03
☐	25	**John Gray**	.30	.15	.03
☐	26	**Larry Pleau**	.60	.30	.06
☐	27	**Poul Popiel**	.50	.25	.05
☐	28	**Renald Leclerc**	.30	.15	.03
☐	29	**Dennis Sobchuk**	.30	.15	.03
☐	30	**Lars-Erik Sjoberg**	.50	.25	.05
☐	31	**Wayne Wood**	.50	.25	.05
☐	32	**Ron Chipperfield**	.30	.15	.03
☐	33	**Tim Sheehy**	.30	.15	.03
☐	34	**Brent Hughes**	.30	.15	.03
☐	35	**Ron Ward**	.30	.15	.03
☐	36	**Ron Huston**	.30	.15	.03
☐	37	**Rosaire Paiement**	.30	.15	.03
☐	38	**Terry Ruskowski**	1.25	.60	.12
☐	39	**Hugh Harris**	.30	.15	.03
☐	40	**J.C. Tremblay**	.75	.35	.07
☐	41	**Rich Leduc**	.30	.15	.03
☐	42	**Peter Sullivan**	.30	.15	.03
☐	43	**Jerry Rollins**	.30	.15	.03
☐	44	**Ken Broderick**	.50	.25	.05
☐	45	**Peter Driscoll**	.30	.15	.03
☐	46	**Joe Noris**	.60	.30	.06
☐	47	**Al McLeod**	.50	.25	.05

			NRMT	VG-E	GOOD
☐	48	Bruce Landon	.30	.15	.03
☐	49	Chris Bordeleau	.50	.25	.05
☐	50	Gordie Howe	24.00	12.00	2.40
☐	51	Thommie Bergman	.50	.25	.05
☐	52	Dave Keon	2.50	1.25	.25
☐	53	Butch Deadmarsh	.30	.15	.03
☐	54	Bryan Maxwell	.30	.15	.03
☐	55	John Garrett	.60	.30	.06
☐	56	Glen Sather	1.75	.85	.17
☐	57	John Miszuk	.30	.15	.03
☐	58	Heikki Riihiranta	.50	.25	.05
☐	59	Richard Grenier	.30	.15	.03
☐	60	Gene Peacosh	.30	.15	.03
☐	61	Joe Daley AS	.50	.25	.05
☐	62	J.C. Tremblay AS	.50	.25	.05
☐	63	Lars-Erik Sjoberg AS	.50	.25	.05
☐	64	Vaclav Nedomansky AS	.50	.25	.05
☐	65	Bobby Hull AS	10.00	5.00	1.00
☐	66	Anders Hedberg AS	.60	.30	.06
☐	67	Chr. Abrahamsson AS	.50	.25	.05
☐	68	Kevin Morrison AS	.50	.25	.05
☐	69	Paul Shmyr AS	.50	.25	.05
☐	70	Andre Lacroix AS	.50	.25	.05
☐	71	Gene Peacosh AS	.50	.25	.05
☐	72	Gordie Howe AS	13.50	6.00	1.00
☐	73	Bob Nevin	.50	.25	.05
☐	74	Richard Lemieux	.30	.15	.03
☐	75	Mike Ford	.30	.15	.03
☐	76	Real Cloutier	.50	.25	.05
☐	77	Al McDonough	.30	.15	.03
☐	78	Del Hall	.30	.15	.03
☐	79	Thommy Abrahamsson	.30	.15	.03
☐	80	Andre Lacroix	.60	.30	.06
☐	81	Frank Hughes	.30	.15	.03
☐	82	Reg Thomas	.30	.15	.03
☐	83	Dave Inkpen	.30	.15	.03
☐	84	Paul Henderson	.50	.25	.05
☐	85	Dave Dryden	.50	.25	.05
☐	86	Lynn Powis	.30	.15	.03
☐	87	Andre Boudrias	.30	.15	.03
☐	88	Veli Pekka Ketola	.30	.15	.03
☐	89	Cam Connor	.50	.25	.05
☐	90	Claude St. Sauveur	.30	.15	.03
☐	91	Garry Swain	.30	.15	.03
☐	92	Ernie Wakely	.50	.25	.05
☐	93	Blair MacDonald	.30	.15	.03
☐	94	Ron Plumb	.50	.25	.05
☐	95	Mark Howe	2.00	1.00	.20
☐	96	Peter Marrin	.30	.15	.03
☐	97	Al Hamilton	.30	.15	.03
☐	98	Paulin Bordeleau	.30	.15	.03
☐	99	Gavin Kirk	.30	.15	.03
☐	100	Bobby Hull	15.00	7.50	1.50

			NRMT	VG-E	GOOD
□ 101	Rick Ley		.75	.35	.07
□ 102	Gary Kurt		.50	.25	.05
□ 103	John McKenzie		.50	.25	.05
□ 104	Al Karlander		.30	.15	.03
□ 105	John French		.30	.15	.03
□ 106	John Hughes		.30	.15	.03
□ 107	Ron Grahame		.50	.25	.05
□ 108	Mark Napier		.75	.35	.07
□ 109	Serge Bernier		.50	.25	.05
□ 110	Christer Abrahamsson		.50	.25	.05
□ 111	Frank Mahovlich		4.00	2.00	.40
□ 112	Ted Green		.75	.35	.07
□ 113	Rick Jodzio		.30	.15	.03
□ 114	Michel Dion		1.50	.75	.15
□ 115	Rich Preston		.30	.15	.03
□ 116	Pekka Rautakallio		.75	.35	.07
□ 117	Checklist Card		3.50	.25	.05
□ 118	Marc Tardif		.75	.35	.07
□ 119	Doug Barrie		.30	.15	.03
□ 120	Vaclav Nedomansky		.60	.30	.06
□ 121	Bill Lesuk		.30	.15	.03
□ 122	Wayne Connelly		.30	.15	.03
□ 123	Pierre Guite		.30	.15	.03
□ 124	Ralph Backstrom		.50	.25	.05
□ 125	Anders Hedberg		.90	.45	.09
□ 126	Norm Ullman		2.50	1.25	.25
□ 127	Steve Sutherland		.30	.15	.03
□ 128	John Schella		.30	.15	.03
□ 129	Don McLeod		.50	.25	.05
□ 130	Canadian Finals		.50	.25	.05
□ 131	U.S. Finals		.50	.25	.05
□ 132	World Trophy Final		2.00	.50	.10

1977-78 O-Pee-Chee NHL

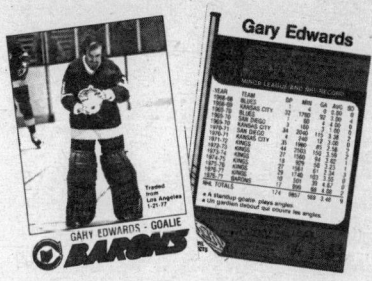

The 1977-78 O-Pee-Chee NHL set consists of 396 color cards portraying NHL players. Card numbers 1 to 264 have nearly identical fronts to the Topps set of this year. Cards 203 and 255 are the only card numbers showing different players in the O-Pee-Chee set compared to the Topps hockey set this year. Cards are 2½" by 3½". The backs, in both French and English, feature the player's NHL record, the card number, and a cartoon-illustrated fact about the player. The cards were printed in Canada. Cards 322-339 have a team logo or emblem on the front with individual player records for that team on the back. There are no key rookie cards in this set.

Le jeu NHL O-Pee-Chee 1977-78 contient 396 cartes en couleurs, représentant les joueurs du NHL. Les cartes 1-264 ont une face quasiment identique à celle du jeu Topps de cette année. Seules les cartes 203 et 255 du jeu O-Pee-Chee représentent des joueurs différents de ceux du jeu Topps de cette année. Les cartes mesurent 2½" x 3½". Le dos, imprimé en français et en anglais, comprend la fiche NHL du joueur, le numéro de carte, et un fait notable concernant le joueur, illustré d'une caricature. Les cartes ont été imprimées au Canada. La face des cartes 322-339 comporte le logo ou emblème de l'équipe, et le dos indique les statistiques des joueurs de cette équipe. Le jeu ne comporte pas de cartes de débutants importants.

			NRMT	VG-E	GOOD
	COMPLETE SET (396)		135.00	65.00	13.50
	COMMON PLAYER (1-396)		.17	.08	.01
☐	1	Goals Leaders	2.00	.50	.10
		Steve Shutt			
		Guy Lafleur			
		Marcel Dionne			

			NRMT	VG-E	GOOD
☐	2	**Assists Leaders**	1.50	.75	.15
		Guy Lafleur			
		Marcel Dionne			
		Larry Robinson			
		Borje Salming			
		Tim Young			
☐	3	**Scoring Leaders**	1.50	.75	.15
		Guy Lafleur			
		Marcel Dionne			
		Steve Shutt			
☐	4	**Penalty Min. Leaders**	.30	.15	.03
		Dave Williams			
		Dennis Polonich			
		Bob Gassoff			
☐	5	**Power Play Goals**	1.00	.50	.10
		Leaders			
		Lanny McDonald			
		Phil Esposito			
		Tom Williams			
☐	6	**Goals Against**	1.00	.50	.10
		Average Leaders			
		Michel Larocque			
		Ken Dryden			
		Glenn Resch			
☐	7	**Game Winning**	1.50	.75	.15
		Goals Leaders			
		Gilbert Perreault			
		Steve Shutt			
		Guy Lafleur			
		Rick MacLeish			
		Peter McNab			
☐	8	**Shutouts Leaders**	1.00	.50	.10
		Ken Dryden			
		Rogatien Vachon			
		Bernie Parent			
		Dunc Wilson			
☐	9	**Brian Spencer**	.17	.08	.01
☐	10	**Denis Potvin AS2**	3.25	1.60	.32
☐	11	**Nick Fotiu**	.17	.08	.01
☐	12	**Bob Murray**	.17	.08	.01
☐	13	**Pete Lopresti**	.17	.08	.01
☐	14	**J. Bob Kelly**	.17	.08	.01
☐	15	**Rick MacLeish**	.50	.25	.05
☐	16	**Terry Harper**	.17	.08	.01
☐	17	**Willi Plett**	.17	.08	.01
☐	18	**Peter McNab**	.17	.08	.01
☐	19	**Wayne Thomas**	.30	.15	.03
☐	20	**Pierre Bouchard**	.17	.08	.01
☐	21	**Dennis Maruk**	.50	.25	.05
☐	22	**Mike Murphy**	.17	.08	.01
☐	23	**Cesare Maniago**	.30	.15	.03
☐	24	**Paul Gardner**	.40	.20	.04
☐	25	**Rod Gilbert**	1.50	.75	.15

			NRMT	VG-E	GOOD
☐	26	Orest Kindrachuk	.17	.08	.01
☐	27	Bill Hajt	.17	.08	.01
☐	28	John Davidson	.30	.15	.03
☐	29	Jean Paul Parise	.17	.08	.01
☐	30	Larry Robinson AS1	1.75	.85	.17
☐	31	Yvon Labre	.17	.08	.01
☐	32	Walt McKechnie	.17	.08	.01
☐	33	Rick Kehoe	.30	.15	.03
☐	34	Randy Holt	.17	.08	.01
☐	35	Garry Unger	.40	.20	.04
☐	36	Lou Nanne	.17	.08	.01
☐	37	Dan Bouchard	.30	.15	.03
☐	38	Darryl Sittler	1.00	.50	.10
☐	39	Bob Murdoch	.17	.08	.01
☐	40	Jean Ratelle	1.35	.65	.13
☐	41	Dave Maloney	.30	.15	.03
☐	42	Danny Gare	.30	.15	.03
☐	43	Jim Watson	.17	.08	.01
☐	44	Tom Williams	.17	.08	.01
☐	45	Serge Savard	1.00	.50	.10
☐	46	Derek Sanderson	.30	.15	.03
☐	47	John Marks	.17	.08	.01
☐	48	Al Cameron	.17	.08	.01
☐	49	Dean Talafous	.17	.08	.01
☐	50	Glenn Resch	1.00	.50	.10
☐	51	Ron Schock	.17	.08	.01
☐	52	Gary Croteau	.17	.08	.01
☐	53	Gerry Meehan	.30	.15	.03
☐	54	Ed Staniowski	.30	.15	.03
☐	55	Phil Esposito	4.00	2.00	.40
☐	56	Dennis Ververgaert	.17	.08	.01
☐	57	Rick Wilson	.17	.08	.01
☐	58	Jim Lorentz	.17	.08	.01
☐	59	Bobby Schmautz	.17	.08	.01
☐	60	Guy Lapointe AS2	.40	.20	.04
☐	61	Ivan Boldirev	.17	.08	.01
☐	62	Bob Nystrom	.30	.15	.03
☐	63	Rick Hampton	.17	.08	.01
☐	64	Jack Valiquette	.17	.08	.01
☐	65	Bernie Parent	2.00	1.00	.20
☐	66	Dave Burrows	.17	.08	.01
☐	67	Butch Goring	.40	.20	.04
☐	68	Checklist 1-132	2.50	.20	.04
☐	69	Murray Wilson	.17	.08	.01
☐	70	Ed Giacomin	1.25	.60	.12
☐	71	Flames Team	.50	.25	.05
☐	72	Bruins Team	.50	.25	.05
☐	73	Sabres Team	.50	.25	.05
☐	74	Blackhawks Team	.50	.25	.05
☐	75	Barons Team	.50	.25	.05
☐	76	Rockies Team	.50	.25	.05
☐	77	Red Wings Team	.50	.25	.05
☐	78	Kings Team	.50	.25	.05

			NRMT	VG-E	GOOD
☐	79	North Stars Team	.50	.25	.05
☐	80	Canadiens Team	.50	.25	.05
☐	81	Islanders Team	.50	.25	.05
☐	82	Rangers Team	.50	.25	.05
☐	83	Flyers Team	.50	.25	.05
☐	84	Penguins Team	.50	.25	.05
☐	85	Blues Team	.50	.25	.05
☐	86	Maple Leafs Team	.50	.25	.05
☐	87	Canucks Team	.50	.25	.05
☐	88	Capitals Team	.50	.25	.05
☐	89	Keith Magnuson	.17	.08	.01
☐	90	Walt Tkaczuk	.30	.15	.03
☐	91	Bill Nyrop	.30	.15	.03
☐	92	Michel Plasse	.30	.15	.03
☐	93	Bob Bourne	.30	.15	.03
☐	94	Lee Fogolin	.17	.08	.01
☐	95	Gregg Sheppard	.17	.08	.01
☐	96	Hartland Monahan	.17	.08	.01
☐	97	Curt Bennett	.17	.08	.01
☐	98	Bob Dailey	.17	.08	.01
☐	99	Bill Goldsworthy	.30	.15	.03
☐	100	Ken Dryden AS1	6.00	3.00	.60
☐	101	Grant Mulvey	.30	.15	.03
☐	102	Pierre Larouche	.40	.20	.04
☐	103	Nick Libett	.17	.08	.01
☐	104	Rick Smith	.17	.08	.01
☐	105	Bryan Trottier	10.00	5.00	1.00
☐	106	Pierre Jarry	.17	.08	.01
☐	107	Red Berenson	.30	.15	.03
☐	108	Jim Schoenfeld	.30	.15	.03
☐	109	Gilles Meloche	.30	.15	.03
☐	110	Lanny McDonald AS2	1.50	.75	.15
☐	111	Don Lever	.17	.08	.01
☐	112	Greg Polis	.17	.08	.01
☐	113	Gary Sargent	.50	.25	.05
☐	114	Earl Anderson	.17	.08	.01
☐	115	Bobby Clarke	1.25	.60	.12
☐	116	Dave Lewis	.17	.08	.01
☐	117	Darcy Rota	.17	.08	.01
☐	118	Andre Savard	.17	.08	.01
☐	119	Denis Herron	.30	.15	.03
☐	120	Steve Shutt AS1	1.00	.50	.10
☐	121	Mel Bridgman	.30	.15	.03
☐	122	Buster Harvey	.17	.08	.01
☐	123	Roland Eriksson	.17	.08	.01
☐	124	Dale Tallon	.17	.08	.01
☐	125	Gilles Gilbert	.30	.15	.03
☐	126	Billy Harris	.17	.08	.01
☐	127	Tom Lysiak	.30	.15	.03
☐	128	Jerry Korab	.17	.08	.01
☐	129	Bob Gainey	1.00	.50	.10
☐	130	Wilf Paiement	.30	.15	.03
☐	131	Tom Bladon	.17	.08	.01

		NRMT	VG-E	GOOD
☐ 132	Ernie Hicke	.17	.08	.01
☐ 133	J.P. Leblanc	.17	.08	.01
☐ 134	Mike Milbury	1.50	.75	.15
☐ 135	Pit Martin	.17	.08	.01
☐ 136	Steve Vickers	.17	.08	.01
☐ 137	Don Awrey	.17	.08	.01
☐ 138	Bernie Wolfe	.17	.08	.01
☐ 139	Doug Jarvis	.30	.15	.03
☐ 140	Borje Salming AS1	.50	.25	.05
☐ 141	Bob MacMillan	.30	.15	.03
☐ 142	Wayne Stephenson	.30	.15	.03
☐ 143	Dave Forbes	.17	.08	.01
☐ 144	Jean Potvin	.17	.08	.01
☐ 145	Guy Charron	.17	.08	.01
☐ 146	Cliff Koroll	.17	.08	.01
☐ 147	Danny Grant	.17	.08	.01
☐ 148	Bill Hogaboam	.17	.08	.01
☐ 149	Al MacAdam	.30	.15	.03
☐ 150	Gerry Desjardins	.30	.15	.03
☐ 151	Yvon Lambert	.17	.08	.01
☐ 152	Rick Lapointe	.30	.15	.03
☐ 153	Ed Westfall	.30	.15	.03
☐ 154	Carol Vadnais	.17	.08	.01
☐ 155	Johnny Bucyk	1.25	.60	.12
☐ 156	J.P. Bordeleau	.17	.08	.01
☐ 157	Ron Stackhouse	.17	.08	.01
☐ 158	Glen Sharpley	.17	.08	.01
☐ 159	Michel Bergeron	.40	.20	.04
☐ 160	Rogatien Vachon AS2	1.00	.50	.10
☐ 161	Fred Stanfield	.17	.08	.01
☐ 162	Gerry Hart	.17	.08	.01
☐ 163	Mario Tremblay	.30	.15	.03
☐ 164	Andre Dupont	.17	.08	.01
☐ 165	Don Marcotte	.17	.08	.01
☐ 166	Wayne Dillon	.17	.08	.01
☐ 167	Claude Larose	.17	.08	.01
☐ 168	Eric Vail	.30	.15	.03
☐ 169	Tom Edur	.17	.08	.01
☐ 170	Tony Esposito	2.00	1.00	.20
☐ 171	Andre St. Laurent	.17	.08	.01
☐ 172	Dan Maloney	.30	.15	.03
☐ 173	Dennis O'Brien	.17	.08	.01
☐ 174	Blair Chapman	.17	.08	.01
☐ 175	Dennis Kearns	.17	.08	.01
☐ 176	Wayne Merrick	.17	.08	.01
☐ 177	Michel Larocque	.40	.20	.04
☐ 178	Bob Kelly	.17	.08	.01
☐ 179	Dave Farrish	.17	.08	.01
☐ 180	Rick Martin AS2	.40	.20	.04
☐ 181	Gary Doak	.17	.08	.01
☐ 182	Jude Drouin	.17	.08	.01
☐ 183	Barry Dean	.17	.08	.01
☐ 184	Gary Smith	.30	.15	.03

		NRMT	VG-E	GOOD
☐ 185	Reggie Leach	.40	.20	.04
☐ 186	Ian Turnbull	.17	.08	.01
☐ 187	Vic Venasky	.17	.08	.01
☐ 188	Wayne Bianchin	.17	.08	.01
☐ 189	Doug Risebrough	.30	.15	.03
☐ 190	Brad Park	1.00	.50	.10
☐ 191	Craig Ramsay	.17	.08	.01
☐ 192	Ken Hodge	.40	.20	.04
☐ 193	Phil Myre	.30	.15	.03
☐ 194	Garry Howatt	.17	.08	.01
☐ 195	Stan Mikita	2.50	1.25	.25
☐ 196	Garnet Bailey	.17	.08	.01
☐ 197	Dennis Hextall	.30	.15	.03
☐ 198	Nick Beverley	.17	.08	.01
☐ 199	Larry Patey	.17	.08	.01
☐ 200	Guy Lafleur AS1	6.00	3.00	.60
☐ 201	Don Edwards	1.00	.50	.10
☐ 202	Gary Dornhoefer	.30	.15	.03
☐ 203	Bob Paradise	.30	.15	.03
☐ 204	Alex Pirus	.17	.08	.01
☐ 205	Peter Mahovlich	.30	.15	.03
☐ 206	Bert Marshall	.17	.08	.01
☐ 207	Gilles Gratton	.30	.15	.03
☐ 208	Alain Daigle	.17	.08	.01
☐ 209	Chris Oddleifson	.17	.08	.01
☐ 210	Gilbert Perreault AS2	1.50	.75	.15
☐ 211	Mike Palmateer	1.00	.50	.10
☐ 212	Billy Lochead	.17	.08	.01
☐ 213	Dick Redmond	.17	.08	.01
☐ 214	Guy Lafleur RB Most Points, RW, Season	2.00	1.00	.20
☐ 215	Ian Turnbull RB Most Goals, Defenseman, Game	.30	.15	.03
☐ 216	Guy Lafleur RB Longest Point Scoring Streak	2.00	1.00	.20
☐ 217	Steve Shutt RB Most Goals, LW, Season	.40	.20	.04
☐ 218	Guy Lafleur RB Most Assists, RW, Season	2.00	1.00	.20
☐ 219	Lorne Henning	.17	.08	.01
☐ 220	Terry O'Reilly	.50	.25	.05
☐ 221	Pat Hickey	.17	.08	.01
☐ 222	Rene Robert	.30	.15	.03
☐ 223	Tim Young	.17	.08	.01
☐ 224	Dunc Wilson	.30	.15	.03
☐ 225	Dennis Hull	.40	.20	.04
☐ 226	Rod Seiling	.17	.08	.01
☐ 227	Bill Barber	1.00	.50	.10

		NRMT	VG-E	GOOD
☐ 228	Dennis Polonich	.17	.08	.01
☐ 229	Billy Smith	1.00	.50	.10
☐ 230	Yvan Cournoyer	1.25	.60	.12
☐ 231	Don Luce	.17	.08	.01
☐ 232	Mike McEwen	.40	.20	.04
☐ 233	Don Saleski	.17	.08	.01
☐ 234	Wayne Cashman	.30	.15	.03
☐ 235	Phil Russell	.17	.08	.01
☐ 236	Mike Corrigan	.17	.08	.01
☐ 237	Guy Chouinard	.30	.15	.03
☐ 238	Steve Jensen	.17	.08	.01
☐ 239	Jim Rutherford	.30	.15	.03
☐ 240	Marcel Dionne AS1	5.50	2.75	.55
☐ 241	Rejean Houle	.30	.15	.03
☐ 242	Jocelyn Guevremont	.17	.08	.01
☐ 243	Jim Harrison	.17	.08	.01
☐ 244	Don Murdoch	.17	.08	.01
☐ 245	Rick Green	1.00	.50	.10
☐ 246	Rick Middleton	1.00	.50	.10
☐ 247	Joe Watson	.17	.08	.01
☐ 248	Syl Apps	.17	.08	.01
☐ 249	Checklist 133-264	2.50	.20	.04
☐ 250	Clark Gillies	.40	.20	.04
☐ 251	Bobby Orr	15.00	7.50	1.50
☐ 252	Nelson Pyatt	.17	.08	.01
☐ 253	Gary McAdam	.30	.15	.03
☐ 254	Jacques Lemaire	1.25	.60	.12
☐ 255	Bob Girard	.17	.08	.01
☐ 256	Ron Greschner	.40	.20	.04
☐ 257	Ross Lonsberry	.17	.08	.01
☐ 258	Dave Gardner	.17	.08	.01
☐ 259	Rick Blight	.17	.08	.01
☐ 260	Gerry Cheevers	1.50	.75	.15
☐ 261	Jean Pronovost	.30	.15	.03
☐ 262	Semi-Finals Canadiens Skate Past Islanders	.50	.25	.05
☐ 263	Semi-Finals Bruins Advance to Finals	.50	.25	.05
☐ 264	Finals Canadiens Win 20th Stanley Cup	1.00	.50	.10
☐ 265	Rick Bowness	.60	.30	.06
☐ 266	George Ferguson	.17	.08	.01
☐ 267	Mike Kitchen	.17	.08	.01
☐ 268	Bob Berry	.30	.15	.03
☐ 269	Greg Smith	.17	.08	.01
☐ 270	Stan Jonathan	.17	.08	.01
☐ 271	Dwight Bialowas	.17	.08	.01
☐ 272	Pete Stemkowski	.17	.08	.01
☐ 273	Greg Joly	.17	.08	.01
☐ 274	Ken Houston	.17	.08	.01

		NRMT	VG-E	GOOD
☐ 275	Brian Glennie	.17	.08	.01
☐ 276	Ed Johnston	.40	.20	.04
☐ 277	John Grisdale	.17	.08	.01
☐ 278	Craig Patrick	.30	.15	.03
☐ 279	Ken Breitenbach	.17	.08	.01
☐ 280	Fred Ahern	.17	.08	.01
☐ 281	Jim Roberts	.17	.08	.01
	St. Louis Blues			
☐ 282	Harvey Bennett	.17	.08	.01
☐ 283	Ab Demarco	.17	.08	.01
☐ 284	Pat Boutette	.17	.08	.01
☐ 285	Bob Plager	.30	.15	.03
☐ 286	Hilliard Graves	.17	.08	.01
☐ 287	Gordie Lane	.17	.08	.01
☐ 288	Ron Andruff	.17	.08	.01
☐ 289	Larry Brown	.17	.08	.01
☐ 290	Mike Fidler	.17	.08	.01
☐ 291	Fred Barrett	.17	.08	.01
☐ 292	Bill Clement	.30	.15	.03
☐ 293	Errol Thompson	.17	.08	.01
☐ 294	Doug Grant	.17	.08	.01
☐ 295	Harold Snepsts	.40	.20	.04
☐ 296	Rick Bragnalo	.17	.08	.01
☐ 297	Bryan Lefley	.17	.08	.01
☐ 298	Gene Carr	.17	.08	.01
☐ 299	Bob Stewart	.17	.08	.01
☐ 300	Lew Morrison	.17	.08	.01
☐ 301	Ed Kea	.17	.08	.01
☐ 302	Scott Garland	.17	.08	.01
☐ 303	Bill Fairbairn	.17	.08	.01
☐ 304	Larry Carriere	.17	.08	.01
☐ 305	Ron Low	.30	.15	.03
☐ 306	Tom Reid	.17	.08	.01
☐ 307	Paul Holmgren	2.25	1.10	.22
☐ 308	Pat Price	.17	.08	.01
☐ 309	Kirk Bowman	.17	.08	.01
☐ 310	Bobby Simpson	.17	.08	.01
☐ 311	Ron Ellis	.17	.08	.01
☐ 312	Rick Bourbonnais UER	.30	.15	.03
	(Photo actually			
	Bernie Federko)			
☐ 313	Bobby Lalonde	.17	.08	.01
☐ 314	Tony White	.17	.08	.01
☐ 315	John Van Boxmeer	.17	.08	.01
☐ 316	Don Kozak	.17	.08	.01
☐ 317	Jim Neilson	.17	.08	.01
☐ 318	Terry Martin	.17	.08	.01
☐ 319	Barry Gibbs	.17	.08	.01
☐ 320	Inge Hammarstrom	.17	.08	.01
☐ 321	Darryl Edestrand	.17	.08	.01
☐ 322	Flames Records	.50	.25	.05
	and Team Logo			
☐ 323	Bruins Records	.50	.25	.05
	and Team Logo			

		NRMT	VG-E	GOOD
☐ 324	Sabres Records and Team Logo	.50	.25	.05
☐ 325	Blackhawks Records and Team Logo	.50	.25	.05
☐ 326	Barons Records and Team Logo	.50	.25	.05
☐ 327	Rockies Records and Team Logo	.50	.25	.05
☐ 328	Red Wings Records and Team Logo	.50	.25	.05
☐ 329	Kings Records and Team Logo	.50	.25	.05
☐ 330	North Stars Records and Team Logo	.50	.25	.05
☐ 331	Canadiens Records and Team Logo	.50	.25	.05
☐ 332	Islanders Records and Team Logo	.50	.25	.05
☐ 333	Rangers Records and Team Logo	.50	.25	.05
☐ 334	Flyers Records and Team Logo	.50	.25	.05
☐ 335	Penguins Records and Team Logo	.50	.25	.05
☐ 336	Blues Records and Team Logo	.50	.25	.05
☐ 337	Leafs Records and Team Logo	.50	.25	.05
☐ 338	Canucks Records and Team Logo	.50	.25	.05
☐ 339	Capitals Records and Team Logo	.50	.25	.05
☐ 340	Chuck Lefley	.17	.08	.01
☐ 341	Garry Monahan	.17	.08	.01
☐ 342	Bryan Watson	.17	.08	.01
☐ 343	Dave Hudson	.17	.08	.01
☐ 344	Neil Komadoski	.17	.08	.01
☐ 345	Gary Edwards	.30	.15	.03
☐ 346	Rey Comeau	.17	.08	.01
☐ 347	Bob Neely	.17	.08	.01
☐ 348	Jean Hamel	.17	.08	.01
☐ 349	Jerry Butler	.17	.08	.01
☐ 350	Mike Walton	.30	.15	.03
☐ 351	Bob Sirois	.17	.08	.01
☐ 352	Jim McElmury	.17	.08	.01
☐ 353	Dave Schultz	.40	.20	.04
☐ 354	Doug Palazzari	.17	.08	.01
☐ 355	David Shand	.17	.08	.01
☐ 356	Stan Weir	.17	.08	.01
☐ 357	Mike Christie	.17	.08	.01
☐ 358	Floyd Thomson	.17	.08	.01
☐ 359	Larry Goodenough	.17	.08	.01

		NRMT	VG-E	GOOD
☐ 360	Bill Riley	.17	.08	.01
☐ 361	Doug Hicks	.17	.08	.01
☐ 362	Dan Newman	.17	.08	.01
☐ 363	Rick Chartraw	.17	.08	.01
☐ 364	Tim Ecclestone	.17	.08	.01
☐ 365	Don Ashby	.17	.08	.01
☐ 366	Jacques Richard	.17	.08	.01
☐ 367	Yves Belanger	.30	.15	.03
☐ 368	Ron Sedlbauer	.17	.08	.01
☐ 369	Jack Lynch UER (Photo actually Bill Collins)	.17	.08	.01
☐ 370	Doug Favell	.30	.15	.03
☐ 371	Bob Murdoch	.30	.15	.03
☐ 372	Ralph Klassen	.17	.08	.01
☐ 373	Richard Mulhern	.17	.08	.01
☐ 374	Jim McKenny	.17	.08	.01
☐ 375	Mike Bloom	.17	.08	.01
☐ 376	Bruce Affleck	.17	.08	.01
☐ 377	Gerry O'Flaherty	.17	.08	.01
☐ 378	Ron Lalonde	.17	.08	.01
☐ 379	Chuck Arnason	.17	.08	.01
☐ 380	Dave Hutchinson	.17	.08	.01
☐ 381A	Checklist ERR (Topps heading)	2.50	.20	.04
☐ 381B	Checklist COR (No Topps heading)	2.50	.20	.04
☐ 382	John Gould	.17	.08	.01
☐ 383	Dave Williams	.30	.15	.03
☐ 384	Len Frig	.17	.08	.01
☐ 385	Pierre Plante	.17	.08	.01
☐ 386	Ralph Stewart	.17	.08	.01
☐ 387	Gord Smith	.17	.08	.01
☐ 388	Denis Dupere	.17	.08	.01
☐ 389	Randy Manery	.17	.08	.01
☐ 390	Lowell MacDonald	.30	.15	.03
☐ 391	Dennis Owchar	.17	.08	.01
☐ 392	Jim Roberts Minnesota North Stars	.17	.08	.01
☐ 393	Mike Veisor	.30	.15	.03
☐ 394	Bob Hess	.17	.08	.01
☐ 395	Curt Ridley	.30	.15	.03
☐ 396	Mike Lampman	.30	.15	.03

1977-78 O-Pee-Chee WHA

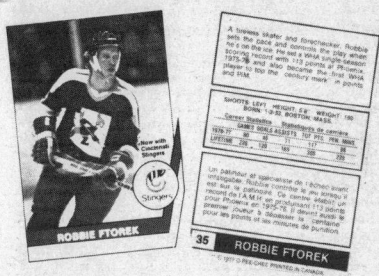

The 1977-78 O-Pee-Chee WHA set consists of 66 color cards featuring WHA players. Cards measure 2½" by 3½". The backs, in both French and English, feature the card number, player statistics, and a short biography of the player portrayed. The cards were printed in Canada. Card number 1 features Gordie Howe's 1000th career goal. There are no key rookie cards in this set.

Le jeu WHA O-Pee-Chee contient 66 cartes en couleurs, représentant des joueurs WHA. Les cartes mesurent 2½" x 3½". Le dos, imprimé en français et en anglais, comprend le numéro de carte, les statistiques du joueur, et une biographie concise. Les cartes ont été imprimées au Canada. La carte numéro 1 représente le 1000ème but de la carrière de Gordie Howe. Le jeu ne comporte pas de cartes de débutants importants.

			NRMT	VG-E	GOOD
	COMPLETE SET (66)		70.00	35.00	7.00
	COMMON PLAYER (1-66)		.40	.20	.04
☐	1	Gordie Howe	25.00	7.50	1.50
☐	2	Jean Bernier	.40	.20	.04
☐	3	Anders Hedberg	.75	.35	.07
☐	4	Ken Broderick	.50	.25	.05
☐	5	Joe Noris	.50	.25	.05
☐	6	Blaine Stoughton	.60	.30	.06
☐	7	Claude St. Sauveur	.40	.20	.04
☐	8	Real Cloutier	.50	.25	.05
☐	9	Joe Daley	.60	.30	.06
☐	10	Ron Chipperfield	.40	.20	.04
☐	11	Wayne Rutledge	.50	.25	.05
☐	12	Mark Napier	.60	.30	.06
☐	13	Rich Leduc	.40	.20	.04
☐	14	Don McLeod	.50	.25	.05

			NRMT	VG-E	GOOD
☐	15	Ulf Nilsson	.75	.35	.07
☐	16	Blair MacDonald	.50	.25	.05
☐	17	Mike Rogers	.75	.35	.07
☐	18	Gary Inness	.50	.25	.05
☐	19	Larry Lund	.40	.20	.04
☐	20	Marc Tardif	.60	.30	.06
☐	21	Lars-Erik Sjoberg	.50	.25	.05
☐	22	Bryan Campbell	.40	.20	.04
☐	23	John Garrett	.60	.30	.06
☐	24	Ron Plumb	.50	.25	.05
☐	25	Mark Howe	2.50	1.25	.25
☐	26	Garry Lariviere	.40	.20	.04
☐	27	Peter Sullivan	.50	.25	.05
☐	28	Dave Dryden	.60	.30	.06
☐	29	Reg Thomas	.40	.20	.04
☐	30	Andre Lacroix	.75	.35	.07
☐	31	Paul Henderson	.60	.30	.06
☐	32	Paulin Bordeleau	.40	.20	.04
☐	33	Juha Widing	.40	.20	.04
☐	34	Mike Antonovich	.40	.20	.04
☐	35	Robbie Ftorek	.75	.35	.07
☐	36	Rosaire Paiement	.40	.20	.04
☐	37	Terry Ruskowski	.60	.30	.06
☐	38	Richard Brodeur	.75	.35	.07
☐	39	Willy Lindstrom	.75	.35	.07
☐	40	Al Hamilton	.40	.20	.04
☐	41	John McKenzie	.50	.25	.05
☐	42	Wayne Wood	.50	.25	.05
☐	43	Claude Larose	.50	.25	.05
☐	44	J.C. Tremblay	.60	.30	.06
☐	45	Gary Bromley	.50	.25	.05
☐	46	Ken Baird	.40	.20	.04
☐	47	Bobby Sheehan	.40	.20	.04
☐	48	Don Larway	.40	.20	.04
☐	49	Al Smith	.50	.25	.05
☐	50	Bobby Hull	15.00	7.50	1.50
☐	51	Peter Marrin	.40	.20	.04
☐	52	Norm Ferguson	.40	.20	.04
☐	53	Dennis Sobchuk	.40	.20	.04
☐	54	Norm Dube	.40	.20	.04
☐	55	Tom Webster	.90	.45	.09
☐	56	Jim Park	.40	.20	.04
☐	57	Dan Labraaten	.75	.35	.07
☐	58	Checklist Card	2.50	.20	.04
☐	59	Paul Shmyr	.50	.25	.05
☐	60	Serge Bernier	.60	.30	.06
☐	61	Frank Mahovlich	2.00	1.00	.20
☐	62	Michel Dion	.60	.30	.06
☐	63	Poul Popiel	.50	.25	.05
☐	64	Lyle Moffat	.40	.20	.04
☐	65	Marty Howe	.60	.30	.06
☐	66	Don Burgess	1.00	.25	.05

1978-79 O-Pee-Chee

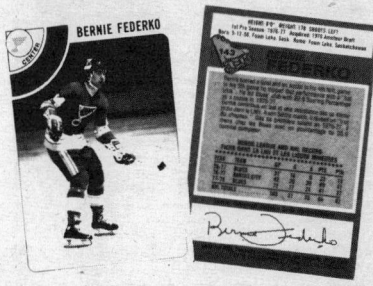

The 1978-79 O-Pee-Chee NHL set consists of 396 color cards of NHL players. The first 264 cards in the set have identical fronts to the Topps cards of this year. Cards 1-5 feature highlights (HL) from the previous season. Cards are 2½" by 3½". The backs, in both French and English, feature the card number (pictured in a hockey skate), year-by-year player career records, a short biography, and a facsimile autograph. The cards were printed in Canada. Card 300 is a special card honoring Bobby Orr's retirement early in the season. The key rookie cards in this set are Mike Bossy, Bernie Federko, and Doug Wilson.

Le jeu NHL O-Pee-Chee 1978-79 contient 396 cartes en couleurs de joueurs NHL. La face des 264 premières cartes du jeu est identique à celle des cartes Topps de cette année. Les cartes 1-5 représentent les moments importants (HL) de la saison précédente. Les cartes mesurent 2½" x 3½". Le dos, imprimé en français et en anglais, comporte le numéro de carte dans un patin de hockey, les statistiques des joueurs par année de carrière, une biographie concise, et une copie d'un autographe. Les cartes ont été imprimées au Canada. La carte numéro 300 honore la retraite de Bobby Orr en début de saison. Les débutants importants de ce jeu sont Mike Bossy, Bernie Federko, et Doug Wilson.

			NRMT	VG-E	GOOD
		COMPLETE SET (396)	150.00	75.00	15.00
		COMMON PLAYER (1-396)	.15	.07	.01
☐	1	**Mike Bossy HL**	8.00	1.50	.30
		Goals by Rookie			
☐	2	**Phil Esposito HL**	1.25	.60	.12
		29th Hat Trick			
☐	3	**Guy Lafleur HL**	1.50	.75	.15
		Scores Against Every Team			

			NRMT	VG-E	GOOD
☐	4	**Darryl Sittler HL**	.50	.25	.05
		Goals in Nine Straight Games			
☐	5	**Garry Unger HL**	.25	.12	.02
		803 Consec. Games			
☐	6	Gary Edwards	.25	.12	.02
☐	7	Rick Blight	.15	.07	.01
☐	8	Larry Patey	.15	.07	.01
☐	9	Craig Ramsay	.15	.07	.01
☐	10	Bryan Trottier AS1	4.00	2.00	.40
☐	11	Don Murdoch	.15	.07	.01
☐	12	Phil Russell	.15	.07	.01
☐	13	Doug Jarvis	.25	.12	.02
☐	14	Gene Carr	.15	.07	.01
☐	15	Bernie Parent	1.50	.75	.15
☐	16	Perry Miller	.15	.07	.01
☐	17	Kent-Erik Andersson	.15	.07	.01
☐	18	Gregg Sheppard	.15	.07	.01
☐	19	Dennis Owchar	.15	.07	.01
☐	20	Rogatien Vachon	.90	.45	.09
☐	21	Dan Maloney	.25	.12	.02
☐	22	Guy Charron	.15	.07	.01
☐	23	Dick Redmond	.15	.07	.01
☐	24	Checklist 1-132	2.00	.15	.03
☐	25	Anders Hedberg	.25	.12	.02
☐	26	Mel Bridgman	.15	.07	.01
☐	27	Lee Fogolin	.15	.07	.01
☐	28	Gilles Meloche	.25	.12	.02
☐	29	Garry Howatt	.15	.07	.01
☐	30	Darryl Sittler AS2	.90	.45	.09
☐	31	Curt Bennett	.15	.07	.01
☐	32	Andre St. Laurent	.15	.07	.01
☐	33	Blair Chapman	.15	.07	.01
☐	34	Keith Magnuson	.15	.07	.01
☐	35	Pierre Larouche	.35	.17	.03
☐	36	Michel Plasse	.25	.12	.02
☐	37	Gary Sargent	.25	.12	.02
☐	38	Mike Walton	.25	.12	.02
☐	39	Robert Picard	.15	.07	.01
☐	40	Terry O'Reilly AS2	.35	.17	.03
☐	41	Dave Farrish	.15	.07	.01
☐	42	Gary McAdam	.25	.12	.02
☐	43	Joe Watson	.15	.07	.01
☐	44	Yves Belanger	.25	.12	.02
☐	45	Steve Jensen	.15	.07	.01
☐	46	Bob Stewart	.15	.07	.01
☐	47	Darcy Rota	.15	.07	.01
☐	48	Dennis Hextall	.25	.12	.02
☐	49	Bert Marshall	.15	.07	.01
☐	50	Ken Dryden AS1	4.50	2.25	.45
☐	51	Peter Mahovlich	.25	.12	.02
☐	52	Dennis Ververgaert	.15	.07	.01
☐	53	Inge Hammarstrom	.15	.07	.01

			NRMT	VG-E	GOOD
☐	54	Doug Favell	.25	.12	.02
☐	55	Steve Vickers	.15	.07	.01
☐	56	Syl Apps	.15	.07	.01
☐	57	Errol Thompson	.15	.07	.01
☐	58	Don Luce	.15	.07	.01
☐	59	Mike Milbury	.35	.17	.03
☐	60	Yvan Cournoyer	1.25	.60	.12
☐	61	Kirk Bowman	.15	.07	.01
☐	62	Billy Smith	.85	.40	.08
☐	63	Goal Leaders	1.50	.75	.15
		Guy Lafleur			
		Mike Bossy			
		Steve Shutt			
☐	64	Assist Leaders	1.50	.75	.15
		Bryan Trottier			
		Guy Lafleur			
		Darryl Sittler			
☐	65	Scoring Leaders	1.50	.75	.15
		Guy Lafleur			
		Bryan Trottier			
		Darryl Sittler			
☐	66	Penalty Minutes Leaders	.25	.12	.02
		Dave Schultz			
		Dave Williams			
		Dennis Polonich			
☐	67	Power Play Goal Leaders	1.50	.75	.15
		Mike Bossy			
		Phil Esposito			
		Steve Shutt			
☐	68	Goals Against Average Leaders	.90	.45	.09
		Ken Dryden			
		Bernie Parent			
		Gilles Gilbert			
☐	69	Game Winning Goal Leaders	1.50	.75	.15
		Guy Lafleur			
		Bill Barber			
		Darryl Sittler			
		Bob Bourne			
☐	70	Shutout Leaders	1.25	.60	.12
		Bernie Parent			
		Ken Dryden			
		Don Edwards			
		Tony Esposito			
		Mike Palmateer			
☐	71	Bob Kelly	.15	.07	.01
☐	72	Ron Stackhouse	.15	.07	.01
☐	73	Wayne Dillon	.15	.07	.01
☐	74	Jim Rutherford	.25	.12	.02
☐	75	Stan Mikita	2.00	1.00	.20

			NRMT	VG-E	GOOD
☐	76	Bob Gainey	.85	.40	.08
☐	77	Gerry Hart	.15	.07	.01
☐	78	Lanny McDonald	1.00	.50	.10
☐	79	Brad Park	1.00	.50	.10
☐	80	Rick Martin	.35	.17	.03
☐	81	Bernie Wolfe	.15	.07	.01
☐	82	Bob MacMillan	.25	.12	.02
☐	83	Brad Maxwell	.15	.07	.01
☐	84	Mike Fidler	.15	.07	.01
☐	85	Carol Vadnais	.15	.07	.01
☐	86	Don Lever	.15	.07	.01
☐	87	Phil Myre	.25	.12	.02
☐	88	Paul Gardner	.25	.12	.02
☐	89	Bob Murray	.15	.07	.01
☐	90	Guy Lafleur AS1	4.50	2.25	.45
☐	91	Bob Murdoch	.15	.07	.01
☐	92	Ron Ellis	.15	.07	.01
☐	93	Jude Drouin	.15	.07	.01
☐	94	Jocelyn Guevremont	.15	.07	.01
☐	95	Gilles Gilbert	.25	.12	.02
☐	96	Bob Sirois	.15	.07	.01
☐	97	Tom Lysiak	.25	.12	.02
☐	98	Andre Dupont	.15	.07	.01
☐	99	Per-Olov Brasar	.15	.07	.01
☐	100	Phil Esposito	3.50	1.75	.35
☐	101	J.P. Bordeleau	.15	.07	.01
☐	102	Pierre Mondou	.60	.30	.06
☐	103	Wayne Bianchin	.15	.07	.01
☐	104	Dennis O'Brien	.15	.07	.01
☐	105	Glenn Resch	.75	.35	.07
☐	106	Dennis Polonich	.15	.07	.01
☐	107	Kris Manery	.15	.07	.01
☐	108	Bill Hajt	.15	.07	.01
☐	109	Jere Gillis	.15	.07	.01
☐	110	Garry Unger	.35	.17	.03
☐	111	Nick Beverley	.15	.07	.01
☐	112	Pat Hickey	.15	.07	.01
☐	113	Rick Middleton	.75	.35	.07
☐	114	Orest Kindrachuk	.15	.07	.01
☐	115	Mike Bossy	50.00	25.00	5.00
☐	116	Pierre Bouchard	.15	.07	.01
☐	117	Alain Daigle	.15	.07	.01
☐	118	Terry Martin	.15	.07	.01
☐	119	Tom Edur	.15	.07	.01
☐	120	Marcel Dionne	4.00	2.00	.40
☐	121	Barry Beck	1.50	.75	.15
☐	122	Billy Lochead	.15	.07	.01
☐	123	Paul Harrison	.15	.07	.01
☐	124	Wayne Cashman	.25	.12	.02
☐	125	Rick MacLeish	.35	.17	.03
☐	126	Bob Bourne	.25	.12	.02
☐	127	Ian Turnbull	.15	.07	.01
☐	128	Gerry Meehan	.25	.12	.02

		NRMT	VG-E	GOOD
☐ 129	Eric Vail	.25	.12	.02
☐ 130	Gilbert Perreault	1.25	.60	.12
☐ 131	Bob Dailey	.15	.07	.01
☐ 132	Dale McCourt	.35	.17	.03
☐ 133	John Wensink	.15	.07	.01
☐ 134	Bill Nyrop	.25	.12	.02
☐ 135	Ivan Boldirev	.15	.07	.01
☐ 136	Lucien Deblois	.25	.12	.02
☐ 137	Brian Spencer	.15	.07	.01
☐ 138	Tim Young	.15	.07	.01
☐ 139	Ron Sedlbauer	.15	.07	.01
☐ 140	Gerry Cheevers	1.25	.60	.12
☐ 141	Dennis Maruk	.25	.12	.02
☐ 142	Barry Dean	.15	.07	.01
☐ 143	Bernie Federko	6.50	3.25	.65
☐ 144	Stefan Persson	.50	.25	.05
☐ 145	Wilf Paiement	.25	.12	.02
☐ 146	Dale Tallon	.15	.07	.01
☐ 147	Yvon Lambert	.15	.07	.01
☐ 148	Greg Joly	.15	.07	.01
☐ 149	Dean Talafous	.15	.07	.01
☐ 150	Don Edwards AS2	.25	.12	.02
☐ 151	Butch Goring	.35	.17	.03
☐ 152	Tom Bladon	.15	.07	.01
☐ 153	Bob Nystrom	.25	.12	.02
☐ 154	Ron Greschner	.25	.12	.02
☐ 155	Jean Ratelle	1.00	.50	.10
☐ 156	Russ Anderson	.15	.07	.01
☐ 157	John Marks	.15	.07	.01
☐ 158	Michel Larocque	.25	.12	.02
☐ 159	Paul Woods	.15	.07	.01
☐ 160	Mike Palmateer	.25	.12	.02
☐ 161	Jim Lorentz	.15	.07	.01
☐ 162	Dave Lewis	.15	.07	.01
☐ 163	Harvey Bennett	.15	.07	.01
☐ 164	Rick Smith	.15	.07	.01
☐ 165	Reggie Leach	.35	.17	.03
☐ 166	Wayne Thomas	.25	.12	.02
☐ 167	Dave Forbes	.15	.07	.01
☐ 168	Doug Wilson	16.00	8.00	1.60
☐ 169	Dan Bouchard	.25	.12	.02
☐ 170	Steve Shutt AS2	.75	.35	.07
☐ 171	Mike Kaszycki	.15	.07	.01
☐ 172	Denis Herron	.25	.12	.02
☐ 173	Rick Bowness	.25	.12	.02
☐ 174	Rick Hampton	.15	.07	.01
☐ 175	Glen Sharpley	.15	.07	.01
☐ 176	Bill Barber	.90	.45	.09
☐ 177	Ron Duguay	1.50	.75	.15
☐ 178	Jim Schoenfeld	.25	.12	.02
☐ 179	Pierre Plante	.15	.07	.01
☐ 180	Jacques Lemaire	1.00	.50	.10
☐ 181	Stan Jonathan	.15	.07	.01

		NRMT	VG-E	GOOD
☐ 182	Billy Harris	.15	.07	.01
☐ 183	Chris Oddleifson	.15	.07	.01
☐ 184	Jean Pronovost	.25	.12	.02
☐ 185	Fred Barrett	.15	.07	.01
☐ 186	Ross Lonsberry	.15	.07	.01
☐ 187	Mike McEwen	.25	.12	.02
☐ 188	Rene Robert	.25	.12	.02
☐ 189	J. Bob Kelly	.15	.07	.01
☐ 190	Serge Savard AS2	.90	.45	.09
☐ 191	Dennis Kearns	.15	.07	.01
☐ 192	Flames Team	.40	.20	.04
☐ 193	Bruins Team	.40	.20	.04
☐ 194	Sabres Team	.40	.20	.04
☐ 195	Blackhawks Team	.40	.20	.04
☐ 196	Rockies Team	.40	.20	.04
☐ 197	Red Wings Team	.40	.20	.04
☐ 198	Kings Team	.40	.20	.04
☐ 199	North Stars Team	.40	.20	.04
☐ 200	Canadiens Team	.40	.20	.04
☐ 201	Islanders Team	.40	.20	.04
☐ 202	Rangers Team	.40	.20	.04
☐ 203	Flyers Team	.40	.20	.04
☐ 204	Penguins Team	.40	.20	.04
☐ 205	Blues Team	.40	.20	.04
☐ 206	Maple Leafs Team	.40	.20	.04
☐ 207	Canucks Team	.40	.20	.04
☐ 208	Capitals Team	.40	.20	.04
☐ 209	Danny Gare	.25	.12	.02
☐ 210	Larry Robinson AS1	1.25	.60	.12
☐ 211	John Davidson	.25	.12	.02
☐ 212	Peter McNab	.15	.07	.01
☐ 213	Rick Kehoe	.25	.12	.02
☐ 214	Terry Harper	.15	.07	.01
☐ 215	Bobby Clarke	2.00	1.00	.20
☐ 216	Bryan Maxwell UER (Photo actually Brad Maxwell)	.15	.07	.01
☐ 217	Ted Bulley	.15	.07	.01
☐ 218	Red Berenson	.25	.12	.02
☐ 219	Ron Grahame	.25	.12	.02
☐ 220	Clark Gillies AS1	.35	.17	.03
☐ 221	Dave Maloney	.25	.12	.02
☐ 222	Derek Smith	.35	.17	.03
☐ 223	Wayne Stephenson	.25	.12	.02
☐ 224	John Van Boxmeer	.15	.07	.01
☐ 225	Dave Schultz	.35	.17	.03
☐ 226	Reed Larson	.50	.25	.05
☐ 227	Rejean Houle	.25	.12	.02
☐ 228	Doug Hicks	.15	.07	.01
☐ 229	Mike Murphy	.15	.07	.01
☐ 230	Pete Lopresti	.15	.07	.01
☐ 231	Jerry Korab	.15	.07	.01
☐ 232	Ed Westfall	.25	.12	.02

		NRMT	VG-E	GOOD
☐ 233	Greg Malone	.15	.07	.01
☐ 234	Paul Holmgren	.50	.25	.05
☐ 235	Walt Tkaczuk	.25	.12	.02
☐ 236	Don Marcotte	.15	.07	.01
☐ 237	Ron Low	.25	.12	.02
☐ 238	Rick Chartraw	.15	.07	.01
☐ 239	Cliff Koroll	.15	.07	.01
☐ 240	Borje Salming AS1	.50	.25	.05
☐ 241	Roland Eriksson	.15	.07	.01
☐ 242	Ric Seiling	.15	.07	.01
☐ 243	Jim Bedard	.25	.12	.02
☐ 244	Peter Lee	.15	.07	.01
☐ 245	Denis Potvin AS2	2.00	1.00	.20
☐ 246	Greg Polis	.15	.07	.01
☐ 247	Jim Watson	.15	.07	.01
☐ 248	Bobby Schmautz	.15	.07	.01
☐ 249	Doug Risebrough	.15	.07	.01
☐ 250	Tony Esposito	1.50	.75	.15
☐ 251	Nick Libett	.15	.07	.01
☐ 252	Ron Zanussi	.15	.07	.01
☐ 253	Andre Savard	.15	.07	.01
☐ 254	Dave Burrows	.15	.07	.01
☐ 255	Ulf Nilsson	.25	.12	.02
☐ 256	Richard Mulhern	.15	.07	.01
☐ 257	Don Saleski	.15	.07	.01
☐ 258	Wayne Merrick	.15	.07	.01
☐ 259	Checklist 133-264	2.00	.15	.03
☐ 260	Guy Lapointe	.35	.17	.03
☐ 261	Grant Mulvey	.25	.12	.02
☐ 262	Stanley Cup: Semis Canadiens Sweep Maple Leafs	.35	.17	.03
☐ 263	Stanley Cup: Semis Bruins Skate Past Flyers	.35	.17	.03
☐ 264	Stanley Cup: Finals Canadiens Win Third Straight Cup	.60	.30	.06
☐ 265	Bob Sauve	.35	.17	.03
☐ 266	Randy Manery	.15	.07	.01
☐ 267	Bill Fairbairn	.15	.07	.01
☐ 268	Garry Monahan	.15	.07	.01
☐ 269	Colin Campbell	.15	.07	.01
☐ 270	Dan Newman	.15	.07	.01
☐ 271	Dwight Foster	.15	.07	.01
☐ 272	Larry Carriere	.15	.07	.01
☐ 273	Michel Bergeron	.35	.17	.03
☐ 274	Scott Garland	.15	.07	.01
☐ 275	Bill McKenzie	.15	.07	.01
☐ 276	Garnet Bailey	.15	.07	.01
☐ 277	Ed Kea	.15	.07	.01
☐ 278	Dave Gardner	.15	.07	.01
☐ 279	Bruce Affleck	.15	.07	.01

		NRMT	VG-E	GOOD
☐ 280	Bruce Boudreau	.15	.07	.01
☐ 281	Jean Hamel	.15	.07	.01
☐ 282	Kurt Walker	.15	.07	.01
☐ 283	Denis Dupere	.15	.07	.01
☐ 284	Gordie Lane	.15	.07	.01
☐ 285	Bobby Lalonde	.15	.07	.01
☐ 286	Pit Martin	.15	.07	.01
☐ 287	Jean Potvin	.15	.07	.01
☐ 288	Jimmy Jones	.15	.07	.01
☐ 289	Dave Hutchinson	.15	.07	.01
☐ 290	Pete Stemkowski	.15	.07	.01
☐ 291	Mike Christie	.15	.07	.01
☐ 292	Bill Riley	.15	.07	.01
☐ 293	Rey Comeau	.15	.07	.01
☐ 294	Jack McIlhargey	.15	.07	.01
☐ 295	Tom Younghans	.15	.07	.01
☐ 296	Mario Faubert	.15	.07	.01
☐ 297	Checklist Card	2.00	.15	.03
☐ 298	Rob Palmer	.15	.07	.01
☐ 299	Dave Hudson	.15	.07	.01
☐ 300	Bobby Orr	21.00	10.50	2.10
☐ 301	Lorne Stamler	.15	.07	.01
☐ 302	Curt Ridley	.25	.12	.02
☐ 303	Greg Smith	.15	.07	.01
☐ 304	Jerry Butler	.15	.07	.01
☐ 305	Gary Doak	.15	.07	.01
☐ 306	Danny Grant	.15	.07	.01
☐ 307	Mark Suzor	.15	.07	.01
☐ 308	Rick Bragnalo	.15	.07	.01
☐ 309	John Gould	.15	.07	.01
☐ 010	Sheldon Kanneglesser	.15	.07	.01
☐ 311	Bobby Sheehan	.15	.07	.01
☐ 312	Randy Carlyle	2.00	1.00	.20
☐ 313	Lorne Henning	.15	.07	.01
☐ 314	Tom Williams	.15	.07	.01
☐ 315	Ron Andruff	.15	.07	.01
☐ 316	Bryan Watson	.15	.07	.01
☐ 317	Willi Plett	.15	.07	.01
☐ 318	John Grisdale	.15	.07	.01
☐ 319	Brian Sutter	4.00	2.00	.40
☐ 320	Trevor Johansen	.25	.12	.02
☐ 321	Vic Venasky	.15	.07	.01
☐ 322	Rick Lapointe	.25	.12	.02
☐ 323	Ron Delorme	.15	.07	.01
☐ 324	Yvon Labre	.15	.07	.01
☐ 325	Bryan Trottier AS	1.25	.60	.12
☐ 326	Guy Lafleur AS	3.00	1.50	.30
☐ 327	Clark Gillies AS	.25	.12	.02
☐ 328	Borje Salming AS	.35	.17	.03
☐ 329	Larry Robinson AS	.50	.25	.05
☐ 330	Ken Dryden AS	3.00	1.50	.30
☐ 331	Darryl Sittler AS	.50	.25	.05
☐ 332	Terry O'Reilly AS	.25	.12	.02

		NRMT	VG-E	GOOD
☐ 333	Steve Shutt AS	.35	.17	.03
☐ 334	Denis Potvin AS	1.25	.60	.12
☐ 335	Serge Savard AS	.35	.17	.03
☐ 336	Don Edwards AS	.25	.12	.02
☐ 337	Glenn Goldup	.15	.07	.01
☐ 338	Mike Kitchen	.15	.07	.01
☐ 339	Bob Girard	.15	.07	.01
☐ 340	Guy Chouinard	.25	.12	.02
☐ 341	Randy Holt	.15	.07	.01
☐ 342	Jim Roberts	.15	.07	.01
☐ 343	Dave Logan	.15	.07	.01
☐ 344	Walt McKechnie	.15	.07	.01
☐ 345	Brian Glennie	.15	.07	.01
☐ 346	Ralph Klassen	.15	.07	.01
☐ 347	Gord Smith	.15	.07	.01
☐ 348	Ken Houston	.15	.07	.01
☐ 349	Bob Manno	.15	.07	.01
☐ 350	Jean Paul Parise	.15	.07	.01
☐ 351	Don Ashby	.15	.07	.01
☐ 352	Fred Stanfield	.15	.07	.01
☐ 353	Dave Taylor	15.00	7.50	1.50
☐ 354	Nelson Pyatt	.15	.07	.01
☐ 355	Blair Stewart	.15	.07	.01
☐ 356	David Shand	.15	.07	.01
☐ 357	Hilliard Graves	.15	.07	.01
☐ 358	Bob Hess	.15	.07	.01
☐ 359	Dave Williams	.25	.12	.02
☐ 360	Larry Wright	.15	.07	.01
☐ 361	Larry Brown	.15	.07	.01
☐ 362	Gary Croteau	.15	.07	.01
☐ 363	Rick Green	.25	.12	.02
☐ 364	Bill Clement	.25	.12	.02
☐ 365	Gerry O'Flaherty	.15	.07	.01
☐ 366	John Baby	.15	.07	.01
☐ 367	Nick Fotiu	.15	.07	.01
☐ 368	Pat Price	.15	.07	.01
☐ 369	Bert Wilson	.15	.07	.01
☐ 370	Bryan Lefley	.15	.07	.01
☐ 371	Ron Lalonde	.15	.07	.01
☐ 372	Bobby Simpson	.15	.07	.01
☐ 373	Doug Grant	.25	.12	.02
☐ 374	Pat Boutette	.15	.07	.01
☐ 375	Bob Paradise	.15	.07	.01
☐ 376	Mario Tremblay	.25	.12	.02
☐ 377	Darryl Edestrand	.15	.07	.01
☐ 378	Andy Spruce	.15	.07	.01
☐ 379	Jack Brownschidle	.15	.07	.01
☐ 380	Harold Snepsts	.35	.17	.03
☐ 381	Al MacAdam	.25	.12	.02
☐ 382	Neil Komadoski	.15	.07	.01
☐ 383	Don Awrey	.15	.07	.01
☐ 384	Ron Schock	.15	.07	.01
☐ 385	Gary Simmons	.25	.12	.02

		NRMT	VG-E	GOOD
☐ 386	Fred Ahern	.15	.07	.01
☐ 387	Larry Bolonchuk	.15	.07	.01
☐ 388	Brad Gassoff	.15	.07	.01
☐ 389	Chuck Arnason	.15	.07	.01
☐ 390	Barry Gibbs	.15	.07	.01
☐ 391	Jack Valiquette	.15	.07	.01
☐ 392	Doug Halward	.15	.07	.01
☐ 393	Hartland Monahan	.15	.07	.01
☐ 394	Rod Seiling	.15	.07	.01
☐ 395	George Ferguson	.15	.07	.01
☐ 396	Al Cameron	.25	.12	.02

1979-80 O-Pee-Chee

The 1979-80 O-Pee-Chee NHL set consists of 396 color cards portraying NHL players. Card numbers 1 to 264 are identical (with a possible exception of a traded line) to the Topps cards of this year. Cards are 2½" by 3½". The fronts feature distinctive blue borders, while the backs, in both French and English, feature the card number, player records, a short biography, and a cartoon-illustrated fact about the player. The cards were printed in Canada. The card of Wayne Gretzky has been illegally reprinted. Most of the reprints were discovered and then destroyed or clearly marked as reprints; however, some are still around. The reprint is difficult to distinguish from the real card; collectors and dealers should be careful when purchasing one or more of these cards. The set features the first hockey card of Wayne Gretzky and the last active card appearance for Bobby Hull and Gordie Howe.

Le jeu NHL O-Pee-Chee 1979-80 contient 396 cartes en couleurs, représentant des joueurs NHL. Les cartes 1-264 sont identiques aux cartes Topps de cette année (avec l'exception possible d'une liste d'échange). Les cartes mesurent 2½" x 3½". Le bord

entourant la face est d'un bleu distinctif, et le dos, imprimé en français et en anglais, comporte le numéro de carte, les statistiques des joueurs, une biographie concise, et un fait notable concernant le joueur, illustré d'une caricature. Les cartes ont été imprimées au Canada. La carte de Wayne Gretzky a été réimprimée illégalement. La plupart des réimpressions ont été découvertes et détruites, ou clairement marquées comme réimpressions; il en existe cependant encore. La réimpression est difficile à distinguer de l'originale; les collectionneurs et négociants doivent être prudents lorsqu'ils achètent ces cartes. Le jeu comporte la première carte de hockey de Wayne Gretzky et les dernières cartes de Bobby Hull et de Gordie Howe.

			MINT	EXC	G-VG
		COMPLETE SET (396)	750.00	375.00	75.00
		COMMON PLAYER (1-396)	.12	.06	.01
☐	1	**Goal Leaders**	2.00	.50	.10
		Mike Bossy			
		Marcel Dionne			
		Guy Lafleur			
☐	2	**Assist Leaders**	1.25	.60	.12
		Bryan Trottier			
		Guy Lafleur			
		Marcel Dionne			
		Bob MacMillan			
☐	3	**Scoring Leaders**	1.25	.60	.12
		Bryan Trottier			
		Marcel Dionne			
		Guy Lafleur			
☐	4	**Penalty Minute Leaders**	.20	.10	.02
		Dave Williams			
		Randy Holt			
		Dave Schultz			
☐	5	**Power Play Goal Leaders**	.75	.35	.07
		Mike Bossy			
		Marcel Dionne			
		Paul Gardner			
		Lanny McDonald			
☐	6	**Goals Against Average Leaders**	1.25	.60	.12
		Ken Dryden			
		Glenn Resch			
		Bernie Parent			
☐	7	**Game Winning Goals Leaders**	1.25	.60	.12
		Guy Lafleur			
		Mike Bossy			
		Bryan Trottier			
		Jean Pronovost			
		Ted Bulley			

			MINT	EXC	G-VG
☐	8	Shutout Leaders	1.00	.50	.10
		Ken Dryden			
		Tony Esposito			
		Mario Lessard			
		Mike Palmateer			
		Bernie Parent			
☐	9	Greg Malone	.12	.06	.01
☐	10	Rick Middleton	.60	.30	.06
☐	11	Greg Smith	.12	.06	.01
☐	12	Rene Robert	.20	.10	.02
☐	13	Doug Risebrough	.12	.06	.01
☐	14	Bob Kelly	.12	.06	.01
☐	15	Walt Tkaczuk	.20	.10	.02
☐	16	John Marks	.12	.06	.01
☐	17	Willie Huber	.12	.06	.01
☐	18	Wayne Gretzky	550.00	275.00	55.00
☐	19	Ron Sedlbauer	.12	.06	.01
☐	20	Glenn Resch AS2	.60	.30	.06
☐	21	Blair Chapman	.12	.06	.01
☐	22	Ron Zanussi	.12	.06	.01
☐	23	Brad Park	.75	.35	.07
☐	24	Yvon Lambert	.12	.06	.01
☐	25	Andre Savard	.12	.06	.01
☐	26	Jim Watson	.12	.06	.01
☐	27	Hal Philipoff	.12	.06	.01
☐	28	Dan Bouchard	.20	.10	.02
☐	29	Bob Sirois	.12	.06	.01
☐	30	Ulf Nilsson	.20	.10	.02
☐	31	Mike Murphy	.12	.06	.01
☐	32	Stefan Persson	.20	.10	.02
☐	33	Garry Unger	.30	.15	.03
☐	34	Rejean Houle	.12	.06	.01
☐	35	Barry Beck	.30	.15	.03
☐	36	Tim Young	.12	.06	.01
☐	37	Rick Dudley	.20	.10	.02
☐	38	Wayne Stephenson	.20	.10	.02
☐	39	Peter McNab	.12	.06	.01
☐	40	Borje Salming AS2	.30	.15	.03
☐	41	Tom Lysiak	.20	.10	.02
☐	42	Don Maloney	1.25	.60	.12
☐	43	Mike Rogers	.20	.10	.02
☐	44	Dave Lewis	.12	.06	.01
☐	45	Peter Lee	.12	.06	.01
☐	46	Marty Howe	.20	.10	.02
☐	47	Serge Bernier	.12	.06	.01
☐	48	Paul Woods	.12	.06	.01
☐	49	Bob Sauve	.20	.10	.02
☐	50	Larry Robinson AS1	1.00	.50	.10
☐	51	Tom Gorence	.12	.06	.01
☐	52	Gary Sargent	.12	.06	.01
☐	53	Thomas Gradin	.50	.25	.05
☐	54	Dean Talafous	.12	.06	.01
☐	55	Bob Murray	.12	.06	.01
☐	56	Bob Bourne	.20	.10	.02

			MINT	EXC	G-VG
☐ 57	Larry Patey		.12	.06	.01
☐ 58	Ross Lonsberry		.12	.06	.01
☐ 59	Rick Smith UER		.12	.06	.01
	(Born Kinston, should be Kingston)				
☐ 60	Guy Chouinard		.20	.10	.02
☐ 61	Danny Gare		.20	.10	.02
☐ 62	Jim Bedard		.20	.10	.02
☐ 63	Dale McCourt UER		.20	.10	.02
	(Pictured in Kings' sweater, but he never played for the Kings)				
☐ 64	Steve Payne		.40	.20	.04
☐ 65	Pat Hughes		.12	.06	.01
☐ 66	Mike McEwen		.20	.10	.02
☐ 67	Reg Kerr		.30	.15	.03
☐ 68	Walt McKechnie		.12	.06	.01
☐ 69	Michel Plasse		.20	.10	.02
☐ 70	Denis Potvin AS1		1.75	.85	.17
☐ 71	Dave Dryden		.20	.10	.02
☐ 72	Gary McAdam		.12	.06	.01
☐ 73	Andre St. Laurent		.12	.06	.01
☐ 74	Jerry Korab		.12	.06	.01
☐ 75	Rick MacLeish		.30	.15	.03
☐ 76	Dennis Kearns		.12	.06	.01
☐ 77	Jean Pronovost		.20	.10	.02
☐ 78	Ron Greschner		.20	.10	.02
☐ 79	Wayne Cashman		.20	.10	.02
☐ 80	Tony Esposito		1.25	.60	.12
☐ 81	Jets Team		.40	.20	.04
☐ 82	Oilers Team		.40	.20	.04
☐ 83	Stanley Cup Finals		.40	.20	.04
	Canadiens Make It Four Straight Cups				
☐ 84	Brian Sutter		.50	.25	.05
☐ 85	Gerry Cheevers		1.00	.50	.10
☐ 86	Pat Hickey		.12	.06	.01
☐ 87	Mike Kaszycki		.12	.06	.01
☐ 88	Grant Mulvey		.20	.10	.02
☐ 89	Derek Smith		.12	.06	.01
☐ 90	Steve Shutt		.60	.30	.06
☐ 91	Robert Picard		.20	.10	.02
☐ 92	Dan Labraaten		.12	.06	.01
☐ 93	Glen Sharpley		.12	.06	.01
☐ 94	Denis Herron		.20	.10	.02
☐ 95	Reggie Leach		.30	.15	.03
☐ 96	John Van Boxmeer		.12	.06	.01
☐ 97	Dave Williams		.20	.10	.02
☐ 98	Butch Goring		.20	.10	.02
☐ 99	Don Marcotte		.12	.06	.01
☐ 100	Bryan Trottier AS1		2.50	1.25	.25
☐ 101	Serge Savard AS2		.75	.35	.07
☐ 102	Cliff Koroll		.12	.06	.01
☐ 103	Gary Smith		.20	.10	.02
☐ 104	Al MacAdam		.20	.10	.02

		MINT	EXC	G-VG
☐ 105	Don Edwards	.20	.10	.02
☐ 106	Errol Thompson	.12	.06	.01
☐ 107	Andre Lacroix	.20	.10	.02
☐ 108	Marc Tardif	.20	.10	.02
☐ 109	Rick Kehoe	.20	.10	.02
☐ 110	John Davidson	.20	.10	.02
☐ 111	Behn Wilson	.30	.15	.03
☐ 112	Doug Jarvis	.20	.10	.02
☐ 113	Tom Rowe	.12	.06	.01
☐ 114	Mike Milbury	.20	.10	.02
☐ 115	Billy Harris	.12	.06	.01
☐ 116	Greg Fox	.12	.06	.01
☐ 117	Curt Fraser	.12	.06	.01
☐ 118	Jean Paul Parise	.12	.06	.01
☐ 119	Ric Seiling	.12	.06	.01
☐ 120	Darryl Sittler	.75	.35	.07
☐ 121	Rick Lapointe	.20	.10	.02
☐ 122	Jim Rutherford	.20	.10	.02
☐ 123	Mario Tremblay	.20	.10	.02
☐ 124	Randy Carlyle	.30	.15	.03
☐ 125	Bobby Clarke	1.75	.85	.17
☐ 126	Wayne Thomas	.20	.10	.02
☐ 127	Ivan Boldirev	.12	.06	.01
☐ 128	Ted Bulley	.12	.06	.01
☐ 129	Dick Redmond	.12	.06	.01
☐ 130	Clark Gillies AS1	.30	.15	.03
☐ 131	Checklist 1-132	1.75	.15	.03
☐ 132	Vaclav Nedomansky	.12	.06	.01
☐ 133	Richard Mulhern	.12	.06	.01
☐ 134	Dave Schultz	.20	.10	.02
☐ 135	Guy Lapointe	.30	.15	.03
☐ 136	Gilles Meloche	.20	.10	.02
☐ 137	Randy Pierce UER	.12	.06	.01
	(Photo actually Ron Delorme)			
☐ 138	Cam Connor	.12	.06	.01
☐ 139	George Ferguson	.12	.06	.01
☐ 140	Bill Barber	.75	.35	.07
☐ 141	Terry Ruskowski UER	.20	.10	.02
	(Misspelled Ruskouski on both sides)			
☐ 142	Wayne Babych	.30	.15	.03
☐ 143	Phil Russell	.12	.06	.01
☐ 144	Bobby Schmautz	.12	.06	.01
☐ 145	Carol Vadnais	.12	.06	.01
☐ 146	John Tonelli	4.50	2.25	.45
☐ 147	Peter Marsh	.30	.15	.03
☐ 148	Thommie Bergman	.12	.06	.01
☐ 149	Rick Martin	.30	.15	.03
☐ 150	Ken Dryden AS1	4.00	2.00	.40
☐ 151	Kris Manery	.12	.06	.01
☐ 152	Guy Charron	.12	.06	.01
☐ 153	Lanny McDonald	.75	.35	.07
☐ 154	Ron Stackhouse	.12	.06	.01
☐ 155	Stan Mikita		.60	.12
☐ 156	Paul Holmgren		.10	.02

		MINT	EXC	G-VG
☐ 157	Perry Miller	.12	.06	.01
☐ 158	Gary Croteau	.12	.06	.01
☐ 159	Dave Maloney	.20	.10	.02
☐ 160	Marcel Dionne AS2	3.50	1.75	.35
☐ 161	Mike Bossy RB	1.75	.85	.17
	Most Goals, RW Season			
☐ 162	Don Maloney RB	.20	.10	.02
	Rookie, Most Points, Playoff Series			
☐ 163	Whalers Team	.40	.20	.04
☐ 164	Brad Park RB	.30	.15	.03
	Most Career Playoff Goals, Defenseman			
☐ 165	Bryan Trottier RB	.75	.35	.07
	Most Points, Period			
☐ 166	Al Hill	.12	.06	.01
☐ 167	Gary Bromley	.20	.10	.02
☐ 168	Don Murdoch	.12	.06	.01
☐ 169	Wayne Merrick	.12	.06	.01
☐ 170	Bob Gainey	.60	.30	.06
☐ 171	Jim Schoenfeld	.20	.10	.02
☐ 172	Gregg Sheppard	.12	.06	.01
☐ 173	Dan Bolduc	.12	.06	.01
☐ 174	Blake Dunlop	.12	.06	.01
☐ 175	Gordie Howe	25.00	12.50	2.50
☐ 176	Richard Brodeur	.40	.20	.04
☐ 177	Tom Younghans	.12	.06	.01
☐ 178	Andre Dupont	.12	.06	.01
☐ 179	Ed Johnstone	.12	.06	.01
☐ 180	Gilbert Perreault	1.00	.50	.10
☐ 181	Bob Lorimer	.12	.06	.01
☐ 182	John Wensink	.12	.06	.01
☐ 183	Lee Fogolin	.12	.06	.01
☐ 184	Greg Carroll	.12	.06	.01
☐ 185	Bobby Hull	22.50	10.00	2.00
☐ 186	Harold Snepsts	.30	.15	.03
☐ 187	Peter Mahovlich	.20	.10	.02
☐ 188	Eric Vail	.20	.10	.02
☐ 189	Phil Myre	.20	.10	.02
☐ 190	Wilf Paiement	.20	.10	.02
☐ 191	Charlie Simmer	3.00	1.50	.30
☐ 192	Per-Olov Brasar	.12	.06	.01
☐ 193	Lorne Henning	.12	.06	.01
☐ 194	Don Luce	.12	.06	.01
☐ 195	Steve Vickers	.12	.06	.01
☐ 196	Bob Miller	.12	.06	.01
☐ 197	Mike Palmateer	.30	.15	.03
☐ 198	Nick Libett	.12	.06	.01
☐ 199	Pat Ribble	.12	.06	.01
☐ 200	Guy Lafleur AS1	4.00	2.00	.40
☐ 201	Mel Bridgman	.12	.06	.01
☐ 202	Morris Lukowich	.50	.25	.05
☐ 203	Don Lever	.12	.06	.01
☐ 204	Tom Bladon	.12	.06	.01
☐ 205	Garry Howatt	.12	.06	.01
☐ 206	Bobby Smith	9.00	4.50	.90

		MINT	EXC	G-VG
☐ 207	Craig Ramsay	.12	.06	.01
☐ 208	Ron Duguay	.20	.10	.02
☐ 209	Gilles Gilbert	.20	.10	.02
☐ 210	Bob MacMillan	.20	.10	.02
☐ 211	Pierre Mondou	.20	.10	.02
☐ 212	J.P. Bordeleau	.12	.06	.01
☐ 213	Reed Larson	.20	.10	.02
☐ 214	Dennis Ververgaert	.12	.06	.01
☐ 215	Bernie Federko	1.00	.50	.10
☐ 216	Mark Howe	.75	.35	.07
☐ 217	Bob Nystrom	.20	.10	.02
☐ 218	Orest Kindrachuk	.12	.06	.01
☐ 219	Mike Fidler	.12	.06	.01
☐ 220	Phil Esposito	2.50	1.25	.25
☐ 221	Bill Hajt	.12	.06	.01
☐ 222	Mark Napier	.20	.10	.02
☐ 223	Dennis Maruk	.20	.10	.02
☐ 224	Dennis Polonich	.12	.06	.01
☐ 225	Jean Ratelle	.75	.35	.07
☐ 226	Bob Dailey	.12	.06	.01
☐ 227	Alain Daigle	.12	.06	.01
☐ 228	Ian Turnbull	.12	.06	.01
☐ 229	Jack Valiquette	.12	.06	.01
☐ 230	Mike Bossy AS2	16.00	8.00	1.60
☐ 231	Brad Maxwell	.12	.06	.01
☐ 232	Dave Taylor	3.00	1.50	.30
☐ 233	Pierre Larouche	.20	.10	.02
☐ 234	Rod Schutt	.12	.06	.01
☐ 235	Rogatien Vachon	.60	.30	.06
☐ 236	Ryan Walter	1.25	.60	.12
☐ 237	Checklist 133-264 UER	1.75	.15	.03
	(245 Buins, should be Bruins)			
☐ 238	Terry O'Reilly	.30	.15	.03
☐ 239	Real Cloutier	.20	.10	.02
☐ 240	Anders Hedberg	.20	.10	.02
☐ 241	Ken Linseman	2.00	1.00	.20
☐ 242	Billy Smith	.70	.35	.07
☐ 243	Rick Chartraw	.12	.06	.01
☐ 244	Flames Team	.40	.20	.04
☐ 245	Bruins Team	.40	.20	.04
☐ 246	Sabres Team	.40	.20	.04
☐ 247	Blackhawks Team	.40	.20	.04
☐ 248	Rockies Team	.40	.20	.04
☐ 249	Red Wings Team	.40	.20	.04
☐ 250	Kings Team	.40	.20	.04
☐ 251	North Stars Team	.40	.20	.04
☐ 252	Canadiens Team	.40	.20	.04
☐ 253	Islanders Team	.40	.20	.04
☐ 254	Rangers Team	.40	.20	.04
☐ 255	Flyers Team	.40	.20	.04
☐ 256	Penguins Team	.40	.20	.04
☐ 257	Blues Team	.40	.20	.04
☐ 258	Maple Leafs Team	.40	.20	.04
☐ 259	Canucks Team	.40	.20	.04

		MINT	EXC	G-VG
☐ 260	Capitals Team	.40	.20	.04
☐ 261	Nordiques Team	.40	.20	.04
☐ 262	Jean Hamel	.12	.06	.01
☐ 263	Stan Jonathan	.12	.06	.01
☐ 264	Russ Anderson	.12	.06	.01
☐ 265	Gordie Roberts	.40	.20	.04
☐ 266	Bill Flett	.12	.06	.01
☐ 267	Robbie Ftorek	.30	.15	.03
☐ 268	Mike Amodeo	.12	.06	.01
☐ 269	Vic Venasky	.12	.06	.01
☐ 270	Bob Manno	.12	.06	.01
☐ 271	Dan Maloney	.20	.10	.02
☐ 272	Al Sims	.12	.06	.01
☐ 273	Greg Polis	.12	.06	.01
☐ 274	Doug Favell	.20	.10	.02
☐ 275	Pierre Plante	.12	.06	.01
☐ 276	Bob Murdoch, Atlanta Flames	.12	.06	.01
☐ 277	Lyle Moffat	.12	.06	.01
☐ 278	Jack Brownschidle	.12	.06	.01
☐ 279	Dave Keon	.75	.35	.07
☐ 280	Darryl Edestrand	.12	.06	.01
☐ 281	Greg Millen	3.00	1.50	.30
☐ 282	John Gould	.12	.06	.01
☐ 283	Rich Leduc	.12	.06	.01
☐ 284	Ron Delorme	.12	.06	.01
☐ 285	Gord Smith	.20	.10	.02
☐ 286	Nick Fotiu	.12	.06	.01
☐ 287	Kevin McCarthy	.12	.06	.01
☐ 288	Jimmy Jones	.12	.06	.01
☐ 289	Pierre Bouchard	.12	.06	.01
☐ 290	Wayne Bianchin	.12	.06	.01
☐ 291	Garry Lariviere	.12	.06	.01
☐ 292	Steve Jensen	.12	.06	.01
☐ 293	John Garrett	.20	.10	.02
☐ 294	Hilliard Graves	.12	.06	.01
☐ 295	Bill Clement	.20	.10	.02
☐ 296	Michel Larocque	.30	.15	.03
☐ 297	Bob Stewart	.12	.06	.01
☐ 298	Doug Patey	.12	.06	.01
☐ 299	Dave Farrish	.12	.06	.01
☐ 300	Al Smith	.12	.06	.01
☐ 301	Billy Lochead	.12	.06	.01
☐ 302	Dave Hutchinson	.12	.06	.01
☐ 303	Bill Riley	.12	.06	.01
☐ 304	Barry Gibbs	.12	.06	.01
☐ 305	Chris Oddleifson	.12	.06	.01
☐ 306	J. Bob Kelly	.20	.10	.02
	(photo actually Bob Kelly)			
☐ 307	Alan Hangsleben	.12	.06	.01
☐ 308	Curt Brackenbury	.12	.06	.01
☐ 309	Rick Green	.20	.10	.02
☐ 310	Ken Houston	.12	.06	.01
☐ 311	Greg Joly	.12	.06	.01
☐ 312	Bill Lesuk	.12	.06	.01

			MINT	EXC	G-VG
☐ 313	Bill Stewart		.12	.06	.01
☐ 314	Rick Ley		.20	.10	.02
☐ 315	Brett Callighen		.20	.10	.02
☐ 316	Michel Dion		.20	.10	.02
☐ 317	Randy Manery		.12	.06	.01
☐ 318	Barry Dean		.12	.06	.01
☐ 319	Pat Boutette		.12	.06	.01
☐ 320	Mark Heaslip		.12	.06	.01
☐ 321	Dave Inkpen		.12	.06	.01
☐ 322	Jere Gillis		.12	.06	.01
☐ 323	Larry Brown		.12	.06	.01
☐ 324	Alain Cote		.12	.06	.01
☐ 325	Gordie Lane		.12	.06	.01
☐ 326	Bobby Lalonde		.12	.06	.01
☐ 327	Ed Staniowski		.20	.10	.02
☐ 328	Ron Plumb		.20	.10	.02
☐ 329	Jude Drouin		.12	.06	.01
☐ 330	Rick Hampton		.12	.06	.01
☐ 331	Stan Weir		.12	.06	.01
☐ 332	Blair Stewart		.12	.06	.01
☐ 333	Mike Polich		.12	.06	.01
☐ 334	Jean Potvin		.12	.06	.01
☐ 335	Jordy Douglas		.12	.06	.01
☐ 336	Joel Quenneville		.12	.06	.01
☐ 337	Glen Hanlon		1.50	.75	.15
☐ 338	Dave Hoyda		.12	.06	.01
☐ 339	Colin Campbell		.12	.06	.01
☐ 340	John Smrke		.12	.06	.01
☐ 341	Brian Glennie		.12	.06	.01
☐ 342	Don Kozak		.12	.06	.01
☐ 343	Yvon Labre		.12	.06	.01
☐ 344	Curt Bennett		.12	.06	.01
☐ 345	Mike Christie		.12	.06	.01
☐ 346	Checklist		1.75	.15	.03
☐ 347	Pat Price		.12	.06	.01
☐ 348	Ron Low		.20	.10	.02
☐ 349	Mike Antonovich		.12	.06	.01
☐ 350	Roland Eriksson		.12	.06	.01
☐ 351	Bob Murdoch		.12	.06	.01
	St. Louis Blues				
☐ 352	Rob Palmer		.12	.06	.01
☐ 353	Brad Gassoff		.12	.06	.01
☐ 354	Bruce Boudreau		.12	.06	.01
☐ 355	Al Hamilton		.12	.06	.01
☐ 356	Blaine Stoughton		.20	.10	.02
☐ 357	John Baby		.12	.06	.01
☐ 358	Gary Inness		.12	.06	.01
☐ 359	Wayne Dillon		.12	.06	.01
☐ 360	Darcy Rota		.12	.06	.01
☐ 361	Brian Engblom		.20	.10	.02
☐ 362	Bill Hogaboam		.12	.06	.01
☐ 363	Dave Debol		.12	.06	.01
☐ 364	Pete Lopresti		.20	.10	.02
☐ 365	Gerry Hart		.12	.06	.01

		MINT	EXC	G-VG
☐ 366	Syl Apps	.12	.06	.01
☐ 367	Jack McIlhargey	.12	.06	.01
☐ 368	Willy Lindstrom	.12	.06	.01
☐ 369	Don Laurence	.12	.06	.01
☐ 370	Chuck Luksa	.12	.06	.01
☐ 371	Dave Semenko	.50	.25	.05
☐ 372	Paul Baxter	.12	.06	.01
☐ 373	Ron Ellis	.12	.06	.01
☐ 374	Leif Svensson	.12	.06	.01
☐ 375	Dennis O'Brien	.12	.06	.01
☐ 376	Glenn Goldup	.12	.06	.01
☐ 377	Terry Richardson	.12	.06	.01
☐ 378	Peter Sullivan	.12	.06	.01
☐ 379	Doug Hicks	.12	.06	.01
☐ 380	Jamie Hislop	.12	.06	.01
☐ 381	Jocelyn Guevremont	.12	.06	.01
☑ 382	Willi Plett	.12	.06	.01
☐ 383	Larry Goodenough	.12	.06	.01
☐ 384	Jim Warner	.12	.06	.01
☐ 385	Rey Comeau	.12	.06	.01
☐ 386	Barry Melrose	.12	.06	.01
☐ 387	Dave Hunter	.40	.20	.04
☐ 388	Wally Weir	.12	.06	.01
☐ 389	Mario Lessard	.75	.35	.07
☐ 390	Ed Kea	.12	.06	.01
☐ 391	Bob Stephenson	.12	.06	.01
☐ 392	Dennis Hextall	.20	.10	.02
☐ 393	Jerry Butler	.12	.06	.01
☐ 394	David Shand	.12	.06	.01
☐ 395	Rick Blight	.12	.06	.01
☐ 396	Lars-Erik Sjoberg	.20	.10	.02

1980-81 O-Pee-Chee

 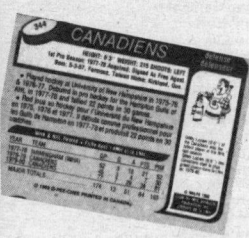

This 396-card set contains the player's name and position (in both English and French) in a hockey puck on the lower right of the front. The team name is listed to the left of the puck. Cards measure 2½" by 3½". Unlike the Topps set of this year, the puck was not issued with a black scratch-off covering. The backs are printed in green and yellowish-green ink with short career milestones listed in both English and French. Career yearly statistics are also included. Short, interesting trivia comments are also contained on the back. A 1980 O-Pee-Chee copyright date is listed on the card. Members of the U.S. Olympic Hockey team are indicated by USO. The key rookie cards in this set are Ray Bourque, Mike Gartner, Michel Goulet, Rod Langway, Mike Liut, Mark Messier, John Ogrodnick, Pete Peeters, and Brian Propp.

Ce jeu de 396 cartes montre le nom et la position du joueur (en anglais et en français) dans un disque de hockey au côté inférieur droit de la face. Le nom de l'équipe est indiqué à gauche du disque. Les cartes mesurent 2½" x 3½". Contrairement au jeu Topps de cette année, la surface noire du disque ne peut pas être enlevée en la grattant. Le dos est imprimé en encre verte et jaune-verte, avec de courtes descriptions d'événements marquants de carrière, en anglais et en français. Il inclut également des statistiques par année de carrière et des courtes histoires anecdotiques. L'an 1980 apparaît comme date de droit d'auteur d'O-Pee-Chee. Les membres de l'équipe olympique des USA sont désignés par les lettres USO. Les débutants importants de ce jeu sont Ray Bourque, Mike Gartner, Michel Goulet, Rod Langway, Mike Liut, Mark Messier, John Ogrodnick, Pete Peeters, et Brian Propp.

		MINT	EXC	G-VG
COMPLETE SET (396)		450.00	225.00	45.00
COMMON PLAYER (1-396)		.10	.05	.01
☐ 1	RB: Flyers Streak .... to 35; Longest in Sports History	.75	.15	.03

			MINT	EXC	G-VG
☐	2	Ray Bourque RB	8.50	4.25	.85
		65 Pts., Record for Rookie Defenseman			
☐	3	Wayne Gretzky RB	33.00	15.00	3.00
		Youngest Ever 50-Goal Scorer			
☐	4	Charlie Simmer RB	.17	.08	.01
		Scores 13th Straight Game, NHL Record			
☐	5	Billy Smith RB	.30	.15	.03
		First Goalie to Score a Goal			
☐	6	Jean Ratelle	.70	.35	.07
☐	7	Dave Maloney	.17	.08	.01
☐	8	Phil Myre	.17	.08	.01
☐	9	Ken Morrow USO	.75	.35	.07
☐	10	Guy Lafleur	3.00	1.50	.30
☐	11	Bill Derlago	.17	.08	.01
☐	12	Doug Wilson	1.25	.60	.12
☐	13	Craig Ramsay	.10	.05	.01
☐	14	Pat Boutette	.10	.05	.01
☐	15	Eric Vail	.17	.08	.01
☐	16	Red Wings Leaders	.17	.08	.01
		Mike Foligno			
☐	17	Bobby Smith	1.00	.50	.10
☐	18	Rick Kehoe	.17	.08	.01
☐	19	Joel Quenneville	.10	.05	.01
☐	20	Marcel Dionne	2.50	1.25	.25
☐	21	Kevin McCarthy	.10	.05	.01
☐	22	Jim Craig USO	.65	.30	.06
☐	23	Steve Vickers	.10	.05	.01
☐	24	Ken Linseman	.30	.15	.03
☐	25	Mike Bossy	6.00	3.00	.60
☐	26	Serge Savard	.60	.30	.06
☐	27	Blackhawks Leaders	.17	.08	.01
		Grant Mulvey			
☐	28	Pat Hickey	.10	.05	.01
☐	29	Peter Sullivan	.10	.05	.01
☐	30	Blaine Stoughton	.17	.08	.01
☐	31	Mike Liut	4.00	2.00	.40
☐	32	Blair MacDonald	.10	.05	.01
☐	33	Rick Green	.17	.08	.01
☐	34	Al MacAdam	.17	.08	.01
☐	35	Robbie Ftorek	.17	.08	.01
☐	36	Dick Redmond	.10	.05	.01
☐	37	Ron Duguay	.17	.08	.01
☐	38	Sabres Leaders	.17	.08	.01
		Danny Gare			
☐	39	Brian Propp	8.00	4.00	.80
☐	40	Bryan Trottier	2.00	1.00	.20
☐	41	Rich Preston	.10	.05	.01
☐	42	Pierre Mondou	.10	.05	.01
☐	43	Reed Larson	.10	.05	.01
☐	44	George Ferguson	.10	.05	.01
☐	45	Guy Chouinard	.17	.08	.01
☐	46	Billy Harris	.10	.05	.01
☐	47	Gilles Meloche	.17	.08	.01

			MINT	EXC	G-VG
☐	48	Blair Chapman	.10	.05	.01
☐	49	Capitals Leaders	.85	.40	.08
		Mike Gartner			
☐	50	Darryl Sittler	.60	.30	.06
☐	51	Rick Martin	.17	.08	.01
☐	52	Ivan Boldirev	.10	.05	.01
☐	53	Craig Norwich	.10	.05	.01
☐	54	Dennis Polonich	.10	.05	.01
☐	55	Bobby Clarke	1.50	.75	.15
☐	56	Terry O'Reilly	.25	.12	.02
☐	57	Carol Vadnais	.10	.05	.01
☐	58	Bob Gainey	.50	.25	.05
☐	59	Whalers Leaders	.17	.08	.01
		Blaine Stoughton			
☐	60	Billy Smith	.60	.30	.06
☐	61	Mike O'Connell	.25	.12	.02
☐	62	Lanny McDonald	.60	.30	.06
☐	63	Lee Fogolin	.10	.05	.01
☐	64	Rocky Saganiuk	.10	.05	.01
☐	65	Rolf Edberg	.10	.05	.01
☐	66	Paul Shmyr	.10	.05	.01
☐	67	Michel Goulet	15.00	7.50	1.50
☐	68	Dan Bouchard	.17	.08	.01
☐	69	Mark Johnson USO	.75	.35	.07
☐	70	Reggie Leach	.25	.12	.02
☐	71	Blues Leaders	.25	.12	.02
		Bernie Federko			
☐	72	Peter Mahovlich	.17	.08	.01
☐	73	Anders Hedberg	.17	.08	.01
☐	74	Brad Park	.60	.30	.06
☐	75	Clark Gillies	.25	.12	.02
☐	76	Doug Jarvis	.17	.08	.01
☐	77	John Garrett	.17	.08	.01
☐	78	Dave Hutchinson	.10	.05	.01
☐	79	John Anderson	.10	.05	.01
☐	80	Gilbert Perreault	1.00	.50	.10
☐	81	Marcel Dionne ASI	1.25	.60	.12
☐	82	Guy Lafleur AS1	1.50	.75	.15
☐	83	Charlie Simmer AS1	.17	.08	.01
☐	84	Larry Robinson AS1	.50	.25	.05
☐	85	Borje Salming AS1	.25	.12	.02
☐	86	Tony Esposito AS1	.75	.35	.07
☐	87	Wayne Gretzky AS2	42.00	20.00	4.00
☐	88	Danny Gare AS2	.17	.08	.01
☐	89	Steve Shutt AS2	.25	.12	.02
☐	90	Barry Beck AS2	.17	.08	.01
☐	91	Mark Howe AS2	.25	.12	.02
☐	92	Don Edwards AS2	.17	.08	.01
☐	93	Tom McCarthy	.17	.08	.01
☐	94	Bruins Leaders	.17	.08	.01
		Peter McNab			
		Rick Middleton			
☐	95	Mike Palmateer	.17	.08	.01

			MINT	EXC	G-VG
☐	96	Jim Schoenfeld	.17	.08	.01
☐	97	Jordy Douglas	.10	.05	.01
☐	98	Keith Brown	.10	.05	.01
☐	99	Dennis Ververgaert	.10	.05	.01
☐	100	Phil Esposito	2.00	1.00	.20
☐	101	Jack Brownschidle	.10	.05	.01
☐	102	Bob Nystrom	.17	.08	.01
☐	103	Steve Christoff USO	.17	.08	.01
☐	104	Rob Palmer	.10	.05	.01
☐	105	Dave Williams	.17	.08	.01
☐	106	Flames Leaders Kent Nilsson	.17	.08	.01
☐	107	Morris Lukowich	.17	.08	.01
☐	108	Jack Valiquette	.10	.05	.01
☐	109	Richie Dunn	.10	.05	.01
☐	110	Rogatien Vachon	.45	.22	.04
☐	111	Mark Napier	.17	.08	.01
☐	112	Gordie Roberts	.10	.05	.01
☐	113	Stan Jonathan	.10	.05	.01
☐	114	Brett Callighen	.10	.05	.01
☐	115	Rick MacLeish	.25	.12	.02
☐	116	Ulf Nilsson	.17	.08	.01
☐	117	Penguins Leaders Rick Kehoe	.17	.08	.01
☐	118	Dan Maloney	.17	.08	.01
☐	119	Terry Ruskowski	.17	.08	.01
☐	120	Denis Potvin	1.50	.75	.15
☐	121	Wayne Stephenson	.17	.08	.01
☐	122	Rich Leduc	.10	.05	.01
☐	123	Checklist 1-132	1.50	.10	.02
☐	124	Don Lever	.10	.05	.01
☐	125	Jim Rutherford	.17	.08	.01
☐	126	Ray Allison	.10	.05	.01
☐	127	Mike Ramsey USO	.45	.22	.04
☐	128	Canucks Leaders Stan Smyl	.17	.08	.01
☐	129	Al Secord	1.50	.75	.15
☐	130	Denis Herron	.17	.08	.01
☐	131	Bob Dailey	.10	.05	.01
☐	132	Dean Talafous	.10	.05	.01
☐	133	Ian Turnbull	.10	.05	.01
☐	134	Ron Sedlbauer	.10	.05	.01
☐	135	Tom Bladon	.10	.05	.01
☐	136	Bernie Federko	.25	.12	.02
☐	137	Dave Taylor	.75	.35	.07
☐	138	Bob Lorimer	.10	.05	.01
☐	139	North Stars Leaders Al MacAdam Steve Payne	.17	.08	.01
☐	140	Ray Bourque	125.00	60.00	12.50
☐	141	Glen Hanlon	.25	.12	.02
☐	142	Willy Lindstrom	.10	.05	.01
☐	143	Mike Rogers	.17	.08	.01

		MINT	EXC	G-VG
☐ 144	Tony McKegney	.50	.25	.05
☐ 145	Behn Wilson	.10	.05	.01
☐ 146	Lucien Deblois	.10	.05	.01
☐ 147	Dave Burrows	.10	.05	.01
☐ 148	Paul Woods	.10	.05	.01
☐ 149	Rangers Leaders	.75	.35	.07
	Phil Esposito			
☐ 150	Tony Esposito	1.25	.60	.12
☐ 151	Pierre Larouche	.17	.08	.01
☐ 152	Brad Maxwell	.10	.05	.01
☐ 153	Stan Weir	.10	.05	.01
☐ 154	Ryan Walter	.17	.08	.01
☐ 155	Dale Hoganson	.10	.05	.01
☐ 156	Anders Kallur	.25	.12	.02
☐ 157	Paul Reinhart	1.25	.60	.12
☐ 158	Greg Millen	.30	.15	.03
☐ 159	Ric Seiling	.10	.05	.01
☐ 160	Mark Howe	.40	.20	.04
☐ 161	Goals Leaders	.17	.08	.01
	Danny Gare (1)			
	Charlie Simmer (1)			
	B. Stoughton (1)			
☐ 162	Assists Leaders	11.00	5.50	1.10
	Wayne Gretzky (1)			
	Marcel Dionne (2)			
	Guy Lafleur (3)			
☐ 163	Scoring Leaders	11.00	5.50	1.10
	Marcel Dionne (1)			
	Wayne Gretzky (1)			
	Guy Lafleur (3)			
☐ 164	Penalty Minutes Leaders	.17	.08	.01
	Jimmy Mann (1)			
	Dave Williams (2)			
	Paul Holmgren (3)			
☐ 165	Power Play Goals Leaders	.25	.12	.02
	Charlie Simmer (1)			
	Marcel Dionne (2)			
	Danny Gare (2)			
	Steve Shutt (2)			
	Darryl Sittler (2)			
☐ 166	Goals Against Avg. Leaders	.17	.08	.01
	Bob Sauve (1)			
	Denis Herron (2)			
	Don Edwards (3)			
☐ 167	Game-Winning Goals Leaders	.17	.08	.01
	Danny Gare (1)			
	Peter McNab (2)			
	Blaine Stoughton (2)			

		MINT	EXC	G-VG
☐ 168	**Shutout Leaders**	.40	.20	.04
	Tony Esposito (1)			
	Gerry Cheevers (2)			
	Bob Sauve (2)			
	Rogatien Vachon (2)			
☐ 169	**Perry Turnbull**	.35	.17	.03
☐ 170	**Barry Beck**	.17	.08	.01
☐ 171	**Kings Leaders**	.17	.08	.01
	Charlie Simmer			
☐ 172	**Paul Holmgren**	.17	.08	.01
☐ 173	**Willie Huber**	.10	.05	.01
☐ 174	**Tim Young**	.10	.05	.01
☐ 175	**Gilles Gilbert**	.17	.08	.01
☐ 176	**Dave Christian USO**...........................	.85	.40	.08
☐ 177	**Lars Lindgren**	.10	.05	.01
☐ 178	**Real Cloutier**	.10	.05	.01
☐ 179	**Laurie Boschman**	.40	.20	.04
☐ 180	**Steve Shutt**....................................	.50	.25	.05
☐ 181	**Bob Murray**	.10	.05	.01
☐ 182	**Oilers Leaders**	20.00	10.00	2.00
	Wayne Gretzky			
☐ 183	**John Van Boxmeer**	.10	.05	.01
☐ 184	**Nick Fotiu**	.10	.05	.01
☐ 185	**Mike McEwen**	.17	.08	.01
☐ 186	**Greg Malone**	.10	.05	.01
☐ 187	**Mike Foligno**	1.00	.50	.10
☐ 188	**Dave Langevin**	.17	.08	.01
☐ 189	**Mel Bridgman**	.10	.05	.01
☐ 190	**John Davidson**	.17	.08	.01
☐ 191	**Mike Milbury**	.17	.08	.01
☐ 192	**Ron Zanussi**	.10	.05	.01
☐ 193	**Maple Leafs Leader**...........................	.35	.17	.03
	Darryl Sittler			
☐ 194	**John Marks**	.10	.05	.01
☐ 195	**Mike Gartner**	15.00	7.50	1.50
☐ 196	**Dave Lewis**.....................................	.10	.05	.01
☐ 197	**Kent Nilsson**	1.50	.75	.15
☐ 198	**Rick Ley**	.17	.08	.01
☐ 199	**Derek Smith**	.10	.05	.01
☐ 200	**Bill Barber**	.60	.30	.06
☐ 201	**Guy Lapointe**	.17	.08	.01
☐ 202	**Vaclav Nedomansky**	.10	.05	.01
☐ 203	**Don Murdoch**...................................	.10	.05	.01
☐ 204	**Islanders Leaders**.............................	1.00	.50	.10
	Mike Bossy			
☐ 205	**Pierre Hamel**	.10	.05	.01
☐ 206	**Mike Eaves**	.10	.05	.01
☐ 207	**Doug Halward**	.10	.05	.01
☐ 208	**Stan Smyl**	.50	.25	.05
☐ 209	**Mike Zuke**	.10	.05	.01
☐ 210	**Borje Salming**	.25	.12	.02
☐ 211	**Walt Tkaczuk**	.17	.08	.01
☐ 212	**Grant Mulvey**	.17	.08	.01

		MINT	EXC	G-VG
☐ 213	Rob Ramage	2.50	1.25	.25
☐ 214	Tom Rowe	.10	.05	.01
☐ 215	Don Edwards	.17	.08	.01
☐ 216	Canadiens Leaders	.50	.25	.05
	Guy Lafleur			
	Pierre Larouche			
☐ 217	Dan Labraaten	.10	.05	.01
☐ 218	Glen Sharpley	.10	.05	.01
☐ 219	Stefan Persson	.17	.08	.01
☐ 220	Peter McNab	.10	.05	.01
☐ 221	Doug Hicks	.10	.05	.01
☐ 222	Bengt Gustafsson	.40	.20	.04
☐ 223	Michel Dion	.17	.08	.01
☐ 224	Jim Watson	.10	.05	.01
☐ 225	Wilf Paiement	.10	.05	.01
☐ 226	Phil Russell	.10	.05	.01
☐ 227	Jets Leaders	.17	.08	.01
	Morris Lukowich			
☐ 228	Ron Stackhouse	.10	.05	.01
☐ 229	Ted Bulley	.10	.05	.01
☐ 230	Larry Robinson	.75	.35	.07
☐ 231	Don Maloney	.17	.08	.01
☐ 232	Rob McClanahan USO	.35	.17	.03
☐ 233	Al Sims	.10	.05	.01
☐ 234	Errol Thompson	.10	.05	.01
☐ 235	Glenn Resch	.50	.25	.05
☐ 236	Bob Miller	.10	.05	.01
☐ 237	Gary Sargent	.10	.05	.01
☐ 238	Nordiques Leaders	.17	.08	.01
	Real Cloutier			
☐ 239	Rene Robert	.17	.08	.01
☐ 240	Charlie Simmer	.35	.17	.03
☐ 241	Thomas Gradin	.17	.08	.01
☐ 242	Rick Vaive	4.00	2.00	.40
☐ 243	Ron Wilson	.10	.05	.01
☐ 244	Brian Sutter	.30	.15	.03
☐ 245	Dale McCourt	.10	.05	.01
☐ 246	Yvon Lambert	.10	.05	.01
☐ 247	Tom Lysiak	.17	.08	.01
☐ 248	Ron Greschner	.17	.08	.01
☐ 249	Flyers Leaders	.17	.08	.01
	Reggie Leach			
☐ 250	Wayne Gretzky	150.00	75.00	15.00
☐ 251	Rick Middleton	.45	.22	.04
☐ 252	Al Smith	.10	.05	.01
☐ 253	Fred Barrett	.10	.05	.01
☐ 254	Butch Goring	.17	.08	.01
☐ 255	Robert Picard	.17	.08	.01
☐ 256	Marc Tardif	.17	.08	.01
☐ 257	Checklist 133-264	1.50	.10	.02
☐ 258	Barry Long	.10	.05	.01
☐ 259	Rockies Leaders	.17	.08	.01
	Rene Robert			

		MINT	EXC	G-VG
☐ 260	Danny Gare	.17	.08	.01
☐ 261	Rejean Houle	.10	.05	.01
☐ 262	Stanley Cup Semi's	.25	.12	.02
	Islanders-Sabres			
☐ 263	Stanley Cup Semi's	.25	.12	.02
	Flyers-North Stars			
☐ 264	Stanley Cup Finals	.40	.20	.04
	Islanders Win 1st			
☐ 265	Bobby Lalonde	.15	.07	.01
☐ 266	Bob Sauve	.25	.12	.02
☐ 267	Bob MacMillan	.25	.12	.02
☐ 268	Greg Fox	.15	.07	.01
☐ 269	Hardy Astrom	.25	.12	.02
☐ 270	Greg Joly	.15	.07	.01
☐ 271	Dave Lumley	.15	.07	.01
☐ 272	Dave Keon	.50	.25	.05
☐ 273	Garry Unger	.25	.12	.02
☐ 274	Steve Payne	.25	.12	.02
☐ 275	Doug Risebrough UER	.25	.12	.02
	(Photo actually Serge Savard)			
☐ 276	Bob Bourne	.25	.12	.02
☐ 277	Ed Johnstone	.15	.07	.01
☐ 278	Peter Lee	.15	.07	.01
☐ 279	Pete Peeters	3.00	1.50	.30
☐ 280	Ron Chipperfield	.15	.07	.01
☐ 281	Wayne Babych	.15	.07	.01
☐ 282	David Shand	.15	.07	.01
☐ 283	Jere Gillis	.15	.07	.01
☐ 284	Dennis Maruk	.25	.12	.02
☐ 285	Jude Drouin	.15	.07	.01
☐ 286	Mike Murphy	.15	.07	.01
☐ 287	Curt Fraser	.15	.07	.01
☐ 288	Gary McAdam	.15	.07	.01
☐ 289	Mark Messier	125.00	60.00	12.50
☐ 290	Vic Venasky	.15	.07	.01
☐ 291	Per-Olov Brasar	.15	.07	.01
☐ 292	Orest Kindrachuk	.15	.07	.01
☐ 293	Dave Hunter	.25	.12	.02
☐ 294	Steve Jensen	.15	.07	.01
☐ 295	Chris Oddleifson	.15	.07	.01
☐ 296	Larry Playfair	.15	.07	.01
☐ 297	Mario Tremblay	.25	.12	.02
☐ 298	Gilles Lupien	.15	.07	.01
☐ 299	Pat Price	.15	.07	.01
☐ 300	Jerry Korab	.15	.07	.01
☐ 301	Darcy Rota	.15	.07	.01
☐ 302	Don Luce	.15	.07	.01
☐ 303	Ken Houston	.15	.07	.01
☐ 304	Brian Engblom	.15	.07	.01
☐ 305	John Tonelli	.50	.25	.05
☐ 306	Doug Sulliman	.15	.07	.01
☐ 307	Rod Schutt	.15	.07	.01
☐ 308	Norm Barnes	.15	.07	.01

			MINT	EXC	G-VG
☐	309	Serge Bernier	.15	.07	.01
☐	310	Larry Patey	.15	.07	.01
☐	311	Dave Farrish	.15	.07	.01
☐	312	Harold Snepsts	.25	.12	.02
☐	313	Bob Sirois	.15	.07	.01
☐	314	Peter Marsh	.15	.07	.01
☐	315	Risto Siltanen	.25	.12	.02
☐	316	Andre St. Laurent	.15	.07	.01
☐	317	Craig Hartsburg	.25	.12	.02
☐	318	Wayne Cashman	.25	.12	.02
☐	319	Lindy Ruff	.25	.12	.02
☐	320	Willi Plett	.15	.07	.01
☐	321	Ron Delorme	.15	.07	.01
☐	322	Gaston Gingras	.25	.12	.02
☐	323	Gordie Lane	.15	.07	.01
☐	324	Doug Soetaert	.25	.12	.02
☐	325	Gregg Sheppard	.15	.07	.01
☐	326	Mike Busniak	.15	.07	.01
☐	327	Jamie Hislop	.15	.07	.01
☐	328	Ed Staniowski	.25	.12	.02
☐	329	Ron Ellis	.15	.07	.01
☐	330	Gary Bromley	.25	.12	.02
☐	331	Mark Lofthouse	.15	.07	.01
☐	332	Dave Hoyda	.15	.07	.01
☐	333	Ron Low	.25	.12	.02
☐	334	Barry Gibbs	.15	.07	.01
☐	335	Gary Edwards	.25	.12	.02
☐	336	Don Marcotte	.15	.07	.01
☐	337	Bill Hajt	.15	.07	.01
☐	338	Brad Marsh	.50	.25	.05
☐	339	J.P. Bordeleau	.15	.07	.01
☐	340	Randy Pierce	.15	.07	.01
☐	341	Eddie Mio	.40	.20	.04
☐	342	Randy Manery	.15	.07	.01
☐	343	Tom Younghans	.15	.07	.01
☐	344	Rod Langway	12.00	6.00	1.20
☐	345	Wayne Merrick	.15	.07	.01
☐	346	Steve Baker	.15	.07	.01
☐	347	Pat Hughes	.15	.07	.01
☐	348	Al Hill	.15	.07	.01
☐	349	Gerry Hart	.15	.07	.01
☐	350	Richard Mulhern	.15	.07	.01
☐	351	Jerry Butler	.15	.07	.01
☐	352	Guy Charron	.15	.07	.01
☐	353	Jimmy Mann	.25	.12	.02
☐	354	Brad McCrimmon	1.75	.85	.17
☐	355	Rick Dudley	.25	.12	.02
☐	356	Pekka Rautakallio	.15	.07	.01
☐	357	Tim Trimper	.15	.07	.01
☐	358	Mike Christie	.15	.07	.01
☐	359	John Ogrodnick	4.00	2.00	.40
☐	360	Dave Semenko	.25	.12	.02
☐	361	Mike Veisor	.25	.12	.02

		MINT	EXC	G-VG
☐ 362	Syl Apps	.15	.07	.01
☐ 363	Mike Polich	.15	.07	.01
☐ 364	Rick Chartraw	.15	.07	.01
☐ 365	Steve Tambellini	.25	.12	.02
☐ 366	Ed Hospodar	.15	.07	.01
☐ 367	Randy Carlyle	.25	.12	.02
☐ 368	Tom Gorence	.15	.07	.01
☐ 369	Pierre Plante	.15	.07	.01
☐ 370	Blake Dunlop	.15	.07	.01
☐ 371	Mike Kaszycki	.15	.07	.01
☐ 372	Rick Blight	.15	.07	.01
☐ 373	Pierre Bouchard	.15	.07	.01
☐ 374	Gary Doak	.15	.07	.01
☐ 375	Andre Savard	.15	.07	.01
☐ 376	Bill Clement	.25	.12	.02
☐ 377	Reg Kerr	.25	.12	.02
☐ 378	Walt McKechnie	.15	.07	.01
☐ 379	George Lyle	.15	.07	.01
☐ 380	Colin Campbell	.15	.07	.01
☐ 381	Dave Debol	.15	.07	.01
☐ 382	Glenn Goldup	.15	.07	.01
☐ 383	Kent-Erik Andersson	.15	.07	.01
☐ 384	Tony Currie	.15	.07	.01
☐ 385	Richard Sevigny	.40	.20	.04
☐ 386	Garry Howatt	.15	.07	.01
☐ 387	Cam Connor	.15	.07	.01
☐ 388	Ross Lonsberry	.15	.07	.01
☐ 389	Frank Bathe	.15	.07	.01
☐ 390	John Wensink	.15	.07	.01
☐ 391	Paul Harrison	.15	.07	.01
☐ 392	Dennis Kearns	.15	.07	.01
☐ 393	Pat Ribble	.15	.07	.01
☐ 394	Markus Mattsson	.25	.12	.02
☐ 395	Chuck Lefley	.15	.07	.01
☐ 396	Checklist 265-396	1.50	.10	.02

1981-82 O-Pee-Chee

LEFT WING AILIER GAUCHE

This 396-card set contains, for the first time, the O-Pee-Chee name within the frame line on the front. The player's name and position are found in the border on the front. The team logo is also contained within the frame line, whereas the team name in bold letters appears across the lower portion of the front. Cards in the set measure 2¹/₂" by 3¹/₂". The backs, printed in black and blue, feature the card number, yearly career statistics, and biographical data in both English and French. A 1981 O-Pee-Chee copyright date is found on the back. Super Action (SA) cards are designated in the list below. The set is essentially numbered in team order; the team leader (TL) card typically pictures the team's leading scorer. The key rookie cards in this set are Glenn Anderson, Don Beaupre, Dino Ciccarelli, Paul Coffey, Reggie Lemelin, Kevin Lowe, Andy Moog, Jari Kurri, Denis Savard, and Peter Stastny.

Ce jeu de 396 cartes indique, pour la première fois, le nom O-Pee-Chee dans la ligne encadrant le bord de la face. Le nom et la position du joueur sont indiqués dans le bord de la face. L'emblème de l'équipe se trouve également dans la ligne encadrant le bord, et le nom de l'équipe apparaît en lettres grasses sur la partie inférieure de la face. Les cartes mesurent 2¹/₂" x 3¹/₂". Le dos, imprimé en noir et bleu, indique le numéro de carte, les statistiques pour chaque année de carrière, et des données biographiques en anglais et en français. Le dos des cartes indique 1981 comme date de droit d'auteur d'O-Pee-Chee. Les cartes "Super Action" (SA) sont indiquées dans la liste ci-dessous. Le jeu est essentiellement numéroté suivant les équipes; la carte du meneur d'équipe (TL) représente généralement le joueur marquant le plus grand nombre de buts pour l'équipe. Les débutants importants de ce jeu sont Glenn Anderson, Don Beaupré, Dino Ciccarelli, Paul Coffey, Reggie Lemelin, Kevin Lowe, Andy Moog, Jari Kurri, Denis Savard, et Peter Stastny.

		MINT	EXC	G-VG
COMPLETE SET (396)		250.00	125.00	25.00
COMMON PLAYER (1-396)		.10	.05	.01
☐ 1	Ray Bourque	20.00	5.00	1.00

			MINT	EXC	G-VG
☐	2	Rick Middleton	.35	.17	.03
☐	3	Dwight Foster	.10	.05	.01
☐	4	Steve Kasper	1.00	.50	.10
☐	5	Peter McNab	.10	.05	.01
☐	6	Mike O'Connell	.10	.05	.01
☐	7	Terry O'Reilly	.20	.10	.02
☐	8	Brad Park	.50	.25	.05
☐	9	Dick Redmond	.10	.05	.01
☐	10	Rogatien Vachon	.40	.20	.04
☐	11	Wayne Cashman	.15	.07	.01
☐	12	Mike Gillis	.10	.05	.01
☐	13	Stan Jonathan	.10	.05	.01
☐	14	Don Marcotte	.10	.05	.01
☐	15	Brad McCrimmon	.15	.07	.01
☐	16	Mike Milbury	.15	.07	.01
☐	17	Ray Bourque SA	4.50	2.25	.45
☐	18	Rick Middleton SA	.15	.07	.01
☐	19	Boston Bruins TL	.15	.07	.01
		Rick Middleton			
☐	20	Danny Gare	.15	.07	.01
☐	21	Don Edwards	.15	.07	.01
☐	22	Tony McKegney	.10	.05	.01
☐	23	Bob Sauve	.15	.07	.01
☐	24	Andre Savard	.10	.05	.01
☐	25	Derek Smith	.10	.05	.01
☐	26	John Van Boxmeer	.10	.05	.01
☐	27	Danny Gare SA	.10	.05	.01
☐	28	Buffalo Sabres TL	.15	.07	.01
		Danny Gare			
☐	29	Richie Dunn	.10	.05	.01
☐	30	Gilbert Perreault	.60	.30	.06
☐	31	Craig Ramsay	.10	.05	.01
☐	32	Ric Seiling	.10	.05	.01
☐	33	Guy Chouinard	.15	.07	.01
☐	34	Kent Nilsson	.20	.10	.02
☐	35	Willi Plett	.10	.05	.01
☐	36	Paul Reinhart	.20	.10	.02
☐	37	Pat Riggin	.85	.40	.08
☐	38	Eric Vail	.15	.07	.01
☐	39	Bill Clement	.15	.07	.01
☐	40	Jamie Hislop	.10	.05	.01
☐	41	Randy Holt	.10	.05	.01
☐	42	Dan Labraaten	.10	.05	.01
☐	43	Kevin Lavallee	.10	.05	.01
☐	44	Rejean Lemelin	3.00	1.50	.30
☐	45	Don Lever	.10	.05	.01
☐	46	Bob MacMillan	.15	.07	.01
☐	47	Brad Marsh	.15	.07	.01
☐	48	Bob Murdoch	.10	.05	.01
☐	49	Jim Peplinski	.40	.20	.04
☐	50	Pekka Rautakallio	.10	.05	.01
☐	51	Phil Russell	.10	.05	.01
☐	52	Kent Nilsson SA	.15	.07	.01

			MINT	EXC	G-VG
☐	53	Calgary Flames TL	.15	.07	.01
		Kent Nilsson			
☐	54	Tony Esposito	.80	.40	.08
☐	55	Keith Brown	.10	.05	.01
☐	56	Ted Bulley	.10	.05	.01
☐	57	Tim Higgins	.10	.05	.01
☐	58	Reg Kerr	.10	.05	.01
☐	59	Tom Lysiak	.15	.07	.01
☐	60	Grant Mulvey	.15	.07	.01
☐	61	Bob Murray	.10	.05	.01
☐	62	Terry Ruskowski	.15	.07	.01
☐	63	Denis Savard	16.00	8.00	1.60
☐	64	Glen Sharpley	.10	.05	.01
☐	65	Darryl Sutter	.60	.30	.06
☐	66	Doug Wilson	.75	.35	.07
☐	67	Tony Esposito SA	.50	.25	.05
☐	68	Murray Bannerman	.60	.30	.06
☐	69	Greg Fox	.10	.05	.01
☐	70	John Marks	.10	.05	.01
☐	71	Peter Marsh	.10	.05	.01
☐	72	Al Secord	.20	.10	.02
☐	73	Chicago Blackhawks TL	.15	.07	.01
		Tom Lysiak			
☐	74	Lucien Deblois	.10	.05	.01
☐	75	Paul Gagne	.10	.05	.01
☐	76	Merlin Malinowski	.10	.05	.01
☐	77	Lanny McDonald	.50	.25	.05
☐	78	Joel Quenneville	.10	.05	.01
☐	79	Rob Ramage	.20	.10	.02
☐	80	Glenn Resch	.35	.17	.03
☐	81	Steve Tambellini	.10	.05	.01
☐	82	Ron Delorme	.10	.05	.01
☐	83	Mike Kitchen	.10	.05	.01
☐	84	Yvon Vautour	.10	.05	.01
☐	85	Colorado Rockies TL	.20	.10	.02
		Lanny McDonald			
☐	86	Dale McCourt	.10	.05	.01
☐	87	Mike Foligno	.15	.07	.01
☐	88	Gilles Gilbert	.15	.07	.01
☐	89	Willie Huber	.10	.05	.01
☐	90	Mark Kirton	.10	.05	.01
☐	91	Jim Korn	.10	.05	.01
☐	92	Reed Larson	.10	.05	.01
☐	93	Gary McAdam	.10	.05	.01
☐	94	Vaclav Nedomansky	.10	.05	.01
☐	95	John Ogrodnick	.25	.12	.02
☐	96	Dale McCourt SA	.10	.05	.01
☐	97	Jean Hamel	.10	.05	.01
☐	98	Glen Hicks	.10	.05	.01
☐	99	Larry Lozinski	.10	.05	.01
☐	100	George Lyle	.10	.05	.01
☐	101	Perry Miller	.10	.05	.01
☐	102	Brad Maxwell	.10	.05	.01

		MINT	EXC	G-VG
☐ 103	Brad Smith	.10	.05	.01
☐ 104	Paul Woods	.10	.05	.01
☐ 105	Detroit Red Wings TL	.15	.07	.01
	Dale McCourt			
☐ 106	Wayne Gretzky	40.00	20.00	4.00
☐ 107	Jari Kurri	25.00	12.50	2.50
☐ 108	Glenn Anderson	6.50	3.25	.65
☐ 109	Curt Brackenbury	.10	.05	.01
☐ 110	Brett Callighen	.10	.05	.01
☐ 111	Paul Coffey	65.00	32.50	6.50
☐ 112	Lee Fogolin	.10	.05	.01
☐ 113	Matti Hagman	.10	.05	.01
☐ 114	Doug Hicks	.10	.05	.01
☐ 115	Dave Hunter	.10	.05	.01
☐ 116	Garry Lariviere	.10	.05	.01
☐ 117	Kevin Lowe	4.50	2.25	.45
☐ 118	Mark Messier	25.00	12.50	2.50
☐ 119	Eddie Mio	.15	.07	.01
☐ 120	Andy Moog	20.00	10.00	2.00
☐ 121	Dave Semenko	.15	.07	.01
☐ 122	Risto Siltanen	.15	.07	.01
☐ 123	Garry Unger	.15	.07	.01
☐ 124	Stan Weir	.10	.05	.01
☐ 125	Wayne Gretzky SA	16.00	8.00	1.60
☐ 126	Edmonton Oilers TL	9.00	4.50	.90
	Wayne Gretzky			
☐ 127	Mike Rogers	.15	.07	.01
☐ 128	Mark Howe	.35	.17	.03
☐ 129	Dave Keon	.50	.25	.05
☐ 130	Warren Miller	.10	.05	.01
☐ 131	Al Sims	.10	.05	.01
☐ 132	Blaine Stoughton	.15	.07	.01
☐ 133	Rick MacLeish	.20	.10	.02
☐ 134	Greg Millen	.20	.10	.02
☐ 135	Mike Rogers SA	.15	.07	.01
☐ 136	Mike Fidler	.10	.05	.01
☐ 137	John Garrett	.15	.07	.01
☐ 138	Don Nachbaur	.10	.05	.01
☐ 139	Tom Rowe	.10	.05	.01
☐ 140	Hartford Whalers TL	.15	.07	.01
	Mike Rogers			
☐ 141	Marcel Dionne	1.25	.60	.12
☐ 142	Charlie Simmer	.20	.10	.02
☐ 143	Dave Taylor	.50	.25	.05
☐ 144	Billy Harris	.10	.05	.01
☐ 145	Jerry Korab	.10	.05	.01
☐ 146	Mario Lessard	.20	.10	.02
☐ 147	Don Luce	.10	.05	.01
☐ 148	Larry Murphy	2.00	1.00	.20
☐ 149	Mike Murphy	.10	.05	.01
☐ 150	Marcel Dionne SA	.65	.30	.06
☐ 151	Charlie Simmer SA	.15	.07	.01
☐ 152	Dave Taylor SA	.30	.15	.03

		MINT	EXC	G-VG
☐ 153	Jim Fox	.15	.07	.01
☐ 154	Steve Jensen	.10	.05	.01
☐ 155	Greg Terrion	.10	.05	.01
☐ 156	Los Angeles Kings TL	.40	.20	.04
	Marcel Dionne			
☐ 157	Bobby Smith	.35	.17	.03
☐ 158	Kent-Erik Andersson	.10	.05	.01
☐ 159	Don Beaupre	4.00	2.00	.40
☐ 160	Steve Christoff	.15	.07	.01
☐ 161	Dino Ciccarelli	8.00	4.00	.80
☐ 162	Craig Hartsburg	.15	.07	.01
☐ 163	Al MacAdam	.15	.07	.01
☐ 164	Tom McCarthy	.10	.05	.01
☐ 165	Gilles Meloche	.15	.07	.01
☐ 166	Steve Payne	.10	.05	.01
☐ 167	Gordie Roberts	.10	.05	.01
☐ 168	Greg Smith	.10	.05	.01
☐ 169	Tim Young	.10	.05	.01
☐ 170	Bobby Smith SA	.20	.10	.02
☐ 171	Mike Eaves	.10	.05	.01
☐ 172	Mike Polich	.10	.05	.01
☐ 173	Tom Younghans	.10	.05	.01
☐ 174	Minn. North Stars TL	.15	.07	.01
	Bobby Smith			
☐ 175	Brian Engblom	.10	.05	.01
☐ 176	Bob Gainey	.35	.17	.03
☐ 177	Guy Lafleur	1.50	.75	.15
☐ 178	Mark Napier	.15	.07	.01
☐ 179	Larry Robinson	.50	.25	.05
☐ 180	Steve Shutt	.35	.17	.03
☐ 181	Keith Acton	.35	.17	.03
☐ 182	Gaston Gingras	.10	.05	.01
☐ 183	Rejean Houle	.10	.05	.01
☐ 184	Doug Jarvis	.15	.07	.01
☐ 185	Yvon Lambert	.10	.05	.01
☐ 186	Rod Langway	.90	.45	.09
☐ 187	Pierre Larouche	.15	.07	.01
☐ 188	Pierre Mondou	.10	.05	.01
☐ 189	Robert Picard	.10	.05	.01
☐ 190	Doug Risebrough	.10	.05	.01
☐ 191	Richard Sevigny	.15	.07	.01
☐ 192	Mario Tremblay	.15	.07	.01
☐ 193	Doug Wickenheiser	.30	.15	.03
☐ 194	Bob Gainey SA	.20	.10	.02
☐ 195	Guy Lafleur SA	.65	.30	.06
☐ 196	Larry Robinson SA	.25	.12	.02
☐ 197	Montreal Canadiens TL	.20	.10	.02
	Steve Shutt			
☐ 198	Mike Bossy	2.75	1.35	.27
☐ 199	Denis Potvin	1.00	.50	.10
☐ 200	Bryan Trottier	1.50	.75	.15
☐ 201	Bob Bourne	.10	.05	.01
☐ 202	Clark Gillies	.20	.10	.02

			MINT	EXC	G-VG
☐ 203	Butch Goring		.15	.07	.01
☐ 204	Anders Kallur		.10	.05	.01
☐ 205	Ken Morrow		.15	.07	.01
☐ 206	Stefan Persson		.15	.07	.01
☐ 207	Billy Smith		.50	.25	.05
☐ 208	Mike Bossy SA		1.25	.60	.12
☐ 209	Denis Potvin SA		.50	.25	.05
☐ 210	Bryan Trottier SA		.60	.30	.06
☐ 211	Duane Sutter		.40	.20	.04
☐ 212	Gordie Lane		.10	.05	.01
☐ 213	Dave Langevin		.10	.05	.01
☐ 214	Bob Lorimer		.10	.05	.01
☐ 215	Mike McEwen		.10	.05	.01
☐ 216	Wayne Merrick		.10	.05	.01
☐ 217	Bob Nystrom		.15	.07	.01
☐ 218	John Tonelli		.25	.12	.02
☐ 219	New York Islanders TL Mike Bossy		.35	.17	.03
☐ 220	Barry Beck		.15	.07	.01
☐ 221	Mike Allison		.15	.07	.01
☐ 222	John Davidson		.15	.07	.01
☐ 223	Ron Duguay		.15	.07	.01
☐ 224	Ron Greschner		.15	.07	.01
☐ 225	Anders Hedberg		.15	.07	.01
☐ 226	Ed Johnstone		.10	.05	.01
☐ 227	Dave Maloney		.15	.07	.01
☐ 228	Don Maloney		.15	.07	.01
☐ 229	Ulf Nilsson		.15	.07	.01
☐ 230	Barry Beck SA		.15	.07	.01
☐ 231	Steve Baker		.15	.07	.01
☐ 232	Jere Gillis		.10	.05	.01
☐ 233	Ed Hospodar		.10	.05	.01
☐ 234	Tom Laidlaw		.15	.07	.01
☐ 235	Dean Talafous		.10	.05	.01
☐ 236	Carol Vadnais		.10	.05	.01
☐ 237	New York Rangers TL Anders Hedberg		.15	.07	.01
☐ 238	Bill Barber		.50	.25	.05
☐ 239	Behn Wilson		.10	.05	.01
☐ 240	Bobby Clarke		1.00	.50	.10
☐ 241	Bob Dailey		.10	.05	.01
☐ 242	Paul Holmgren		.15	.07	.01
☐ 243	Reggie Leach		.15	.07	.01
☐ 244	Ken Linseman		.20	.10	.02
☐ 245	Pete Peeters		.50	.25	.05
☐ 246	Brian Propp		1.25	.60	.12
☐ 247	Bill Barber SA		.20	.10	.02
☐ 248	Mel Bridgman		.10	.05	.01
☐ 249	Mike Busniuk		.10	.05	.01
☐ 250	Tom Gorence		.10	.05	.01
☐ 251	Tim Kerr		6.50	3.25	.65
☐ 252	Rick St. Croix		.20	.10	.02
☐ 253	Philadelphia Flyers TL Bill Barber		.20	.10	.02

		MINT	EXC	G-VG
☐ 254	Rick Kehoe	.15	.07	.01
☐ 255	Pat Boutette	.10	.05	.01
☐ 256	Randy Carlyle	.15	.07	.01
☐ 257	Paul Gardner	.15	.07	.01
☐ 258	Peter Lee	.10	.05	.01
☐ 259	Rod Schutt	.10	.05	.01
☐ 260	Rick Kehoe SA	.15	.07	.01
☐ 261	Mario Faubert	.10	.05	.01
☐ 262	George Ferguson	.10	.05	.01
☐ 263	Ross Lonsberry	.10	.05	.01
☐ 264	Greg Malone	.10	.05	.01
☐ 265	Pat Price	.10	.05	.01
☐ 266	Ron Stackhouse	.10	.05	.01
☐ 267	Pittsburgh Penguins TL	.15	.07	.01
	Rick Kehoe			
☐ 268	Jacques Richard	.10	.05	.01
☐ 269	Peter Stastny	16.00	8.00	1.60
☐ 270	Dan Bouchard	.15	.07	.01
☐ 271	Kim Clackson	.10	.05	.01
☐ 272	Alain Cote	.10	.05	.01
☐ 273	Andre Dupont	.10	.05	.01
☐ 274	Robbie Ftorek	.15	.07	.01
☐ 275	Michel Goulet	2.50	1.25	.25
☐ 276	Dale Hoganson	.10	.05	.01
☐ 277	Dale Hunter	.60	.30	.06
☐ 278	Pierre Lacroix	.10	.05	.01
☐ 279	Mario Marois	.40	.20	.04
☐ 280	Dave Pichette	.10	.05	.01
☐ 281	Michel Plasse	.15	.07	.01
☐ 282	Anton Stastny	.75	.35	.07
☐ 283	Marc Tardif	.15	.07	.01
☐ 284	Wally Weir	.10	.05	.01
☐ 285	Jacques Richard SA	.10	.05	.01
☐ 286	Peter Stastny SA	3.50	1.75	.35
☐ 287	Quebec Nordiques TL	1.00	.50	.10
	Peter Stastny			
☐ 288	Bernie Federko	.20	.10	.02
☐ 289	Mike Liut	.75	.35	.07
☐ 290	Wayne Babych	.10	.05	.01
☐ 291	Blair Chapman	.10	.05	.01
☐ 292	Tony Currie	.10	.05	.01
☐ 293	Blake Dunlop	.10	.05	.01
☐ 294	Ed Kea	.10	.05	.01
☐ 295	Rick Lapointe	.10	.05	.01
☐ 296	Jorgen Pettersson	.35	.17	.03
☐ 297	Brian Sutter	.20	.10	.02
☐ 298	Perry Turnbull	.15	.07	.01
☐ 299	Mike Zuke	.10	.05	.01
☐ 300	Bernie Federko SA	.15	.07	.01
☐ 301	Mike Liut SA	.20	.10	.02
☐ 302	Jack Brownschidle	.10	.05	.01
☐ 303	Larry Patey	.10	.05	.01

		MINT	EXC	G-VG
☐ 304	St. Louis Blues TL	.15	.07	.01
	Bernie Federko			
☐ 305	Bill Derlago	.10	.05	.01
☐ 306	Wilf Paiement	.10	.05	.01
☐ 307	Borje Salming	.25	.12	.02
☐ 308	Darryl Sittler	.45	.22	.04
☐ 309	Ian Turnbull	.10	.05	.01
☐ 310	Rick Vaive	.40	.20	.04
☐ 311	Wilf Paiement SA	.10	.05	.01
☐ 312	Darryl Sittler SA	.25	.12	.02
☐ 313	John Andersson	.10	.05	.01
☐ 314	Laurie Boschman	.10	.05	.01
☐ 315	Jiri Crha	.30	.15	.03
☐ 316	Vitezslav Duris	.10	.05	.01
☐ 317	Dave Farrish	.10	.05	.01
☐ 318	Pat Hickey	.10	.05	.01
☐ 319	Michel Larocque	.20	.10	.02
☐ 320	Dan Maloney	.15	.07	.01
☐ 321	Terry Martin	.10	.05	.01
☐ 322	Rene Robert	.15	.07	.01
☐ 323	Rocky Saganiuk	.10	.05	.01
☐ 324	Ron Sedlbauer	.10	.05	.01
☐ 325	Ron Zanussi	.10	.05	.01
☐ 326	Toronto Maple Leafs TL	.15	.07	.01
	Wilf Paiement			
☐ 327	Thomas Gradin	.15	.07	.01
☐ 328	Stan Smyl	.10	.05	.01
☐ 329	Ivan Boldirev	.10	.05	.01
☐ 330	Per-Olov Brasar UER	.10	.05	.01
	(Photo actually Brent Ashton)			
☐ 331	Richard Brodeur	.20	.10	.02
☐ 332	Jerry Butler	.10	.05	.01
☐ 333	Colin Campbell	.10	.05	.01
☐ 334	Curt Fraser	.10	.05	.01
☐ 335	Doug Halward	.10	.05	.01
☐ 336	Glen Hanlon	.20	.10	.02
☐ 337	Dennis Kearns	.10	.05	.01
☐ 338	Rick Lanz UER	.10	.05	.01
	(Photo actually Thomas Gradin)			
☐ 339	Pat Ribble	.10	.05	.01
☐ 340	Blair MacDonald	.10	.05	.01
☐ 341	Kevin McCarthy	.10	.05	.01
☐ 342	Gerry Minor	.10	.05	.01
☐ 343	Darcy Rota	.10	.05	.01
☐ 344	Harold Snepsts	.20	.10	.02
☐ 345	Dave Williams	.15	.07	.01
☐ 346	Vancouver Canucks TL	.15	.07	.01
	Thomas Gradin			
☐ 347	Mike Gartner	2.50	1.25	.25
☐ 348	Rick Green	.15	.07	.01
☐ 349	Bob Kelly	.10	.05	.01
☐ 350	Dennis Maruk	.15	.07	.01
☐ 351	Mike Palmateer	.15	.07	.01

			MINT	EXC	G-VG
☐ 352	Ryan Walter		.15	.07	.01
☐ 353	Bengt Gustafsson		.15	.07	.01
☐ 354	Al Hangsleben		.10	.05	.01
☐ 355	Jean Pronovost		.15	.07	.01
☐ 356	Dennis Ververgaert		.10	.05	.01
☐ 357	Washington Capitols TL		.15	.07	.01
	Dennis Maruk				
☐ 358	Dave Babych		.75	.35	.07
☐ 359	Dave Christian		.15	.07	.01
☐ 360	Dave Christian SA		.15	.07	.01
☐ 361	Rick Bowness		.20	.10	.02
☐ 362	Rick Dudley		.15	.07	.01
☐ 363	Norm Dupont		.10	.05	.01
☐ 364	Dan Geoffrion		.10	.05	.01
☐ 365	Pierre Hamel		.10	.05	.01
☐ 366	Dave Hoyda UER		.10	.05	.01
	(Photo actually Doug Lecuyer)				
☐ 367	Doug Lecuyer		.10	.05	.01
☐ 368	Willy Lindstrom		.10	.05	.01
☐ 369	Barry Long		.10	.05	.01
☐ 370	Morris Lukowich		.15	.07	.01
☐ 371	Kris Manery		.10	.05	.01
☐ 372	Jimmy Mann		.10	.05	.01
☐ 373	Moe Mantha		.40	.20	.04
☐ 374	Markus Mattsson		.15	.07	.01
☐ 375	Don Spring		.10	.05	.01
☐ 376	Tim Trimper		.10	.05	.01
☐ 377	Ron Wilson		.10	.05	.01
☐ 378	Winnipeg Jets TL		.15	.07	.01
	Dave Christian				
☐ 379	Checklist 1-132		.90	.07	.01
☐ 380	Checklist 133-264		.90	.07	.01
☐ 381	Checklist 265-396		.90	.07	.01
☐ 382	Goal Leader		1.00	.50	.10
	Mike Bossy				
☐ 383	Assist Leader		7.50	3.75	.75
	Wayne Gretzky				
☐ 384	Scoring Leader		7.50	3.75	.75
	Wayne Gretzky				
☐ 385	Penalty Leader		.15	.07	.01
	Dave Williams				
☐ 386	Power Play Leader		1.00	.50	.10
	Mike Bossy				
☐ 387	Goals Against Leader		.15	.07	.01
	Richard Sevigny				
☐ 388	Game Winning Goal Leader		1.00	.50	.10
	Mike Bossy				
☐ 389	Shutout Leaders		.20	.10	.02
	Don Edwards				
	Glenn Resch				
☐ 390	Mike Bossy RB		1.00	.50	.10
	Eight hat tricks in one season				

			MINT	EXC	G-VG
☐ 391	**Marcel Dionne,**		.50	.25	.05
	Charlie Simmer,				
	Dave Taylor RB				
	100 points each				
☐ 392	**Wayne Gretzky RB**		8.00	4.00	.80
	Season scoring record				
☐ 393	**Larry Murphy RB**		.20	.10	.02
	Highest scoring rookie defenseman				
☐ 394	**Mike Palmateer RB**		.15	.07	.01
	Seventh assist, new goalie record				
☐ 395	**Peter Stastny RB**		1.00	.50	.10
	Rookie scoring record				
☐ 396	**Bob Manno**		.15	.07	.01

1982-83 O-Pee-Chee

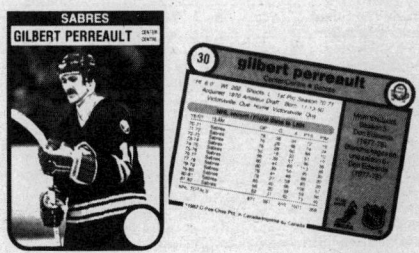

This 396-card set features the team logo within the frame line, but the O-Pee-Chee logo within the frame line of In Action and special cards. Cards are 2½" by 3½". The backs are printed in light and dark purple ink on a white card stock. Highlight cards (HL cards 1-5), team scoring leaders cards, league leaders cards, and In Action cards are contained within the set, in addition to individual player cards. Topps did not produce a hockey card set this year. The key rookie cards in this set are Neal Broten, Ron Francis, Grant Fuhr, Dale Hawerchuk, and Joey Mullen.

Ce jeu de 396 cartes représente l'emblème de l'équipe dans la ligne encadrant le bord, mais les cartes "in Action" ou les cartes spéciales comportent l'emblème O-Pee-Chee dans cette ligne. Les cartes mesurent 2½" x 3½". Le dos est imprimé en pourpre clair et foncé sur une pâte de papier blanche. En plus des cartes représentant les joueurs individuels, le jeu contient des cartes illustrant les moments importants (cartes HL 1-5), les joueurs marquant le plus grand nombre de buts pour l'équipe, les champions, et les

cartes "In Action". Topps n'a pas produit de jeu de cartes de hockey cette année. Les débutants importants de ce jeu sont Neal Broten, Ron Francis, Grant Fuhr, Dale Hawerchuk, et Joey Mullen.

			MINT	EXC	G-VG
		COMPLETE SET (396)	130.00	65.00	13.00
		COMMON PLAYER (1-396)	.08	.04	.01
☐	1	Wayne Gretzky HL .... More Records	10.00	2.50	.50
☐	2	Mike Bossy HL .... Record 147 Points	.75	.35	.07
☐	3	Dale Hawerchuk HL .... Rookie Record	3.00	1.50	.30
☐	4	Mikko Leinonen HL .... Six Assists One Game	.14	.07	.01
☐	5	Bryan Trottier HL .... Sets Assist Mark	.60	.30	.06
☐	6	Bruins Scoring: .... Rick Middleton	.14	.07	.01
☐	7	Ray Bourque	6.00	3.00	.60
☐	8	Wayne Cashman	.14	.07	.01
☐	9	Bruce Crowder	.08	.04	.01
☐	10	Keith Crowder	.25	.12	.02
☐	11	Tom Fergus	.35	.17	.03
☐	12	Steve Kasper	.14	.07	.01
☐	13	Normand Leveille	.08	.04	.01
☐	14	Don Marcotte	.08	.04	.01
☐	15	Rick Middleton	.30	.15	.03
☐	16	Peter McNab	.08	.04	.01
☐	17	Mike O'Connell	.08	.04	.01
☐	18	Terry O'Reilly	.20	.10	.02
☐	19	Brad Park	.40	.20	.04
☐	20	Barry Pederson	.60	.30	.06
☐	21	Brad Palmer	.08	.04	.01
☐	22	Pete Peeters	.30	.15	.03
☐	23	Rogatien Vachon	.35	.17	.03
☐	24	Ray Bourque IA	1.75	.85	.17
☐	25	Sabres Scoring: .... Gilbert Perreault	.25	.12	.02
☐	26	Mike Foligno	.14	.07	.01
☐	27	Yvon Lambert	.08	.04	.01
☐	28	Dale McCourt	.08	.04	.01
☐	29	Tony McKegney	.08	.04	.01
☐	30	Gilbert Perreault	.60	.30	.06
☐	31	Lindy Ruff	.08	.04	.01
☐	32	Mike Ramsey	.08	.04	.01
☐	33	J.F. Sauve	.08	.04	.01
☐	34	Bob Sauve	.14	.07	.01
☐	35	Ric Seiling	.08	.04	.01
☐	36	John Van Boxmeer	.08	.04	.01
☐	37	John Van Boxmeer IA	.08	.04	.01

			MINT	EXC	G-VG
☐	38	Calgary Flames	.14	.07	.01
		Scoring Leaders:			
		Lanny McDonald			
☐	39	Mel Bridgman	.08	.04	.01
☐	40	Mel Bridgman IA	.08	.04	.01
☐	41	Guy Chouinard	.08	.04	.01
☐	42	Steve Christoff	.08	.04	.01
☐	43	Denis Cyr	.08	.04	.01
☐	44	Bill Clement	.14	.07	.01
☐	45	Richie Dunn	.08	.04	.01
☐	46	Don Edwards	.14	.07	.01
☐	47	Jamie Hislop	.08	.04	.01
☐	48	Steve Konroyd	.08	.04	.01
☐	49	Kevin Lavallee	.08	.04	.01
☐	50	Rejean Lemelin	.40	.20	.04
☐	51	Lanny McDonald	.40	.20	.04
☐	52	Lanny McDonald IA	.20	.10	.02
☐	53	Bob Murdoch	.08	.04	.01
☐	54	Kent Nilsson	.14	.07	.01
☐	55	Jim Peplinski	.14	.07	.01
☐	56	Paul Reinhart	.14	.07	.01
☐	57	Doug Risebrough	.14	.07	.01
☐	58	Phil Russell	.08	.04	.01
☐	59	Howard Walker	.08	.04	.01
☐	60	Blackhawks Scoring:	.14	.07	.01
		Al Secord			
☐	61	Murray Bannerman	.14	.07	.01
☐	62	Keith Brown	.08	.04	.01
☐	63	Doug Crossman	.65	.30	.06
☐	64	Tony Esposito	.65	.30	.06
☐	65	Greg Fox	.08	.04	.01
☐	66	Tim Higgins	.08	.04	.01
☐	67	Reg Kerr	.08	.04	.01
☐	68	Tom Lysiak	.14	.07	.01
☐	69	Grant Mulvey	.14	.07	.01
☐	70	Bob Murray	.08	.04	.01
☐	71	Rich Preston	.08	.04	.01
☐	72	Terry Ruskowski	.14	.07	.01
☐	73	Denis Savard	4.50	2.25	.45
☐	74	Al Secord	.14	.07	.01
☐	75	Glen Sharpley	.08	.04	.01
☐	76	Darryl Sutter	.14	.07	.01
☐	77	Doug Wilson	.50	.25	.05
☐	78	Doug Wilson IA	.25	.12	.02
☐	79	Red Wings Scoring:	.14	.07	.01
		John Ogrodnick			
☐	80	John Barrett	.08	.04	.01
☐	81	Mike Blaisdell	.08	.04	.01
☐	82	Colin Campbell	.08	.04	.01
☐	83	Danny Gare	.14	.07	.01
☐	84	Gilles Gilbert	.14	.07	.01
☐	85	Willie Huber	.08	.04	.01
☐	86	Greg Joly	.08	.04	.01

			MINT	EXC	G-VG
☐	87	Mark Kirton	.08	.04	.01
☐	88	Reed Larson	.08	.04	.01
☐	89	Reed Larson IA	.08	.04	.01
☐	90	Reggie Leach	.14	.07	.01
☐	91	Walt McKechnie	.08	.04	.01
☐	92	John Ogrodnick	.20	.10	.02
☐	93	Mark Osborne	.40	.20	.04
☐	94	Jim Schoenfeld	.14	.07	.01
☐	95	Derek Smith	.08	.04	.01
☐	96	Greg Smith	.08	.04	.01
☐	97	Eric Vail	.14	.07	.01
☐	98	Paul Woods	.08	.04	.01
☐	99	Edmonton Scoring: Wayne Gretzky	7.50	3.75	.75
☐	100	Glenn Anderson	1.25	.60	.12
☐	101	Paul Coffey	12.00	6.00	1.20
☐	102	Paul Coffey IA	3.00	1.50	.30
☐	103	Brett Callighen	.08	.04	.01
☐	104	Lee Fogolin	.08	.04	.01
☐	105	Grant Fuhr	12.50	6.25	1.25
☐	106	Wayne Gretzky	25.00	12.50	2.50
☐	107	Wayne Gretzky IA	11.00	5.50	1.10
☐	108	Matti Hagman	.08	.04	.01
☐	109	Pat Hughes	.08	.04	.01
☐	110	Dave Hunter	.14	.07	.01
☐	111	Jari Kurri	5.00	2.50	.50
☐	112	Ron Low	.14	.07	.01
☐	113	Kevin Lowe	.65	.30	.06
☐	114	Dave Lumley	.08	.04	.01
☐	115	Ken Linseman	.14	.07	.01
☐	116	Garry Lariviere	.08	.04	.01
☐	117	Mark Messier	8.00	4.00	.80
☐	118	Tom Roulston	.08	.04	.01
☐	119	Dave Semenko	.14	.07	.01
☐	120	Garry Unger	.14	.07	.01
☐	121	Checklist 1-132	.50	.05	.01
☐	122	Hartford Whalers Scoring Leaders: Blaine Stoughton	.14	.07	.01
☐	123	Ron Francis	12.00	6.00	1.20
☐	124	Chris Kotsopoulos	.08	.04	.01
☐	125	Pierre Larouche	.14	.07	.01
☐	126	Greg Millen	.14	.07	.01
☐	127	Warren Miller	.08	.04	.01
☐	128	Merlin Malinowski	.08	.04	.01
☐	129	Risto Siltanen	.08	.04	.01
☐	130	Blaine Stoughton	.08	.04	.01
☐	131	Blaine Stoughton IA	.08	.04	.01
☐	132	Doug Sulliman	.08	.04	.01
☐	133	Blake Wesley	.08	.04	.01
☐	134	New Jersey Devils Scoring Leaders: Steve Tambellini	.14	.07	.01

		MINT	EXC	G-VG
☐ 135	Brent Ashton	.08	.04	.01
☐ 136	Aaron Broten	.08	.04	.01
☐ 137	Joe Cirella	.35	.17	.03
☐ 138	Dwight Foster	.08	.04	.01
☐ 139	Paul Gagne	.08	.04	.01
☐ 140	Garry Howatt	.08	.04	.01
☐ 141	Don Lever	.08	.04	.01
☐ 142	Bob Lorimer	.08	.04	.01
☐ 143	Bob MacMillan	.14	.07	.01
☐ 144	Rick Meagher	.40	.20	.04
☐ 145	Glenn Resch	.30	.15	.03
☐ 146	Glenn Resch IA	.20	.10	.02
☐ 147	Steve Tambellini	.08	.04	.01
☐ 148	Carol Vadnais	.08	.04	.01
☐ 149	LA Kings Scoring: Marcel Dionne	.30	.15	.03
☐ 150	Dan Bonar	.08	.04	.01
☐ 151	Steve Bozek	.20	.10	.02
☐ 152	Marcel Dionne	1.00	.50	.10
☐ 153	Marcel Dionne IA	.50	.25	.05
☐ 154	Jim Fox	.08	.04	.01
☐ 155	Mark Hardy	.08	.04	.01
☐ 156	Mario Lessard	.14	.07	.01
☐ 157	Dave Lewis	.08	.04	.01
☐ 158	Larry Murphy	.14	.07	.01
☐ 159	Charlie Simmer	.20	.10	.02
☐ 160	Doug Smith	.08	.04	.01
☐ 161	Dave Taylor	.25	.12	.02
☐ 162	North Stars Scoring: Dino Ciccarelli	.20	.10	.02
☐ 163	Don Beaupre	.25	.12	.02
☐ 164	Neal Broten	4.00	2.00	.40
☐ 165	Dino Ciccarelli	1.50	.75	.15
☐ 166	Curt Giles	.08	.04	.01
☐ 167	Craig Hartsburg	.14	.07	.01
☐ 168	Brad Maxwell	.08	.04	.01
☐ 169	Tom McCarthy	.08	.04	.01
☐ 170	Gilles Meloche	.14	.07	.01
☐ 171	Al MacAdam	.14	.07	.01
☐ 172	Steve Payne	.08	.04	.01
☐ 173	Willi Plett	.08	.04	.01
☐ 174	Gordie Roberts	.08	.04	.01
☐ 175	Bobby Smith	.30	.15	.03
☐ 176	Bobby Smith IA	.15	.07	.01
☐ 177	Tim Young	.08	.04	.01
☐ 178	Montreal Scoring: Mark Napier	.14	.07	.01
☐ 179	Keith Acton	.14	.07	.01
☐ 180	Keith Acton IA	.14	.07	.01
☐ 181	Bob Gainey	.30	.15	.03
☐ 182	Gaston Gingras	.14	.07	.01
☐ 183	Rick Green	.14	.07	.01
☐ 184	Rejean Houle	.08	.04	.01

		MINT	EXC	G-VG
☐ 185	Mark Hunter	.35	.17	.03
☐ 186	Guy Lafleur	1.50	.75	.15
☐ 187	Guy Lafleur IA	.60	.30	.06
☐ 188	Pierre Mondou	.08	.04	.01
☐ 189	Mark Napier	.14	.07	.01
☐ 190	Robert Picard	.08	.04	.01
☐ 191	Larry Robinson	.40	.20	.04
☐ 192	Steve Shutt	.30	.15	.03
☐ 193	Mario Tremblay	.14	.07	.01
☐ 194	Ryan Walter	.14	.07	.01
☐ 195	Rick Wamsley	.60	.30	.06
☐ 196	Doug Wickenheiser	.14	.07	.01
☐ 197	Islanders Scoring: Mike Bossy	.50	.25	.05
☐ 198	Bob Bourne	.08	.04	.01
☐ 199	Mike Bossy	2.00	1.00	.20
☐ 200	Butch Goring	.14	.07	.01
☐ 201	Clark Gillies	.20	.10	.02
☐ 202	Tomas Jonsson	.20	.10	.02
☐ 203	Anders Kallur	.08	.04	.01
☐ 204	Dave Langevin	.08	.04	.01
☐ 205	Wayne Merrick	.08	.04	.01
☐ 206	Ken Morrow	.14	.07	.01
☐ 207	Mike McEwen	.14	.07	.01
☐ 208	Bob Nystrom	.14	.07	.01
☐ 209	Stefan Persson	.14	.07	.01
☐ 210	Denis Potvin	.75	.35	.07
☐ 211	Billy Smith	.35	.17	.03
☐ 212	Duane Sutter	.14	.07	.01
☐ 213	John Tonelli	.20	.10	.02
☐ 214	Bryan Trottier	.75	.35	.07
☐ 215	Bryan Trottier IA	.45	.22	.04
☐ 216	Brent Sutter	1.25	.60	.12
☐ 217	Rangers Scoring: Ron Duguay	.14	.07	.01
☐ 218	Kent-Erik Andersson	.08	.04	.01
☐ 219	Barry Beck	.14	.07	.01
☐ 220	Barry Beck IA	.14	.07	.01
☐ 221	Ron Duguay	.14	.07	.01
☐ 222	Nick Fotiu	.08	.04	.01
☐ 223	Robbie Ftorek	.14	.07	.01
☐ 224	Ron Greschner	.14	.07	.01
☐ 225	Anders Hedberg	.14	.07	.01
☐ 226	Ed Johnstone	.08	.04	.01
☐ 227	Tom Laidlaw	.08	.04	.01
☐ 228	Dave Maloney	.14	.07	.01
☐ 229	Don Maloney	.14	.07	.01
☐ 230	Eddie Mio	.14	.07	.01
☐ 231	Mark Pavelich	.20	.10	.02
☐ 232	Mike Rogers	.14	.07	.01
☐ 233	Reijo Ruotsalainen	.60	.30	.06
☐ 234	Steve Weeks	.30	.15	.03

		MINT	EXC	G-VG
☐ 235	Goals Leader (Wayne Gretzky)	6.00	3.00	.60
☐ 236	Power Play Leader (Paul Gardner)	.14	.07	.01
☐ 237	Shorthanded Goal Leader (Wayne Gretzky and Michel Goulet)	4.00	2.00	.40
☐ 238	Penalty Minutes Leader (Paul Baxter)	.14	.07	.01
☐ 239	Goals Against Leader (Denis Herron)	.14	.07	.01
☐ 240	Assist Leader (Wayne Gretzky)	6.00	3.00	.60
☐ 241	Shutout Leader (Denis Herron)	.14	.07	.01
☐ 242	Winning Goal Leader (Wayne Gretzky)	6.00	3.00	.60
☐ 243	Scoring Leader (Wayne Gretzky)	6.00	3.00	.60
☐ 244	Flyers Scoring: Bill Barber	.20	.10	.02
☐ 245	Fred Arthur	.08	.04	.01
☐ 246	Bill Barber	.40	.20	.04
☐ 247	Bill Barber IA	.20	.10	.02
☐ 248	Bobby Clarke	.80	.40	.08
☐ 249	Ron Flockhart	.08	.04	.01
☐ 250	Tom Gorence	.08	.04	.01
☐ 251	Paul Holmgren	.14	.07	.01
☐ 252	Mark Howe	.25	.12	.02
☐ 253	Tim Kerr	.75	.35	.07
☐ 254	Brad Marsh	.14	.07	.01
☐ 255	Brad McCrimmon	.14	.07	.01
☐ 256	Brian Propp	.50	.25	.05
☐ 257	Darryl Sittler	.40	.20	.04
☐ 258	Rick St. Croix	.08	.04	.01
☐ 259	Jim Watson	.08	.04	.01
☐ 260	Behn Wilson	.08	.04	.01
☐ 261	Checklist 133-264	.50	.05	.01
☐ 262	Penguins Scoring: Mike Bullard	.14	.07	.01
☐ 263	Pat Boutette	.08	.04	.01
☐ 264	Mike Bullard	1.50	.75	.15
☐ 265	Randy Carlyle	.14	.07	.01
☐ 266	Randy Carlyle IA	.14	.07	.01
☐ 267	Michel Dion	.14	.07	.01
☐ 268	George Ferguson	.08	.04	.01
☐ 269	Paul Gardner	.14	.07	.01
☐ 270	Denis Herron	.14	.07	.01
☐ 271	Rick Kehoe	.14	.07	.01
☐ 272	Greg Malone	.08	.04	.01
☐ 273	Rick MacLeish	.20	.10	.02
☐ 274	Pat Price	.08	.04	.01
☐ 275	Ron Stackhouse	.08	.04	.01

		MINT	EXC	G-VG
☐ 276	Quebec Nordiques Scoring Leaders: Peter Stastny	.30	.15	.03
☐ 277	Pierre Aubry	.08	.04	.01
☐ 278	Dan Bouchard	.14	.07	.01
☐ 279	Real Cloutier	.08	.04	.01
☐ 280	Real Cloutier IA	.08	.04	.01
☐ 281	Alain Cote	.08	.04	.01
☐ 282	Andre Dupont	.08	.04	.01
☐ 283	John Garrett	.14	.07	.01
☐ 284	Michel Goulet	1.00	.50	.10
☐ 285	Dale Hunter	.14	.07	.01
☐ 286	Pierre Lacroix	.08	.04	.01
☐ 287	Mario Marois	.08	.04	.01
☐ 288	Wilf Paiement	.08	.04	.01
☐ 289	Dave Pichette	.08	.04	.01
☐ 290	Jacques Richard	.08	.04	.01
☐ 291	Normand Rochefort	.08	.04	.01
☐ 292	Peter Stastny	4.50	2.25	.45
☐ 293	Peter Stastny IA	.60	.30	.06
☐ 294	Anton Stastny	.14	.07	.01
☐ 295	Marian Stastny	.30	.15	.03
☐ 296	Marc Tardif	.14	.07	.01
☐ 297	Wally Weir	.08	.04	.01
☐ 298	Blues Scoring: Brian Sutter	.14	.07	.01
☐ 299	Wayne Babych	.08	.04	.01
☐ 300	Jack Brownschidle	.08	.04	.01
☐ 301	Blake Dunlop	.08	.04	.01
☐ 302	Bernie Federko	.20	.10	.02
☐ 303	Bernie Federko IA	.14	.07	.01
☐ 304	Pat Hickey	.08	.04	.01
☐ 305	Guy Lapointe	.14	.07	.01
☐ 306	Mike Liut	.35	.17	.03
☐ 307	Joe Mullen	6.00	3.00	.60
☐ 308	Larry Patey	.08	.04	.01
☐ 309	Jorgen Pettersson	.14	.07	.01
☐ 310	Rob Ramage	.14	.07	.01
☐ 311	Brian Sutter	.14	.07	.01
☐ 312	Perry Turnbull	.14	.07	.01
☐ 313	Mike Zuke	.08	.04	.01
☐ 314	Toronto Scoring: Rick Vaive	.14	.07	.01
☐ 315	John Anderson	.08	.04	.01
☐ 316	Normand Aubin	.08	.04	.01
☐ 317	Jim Benning	.25	.12	.02
☐ 318	Fred Boimistruck	.08	.04	.01
☐ 319	Bill Derlago	.08	.04	.01
☐ 320	Bill Derlago IA	.08	.04	.01
☐ 321	Miroslav Frycer	.08	.04	.01
☐ 322	Billy Harris	.08	.04	.01
☐ 323	Jim Korn	.08	.04	.01
☐ 324	Michel Larocque	.20	.10	.02

		MINT	EXC	G-VG
☐ 325	Bob Manno	.08	.04	.01
☐ 326	Dan Maloney	.14	.07	.01
☐ 327	Bob McGill	.08	.04	.01
☐ 328	Barry Melrose	.08	.04	.01
☐ 329	Terry Martin	.08	.04	.01
☐ 330	Rene Robert	.14	.07	.01
☐ 331	Rocky Saganiuk	.08	.04	.01
☐ 332	Borje Salming	.20	.10	.02
☐ 333	Greg Terrion	.08	.04	.01
☐ 334	Vincent Tremblay	.08	.04	.01
☐ 335	Rick Vaive	.14	.07	.01
☐ 336	Rick Vaive IA	.14	.07	.01
☐ 337	Vancouver Canucks	.14	.07	.01
	Scoring Leaders:			
	Thomas Gradin			
☐ 338	Ivan Boldirev	.08	.04	.01
☐ 339	Richard Brodeur	.14	.07	.01
☐ 340	Richard Brodeur IA	.14	.07	.01
☐ 341	Tony Currie	.08	.04	.01
☐ 342	Marc Crawford	.08	.04	.01
☐ 343	Curt Fraser	.08	.04	.01
☐ 344	Thomas Gradin	.14	.07	.01
☐ 345	Thomas Gradin IA	.14	.07	.01
☐ 346	Ivan Hlinka UER	.14	.07	.01
	(Photo actually Jiri Bubla)			
☐ 347	Ron Delorme	.08	.04	.01
☐ 348	Rick Lanz	.08	.04	.01
☐ 349	Lars Lindgren	.08	.04	.01
☐ 350	Blair MacDonald	.08	.04	.01
☐ 351	Kevin McCarthy	.08	.04	.01
☐ 352	Gerry Minor	.08	.04	.01
☐ 353	Lars Molin	.08	.04	.01
☐ 354	Gary Lupul	.08	.04	.01
☐ 355	Darcy Rota	.08	.04	.01
☐ 356	Stan Smyl	.08	.04	.01
☐ 357	Harold Snepsts	.14	.07	.01
☐ 358	Dave Williams	.14	.07	.01
☐ 359	Washington Capitals	.14	.07	.01
	Scoring Leaders:			
	Dennis Maruk			
☐ 360	Ted Bulley	.08	.04	.01
☐ 361	Bob Carpenter	1.75	.85	.17
☐ 362	Brian Engblom	.08	.04	.01
☐ 363	Mike Gartner	1.00	.50	.10
☐ 364	Bengt Gustafsson	.14	.07	.01
☐ 365	Doug Hicks	.08	.04	.01
☐ 366	Ken Houston	.08	.04	.01
☐ 367	Doug Jarvis	.14	.07	.01
☐ 368	Rod Langway	.50	.25	.05
☐ 369	Dennis Maruk	.14	.07	.01
☐ 370	Dennis Maruk IA	.14	.07	.01
☐ 371	Dave Parro	.08	.04	.01
☐ 372	Pat Riggin	.20	.10	.02

		MINT	EXC	G-VG
☐ 373	Chris Valentine	.08	.04	.01
☐ 374	Winnipeg Jets Scoring Leaders: Dale Hawerchuk	1.50	.75	.15
☐ 375	Dave Babych	.20	.10	.02
☐ 376	Dave Babych IA	.14	.07	.01
☐ 377	Dave Christian	.14	.07	.01
☐ 378	Norm Dupont	.08	.04	.01
☐ 379	Lucien Deblois	.08	.04	.01
☐ 380	Dale Hawerchuk	12.50	6.25	1.25
☐ 381	Dale Hawerchuk IA	3.50	1.75	.35
☐ 382	Craig Levie	.14	.07	.01
☐ 383	Morris Lukowich	.14	.07	.01
☐ 384	Willy Lindstrom	.08	.04	.01
☐ 385	Bengt Lundholm	.08	.04	.01
☐ 386	Paul MacLean	.75	.35	.07
☐ 387	Bryan Maxwell	.08	.04	.01
☐ 388	Doug Smail	.60	.30	.06
☐ 389	Doug Soetaert	.14	.07	.01
☐ 390	Serge Savard	.50	.25	.05
☐ 391	Thomas Steen	1.75	.85	.17
☐ 392	Don Spring	.08	.04	.01
☐ 393	Ed Staniowski	.14	.07	.01
☐ 394	Tim Trimper	.08	.04	.01
☐ 395	Tim Walters	.08	.04	.01
☐ 396	Checklist 265-396	.50	.05	.01

1983-84 O-Pee-Chee

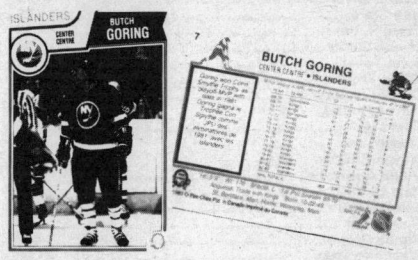

This 396-card set features players of the NHL. Cards measure 2¹/₂" by 3¹/₂". A 1983 copyright date is found on the backs of the cards. Backs are written in both French and English. Each team has a Highlight (HL) card featuring one or two players. The key rookie cards in this set are Brian Bellows, Phil Housley, Steve Larmer, Pelle Lindbergh, Mats Naslund, Bernie Nicholls, and Scott Stevens.

Ce jeu de 396 cartes représente des joueurs de la NHL. Les cartes mesurent 2¹/₂" x 3¹/₂". Le dos comporte l'année 1983 comme date de droit d'auteur, et est imprimé en français et en anglais. Chaque équipe a une carte des moments marquants (HL), mettant un ou deux joueurs en vedette. Les débutants importants de ce jeu sont Brian Bellows, Phil Housley, Steve Larmer, Pelle Lindbergh, Mats Naslund, Bernie Nicholls, et Scott Stevens.

			MINT	EXC	G-VG
		COMPLETE SET (396)	130.00	65.00	13.00
		COMMON PLAYER (1-396)	.08	.04	.01
☐	1	Islanders Leaders:	.75	.20	.04
		Mike Bossy			
☐	2	Islanders HL:	.30	.15	.03
		Denis Potvin			
☐	3	Mike Bossy....................	1.50	.75	.15
☐	4	Bob Bourne	.08	.04	.01
☐	5	Billy Carroll	.08	.04	.01
☐	6	Clark Gillies	.20	.10	.02
☐	7	Butch Goring	.14	.07	.01
☐	8	Mats Hallin	.08	.04	.01
☐	9	Tomas Jonsson	.08	.04	.01
☐	10	Gordie Lane	.08	.04	.01
☐	11	Dave Langevin	.08	.04	.01

			MINT	EXC	G-VG
☐	12	Rollie Melanson	.50	.25	.05
☐	13	Ken Morrow	.14	.07	.01
☐	14	Bob Nystrom	.14	.07	.01
☐	15	Stefan Persson	.14	.07	.01
☐	16	Denis Potvin	.75	.35	.07
☐	17	Billy Smith	.35	.17	.03
☐	18	Brent Sutter	.25	.12	.02
☐	19	Duane Sutter	.14	.07	.01
☐	20	John Tonelli	.20	.10	.02
☐	21	Bryan Trottier	.75	.35	.07
☐	22	Oilers Leaders: Wayne Gretzky	8.00	4.00	.80
☐	23	Oilers HL: Mark Messier Wayne Gretzky	12.00	6.00	1.20
☐	24	Glenn Anderson	.75	.35	.07
☐	25	Paul Coffey	6.00	3.00	.60
☐	26	Lee Fogolin	.08	.04	.01
☐	27	Grant Fuhr	4.00	2.00	.40
☐	28	Randy Gregg	.90	.45	.09
☐	29	Wayne Gretzky	21.00	10.50	2.10
☐	30	Charlie Huddy	.90	.45	.09
☐	31	Pat Hughes	.08	.04	.01
☐	32	Dave Hunter	.14	.07	.01
☐	33	Don Jackson	.08	.04	.01
☐	34	Jari Kurri	3.00	1.50	.30
☐	35	Willy Lindstrom	.08	.04	.01
☐	36	Ken Linseman	.14	.07	.01
☐	37	Kevin Lowe	.40	.20	.04
☐	38	Dave Lumley	.08	.04	.01
☐	39	Mark Messier	6.00	3.00	.60
☐	40	Andy Moog	2.50	1.25	.25
☐	41	Jaroslav Pouzar	.08	.04	.01
☐	42	Tom Roulston	.08	.04	.01
☐	43	Bruins Leaders: Rick Middleton	.14	.07	.01
☐	44	Bruins HL: Pete Peeters	.14	.07	.01
☐	45	Ray Bourque	5.00	2.50	.50
☐	46	Bruce Crowder	.08	.04	.01
☐	47	Keith Crowder	.08	.04	.01
☐	48	Luc Dufour	.08	.04	.01
☐	49	Tom Fergus	.08	.04	.01
☐	50	Steve Kasper	.14	.07	.01
☐	51	Gord Kluzak	.40	.20	.04
☐	52	Mike Krushelnyski	1.00	.50	.10
☐	53	Peter McNab	.08	.04	.01
☐	54	Rick Middleton	.25	.12	.02
☐	55	Mike Milbury	.14	.07	.01
☐	56	Mike O'Connell	.08	.04	.01
☐	57	Barry Pederson	.14	.07	.01
☐	58	Pete Peeters	.25	.12	.02
☐	59	Jim Schoenfeld	.14	.07	.01

			MINT	EXC	G-VG
☐	60	Sabres Leaders:	.14	.07	.01
		Tony McKegney			
☐	61	Sabres HL:	.14	.07	.01
		Bob Sauve			
☐	62	Real Cloutier	.08	.04	.01
☐	63	Mike Foligno	.08	.04	.01
☐	64	Bill Hajt	.08	.04	.01
☐	65	Phil Housley	6.50	3.25	.65
☐	66	Dale McCourt	.08	.04	.01
☐	67	Gilbert Perreault	.60	.30	.06
☐	68	Brent Peterson	.08	.04	.01
☐	69	Craig Ramsay	.08	.04	.01
☐	70	Mike Ramsey	.08	.04	.01
☐	71	Bob Sauve	.14	.07	.01
☐	72	Ric Seiling	.08	.04	.01
☐	73	John Van Boxmeer	.08	.04	.01
☐	74	Flames Leaders:	.14	.07	.01
		Lanny McDonald			
☐	75	Flames HL:	.14	.07	.01
		Lanny McDonald			
☐	76	Ed Beers	.25	.12	.02
☐	77	Steve Bozek	.08	.04	.01
☐	78	Guy Chouinard	.14	.07	.01
☐	79	Mike Eaves	.08	.04	.01
☐	80	Don Edwards	.14	.07	.01
☐	81	Kari Eloranta	.08	.04	.01
☐	82	Dave Hindmarch	.08	.04	.01
☐	83	Jamie Hislop	.08	.04	.01
☐	84	Jim Jackson	.08	.04	.01
☐	85	Steve Konroyd	.08	.04	.01
☐	86	Rejean Lemelin	.30	.15	.03
☐	87	Lanny McDonald	.35	.17	.03
☐	88	Greg Meredith	.08	.04	.01
☐	89	Kent Nilsson	.14	.07	.01
☐	90	Jim Peplinski	.08	.04	.01
☐	91	Paul Reinhart	.14	.07	.01
☐	92	Doug Risebrough	.14	.07	.01
☐	93	Steve Tambellini	.08	.04	.01
☐	94	Mickey Volcan	.08	.04	.01
☐	95	Blackhawks Leaders:	.14	.07	.01
		Al Secord			
☐	96	Blackhawks HL:	.40	.20	.04
		Denis Savard			
☐	97	Murray Bannerman	.14	.07	.01
☐	98	Keith Brown	.08	.04	.01
☐	99	Tony Esposito	.65	.30	.06
☐	100	Dave Feamster	.08	.04	.01
☐	101	Greg Fox	.08	.04	.01
☐	102	Curt Fraser	.08	.04	.01
☐	103	Bill Gardner	.08	.04	.01
☐	104	Tim Higgins	.08	.04	.01
☐	105	Steve Larmer UER	15.00	7.50	1.50
		(Photo actually Steve Ludzik)			

		MINT	EXC	G-VG
☐ 106	Steve Ludzik UER	3.00	1.50	.30
	(Photo actually Steve Larmer)			
☐ 107	Tom Lysiak	.14	.07	.01
☐ 108	Bob Murray	.08	.04	.01
☐ 109	Rick Paterson	.08	.04	.01
☐ 110	Rich Preston	.08	.04	.01
☐ 111	Denis Savard	2.50	1.25	.25
☐ 112	Al Secord	.14	.07	.01
☐ 113	Darryl Sutter	.14	.07	.01
☐ 114	Doug Wilson	.50	.25	.05
☐ 115	Red Wings Leaders:	.14	.07	.01
	John Ogrodnick			
☐ 116	Red Wings HL:	.14	.07	.01
	Corrado Micalef			
☐ 117	John Barrett	.08	.04	.01
☐ 118	Ivan Boldirev	.08	.04	.01
☐ 119	Colin Campbell	.08	.04	.01
☐ 120	Murray Craven	1.00	.50	.10
☐ 121	Ron Duguay	.14	.07	.01
☐ 122	Dwight Foster	.08	.04	.01
☐ 123	Danny Gare	.14	.07	.01
☐ 124	Ed Johnstone	.08	.04	.01
☐ 125	Reed Larson	.08	.04	.01
☐ 126	Corrado Micalef	.14	.07	.01
☐ 127	Eddie Mio	.14	.07	.01
☐ 128	John Ogrodnick	.14	.07	.01
☐ 129	Brad Park	.35	.17	.03
☐ 130	Greg Smith	.08	.04	.01
☐ 131	Ken Solheim	.08	.04	.01
☐ 132	Bob Manno	.08	.04	.01
☐ 133	Paul Woods	.08	.04	.01
☐ 134	Checklist 1-132	.45	.05	.01
☐ 135	Whalers Leaders:	.14	.07	.01
	Blaine Stoughton			
☐ 136	Whalers HL:	.14	.07	.01
	Blaine Stoughton			
☐ 137	Richie Dunn	.08	.04	.01
☐ 138	Ron Francis	3.50	1.75	.35
☐ 139	Marty Howe	.14	.07	.01
☐ 140	Mark Johnson	.14	.07	.01
☐ 141	Paul Lawless	.08	.04	.01
☐ 142	Merlin Malinowski	.08	.04	.01
☐ 143	Greg Millen	.14	.07	.01
☐ 144	Ray Neufeld	.08	.04	.01
☐ 145	Joel Quenneville	.08	.04	.01
☐ 146	Risto Siltanen	.08	.04	.01
☐ 147	Blaine Stoughton	.14	.07	.01
☐ 148	Doug Sulliman	.08	.04	.01
☐ 149	Bob Sullivan	.08	.04	.01
☐ 150	Kings Leaders:	.40	.20	.04
	Marcel Dionne			
☐ 151	Kings HL:	.40	.20	.04
	Marcel Dionne			

		MINT	EXC	G-VG
☐ 152	Marcel Dionne	1.00	.50	.10
☐ 153	Daryl Evans	.08	.04	.01
☐ 154	Jim Fox	.08	.04	.01
☐ 155	Mark Hardy	.08	.04	.01
☐ 156	Gary Laskoski	.08	.04	.01
☐ 157	Kevin Lavallee	.08	.04	.01
☐ 158	Dave Lewis	.08	.04	.01
☐ 159	Larry Murphy	.14	.07	.01
☐ 160	Bernie Nicholls	16.00	8.00	1.60
☐ 161	Terry Ruskowski	.14	.07	.01
☐ 162	Charlie Simmer	.20	.10	.02
☐ 163	Dave Taylor	.25	.12	.02
☐ 164	North Stars Leaders: Dino Ciccarelli	.20	.10	.02
☐ 165	North Stars HL: Brian Bellows	1.00	.50	.10
☐ 166	Don Beaupre	.20	.10	.02
☐ 167	Brian Bellows	10.00	5.00	1.00
☐ 168	Neal Broten	.75	.35	.07
☐ 169	Steve Christoff	.08	.04	.01
☐ 170	Dino Ciccarelli	.75	.35	.07
☐ 171	George Ferguson	.08	.04	.01
☐ 172	Craig Hartsburg	.08	.04	.01
☐ 173	Al MacAdam	.08	.04	.01
☐ 174	Dennis Maruk	.14	.07	.01
☐ 175	Brad Maxwell	.08	.04	.01
☐ 176	Tom McCarthy	.08	.04	.01
☐ 177	Gilles Meloche	.14	.07	.01
☐ 178	Steve Payne	.08	.04	.01
☐ 179	Willi Plett	.08	.04	.01
☐ 180	Gordie Roberts	.08	.04	.01
☐ 181	Bobby Smith	.30	.15	.03
☐ 182	Canadiens Leaders: Mark Napier	.14	.07	.01
☐ 183	Canadiens HL: Guy Lafleur	.40	.20	.04
☐ 184	Keith Acton	.08	.04	.01
☐ 185	Guy Carbonneau	1.25	.60	.12
☐ 186	Gilbert Delorme	.08	.04	.01
☐ 187	Bob Gainey	.30	.15	.03
☐ 188	Rick Green	.14	.07	.01
☐ 189	Guy Lafleur	1.50	.75	.15
☐ 190	Craig Ludwig	.50	.25	.05
☐ 191	Pierre Mondou	.08	.04	.01
☐ 192	Mark Napier	.14	.07	.01
☐ 193	Mats Naslund	3.50	1.75	.35
☐ 194	Chris Nilan	.60	.30	.06
☐ 195	Larry Robinson	.40	.20	.04
☐ 196	Bill Root	.08	.04	.01
☐ 197	Richard Sevigny	.14	.07	.01
☐ 198	Steve Shutt	.30	.15	.03
☐ 199	Mario Tremblay	.14	.07	.01
☐ 200	Ryan Walter	.14	.07	.01

		MINT	EXC	G-VG
☐ 201	Rick Wamsley	.14	.07	.01
☐ 202	Doug Wickenheiser	.14	.07	.01
☐ 203	Hart Trophy (Wayne Gretzky)	6.00	3.00	.60
☐ 204	Ross Trophy (Wayne Gretzky)	6.00	3.00	.60
☐ 205	Lady Byng Trophy (Mike Bossy)	.85	.40	.08
☐ 206	Calder Trophy (Steve Larmer)	2.50	1.25	.25
☐ 207	Norris Trophy (Rod Langway)	.20	.10	.02
☐ 208	Masterton Trophy (Lanny McDonald)	.25	.12	.02
☐ 209	Vezina Trophy (Pete Peeters)	.20	.10	.02
☐ 210	Mike Bossy RB Scores 50 goals, first six seasons	.65	.30	.06
☐ 211	Marcel Dionne RB Scores 100 points in seven seasons	.40	.20	.04
☐ 212	Wayne Gretzky RB Scores in 30 consecutive games	6.00	3.00	.60
☐ 213	Pat Hughes RB Two short-handed goals within 25 seconds	.14	.07	.01
☐ 214	Rick Middleton RB 19 points in one playoff series	.14	.07	.01
☐ 215	Goal Leaders Wayne Gretzky	6.00	3.00	.60
☐ 216	Assists Leaders Wayne Gretzky	6.00	3.00	.60
☐ 217	Scoring Leaders Wayne Gretzky	6.00	3.00	.60
☐ 218	Game Winning Goal Leaders Brian Propp	.20	.10	.02
☐ 219	Power Play Goal Leaders Paul Gardner Al Secord	.14	.07	.01
☐ 220	Penalty Min. Leaders Randy Holt	.14	.07	.01
☐ 221	Goals Against Average Leaders Pete Peeters	.20	.10	.02
☐ 222	Shutout Leaders Pete Peeters	.20	.10	.02
☐ 223	Devils Leaders: Steve Tambellini	.14	.07	.01
☐ 224	Devils HL: Don Lever	.14	.07	.01
☐ 225	Brent Ashton	.08	.04	.01
☐ 226	Mel Bridgman	.08	.04	.01
☐ 227	Aaron Broten	.08	.04	.01

		MINT	EXC	G-VG
☐ 228	Murray Brumwell	.08	.04	.01
☐ 229	Garry Howatt	.08	.04	.01
☐ 230	Jeff Larmer	.08	.04	.01
☐ 231	Don Lever	.08	.04	.01
☐ 232	Bob Lorimer	.08	.04	.01
☐ 233	Ron Low	.14	.07	.01
☐ 234	Bob MacMillan	.14	.07	.01
☐ 235	Hector Marini	.08	.04	.01
☐ 236	Glenn Resch	.30	.15	.03
☐ 237	Phil Russell	.08	.04	.01
☐ 238	Rangers Leaders: Mark Pavelich	.14	.07	.01
☐ 239	Rangers HL: Mark Pavelich	.14	.07	.01
☐ 240	Bill Baker	.08	.04	.01
☐ 241	Barry Beck	.14	.07	.01
☐ 242	Mike Blaisdell	.08	.04	.01
☐ 243	Nick Fotiu	.08	.04	.01
☐ 244	Robbie Ftorek	.14	.07	.01
☐ 245	Anders Hedberg	.14	.07	.01
☐ 246	Willie Huber	.08	.04	.01
☐ 247	Tom Laidlaw	.08	.04	.01
☐ 248	Mikko Leinonen	.14	.07	.01
☐ 249	Dave Maloney	.14	.07	.01
☐ 250	Don Maloney	.14	.07	.01
☐ 251	Rob McClanahan	.08	.04	.01
☐ 252	Mark Osborne	.14	.07	.01
☐ 253	Mark Pavelich	.14	.07	.01
☐ 254	Mike Rogers	.14	.07	.01
☐ 255	Reijo Ruotsalainen	.14	.07	.01
☐ 256	Checklist 133-264	.45	.05	.01
☐ 257	Flyers Leaders: Darryl Sittler	.25	.12	.02
☐ 258	Flyers HL: Darryl Sittler	.25	.12	.02
☐ 259	Ray Allison	.08	.04	.01
☐ 260	Bill Barber	.40	.20	.04
☐ 261	Lindsay Carson	.08	.04	.01
☐ 262	Bobby Clarke	.80	.40	.08
☐ 263	Doug Crossman	.14	.07	.01
☐ 264	Ron Flockhart	.08	.04	.01
☐ 265	Bob Froese	1.50	.75	.15
☐ 266	Paul Holmgren	.14	.07	.01
☐ 267	Mark Howe	.25	.12	.02
☐ 268	Pelle Lindbergh	13.50	6.00	1.00
☐ 269	Brad Marsh	.14	.07	.01
☐ 270	Brad McCrimmon	.14	.07	.01
☐ 271	Brian Propp	.40	.20	.04
☐ 272	Darryl Sittler	.35	.17	.03
☐ 273	Mark Taylor	.08	.04	.01
☐ 274	Penguins Leaders: Rick Kehoe	.14	.07	.01

		MINT	EXC	G-VG
☐ 275	Penguins HL: .... Paul Gardner	.14	.07	.01
☐ 276	Pat Boutette	.08	.04	.01
☐ 277	Mike Bullard	.20	.10	.02
☐ 278	Randy Carlyle	.14	.07	.01
☐ 279	Michel Dion	.14	.07	.01
☐ 280	Paul Gardner	.14	.07	.01
☐ 281	Dave Hannan..............................	.08	.04	.01
☐ 282	Rick Kehoe.................................	.14	.07	.01
☐ 283	Randy Boyd	.08	.04	.01
☐ 284	Greg Malone	.08	.04	.01
☐ 285	Doug Shedden	.20	.10	.02
☐ 286	Andre St. Laurent	.08	.04	.01
☐ 287	Nordiques Leaders: .... Michel Goulet	.25	.12	.02
☐ 288	Nordiques HL: .... Michel Goulet	.30	.15	.03
☐ 289	Pierre Aubrey.............................	.08	.04	.01
☐ 290	Dan Bouchard	.14	.07	.01
☐ 291	Alain Cote	.08	.04	.01
☐ 292	Michel Goulet	.60	.30	.06
☐ 293	Dale Hunter	.14	.07	.01
☐ 294	Rick Lapointe	.08	.04	.01
☐ 295	Mario Marois	.08	.04	.01
☐ 296	Tony McKegney	.08	.04	.01
☐ 297	Randy Moller	.14	.07	.01
☐ 298	Wilf Paiement	.08	.04	.01
☐ 299	Dave Pichette	.08	.04	.01
☐ 300	Normand Rochefort......................	.08	.04	.01
☐ 301	Louis Sleigher	.08	.04	.01
☐ 302	Anton Stastny	.14	.07	.01
☐ 303	Marian Stastny	.14	.07	.01
☐ 304	Peter Stastny.............................	2.50	1.25	.25
☐ 305	Marc Tardif.................................	.14	.07	.01
☐ 306	Wally Weir	.08	.04	.01
☐ 307	Blake Wesley	.08	.04	.01
☐ 308	Blues Leaders: .... Brian Sutter	.14	.07	.01
☐ 309	Blues HL: .... Mike Liut	.14	.07	.01
☐ 310	Wayne Babych	.08	.04	.01
☐ 311	Jack Brownschidle	.08	.04	.01
☐ 312	Mike Crombeen	.08	.04	.01
☐ 313	Andre Dore	.08	.04	.01
☐ 314	Blake Dunlop	.08	.04	.01
☐ 315	Bernie Federko	.20	.10	.02
☐ 316	Mike Liut....................................	.30	.15	.03
☐ 317	Joe Mullen	1.25	.60	.12
☐ 318	Jorgen Pettersson	.14	.07	.01
☐ 319	Rob Ramage	.14	.07	.01
☐ 320	Brian Sutter	.14	.07	.01
☐ 321	Perry Turnbull	.14	.07	.01
☐ 322	Mike Zuke	.08	.04	.01

		MINT	EXC	G-VG
☐ 323	**Maple Leafs Leaders:**	.14	.07	.01
	Rick Vaive			
☐ 324	**Maple Leafs HL:**	.14	.07	.01
	Rick Vaive			
☐ 325	**John Anderson**	.08	.04	.01
☐ 326	**Jim Benning**	.08	.04	.01
☐ 327	**Bill Derlago**	.08	.04	.01
☐ 328	**Dan Daoust**	.08	.04	.01
☐ 329	**Dave Farrish**	.08	.04	.01
☐ 330	**Miroslav Frycer**	.08	.04	.01
☐ 331	**Stewart Gavin**	.50	.25	.05
☐ 332	**Gaston Gingras**	.08	.04	.01
☐ 333	**Billy Harris**	.08	.04	.01
☐ 334	**Peter Inhacek**	.08	.04	.01
☐ 335	**Jim Korn**	.08	.04	.01
☐ 336	**Terry Martin**	.08	.04	.01
☐ 337	**Frank Nigro**	.08	.04	.01
☐ 338	**Mike Palmateer**	.14	.07	.01
☐ 339	**Walt Poddubny**	1.75	.85	.17
☐ 340	**Rick St. Croix**	.08	.04	.01
☐ 341	**Borje Salming**	.20	.10	.02
☐ 342	**Greg Terrion**	.08	.04	.01
☐ 343	**Rick Vaive**	.14	.07	.01
☐ 344	**Canucks Leaders:**	.14	.07	.01
	Darcy Rota			
☐ 345	**Canucks HL:**	.14	.07	.01
	Darcy Rota			
☐ 346	**Richard Brodeur**	.14	.07	.01
☐ 347	**Jiri Bubla**	.20	.10	.02
☐ 348	**Ron Delorme**	.08	.04	.01
☐ 349	**John Garrett**	.14	.07	.01
☐ 350	**Thomas Gradin**	.14	.07	.01
☐ 351	**Doug Halward**	.08	.04	.01
☐ 352	**Mark Kirton**	.08	.04	.01
☐ 353	**Rick Lanz**	.08	.04	.01
☐ 354	**Lars Lindgren**	.08	.04	.01
☐ 355	**Gary Lupul**	.08	.04	.01
☐ 356	**Kevin McCarthy**	.08	.04	.01
☐ 357	**Jim Nill**	.08	.04	.01
☐ 358	**Darcy Rota**	.08	.04	.01
☐ 359	**Stan Smyl**	.14	.07	.01
☐ 360	**Harold Snepsts**	.14	.07	.01
☐ 361	**Patrik Sundstrom**	1.75	.85	.17
☐ 362	**Tony Tanti**	1.75	.85	.17
☐ 363	**Dave Williams**	.14	.07	.01
☐ 364	**Capitals Leaders:**	.30	.15	.03
	Mike Gartner			
☐ 365	**Capitals HL:**	.20	.10	.02
	Rod Langway			
☐ 366	**Bob Carpenter**	.35	.17	.03
☐ 367	**Dave Christian**	.14	.07	.01
☐ 368	**Brian Engblom**	.08	.04	.01
☐ 369	**Mike Gartner**	.60	.30	.06

		MINT	EXC	G-VG
□ 370	Bengt Gustafsson	.08	.04	.01
□ 371	Ken Houston	.08	.04	.01
□ 372	Doug Jarvis	.14	.07	.01
□ 373	Al Jensen	.35	.17	.03
□ 374	Rod Langway	.40	.20	.04
□ 375	Craig Laughlin	.08	.04	.01
□ 376	Scott Stevens	7.50	3.75	.75
□ 377	Jets Leaders:	.35	.17	.03
	Dale Hawerchuk			
□ 378	Jets HL:	.14	.07	.01
	Lucien Deblois			
□ 379	Scott Arniel	.30	.15	.03
□ 380	Dave Babych	.14	.07	.01
□ 381	Laurie Boschman	.08	.04	.01
□ 382	Wade Campbell	.08	.04	.01
□ 383	Lucien Deblois	.08	.04	.01
□ 384	Murray Eaves	.08	.04	.01
□ 385	Dale Hawerchuk	3.50	1.75	.35
□ 386	Morris Lukowich	.08	.04	.01
□ 387	Bengt Lundholm	.08	.04	.01
□ 388	Paul MacLean	.25	.12	.02
□ 389	Brian Mullen	1.25	.60	.12
□ 390	Doug Smail	.14	.07	.01
□ 391	Doug Soetaert	.14	.07	.01
□ 392	Don Spring	.08	.04	.01
□ 393	Thomas Steen	.14	.07	.01
□ 394	Tim Watters	.08	.04	.01
□ 395	Tim Young	.08	.04	.01
□ 396	Checklist 265-396	.45	.05	.01

1984-85 O-Pee-Chee

This 396-card set features players of the NHL. Cards measure 2½" by 3½". A 1984 copyright date is found on the backs of the cards. Backs are written in both French and English. Backs are printed in blue, pink, and purple on off-white card stock. All-Stars are featured on cards 207-218. Cards 352-372 feature each team's leading goal scorer on the front and team individual scoring statistics on the back. The key rookie cards in this set are Tom Barrasso, Chris Chelios, Doug Gilmour, Pat LaFontaine, Gary Leeman, Cam Neely, Pat Verbeek, and Steve Yzerman.

Ce jeu de 396 cartes représente des joueurs de la NHL. Les cartes mesurent 2½" x 3½". Le dos comporte l'année 1984 comme date de droit d'auteur, et est imprimé en français et en anglais en encre bleu, rose et pourpre sur une pâte couleur blanc-cassé. Les cartes 207-218 représentent les All-Stars. Les cartes 352-372 représentent, du côté face, le joueur marquant le plus de buts pour son équipe, et, au dos, les statistiques des buts individuels des joueurs de l'équipe. Les débutants importants de ce jeu sont Tom Barrasso, Chris Chelios, Doug Gilmour, Pat LaFontaine, Gary Leeman, Cam Neely, Pat Verbeek, et Steve Yzerman.

			MINT	EXC	G-VG
	COMPLETE SET (396)		165.00	75.00	15.00
	COMMON PLAYER (1-396)		.08	.04	.01
☐	1	Ray Bourque	4.00	1.00	.20
☐	2	Keith Crowder	.08	.04	.01
☐	3	Luc Dufour	.08	.04	.01
☐	4	Tom Fergus	.08	.04	.01
☐	5	Doug Keans	.30	.15	.03
☐	6	Gord Kluzak	.14	.07	.01
☐	7	Ken Linseman	.14	.07	.01
☐	8	Nevin Markwart	.08	.04	.01
☐	9	Rick Middleton	.25	.12	.02

			MINT	EXC	G-VG
☐	10	Mike Milbury	.14	.07	.01
☐	11	Jim Nill	.08	.04	.01
☐	12	Mike O'Connell	.08	.04	.01
☐	13	Terry O'Reilly	.20	.10	.02
☐	14	Barry Pederson	.14	.07	.01
☐	15	Pete Peeters	.20	.10	.02
☐	16	Dave Silk	.14	.07	.01
☐	17	Dave Andreychuk	2.50	1.25	.25
☐	18	Tom Barrasso	4.50	2.25	.45
☐	19	Real Cloutier	.08	.04	.01
☐	20	Mike Foligno	.08	.04	.01
☐	21	Bill Hajt	.08	.04	.01
☐	22	Gilles Hamel	.08	.04	.01
☐	23	Phil Housley	.75	.35	.07
☐	24	Gilbert Perreault	.45	.22	.04
☐	25	Brent Peterson	.08	.04	.01
☐	26	Larry Playfair	.08	.04	.01
☐	27	Craig Ramsay	.08	.04	.01
☐	28	Mike Ramsey	.08	.04	.01
☐	29	Lindy Ruff	.08	.04	.01
☐	30	Bob Sauve	.14	.07	.01
☐	31	Ric Seiling	.08	.04	.01
☐	32	Murray Bannerman	.14	.07	.01
☐	33	Keith Brown	.08	.04	.01
☐	34	Curt Fraser	.08	.04	.01
☐	35	Bill Gardner	.08	.04	.01
☐	36	Jeff Larmer	.08	.04	.01
☐	37	Steve Larmer	4.00	2.00	.40
☐	38	Steve Ludzik	.08	.04	.01
☐	39	Tom Lysiak	.14	.07	.01
☐	40	Bob MacMillan	.14	.07	.01
☐	41	Bob Murray	.08	.04	.01
☐	42	Troy Murray	1.00	.50	.10
☐	43	Jack O'Callahan	.14	.07	.01
☐	44	Rick Paterson	.08	.04	.01
☐	45	Denis Savard	1.50	.75	.15
☐	46	Al Secord	.14	.07	.01
☐	47	Darryl Sutter	.14	.07	.01
☐	48	Doug Wilson	.35	.17	.03
☐	49	John Barrett	.14	.07	.01
☐	50	Ivan Boldirev	.08	.04	.01
☐	51	Colin Campbell	.08	.04	.01
☐	52	Ron Duguay	.14	.07	.01
☐	53	Dwight Foster	.08	.04	.01
☐	54	Danny Gare	.14	.07	.01
☐	55	Ed Johnstone	.08	.04	.01
☐	56	Kelly Kisio	.85	.40	.08
☐	57	Lane Lambert	.08	.04	.01
☐	58	Reed Larson	.08	.04	.01
☐	59	Bob Manno	.08	.04	.01
☐	60	Randy Ladouceur	.08	.04	.01
☐	61	Eddie Mio	.14	.07	.01
☐	62	John Ogrodnick	.14	.07	.01

			MINT	EXC	G-VG
☐	63	Brad Park	.35	.17	.03
☐	64	Greg Smith	.08	.04	.01
☐	65	Greg Stefan	.60	.30	.06
☐	66	Paul Woods	.08	.04	.01
☐	67	Steve Yzerman	45.00	22.50	4.50
☐	68	Bob Crawford	.14	.07	.01
☐	69	Richie Dunn	.08	.04	.01
☐	70	Ron Francis	1.75	.85	.17
☐	71	Marty Howe	.14	.07	.01
☐	72	Mark Johnson	.14	.07	.01
☐	73	Chris Kotsopoulos	.08	.04	.01
☐	74	Greg Malone	.08	.04	.01
☐	75	Greg Millen	.14	.07	.01
☐	76	Ray Neufeld	.08	.04	.01
☐	77	Joel Quenneville	.08	.04	.01
☐	78	Risto Siltanen	.08	.04	.01
☐	79	Sylvain Turgeon	.85	.40	.08
☐	80	Mike Zuke	.08	.04	.01
☐	81	Steve Christoff	.08	.04	.01
☐	82	Marcel Dionne	.80	.40	.08
☐	83	Brian Engblom	.08	.04	.01
☐	84	Jim Fox	.08	.04	.01
☐	85	Anders Hakansson	.08	.04	.01
☐	86	Mark Hardy	.08	.04	.01
☐	87	Brian MacLellan	.35	.17	.03
☐	88	Bernie Nicholls	5.00	2.50	.50
☐	89	Terry Ruskowski	.14	.07	.01
☐	90	Charlie Simmer	.14	.07	.01
☐	91	Doug Smith	.08	.04	.01
☐	92	Dave Taylor	.20	.10	.02
☐	93	Keith Acton	.08	.04	.01
☐	94	Don Beaupre	.20	.10	.02
☐	95	Brian Bellows	2.25	1.10	.22
☐	96	Neal Broten	.40	.20	.04
☐	97	Dino Ciccarelli	.40	.20	.04
☐	98	Craig Hartsburg	.08	.04	.01
☐	99	Tom Hirsch	.08	.04	.01
☐	100	Paul Holmgren	.14	.07	.01
☐	101	Dennis Maruk	.14	.07	.01
☐	102	Brad Maxwell	.08	.04	.01
☐	103	Tom McCarthy	.08	.04	.01
☐	104	Gilles Meloche	.14	.07	.01
☐	105	Mark Napier	.14	.07	.01
☐	106	Steve Payne	.08	.04	.01
☐	107	Gordie Roberts	.08	.04	.01
☐	108	Harold Snepsts	.14	.07	.01
☐	109	Mel Bridgman	.08	.04	.01
☐	110	Joe Cirella	.14	.07	.01
☐	111	Tim Higgins	.08	.04	.01
☐	112	Don Lever	.08	.04	.01
☐	113	Dave Lewis	.08	.04	.01
☐	114	Bob Lorimer	.08	.04	.01
☐	115	Ron Low	.14	.07	.01

		MINT	EXC	G-VG
☐ 116	Jan Ludvig	.08	.04	.01
☐ 117	Gary McAdam	.08	.04	.01
☐ 118	Rich Preston	.08	.04	.01
☐ 119	Glenn Resch	.30	.15	.03
☐ 120	Phil Russell	.08	.04	.01
☐ 121	Pat Verbeek	5.00	2.50	.50
☐ 122	Mike Bossy	1.25	.60	.12
☐ 123	Bob Bourne	.08	.04	.01
☐ 124	Pat Flatley	.65	.30	.06
☐ 125	Greg Gilbert	.65	.30	.06
☐ 126	Clark Gillies	.20	.10	.02
☐ 127	Butch Goring	.14	.07	.01
☐ 128	Tomas Jonsson	.08	.04	.01
☐ 129	Pat LaFontaine	20.00	10.00	2.00
☐ 130	Rollie Melanson	.14	.07	.01
☐ 131	Ken Morrow	.14	.07	.01
☐ 132	Bob Nystrom	.14	.07	.01
☐ 133	Stefan Persson	.14	.07	.01
☐ 134	Denis Potvin	.65	.30	.06
☐ 135	Billy Smith	.30	.15	.03
☐ 136	Brent Sutter	.20	.10	.02
☐ 137	Duane Sutter	.14	.07	.01
☐ 138	John Tonelli	.20	.10	.02
☐ 139	Bryan Trottier	.75	.35	.07
☐ 140	Barry Beck	.14	.07	.01
☐ 141	Ron Greschner	.14	.07	.01
☐ 142	Glen Hanlon	.14	.07	.01
☐ 143	Anders Hedberg	.14	.07	.01
☐ 144	Tom Laidlaw	.08	.04	.01
☐ 145	Pierre Larouche	.14	.07	.01
☐ 146	Dave Maloney	.14	.07	.01
☐ 147	Don Maloney	.14	.07	.01
☐ 148	Mark Osborne	.08	.04	.01
☐ 149	Larry Patey	.08	.04	.01
☐ 150	James Patrick	1.00	.50	.10
☐ 151	Mark Pavelich	.14	.07	.01
☐ 152	Mike Rogers	.14	.07	.01
☐ 153	Reijo Ruotsalainen	.14	.07	.01
☐ 154	Blaine Stoughton	.14	.07	.01
☐ 155	Peter Sundstrom	.45	.22	.04
☐ 156	Bill Barber	.30	.15	.03
☐ 157	Doug Crossman	.14	.07	.01
☐ 158	Thomas Eriksson	.08	.04	.01
☐ 159	Bob Froese	.35	.17	.03
☐ 160	Paul Guay	.08	.04	.01
☐ 161	Mark Howe	.35	.17	.03
☐ 162	Tim Kerr	.25	.12	.02
☐ 163	Brad Marsh	.14	.07	.01
☐ 164	Brad McCrimmon	.14	.07	.01
☐ 165	Dave Poulin	1.00	.50	.10
☐ 166	Brian Propp	.35	.17	.03
☐ 167	Ilkka Sinisalo	.75	.35	.07
☐ 168	Darryl Sittler	.35	.17	.03

		MINT	EXC	G-VG
☐ 169	Rich Sutter	.35	.17	.03
☐ 170	Ron Sutter	.50	.25	.05
☐ 171	Pat Boutette	.08	.04	.01
☐ 172	Mike Bullard	.14	.07	.01
☐ 173	Michel Dion	.14	.07	.01
☐ 174	Ron Flockhart	.08	.04	.01
☐ 175	Greg Fox	.08	.04	.01
☐ 176	Denis Herron	.14	.07	.01
☐ 177	Rick Kehoe	.14	.07	.01
☐ 178	Kevin McCarthy	.08	.04	.01
☐ 179	Tom Roulston	.08	.04	.01
☐ 180	Mark Taylor	.08	.04	.01
☐ 181	Wayne Babych	.08	.04	.01
☐ 182	Tim Bothwell	.14	.07	.01
☐ 183	Kevin Lavallee	.08	.04	.01
☐ 184	Bernie Federko	.20	.10	.02
☐ 185	Doug Gilmour	3.00	1.50	.30
☐ 186	Terry Johnson	.08	.04	.01
☐ 187	Mike Liut	.25	.12	.02
☐ 188	Joey Mullen	.60	.30	.06
☐ 189	Jorgen Pettersson	.14	.07	.01
☐ 190	Rob Ramage	.14	.07	.01
☐ 191	Dwight Schofield	.08	.04	.01
☐ 192	Brian Sutter	.14	.07	.01
☐ 193	Doug Wickenheiser	.08	.04	.01
☐ 194	Bob Carpenter	.20	.10	.02
☐ 195	Dave Christian	.14	.07	.01
☐ 196	Bob Gould	.08	.04	.01
☐ 197	Mike Gartner	.40	.20	.04
☐ 198	Bengt Gustafsson	.08	.04	.01
☐ 199	Alan Haworth	.08	.04	.01
☐ 200	Doug Jarvis	.14	.07	.01
☐ 201	Al Jensen	.14	.07	.01
☐ 202	Rod Langway	.20	.10	.02
☐ 203	Craig Laughlin	.08	.04	.01
☐ 204	Larry Murphy	.14	.07	.01
☐ 205	Pat Riggin	.14	.07	.01
☐ 206	Scott Stevens	1.25	.60	.12
☐ 207	Michel Goulet AS	.30	.15	.03
☐ 208	Wayne Gretzky AS	6.00	3.00	.60
☐ 209	Mike Bossy AS	.75	.35	.07
☐ 210	Rod Langway AS	.20	.10	.02
☐ 211	Ray Bourque AS	2.00	1.00	.20
☐ 212	Tom Barrasso AS	.45	.22	.04
☐ 213	Mark Messier AS	2.00	1.00	.20
☐ 214	Bryan Trottier AS	.35	.17	.03
☐ 215	Jari Kurri AS	.75	.35	.07
☐ 216	Denis Potvin AS	.45	.22	.04
☐ 217	Paul Coffey AS	1.75	.85	.17
☐ 218	Pat Riggin AS	.14	.07	.01
☐ 219	Ed Beers	.08	.04	.01
☐ 220	Steve Bozek	.08	.04	.01
☐ 221	Mike Eaves	.08	.04	.01

			MINT	EXC	G-VG
☐ 222	Don Edwards		.14	.07	.01
☐ 223	Kari Eloranta		.08	.04	.01
☐ 224	Dave Hindmarch		.08	.04	.01
☐ 225	Jim Jackson		.08	.04	.01
☐ 226	Steve Konroyd		.08	.04	.01
☐ 227	Richard Kromm		.08	.04	.01
☐ 228	Rejean Lemelin		.25	.12	.02
☐ 229	Hakan Loob		1.50	.75	.15
☐ 230	Jamie Macoun		.60	.30	.06
☐ 231	Lanny McDonald		.30	.15	.03
☐ 232	Kent Nilsson		.14	.07	.01
☐ 233	Jim Peplinski		.08	.04	.01
☐ 234	Dan Quinn		1.25	.60	.12
☐ 235	Paul Reinhart		.14	.07	.01
☐ 236	Doug Risebrough		.14	.07	.01
☐ 237	Steve Tambellini		.08	.04	.01
☐ 238	Glenn Anderson		.50	.25	.05
☐ 239	Paul Coffey		3.00	1.50	.30
☐ 240	Lee Fogolin		.08	.04	.01
☐ 241	Grant Fuhr		2.00	1.00	.20
☐ 242	Randy Gregg		.20	.10	.02
☐ 243	Wayne Gretzky		16.00	8.00	1.60
☐ 244	Charlie Huddy		.20	.10	.02
☐ 245	Pat Hughes		.08	.04	.01
☐ 246	Dave Hunter		.14	.07	.01
☐ 247	Don Jackson		.08	.04	.01
☐ 248	Mike Krushelnyski		.20	.10	.02
☐ 249	Jari Kurri		2.00	1.00	.20
☐ 250	Willy Lindstrom		.08	.04	.01
☐ 251	Kevin Lowe		.25	.12	.02
☐ 252	Dave Lumley		.08	.04	.01
☐ 253	Kevin McClelland		.08	.04	.01
☐ 254	Mark Messier		4.00	2.00	.40
☐ 255	Andy Moog		1.25	.60	.12
☐ 256	Jaroslav Pouzar		.08	.04	.01
☐ 257	Guy Carbonneau		.25	.12	.02
☐ 258	John Chabot		.25	.12	.02
☐ 259	Chris Chelios		12.00	6.00	1.20
☐ 260	Lucien Deblois		.08	.04	.01
☐ 261	Bob Gainey		.25	.12	.02
☐ 262	Rick Green		.08	.04	.01
☐ 263	Jean Hamel		.08	.04	.01
☐ 264	Guy Lafleur		1.00	.50	.10
☐ 265	Craig Ludwig		.14	.07	.01
☐ 266	Pierre Mondou		.08	.04	.01
☐ 267	Mats Naslund		.50	.25	.05
☐ 268	Chris Nilan		.20	.10	.02
☐ 269	Steve Penney		.35	.17	.03
☐ 270	Larry Robinson		.35	.17	.03
☐ 271	Bill Root		.08	.04	.01
☐ 272	Steve Shutt		.25	.12	.02
☐ 273	Bobby Smith		.20	.10	.02
☐ 274	Mario Tremblay		.14	.07	.01

		MINT	EXC	G-VG
☐ 275	Ryan Walter	.14	.07	.01
☐ 276	Bo Berglund	.08	.04	.01
☐ 277	Dan Bouchard	.14	.07	.01
☐ 278	Alain Cote	.08	.04	.01
☐ 279	Andre Dore	.08	.04	.01
☐ 280	Michel Goulet	.40	.20	.04
☐ 281	Dale Hunter	.14	.07	.01
☐ 282	Mario Marois	.08	.04	.01
☐ 283	Tony McKegney	.08	.04	.01
☐ 284	Randy Moller	.08	.04	.01
☐ 285	Wilf Paiement	.08	.04	.01
☐ 286	Pat Price	.08	.04	.01
☐ 287	Normand Rochefort	.08	.04	.01
☐ 288	Andre Savard	.08	.04	.01
☐ 289	Richard Sevigny	.14	.07	.01
☐ 290	Louis Sleigher	.08	.04	.01
☐ 291	Anton Stastny	.14	.07	.01
☐ 292	Marian Stastny	.14	.07	.01
☐ 293	Peter Stastny	1.50	.75	.15
☐ 294	Blake Wesley	.08	.04	.01
☐ 295	John Anderson	.08	.04	.01
☐ 296	Jim Benning	.08	.04	.01
☐ 297	Allan Bester	.60	.30	.06
☐ 298	Rich Costello	.08	.04	.01
☐ 299	Dan Daoust	.08	.04	.01
☐ 300	Bill Derlago	.08	.04	.01
☐ 301	Dave Farrish	.08	.04	.01
☐ 302	Stewart Gavin	.14	.07	.01
☐ 303	Gaston Gingras	.08	.04	.01
☐ 304	Jim Korn	.08	.04	.01
☐ 305	Gary Leeman	3.00	1.50	.30
☐ 306	Terry Martin	.08	.04	.01
☐ 307	Gary Nylund	.08	.04	.01
☐ 308	Mike Palmateer	.14	.07	.01
☐ 309	Walt Poddubny	.14	.07	.01
☐ 310	Rick St. Croix	.08	.04	.01
☐ 311	Borje Salming	.20	.10	.02
☐ 312	Greg Terrion	.08	.04	.01
☐ 313	Rick Vaive	.14	.07	.01
☐ 314	Richard Brodeur	.14	.07	.01
☐ 315	Jiri Bubla	.14	.07	.01
☐ 316	Ron Delorme	.08	.04	.01
☐ 317	John Garrett	.14	.07	.01
☐ 318	Jere Gillis	.08	.04	.01
☐ 319	Thomas Gradin	.14	.07	.01
☐ 320	Doug Halward	.08	.04	.01
☐ 321	Rick Lanz	.08	.04	.01
☐ 322	Moe Lemay	.08	.04	.01
☐ 323	Gary Lupul	.08	.04	.01
☐ 324	Al MacAdam	.14	.07	.01
☐ 325	Rob McClanahan	.08	.04	.01
☐ 326	Peter McNab	.08	.04	.01
☐ 327	Cam Neely	45.00	22.50	4.50

		MINT	EXC	G-VG
☐ 328	Darcy Rota	.08	.04	.01
☐ 329	Andy Schliebener	.08	.04	.01
☐ 330	Stan Smyl	.14	.07	.01
☐ 331	Patrik Sundstrom	.20	.10	.02
☐ 332	Tony Tanti	.20	.10	.02
☐ 333	Scott Arniel	.08	.04	.01
☐ 334	Dave Babych	.14	.07	.01
☐ 335	Laurie Boschman	.08	.04	.01
☐ 336	Wade Campbell	.08	.04	.01
☐ 337	Randy Carlyle	.14	.07	.01
☐ 338	Jordy Douglas	.08	.04	.01
☐ 339	Dale Hawerchuk	1.75	.85	.17
☐ 340	Morris Lukowich	.08	.04	.01
☐ 341	Bengt Lundholm	.08	.04	.01
☐ 342	Paul MacLean	.20	.10	.02
☐ 342	Andrew McBain	.08	.04	.01
☐ 344	Brian Mullen	.20	.10	.02
☐ 345	Robert Picard	.08	.04	.01
☐ 346	Doug Smail	.14	.07	.01
☐ 347	Doug Soetaert	.14	.07	.01
☐ 348	Thomas Steen	.14	.07	.01
☐ 349	Perry Turnbull	.14	.07	.01
☐ 350	Tim Watters	.08	.04	.01
☐ 351	Tim Young	.08	.04	.01
☐ 352	Boston Bruins Rick Middleton	.14	.07	.01
☐ 353	Buffalo Sabres Dave Andreychuk	.20	.10	.02
☐ 354	Calgary Flames Ed Beers	.14	.07	.01
☐ 355	Chicago Blackhawks Denis Savard	.25	.12	.02
☐ 356	Detroit Red Wings John Ogrodnick	.14	.07	.01
☐ 357	Edmonton Oilers Wayne Gretzky	4.00	2.00	.40
☐ 358	Los Angeles Kings Charlie Simmer	.14	.07	.01
☐ 359	Minnesota North Stars Brian Bellows	.25	.12	.02
☐ 360	Montreal Canadiens Guy Lafleur	.50	.25	.05
☐ 361	New Jersey Devils Mel Bridgman	.14	.07	.01
☐ 362	New York Islanders Mike Bossy	.50	.25	.05
☐ 363	New York Rangers Pierre Larouche	.14	.07	.01
☐ 364	Philadelphia Flyers Tim Kerr	.14	.07	.01
☐ 365	Pittsburgh Penguins Mike Bullard	.14	.07	.01
☐ 366	Quebec Nordiques Michel Goulet	.25	.12	.02

		MINT	EXC	G-VG
☐ 367	**St. Louis Blues UER** .... Bernie Federko Joe Mullen (Names reversed)	.20	.10	.02
☐ 368	**Toronto Maple Leafs** .... Rick Vaive	.14	.07	.01
☐ 369	**Vancouver Canucks** .... Tony Tanti	.14	.07	.01
☐ 370	**Washington Capitals** .... Mike Gartner	.25	.12	.02
☐ 371	**Winnipeg Jets** .... Paul MacLean	.14	.07	.01
☐ 372	**Hartford Whalers** .... Sylvain Turgeon	.14	.07	.01
☐ 373	**Art Ross Trophy** .... Wayne Gretzky	4.00	2.00	.40
☐ 374	**Hart Trophy** .... Wayne Gretzky	4.00	2.00	.40
☐ 375	**Calder Trophy** .... Tom Barasso	.35	.17	.03
☐ 376	**Lady Byng Trophy** .... Mike Bossy	.50	.25	.05
☐ 377	**Norris Trophy** .... Rod Langway	.20	.10	.02
☐ 378	**Masterson Trophy** .... Brad Park	.25	.12	.02
☐ 379	**Vezina Trophy** .... Tom Barasso	.35	.17	.03
☐ 380	**Scoring Leaders:** .... Wayne Gretzky	4.00	2.00	.40
☐ 381	**Goals Leaders** .... Wayne Gretzky	4.00	2.00	.40
☐ 382	**Assists Leaders** .... Wayne Gretzky	4.00	2.00	.40
☐ 383	**Power Play** .... **Goal Leaders** Wayne Gretzky	4.00	2.00	.40
☐ 384	**Game Winning** .... **Goal Leaders** Michel Goulet	.20	.10	.02
☐ 385	**Rookie Scoring** .... **Leaders** Steve Yzerman	4.00	2.00	.40
☐ 386	**Goals Against** .... **Average Leaders** Pat Riggin	.14	.07	.01
☐ 387	**Save Percentage** .... **Leaders** Rollie Melanson	.14	.07	.01
☐ 388	**Wayne Gretzky RB** .... Scores in 51 Straight Games	4.00	2.00	.40

			MINT	EXC	G-VG
☐ 389	**Denis Potvin RB**		.35	.17	.03
	20 Goals, Eight Seasons, Defenseman				
☐ 390	**Brad Park RB**...................................		.25	.12	.02
	Most Career Assists, Defenseman				
☐ 391	**Michel Goulet RB**		.20	.10	.02
	Most Points, Season, Left Wing				
☐ 392	**Pat LaFontaine RB**		3.00	1.50	.30
	Rookie Scoring Mark				
☐ 393	**Dale Hawerchuk RB**		.50	.25	.05
	Five Assists, Period				
☐ 394	**Checklist 1-132**		.40	.04	.01
☐ 395	**Checklist 133-264**..............................		.40	.04	.01
☐ 396	**Checklist 265-396**..............................		.40	.04	.01

1985-86 O-Pee-Chee

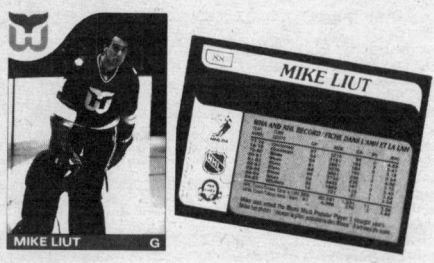

This 264-card set features players of the NHL. Cards measure 2¹/₂" by 3¹/₂". A 1985 copyright date is found on the backs of the cards. Backs are written in both French and English. The wax boxes had cards printed on the bottom with four players per box; these wax box cards are "lettered" A-P rather than numbered. The set is considered complete without these wax box cards. The key rookies in this set are Mario Lemieux and Al MacInnis. Other notable rookie cards include Kevin Dineen, Brian Hayward, Kelly Hrudey, Al Iafrate, Kirk Muller, Ed Olczyk, Tomas Sandstrom, and Peter Zezel.

Ce jeu de 264 cartes représente des joueurs de la NHL. Les cartes mesurent 2¹/₂" x 3¹/₂". Le dos comporte l'année 1985 comme date de droit d'auteur, et est imprimé en français et en anglais. Les boîtes paraffinées avaient des cartes imprimées sur le fond, avec quatre joueurs par boîte; ces cartes se distinguent par les lettres A-P au lieu d'être numérotées. Le jeu est considéré comme complet sans ces cartes. Les débutants importants de ce jeu sont Mario Lemieux et Al MacInnis. D'autres cartes notables de

débutants représentent Kevin Dineen, Brian Hayward, Kelly Hrudey, Al Iafrate, Kirk Muller, Ed Olczyk, Tomas Sandstrom, et Peter Zezel.

			MINT	EXC	G-VG
		COMPLETE SET (264)	275.00	135.00	27.00
		COMMON PLAYER (1-264)	.08	.04	.01
☐	1	Lanny McDonald	.50	.10	.02
☐	2	Mike O'Connell	.08	.04	.01
☐	3	Curt Fraser	.08	.04	.01
☐	4	Steve Penney	.14	.07	.01
☐	5	Brian Engblom	.08	.04	.01
☐	6	Ron Sutter	.14	.07	.01
☐	7	Joe Mullen	.35	.17	.03
☐	8	Rod Langway	.20	.10	.02
☐	9	Mario Lemieux	135.00	65.00	13.50
☐	10	Dave Babych	.14	.07	.01
☐	11	Bob Nystrom	.08	.04	.01
☐	12	Andy Moog	.75	.35	.07
☐	13	Dino Ciccarelli	.30	.15	.03
☐	14	Dwight Foster	.08	.04	.01
☐	15	James Patrick	.25	.12	.02
☐	16	Thomas Gradin	.14	.07	.01
☐	17	Mike Foligno	.08	.04	.01
☐	18	Mario Gosselin	.65	.30	.06
☐	19	Mike Zuke	.08	.04	.01
☐	20	John Anderson	.08	.04	.01
☐	21	Dave Pichette	.08	.04	.01
☐	22	Nick Fotiu	.08	.04	.01
☐	23	Tom Lysiak	.14	.07	.01
☐	24	Peter Zezel	2.00	1.00	.20
☐	25	Denis Potvin	.50	.25	.05
☐	26	Bob Carpenter	.20	.10	.02
☐	27	Murray Bannerman	.14	.07	.01
☐	28	Gordie Roberts	.08	.04	.01
☐	29	Steve Yzerman	16.00	8.00	1.60
☐	30	Phil Russell	.08	.04	.01
☐	31	Peter Stastny	1.00	.50	.10
☐	32	Craig Ramsay	.08	.04	.01
☐	33	Terry Ruskowski	.08	.04	.01
☐	34	Kevin Dineen	3.50	1.75	.35
☐	35	Mark Howe	.25	.12	.02
☐	36	Glenn Resch	.20	.10	.02
☐	37	Danny Gare	.14	.07	.01
☐	38	Doug Bodger	.60	.30	.06
☐	39	Mike Rogers	.14	.07	.01
☐	40	Ray Bourque	3.00	1.50	.30
☐	41	John Tonelli	.20	.10	.02
☐	42	Mel Bridgman	.08	.04	.01
☐	43	Sylvain Turgeon	.14	.07	.01
☐	44	Mark Johnson	.14	.07	.01
☐	45	Doug Wilson	.30	.15	.03
☐	46	Mike Gartner	.35	.17	.03

			MINT	EXC	G-VG
☐	47	Brent Peterson	.08	.04	.01
☐	48	Paul Reinhart	.14	.07	.01
☐	49	Mike Krushelnyski	.14	.07	.01
☐	50	Brian Bellows	.75	.35	.07
☐	51	Chris Chelios	2.00	1.00	.20
☐	52	Barry Pederson	.14	.07	.01
☐	53	Murray Craven	.25	.12	.02
☐	54	Pierre Larouche	.14	.07	.01
☐	55	Reed Larson	.08	.04	.01
☐	56	Pat Verbeek	.50	.25	.05
☐	57	Randy Carlyle	.14	.07	.01
☐	58	Ray Neufeld	.08	.04	.01
☐	59	Keith Brown	.08	.04	.01
☐	60	Bryan Trottier	.50	.25	.05
☐	61	Jim Fox	.08	.04	.01
☐	62	Scott Stevens	.50	.25	.05
☐	63	Phil Housley	.30	.15	.03
☐	64	Rick Middleton	.20	.10	.02
☐	65	Steve Payne	.08	.04	.01
☐	66	Dave Lewis	.08	.04	.01
☐	67	Mike Bullard	.14	.07	.01
☐	68	Stan Smyl	.14	.07	.01
☐	69	Mark Pavelich	.14	.07	.01
☐	70	John Ogrodnick	.14	.07	.01
☐	71	Bill Derlago	.08	.04	.01
☐	72	Brad Marsh	.08	.04	.01
☐	73	Denis Savard	1.00	.50	.10
☐	74	Mark Fusco	.08	.04	.01
☐	75	Pete Peeters	.14	.07	.01
☐	76	Doug Gilmour	.35	.17	.03
☐	77	Mike Ramsey	.08	.04	.01
☐	78	Anton Stastny	.14	.07	.01
☐	79	Steve Kasper	.14	.07	.01
☐	80	Bryan Erickson	.14	.07	.01
☐	81	Clark Gillies	.14	.07	.01
☐	82	Keith Acton	.08	.04	.01
☐	83	Pat Flatley	.14	.07	.01
☐	84	Kirk Muller	4.00	2.00	.40
☐	85	Paul Coffey	2.00	1.00	.20
☐	86	Ed Olczyk	4.00	2.00	.40
☐	87	Charlie Simmer	.14	.07	.01
☐	88	Mike Liut	.20	.10	.02
☐	89	Dave Maloney	.14	.07	.01
☐	90	Marcel Dionne	.65	.30	.06
☐	91	Tim Kerr	.25	.12	.02
☐	92	Ivan Boldirev	.08	.04	.01
☐	93	Ken Morrow	.14	.07	.01
☐	94	Don Maloney	.14	.07	.01
☐	95	Rejean Lemelin	.20	.10	.02
☐	96	Curt Giles	.08	.04	.01
☐	97	Bob Bourne	.08	.04	.01
☐	98	Joe Cirella	.14	.07	.01
☐	99	Dave Christian	.14	.07	.01

		MINT	EXC	G-VG
☐ 100	Darryl Sutter	.14	.07	.01
☐ 101	Kelly Kisio	.20	.10	.02
☐ 102	Mats Naslund	.35	.17	.03
☐ 103	Joel Quenneville	.08	.04	.01
☐ 104	Bernie Federko	.20	.10	.02
☐ 105	Tom Barrasso	.40	.20	.04
☐ 106	Rick Vaive	.14	.07	.01
☐ 107	Brent Sutter	.14	.07	.01
☐ 108	Wayne Babych	.08	.04	.01
☐ 109	Dale Hawerchuk	1.00	.50	.10
☐ 110	Pelle Lindbergh	7.50	3.75	.75
☐ 111	Dennis Maruk	.14	.07	.01
☐ 112	Reijo Ruotsalainen	.14	.07	.01
☐ 113	Tom Fergus	.08	.04	.01
☐ 114	Bob Murray	.08	.04	.01
☐ 115	Patrik Sundstrom	.14	.07	.01
☐ 116	Ron Duguay	.14	.07	.01
☐ 117	Alan Haworth	.08	.04	.01
☐ 118	Greg Malone	.08	.04	.01
☐ 119	Bill Hajt	.08	.04	.01
☐ 120	Wayne Gretzky	16.00	8.00	1.60
☐ 121	Craig Redmond	.08	.04	.01
☐ 122	Kelly Hrudey	6.00	3.00	.60
☐ 123	Tomas Sandstrom	12.50	6.25	1.25
☐ 124	Neal Broten	.20	.10	.02
☐ 125	Moe Mantha	.14	.07	.01
☐ 126	Greg Gilbert	.14	.07	.01
☐ 127	Bruce Driver	.65	.30	.06
☐ 128	Dave Poulin	.20	.10	.02
☐ 129	Morris Lukowich	.08	.04	.01
☐ 130	Mike Bossy	1.00	.50	.10
☐ 131	Larry Playfair	.08	.04	.01
☐ 132	Steve Larmer	1.25	.60	.12
☐ 133	Doug Keans	.14	.07	.01
☐ 134	Bob Manno	.08	.04	.01
☐ 135	Brian Sutter	.14	.07	.01
☐ 136	Pat Riggin	.14	.07	.01
☐ 137	Pat LaFontaine	4.00	2.00	.40
☐ 138	Barry Beck	.14	.07	.01
☐ 139	Rich Preston	.08	.04	.01
☐ 140	Ron Francis	1.00	.50	.10
☐ 141	Brian Propp	.30	.15	.03
☐ 142	Don Beaupre	.20	.10	.02
☐ 143	Dave Andreychuk	.30	.15	.03
☐ 144	Ed Beers	.08	.04	.01
☐ 145	Paul MacLean	.14	.07	.01
☐ 146	Troy Murray	.14	.07	.01
☐ 147	Larry Robinson	.30	.15	.03
☐ 148	Bernie Nicholls	1.50	.75	.15
☐ 149	Glen Hanlon	.14	.07	.01
☐ 150	Michel Goulet	.35	.17	.03
☐ 151	Doug Jarvis	.14	.07	.01
☐ 152	Warren Young	.40	.20	.04

		MINT	EXC	G-VG
☐ 153	Tony Tanti	.20	.10	.02
☐ 154	Tomas Jonsson	.08	.04	.01
☐ 155	Jari Kurri	1.00	.50	.10
☐ 156	Tony McKegney	.08	.04	.01
☐ 157	Greg Stefan	.14	.07	.01
☐ 158	Brad McCrimmon	.14	.07	.01
☐ 159	Keith Crowder	.08	.04	.01
☐ 160	Gilbert Perreault	.40	.20	.04
☐ 161	Tim Bothwell	.08	.04	.01
☐ 162	Bob Crawford	.08	.04	.01
☐ 163	Paul Gagne	.08	.04	.01
☐ 164	Dan Daoust	.08	.04	.01
☐ 165	Checklist 1-132	.40	.04	.01
☐ 166	Tim Bernhardt	.14	.07	.01
☐ 167	Gord Kluzak	.14	.07	.01
☐ 168	Glenn Anderson	.40	.20	.04
☐ 169	Bob Gainey	.25	.12	.02
☐ 170	Brent Ashton	.08	.04	.01
☐ 171	Ron Flockhart	.08	.04	.01
☐ 172	Gary Nylund	.08	.04	.01
☐ 173	Moe Lemay	.08	.04	.01
☐ 174	Bob Sauve	.14	.07	.01
☐ 175	Doug Smail	.14	.07	.01
☐ 176	Dan Quinn	.25	.12	.02
☐ 177	Mark Messier	3.00	1.50	.30
☐ 178	Jay Wells	.08	.04	.01
☐ 179	Dale Hunter	.14	.07	.01
☐ 180	Richard Brodeur	.14	.07	.01
☐ 181	Bobby Smith	.20	.10	.02
☐ 182	Ron Greschner	.14	.07	.01
☐ 183	Don Edwards	.14	.07	.01
☐ 184	Hakan Loob	.25	.12	.02
☐ 185	Dave Ellett	.85	.40	.08
☐ 186	Denis Herron	.14	.07	.01
☐ 187	Charlie Huddy	.14	.07	.01
☐ 188	Ilkka Sinisalo	.14	.07	.01
☐ 189	Doug Halward	.08	.04	.01
☐ 190	Craig Laughlin	.08	.04	.01
☐ 191	Carey Wilson	.60	.30	.06
☐ 192	Craig Ludwig	.14	.07	.01
☐ 193	Bob MacMillan	.14	.07	.01
☐ 194	Mario Marois	.08	.04	.01
☐ 195	Brian Mullen	.14	.07	.01
☐ 196	Rob Ramage	.14	.07	.01
☐ 197	Rick Lanz	.08	.04	.01
☐ 198	Miroslav Frycer	.08	.04	.01
☐ 199	Randy Gregg	.14	.07	.01
☐ 200	Corrado Micalef	.08	.04	.01
☐ 201	Jamie Macoun	.14	.07	.01
☐ 202	Bob Brooke	.08	.04	.01
☐ 203	Billy Carroll	.08	.04	.01
☐ 204	Brian MacLellan	.08	.04	.01
☐ 205	Alain Cote	.08	.04	.01

		MINT	EXC	G-VG
☐ 206	Thomas Steen	.14	.07	.01
☐ 207	Grant Fuhr	1.50	.75	.15
☐ 208	Rich Sutter	.14	.07	.01
☐ 209	Al MacAdam	.14	.07	.01
☐ 210	Al Iafrate	4.00	2.00	.40
☐ 211	Pierre Mondou	.08	.04	.01
☐ 212	Randy Hillier	.08	.04	.01
☐ 213	Mike Eaves	.08	.04	.01
☐ 214	Dave Taylor	.20	.10	.02
☐ 215	Robert Picard	.08	.04	.01
☐ 216	Randy Ladouceur	.08	.04	.01
☐ 217	Willy Lindstrom	.08	.04	.01
☐ 218	Torrie Robertson	.14	.07	.01
☐ 219	Tom Kurvers	.50	.25	.05
☐ 220	John Garrett	.14	.07	.01
☐ 221	Greg Millen	.14	.07	.01
☐ 222	Richard Kromm	.08	.04	.01
☐ 223	Bob Janecyk	.35	.17	.03
☐ 224	Brad Maxwell	.08	.04	.01
☐ 225	Mike McPhee	1.25	.60	.12
☐ 226	Brian Hayward	1.75	.85	.17
☐ 227	Duane Sutter	.14	.07	.01
☐ 228	Cam Neely	16.00	8.00	1.60
☐ 229	Doug Wickenheiser	.08	.04	.01
☐ 230	Rollie Melanson	.14	.07	.01
☐ 231	Bruce Bell	.08	.04	.01
☐ 232	Harold Snepsts	.14	.07	.01
☐ 233	Guy Carbonneau	.20	.10	.02
☐ 234	Doug Sulliman	.08	.04	.01
☐ 235	Lee Fogolin	.08	.04	.01
☐ 236	Larry Murphy	.14	.07	.01
☐ 237	Al MacInnis	35.00	17.50	3.50
☐ 238	Don Lever	.08	.04	.01
☐ 239	Kevin Lowe	.25	.12	.02
☐ 240	Randy Moller	.08	.04	.01
☐ 241	Doug Lidster	.20	.10	.02
☐ 242	Craig Hartsburg	.08	.04	.01
☐ 243	Doug Risebrough	.14	.07	.01
☐ 244	John Chabot	.08	.04	.01
☐ 245	Mario Tremblay	.14	.07	.01
☐ 246	Dan Bouchard	.14	.07	.01
☐ 247	Doug Shedden	.14	.07	.01
☐ 248	Borje Salming	.20	.10	.02
☐ 249	Aaron Broten	.08	.04	.01
☐ 250	Jim Benning	.08	.04	.01
☐ 251	Laurie Boschman	.08	.04	.01
☐ 252	George McPhee	.25	.12	.02
☐ 253	Mark Napier	.14	.07	.01
☐ 254	Perry Turnbull	.14	.07	.01
☐ 255	Warren Skorodenski	.35	.17	.03
☐ 256	Checklist 133-264	.40	.04	.01
☐ 257	Goal Leaders	5.00	2.50	.50
	Wayne Gretzky			

			MINT	EXC	G-VG
☐ 258	**Assist Leaders**		5.00	2.50	.50
	Wayne Gretzky				
☐ 259	**Scoring Leaders**		5.00	2.50	.50
	Wayne Gretzky				
☐ 260	**Power Play Goals**		.14	.07	.01
	Leaders				
	Tim Kerr				
☐ 261	**Game Winning Goals**		.45	.22	.04
	Leaders				
	Jari Kurri				
☐ 262	**Rookie Scoring**		33.00	15.00	3.00
	Leaders				
	Mario Lemieux				
☐ 263	**Goals Against Average**		.20	.10	.02
	Leaders				
	Tom Barrasso				
☐ 264	**Save Pctg. Leaders**		.20	.10	.02
	Warren Skorodenski				

1986-87 O-Pee-Chee

This 264-card set features players of the NHL. Cards measure 2¹/₂" by 3¹/₂". A 1986 copyright date is found on the backs of the cards. Backs are written in both French and English and are printed in blue and black ink on white card stock. There were also 16 cards printed on the bottom of the wax pack boxes, four to a box. These cards are "lettered" rather than numbered and are not considered part of the complete set. The key rookie in this set is Patrick Roy. Other notable rookie cards include Russ Courtnall, Petr Klima, John MacLean, Gary Suter, and John Vanbiesbrouck.

Ce jeu de 264 cartes représente des joueurs de la NHL. Les cartes mesurent 2¹/₂" x 3¹/₂". Le dos comporte l'année 1986 comme date de droit d'auteur, et est imprimé en

français et en anglais en encre bleue et noire sur de la pâte blanche. Seize cartes ont été imprimées sur les fonds de boîtes paraffinées, quatre cartes par boîte. Ces cartes se distinguent par des lettres au lieu d'être numérotées, et ne sont pas considérées comme faisant partie du jeu complet. Le débutant prometteur du jeu est Patrick Roy. D'autres cartes notables de débutants représentent Russ Courtnall, Petr Klima, John MacLean, Gary Suter, et John Vanbiesbrouck.

			MINT	EXC	G-VG
		COMPLETE SET (264)	140.00	70.00	14.00
		COMMON PLAYER (1-264)	.07	.03	.01
☐	1	Ray Bourque	2.00	.50	.10
☐	2	Pat LaFontaine	1.75	.85	.17
☐	3	Wayne Gretzky	13.50	6.00	1.00
☐	4	Lindy Ruff	.07	.03	.01
☐	5	Brad McCrimmon	.07	.03	.01
☐	6	Dave Williams	.12	.06	.01
☐	7	Denis Savard	.75	.35	.07
☐	8	Lanny McDonald	.30	.15	.03
☐	9	John Vanbiesbrouck	3.00	1.50	.30
☐	10	Greg Adams	.60	.30	.06
		New Jersey Devils			
☐	11	Steve Yzerman	10.00	5.00	1.00
☐	12	Craig Hartsburg	.07	.03	.01
☐	13	John Anderson	.07	.03	.01
☐	14	Bob Bourne	.07	.03	.01
☐	15	Kjell Dahlin	.50	.25	.05
☐	16	Dave Andreychuk	.12	.06	.01
☐	17	Rob Ramage	.12	.06	.01
☐	18	Ron Greschner	.12	.06	.01
☐	19	Bruce Driver	.12	.06	.01
☐	20	Peter Stastny	.75	.35	.07
☐	21	Dave Christian	.12	.06	.01
☐	22	Doug Keans	.12	.06	.01
☐	23	Scott Bjugstad	.07	.03	.01
☐	24	Doug Bodger	.12	.06	.01
☐	25	Troy Murray	.12	.06	.01
☐	26	Al Iafrate	.50	.25	.05
☐	27	Kelly Hrudey	.75	.35	.07
☐	28	Doug Jarvis	.12	.06	.01
☐	29	Rich Sutter	.12	.06	.01
☐	30	Marcel Dionne	.60	.30	.06
☐	31	Curt Fraser	.07	.03	.01
☐	32	Doug Lidster	.12	.06	.01
☐	33	Brian MacLellan	.07	.03	.01
☐	34	Barry Pederson	.12	.06	.01
☐	35	Craig Laughlin	.07	.03	.01
☐	36	Ilkka Sinisalo	.12	.06	.01
☐	37	John MacLean	6.50	3.25	.65
☐	38	Brian Mullen	.15	.07	.01
☐	39	Duane Sutter	.12	.06	.01
☐	40	Brian Engblom	.07	.03	.01
☐	41	Chris Cichocki	.07	.03	.01

		MINT	EXC	G-VG
☐ 42	Gordie Roberts	.07	.03	.01
☐ 43	Ron Francis	.65	.30	.06
☐ 44	Joe Mullen	.25	.12	.02
☐ 45	Moe Mantha	.07	.03	.01
☐ 46	Pat Verbeek	.25	.12	.02
☐ 47	Clint Malarchuk	.75	.35	.07
☐ 48	Bob Brooke	.07	.03	.01
☐ 49	Darryl Sutter	.12	.06	.01
☐ 50	Stan Smyl	.12	.06	.01
☐ 51	Greg Stefan	.12	.06	.01
☐ 52	Bill Hajt	.07	.03	.01
☐ 53	Patrick Roy	40.00	20.00	4.00
☐ 54	Gord Kluzak	.12	.06	.01
☐ 55	Bob Froese	.15	.07	.01
☐ 56	Grant Fuhr	1.00	.50	.10
☐ 57	Mark Hunter	.12	.06	.01
☐ 58	Dana Murzyn	.20	.10	.02
☐ 59	Mike Gartner	.30	.15	.03
☐ 60	Dennis Maruk	.12	.06	.01
☐ 61	Rich Preston	.07	.03	.01
☐ 62	Larry Robinson	.25	.12	.02
☐ 63	Dave Taylor	.15	.07	.01
☐ 64	Bob Murray	.07	.03	.01
☐ 65	Ken Morrow	.12	.06	.01
☐ 66	Mike Ridley	1.00	.50	.10
☐ 67	John Tucker	.25	.12	.02
☐ 68	Miroslav Frycer	.07	.03	.01
☐ 69	Danny Gare	.12	.06	.01
☐ 70	Randy Burridge	.30	.15	.03
☐ 71	Dave Poulin	.15	.07	.01
☐ 72	Brian Sutter	.12	.06	.01
☐ 73	Dave Babych	.12	.06	.01
☐ 74	Dale Hawerchuk	.65	.30	.06
☐ 75	Brian Bellows	.50	.25	.05
☐ 76	Dave Pasin	.07	.03	.01
☐ 77	Pete Peeters	.15	.07	.01
☐ 78	Tomas Jonsson	.07	.03	.01
☐ 79	Gilbert Perreault	.30	.15	.03
☐ 80	Glenn Anderson	.35	.17	.03
☐ 81	Don Maloney	.12	.06	.01
☐ 82	Ed Olczyk	.50	.25	.05
☐ 83	Mike Bullard	.12	.06	.01
☐ 84	Tom Fergus	.07	.03	.01
☐ 85	Dave Lewis	.07	.03	.01
☐ 86	Brian Propp	.25	.12	.02
☐ 87	John Ogrodnick	.12	.06	.01
☐ 88	Kevin Dineen	.40	.20	.04
☐ 89	Don Beaupre	.15	.07	.01
☐ 90	Mike Bossy	1.00	.50	.10
☐ 91	Tom Barrasso	.25	.12	.02
☐ 92	Michel Goulet	.30	.15	.03
☐ 93	Doug Gilmour	.20	.10	.02
☐ 94	Kirk Muller	.50	.25	.05

			MINT	EXC	G-VG
☐	95	Larry Melnyk	.07	.03	.01
☐	96	Bob Gainey	.20	.10	.02
☐	97	Steve Kasper	.12	.06	.01
☐	98	Petr Klima	6.00	3.00	.60
☐	99	Neal Broten	.15	.07	.01
☐	100	Al Secord	.12	.06	.01
☐	101	Bryan Erickson	.07	.03	.01
☐	102	Rejean Lemelin	.15	.07	.01
☐	103	Sylvain Turgeon	.12	.06	.01
☐	104	Bob Nystrom	.07	.03	.01
☐	105	Bernie Federko	.15	.07	.01
☐	106	Doug Wilson	.30	.15	.03
☐	107	Alan Haworth	.07	.03	.01
☐	108	Jari Kurri	.85	.40	.08
☐	109	Ron Sutter	.12	.06	.01
☐	110	Reed Larson	.07	.03	.01
☐	111	Terry Ruskowski	.07	.03	.01
☐	112	Mark Johnson	.12	.06	.01
☐	113	James Patrick	.12	.06	.01
☐	114	Paul MacLean	.12	.06	.01
☐	115	Mike Ramsey	.07	.03	.01
☐	116	Kelly Kisio	.12	.06	.01
☐	117	Brent Sutter	.12	.06	.01
☐	118	Joel Quenneville	.07	.03	.01
☐	119	Curt Giles	.07	.03	.01
☐	120	Tony Tanti	.12	.06	.01
☐	121	Doug Sulliman	.07	.03	.01
☐	122	Mario Lemieux	45.00	22.50	4.50
☐	123	Mark Howe	.20	.10	.02
☐	124	Bob Sauve	.12	.06	.01
☐	125	Anton Stastny	.12	.06	.01
☐	126	Scott Stevens	.35	.17	.03
☐	127	Mike Foligno	.07	.03	.01
☐	128	Reijo Ruotsalainen	.07	.03	.01
☐	129	Denis Potvin	.45	.22	.04
☐	130	Keith Crowder	.07	.03	.01
☐	131	Bob Janecyk	.12	.06	.01
☐	132	John Tonelli	.15	.07	.01
☐	133	Mike Liut	.20	.10	.02
☐	134	Tim Kerr	.20	.10	.02
☐	135	Al Jensen	.12	.06	.01
☐	136	Mel Bridgman	.07	.03	.01
☐	137	Paul Coffey	1.25	.60	.12
☐	138	Dino Ciccarelli	.25	.12	.02
☐	139	Steve Larmer	.75	.35	.07
☐	140	Mike O'Connell	.07	.03	.01
☐	141	Clark Gillies	.15	.07	.01
☐	142	Phil Russell	.07	.03	.01
☐	143	Dirk Graham	.25	.12	.02
☐	144	Randy Carlyle	.12	.06	.01
☐	145	Charlie Simmer	.15	.07	.01
☐	146	Ron Flockhart	.07	.03	.01
☐	147	Tom Laidlaw	.07	.03	.01

		MINT	EXC	G-VG
☐ 148	Dave Tippett	.25	.12	.02
☐ 149	Wendel Clark	2.00	1.00	.20
☐ 150	Bob Carpenter	.15	.07	.01
☐ 151	Bill Watson	.07	.03	.01
☐ 152	Roberto Romano	.12	.06	.01
☐ 153	Doug Shedden	.12	.06	.01
☐ 154	Phil Housley	.25	.12	.02
☐ 155	Bryan Trottier	.45	.22	.04
☐ 156	Patrik Sundstrom	.15	.07	.01
☐ 157	Rick Middleton	.20	.10	.02
☐ 158	Glenn Resch	.20	.10	.02
☐ 159	Bernie Nicholls	.90	.45	.09
☐ 160	Ray Ferraro	.50	.25	.05
☐ 161	Mats Naslund	.25	.12	.02
☐ 162	Pat Flatley	.12	.06	.01
☐ 163	Joe Cirella	.12	.06	.01
☐ 164	Rod Langway	.20	.10	.02
☐ 165	Checklist 1-132	.30	.03	.01
☐ 166	Carey Wilson	.15	.07	.01
☐ 167	Murray Craven	.12	.06	.01
☐ 168	Paul Gillis	.07	.03	.01
☐ 169	Borje Salming	.20	.10	.02
☐ 170	Perry Turnbull	.12	.06	.01
☐ 171	Chris Chelios	1.00	.50	.10
☐ 172	Keith Acton	.07	.03	.01
☐ 173	Al MacInnis	10.00	5.00	1.00
☐ 174	Russ Courtnall	6.00	3.00	.60
☐ 175	Brad Marsh	.07	.03	.01
☐ 176	Guy Carbonneau	.15	.07	.01
☐ 177	Ray Neufeld	.07	.03	.01
☐ 178	Craig MacTavish	.60	.30	.06
☐ 179	Rick Lanz	.07	.03	.01
☐ 180	Murray Bannerman	.12	.06	.01
☐ 181	Brent Ashton	.07	.03	.01
☐ 182	Jim Peplinski	.07	.03	.01
☐ 183	Mark Napier	.12	.06	.01
☐ 184	Laurie Boschman	.07	.03	.01
☐ 185	Larry Murphy	.12	.06	.01
☐ 186	Mark Messier	2.00	1.00	.20
☐ 187	Risto Siltanen	.12	.06	.01
☐ 188	Bobby Smith	.20	.10	.02
☐ 189	Gary Suter	3.00	1.50	.30
☐ 190	Peter Zezel	.25	.12	.02
☐ 191	Rick Vaive	.12	.06	.01
☐ 192	Dale Hunter	.12	.06	.01
☐ 193	Mike Krushelnyski	.12	.06	.01
☐ 194	Scott Arniel	.07	.03	.01
☐ 195	Larry Playfair	.07	.03	.01
☐ 196	Doug Risebrough	.12	.06	.01
☐ 197	Kevin Lowe	.25	.12	.02
☐ 198	Checklist 133-264	.30	.03	.01
☐ 199	Chris Nilan	.15	.07	.01
☐ 200	Paul Cyr	.07	.03	.01

		MINT	EXC	G-VG
□ 201	Ric Seiling	.07	.03	.01
□ 202	Doug Smith	.07	.03	.01
□ 203	Jamie Macoun	.12	.06	.01
□ 204	Dan Quinn	.15	.07	.01
□ 205	Paul Reinhart	.12	.06	.01
□ 206	Keith Brown	.07	.03	.01
□ 207	Jack O'Callahan	.07	.03	.01
□ 208	Steve Richmond	.07	.03	.01
□ 209	Warren Young	.15	.07	.01
□ 210	Lee Fogolin	.07	.03	.01
□ 211	Charlie Huddy	.15	.07	.01
□ 212	Andy Moog	.60	.30	.06
□ 213	Wayne Babych	.07	.03	.01
□ 214	Torrie Robertson	.07	.03	.01
□ 215	Jim Fox	.07	.03	.01
□ 216	Phil Sykes	.07	.03	.01
□ 217	Jay Wells	.07	.03	.01
□ 218	Dave Langevin	.07	.03	.01
□ 219	Steve Payne	.07	.03	.01
□ 220	Craig Ludwig	.12	.06	.01
□ 221	Mike McPhee	.25	.12	.02
□ 222	Steve Penney	.12	.06	.01
□ 223	Mario Tremblay	.12	.06	.01
□ 224	Ryan Walter	.12	.06	.01
□ 225	Alain Chevrier	.65	.30	.06
□ 226	Uli Hiemer	.07	.03	.01
□ 227	Tim Higgins	.07	.03	.01
□ 228	Billy Smith	.25	.12	.02
□ 229	Richard Kromm	.07	.03	.01
□ 230	Tomas Sandstrom	2.50	1.25	.25
□ 231	Jim Johnson	.30	.15	.03
□ 232	Willy Lindstrom	.07	.03	.01
□ 233	Alain Cote	.07	.03	.01
□ 234	Gilbert Delorme	.07	.03	.01
□ 235	Mario Gosselin	.25	.12	.02
□ 236	David Shaw	.07	.03	.01
□ 237	Dave Barr	.35	.17	.03
□ 238	Ed Beers	.07	.03	.01
□ 239	Charlie Bourgeois	.07	.03	.01
□ 240	Rick Wamsley	.15	.07	.01
□ 241	Dan Daoust	.07	.03	.01
□ 242	Brad Maxwell	.07	.03	.01
□ 243	Gary Nylund	.07	.03	.01
□ 244	Greg Terrion	.07	.03	.01
□ 245	Steve Thomas	.80	.40	.08
□ 246	Richard Brodeur	.12	.06	.01
□ 247	Joel Otto UER	.40	.20	.04
	(Photo actually Moe Lemay)			
□ 248	Doug Halward	.07	.03	.01
□ 249	Moe Lemay UER	.12	.06	.01
	(Photo actually Joel Otto)			
□ 250	Cam Neely	10.00	5.00	1.00
□ 251	Brent Peterson	.07	.03	.01

		MINT	EXC	G-VG
☐ 252	Petri Skriko	.50	.25	.05
☐ 253	Greg C. Adams Washington Capitals	.25	.12	.02
☐ 254	Bill Derlago	.07	.03	.01
☐ 255	Brian Hayward	.25	.12	.02
☐ 256	Doug Smail	.12	.06	.01
☐ 257	Thomas Steen	.12	.06	.01
☐ 258	Goals Leaders Jari Kurri	.40	.20	.04
☐ 259	Assists Leaders Wayne Gretzky	5.00	2.50	.50
☐ 260	Points Leaders Wayne Gretzky	5.00	2.50	.50
☐ 261	Power Play Goal Leaders Tim Kerr	.12	.06	.01
☐ 262	Rookie Leaders Kjell Dahlin	.15	.07	.01
☐ 263	Goals Against Average Leaders Bob Froese	.12	.06	.01
☐ 264	Save Pct. Leaders Bob Froese	.15	.07	.01

1987-88 O-Pee-Chee

The 1987-88 O-Pee-Chee hockey set contains 264 standard size (2½" by 3½") cards. The fronts feature color photos with white borders. The backs are a mauve tint and show career statistics and highlights. There were cards printed on the bottoms of the wax boxes; these cards are similar to the regular issue cards but are "lettered" A-P rather than numbered. These wax box cards are not considered part of the complete

set price below, as they are usually offered separately or as an extra. The key rookies in this set are Daniel Berthiaume, Jimmy Carson, Vin Damphousse, Kevin Hatcher, Ron Hextall, Claude Lemieux, Marty McSorley, Adam Oates, Stephan Richer, Luc Robitaille, Craig Simpson, Esa Tikkanen, Rick Tocchet, and Mike Vernon.

Le jeu de cartes de hockey O-Pee-Chee 1987-88 contient 264 cartes de format standard (2¹/₂" x 3¹/₂"). La face comporte une photo en couleurs bordée de blanc. Le dos, d'une teinte mauve, indique les statistiques et dates marquantes. Des cartes ont été imprimées sur les fonds de boîtes paraffinées; elles ressemblent aux cartes de l'édition régulière, mais portent les lettres Á-P au lieu d'être numérotées. Ces cartes imprimées sur boîte ne sont pas considérées comme faisant partie du jeu complet évalué ci-dessous, étant généralement offertes séparément ou en prime. Les débutants importants de ce jeu sont Daniel Berthiaume, Jimmy Carson, Vin Damphousse, Kevin Hatcher, Ron Hextall, Claude Lemieux, Marty McSorley, Adam Oates, Stephan Richer, Luc Robitaille, Craig Simpson, Esa Tikkanen, Rick Tocchet, et Mike Vernon.

			MINT	EXC	G-VG
		COMPLETE SET (264)	140.00	70.00	14.00
		COMMON PLAYER (1-264)	.06	.03	.00
☐	1	Denis Potvin	.60	.12	.02
☐	2	Rick Tocchet	16.00	8.00	1.60
☐	3	Dave Andreychuk	.15	.07	.01
☐	4	Stan Smyl	.10	.05	.01
☐	5	Dave Babych	.10	.05	.01
☐	6	Pat Verbeek	.20	.10	.02
☐	7	Esa Tikkanen	8.00	4.00	.80
☐	8	Mike Ridley	.15	.07	.01
☐	9	Randy Carlyle	.10	.05	.01
☐	10	Greg Paslawski	.15	.07	.01
☐	11	Neal Broten	.15	.07	.01
☐	12	Wendel Clark	.25	.12	.02
☐	13	Bill Ranford	2.50	1.25	.25
☐	14	Doug Wilson	.25	.12	.02
☐	15	Mario Lemieux	20.00	10.00	2.00
☐	16	Mats Naslund	.20	.10	.02
☐	17	Mel Bridgman	.06	.03	.00
☐	18	James Patrick	.10	.05	.01
☐	19	Rollie Melanson	.15	.07	.01
☐	20	Lanny McDonald	.25	.12	.02
☐	21	Peter Stastny	.60	.30	.06
☐	22	Murray Craven	.10	.05	.01
☐	23	Ulf Samuelsson	1.00	.50	.10
☐	24	Mike Thelvin	.10	.05	.01
☐	25	Scott Stevens	.25	.12	.02
☐	26	Petr Klima	1.00	.50	.10
☐	27	Brent Sutter	.10	.05	.01
☐	28	Tomas Sandstrom	1.00	.50	.10
☐	29	Tim Bothwell	.06	.03	.00
☐	30	Bob Carpenter	.10	.05	.01
☐	31	Brian MacLellan	.06	.03	.00
☐	32	John Chabot	.06	.03	.00
☐	33	Phil Housley	.20	.10	.02

			MINT	EXC	G-VG
☐	34	Patrik Sundstrom	.10	.05	.01
☐	35	Dave Ellett	.15	.07	.01
☐	36	John Vanbiesbrouck	.50	.25	.05
☐	37	Dave Lewis	.06	.03	.00
☐	38	Tom McCarthy	.06	.03	.00
☐	39	Dave Poulin	.10	.05	.01
☐	40	Mike Foligno	.06	.03	.00
☐	41	Gordie Roberts	.06	.03	.00
☐	42	Luc Robitaille	30.00	15.00	3.00
☐	43	Duane Sutter	.10	.05	.01
☐	44	Pete Peeters	.10	.05	.01
☐	45	John Anderson	.06	.03	.00
☐	46	Aaron Broten	.06	.03	.00
☐	47	Keith Brown	.06	.03	.00
☐	48	Bobby Smith	.20	.10	.02
☐	49	Don Maloney	.10	.05	.01
☐	50	Mark Hunter	.10	.05	.01
☐	51	Moe Mantha	.06	.03	.00
☐	52	Charlie Simmer	.10	.05	.01
☐	53	Wayne Gretzky	12.50	6.25	1.25
☐	54	Mark Howe	.20	.10	.02
☐	55	Bob Gould	.06	.03	.00
☐	56	Steve Yzerman	5.00	2.50	.50
☐	57	Larry Playfair	.06	.03	.00
☐	58	Alain Chevrier	.15	.07	.01
☐	59	Steve Larmer	.45	.22	.04
☐	60	Bryan Trottier	.40	.20	.04
☐	61	Stewart Gavin	.10	.05	.01
☐	62	Russ Courtnall	1.00	.50	.10
☐	63	Mike Ramsey	.06	.03	.00
☐	64	Bob Brooke	.06	.03	.00
☐	65	Rick Wamsley	.15	.07	.01
☐	66	Ken Morrow	.10	.05	.01
☐	67	Gerard Gallant	2.00	1.00	.20
☐	68	Kevin Hatcher	3.00	1.50	.30
☐	69	Cam Neely	5.00	2.50	.50
☐	70	Sylvain Turgeon	.10	.05	.01
☐	71	Peter Zezel	.15	.07	.01
☐	72	Al MacInnis	4.00	2.00	.40
☐	73	Terry Ruskowski	.06	.03	.00
☐	74	Troy Murray	.10	.05	.01
☐	75	Jim Fox	.06	.03	.00
☐	76	Kelly Kisio	.10	.05	.01
☐	77	Michel Goulet	.20	.10	.02
☐	78	Tom Barrasso	.20	.10	.02
☐	79	Bruce Driver	.10	.05	.01
☐	80	Craig Simpson	2.50	1.25	.25
☐	81	Dino Ciccarelli	.20	.10	.02
☐	82	Gary Nylund	.06	.03	.00
☐	83	Bernie Federko	.15	.07	.01
☐	84	John Tonelli	.10	.05	.01
☐	85	Brad McCrimmon	.06	.03	.00
☐	86	Dave Tippett	.06	.03	.00

		MINT	EXC	G-VG
☐ 87	Ray Bourque	1.50	.75	.15
☐ 88	Dave Christian	.06	.03	.00
☐ 89	Glen Hanlon	.10	.05	.01
☐ 90	Brian Curran	.10	.05	.01
☐ 91	Paul MacLean	.10	.05	.01
☐ 92	Jimmy Carson	2.50	1.25	.25
☐ 93	Willie Huber	.06	.03	.00
☐ 94	Brian Bellows	.35	.17	.03
☐ 95	Doug Jarvis	.10	.05	.01
☐ 96	Clark Gillies	.10	.05	.01
☐ 97	Tony Tanti	.10	.05	.01
☐ 98	Pelle Eklund	1.50	.75	.15
☐ 99	Paul Coffey	1.00	.50	.10
☐ 100	Brent Ashton	.06	.03	.00
☐ 101	Mark Johnson	.06	.03	.00
☐ 102	Greg Johnston	.06	.03	.00
☐ 103	Ron Flockhart	.06	.03	.00
☐ 104	Ed Olczyk	.30	.15	.03
☐ 105	Mike Bossy	.75	.35	.07
☐ 106	Chris Chelios	.45	.22	.04
☐ 107	Gilles Meloche	.10	.05	.01
☐ 108	Rod Langway	.15	.07	.01
☐ 109	Ray Ferraro	.10	.05	.01
☐ 110	Ron Duguay	.10	.05	.01
☐ 111	Al Secord	.10	.05	.01
☐ 112	Mark Messier	1.50	.75	.15
☐ 113	Ron Sutter	.10	.05	.01
☐ 114	Darren Veitch	.15	.07	.01
☐ 115	Rick Middleton	.15	.07	.01
☐ 116	Doug Sulliman	.06	.03	.00
☐ 117	Dennis Maruk	.10	.05	.01
☐ 118	Dave Taylor	.15	.07	.01
☐ 119	Kelly Hrudey	.35	.17	.03
☐ 120	Tom Fergus	.06	.03	.00
☐ 121	Christian Ruuttu	.50	.25	.05
☐ 122	Brian Benning	.30	.15	.03
☐ 123	Adam Oates	30.00	15.00	3.00
☐ 124	Kevin Dineen	.25	.12	.02
☐ 125	Doug Bodger	.10	.05	.01
☐ 126	Joe Mullen	.20	.10	.02
☐ 127	Denis Savard	.60	.30	.06
☐ 128	Brad Marsh	.06	.03	.00
☐ 129	Marcel Dionne	.50	.25	.05
☐ 130	Bryan Erickson	.06	.03	.00
☐ 131	Reed Larson	.06	.03	.00
☐ 132	Don Beaupre	.15	.07	.01
☐ 133	Larry Murphy	.10	.05	.01
☐ 134	John Ogrodnick	.10	.05	.01
☐ 135	Greg Adams	.15	.07	.01
	New Jersey Devils			
☐ 136	Pat Flatley	.10	.05	.01
☐ 137	Scott Arniel	.06	.03	.00
☐ 138	Dana Murzyn	.06	.03	.00

			MINT	EXC	G-VG
☐ 139	Greg C. Adams		.06	.03	.00
	Washington Capitals				
☐ 140	Bob Sauve		.10	.05	.01
☐ 141	Mike O'Connell		.06	.03	.00
☐ 142	Walt Poddubny		.10	.05	.01
☐ 143	Paul Reinhart		.10	.05	.01
☐ 144	Tim Kerr		.20	.10	.02
☐ 145	Brian Lawton		.20	.10	.02
☐ 146	Gino Cavallini		.35	.17	.03
☐ 147	Doug Keans		.10	.05	.01
☐ 148	Jari Kurri		.65	.30	.06
☐ 149	Dale Hawerchuk		.50	.25	.05
☐ 150	Randy Cunneyworth		.40	.20	.04
☐ 151	Jay Wells		.06	.03	.00
☐ 152	Mike Liut		.20	.10	.02
☐ 153	Steve Konroyd		.06	.03	.00
☐ 154	John Tucker		.06	.03	.00
☐ 155	Rick Vaive		.10	.05	.01
☐ 156	Bob Murray		.06	.03	.00
☐ 157	Kirk Muller		.15	.07	.01
☐ 158	Brian Propp		.20	.10	.02
☐ 159	Ron Greschner		.10	.05	.01
☐ 160	Rob Ramage		.10	.05	.01
☐ 161	Craig Laughlin		.06	.03	.00
☐ 162	Steve Kasper		.10	.05	.01
☐ 163	Patrick Roy		7.00	3.50	.70
☐ 164	Shawn Burr		.35	.17	.03
☐ 165	Craig Hartsburg		.06	.03	.00
☐ 166	Dean Evason		.25	.12	.02
☐ 167	Bob Bourne		.06	.03	.00
☐ 168	Mike Gartner		.20	.10	.02
☐ 169	Ron Hextall		3.50	1.75	.35
☐ 170	Joe Cirella		.10	.05	.01
☐ 171	Dan Quinn		.10	.05	.01
☐ 172	Tony McKegney		.06	.03	.00
☐ 173	Pat LaFontaine		1.25	.60	.12
☐ 174	Allen Pedersen		.06	.03	.00
☐ 175	Doug Gilmour		.15	.07	.01
☐ 176	Gary Suter		.50	.25	.05
☐ 177	Barry Pederson		.10	.05	.01
☐ 178	Grant Fuhr		.90	.45	.09
☐ 179	Wayne Presley		.40	.20	.04
☐ 180	Wilf Paiement		.06	.03	.00
☐ 181	Doug Smail		.10	.05	.01
☐ 182	Doug Crossman		.10	.05	.01
☐ 183	Bernie Nichols		.65	.30	.06
☐ 184	Dirk Graham		.10	.05	.01
☐ 185	Anton Stastny		.10	.05	.01
☐ 186	Greg Stefan		.10	.05	.01
☐ 187	Ron Francis		.50	.25	.05
☐ 188	Steve Thomas		.20	.10	.02
☐ 189	Kelly Miller		.60	.30	.06
☐ 190	Tomas Jonsson		.06	.03	.00

		MINT	EXC	G-VG
☐ 191	John MacLean	1.25	.60	.12
☐ 192	Larry Robinson	.20	.10	.02
☐ 193	Doug Wickenheiser	.06	.03	.00
☐ 194	Keith Crowder	.06	.03	.00
☐ 195	Bob Froese	.10	.05	.01
☐ 196	Jim Johnson	.06	.03	.00
☐ 197	Checklist 1-132	.15	.01	.00
☐ 198	Checklist 133-264	.15	.01	.00
☐ 199	Glenn Anderson	.25	.12	.02
☐ 200	Kevin Lowe	.20	.10	.02
☐ 201	Kevin McClelland	.06	.03	.00
☐ 202	Mike Krushelnyski	.10	.05	.01
☐ 203	Craig MacTavish	.10	.05	.01
☐ 204	Andy Moog	.40	.20	.04
☐ 205	Marty McSorley	3.00	1.50	.30
☐ 206	Craig Muni	.25	.12	.02
☐ 207	Charlie Huddy	.15	.07	.01
☐ 208	Hakan Loob	.15	.07	.01
☐ 209	Jim Peplinski	.06	.03	.00
☐ 210	Mike Bullard	.10	.05	.01
☐ 211	Carey Wilson	.10	.05	.01
☐ 212	Joel Otto	.10	.05	.01
☐ 213	Neil Sheehy	.25	.12	.02
☐ 214	Jamie Macoun	.10	.05	.01
☐ 215	Mike Vernon	3.50	1.75	.35
☐ 216	Steve Bozek	.06	.03	.00
☐ 217	Daniel Berthiaume	3.00	1.50	.30
☐ 218	Gilles Hamel	.06	.03	.00
☐ 219	Tim Watters	.06	.03	.00
☐ 220	Mario Marois	.06	.03	.00
☐ 221	Thomas Steen	.10	.05	.01
☐ 222	Laurie Boschman	.06	.03	.00
☐ 223	Steve Rooney	.10	.05	.01
☐ 224	Ron Wilson	.06	.03	.00
☐ 225	Fredrik Olausson	.45	.22	.04
☐ 226	Jim Kyte	.15	.07	.01
☐ 227	Claude Lemieux	2.50	1.25	.25
☐ 228	Bob Gainey	.20	.10	.02
☐ 229	Gaston Gingras	.06	.03	.00
☐ 230	Brian Hayward	.15	.07	.01
☐ 231	Ryan Walter	.10	.05	.01
☐ 232	Guy Carbonneau	.15	.07	.01
☐ 233	Stephane Richer	7.00	3.50	.70
☐ 234	Rick Green	.06	.03	.00
☐ 235	Brian Skrudland	.65	.30	.06
☐ 236	Allan Bester	.20	.10	.02
☐ 237	Borje Salming	.15	.07	.01
☐ 238	Al Iafrate	.20	.10	.02
☐ 239	Rick Lanz	.06	.03	.00
☐ 240	Gary Leeman	.20	.10	.02
☐ 241	Greg Terrion	.06	.03	.00
☐ 242	Ken Wregget	.75	.35	.07
☐ 243	Vincent Damphousse	5.50	2.75	.55

		MINT	EXC	G-VG
☐ 244	Chris Kotsopoulos	.06	.03	.00
☐ 245	Dale Hunter	.10	.05	.01
☐ 246	Clint Malarchuk	.20	.10	.02
☐ 247	Paul Gillis	.06	.03	.00
☐ 248	Robert Picard	.06	.03	.00
☐ 249	Doug Shedden	.06	.03	.00
☐ 250	Mario Gosselin	.15	.07	.01
☐ 251	Randy Moller	.06	.03	.00
☐ 252	David Shaw	.06	.03	.00
☐ 253	Mike Eagles	.06	.03	.00
☐ 254	Alain Cote	.06	.03	.00
☐ 255	Petri Skriko	.15	.07	.01
☐ 256	Doug Lidster	.10	.05	.01
☐ 257	Richard Brodeur	.10	.05	.01
☐ 258	Rich Sutter	.10	.05	.01
☐ 259	Steve Tambellini	.06	.03	.00
☐ 260	Jim Benning	.06	.03	.00
☐ 261	Dave Richter	.06	.03	.00
☐ 262	Michael Petit	.25	.12	.02
☐ 263	Brent Peterson	.06	.03	.00
☐ 264	Jim Sandlak	.20	.10	.02

1988-89 O-Pee-Chee

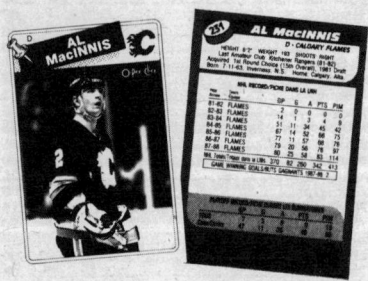

The 1988-89 O-Pee-Chee hockey set contains 264 standard size (2½" by 3½") cards. The fronts feature color photos with various colored borders and each player's team logo. The backs are amber and show career statistics and highlights. There were cards printed on the bottoms of the wax boxes; these cards are similar to the regular issue cards but are "lettered" A-P rather than numbered. These wax box cards are not considered part of the complete set price below, as they are usually offered separately or as an extra. The key rookie cards in this set are Jeff Brown, Rob Brown, Dave Gagner,

Brett Hull, Joe Nieuwendyk, Bob Probert, Steve Smith, and Pierre Turgeon.

Le jeu de cartes de hockey O-Pee-Chee 1988-89 contient 264 cartes de format standard (2¹/₂" x 3¹/₂"). La face comporte une photo en couleurs bordée de couleurs différentes, et l'emblème de l'équipe de chaque joueur. Le dos est de couleur ambre, et indique les statistiques et dates marquantes. Des cartes ont été imprimées sur les fonds de boîtes paraffinées. Elles ressemblent aux cartes de l'édition régulière, mais portent les lettres A-P au lieu d'être numérotées. Ces cartes imprimées sur boîte ne sont pas considérées comme faisant partie du jeu complet évalué ci-dessous, étant généralement offertes séparément ou en prime. Les débutants importants de ce jeu sont Jeff Brown, Rob Brown, Dave Gagner, Brett Hull, Joe Nieuwendijk, Bob Probert, Steve Smith, et Pierre Turgeon.

			MINT	EXC	G-VG
		COMPLETE SET (264)	175.00	85.00	18.00
		COMMON PLAYER (1-264)	.05	.02	.00
☐	1	Mario Lemieux	10.00	2.50	.50
☐	2	Bob Joyce	.50	.25	.05
☐	3	Joel Quenneville	.05	.02	.00
☐	4	Tony McKegney	.05	.02	.00
☐	5	Stephane Richer	1.50	.75	.15
☐	6	Mark Howe	.15	.07	.01
☐	7	Brent Sutter	.10	.05	.01
☐	8	Gilles Meloche	.10	.05	.01
☐	9	Jimmy Carson	.40	.20	.04
☐	10	John MacLean	.60	.30	.06
☐	11	Gary Leeman	.15	.07	.01
☐	12	Gerard Gallant	.40	.20	.04
☐	13	Marcel Dionne	.40	.20	.04
☐	14	Dave Christian	.05	.02	.00
☐	15	Gary Nylund	.05	.02	.00
☐	16	Joe Nieuwendyk	15.00	7.50	1.50
☐	17	Billy Smith	.15	.07	.01
☐	18	Christian Ruutu	.10	.05	.01
☐	19	Randy Cunneyworth	.05	.02	.00
☐	20	Brian Lawton	.05	.02	.00
☐	21	Scott Mellanby	.40	.20	.04
☐	22	Peter Stastny	.45	.22	.04
☐	23	Gord Kluzak	.05	.02	.00
☐	24	Sylvain Turgeon	.05	.02	.00
☐	25	Clint Malarchuk	.15	.07	.01
☐	26	Denis Savard	.50	.25	.05
☐	27	Craig Simpson	.40	.20	.04
☐	28	Petr Klima	.50	.25	.05
☐	29	Pat Verbeek	.15	.07	.01
☐	30	Moe Mantha	.05	.02	.00
☐	31	Chris Nilan	.05	.02	.00
☐	32	Barry Pederson	.05	.02	.00
☐	33	Randy Burridge	.05	.02	.00
☐	34	Ron Hextall	.85	.40	.08
☐	35	Gaston Gingras	.05	.02	.00
☐	36	Kevin Dineen	.15	.07	.01

			MINT	EXC	G-VG
☐	37	Tom Laidlaw	.05	.02	.00
☐	38	Paul MacLean	.10	.05	.01
☐	39	John Chabot	.05	.02	.00
☐	40	Lindy Ruff	.05	.02	.00
☐	41	Dan Quinn	.10	.05	.01
☐	42	Don Beaupre	.10	.05	.01
☐	43	Gary Suter	.30	.15	.03
☐	44	Mikko Makela	.15	.07	.01
☐	45	Mark Johnson	.05	.02	.00
☐	46	Dave Taylor	.15	.07	.01
☐	47	Ulf Dahlen	.25	.12	.02
☐	48	Jeff Sharples	.15	.07	.01
☐	49	Chris Chelios	.30	.15	.03
☐	50	Mike Gartner	.20	.10	.02
☐	51	Darren Pang	.35	.17	.03
☐	52	Ron Francis	.40	.20	.04
☐	53	Ken Morrow	.05	.02	.00
☐	54	Michel Goulet	.20	.10	.02
☐	55	Ray Sheppard	1.00	.50	.10
☐	56	Doug Gilmour	.15	.07	.01
☐	57	David Shaw	.05	.02	.00
☐	58	Cam Neely	1.50	.75	.15
☐	59	Grant Fuhr	.60	.30	.06
☐	60	Scott Stevens	.20	.10	.02
☐	61	Bob Brooke	.05	.02	.00
☐	62	Dave Hunter	.05	.02	.00
☐	63	Alan Kerr	.05	.02	.00
☐	64	Brad Marsh	.05	.02	.00
☐	65	Dale Hawerchuk	.45	.22	.04
☐	66	Brett Hull	100.00	50.00	10.00
☐	67	Patrik Sundstrom	.10	.05	.01
☐	68	Greg Stefan	.10	.05	.01
☐	69	James Patrick	.10	.05	.01
☐	70	Dale Hunter	.05	.02	.00
☐	71	Al Iafrate	.15	.07	.01
☐	72	Bob Carpenter	.10	.05	.01
☐	73	Ray Bourque	1.00	.50	.10
☐	74	John Tucker	.05	.02	.00
☐	75	Carey Wilson	.05	.02	.00
☐	76	Joe Mullen	.20	.10	.02
☐	77	Rick Vaive	.10	.05	.01
☐	78	Shawn Burr	.05	.02	.00
☐	79	Murray Craven	.10	.05	.01
☐	80	Clark Gillies	.10	.05	.01
☐	81	Bernie Federko	.10	.05	.01
☐	82	Tony Tanti	.10	.05	.01
☐	83	Greg Gilbert	.10	.05	.01
☐	84	Kirk Muller	.20	.10	.02
☐	85	Dave Tippett	.05	.02	.00
☐	86	Kevin Hatcher	.40	.20	.04
☐	87	Rick Middleton	.15	.07	.01
☐	88	Bobby Smith	.20	.10	.02
☐	89	Doug Wilson	.25	.12	.02

			MINT	EXC	G-VG
☐	90	Scott Arniel	.05	.02	.00
☐	91	Brian Mullen	.10	.05	.01
☐	92	Mike O'Connell	.05	.02	.00
☐	93	Mark Messier	1.00	.50	.10
☐	94	Sean Burke	1.00	.50	.10
☐	95	Brian Bellows	.30	.15	.03
☐	96	Doug Bodger	.05	.02	.00
☐	97	Bryan Trottier	.30	.15	.03
☐	98	Anton Stastny	.10	.05	.01
☐	99A	Checklist 1-99	.15	.01	.00
		(found in vending cases)			
☐	99B	Checklist 1-132	.15	.01	.00
		(found in wax cases)			
☐	100	Dave Poulin	.10	.05	.01
☐	101	Bob Bourne	.05	.02	.00
☐	102	John Vanbiesbrouck	.20	.10	.02
☐	103	Allen Pedersen	.05	.02	.00
☐	104	Mike Ridley	.10	.05	.01
☐	105	Andrew McBain	.05	.02	.00
☐	106	Troy Murray	.10	.05	.01
☐	107	Tom Barrasso	.20	.10	.02
☐	108	Tomas Jonsson	.05	.02	.00
☐	109	Rob Brown	5.00	2.50	.50
☐	110	Hakan Loob	.15	.07	.01
☐	111	Ilkka Sinisalo	.10	.05	.01
☐	112	Dave Archibald	.25	.12	.02
☐	113	Doug Halward	.05	.02	.00
☐	114	Ray Ferraro	.10	.05	.01
☐	115	Doug Brown	.15	.07	.01
☐	116	Patrick Roy	2.50	1.25	.25
☐	117	Greg Millen	.10	.05	.01
☐	118	Ken Linseman	.10	.05	.01
☐	119	Phil Housley	.20	.10	.02
☐	120	Wayne Gretzky UER	10.00	5.00	1.00
		(No position on front)			
☐	121	Tomas Sandstrom	.35	.17	.03
☐	122	Brendan Shanahan	2.50	1.25	.25
☐	123	Pat LaFontaine	.65	.30	.06
☐	124	Luc Robitaille	5.00	2.50	.50
☐	125	Ed Olczyk	.20	.10	.02
☐	126	Ron Sutter	.10	.05	.01
☐	127	Mike Liut	.15	.07	.01
☐	128	Brent Ashton	.05	.02	.00
☐	129	Tony Hrkac	.45	.22	.04
☐	130	Kelly Miller	.10	.05	.01
☐	131	Alan Haworth	.05	.02	.00
☐	132	Dave McIlwain	.25	.12	.02
☐	133	Mike Ramsey	.05	.02	.00
☐	134	Bob Sweeney	.25	.12	.02
☐	135	Dirk Graham	.05	.02	.00
☐	136	Ulf Samuelsson	.15	.07	.01
☐	137	Petri Skriko	.10	.05	.01
☐	138	Aaron Broten	.05	.02	.00

		MINT	EXC	G-VG
☐ 139	Jim Fox	.05	.02	.00
☐ 140	Randy Wood	.15	.07	.01
☐ 141	Larry Murphy	.10	.05	.01
☐ 142	Daniel Berthiaume	.40	.20	.04
☐ 143	Kelly Kisio	.10	.05	.01
☐ 144	Neal Broten	.10	.05	.01
☐ 145	Reed Larson	.05	.02	.00
☐ 146	Peter Zezel	.10	.05	.01
☐ 147	Jari Kurri	.50	.25	.05
☐ 148	Jim Johnson	.05	.02	.00
☐ 149	Gino Cavallini	.10	.05	.01
☐ 150	Glen Hanlon	.10	.05	.01
☐ 151	Bengt Gustafsson	.05	.02	.00
☐ 152	Mike Bullard	.10	.05	.01
☐ 153	John Ogrodnick	.10	.05	.01
☐ 154	Steve Larmer	.30	.15	.03
☐ 155	Kelly Hrudey	.25	.12	.02
☐ 156	Mats Naslund	.20	.10	.02
☐ 157	Bruce Driver	.10	.05	.01
☐ 158	Randy Hillier	.05	.02	.00
☐ 159	Craig Hartsburg	.05	.02	.00
☐ 160	Rollie Melanson	.10	.05	.01
☐ 161	Adam Oates	5.00	2.50	.50
☐ 162	Greg Adams	.10	.05	.01
	Vancouver Canucks			
☐ 163	Dave Andreychuk	.10	.05	.01
☐ 164	Dave Babych	.10	.05	.01
☐ 165	Brian Noonan	.10	.05	.01
☐ 166	Glen Wesley	1.00	.50	.10
☐ 167	Dave Ellett	.10	.05	.01
☐ 168	Brian Propp	.15	.07	.01
☐ 169	Bernie Nicholls	.40	.20	.04
☐ 170	Walt Poddubny	.10	.05	.01
☐ 171	Steve Konroyd	.05	.02	.00
☐ 172	Doug Sulliman	.05	.02	.00
☐ 173	Mario Gosselin	.15	.07	.01
☐ 174	Brian Benning	.05	.02	.00
☐ 175	Dino Ciccarelli	.20	.10	.02
☐ 176	Steve Kasper	.10	.05	.01
☐ 177	Rick Tocchet	2.75	1.35	.27
☐ 178	Brad McCrimmon	.05	.02	.00
☐ 179	Paul Coffey	.75	.35	.07
☐ 180	Pete Peeters	.10	.05	.01
☐ 181	Bob Probert	4.00	2.00	.40
☐ 182	Steve Duchesne	2.50	1.25	.25
☐ 183	Russ Courtnall	.25	.12	.02
☐ 184	Mike Foligno	.05	.02	.00
☐ 185	Wayne Presley	.05	.02	.00
☐ 186	Rejean Lemelin	.15	.07	.01
☐ 187	Mark Hunter	.05	.02	.00
☐ 188	Joe Cirella	.10	.05	.01
☐ 189	Glenn Anderson	.25	.12	.02
☐ 190	John Anderson	.05	.02	.00

		MINT	EXC	G-VG
☐ 191	Pat Flatley	.05	.02	.00
☐ 192	Rod Langway	.15	.07	.01
☐ 193	Brian MacLellan	.05	.02	.00
☐ 194	Pierre Turgeon	11.00	5.50	1.10
☐ 195	Brian Hayward	.15	.07	.01
☐ 196	Steve Yzerman	1.50	.75	.15
☐ 197	Doug Crossman	.10	.05	.01
☐ 198A	Checklist 100-198	.15	.01	.00
	(found in vending cases)			
☐ 198B	Checklist 133-264	.15	.01	.00
	(found in wax cases)			
☐ 199	Greg C. Adams	.05	.02	.00
	Edmonton Oilers			
☐ 200	Laurie Boschman	.05	.02	.00
☐ 201	Jeff Brown	1.50	.75	.15
☐ 202	Garth Butcher	.50	.25	.05
☐ 203	Guy Carbonneau	.15	.07	.01
☐ 204	Randy Carlyle	.10	.05	.01
☐ 205	Alain Cote	.05	.02	.00
☐ 206	Keith Crowder	.05	.02	.00
☐ 207	Vincent Damphousse	1.00	.50	.10
☐ 208	Gaetan Duchesne	.35	.17	.03
☐ 209	Iain Duncan	.05	.02	.00
☐ 210	Tommy Albelin	.15	.07	.01
☐ 211	Pelle Eklund	.15	.07	.01
☐ 212	Jan Erixon	.20	.10	.02
☐ 213	Paul Fenton	.20	.10	.02
☐ 214	Tom Fergus	.05	.02	.00
☐ 215	Dave Gagner	5.00	2.50	.50
☐ 216	Bob Gainey	.15	.07	.01
☐ 217	Stewart Gavin	.10	.05	.01
☐ 218	Charlie Huddy	.10	.05	.01
☐ 219	Jeff Jackson	.15	.07	.01
☐ 220	Uwe Krupp	.50	.25	.05
☐ 221	Mike Krushelnyski	.10	.05	.01
☐ 222	Tom Kurvers	.05	.02	.00
☐ 223	Jason Lambert	.05	.02	.00
☐ 224	Lane Lambert	.05	.02	.00
☐ 225	Rick Lanz	.05	.02	.00
☐ 226	Brad Lauer	.10	.05	.01
☐ 227	Claude Lemieux	.40	.20	.04
☐ 228	Doug Lidster	.05	.02	.00
☐ 229	Kevin Lowe UER	.20	.10	.02
	(Has Gretzky's stats)			
☐ 230	Craig Ludwig	.05	.02	.00
☐ 231	Al MacInnis	1.50	.75	.15
☐ 232	Craig MacTavish	.10	.05	.01
☐ 233	Mario Marois	.05	.02	.00
	(misspelled Marios on checklist 198)			
☐ 234	Lanny McDonald	.25	.12	.02
☐ 235	Rick Meagher	.10	.05	.01
☐ 236	Craig Muni	.10	.05	.01
☐ 237	Mike McPhee	.15	.07	.01

			MINT	EXC	G-VG
☐	238	Ric Nattress	.10	.05	.01
☐	239	Ray Neufeld	.05	.02	.00
☐	240	Lee Norwood	.10	.05	.01
☐	241	Mark Osborne UER	.10	.05	.01
		(Misspelled Osbourne on both sides)			
☐	242	Joel Otto	.10	.05	.01
☐	243	Jim Peplinski	.05	.02	.00
☐	244	Rob Ramage	.10	.05	.01
☐	245	Luke Richardson	.20	.10	.02
☐	246	Larry Robinson	.20	.10	.02
☐	247	Borje Salming	.15	.07	.01
☐	248	David Saunders	.05	.02	.00
☐	249	Al Secord	.10	.05	.01
☐	250	Charlie Simmer	.10	.05	.01
☐	251	Doug Smail	.10	.05	.01
☐	252	Steve Smith	1.75	.85	.17
☐	253	Stan Smyl	.10	.05	.01
☐	254	Thomas Steen	.10	.05	.01
☐	255	Rich Sutter	.10	.05	.01
☐	256	Petr Svoboda	.50	.25	.05
☐	257	Peter Taglianetti	.25	.12	.02
☐	258	Steve Tambellini	.05	.02	.00
☐	259	Steve Thomas	.10	.05	.01
☐	260	Esa Tikkanen	1.25	.60	.12
☐	261	Mike Vernon	.75	.35	.07
☐	262	Ryan Walter	.10	.05	.01
☐	263	Doug Wickenheiser	.05	.02	.00
☐	264	Ken Wregget	.25	.12	.02

1989-90 O-Pee-Chee

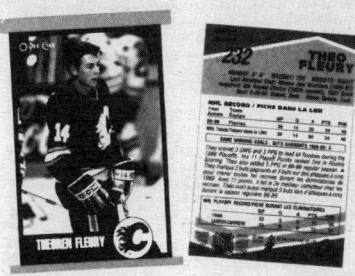

The 1989-90 O-Pee-Chee hockey set contains 330 cards, each measuring the standard size, 2¹/₂" by 3¹/₂". The fronts feature color action photos with various color borders and each player's team logo at the lower right hand corner. Aqua-blue stripes appear at the top and bottom on the card face, with marble gray background along the sides. The backs are tinted red with black letters, and provide career statistics and highlights. The team cards in the set (298-318) are actually action scenes with no players explicitly identified; the team card backs provide for and against power play stats for the team's previous season. This set was produced in unprecedented quantities for O-Pee-Chee, as they allowed reorders from dealers and went back to press for a second printing. Most dealers consider that this O-Pee-Chee set was produced in an amount much greater than the Topps production of this year, whose production was considered rather normal or typical for Topps hockey.

Le jeu O-Pee-Chee 1989-90 contient 330 cartes de format standard, 2¹/₂" x 3¹/₂". La face représente une photo d'action en couleurs, entourée d'un bord de couleurs variées, et comportant l'emblème de l'équipe de chaque joueur au coin inférieur droit. Des rayures bleues-vertes soulignent le haut et le bas de la face, avec un fond gris marbré longeant les côtés. Le dos est d'une teinte rouge avec des lettres noires, et présente des statistiques et des moments importants de la carrière.

			MINT	EXC	G-VG
	COMPLETE SET (330)		24.00	12.00	2.40
	COMMON PLAYER (1-330)		.03	.01	.00
☐	1	Mario Lemieux	2.00	.50	.10
☐	2	Ulf Dahlen	.06	.03	.00
☐	3	Terry Carkner	.10	.05	.01
☐	4	Tony McKegney	.03	.01	.00
☐	5	Dennis Savard	.20	.10	.02
☐	6	Derek King	.10	.05	.01

			MINT	EXC	G-VG
☐	7	Lanny McDonald	.10	.05	.01
☐	8	John Tonelli	.06	.03	.00
☐	9	Tom Kurvers	.03	.01	.00
☐	10	David Archibald	.03	.01	.00
☐	11	Peter Sidorkiewicz	.30	.15	.03
☐	12	Esa Tikkanen	.25	.12	.02
☐	13	Dave Barr	.03	.01	.00
☐	14	Brent Sutter	.06	.03	.00
☐	15	Cam Neely	.40	.20	.04
☐	16	Calle Johansson	.10	.05	.01
☐	17	Patrick Roy	.40	.20	.04
☐	18	Dale DeGray	.10	.05	.01
☐	19	Phil Bourque	.20	.10	.02
☐	20	Kevin Dineen	.08	.04	.01
☐	21	Mike Bullard	.03	.01	.00
☐	22	Gary Leeman	.08	.04	.01
☐	23	Greg Stefan	.06	.03	.00
☐	24	Brian Mullen	.06	.03	.00
☐	25	Pierre Turgeon	.65	.30	.06
☐	26	Bob Rouse	.10	.05	.01
☐	27	Peter Zezel	.06	.03	.00
☐	28	Jeff Brown	.15	.07	.01
☐	29	Andy Brickley	.10	.05	.01
☐	30	Mike Gartner	.10	.05	.01
☐	31	Darren Pang	.08	.04	.01
☐	32	Pat Verbeek	.08	.04	.01
☐	33	Petri Skriko	.03	.01	.00
☐	34	Tom Laidlaw	.03	.01	.00
☐	35	Randy Wood	.03	.01	.00
☐	36	Tom Barrasso	.08	.04	.01
☐	37	John Tucker	.03	.01	.00
☐	38	Andrew McBain	.03	.01	.00
☐	39	David Shaw	.03	.01	.00
☐	40	Rejean Lemelin	.08	.04	.01
☐	41	Dino Ciccarelli	.10	.05	.01
☐	42	Jeff Sharples	.03	.01	.00
☐	43	Jari Kurri	.25	.12	.02
☐	44	Murray Craven	.06	.03	.00
☐	45	Cliff Ronning	.60	.30	.06
☐	46	Dave Babych	.03	.01	.00
☐	47	Bernie Nicholls	.20	.10	.02
☐	48	Jon Casey	1.00	.50	.10
☐	49	Al MacInnis	.20	.10	.02
☐	50	Bob Errey	.10	.05	.01
☐	51	Glen Wesley	.08	.04	.01
☐	52	Dirk Graham	.03	.01	.00
☐	53	Guy Carbonneau	.06	.03	.00
☐	54	Tomas Sandstrom	.10	.05	.01
☐	55	Rod Langway	.08	.04	.01
☐	56	Patrik Sundstrom	.06	.03	.00
☐	57	Michel Goulet	.10	.05	.01
☐	58	Dave Taylor	.08	.04	.01
☐	59	Phil Housley	.08	.04	.01

			MINT	EXC	G-VG
☐	60	Pat LaFontaine	.25	.12	.02
☐	61	Kirk McLean	.40	.20	.04
☐	62	Ken Linseman	.03	.01	.00
☐	63	Randy Cunneyworth	.03	.01	.00
☐	64	Tony Hrkac	.03	.01	.00
☐	65	Mark Messier	.40	.20	.04
☐	66	Carey Wilson	.03	.01	.00
☐	67	Stephen Leach	.20	.10	.02
☐	68	Christian Ruuttu	.03	.01	.00
☐	69	Dave Ellett	.03	.01	.00
☐	70	Ray Ferraro	.03	.01	.00
☐	71	Colin Patterson	.10	.05	.01
☐	72	Tim Kerr	.08	.04	.01
☐	73	Bob Joyce	.06	.03	.00
☐	74	Doug Gilmour	.08	.04	.01
☐	75	Lee Norwood	.03	.01	.00
☐	76	Dale Hunter	.03	.01	.00
☐	77	Jim Johnson	.03	.01	.00
☐	78	Mike Foligno	.03	.01	.00
☐	79	Al Iafrate	.06	.03	.00
☐	80	Rick Tocchet	.30	.15	.03
☐	81	Greg Hawgood	.15	.07	.01
☐	82	Steve Thomas	.06	.03	.00
☐	83	Steve Yzerman	.40	.20	.04
☐	84	Mike McPhee	.06	.03	.00
☐	85	Dave Volek	.40	.20	.04
☐	86	Brian Benning	.03	.01	.00
☐	87	Neal Broten	.06	.03	.00
☐	88	Luc Robitaille	.45	.22	.04
☐	89	Trevor Linden	1.50	.75	.15
☐	90	James Patrick	.06	.03	.00
☐	91	Brian Lawton	.03	.01	.00
☐	92	Sean Burke	.12	.06	.01
☐	93	Scott Stevens	.10	.05	.01
☐	94	Pat Elynuik	.50	.25	.05
☐	95	Paul Coffey	.30	.15	.03
☐	96	Jan Erixon	.03	.01	.00
☐	97	Mike Liut	.08	.04	.01
☐	98	Wayne Presley	.03	.01	.00
☐	99	Craig Simpson	.15	.07	.01
☐	100	Kjell Samuelsson	.15	.07	.01
☐	101	Shawn Burr	.03	.01	.00
☐	102	John MacLean	.10	.05	.01
☐	103	Tom Fergus	.03	.01	.00
☐	104	Mike Krushelnyski	.03	.01	.00
☐	105	Gary Nylund	.03	.01	.00
☐	106	Dave Andreychuk	.06	.03	.00
☐	107	Bernie Federko	.06	.03	.00
☐	108	Gary Suter	.10	.05	.01
☐	109	Dave Gagner	.25	.12	.02
☐	110	Ray Bourque	.35	.17	.03
☐	111	Geoff Courtnall	1.00	.50	.10
☐	112	Doug Wilson	.10	.05	.01

		MINT	EXC	G-VG
☐ 113	Joe Sakic	6.00	3.00	.60
☐ 114	John Vanbiesbrouck	.10	.05	.01
☐ 115	Dave Poulin	.06	.03	.00
☐ 116	Rick Meagher	.03	.01	.00
☐ 117	Kirk Muller	.08	.04	.01
☐ 118	Mats Naslund	.08	.04	.01
☐ 119	Ray Sheppard	.03	.01	.00
☐ 120	Jeff Norton	.15	.07	.01
☐ 121	Randy Burridge	.03	.01	.00
☐ 122	Dale Hawerchuk	.15	.07	.01
☐ 123	Steve Duchesne	.15	.07	.01
☐ 124	John Anderson	.03	.01	.00
☐ 125	Rick Vaive	.06	.03	.00
☐ 126	Randy Hillier	.03	.01	.00
☐ 127	Jimmy Carson	.20	.10	.02
☐ 128	Larry Murphy	.06	.03	.00
☐ 129	Paul MacLean	.06	.03	.00
☐ 130	Joe Cirella	.06	.03	.00
☐ 131	Kelly Miller	.06	.03	.00
☐ 132	Alain Chevrier	.06	.03	.00
☐ 133	Ed Olczyk	.08	.04	.01
☐ 134	Dave Tippett	.03	.01	.00
☐ 135	Bob Sweeney	.03	.01	.00
☐ 136	Brian Leetch	2.00	1.00	.20
☐ 137	Greg Millen	.06	.03	.00
☐ 138	Joe Nieuwendyk	.75	.35	.07
☐ 139	Brian Propp	.08	.04	.01
☐ 140	Mike Ramsey	.03	.01	.00
☐ 141	Mike Allison	.03	.01	.00
☐ 142	Shawn Chambers	.12	.06	.01
☐ 143	Peter Stastny	.15	.07	.01
☐ 144	Glen Hanlon	.06	.03	.00
☐ 145	John Cullen	1.50	.75	.15
☐ 146	Kevin Hatcher	.15	.07	.01
☐ 147	Brendan Shanahan	.15	.07	.01
☐ 148	Paul Reinhart	.06	.03	.00
☐ 149	Bryan Trottier	.20	.10	.02
☐ 150	Dave Manson	.15	.07	.01
☐ 151	Marc Habscheid	.10	.05	.01
☐ 152	Dan Quinn	.06	.03	.00
☐ 153	Stephane Richer	.25	.12	.02
☐ 154	Doug Bodger	.03	.01	.00
☐ 155	Ron Hextall	.25	.12	.02
☐ 156	Wayne Gretzky	2.25	1.10	.22
☐ 157	Steve Tuttle	.10	.05	.01
☐ 158	Charlie Huddy	.06	.03	.00
☐ 159	Dave Christian	.03	.01	.00
☐ 160	Andy Moog	.15	.07	.01
☐ 161	Tony Granato	.75	.35	.07
☐ 162	Sylvain Cote	.10	.05	.01
☐ 163	Mike Vernon	.25	.12	.02
☐ 164	Steve Chiasson	.15	.07	.01
☐ 165	Mike Ridley	.06	.03	.00

		MINT	EXC	G-VG
☐ 166	Kelly Hrudey	.08	.04	.01
☐ 167	Bobby Carpenter	.06	.03	.00
☐ 168	Zarley Zalapski	.40	.20	.04
☐ 169	Derek Laxdal	.10	.05	.01
☐ 170	Clint Malarchuk	.06	.03	.00
☐ 171	Kelly Kisio	.03	.01	.00
☐ 172	Gerard Gallant	.12	.06	.01
☐ 173	Ron Sutter	.06	.03	.00
☐ 174	Chris Chelios	.15	.07	.01
☐ 175	Ron Francis	.15	.07	.01
☐ 176	Gino Cavallini	.06	.03	.00
☐ 177	Brian Bellows	.15	.07	.01
☐ 178	Greg C. Adams	.06	.03	.00
	Vancouver Canucks			
☐ 179	Steve Larmer	.15	.07	.01
☐ 180	Aaron Broten	.03	.01	.00
☐ 181	Brent Ashton	.03	.01	.00
☐ 182	Gerald Diduck	.10	.05	.01
☐ 183	Paul MacDermid	.10	.05	.01
☐ 184	Walt Poddubny	.06	.03	.00
☐ 185	Adam Oates	.45	.22	.04
☐ 186	Brett Hull	6.00	3.00	.60
☐ 187	Scott Arniel	.03	.01	.00
☐ 188	Bobby Smith	.08	.04	.01
☐ 189	Guy Lafleur	.30	.15	.03
☐ 190	Craig Janney	1.50	.75	.15
☐ 191	Mark Howe	.08	.04	.01
☐ 192	Grant Fuhr	.20	.10	.02
☐ 193	Rob Brown	.30	.15	.03
☐ 194	Steve Kasper	.06	.03	.00
☐ 195	Pete Peeters	.08	.04	.01
☐ 196	Joe Mullen	.08	.04	.01
☐ 197	Checklist 1-99	.08	.01	.00
☐ 198	Checklist 100-198	.08	.01	.00
☐ 199	Keith Crowder	.03	.01	.00
☐ 200	Daren Puppa	.75	.35	.07
☐ 201	Benoit Hogue	.25	.12	.02
☐ 202	Gary Roberts	.25	.12	.02
☐ 203	Brad McCrimmon	.03	.01	.00
☐ 204	Rick Wamsley	.08	.04	.01
☐ 205	Joel Otto	.06	.03	.00
☐ 206	Jim Peplinski	.03	.01	.00
☐ 207	Jamie Macoun	.06	.03	.00
☐ 208	Brian MacLellan	.03	.01	.00
☐ 209	Scott Young	.30	.15	.03
☐ 210	Ulf Samuelsson	.10	.05	.01
☐ 211	Joel Quenneville UER	.03	.01	.00
	(Misspelled Quennville on card back)			
☐ 212	Tim Watters	.03	.01	.00
☐ 213	Curt Giles	.03	.01	.00
☐ 214	Stewart Gavin	.06	.03	.00
☐ 215	Bob Brooke	.03	.01	.00
☐ 216	Basil McRae	.25	.12	.02

			MINT	EXC	G-VG
☐ 217	Frantisek Musil		.10	.05	.01
☐ 218	Adam Creighton		.25	.12	.02
☐ 219	Troy Murray		.08	.04	.01
☐ 220	Steve Konroyd		.03	.01	.00
☐ 221	Duane Sutter		.06	.03	.00
☐ 222	Trent Yawney		.12	.06	.01
☐ 223	Mike O'Connell		.03	.01	.00
☐ 224	Jim Nill		.03	.01	.00
☐ 225	John Chabot		.03	.01	.00
☐ 226	Glenn Anderson		.10	.05	.01
☐ 227	Kevin Lowe		.10	.05	.01
☐ 228	Steve Smith		.15	.07	.01
☐ 229	Randy Gregg		.06	.03	.00
☐ 230	Craig MacTavish		.06	.03	.00
☐ 231	Craig Muni		.03	.01	.00
☐ 232	Theoren Fleury		6.00	3.00	.60
☐ 233	Bill Ranford		.25	.12	.02
☐ 234	Claude Lemieux		.15	.07	.01
☐ 235	Larry Robinson		.10	.05	.01
☐ 236	Craig Ludwig		.03	.01	.00
☐ 237	Brian Hayward		.08	.04	.01
☐ 238	Petr Svoboda		.08	.04	.01
☐ 239	Russ Courtnall		.08	.04	.01
☐ 240	Ryan Walter		.06	.03	.00
☐ 241	Tommy Albelin		.03	.01	.00
☐ 242	Doug Brown		.03	.01	.00
☐ 243	Ken Daneyko		.10	.05	.01
☐ 244	Mark Johnson		.03	.01	.00
☐ 245	Randy Velischek		.10	.05	.01
☐ 246	Brad Dalgarno		.10	.05	.01
☐ 247	Mikko Makela		.03	.01	.00
☐ 248	Shayne Corson		.75	.35	.07
☐ 249	Marc Bergevin		.10	.05	.01
☐ 250	Patrick Flatley		.03	.01	.00
☐ 251	Michel Petit		.06	.03	.00
☐ 252	Mark Hardy		.03	.01	.00
☐ 253	Scott Mellanby		.06	.03	.00
☐ 254	Keith Acton		.03	.01	.00
☐ 255	Ken Wregget		.12	.06	.01
☐ 256	Gord Dineen		.10	.05	.01
☐ 257	Dave Hannan		.03	.01	.00
☐ 258	Mario Gosselin		.08	.04	.01
☐ 259	Randy Moller		.03	.01	.00
☐ 260	Mario Marois		.03	.01	.00
☐ 261	Robert Picard		.03	.01	.00
☐ 262	Marc Fortier		.10	.05	.01
☐ 263	Ron Tugnutt		.35	.17	.03
☐ 264	Iiro Jarvi		.10	.05	.01
☐ 265	Paul Gillis		.03	.01	.00
☐ 266	Mike Hough		.10	.05	.01
☐ 267	Jim Sandlak		.03	.01	.00
☐ 268	Greg Paslawski		.03	.01	.00
☐ 269	Paul Cavallini		.40	.20	.04

		MINT	EXC	G-VG
☐ 270	Gaston Gingras	.03	.01	.00
☐ 271	Allan Bester	.06	.03	.00
☐ 272	Vincent Damphousse	.20	.10	.02
☐ 273	Daniel Marois	.50	.25	.05
☐ 274	Mark Osbourne UER	.03	.01	.00
	(Misspelled Osbourne on card front)			
☐ 275	Craig Laughlin	.03	.01	.00
☐ 276	Brad Marsh	.03	.01	.00
☐ 277	Dan Daoust	.03	.01	.00
☐ 278	Borje Salming	.08	.04	.01
☐ 279	Chris Kotsopoulos	.03	.01	.00
☐ 280	Tony Tanti	.06	.03	.00
☐ 281	Barry Pederson	.03	.01	.00
☐ 282	Rich Sutter	.06	.03	.00
☐ 283	Stan Smyl	.06	.03	.00
☐ 284	Doug Lidster	.03	.01	.00
☐ 285	Steve Weeks	.06	.03	.00
☐ 286	Harold Snepsts	.06	.03	.00
☐ 287	Brian Bradley	.10	.05	.01
☐ 288	Larry Melnyk	.03	.01	.00
☐ 289	Bob Gould	.03	.01	.00
☐ 290	Thomas Steen	.06	.03	.00
☐ 291	Randy Carlyle	.06	.03	.00
☐ 292	Hannu Jarvenpaa UER	.10	.05	.01
	(Misspelled Jaryenpaa on card front)			
☐ 293	Iain Duncan	.03	.01	.00
☐ 294	Doug Smail	.06	.03	.00
☐ 295	Jim Kyte	.03	.01	.00
☐ 296	Daniel Berthiaume	.08	.04	.01
☐ 297	Peter Taglianetti	.03	.01	.00
☐ 298	Boston Bruins	.06	.03	.00
	Action Scene			
☐ 299	Buffalo Sabres	.06	.03	.00
	Action Scene			
☐ 300	Calgary Flames	.06	.03	.00
	Action Scene			
☐ 301	Chicago Blackhawks	.06	.03	.00
	Action Scene			
☐ 302	Detroit Red Wings	.06	.03	.00
	Action Scene			
☐ 303	Edmonton Oilers	.06	.03	.00
	Action Scene			
☐ 304	Hartford Whalers	.06	.03	.00
	Action Scene			
☐ 305	Los Angeles Kings	.06	.03	.00
	Action Scene			
☐ 306	Minnesota North Stars	.06	.03	.00
	Action Scene			
☐ 307	Montreal Canadians	.06	.03	.00
	Action Scene			
	(Chris Chelios' back)			
☐ 308	New Jersey Devils	.06	.03	.00
	Action Scene			

		MINT	EXC	G-VG
☐ 309	**New York Islanders** Action Scene	.06	.03	.00
☐ 310	**New York Rangers** Action Scene	.06	.03	.00
☐ 311	**Philadelphia Flyers** Action Scene	.06	.03	.00
☐ 312	**Pittsburgh Penguins** Action Scene Mario Lemieux	.30	.15	.03
☐ 313	**Quebec Nordiques** Action Scene Joe Sakic	.50	.25	.05
☐ 314	**St. Louis Blues** Action Scene	.06	.03	.00
☐ 315	**Toronto Maple Leafs** Action Scene	.06	.03	.00
☐ 316	**Vancouver Canucks** Action Scene (Ray Bourque defending)	.10	.05	.01
☐ 317	**Washington Capitals** Action Scene	.06	.03	.00
☐ 318	**Winnipeg Jets** Action Scene	.06	.03	.00
☐ 319	**Art Ross Trophy** Mario Lemieux	.30	.15	.03
☐ 320	**Hart Trophy** Wayne Gretzky	.50	.25	.05
☐ 321	**Calder Trophy** Brian Leetch	.30	.15	.03
☐ 322	**Vezina Trophy** Patrick Roy	.20	.10	.02
☐ 323	**Norris Trophy** Chris Chelios	.10	.05	.01
☐ 324	**Lady Byng Trophy** Joe Mullen	.06	.03	.00
☐ 325	**1988-89 Highlight** Wayne Gretzky	.50	.25	.05
☐ 326	**1988-89 Highlight** Brian Leetch UER (Photo actually David Shaw)	.30	.15	.03
☐ 327	**1988-89 Highlight** Mario Lemieux	.30	.15	.03
☐ 328	**1988-89 Highlight** Esa Tikkanen	.08	.04	.01
☐ 329	**Coupe Stanley Cup** Calgary Flames	.10	.05	.01
☐ 330	**Checklist 221-330**	.10	.01	.00

1990-91 O-Pee-Chee

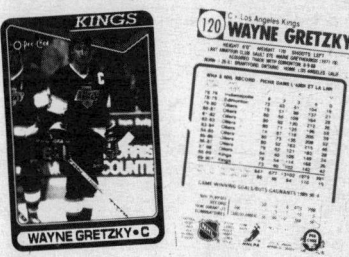

The 1990-91 O-Pee-Chee hockey set contains 528 cards, each measuring the standard size, 2½" by 3½". The fronts feature color action photos with borders in two different colors per card. A hockey stick is superimposed over the picture at the top border. The backs have blue lettering on a pale green background, and have biographical information and career statistics. The team cards are actually unidentified and uncaptioned action scenes with the team's previous season standings and power play stats on the card back.

Le jeu O-Pee-Chee 1990-91 contient 528 cartes de format standard, 2½" x 3½". La face représente une photo d'action en couleurs, entourée d'un bord bicolore, différent pour chaque carte. Un stick de hockey est superposé à la photo au bord supérieur. Le dos est imprimé en lettres bleues sur un fond vert pale, et présente des données biographiques et des statistiques de carrière.

			MINT	EXC	G-VG
	COMPLETE SET (528)		25.00	12.50	2.50
	COMMON PLAYER (1-528)		.03	.01	.00
☐	1	Gretzky Tribute	.50	.15	.03
		Indianapolis Racers			
☐	2	Gretzky Tribute	.30	.15	.03
		Edmonton Oilers			
☐	3	Gretzky Tribute	.30	.15	.03
		Los Angeles Kings			
☐	4	Brett Hull HL	.25	.12	.02
☐	5	Jari Kurri HL	.08	.04	.01
		(Jari, not Jarri)			
☐	6	Bryan Trottier HL	.08	.04	.01
☐	7	Jeremy Roenick	1.75	.85	.17
☐	8	Brian Propp	.08	.04	.01

			MINT	EXC	G-VG
☐	9	Jim Hrivnak	.10	.05	.01
☐	10	Mick Vukota	.10	.05	.01
☐	11	Tom Kurvers	.03	.01	.00
☐	12	Ulf Dahlen	.06	.03	.00
☐	13	Bernie Nicholls	.15	.07	.01
☐	14	Peter Sidorkiewicz	.08	.04	.01
☐	15	Peter Zezel	.06	.03	.00
☐	16	Mike Hartman	.10	.05	.01
☐	17	Kings Team	.06	.03	.00
☐	18	Jim Sandlak	.03	.01	.00
☐	19	Rob Brown	.15	.07	.01
☐	20	Paul Ranheim	.25	.12	.02
☐	21	Rick Zombo	.12	.06	.01
☐	22	Paul Gillis	.03	.01	.00
☐	23	Brian Hayward	.06	.03	.00
☐	24	Brent Ashton	.03	.01	.00
☐	25	Mark Lamb	.15	.07	.01
☐	26	Rick Tocchet	.20	.10	.02
☐	27	Viacheslav Fetisov	.25	.12	.02
☐	28	Denis Savard	.15	.07	.01
☐	29	Chris Chelios	.10	.05	.01
☐	30	Janne Ojanen	.10	.05	.01
☐	31	Don Maloney	.03	.01	.00
☐	32	Allan Bester	.06	.03	.00
☐	33	Geoff Smith	.12	.06	.01
☐	34	Daniel Shank	.12	.06	.01
☐	35	Mikael Andersson	.10	.05	.01
☐	36	Gino Cavallini	.06	.03	.00
☐	37	Rob Murphy	.10	.05	.01
☐	38	Flames Team	.06	.03	.00
☐	39	Laurie Boschman	.03	.01	.00
☐	40	Craig Wolanin	.12	.06	.01
☐	41	Phil Bourque	.03	.01	.00
☐	42	Alexander Mogilny	.60	.30	.06
☐	43	Ray Bourque	.35	.17	.03
☐	44	Mike Liut	.06	.03	.00
☐	45	Ron Sutter	.06	.03	.00
☐	46	Bob Kudelski	.20	.10	.02
☐	47	Larry Murphy	.03	.01	.00
☐	48	Darren Turcotte	1.00	.50	.10
☐	49	Paul Ysebaert	.30	.15	.03
☐	50	Alan Kerr	.03	.01	.00
☐	51	Randy Carlyle	.03	.01	.00
☐	52	Iiro Jarvi	.06	.03	.00
☐	53	Don Barber	.10	.05	.01
☐	54	Carey Wilson UER	.03	.01	.00
		(Misspelled Cary on both sides)			
☐	55	Joe Kocur	.15	.07	.01
☐	56	Steve Larmer	.15	.07	.01
☐	57	Paul Cavallini	.06	.03	.00
☐	58	Shayne Corson	.12	.06	.01
☐	59	Canucks Team	.06	.03	.00
☐	60	Sergei Makarov	.50	.25	.05

			MINT	EXC	G-VG
☐	61	Kjell Samuelson	.03	.01	.00
☐	62	Tony Granato	.25	.12	.02
☐	63	Tom Fergus	.03	.01	.00
☐	64	Martin Gelinas	.35	.17	.03
☐	65	Tom Barrasso	.08	.04	.01
☐	66	Pierre Turgeon	.45	.22	.04
☐	67	Randy Cunneyworth	.03	.01	.00
☐	68	Michal Pivonka	.15	.07	.01
☐	69	Cam Neely	.35	.17	.03
☐	70	Brian Bellows	.12	.06	.01
☐	71	Pat Elynuik	.10	.05	.01
☐	72	Doug Crossman	.03	.01	.00
☐	73	Sylvain Turgeon	.03	.01	.00
☐	74	Shawn Burr	.03	.01	.00
☐	75	John Vanbiesbrouck	.12	.06	.01
☐	76	Steve Bozek	.03	.01	.00
☐	77	Brett Hull	1.00	.50	.10
☐	78	Zarley Zalapski	.08	.04	.01
☐	79	Wendel Clark	.06	.03	.00
☐	80	Flyers Team	.06	.03	.00
☐	81	Kelly Miller	.06	.03	.00
☐	82	Mark Pederson	.15	.07	.01
☐	83	Adam Creighton	.08	.04	.01
☐	84	Scott Young	.08	.04	.01
☐	85	Petr Klima	.12	.06	.01
☐	86	Steve Duchesne	.06	.03	.00
☐	87	Joe Nieuwendyk	.45	.22	.04
☐	88	Andy Brickley	.03	.01	.00
☐	89	Phil Housley	.08	.04	.01
☐	90	Neal Broten	.06	.03	.00
☐	91	Al Iafrate	.06	.03	.00
☐	92	Steve Thomas	.06	.03	.00
☐	93	Guy Carbonneau	.06	.03	.00
☐	94	Steve Chiasson	.06	.03	.00
☐	95	Mike Tomlak	.10	.05	.01
☐	96	Roger Johansson	.08	.04	.01
☐	97	Randy Wood	.03	.01	.00
☐	98	Jim Johnson	.03	.01	.00
☐	99	Bob Sweeney	.03	.01	.00
☐	100	Dino Ciccarelli	.10	.05	.01
☐	101	Rangers Team	.06	.03	.00
☐	102	Mike Ramsey	.03	.01	.00
☐	103	Kelly Hrudey	.08	.04	.01
☐	104	Dave Ellett	.03	.01	.00
☐	105	Bob Brooke	.03	.01	.00
☐	106	Greg Adams	.03	.01	.00
		Vancouver Canucks			
☐	107	Joe Cirella	.03	.01	.00
☐	108	Jari Kurri	.20	.10	.02
☐	109	Pete Peeters	.08	.04	.01
☐	110	Paul MacLean	.06	.03	.00
☐	111	Doug Wilson	.10	.05	.01
☐	112	Pat Verbeek	.08	.04	.01

			MINT	EXC	G-VG
☐ 113	Bob Beers		.12	.06	.01
☐ 114	Mike O'Connell		.03	.01	.00
☐ 115	Brian Bradley		.03	.01	.00
☐ 116	Paul Coffey		.30	.15	.03
☐ 117	Doug Brown		.03	.01	.00
☐ 118	Aaron Broten		.03	.01	.00
☐ 119	Bob Essensa		.25	.12	.02
☐ 120	Wayne Gretzky UER		1.25	.60	.12
	(1302 career assists, not 13102)				
☐ 121	Vincent Damphousse		.10	.05	.01
☐ 122	Nordiques Team		.06	.03	.00
☐ 123	Mike Foligno		.03	.01	.00
☐ 124	Russ Courtnall		.06	.03	.00
☐ 125	Rick Meagher		.03	.01	.00
☐ 126	Craig Fisher		.20	.10	.02
☐ 127	Al MacInnis		.20	.10	.02
☐ 128	Derek King		.03	.01	.00
☐ 129	Dale Hunter		.03	.01	.00
☐ 130	Mark Messier UER		.35	.17	.03
	(Position LW, should be C)				
☐ 131	James Patrick		.03	.01	.00
	(Blue border, should be orange)				
☐ 132	Checklist Card UER		.06	.01	.00
	(132 Cary Wilson, should be Carey)				
☐ 133	Red Wings Team		.06	.03	.00
☐ 134	Barry Pederson		.03	.01	.00
☐ 135	Gary Leeman		.06	.03	.00
☐ 136	Doug Gilmour		.06	.03	.00
☐ 137	Mike McPhee		.06	.03	.00
☐ 138	Bob Murray		.03	.01	.00
☐ 139	Bob Carpenter		.06	.03	.00
☐ 140	Sean Burke		.08	.04	.01
☐ 141	Dale Hawerchuk		.15	.07	.01
☐ 142	Guy Lafleur		.20	.10	.02
☐ 143	Lindy Ruff		.03	.01	.00
☐ 144	Whalers Team		.06	.03	.00
☐ 145	Glenn Anderson		.08	.04	.01
☐ 146	Dave Chyzowski		.10	.05	.01
☐ 147	Kevin Hatcher		.08	.04	.01
☐ 148	Rick Vaive		.06	.03	.00
☐ 149	Adam Oates		.25	.12	.02
☐ 150	Garth Butcher		.08	.04	.01
☐ 151	Basil McRae		.08	.04	.01
☐ 152	Ilkka Sinisalo		.03	.01	.00
☐ 153	Steve Kasper		.06	.03	.00
☐ 154	Greg Paslawski		.03	.01	.00
☐ 155	Brad Marsh		.03	.01	.00
☐ 156	Esa Tikkanen		.15	.07	.01
☐ 157	Tony Tanti		.06	.03	.00
☐ 158	Mario Marois		.03	.01	.00
	(On front, oi in Marois is out of line)				
☐ 159	Sylvain Lefebvre		.15	.07	.01
☐ 160	Troy Murray		.06	.03	.00

			MINT	EXC	G-VG
☐ 161	Gary Roberts		.06	.03	.00
☐ 162	Randy Ladouceur		.03	.01	.00
☐ 163	John Chabot		.03	.01	.00
☐ 164	Calle Johansson		.03	.01	.00
☐ 165	Bruins Team		.06	.03	.00
☐ 166	Jeff Norton		.03	.01	.00
☐ 167	Mike Krushelnyski		.03	.01	.00
☐ 168	Dave Gagner		.15	.07	.01
☐ 169	Dave Andreychuk		.06	.03	.00
☐ 170	Dave Capuano		.12	.06	.01
☐ 171	Curtis Joseph		.25	.12	.02
☐ 172	Bruce Driver		.03	.01	.00
☐ 173	Scott Mellanby		.06	.03	.00
☐ 174	John Ogrodnick		.06	.03	.00
☐ 175	Mario Lemieux		1.00	.50	.10
☐ 176	Marc Fortier		.06	.03	.00
☐ 177	Vincent Riendeau		.30	.15	.03
☐ 178	Mark Johnson		.03	.01	.00
☐ 179	Dirk Graham		.03	.01	.00
☐ 180	Jets Team		.06	.03	.00
☐ 181	Robb Stauber		.20	.10	.02
☐ 182	Christian Ruuttu		.03	.01	.00
☐ 183	Dave Tippett		.03	.01	.00
☐ 184	Pat LaFontaine		.20	.10	.02
☐ 185	Mark Howe		.06	.03	.00
☐ 186	Stephane Richer		.12	.06	.01
☐ 187	Jan Erixon		.03	.01	.00
☐ 188	Neil Sheehy		.03	.01	.00
☐ 189	Craig MacTavish		.03	.01	.00
☐ 190	Randy Burridge		.03	.01	.00
☐ 191	Bernie Federko		.06	.03	.00
☐ 192	Shawn Chambers		.06	.03	.00
☐ 193	Mark Messier AS1		.15	.07	.01
☐ 194	Luc Robitaille AS1		.15	.07	.01
☐ 195	Brett Hull AS1		.45	.22	.04
☐ 196	Ray Bourque AS1		.15	.07	.01
☐ 197	Al MacInnis AS1		.10	.05	.01
☐ 198	Patrick Roy AS1		.15	.07	.01
☐ 199	Wayne Gretzky AS2		.50	.25	.05
☐ 200	Brian Bellows AS2		.10	.05	.01
☐ 201	Cam Neely AS2		.15	.07	.01
☐ 202	Paul Coffey AS2		.15	.07	.01
☐ 203	Doug Wilson AS2		.08	.04	.01
☐ 204	Daren Puppa AS2		.10	.05	.01
☐ 205	Gary Suter		.10	.05	.01
☐ 206	Ed Olczyk		.08	.04	.01
☐ 207	Doug Lidster		.03	.01	.00
☐ 208	John Cullen		.30	.15	.03
☐ 209	Luc Robitaille		.25	.12	.02
☐ 210	Tim Kerr		.08	.04	.01
☐ 211	Scott Stevens		.08	.04	.01
☐ 212	Craig Janney		.35	.17	.03
☐ 213	Kevin Dineen		.06	.03	.00

			MINT	EXC	G-VG
☐ 214	Jim Waite		.12	.06	.01
☐ 215	Benoit Hogue		.08	.04	.01
☐ 216	Curtis Leschyshyn		.12	.06	.01
☐ 217	Brad Lauer		.03	.01	.00
☐ 218	Joe Mullen		.08	.04	.01
☐ 219	Patrick Roy		.25	.12	.02
☐ 220	Blues Team		.06	.03	.00
☐ 221	Brian Leetch		.60	.30	.06
☐ 222	Steve Yzerman		.35	.17	.03
☐ 223	Steph Beauregard		.20	.10	.02
☐ 224	John MacLean		.08	.04	.01
☐ 225	Trevor Linden		.30	.15	.03
☐ 226	Bill Ranford		.15	.07	.01
☐ 227	Mark Osborne		.03	.01	.00
☐ 228	Curt Giles		.03	.01	.00
☐ 229	Mikko Makela		.03	.01	.00
☐ 230	Bob Errey		.03	.01	.00
☐ 231	Jimmy Carson		.15	.07	.01
☐ 232	Kay Whitmore		.15	.07	.01
☐ 233	Gary Nylund		.03	.01	.00
☐ 234	Jiri Hrdina		.10	.05	.01
☐ 235	Stephan Leach		.03	.01	.00
☐ 236	Greg Hawgood UER		.03	.01	.00
	(Photo actually Don Sweeney)				
☐ 237	Jocelyn Lemieux		.12	.06	.01
☐ 238	Daren Puppa		.15	.07	.01
☐ 239	Kelly Kisio		.03	.01	.00
☐ 240	Craig Simpson		.12	.06	.01
☐ 241	Maple Leafs Team		.06	.03	.00
☐ 242	Frederik Olausson		.03	.01	.00
☐ 243	Ron Hextall		.15	.07	.01
☐ 244	Sergio Momesso		.15	.07	.01
☐ 245	Kirk Muller		.08	.04	.01
☐ 246	Petr Svoboda		.03	.01	.00
☐ 247	Daniel Berthiaume		.08	.04	.01
☐ 248	Andrew McBain		.03	.01	.00
☐ 249	Jeff Jackson		.03	.01	.00
	('89-'90 stats should be 65, not 0)				
☐ 250	Randy Gilhen		.10	.05	.01
☐ 251	Oilers Team		.06	.03	.00
☐ 252	Rick Bennett		.10	.05	.01
☐ 253	Don Beaupre		.06	.03	.00
☐ 254	Pelle Eklund		.06	.03	.00
☐ 255	Greg Gilbert		.03	.01	.00
☐ 256	Gordie Roberts		.03	.01	.00
☐ 257	Kirk McLean		.08	.04	.01
☐ 258	Brent Sutter		.06	.03	.00
☐ 259	Brendan Shanahan		.08	.04	.01
☐ 260	Todd Krygier		.12	.06	.01
☐ 261	Larry Robinson UER		.10	.05	.01
	('80-'81 season stats missing, making career totals wrong)				
☐ 262	Sabres Team		.06	.03	.00

		MINT	EXC	G-VG
☐ 263	Dave Christian	.06	.03	.00
☐ 264	Checklist Card	.06	.01	.00
☐ 265	Jamie Macoun	.06	.03	.00
☐ 266	Glen Hanlon	.06	.03	.00
☐ 267	Daniel Marois	.12	.06	.01
☐ 268	Doug Smail	.06	.03	.00
☐ 269	Jon Casey	.15	.07	.01
☐ 270	Brian Skrudland	.06	.03	.00
☐ 271	Michel Petit	.03	.01	.00
☐ 272	Dan Quinn	.06	.03	.00
☐ 273	Geoff Courtnall	.15	.07	.01
☐ 274	Mike Bullard	.03	.01	.00
☐ 275	Randy Gregg	.06	.03	.00
☐ 276	Keith Brown	.03	.01	.00
☐ 277	Troy Mallette	.12	.06	.01
☐ 278	Steve Tuttle	.03	.01	.00
☐ 279	Brad Shaw	.12	.06	.01
☐ 280	Mark Recchi	2.25	1.10	.22
☐ 281	John Tonelli	.06	.03	.00
☐ 282	Doug Bodger	.03	.01	.00
☐ 283	Thomas Steen	.06	.03	.00
☐ 284	Devils Team	.06	.03	.00
☐ 285	Lee Norwood	.03	.01	.00
☐ 286	Brian MacLellan	.03	.01	.00
☐ 287	Bobby Smith	.10	.05	.01
☐ 288	Robert Cimetta	.15	.07	.01
☐ 289	Rob Zettler	.10	.05	.01
☐ 290	David Reid	.15	.07	.01
☐ 291	Bryan Trottier	.15	.07	.01
☐ 292	Brian Mullen	.06	.03	.00
☐ 293	Paul Reinhart	.06	.03	.00
☐ 294	Andy Moog	.15	.07	.01
☐ 295	Jeff Brown	.06	.03	.00
☐ 296	Ryan Walter	.06	.03	.00
☐ 297	Trent Yawney	.06	.03	.00
☐ 298	John Druce	.30	.15	.03
☐ 299	Dave McLlwain	.03	.01	.00
☐ 300	David Volek	.06	.03	.00
☐ 301	Tomas Sandstrom	.10	.05	.01
☐ 302	Gord Murphy	.15	.07	.01
☐ 303	Lou Franceschetti	.12	.06	.01
☐ 304	Dana Murzyn	.03	.01	.00
☐ 305	North Stars Team	.06	.03	.00
☐ 306	Patrik Sundstrom	.06	.03	.00
☐ 307	Kevin Lowe	.08	.04	.01
☐ 308	Dave Barr	.03	.01	.00
☐ 309	Wendell Young	.12	.06	.01
☐ 310	Darrin Shannon	.12	.06	.01
☐ 311	Ron Francis	.15	.07	.01
☐ 312	Stephane Fiset	.15	.07	.01
☐ 313	Paul Fenton	.06	.03	.00
☐ 314	Dave Taylor	.08	.04	.01
☐ 315	Islanders Team	.06	.03	.00

			MINT	EXC	G-VG
☐ 316	Petri Skriko		.03	.01	.00
☐ 317	Rob Ramage		.06	.03	.00
☐ 318	Murray Craven		.06	.03	.00
☐ 319	Gaetan Duchesne		.06	.03	.00
☐ 320	Brad McCrimmon		.03	.01	.00
☐ 321	Grant Fuhr		.15	.07	.01
☐ 322	Gerard Gallant		.10	.05	.01
☐ 323	Tommy Albelin		.03	.01	.00
☐ 324	Scott Arniel		.03	.01	.00
☐ 325	Mike Keane		.10	.05	.01
☐ 326	Penguins Team		.06	.03	.00
☐ 327	Mike Ridley		.03	.01	.00
☐ 328	Dave Babych		.06	.03	.00
☐ 329	Michel Goulet		.10	.05	.01
☐ 330	Mike Richter		.50	.25	.05
☐ 331	Garry Galley		.12	.06	.01
☐ 332	Rob Brind'Amour		.50	.25	.05
☐ 333	Tony McKegeny		.03	.01	.00
☐ 334	Peter Stastny		.15	.07	.01
☐ 335	Greg Millen		.06	.03	.00
☐ 336	Ray Ferraro		.03	.01	.00
☐ 337	Miloslav Horava		.10	.05	.01
☐ 338	Paul MacDermid		.03	.01	.00
☐ 339	Craig Coxe		.10	.05	.01
☐ 340	Dave Snuggerud		.12	.06	.01
☐ 341	Mike Lalor		.10	.05	.01
☐ 342	Marc Habscheid		.03	.01	.00
☐ 343	Rejean Lemelin		.06	.03	.00
☐ 344	Charlie Huddy		.06	.03	.00
☐ 345	Ken Linseman		.03	.01	.00
☐ 346	Canadiens Team		.06	.03	.00
☐ 347	Troy Loney		.12	.06	.01
☐ 348	Mike Modano		1.25	.60	.12
☐ 349	Jeff Reese		.15	.07	.01
☐ 350	Patrick Flatley		.03	.01	.00
☐ 351	Mike Vernon		.20	.10	.02
☐ 352	Todd Elik		.25	.12	.02
☐ 353	Rod Langway		.06	.03	.00
☐ 354	Moe Mantha		.03	.01	.00
☐ 355	Keith Acton		.03	.01	.00
☐ 356	Scott Pearson		.25	.12	.02
☐ 357	Perry Berezan		.10	.05	.01
☐ 358	Alexei Kasatonov		.15	.07	.01
☐ 359	Igor Larionov		.15	.07	.01
☐ 360	Kevin Stevens		1.25	.60	.12
☐ 361	Yves Racine		.15	.07	.01
☐ 362	Dave Poulin		.06	.03	.00
☐ 363	Blackhawks Team		.06	.03	.00
☐ 364	Yvon Corriveau		.10	.05	.01
☐ 365	Brian Benning		.03	.01	.00
☐ 366	Hubie McDonough		.10	.05	.01
☐ 367	Ron Tugnutt		.10	.05	.01
☐ 368	Steve Smith		.08	.04	.01

		MINT	EXC	G-VG
☐ 369	Joel Otto	.03	.01	.00
☐ 370	Dave Lowry	.12	.06	.01
☐ 371	Clint Malarchuk	.06	.03	.00
☐ 372	Mathieu Schneider	.30	.15	.03
☐ 373	Mike Gartner	.10	.05	.01
☐ 374	John Tucker	.03	.01	.00
☐ 375	Chris Terreri	.35	.17	.03
☐ 376	Dean Evason	.03	.01	.00
☐ 377	Jamie Leach	.20	.10	.02
☐ 378	Jacques Cloutier	.12	.06	.01
☐ 379	Glen Wesley	.06	.03	.00
☐ 380	Vladimir Krutov	.15	.07	.01
☐ 381	Terry Carkner	.03	.01	.00
☐ 382	John McIntyre	.15	.07	.01
☐ 383	Ville Siren	.08	.04	.01
☐ 384	Joe Sakic	1.00	.50	.10
☐ 385	Teppo Numminen	.10	.05	.01
☐ 386	Theo Fleury	1.00	.50	.10
☐ 387	Glen Featherstone	.10	.05	.01
☐ 388	Stephan Lebeau	.50	.25	.05
☐ 389	Kevin McClelland	.03	.01	.00
☐ 390	Uwe Krupp	.03	.01	.00
☐ 391	Mark Janssens	.08	.04	.01
☐ 392	Marty McSorley	.10	.05	.01
☐ 393	Vladimir Ruzicka	.35	.17	.03
☐ 394	Capitals Team	.06	.03	.00
☐ 395	Mark Fitzpatrick	.10	.05	.01
☐ 396	Checklist Card	.06	.01	.00
☐ 397	Dave Manson	.06	.03	.00
☐ 398	Bob Gould	.03	.01	.00
☐ 399	Bill Houlder	.10	.05	.01
☐ 400	Glenn Healy	.12	.06	.01
☐ 401	John Kordic UER	.12	.06	.01
	(Listed as Defense, should be LW)			
☐ 402	Stewart Gavin	.06	.03	.00
☐ 403	David Shaw	.03	.01	.00
☐ 404	Ed Kastelic	.08	.04	.01
☐ 405	Rich Sutter	.06	.03	.00
☐ 406	Grant Ledyard	.12	.06	.01
☐ 407	Steve Weeks	.06	.03	.00
☐ 408	Randy Hillier	.03	.01	.00
☐ 409	Rick Wamsley	.06	.03	.00
☐ 410	Doug Houda	.10	.05	.01
☐ 411	Ken McRae	.10	.05	.01
☐ 412	Craig Ludwig	.03	.01	.00
☐ 413	Doug Evans	.10	.05	.01
☐ 414	Ken Baumgartner	.12	.06	.01
☐ 415	Ken Wregget	.10	.05	.01
☐ 416	Eric Weinrich	.35	.17	.03
☐ 417	Mike Allison	.03	.01	.00
☐ 418	Joel Quenneville	.03	.01	.00
☐ 419	Larry Melnyk	.03	.01	.00
☐ 420	Colin Patterson	.03	.01	.00

			MINT	EXC	G-VG
☐ 421	Gerald Diduck		.03	.01	.00
☐ 422	Brent Gilchrist		.12	.06	.01
☐ 423	Craig Muni		.03	.01	.00
☐ 424	Mike Hudson		.15	.07	.01
☐ 425	Eric Desjardins		.15	.07	.01
☐ 426	Walt Poddubny		.03	.01	.00
☐ 427	Mike Hough		.03	.01	.00
☐ 428	Luke Richardson		.03	.01	.00
☐ 429	Joe Murphy		.35	.17	.03
☐ 430	Tim Cheveldae		.30	.15	.03
☐ 431	Adam Burt		.12	.06	.01
☐ 432	Kelly Chase		.10	.05	.01
☐ 433	Robert Nordmark		.08	.04	.01
☐ 434	Tim Hunter		.12	.06	.01
☐ 435	Peter Taglianetti		.03	.01	.00
☐ 436	Alain Chevrier		.06	.03	.00
☐ 437	Darin Kimble		.12	.06	.01
☐ 438	Dave Maley		.12	.06	.01
☐ 439	Jim Wiemer		.08	.04	.01
☐ 440	Nick Kypreos		.08	.04	.01
☐ 441	Lucien Deblois		.03	.01	.00
☐ 442	Mario Gosselin		.06	.03	.00
☐ 443	Neil Wilkinson		.15	.07	.01
☐ 444	Mark Kumpel		.08	.04	.01
☐ 445	Sergei Mylnikov		.20	.10	.02
☐ 446	Ray Sheppard		.03	.01	.00
☐ 447	Ron Greschner		.06	.03	.00
☐ 448	Craig Berube		.15	.07	.01
☐ 449	Dave Hannan		.03	.01	.00
☐ 450	Jim Korn UER		.06	.03	.00
	(Photo actually Paul Ranheim)				
☐ 451	Claude Lemieux		.10	.05	.01
☐ 452	Eldon Reddick		.15	.07	.01
☐ 453	Randy Velischek		.03	.01	.00
☐ 454	Chris Nilan		.06	.03	.00
☐ 455	Jim Benning		.03	.01	.00
☐ 456	Wayne Presley		.03	.01	.00
☐ 457	Jon Morris		.10	.05	.01
☐ 458	Clark Donatelli		.10	.05	.01
☐ 459	Ric Nattress		.03	.01	.00
☐ 460	Rob Murray		.15	.07	.01
☐ 461	Tim Watters		.03	.01	.00
☐ 462	Checklist Card		.06	.01	.00
☐ 463	Derrick Smith		.08	.04	.01
☐ 464	Lyndon Byers		.10	.05	.01
☐ 465	Jeff Chychrun		.10	.05	.01
☐ 466	Duane Sutter		.06	.03	.00
☐ 467	Conn Smythe Trophy		.06	.03	.00
☐ 468	Anatoli Semenov		.50	.25	.05
☐ 469	Konstantin Kurashov		.15	.07	.01
☐ 470	Gord Dineen		.03	.01	.00
☐ 471	Jeff Beukeboom		.12	.06	.01
☐ 472	Andrei Lomakin		.10	.05	.01

		MINT	EXC	G-VG
☐ 473	Doug Sulliman	.03	.01	.00
☐ 474	Alexander Kerch	.10	.05	.01
☐ 475	Norris Trophy	.06	.03	.00
☐ 476	Keith Crowder	.03	.01	.00
☐ 477	Oleg Znarok	.10	.05	.01
☐ 478	Dimitri Zinovyev	.10	.05	.01
☐ 479	Igor Esmantovich	.10	.05	.01
☐ 480	Adam Graves	.35	.17	.03
☐ 481	Petr Prajsler	.10	.05	.01
☐ 482	Sergei Yashin	.10	.05	.01
☐ 483	Jeff Bloemberg	.10	.05	.01
☐ 484	Yuri Strakhov	.10	.05	.01
☐ 485	Sergei B. Makarov	.12	.06	.01
☐ 486	Jennings Trophy	.06	.03	.00
☐ 487	Sergei Zaltsev	.10	.05	.01
☐ 488	Selke Trophy	.06	.03	.00
☐ 489	Yuri Kusnetsov	.15	.07	.01
☐ 490	Tom Chorske	.10	.05	.01
☐ 491	Igor Akulinin	.10	.05	.01
☐ 492	Mikhail Panin	.10	.05	.01
☐ 493	Sergei Nemchinov	.10	.05	.01
☐ 494	Vladimir Yurzinov	.10	.05	.01
☐ 495	Gord Kluzak	.03	.01	.00
☐ 496	Sergei Skosyrev	.10	.05	.01
☐ 497	Jeff Parker	.12	.06	.01
☐ 498	Tom Tilley	.10	.05	.01
☐ 499	Alexander Smirnov	.20	.10	.02
☐ 500	Alexander Lysenko	.20	.10	.02
☐ 501	Artur Irbe	.50	.25	.05
☐ 502	Alexei Frolikov	.10	.05	.01
☐ 503	Calder Trophy	.06	.03	.00
☐ 504	Nikolai Varjanov	.10	.05	.01
☐ 505	Allen Pedersen	.03	.01	.00
☐ 506	Vladimir Shashov	.10	.05	.01
☐ 507	Tim Bergland	.10	.05	.01
☐ 508	Gennady Lebedev	.10	.05	.01
☐ 509	Rod Buskas	.10	.05	.01
☐ 510	Grant Jennings	.15	.07	.01
☐ 511	Ulf Samuelsson	.06	.03	.00
☐ 512	Vezina Trophy	.06	.03	.00
☐ 513	Lady Byng Trophy	.06	.03	.00
☐ 514	Dimitri Mironov	.10	.05	.01
☐ 515	Randy Moller	.03	.01	.00
☐ 516	Kerry Huffman	.15	.07	.01
☐ 517	Gilbert Delorme	.03	.01	.00
☐ 518	Greg C. Adams	.03	.01	.00
☐ 519	Hart Trophy	.06	.03	.00
☐ 520	Sheldon Kennedy	.10	.05	.01
☐ 521	Harijs Vitolins	.10	.05	.01
☐ 522	Art Ross Trophy	.06	.03	.00
☐ 523	Dmitri Frolov	.10	.05	.01
☐ 524	Tom Laidlaw	.03	.01	.00
☐ 525	Oleg Bratash	.10	.05	.01

		MINT	EXC	G-VG
☐ 526	Kris King	.10	.05	.01
☐ 527	Wayne Van Dorp	.12	.06	.01
☐ 528	Chris Dahlquist	.12	.06	.01

1990-91 O-Pee-Chee Premier

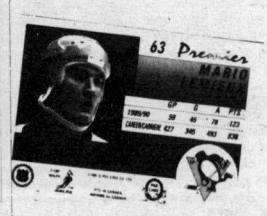

The 1990-91 O-Pee-Chee Premier hockey set contains 132 cards measuring the standard size (2½" by 3½"). The fronts feature color action photos of the players and have the words "O-Pee-Chee Premier" in the gold band above the picture. Each card has a different color border that shades from dark to light. The backs are horizontally oriented and have a head and shoulders shot of the player in the upper left hand corner, with biographical and statistical information in various color panels.

Le jeu O-Pee-Chee Première 1990-91 contient 132 cartes de format standard (2½" x 3½"). La face représente une photo d'action du joueur en couleurs, et comportent les mots "O-Pee-Chee Première" dans la bande dorée au-dessus de la photo. Chaque carte est encadrée d'un bord de couleur différente, allant du sombre au clair. Le dos est orienté horizontalement, et présente une photo de la tête et des épaules du joueur dans le coin supérieur gauche, avec des données biographiques et statistiques contenues dans les panneaux de couleurs différentes.

			MINT	EXC	G-VG
		COMPLETE SET (132)	150.00	75.00	15.00
		COMMON PLAYER (1-132)	.25	.12	.02
☐	1	Scott Arniel	.25	.12	.02
☐	2	Jergus Baca	.50	.25	.05
☐	3	Brian Bellows	.50	.25	.05
☐	4	Jean-Claude Bergeron	.50	.25	.05

			MINT	EXC	G-VG
☐	5	Daniel Berthiaume	.35	.17	.03
☐	6	Rob Blake	3.00	1.50	.30
☐	7	Peter Bondra	2.00	1.00	.20
☐	8	Laurie Boschman	.25	.12	.02
☐	9	Ray Bourque	1.00	.50	.10
☐	10	Aaron Broten	.25	.12	.02
☐	11	Greg Brown	.50	.25	.05
☐	12	Jimmy Carson	.40	.20	.04
☐	13	Chris Chelios	.45	.22	.04
☐	14	Dino Ciccarelli	.35	.17	.03
☐	15	Zdeno Ciger	.50	.25	.05
☐	16	Paul Coffey	.75	.35	.07
☐	17	Danton Cole	.35	.17	.03
☐	18	Geoff Courtnall	.40	.20	.04
☐	19	Mike Craig	1.50	.75	.15
		(Played Juniors at Oshawa, not Minors)			
☐	20	John Cullen	.75	.35	.07
☐	21	Vincent Damphousse	.35	.17	.03
☐	22	Gerald Diduck	.25	.12	.02
☐	23	Kevin Dineen	.35	.17	.03
☐	24	Per Olav Djoos	.40	.20	.04
		(Photo shoots right, back says shoots left)			
☐	25	Tie Domi	.40	.20	.04
☐	26	Peter Douris	.35	.17	.03
☐	27	Rob DiMaio	.35	.17	.03
☐	28	Pat Elynuik	.35	.17	.03
☐	29	Bob Essensa	.35	.17	.03
☐	30	Sergei Fedorov	30.00	15.00	3.00
☐	31	Brent Fedyk	.75	.35	.07
☐	32	Ron Francis	.35	.17	.03
☐	33	Link Gaetz	.45	.22	.04
☐	34	Troy Gamble	1.50	.75	.15
☐	35	Johan Garpenlov	1.50	.75	.15
☐	36	Mike Gartner	.35	.17	.03
☐	37	Rick Green	.25	.12	.02
☐	38	Wayne Gretzky	7.50	3.75	.75
☐	39	Jeff Hackett	.75	.35	.07
☐	40	Dale Hawerchuk UER	.35	.17	.03
		(Misspelled Hawerchuck)			
☐	41	Ron Hextall	.35	.17	.03
☐	42	Bruce Hoffort	.40	.20	.04
☐	43	Bobby Holik	3.50	1.75	.35
☐	44	Martin Hostak	.40	.20	.04
☐	45	Phil Housley	.40	.20	.04
☐	46	Jody Hull	.40	.20	.04
☐	47	Brett Hull	7.50	3.75	.75
☐	48	Al Iafrate	.35	.17	.03
☐	49	Peter Ing	1.00	.50	.10
☐	50	Jaromir Jagr	16.00	8.00	1.60
☐	51	Curtis Joseph	.40	.20	.04
☐	52	Robert Kron	.75	.35	.07
☐	53	Frantisek Kucera	.35	.17	.03
☐	54	Dale Kushner	.35	.17	.03

			MINT	EXC	G-VG
☐	55	Guy Lafleur	.50	.25	.05
☐	56	Pat LaFontaine	.40	.20	.04
☐	57	Mike Lalor	.25	.12	.02
☐	58	Steve Larmer	.35	.17	.03
☐	59	Jiri Latal	.50	.25	.05
☐	60	Jamie Leach	.40	.20	.04
☐	61	Brian Leetch	1.00	.50	.10
☐	62	Claude Lemieux	.35	.17	.03
☐	63	Mario Lemieux	4.00	2.00	.40
☐	64	Craig Ludwig	.25	.12	.02
☐	65	Al MacInnis	.45	.22	.04
☐	66	Mikko Makela	.25	.12	.02
☐	67	Dave Marcinyshyn	.35	.17	.03
☐	68	Stephane Matteau	.90	.45	.09
☐	69	Brad McCrimmon	.25	.12	.02
☐	70	Kirk McLean	.35	.17	.03
☐	71	Mark Messier	1.00	.50	.10
☐	72	Kelly Miller	.35	.17	.03
☐	73	Kevin Miller	1.00	.50	.10
☐	74	Mike Modano	4.00	2.00	.40
☐	75	Alexander Mogilny	1.50	.75	.15
☐	76	Andy Moog	.40	.20	.04
☐	77	Joe Mullen	.35	.17	.03
☐	78	Kirk Muller	.35	.17	.03
☐	79	Pat Murray	.35	.17	.03
☐	80	Jarmo Myllys	.35	.17	.03
☐	81	Petr Nedved	3.00	1.50	.30
☐	82	Cam Neely	.75	.35	.07
☐	83	Bernie Nicholls	.40	.20	.04
☐	84	Joe Nieuwendyk	.90	.45	.09
☐	85	Chris Nilan	.25	.12	.02
☐	86	Owen Nolan	2.00	1.00	.20
☐	87	Brian Noonan	.25	.12	.02
☐	88	Adam Oates	.75	.35	.07
☐	89	Greg Parks UER	.35	.17	.03
		(Back photo actually Scott Arniel)			
☐	90	Adrien Plavsic	.35	.17	.03
☐	91	Keith Primeau	1.50	.75	.15
☐	92	Brian Propp	.35	.17	.03
☐	93	Dan Quinn	.25	.12	.02
☐	94	Bill Ranford	.35	.17	.03
☐	95	Robert Reichel	2.00	1.00	.20
☐	96	Mike Ricci	5.00	2.50	.50
		(Born 11/27/71, should be October)			
☐	97	Steve Rice	2.50	1.25	.25
		(Played Juniors at Kitchener, not Minors)			
☐	98	Stephane Richer	.40	.20	.04
☐	99	Luc Robitaille	.75	.35	.07
☐	100	Jeremy Roenick	7.50	3.75	.75
☐	101	Patrick Roy	.75	.35	.07
☐	102	Joe Sakic	3.00	1.50	.30
☐	103	Denis Savard	.40	.20	.04
☐	104	Anatoli Semenov	.75	.35	.07

			MINT	EXC	G-VG
☐	105	Brendan Shanahan	.35	.17	.03
☐	106	Ray Sheppard	.25	.12	.02
☐	107	Mike Sillinger	1.50	.75	.15
		(Played Juniors at Regina, not Minors)			
☐	108	Ilkka Sinisalo	.25	.12	.02
☐	109	Bobby Smith	.35	.17	.03
☐	110	Paul Stanton	.50	.25	.05
☐	111	Kevin Stevens	4.00	2.00	.40
☐	112	Scott Stevens	.35	.17	.03
☐	113	Alan Stewart	.35	.17	.03
☐	114	Mats Sundin	5.00	2.50	.50
☐	115	Brent Sutter	.35	.17	.03
☐	116	Tim Sweeney	.35	.17	.03
☐	117	Peter Taglianetti	.25	.12	.02
☐	118	John Tanner	.50	.25	.05
☐	119	Dave Tippett	.25	.12	.02
☐	120	Rick Tocchet	.45	.22	.04
☐	121	Bryan Trottier	.50	.25	.05
☐	122	John Tucker	.25	.12	.02
☐	123	Darren Turcotte	1.50	.75	.15
☐	124	Pierre Turgeon	.75	.35	.07
☐	125	Randy Velischek	.25	.12	.02
☐	126	Mike Vernon	.40	.20	.04
☐	127	Wes Walz	.75	.35	.07
☐	128	Carey Wilson	.25	.12	.02
☐	129	Doug Wilson	.35	.17	.03
☐	130	Steve Yzerman	1.00	.50	.10
☐	131	Peter Zezel	.35	.17	.03
☐	132	Checklist Card	.30	.12	.02

1951-52 Parkhurst

FLOYD 'BUSHER' CURRY —Mont Canadiens
Right Wing. 1950-51 Record —Goals 13
Assists 14, Points 27, Min. in Penalty 23
Born: Chapleau, Ontario, Aug. 11, 1925
NO.:12 PARKIE 1951-52 Hockey Series

The 1951-52 Parkhurst set contains 105 relatively small cards in somewhat crude color. Cards are 1³/₄" by 2¹/₂". The player's name, team, number, and 1950-51 statistics all appear on the front of the card. The backs of the cards are blank. The cards feature players from each of the six NHL teams. The set numbering is basically according to teams, i.e., Montreal Canadiens (1-18), Boston Bruins (19-35), Chicago Blackhawks (36-51 and 53), Detroit Red Wings (54-69), Toronto Maple Leafs (70-88), and New York Rangers (89-105). The set features the first cards of hockey greats, Gordie Howe and Maurice Richard. Other notable rookie cards in this set are Alex Delvecchio, Boom Boom Geoffrion, Doug Harvey, Red Kelly, Ted Lindsay, and Terry Sawchuck.

Le jeu Parkhurst 1951-52 contient 105 cartes de taille plutôt petite, et de couleurs relativement médiocres . Les cartes mesurent 1³/₄" x 2¹/₂". La face de la carte indique le nom du joueur, l'équipe, le numéro, et les statistiques pour 1950-51. Le dos est vierge. Les cartes représentent des joueurs des six équipes NHL. Elles sont numérotées suivant les équipes, c'est à dire, Montréal Canadiens (1-18), Boston Bruins (19-35), Chicago Blackhawks (36-51 et 53), Detroit Red Wings (54-69), Toronto Maple Leafs (70-88), et New York Rangers (89-105). Le jeu inclut les premières cartes des étoiles du hockey, Gordie Howe et Maurice Richard. Le jeu inclut d'autres débutants importants notables, comme Alex Delvecchio, Boom Boom Geoffrion, Doug Harvey, Red Kelly, Ted Lindsay, et Terry Sawchuck.

			NRMT	VG-E	GOOD
	COMPLETE SET (105)		5500.00	2500.00	550.00
	COMMON PLAYER (1-105)		18.00	9.00	1.80
☐	1	Elmer Lach	125.00	25.00	5.00
☐	2	Paul Meger	18.00	9.00	1.80
☐	3	Butch Bouchard	45.00	22.50	4.50

			NRMT	VG-E	GOOD
☐	4	Maurice Richard	750.00	375.00	75.00
☐	5	Bert Olmstead	42.00	20.00	4.00
☐	6	Bud MacPherson	18.00	9.00	1.80
☐	7	Tom Johnson	42.00	20.00	4.00
☐	8	Paul Masnick	18.00	9.00	1.80
☐	9	Calum Mackay	18.00	9.00	1.80
☐	10	Doug Harvey	120.00	60.00	12.00
☐	11	Ken Mosdell	25.00	12.50	2.50
☐	12	Busher Curry	25.00	12.50	2.50
☐	13	Billy Reay	25.00	12.50	2.50
☐	14	Boom Boom Geoffrion	180.00	90.00	18.00
☐	15	Gerry McNeil	25.00	12.50	2.50
☐	16	Dick Gamble	18.00	9.00	1.80
☐	17	Gerry Couture	18.00	9.00	1.80
☐	18	Ross Robert Lowe	18.00	9.00	1.80
☐	19	Jim Henry	25.00	12.50	2.50
☐	20	Victor Ivan Lynn	18.00	9.00	1.80
☐	21	Walter Gus Kyle	18.00	9.00	1.80
☐	22	Ed Sandford	18.00	9.00	1.80
☐	23	John Henderson	25.00	12.50	2.50
☐	24	Dunc Fisher	18.00	9.00	1.80
☐	25	Hal Laycoe	18.00	9.00	1.80
☐	26	Bill Quackenbush	42.00	20.00	4.00
☐	27	George Sullivan	18.00	9.00	1.80
☐	28	Woody Dumart	18.00	9.00	1.80
☐	29	Milt Schmidt	65.00	32.50	6.50
☐	30	Adam Brown	18.00	9.00	1.80
☐	31	Pentti Lund	18.00	9.00	1.80
☐	32	Ray Barry	18.00	9.00	1.80
☐	33	Ed Kryzanowski	18.00	9.00	1.80
☐	34	Johnny Pierson	18.00	9.00	1.80
☐	35	Lorne Ferguson	18.00	9.00	1.80
☐	36	Clare Rags Raglan	18.00	9.00	1.80
☐	37	Bill Gadsby	42.00	20.00	4.00
☐	38	Al Dewsbury	18.00	9.00	1.80
☐	39	George Clare Martin	18.00	9.00	1.80
☐	40	Gus Bodnar	18.00	9.00	1.80
☐	41	Jim Peters	18.00	9.00	1.80
☐	42	Bep Guidolin	18.00	9.00	1.80
☐	43	George Gee	18.00	9.00	1.80
☐	44	Jim McFadden	18.00	9.00	1.80
☐	45	Fred Hucul	18.00	9.00	1.80
☐	46	John Lee Fogolin	18.00	9.00	1.80
☐	47	Harry Lumley	50.00	25.00	5.00
☐	48	Doug Bentley	45.00	22.50	4.50
☐	49	Bill Mosienko	42.00	20.00	4.00
☐	50	Roy Conacher	25.00	12.50	2.50
☐	51	Pete Babando	18.00	9.00	1.80
☐	52	The Winning Goal	30.00	15.00	3.00
☐	53	Jack Stewart	25.00	12.50	2.50
☐	54	Marty Pavelich	18.00	9.00	1.80
☐	55	Red Kelly	100.00	50.00	10.00
☐	56	Ted Lindsay	100.00	50.00	10.00

			NRMT	VG-E	GOOD
☐	57	Glen Skov	18.00	9.00	1.80
☐	58	Benny Woit	18.00	9.00	1.80
☐	59	Tony Leswick	18.00	9.00	1.80
☐	60	Frederick Glover	18.00	9.00	1.80
☐	61	Terry Sawchuk	400.00	200.00	40.00
☐	62	Vic Stasiuk	18.00	9.00	1.80
☐	63	Alex Delvecchio	100.00	50.00	10.00
☐	64	Sid Abel	45.00	22.50	4.50
☐	65	Metro Prystai	18.00	9.00	1.80
☐	66	Gordie Howe	1500.00	500.00	125.00
☐	67	Bob Goldham	18.00	9.00	1.80
☐	68	Marcel Pronovost	45.00	22.50	4.50
☐	69	Leo Reise	18.00	9.00	1.80
☐	70	Harry Watson	30.00	15.00	3.00
☐	71	Danny Lewicki	18.00	9.00	1.80
☐	72	Howie Meeker	30.00	15.00	3.00
☐	73	Gus Mortson	18.00	9.00	1.80
☐	74	Joe Klukay	18.00	9.00	1.80
☐	75	Turk Broda	75.00	37.50	7.50
☐	76	Al Rollins	25.00	12.50	2.50
☐	77	Bill Juzda	18.00	9.00	1.80
☐	78	Ray Timgren	18.00	9.00	1.80
☐	79	Hugh Bolton	18.00	9.00	1.80
☐	80	Fern Flaman	42.00	20.00	4.00
☐	81	Max Bentley	45.00	22.50	4.50
☐	82	Jim Thomson	18.00	9.00	1.80
☐	83	Fleming Mackell	18.00	9.00	1.80
☐	84	Sid Smith	18.00	9.00	1.80
☐	85	Cal Gardner	18.00	9.00	1.80
☐	86	Teeder Kennedy	42.00	20.00	4.00
☐	87	Tod Sloan	18.00	9.00	1.80
☐	88	Bob Solinger	18.00	9.00	1.80
☐	89	Frank Eddolls	18.00	9.00	1.80
☐	90	Jack Evans	18.00	9.00	1.80
☐	91	Hy Buller	18.00	9.00	1.80
☐	92	Steve Kraftcheck	18.00	9.00	1.80
☐	93	Bones Raleigh	18.00	9.00	1.80
☐	94	Allan Stanley	42.00	20.00	4.00
☐	95	Paul Ronty	18.00	9.00	1.80
☐	96	Edgar Laprade	18.00	9.00	1.80
☐	97	Nick Mickoski	18.00	9.00	1.80
☐	98	Jack McLeod	18.00	9.00	1.80
☐	99	Gaye Stewart	18.00	9.00	1.80
☐	100	Wally Hergesheimer	18.00	9.00	1.80
☐	101	Ed Kullman	18.00	9.00	1.80
☐	102	Ed Slowinski	18.00	9.00	1.80
☐	103	Reggie Sinclair	18.00	9.00	1.80
☐	104	Chuck Rayner	42.00	20.00	4.00
☐	105	Jim Conacher	50.00	12.00	2.50

1952-53 Parkhurst

The 1952-53 Parkhurst set contains 105 color, line-drawing cards. Cards are approximately 1¹⁵/₁₆" by 2¹⁵/₁₆". The obverse contains a facsimile autograph of the player pictured while the backs contain a short biography in English and 1951-52 statistics. The backs also contain the card number and a special album (for holding a set of cards) offer. The cards feature players from each of the six NHL teams. The set numbering is roughly according to teams, i.e., Montreal Canadiens (1-15, 52, 93), Boston Bruins (68-85), Chicago Blackhawks (16-17, 26-27, 29-33, 35-41, 55-56), Detroit Red Wings (53, 60-67, 86-92, 104), Toronto Maple Leafs (28, 34, 42-48, 50-51, 54, 58-59, 94-96, 105), and New York Rangers (18-25, 49, 57, 97-103). The key rookie cards in this set are George Armstrong, Tim Horton, and Dickie Moore.

Le jeu Parkhurst 1952-53 contient 105 cartes dessinées et en couleurs. Les cartes mesurent approximativement 1¹⁵/₁₆" x 2¹⁵/₁₆". La face comprend une copie de l'autographe du joueur, tandis que le dos offre une biographie concise en anglais, et les statistiques pour 1951-52. Le dos comporte également le numéro de carte et une offre pour un album spécial (pouvant contenir un jeu de cartes). Les cartes représentent des joueurs des six équipes NHL. Le jeu est numéroté plus ou moins suivant les équipes, c'est à dire, Montréal Canadiens (1-15, 52, 93), Boston Bruins (68-85), Chicago Blackhawks (16-17, 26-27, 29-33, 35-41, 55-56), Detroit Red Wings (53, 60-67, 86-92, 104), Toronto Maple Leafs (28, 34, 42-48, 50-51, 54, 58-59, 94-96, 105), et New York Rangers (18-25, 49, 57, 97-103). Les débutants importants représentées dans ce jeu sont George Armstrong, Tim Horton, et Dickie Moore.

			NRMT	VG-E	GOOD
	COMPLETE SET (105)		4000.00	1900.00	400.00
	COMMON PLAYER (1-105)		18.00	9.00	1.80
☐	1	Maurice Richard	650.00	200.00	40.00
☐	2	Billy Reay	22.00	11.00	2.20
☐	3	Boom Boom Geoffrion	80.00	40.00	8.00

			NRMT	VG-E	GOOD
☐	4	Paul Meger	18.00	9.00	1.80
☐	5	Dick Gamble	18.00	9.00	1.80
☐	6	Elmer Lach	30.00	15.00	3.00
☐	7	Floyd Curry	22.00	11.00	2.20
☐	8	Ken Mosdell	18.00	9.00	1.80
☐	9	Tom Johnson	30.00	15.00	3.00
☐	10	Dickie Moore	55.00	27.50	5.50
☐	11	Bud MacPherson	18.00	9.00	1.80
☐	12	Gerry McNeil	18.00	9.00	1.80
☐	13	Butch Bouchard	30.00	15.00	3.00
☐	14	Doug Harvey	50.00	25.00	5.00
☐	15	Goose McCormack	18.00	9.00	1.80
☐	16	Pete Babando	18.00	9.00	1.80
☐	17	Al Dewsbury	18.00	9.00	1.80
☐	18	Ed Kullman	18.00	9.00	1.80
☐	19	Ed Slowinski	18.00	9.00	1.80
☐	20	Wally Hergesheimer	18.00	9.00	1.80
☐	21	Allan Stanley	30.00	15.00	3.00
☐	22	Chuck Rayner	30.00	15.00	3.00
☐	23	Steve Kraftcheck	18.00	9.00	1.80
☐	24	Paul Ronty	18.00	9.00	1.80
☐	25	Gaye Stewart	18.00	9.00	1.80
☐	26	Fred Hucul	18.00	9.00	1.80
☐	27	Bill Mosienko	30.00	15.00	3.00
☐	28	Jim Morrison	18.00	9.00	1.80
☐	29	Ted Kryzanowski	18.00	9.00	1.80
☐	30	Cal Gardner	18.00	9.00	1.80
☐	31	Al Rollins	22.00	11.00	2.20
☐	32	Enio Sclisizzi	18.00	9.00	1.80
☐	33	Pete Conacher	22.00	11.00	2.20
☐	34	Leo Boivin	42.00	20.00	4.00
☐	35	Jim Peters	18.00	9.00	1.80
☐	36	George Gee	18.00	9.00	1.80
☐	37	Gus Bodnar	18.00	9.00	1.80
☐	38	Jim McFadden	18.00	9.00	1.80
☐	39	Gus Mortson	18.00	9.00	1.80
☐	40	Freddy Glover	18.00	9.00	1.80
☐	41	Gerry Couture	18.00	9.00	1.80
☐	42	Howie Meeker	22.00	11.00	2.20
☐	43	Jim Thomson	18.00	9.00	1.80
☐	44	Ted Kennedy	30.00	15.00	3.00
☐	45	Sid Smith	18.00	9.00	1.80
☐	46	Harry Watson	22.00	11.00	2.20
☐	47	Fern Flaman	30.00	15.00	3.00
☐	48	Tod Sloan	18.00	9.00	1.80
☐	49	Leo Reise	18.00	9.00	1.80
☐	50	Bob Solinger	18.00	9.00	1.80
☐	51	George Armstrong	55.00	27.50	5.50
☐	52	Dollard St. Laurent	22.00	11.00	2.20
☐	53	Alex Delvecchio	40.00	20.00	4.00
☐	54	Gord Hannigan	18.00	9.00	1.80
☐	55	Lee Fogolin	18.00	9.00	1.80
☐	56	Bill Gadsby	30.00	15.00	3.00

		NRMT	VG-E	GOOD
☐ 57	Herb Dickenson	22.00	11.00	2.20
☐ 58	Tim Horton	100.00	50.00	10.00
☐ 59	Harry Lumley	30.00	15.00	3.00
☐ 60	Metro Prystai	18.00	9.00	1.80
☐ 61	Marcel Pronovost	30.00	15.00	3.00
☐ 62	Benny Woit	18.00	9.00	1.80
☐ 63	Glen Skov	18.00	9.00	1.80
☐ 64	Bob Goldham	18.00	9.00	1.80
☐ 65	Tony Leswick	18.00	9.00	1.80
☐ 66	Marty Pavelich	18.00	9.00	1.80
☐ 67	Red Kelly	40.00	20.00	4.00
☐ 68	Bill Quackenbush	30.00	15.00	3.00
☐ 69	Ed Sandford	18.00	9.00	1.80
☐ 70	Milt Schmidt	35.00	17.50	3.50
☐ 71	Hal Laycoe	18.00	9.00	1.80
☐ 72	Woody Dumart	18.00	9.00	1.80
☐ 73	Jerry Toppazzini	18.00	9.00	1.80
☐ 74	Jim Henry	22.00	11.00	2.20
☐ 75	Joe Klukay	18.00	9.00	1.80
☐ 76	Dave Creighton	22.00	11.00	2.20
☐ 77	Jack McIntyre	18.00	9.00	1.80
☐ 78	Johnny Pierson	18.00	9.00	1.80
☐ 79	George Sullivan	18.00	9.00	1.80
☐ 80	Real Chevrefils	22.00	11.00	2.20
☐ 81	Leo Labine	18.00	9.00	1.80
☐ 82	Fleming Mackell	18.00	9.00	1.80
☐ 83	Pentti Lund	18.00	9.00	1.80
☐ 84	Bob Armstrong	18.00	9.00	1.80
☐ 85	Warren Godfrey	18.00	9.00	1.80
☐ 86	Terry Sawchuk	200.00	100.00	20.00
☐ 87	Ted Lindsay	40.00	20.00	4.00
☐ 88	Gordie Howe	900.00	450.00	90.00
☐ 89	Johnny Wilson	18.00	9.00	1.80
☐ 90	Vic Stasiuk	18.00	9.00	1.80
☐ 91	Larry Zeidel	18.00	9.00	1.80
☐ 92	Larry Wilson	18.00	9.00	1.80
☐ 93	Bert Olmstead	30.00	15.00	3.00
☐ 94	Ron Stewart	18.00	9.00	1.80
☐ 95	Max Bentley	30.00	15.00	3.00
☐ 96	Rudy Migay	18.00	9.00	1.80
☐ 97	Jack Stoddard	18.00	9.00	1.80
☐ 98	Hy Buller	18.00	9.00	1.80
☐ 99	Bones Raleigh	18.00	9.00	1.80
☐ 100	Edgar Laprade	18.00	9.00	1.80
☐ 101	Nick Mickoski	18.00	9.00	1.80
☐ 102	Jack McLeod	18.00	9.00	1.80
☐ 103	Jim Conacher	22.00	11.00	2.20
☐ 104	Reginald Sinclair	18.00	9.00	1.80
☐ 105	Bob Hassard	40.00	12.00	2.50

1953-54 Parkhurst

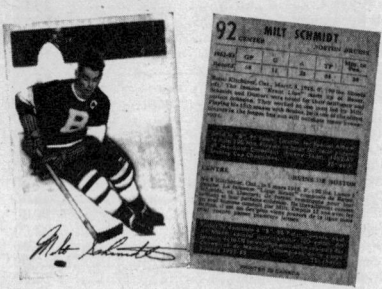

The 1953-54 Parkhurst set contains 100 cards in full color. Cards measure 2½" by 3⅝". The size of the card increased from the previous year and the picture and color show marked improvement. A facsimile autograph of the player is found on the front. The backs contain the card number, 1952-53 statistics, a short biography, and an album offer. The back data is presented in both English and French. The cards feature players from each of the six NHL teams. The set numbering is basically according to teams, i.e., Toronto Maple Leafs (1-17), Montreal Canadiens (18-35), Detroit Red Wings (36-52), New York Rangers (53-68), Chicago Blackhawks (69-84), and Boston Bruins (85-100). The key rookie cards in this set are Al Arbour, Andy Bathgate, Jean Beliveau, Harry Howell, and Gump Worsley.

Le jeu Parkhurst 1953-54 contient 100 cartes en couleurs, mesurant 2½' x 3⅝'. Les cartes sont plus grandes que l'année précédente, et la qualité de la photo et des couleurs a bien améliorée. Une copie de la signature du joueur se trouve à la face. Le dos comprend le numéro de carte, les statistiques pour 1952-53, une biographie concise, et une offre d'album. Les données au dos sont imprimées en anglais et en français. Les cartes représentent des joueurs des six équipes NHL. Le jeu est essentiellement numéroté selon les équipes, c'est à dire, Toronto Maple Leafs (1-17), Montréal Canadiens (18-35), Detroit Red Wings (36-52), New York Rangers (53-68), Chicago Blackhawks (69-84), et Boston Bruins (85-100). Les débutants importants du jeu sont Al Arbour, Andy Bathgate, Jean Beliveau, Harry Howell, et Gump Worsley.

			NRMT	VG-E	GOOD
	COMPLETE SET (100)		2500.00	1100.00	250.00
	COMMON PLAYER (1-100)		10.00	5.00	1.00
☐	1	Harry Lumley	45.00	10.00	2.00
☐	2	Sid Smith	10.00	5.00	1.00
☐	3	Gord Hannigan	10.00	5.00	1.00
☐	4	Bob Hassard	10.00	5.00	1.00

	#	Player	NRMT	VG-E	GOOD
☐	5	Tod Sloan	10.00	5.00	1.00
☐	6	Leo Boivin	16.00	8.00	1.60
☐	7	Ted Kennedy	16.00	8.00	1.60
☐	8	Jim Thomson	10.00	5.00	1.00
☐	9	Ron Stewart	10.00	5.00	1.00
☐	10	Eric Nesterenko	20.00	10.00	2.00
☐	11	George Armstrong	20.00	10.00	2.00
☐	12	Harry Watson	13.50	6.50	1.20
☐	13	Tim Horton	40.00	20.00	4.00
☐	14	Fern Flaman	16.00	8.00	1.60
☐	15	Jim Morrison	10.00	5.00	1.00
☐	16	Bob Solinger	10.00	5.00	1.00
☐	17	Rudy Migay	10.00	5.00	1.00
☐	18	Dick Gamble	10.00	5.00	1.00
☐	19	Bert Olmstead	16.00	8.00	1.60
☐	20	Eddie Mazur	10.00	5.00	1.00
☐	21	Paul Meger	10.00	5.00	1.00
☐	22	Bud MacPherson	10.00	5.00	1.00
☐	23	Dollard St. Laurent	10.00	5.00	1.00
☐	24	Maurice Richard	250.00	125.00	25.00
☐	25	Gerry McNeil	11.00	5.50	1.10
☐	26	Doug Harvey	33.00	16.00	3.00
☐	27	Jean Beliveau	250.00	125.00	25.00
☐	28	Dickie Moore	20.00	10.00	2.00
☐	29	Boom Boom Geoffrion	50.00	25.00	5.00
☐	30	Lach/Richard	60.00	30.00	6.00
☐	31	Elmer Lach	16.00	8.00	1.60
☐	32	Butch Bouchard	16.00	8.00	1.60
☐	33	Ken Mosdell	10.00	5.00	1.00
☐	34	John McCormack	10.00	5.00	1.00
☐	35	Floyd Curry	11.00	5.50	1.10
☐	36	Earl Reibel	10.00	5.00	1.00
☐	37	Bill Dineen UER (Photo actually Al Arbour)	20.00	10.00	2.00
☐	38	Al Arbour UER (Photo actually Bill Dineen)	20.00	10.00	2.00
☐	39	Vic Stasiuk	10.00	5.00	1.00
☐	40	Red Kelly	30.00	15.00	3.00
☐	41	Marcel Pronovost	16.00	8.00	1.60
☐	42	Metro Prystai	10.00	5.00	1.00
☐	43	Tony Leswick	10.00	5.00	1.00
☐	44	Marty Pavelich	10.00	5.00	1.00
☐	45	Benny Woit	10.00	5.00	1.00
☐	46	Terry Sawchuk	110.00	55.00	11.00
☐	47	Alex Delvecchio	30.00	15.00	3.00
☐	48	Glen Skov	10.00	5.00	1.00
☐	49	Bob Goldham	10.00	5.00	1.00
☐	50	Gordie Howe	500.00	250.00	50.00
☐	51	Johnny Wilson	10.00	5.00	1.00
☐	52	Ted Lindsay	30.00	15.00	3.00
☐	53	Gump Worsley	135.00	65.00	13.50
☐	54	Jack Evans	10.00	5.00	1.00
☐	55	Max Bentley	16.00	8.00	1.60

		NRMT	VG-E	GOOD
☐ 56	Andy Bathgate	55.00	27.50	5.50
☐ 57	Harry Howell	50.00	25.00	5.00
☐ 58	Hy Buller	10.00	5.00	1.00
☐ 59	Chuck Rayner	16.00	8.00	1.60
☐ 60	Jack Stoddard	10.00	5.00	1.00
☐ 61	Ed Kullman	10.00	5.00	1.00
☐ 62	Nick Mickoski	10.00	5.00	1.00
☐ 63	Paul Ronty	10.00	5.00	1.00
☐ 64	Allan Stanley	16.00	8.00	1.60
☐ 65	Leo Reise	10.00	5.00	1.00
☐ 66	Aldo Guidolin	10.00	5.00	1.00
☐ 67	Wally Hergesheimer	10.00	5.00	1.00
☐ 68	Don Raleigh	10.00	5.00	1.00
☐ 69	Jim Peters	10.00	5.00	1.00
☐ 70	Pete Conacher	11.00	5.50	1.10
☐ 71	Fred Hucul	10.00	5.00	1.00
☐ 72	Lee Fogolin	10.00	5.00	1.00
☐ 73	Larry Zeidel	10.00	5.00	1.00
☐ 74	Larry Wilson	10.00	5.00	1.00
☐ 75	Gus Bodnar	10.00	5.00	1.00
☐ 76	Bill Gadsby	16.00	8.00	1.60
☐ 77	Jim McFadden	10.00	5.00	1.00
☐ 78	Al Dewsbury	10.00	5.00	1.00
☐ 79	Rags Raglan	10.00	5.00	1.00
☐ 80	Bill Mosienko	16.00	8.00	1.60
☐ 81	Gus Mortson	10.00	5.00	1.00
☐ 82	Al Rollins	11.00	5.50	1.10
☐ 83	George Gee	10.00	5.00	1.00
☐ 84	Gerry Couture	10.00	5.00	1.00
☐ 85	Dave Creighton	10.00	5.00	1.00
☐ 86	Jim Henry	11.00	5.50	1.10
☐ 87	Hal Laycoe	10.00	5.00	1.00
☐ 88	Johnny Pierson	10.00	5.00	1.00
☐ 89	Real Chevrefils	10.00	5.00	1.00
☐ 90	Ed Sandford	10.00	5.00	1.00
☐ 91A	Fleming Mackell ERR (No bio)	11.00	5.50	1.10
☐ 91B	Fleming Mackell COR	11.00	5.50	1.10
☐ 92	Milt Schmidt	18.00	9.00	1.80
☐ 93	Leo Labine	10.00	5.00	1.00
☐ 94	Joe Klukay	10.00	5.00	1.00
☐ 95	Warren Godfrey	10.00	5.00	1.00
☐ 96	Woody Dumart	10.00	5.00	1.00
☐ 97	Frank Martin	10.00	5.00	1.00
☐ 98	Jerry Toppazzini	10.00	5.00	1.00
☐ 99	Cal Gardner	10.00	5.00	1.00
☐ 100	Bill Quackenbush	30.00	10.00	2.00

1954-55 Parkhurst

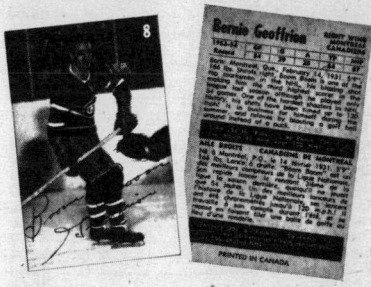

The 1954-55 Parkhurst set contains 100 cards in full color with both the card and the number and a facsimile autograph on the fronts. Cards in the set measure approximately 2½" by 3⅝". The backs, in both English and French, contain 1953-54 statistics, a short player biography, and an album offer (contained only on cards 1-88). Cards 1-88 feature players from each of the six NHL teams and the remaining cards are action scenes. The player/set numbering is basically according to teams, i.e., Montreal Canadiens (1-15), Toronto Maple Leafs (16-32), Detroit Red Wings (33-48), Boston Bruins (49-64), New York Rangers (65-76), and Chicago Blackhawks (77-88), and All-Star selections from the previous season are denoted discreetly on the card front by a red star (first team selection) or blue star (second team). The best rookie card in this set is Johnny Bower.

Le jeu Parkhurst 1954-55 contient 100 cartes en couleurs, avec, du côté face, le numéro de carte et une copie de l'autographe du joueur. Les cartes de ce jeu mesurent à peu près 2½" x 3⅝". Le dos, imprimé en anglais et en français, présente les statistiques pour 1953-54, une biographie concise, et une offre d'album (présentée seulement sur les cartes 1-88). Les cartes 1-88 représentent des joueurs des six équipes NHL, et les autres cartes montrent des scènes d'action. Le numérotage des joueurs et du jeu est essentiellement effectué selon les équipes, c'est à dire, Montréal Canadiens (1-15), Toronto Maple Leafs (16-32), Detroit Red Wings (33-48), Boston Bruins (49-64), New York Rangers (65-76), et Chicago Blackhawks (77-88). Les sélections All-Star de la saison précédente sont discrètement indiquées à la face de la carte par une étoile rouge (sélection première équipe) ou bleue (deuxième équipe). Johnny Bower est le débutant prometteur de ce jeu.

			NRMT	VG-E	GOOD
		COMPLETE SET (100)	2200.00	1000.00	200.00
		COMMON PLAYER (1-100)	10.00	5.00	1.00
☐	1	Gerry McNeil	22.00	6.00	1.20
☐	2	Dickie Moore	16.00	8.00	1.60
☐	3	Jean Beliveau	110.00	55.00	11.00
☐	4	Eddie Mazur	10.00	5.00	1.00
☐	5	Bert Olmstead	16.00	8.00	1.60
☐	6	Butch Bouchard	16.00	8.00	1.60
☐	7	Maurice Richard	200.00	100.00	20.00
☐	8	Boom Boom Geoffrion	50.00	25.00	5.00
☐	9	John McCormack	10.00	5.00	1.00
☐	10	Tom Johnson	16.00	8.00	1.60
☐	11	Calum Mackay	10.00	5.00	1.00
☐	12	Ken Mosdell	10.00	5.00	1.00
☐	13	Paul Masnick	10.00	5.00	1.00
☐	14	Doug Harvey	33.00	16.00	3.00
☐	15	Floyd Curry	11.00	5.50	1.10
☐	16	Harry Lumley	16.00	8.00	1.60
☐	17	Harry Watson	12.50	6.25	1.25
☐	18	Jim Morrison	10.00	5.00	1.00
☐	19	Eric Nesterenko	12.50	6.25	1.25
☐	20	Fern Flaman	16.00	8.00	1.60
☐	21	Rudy Migay	10.00	5.00	1.00
☐	22	Sid Smith	10.00	5.00	1.00
☐	23	Ron Stewart	10.00	5.00	1.00
☐	24	George Armstrong	17.00	8.50	1.70
☐	25	Earl Balfour	12.50	6.25	1.25
☐	26	Leo Boivin	16.00	8.00	1.60
☐	27	Gord Hannigan	10.00	5.00	1.00
☐	28	Bob Bailey	10.00	5.00	1.00
☐	29	Ted Kennedy	16.00	8.00	1.60
☐	30	Tod Sloan	10.00	5.00	1.00
☐	31	Tim Horton	30.00	15.00	3.00
☐	32	Jim Thomson	10.00	5.00	1.00
☐	33	Terry Sawchuk	85.00	42.50	8.50
☐	34	Marcel Pronovost	16.00	8.00	1.60
☐	35	Metro Prystai	10.00	5.00	1.00
☐	36	Alex Delvecchio	25.00	12.50	2.50
☐	37	Earl Reibel	10.00	5.00	1.00
☐	38	Benny Woit	10.00	5.00	1.00
☐	39	Bob Goldham	10.00	5.00	1.00
☐	40	Glen Skov	10.00	5.00	1.00
☐	41	Gordie Howe	400.00	200.00	40.00
☐	42	Red Kelly	25.00	12.50	2.50
☐	43	Marty Pavelich	10.00	5.00	1.00
☐	44	Johnny Wilson	10.00	5.00	1.00
☐	45	Tony Leswick	10.00	5.00	1.00
☐	46	Ted Lindsay	25.00	12.50	2.50
☐	47	Keith Allan	10.00	5.00	1.00
☐	48	Bill Dineen	11.00	5.50	1.10
☐	49	Jim Henry	11.00	5.50	1.10

			NRMT	VG-E	GOOD
☐	50	Fleming Mackell	10.00	5.00	1.00
☐	51	Bill Quackenbush	16.00	8.00	1.60
☐	52	Hal Laycoe	10.00	5.00	1.00
☐	53	Cal Gardner	10.00	5.00	1.00
☐	54	Joe Klukay	10.00	5.00	1.00
☐	55	Bob Armstrong	10.00	5.00	1.00
☐	56	Warren Godfrey	10.00	5.00	1.00
☐	57	Doug Mohns	20.00	10.00	2.00
☐	58	Dave Creighton	10.00	5.00	1.00
☐	59	Milt Schmidt	16.00	8.00	1.60
☐	60	Johnny Pierson	10.00	5.00	1.00
☐	61	Leo Labine	10.00	5.00	1.00
☐	62	Gus Bodnar	10.00	5.00	1.00
☐	63	Real Chevrefils	10.00	5.00	1.00
☐	64	Ed Sandford	10.00	5.00	1.00
☐	65	Johnny Bower UER	110.00	55.00	11.00
		(Misspelled Bowers)			
☐	66	Paul Ronty	10.00	5.00	1.00
☐	67	Leo Reise	10.00	5.00	1.00
☐	68	Don Raleigh	10.00	5.00	1.00
☐	69	Bob Chrystal	10.00	5.00	1.00
☐	70	Harry Howell	20.00	10.00	2.00
☐	71	Wally Hergesheimer	10.00	5.00	1.00
☐	72	Jack Evans	10.00	5.00	1.00
☐	73	Camille Henry	15.00	7.50	1.50
☐	74	Dean Prentice	20.00	10.00	2.00
☐	75	Nick Mickoski	10.00	5.00	1.00
☐	76	Ron Murphy	10.00	5.00	1.00
☐	77	Al Rollins	11.00	5.50	1.10
☐	78	Al Dewsbury	10.00	5.00	1.00
☐	79	Lou Jankowski	10.00	5.00	1.00
☐	80	George Gee	10.00	5.00	1.00
☐	81	Gus Mortson	10.00	5.00	1.00
☐	82	Fred Sasakamoose	10.00	5.00	1.00
☐	83	Ike Hildebrand	10.00	5.00	1.00
☐	84	Lee Fogolin	10.00	5.00	1.00
☐	85	Larry Wilson	10.00	5.00	1.00
☐	86	Pete Conacher	10.00	5.00	1.00
☐	87	Bill Gadsby	16.00	8.00	1.60
☐	88	Jack McIntyre	10.00	5.00	1.00
☐	89	Busher Curry goes up and over	11.00	5.50	1.10
☐	90	Delvecchio finds Leaf defense hard to crack	16.00	8.00	1.60
☐	91	Battle of All-Stars (Red Kelly and Harry Lumley)	18.00	9.00	1.80
☐	92	Lum stops Howe With help of Stewart's stick	50.00	25.00	5.00
☐	93	Net-minders nightmare (Harry Lumley and others)	12.00	6.00	1.20
☐	94	Meger goes down and under	11.00	5.50	1.10

			NRMT	VG-E	GOOD
☐	95	Harvey takes nosedive	18.00	9.00	1.80
☐	96	Terry boots out	35.00	17.50	3.50
		Teeder's blast			
☐	97	Reibel tests Habs	11.00	5.50	1.10
		Rookie "Mr. Zero"			
☐	98	Plante protects	30.00	15.00	3.00
		against slippery Sloan			
☐	99	Placid Plante foils	30.00	15.00	3.00
		tireless Teeder			
☐	100	Sawchuck stops	75.00	37.50	7.50
		Boom Boom			

1955-56 Parkhurst

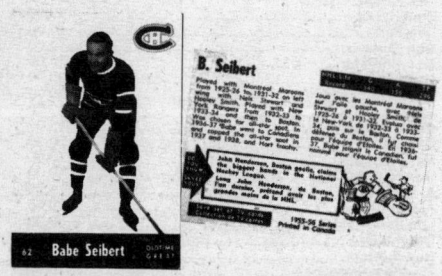

The 1955-56 Parkhurst set contains 79 cards in full color with the number and team insignia on the fronts. Cards in the set measure approximately 2¹/₂" by 3⁹/₁₆". The set features players from Montreal and Toronto only, current players as well as All-Time Greats. The All-Time Great selections are numbers 21-32 and 55-66. The backs, printed in red ink, in both English and French, contain 1954-55 statistics, a short biography, a "Do You Know" information section, and an album offer. The key rookie card in this set is Jacques Plante. The same 79 cards can also be found with Quaker Oats backs, i.e., green printing on back. The Quaker Oats version is much tougher to locate and the values are approximately five times the value of the corresponding Parkhurst player's card.

Le jeu Parkhurst 1955-56 contient 79 cartes en couleurs, avec le numéro et l'emblème de l'équipe à la face. Les cartes de ce jeu mesurent à peu près 2¹/₂" x 3⁹/₁₆". Le jeu ne représente que des joueurs de Montréal et de Toronto - joueurs actifs ainsi qu'étoiles All-Time. Les sélections étoiles All-Time sont numérotées 21-32 et 55-66. Le dos, imprimé en encre rouge en anglais et en français, offre les statistiques pour 1954-55, une biographie concise, une section informative intitulée "Savez-vous?...", et une offre

d'album. Ces mêmes 79 cartes existent également avec un dos Quaker Oats, c'est à dire, imprimé en vert. La version Quaker Oats est bien plus difficile à trouver, et vaut à peu près le double des cartes Parkhurst correspondantes. Le débutant prometteur de ce jeu est Jacques Plante.

			NRMT	VG-E	GOOD
		COMPLETE SET (79)	1650.00	800.00	175.00
		COMMON PLAYER (1-79)	10.00	5.00	1.00
☐	1	**Harry Lumley**	45.00	10.00	2.00
☐	2	**Sid Smith**	10.00	5.00	1.00
☐	3	**Tim Horton**	30.00	15.00	3.00
☐	4	**George Armstrong**	17.00	8.50	1.70
☐	5	**Ron Stewart**	10.00	5.00	1.00
☐	6	**Joe Klukay**	10.00	5.00	1.00
☐	7	**Marc Reaume**	10.00	5.00	1.00
☐	8	**Jim Morrison**	10.00	5.00	1.00
☐	9	**Parker MacDonald**	10.00	5.00	1.00
☐	10	**Tod Sloan**	10.00	5.00	1.00
☐	11	**Jim Thomson**	10.00	5.00	1.00
☐	12	**Rudy Migay**	10.00	5.00	1.00
☐	13	**Brian Cullen**	14.00	7.00	1.40
☐	14	**Hugh Bolton**	10.00	5.00	1.00
☐	15	**Eric Nesterenko**	12.50	6.25	1.25
☐	16	**Larry Cahan**	10.00	5.00	1.00
☐	17	**Willie Marshall**	10.00	5.00	1.00
☐	18	**Dick Duff**	14.00	7.00	1.40
☐	19	**Jack Caffery**	10.00	5.00	1.00
☐	20	**Billy Harris**	10.00	5.00	1.00
☐	21	**Lorne Chabot**	11.00	5.50	1.10
☐	22	**Harvey Jackson**	14.00	7.00	1.40
☐	23	**Turk Broda**	20.00	10.00	2.00
☐	24	**Joe Primeau**	14.00	7.00	1.40
☐	25	**Gordie Drillon**	14.00	7.00	1.40
☐	26	**Chuck Conacher**	14.00	7.00	1.40
☐	27	**Sweeney Schriner**	14.00	7.00	1.40
☐	28	**Syl Apps**	15.00	7.50	1.50
☐	29	**Teeder Kennedy**	16.00	8.00	1.60
☐	30	**Ace Bailey**	16.00	8.00	1.60
☐	31	**Babe Pratt**	14.00	7.00	1.40
☐	32	**Harold Cotton**	11.00	5.50	1.10
☐	33	**King Clancy**	20.00	10.00	2.00
☐	34	**Hap Day**	14.00	7.00	1.40
☐	35	**Don Marshall**	20.00	10.00	2.00
☐	36	**Jack LeClair**	14.00	7.00	1.40
☐	37	**Maurice Richard**	175.00	85.00	18.00
☐	38	**Dickie Moore**	16.00	8.00	1.60
☐	39	**Ken Mosdell**	10.00	5.00	1.00
☐	40	**Floyd Curry**	11.00	5.50	1.10
☐	41	**Calum Mackay**	10.00	5.00	1.00
☐	42	**Bert Olmstead**	16.00	8.00	1.60
☐	43	**Boom Boom Geoffrion**	42.00	20.00	4.00
☐	44	**Jean Beliveau**	75.00	37.50	7.50

			NRMT	VG-E	GOOD
☐	45	Doug Harvey	25.00	12.50	2.50
☐	46	Butch Bouchard	16.00	8.00	1.60
☐	47	Bud MacPherson	10.00	5.00	1.00
☐	48	Dollard St. Laurent	10.00	5.00	1.00
☐	49	Tom Johnson	16.00	8.00	1.60
☐	50	Jacques Plante	300.00	150.00	30.00
☐	51	Paul Meger	10.00	5.00	1.00
☐	52	Gerry McNeil	11.00	5.50	1.10
☐	53	Jean Guy Talbot	10.00	5.00	1.00
☐	54	Bob Turner	10.00	5.00	1.00
☐	55	Newsy Lalonde	17.00	8.50	1.70
☐	56	Georges Vezina	30.00	15.00	3.00
☐	57	Howie Morenz	35.00	17.50	3.50
☐	58	Aurel Joliat	20.00	10.00	2.00
☐	59	George Hainsworth	14.00	7.00	1.40
☐	60	Sylvio Mantha	14.00	7.00	1.40
☐	61	Battleship Leduc	11.00	5.50	1.10
☐	62	Babe Siebert	14.00	7.00	1.40
☐	63	Bill Durnan	16.00	8.00	1.60
☐	64	Ken Reardon	16.00	8.00	1.60
☐	65	Johnny Gagnon	11.00	5.50	1.10
☐	66	Billy Reay	11.00	5.50	1.10
☐	67	Toe Blake	14.00	7.00	1.40
☐	68	Frank Selke	14.00	7.00	1.40
☐	69	Hugh beats Hodge	11.00	5.50	1.10
☐	70	Lum stops Boom Boom	20.00	10.00	2.00
☐	71	Plante is protected	25.00	12.50	2.50
☐	72	Rocket roars through	40.00	20.00	4.00
☐	73	Richard tests Lumley	40.00	20.00	4.00
☐	74	Beliveau bats puck	20.00	10.00	2.00
☐	75	Leaf speedsters attack (Eric Nesterenko, Sid Smith, and Jacques Plante)	20.00	10.00	2.00
☐	76	Curry scores again	11.00	5.50	1.10
☐	77	Jammed on the boards (Tod Sloan, Parker MacDonald, Doug Harvey, and Jean Beliveau)	20.00	10.00	2.00
☐	78	The Montreal Forum	12.00	6.00	1.20
☐	79	Maple Leafs Garden	40.00	7.50	1.50

1957-58 Parkhurst

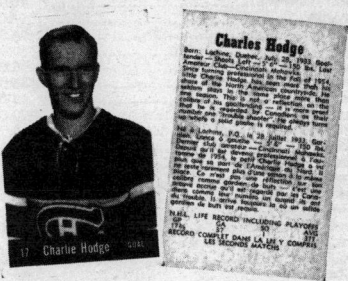

The 1957-58 Parkhurst set contains 50 color cards featuring Montreal and Toronto players. Cards are approximately 2⁷/₁₆" by 3⅝". There are card numbers 1 to 25 for Montreal and card numbers 1 to 25 for Toronto. The checklist below renumbers the Maple Leaf players starting with number 26, while the Montreal Canadiens have the numbers 1-25. The cards are numbered on the fronts and the backs feature resumes in both French and English. The card number, the player's name, and his position appear in a red rectangle on the front. The backs are printed in blue ink. The key rookie cards in this set are Frank Mahovlich and Henri Richard. There was no Parkhurst hockey set in 1956-57.

Le jeu Parkhurst 1957-58 contient 50 cartes en couleurs représentant des joueurs de Montréal et de Toronto. Les cartes mesurent approximativement 2⁷/₁₆" x 3⅝". Il existe des cartes numérotées de 1 à 25 pour Montréal, et de 1 à 25 pour Toronto. La liste ci-dessous recommence le numérotage des joueurs Maple Leaf avec le numéro 26, alors que les joueurs Montréal Canadiens sont numérotés de 1 à 25. Les cartes sont numérotées à la face, et le dos présente de brèves descriptions en français et en anglais. Le numéro de carte, le nom du joueur et sa position apparaissent dans un rectangle rouge à la face. Le dos est imprimé en encre bleue. Les débutants importants de ce jeu sont Frank Mahovlich et Henri Richard. Il n'existait pas de jeu Parkhurst en 1956-57.

			NRMT	VG-E	GOOD
	COMPLETE SET (50)		1200.00	600.00	125.00
	COMMON PLAYER (1-50)		10.00	5.00	1.00
☐	1	Doug Harvey	60.00	12.00	2.50
☐	2	Boom Boom Geoffrion	35.00	17.50	3.50
☐	3	Jean Beliveau	75.00	37.50	7.50
☐	4	Henri Richard	100.00	50.00	10.00
☐	5	Maurice Richard	150.00	75.00	15.00
☐	6	Tom Johnson	16.00	8.00	1.60

			NRMT	VG-E	GOOD
☐	7	Andre Pronovost	12.50	6.25	1.25
☐	8	Don Marshall	11.00	5.50	1.10
☐	9	Jean Guy Talbot	10.00	5.00	1.00
☐	10	Dollard St. Laurent	10.00	5.00	1.00
☐	11	Phil Goyette	14.00	7.00	1.40
☐	12	Claude Provost	14.00	7.00	1.40
☐	13	Bob Turner	10.00	5.00	1.00
☐	14	Dickie Moore	16.00	8.00	1.60
☐	15	Jacques Plante	135.00	65.00	13.50
☐	16	Toe Blake	15.00	7.50	1.50
☐	17	Charlie Hodge	20.00	10.00	2.00
☐	18	Marcel Bonin	10.00	5.00	1.00
☐	19	Bert Olmstead	16.00	8.00	1.60
☐	20	Floyd Curry	11.00	5.50	1.10
☐	21	Canadiens on guard	11.00	5.50	1.10
		(Len Broderick)			
☐	22	B. Cullen scores	11.00	5.50	1.10
☐	23	Puck and sticks high	14.00	7.00	1.40
		(Len Broderick and Doug Harvey)			
☐	24	Geoffrion side-steps Chadwick	20.00	10.00	2.00
☐	25	Olmstead beats Chadwick	12.00	6.00	1.20
☐	26	George Armstrong	16.00	8.00	1.60
☐	27	Ed Chadwick	14.00	7.00	1.40
☐	28	Dick Duff	10.00	5.00	1.00
☐	29	Bob Pulford	30.00	15.00	3.00
☐	30	Tod Sloan	10.00	5.00	1.00
☐	31	Rudy Migay	10.00	5.00	1.00
☐	32	Ron Stewart	10.00	5.00	1.00
☐	33	Gerry James	10.00	5.00	1.00
☐	34	Brian Cullen	10.00	5.00	1.00
☐	35	Sid Smith	10.00	5.00	1.00
☐	36	Jim Morrison	10.00	5.00	1.00
☐	37	Marc Reaume	10.00	5.00	1.00
☐	38	Hugh Bolton	10.00	5.00	1.00
☐	39	Pete Conacher	10.00	5.00	1.00
☐	40	Billy Harris	10.00	5.00	1.00
☐	41	Mike Nykoluk	10.00	5.00	1.00
☐	42	Frank Mahovlich	165.00	75.00	15.00
☐	43	Ken Girard	10.00	5.00	1.00
☐	44	Al McNeil	10.00	5.00	1.00
☐	45	Bob Baun	14.00	7.00	1.40
☐	46	Barry Cullen	10.00	5.00	1.00
☐	47	Tim Horton	28.00	14.00	2.80
☐	48	Gary Collins	10.00	5.00	1.00
☐	49	Gary Aldcorn	10.00	5.00	1.00
☐	50	Billy Reay	18.00	6.00	1.20

1958-59 Parkhurst

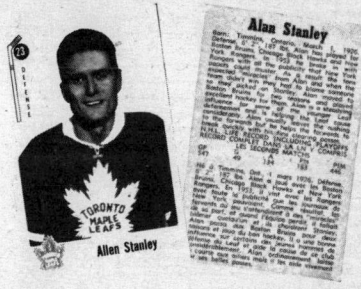

The 1958-59 Parkhurst set contains 50 color cards of Montreal and Toronto players. Cards are approximately 2⁷/₁₆" by 3⁵/₈". In contrast to the 1957-58 Parkhurst set, the cards, numbered on the fronts, are numbered continuously from 1 to 50. Resumes on the backs of the cards are in both French and English. The player's name and the team logo appear in a yellow rectangle at the bottom on the front. The number, position, and (usually) a hockey stick appear on the front at the upper left. The backs are printed in black ink. The best rookie card in this set is Ralph Backstrom.

Le jeu Parkhurst 1958-59 contient 50 cartes en couleurs de joueurs de Montréal et de Toronto. Les cartes mesurent à peu près 2⁷/₁₆" x 3⁵/₈". Contrairement au jeu Parkhurst de 1957-58, la face des cartes est numérotée de 1 à 50 sans interruption. Les descriptions sommaires au dos sont en français et en anglais. Le nom du joueur et l'emblème de l'équipe apparaissent dans un rectangle jaune à la partie inférieure de la face. La face montre le numéro, la position et (généralement) un stick de hockey au côté supérieur gauche. Le dos est imprimé en encre noire. La carte du débutant important représente Ralph Backstrom.

			NRMT	VG-E	GOOD
		COMPLETE SET (50)	1000.00	500.00	100.00
		COMMON PLAYER (1-50)	10.00	5.00	1.00
☐	1	Pulford comes close	20.00	7.50	1.50
☐	2	Henri Richard	30.00	15.00	3.00
☐	3	Andre Pronovost	10.00	5.00	1.00
☐	4	Billy Harris	10.00	5.00	1.00
☐	5	Albert Langlois	10.00	5.00	1.00
☐	6	Noel Price	10.00	5.00	1.00
☐	7	Armstrong breaks through	12.00	6.00	1.20
☐	8	Dickie Moore	15.00	7.50	1.50

		NRMT	VG-E	GOOD
☐ 9	Toe Blake	14.00	7.00	1.40
☐ 10	Tom Johnson	14.00	7.00	1.40
☐ 11	An object of interest	20.00	10.00	2.00
	(Jacques Plante and George Armstrong)			
☐ 12	Ed Chadwick	11.00	5.50	1.10
☐ 13	Bob Nevin	10.00	5.00	1.00
☐ 14	Ron Stewart	10.00	5.00	1.00
☐ 15	Bob Baun	11.00	5.50	1.10
☐ 16	Ralph Backstrom	14.00	7.00	1.40
☐ 17	Charlie Hodge	12.00	6.00	1.20
☐ 18	Gary Aldcorn	10.00	5.00	1.00
☐ 19	Willie Marshall	10.00	5.00	1.00
☐ 20	Marc Reaume	10.00	5.00	1.00
☐ 21	All eyes on puck	14.00	7.00	1.40
	(Jacques Plante and others)			
☐ 22	Jacques Plante	90.00	45.00	9.00
☐ 23	Allan Stanley	14.00	7.00	1.40
☐ 24	Ian Cushenan	10.00	5.00	1.00
☐ 25	Billy Reay CO	11.00	5.50	1.10
☐ 26	Plante catches a shot	14.00	7.00	1.40
☐ 27	Bert Olmstead	14.00	7.00	1.40
☐ 28	Boom Boom Geoffrion	35.00	17.50	3.50
☐ 29	Dick Duff	10.00	5.00	1.00
☐ 30	Ab McDonald	10.00	5.00	1.00
☐ 31	Barry Cullen	10.00	5.00	1.00
☐ 32	Marcel Bonin	10.00	5.00	1.00
☐ 33	Frank Mahovlich	70.00	35.00	7.00
☐ 34	Jean Beliveau	65.00	32.50	6.50
☐ 35	Canadiens on guard	11.00	5.50	1.10
☐ 36	B. Cullen shoots	11.00	5.50	1.10
☐ 37	Steve Kraftcheck	10.00	5.00	1.00
☐ 38	Maurice Richard	150.00	75.00	15.00
☐ 39	Action around the net	14.00	7.00	1.40
	(Jacques Plante and others)			
☐ 40	Bob Turner	10.00	5.00	1.00
☐ 41	Jean Guy Talbot	10.00	5.00	1.00
☐ 42	Tim Horton	25.00	12.50	2.50
☐ 43	Claude Provost	10.00	5.00	1.00
☐ 44	Don Marshall	11.00	5.50	1.10
☐ 45	Bob Pulford	16.00	8.00	1.60
☐ 46	Johnny Bower	25.00	12.50	2.50
☐ 47	Phil Goyette	11.00	5.50	1.10
☐ 48	George Armstrong	15.00	7.50	1.50
☐ 49	Doug Harvey	25.00	12.50	2.50
☐ 50	Brian Cullen	18.00	6.00	1.20

1959-60 Parkhurst

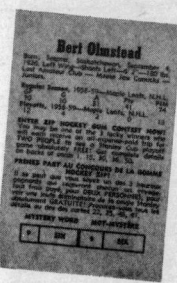

Bert Olmstead

The 1959-60 Parkhurst set contains 50 color cards of Montreal and Toronto players. Cards are approximately 2⁷/₁₆" by 3⁵/₈". The cards are numbered on the fronts, and the backs, which contain 1958-59 statistics, a short biography, and a Hockey Gum contest ad, are written in both French and English. The best rookie card in this set is Carl Brewer.

Le jeu Parkhurst 1959-60 contient 50 cartes en couleurs de joueurs de Montréal et de Toronto. Les cartes mesurent approximativement 2⁷/₁₆" x 3⁵/₈". Elles sont numérotées à la face, et le dos, imprimé en français et en anglais, présente des statistiques pour 1958-59, une biographie concise, et un concours organisé par la Gomme Hockey. La carte du débutant important de ce jeu représente Carl Brewer.

			NRMT	VG-E	GOOD
	COMPLETE SET (50)		900.00	450.00	90.00
	COMMON PLAYER (1-50)		9.00	4.50	.90
☐	1	Canadiens on guard	30.00	7.50	1.50
☐	2	Maurice Richard	150.00	75.00	15.00
☐	3	Carl Brewer	14.00	7.00	1.40
☐	4	Phil Goyette	10.00	5.00	1.00
☐	5	Ed Chadwick	10.00	5.00	1.00
☐	6	Jean Beliveau	60.00	30.00	6.00
☐	7	George Armstrong	15.00	7.50	1.50
☐	8	Doug Harvey	24.00	12.00	2.40
☐	9	Billy Harris	9.00	4.50	.90
☐	10	Tom Johnson	14.00	7.00	1.40
☐	11	Marc Reaume	9.00	4.50	.90
☐	12	Marcel Bonin	9.00	4.50	.90
☐	13	Johnny Wilson	9.00	4.50	.90
☐	14	Dickie Moore	15.00	7.50	1.50

			NRMT	VG-E	GOOD
☐	15	Punch Imlach	12.00	6.00	1.20
☐	16	Charlie Hodge	11.00	5.50	1.10
☐	17	Larry Regan	10.00	5.00	1.00
☐	18	Claude Provost	9.00	4.50	.90
☐	19	Gerry Ehman	9.00	4.50	.90
☐	20	Ab McDonald	9.00	4.50	.90
☐	21	Bob Baun	10.00	5.00	1.00
☐	22	Kenneth Reardon	12.00	6.00	1.20
☐	23	Tim Horton	24.00	12.00	2.40
☐	24	Frank Mahovlich	50.00	25.00	5.00
☐	25	Johnny Bower IA	14.00	7.00	1.40
☐	26	Ron Stewart	9.00	4.50	.90
☐	27	Toe Blake	12.00	6.00	1.20
☐	28	Bob Pulford	14.00	7.00	1.40
☐	29	Ralph Backstrom	10.00	5.00	1.00
☐	30	Action around the net	10.00	5.00	1.00
☐	31	Bill Hicke	9.00	4.50	.90
☐	32	Johnny Bower	22.00	11.00	2.20
☐	33	Boom Boom Geoffrion	33.00	16.00	3.00
☐	34	Ted Hampson	9.00	4.50	.90
☐	35	Andre Pronovost	9.00	4.50	.90
☐	36	Stafford Smythe	10.00	5.00	1.00
☐	37	Don Marshall	10.00	5.00	1.00
☐	38	Dick Duff	9.00	4.50	.90
☐	39	Henri Richard	22.00	11.00	2.20
☐	40	Bert Olmstead	14.00	7.00	1.40
☐	41	Jacques Plante	75.00	37.50	7.50
☐	42	Noel Price	9.00	4.50	.90
☐	43	Bob Turner	9.00	4.50	.90
☐	44	Allan Stanley	14.00	7.00	1.40
☐	45	Albert Langlois	9.00	4.50	.90
☐	46	Officials intervene	10.00	5.00	1.00
☐	47	Frank Selke	10.00	5.00	1.00
☐	48	Gary Edmundson	9.00	4.50	.90
☐	49	Jean Guy Talbot	9.00	4.50	.90
☐	50	King Clancy	25.00	8.00	1.60

1960-61 Parkhurst

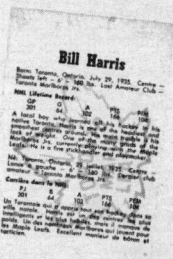

The 1960-61 Parkhurst set of 61 color cards, numbered on the fronts, contains players from Montreal, Toronto, and Detroit. The numbering of the players in the set is basically by teams, i.e., Toronto Maple Leafs (1-19), Detroit Red Wings (20-37), and Montreal Canadiens (38-55). Cards in the set are $2^7/_{16}$" by $3^5/_8$". The backs, in both French and English, are printed in blue ink and contain NHL lifetime records, vital statistics, and biographical data of the player. This set contains the last card of Maurice "Rocket" Richard. The best rookie card in this set is John McKenzie.

Le jeu Parkhurst 1960-61 contient 61 cartes en couleurs, numérotées à la face, représentant des joueurs de Montréal, de Toronto et de Detroit. Les joueurs de ce jeu sont essentiellement numérotés par équipe, c'est à dire, Toronto Maple Leafs (1-19), Detroit Red Wings (20-37), et Montréal Canadiens (38-55). Les cartes mesurent $2^7/_{16}$" x $3^5/_8$". Le dos est imprimé en français et en anglais en encre bleue, et contient les statistiques de carrière NHL, et les données personnelles et biographiques du joueur. Ce jeu contient la dernière carte de Maurice Richard, dit "Rocket". La carte du débutant important de ce jeu représente John McKenzie.

			NRMT	VG-E	GOOD
	COMPLETE SET (61)		1100.00	500.00	100.00
	COMMON PLAYER (1-61)		7.50	3.75	.75
☐	1	Tim Horton	30.00	10.00	2.00
☐	2	Frank Mahovlich	40.00	20.00	4.00
☐	3	Johnny Bower	20.00	10.00	2.00
☐	4	Bert Olmstead	12.50	6.25	1.25
☐	5	Gary Edmundson	7.50	3.75	.75
☐	6	Ron Stewart	7.50	3.75	.75
☐	7	Gerry James	7.50	3.75	.75
☐	8	Gerry Ehman	7.50	3.75	.75
☐	9	Red Kelly	16.00	8.00	1.60
☐	10	Dave Creighton	7.50	3.75	.75
☐	11	Bob Baun	7.50	3.75	.75

			NRMT	VG-E	GOOD
☐	12	Dick Duff	7.50	3.75	.75
☐	13	Larry Regan	7.50	3.75	.75
☐	14	Johnny Wilson	7.50	3.75	.75
☐	15	Billy Harris	7.50	3.75	.75
☐	16	Allan Stanley	12.50	6.25	1.25
☐	17	George Armstrong	13.50	6.50	1.25
☐	18	Carl Brewer	7.50	3.75	.75
☐	19	Bob Pulford	12.50	6.25	1.25
☐	20	Gordie Howe	250.00	125.00	25.00
☐	21	Val Fonteyne	7.50	3.75	.75
☐	22	Murray Oliver	7.50	3.75	.75
☐	23	Sid Abel CO	10.00	5.00	1.00
☐	24	Jack McIntyre	7.50	3.75	.75
☐	25	Marc Reaume	7.50	3.75	.75
☐	26	Norm Ullman	16.00	8.00	1.60
☐	27	Brian Smith	7.50	3.75	.75
☐	28	Jerry Melnyk	7.50	3.75	.75
☐	29	Marcel Pronovost	12.50	6.25	1.25
☐	30	Warren Godfrey	7.50	3.75	.75
☐	31	Terry Sawchuk	50.00	25.00	5.00
☐	32	Barry Cullen	7.50	3.75	.75
☐	33	Gary Aldcorn	7.50	3.75	.75
☐	34	Pete Goegan	7.50	3.75	.75
☐	35	Len Lunde	7.50	3.75	.75
☐	36	Alex Delvecchio	16.00	8.00	1.60
☐	37	John McKenzie	12.50	6.25	1.25
☐	38	Dickie Moore	12.50	6.25	1.25
☐	39	Albert Langlois	7.50	3.75	.75
☐	40	Bill Hicke	7.50	3.75	.75
☐	41	Ralph Backstrom	7.50	3.75	.75
☐	42	Don Marshall	7.50	3.75	.75
☐	43	Bob Turner	7.50	3.75	.75
☐	44	Tom Johnson	12.50	6.25	1.25
☐	45	Maurice Richard	125.00	60.00	12.50
☐	46	Boom Boom Geoffrion	30.00	15.00	3.00
☐	47	Henri Richard	18.00	9.00	1.80
☐	48	Doug Harvey	22.00	11.00	2.20
☐	49	Jean Beliveau	50.00	25.00	5.00
☐	50	Phil Goyette	7.50	3.75	.75
☐	51	Marcel Bonin	7.50	3.75	.75
☐	52	Jean Guy Talbot	7.50	3.75	.75
☐	53	Jacques Plante	65.00	32.50	6.50
☐	54	Claude Provost	7.50	3.75	.75
☐	55	Andre Pronovost	7.50	3.75	.75
☐	56	Line: Hicke, McDonald, Backstrom	9.00	4.50	.90
☐	57	Line: Marshall, Moore, H. Richard	16.00	8.00	1.60
☐	58	Line: Provost, Pronovost, Goyette	9.00	4.50	.90
☐	59	Line: Geoffrion, Marshall, Beliveau	21.00	10.50	2.10
☐	60	Ab McDonald	7.50	3.75	.75
☐	61	Jim Morrison	14.00	4.50	.90

1961-62 Parkhurst

The 1961-62 Parkhurst set contains 51 cards in full color, numbered on the fronts. Cards are 2⁷/₁₆" by 3⁵/₈". The backs contain 1960-61 statistics and a cartoon; the punch line for which could be seen by rubbing the card with a penny. The cards contain players from Montreal, Toronto, and Detroit. The numbering of the players in the set is basically by teams, i.e., Toronto Maple Leafs (1-18), Detroit Red Wings (19-34), and Montreal Canadiens (35-51). The backs are in both French and English. The best rookie card in this set is Dave Keon.

Le jeu Parkhurst 1961-62 contient 51 cartes en couleurs, numérotées à la face. Les cartes mesurent 2⁷/₁₆" x 3⁵/₈". Le dos comporte les statistiques pour 1960-61 et une caricature dont l'astuce est découverte en grattant la carte avec une pièce de monnaie. Les cartes représentent des joueurs de Montréal, de Toronto, et de Detroit. Les joueurs de ce jeu sont essentiellement numérotés par équipe, c.à.d., Toronto Maple Leafs (1-18), Detroit Red Wings (19-34), et Montréal Canadiens (35-51). Le dos est imprimé en français et en anglais. La carte du débutant important de ce jeu représente Dave Keon.

			NRMT	VG-E	GOOD
	COMPLETE SET (51)		900.00	450.00	90.00
	COMMON PLAYER (1-51)		7.50	3.75	.75
☐	1	Tim Horton	28.00	9.00	1.80
☐	2	Frank Mahovlich	36.00	18.00	3.60
☐	3	Johnny Bower	18.00	9.00	1.80
☐	4	Bert Olmstead	11.00	5.50	1.10
☐	5	Dave Keon	65.00	32.50	6.50
☐	6	Ron Stewart	7.50	3.75	.75
☐	7	Eddie Shack	11.00	5.50	1.10
☐	8	Bob Pulford	11.00	5.50	1.10
☐	9	Red Kelly	16.00	8.00	1.60
☐	10	Bob Nevin	7.50	3.75	.75

			NRMT	VG-E	GOOD
☐	11	Bob Baun	7.50	3.75	.75
☐	12	Dick Duff	7.50	3.75	.75
☐	13	Larry Keenan	7.50	3.75	.75
☐	14	Larry Hillman	7.50	3.75	.75
☐	15	Billy Harris	7.50	3.75	.75
☐	16	Allan Stanley	11.00	5.50	1.10
☐	17	George Armstrong	12.50	6.25	1.25
☐	18	Carl Brewer	7.50	3.75	.75
☐	19	Howie Glover	7.50	3.75	.75
☐	20	Gordie Howe	200.00	100.00	20.00
☐	21	Val Fonteyne	7.50	3.75	.75
☐	22	Al Johnson	7.50	3.75	.75
☐	23	Pete Goegan	7.50	3.75	.75
☐	24	Len Lunde	7.50	3.75	.75
☐	25	Alex Delvecchio	16.00	8.00	1.60
☐	26	Norm Ullman	14.00	7.00	1.40
☐	27	Bill Gadsby	11.00	5.50	1.10
☐	28	Ed Litzenberger	7.50	3.75	.75
☐	29	Marcel Pronovost	11.00	5.50	1.10
☐	30	Warren Godfrey	7.50	3.75	.75
☐	31	Terry Sawchuk	50.00	25.00	5.00
☐	32	Vic Stasiuk	7.50	3.75	.75
☐	33	Leo Labine	7.50	3.75	.75
☐	34	John McKenzie	7.50	3.75	.75
☐	35	Boom Boom Geoffrion	28.00	14.00	2.80
☐	36	Dickie Moore	12.50	6.25	1.25
☐	37	Albert Langlois	7.50	3.75	.75
☐	38	Bill Hicke	7.50	3.75	.75
☐	39	Ralph Backstrom	7.50	3.75	.75
☐	40	Don Marshall	7.50	3.75	.75
☐	41	Bob Turner	7.50	3.75	.75
☐	42	Tom Johnson	11.00	5.50	1.10
☐	43	Henri Richard	16.00	8.00	1.60
☐	44	Wayne Connelly	10.00	5.00	1.00
☐	45	Jean Beliveau	45.00	22.50	4.50
☐	46	Phil Goyette	7.50	3.75	.75
☐	47	Marcel Bonin	7.50	3.75	.75
☐	48	Jean Guy Talbot	7.50	3.75	.75
☐	49	Jacques Plante	60.00	30.00	6.00
☐	50	Claude Provost	7.50	3.75	.75
☐	51	Andre Pronovost UER	12.50	4.00	.80
		(Shown as Montreal, should be Boston)			

1962-63 Parkhurst

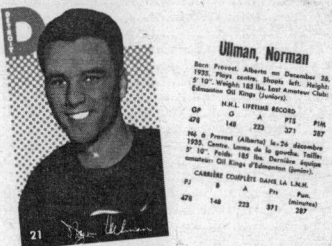

The 1962-63 Parkhurst set contains 54 cards in full color, with the card number and a facsimile autograph of the player contained in a panel at the bottom of the front of the card. Cards are approximately 2⁷/₁₆" by 3⁵/₈". The backs, in both French and English, contain player lifetime statistics and player vital statistics in paragraph form. An unnumbered checklist card was issued as well as an unnumbered game or tally card. Both of these are considered rather difficult to obtain. There are several different styles or designs within this set, depending on card number; e.g., some cards have a giant puck as background for their photo on the front. The numbering of the players in the set is basically by teams, i.e., Toronto Maple Leafs (1-18), Detroit Red Wings (19-36), and Montreal Canadiens (37-54). The notable rookie cards in this set are Bobby Rousseau, Gilles Trembley, and J.C. Trembley.

Le jeu Parkhurst 1962-63 contient 54 cartes en couleurs, avec le numéro de carte et une copie de l'autographe du joueur dans un panneau situé au bas de la face. Les cartes mesurent approximativement 2⁷/₁₆" x 3⁵/₈". Le dos, imprimé en français et en anglais, présente, sous forme de paragraphes, les statistiques de la carrière et les données personnelles du joueur. Une carte de vérification non-numérotée fut omise, mais est considérée plutôt difficile à obtenir. Ce jeu comprend plusieurs styles ou motifs, suivant le numéro de la carte; par exemple, certaines cartes ont un disque de hockey géant comme arrière-plan pour la photo à l'avant-plan. Les joueurs de ce jeu sont numérotés essentiellement par équipe, c.à.d., Toronto Maple Leafs (1- 18), Detroit Red Wings (19-36), et Montréal Canadiens (37- 54). Les débutants importants de ce jeu sont Bobby Rousseau, Gilles Trembley et J.C. Trembley.

			NRMT	VG-E	GOOD
	COMPLETE SET (54)	....	1000.00	500.00	100.00
	COMMON PLAYER (1-54)	....	7.50	3.75	.75
☐	1	Billy Harris	12.50	4.50	.90
☐	2	Dick Duff	7.50	3.75	.75

			NRMT	VG-E	GOOD
☐	3	Bob Baun	7.50	3.75	.75
☐	4	Frank Mahovlich	36.00	18.00	3.60
☐	5	Red Kelly	16.00	8.00	1.60
☐	6	Ron Stewart	7.50	3.75	.75
☐	7	Tim Horton	20.00	10.00	2.00
☐	8	Carl Brewer	7.50	3.75	.75
☐	9	Allan Stanley	11.00	5.50	1.10
☐	10	Bob Nevin	7.50	3.75	.75
☐	11	Bob Pulford	11.00	5.50	1.10
☐	12	Ed Litzenberger	7.50	3.75	.75
☐	13	George Armstrong	12.00	6.00	1.20
☐	14	Eddie Shack	10.00	5.00	1.00
☐	15	Dave Keon	22.00	11.00	2.20
☐	16	Johnny Bower	16.00	8.00	1.60
☐	17	Larry Hillman	7.50	3.75	.75
☐	18	Frank Mahovlich	36.00	18.00	3.60
☐	19	Hank Bassen	7.50	3.75	.75
☐	20	Gerry Odrowski	7.50	3.75	.75
☐	21	Norm Ullman	12.50	6.25	1.25
☐	22	Vic Stasiuk	7.50	3.75	.75
☐	23	Bruce MacGregor	7.50	3.75	.75
☐	24	Claude LaForge	7.50	3.75	.75
☐	25	Bill Gadsby	11.00	5.50	1.10
☐	26	Leo Labine	7.50	3.75	.75
☐	27	Val Fonteyne	7.50	3.75	.75
☐	28	Howie Glover	7.50	3.75	.75
☐	29	Marc Boileau	7.50	3.75	.75
☐	30	Gordie Howe	160.00	80.00	16.00
☐	31	Gordie Howe	160.00	80.00	16.00
☐	32	Alex Delvecchio	16.00	8.00	1.60
☐	33	Marcel Pronovost	11.00	5.50	1.10
☐	34	Sid Abel	10.00	5.00	1.00
☐	35	Len Lunde	7.50	3.75	.75
☐	36	Warren Godfrey	7.50	3.75	.75
☐	37	Phil Goyette	7.50	3.75	.75
☐	38	Henri Richard	16.00	8.00	1.60
☐	39	Jean Beliveau	40.00	20.00	4.00
☐	40	Bill Hicke	7.50	3.75	.75
☐	41	Claude Provost	7.50	3.75	.75
☐	42	Dickie Moore	12.50	6.25	1.25
☐	43	Don Marshall	7.50	3.75	.75
☐	44	Ralph Backstrom	7.50	3.75	.75
☐	45	Marcel Bonin	7.50	3.75	.75
☐	46	Gilles Tremblay	12.50	6.25	1.25
☐	47	Bobby Rousseau	12.50	6.25	1.25
☐	48	Boom Boom Geoffrion	25.00	12.50	2.50
☐	49	Jacques Plante	50.00	25.00	5.00
☐	50	Tom Johnson	11.00	5.50	1.10
☐	51	Jean Guy Talbot	7.50	3.75	.75
☐	52	Lou Fontinato	7.50	3.75	.75
☐	53	Boom Boom Geoffrion	25.00	12.50	2.50
☐	54	J.C. Tremblay	17.00	6.00	1.20

			NRMT	**VG-E**	**GOOD**
☐	xx	**Checklist Card**	150.00	50.00	10.00
		(Unnumbered)			
☐	xx	**Tally Game Card**	150.00	50.00	10.00
		(Unnumbered)			

1963-64 Parkhurst

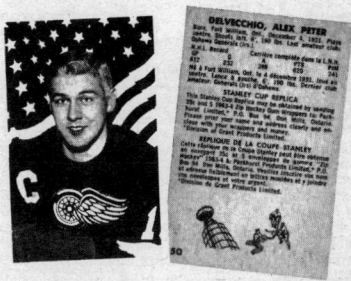

The 1963-64 Parkhurst set contains 99 color cards. Cards measure 2⁷/₁₆" by 3⁵/₈". The fronts of the cards feature the player with a background of either thin stripes or the Canadian or American flag, depending upon whether the player is on the Detroit (American flag), Toronto (Canadian flag), or Montreal (multi-color striped background) team. The numbering of the players in the set is basically by teams, i.e., Toronto Maple Leafs (1-20 and 61-79), Detroit Red Wings (41-60), and Montreal Canadiens (21-40 and 80-99). The backs, in both French and English, contain the card number, player lifetime NHL statistics, player vital statistics, and a Stanley Cup replica offer. The set includes two cards of each Montreal and Toronto player and only one of each Detroit player, with the following exceptions: numbers 15, 20, and 75 (single card Maple Leafs). Each Toronto player's double is obtained by adding 60, e.g., 1 and 61, 2 and 62, 3 and 63, etc., are the same player. Each Montreal player's double is obtained by adding 59, e.g., 21 and 80, 22 and 81, 23 and 82, etc., are the same player. The key rookie cards in the set are Red Berenson, Jacques Laperriere, and Cesare Maniago.

Le jeu Parkhurst 1963-64 contient 99 cartes en couleurs, mesurant 2⁷/₁₆" x 3⁵/₈". La face des cartes représente les joueurs sur un arrière-plan constitué de fines rayures (équipe de Montréal), d'un drapeau canadien (équipe de Toronto), ou d'un drapeau américain (équipe de Detroit). Les joueurs de ce jeu sont numérotés essentiellement par équipe, c.à.d., Toronto Maple Leafs (1-20 et 61-79), Detroit Red Wings (41-60), et Montréal Canadiens (21-40 et 80-99). Le dos, imprimé en français et en anglais, comprend le numéro de carte, les statistiques de carrière NHL du joueur, et une offre pour une réplique de la coupe Stanley. Le jeu inclut deux cartes de chaque joueur de Montréal et de Toronto, et seulement une carte de chaque joueur de Detroit (sauf les

numéros suivants: 15, 20, et 75 (Maple Leafs à carte simple). Le double des joueurs de Toronto est obtenu en ajoutant 60; c.à.d., 1 et 61, 2 et 62, 3 et 63, etc. représentent le même joueur. Le double des joueurs de Montréal est obtenu en ajoutant 59; c.à.d., les numéros 21 et 80, 22 et 81, 23 et 82, représentent le même joueur. Les débutants importants de ce jeu sont Red Berenson, Jacques Laperriere, et Cesare Maniago.

			NRMT	VG-E	GOOD
		COMPLETE SET (99)	1200.00	600.00	125.00
		COMMON PLAYER (1-99)	7.00	3.50	.70
☐	1	Allan Stanley	21.00	7.00	1.40
☐	2	Don Simmons	7.00	3.50	.70
☐	3	Red Kelly	15.00	7.50	1.50
☐	4	Dick Duff	7.00	3.50	.70
☐	5	Johnny Bower	15.00	7.50	1.50
☐	6	Ed Litzenberger	7.00	3.50	.70
☐	7	Kent Douglas	7.00	3.50	.70
☐	8	Carl Brewer	7.00	3.50	.70
☐	9	Eddie Shack	9.00	4.50	.90
☐	10	Bob Nevin	7.00	3.50	.70
☐	11	Billy Harris	7.00	3.50	.70
☐	12	Bob Pulford	10.00	5.00	1.00
☐	13	George Armstrong	10.00	5.00	1.00
☐	14	Ron Stewart	7.00	3.50	.70
☐	15	John McMillan	7.00	3.50	.70
☐	16	Tim Horton	18.00	9.00	1.80
☐	17	Frank Mahovlich	35.00	17.50	3.50
☐	18	Bob Baun	7.00	3.50	.70
☐	19	Punch Imlach	9.00	4.50	.90
☐	20	King Clancy	11.00	5.50	1.10
☐	21	Gilles Tremblay	7.00	3.50	.70
☐	22	Jean Guy Talbot	7.00	3.50	.70
☐	23	Henri Richard	15.00	7.50	1.50
☐	24	Ralph Backstrom	7.00	3.50	.70
☐	25	Bill Hicke	7.00	3.50	.70
☐	26	Red Berenson	16.00	8.00	1.60
☐	27	Jacques Laperriere	22.00	11.00	2.20
☐	28	Jean Gauthier	7.00	3.50	.70
☐	29	Boom Boom Geoffrion	24.00	12.00	2.40
☐	30	Jean Beliveau	36.00	18.00	3.60
☐	31	J.C. Tremblay	8.00	4.00	.80
☐	32	Terry Harper	10.00	5.00	1.00
☐	33	John Ferguson	12.00	6.00	1.20
☐	34	Toe Blake	10.00	5.00	1.00
☐	35	Bobby Rousseau	7.00	3.50	.70
☐	36	Claude Provost	7.00	3.50	.70
☐	37	Marc Reaume	7.00	3.50	.70
☐	38	Dave Balon	7.00	3.50	.70
☐	39	Gump Worsley	17.00	8.50	1.70
☐	40	Cesare Maniago	10.00	5.00	1.00
☐	41	Bruce MacGregor	7.00	3.50	.70
☐	42	Alex Faulkner	7.00	3.50	.70
☐	43	Pete Goegan	7.00	3.50	.70

			NRMT	VG-E	GOOD
☐	44	Parker MacDonald	7.00	3.50	.70
☐	45	Andre Pronovost	7.00	3.50	.70
☐	46	Marcel Pronovost	10.00	5.00	1.00
☐	47	Bob Dillabough	7.00	3.50	.70
☐	48	Larry Jeffrey	7.00	3.50	.70
☐	49	Ian Cushenan	7.00	3.50	.70
☐	50	Alex Delvecchio	15.00	7.50	1.50
☐	51	Hank Ciesla	7.00	3.50	.70
☐	52	Norm Ullman	12.00	6.00	1.20
☐	53	Terry Sawchuk	45.00	22.50	4.50
☐	54	Ron Ingram	7.00	3.50	.70
☐	55	Gordie Howe	150.00	75.00	15.00
☐	56	Billy McNeil	7.00	3.50	.70
☐	57	Floyd Smith	7.00	3.50	.70
☐	58	Vic Stasiuk	7.00	3.50	.70
☐	59	Bill Gadsby	10.00	5.00	1.00
☐	60	Doug Barkley	7.00	3.50	.70
☐	61	Allan Stanley	10.00	5.00	1.00
☐	62	Don Simmons	7.00	3.50	.70
☐	63	Red Kelly	15.00	7.50	1.50
☐	64	Dick Duff	7.00	3.50	.70
☐	65	Johnny Bower	15.00	7.50	1.50
☐	66	Ed Litzenberger	7.00	3.50	.70
☐	67	Kent Douglas	7.00	3.50	.70
☐	68	Carl Brewer	7.00	3.50	.70
☐	69	Eddie Shack	9.00	4.50	.90
☐	70	Bob Nevin	7.00	3.50	.70
☐	71	Billy Harris	7.00	3.50	.70
☐	72	Bob Pulford	10.00	5.00	1.00
☐	73	George Armstrong	10.00	5.00	1.00
☐	74	Ron Stewart	7.00	3.50	.70
☐	75	Dave Keon	17.00	8.50	1.70
☐	76	Tim Horton	18.00	9.00	1.80
☐	77	Frank Mahovlich	35.00	17.50	3.50
☐	78	Bob Baun	7.00	3.50	.70
☐	79	Punch Imlach	9.00	4.50	.90
☐	80	Gilles Tremblay	7.00	3.50	.70
☐	81	Jean Guy Talbot	7.00	3.50	.70
☐	82	Henri Richard	15.00	7.50	1.50
☐	83	Ralph Backstrom	7.00	3.50	.70
☐	84	Bill Hicke	7.00	3.50	.70
☐	85	Red Berenson	16.00	8.00	1.60
☐	86	Jacques Laperriere	22.00	11.00	2.20
☐	87	Jean Gauthier	7.00	3.50	.70
☐	88	Boom Boom Geoffrion	24.00	12.00	2.40
☐	89	Jean Beliveau	36.00	18.00	3.60
☐	90	J.C. Tremblay	8.00	4.00	.80
☐	91	Terry Harper	10.00	5.00	1.00
☐	92	John Ferguson	12.00	6.00	1.20
☐	93	Toe Blake	10.00	5.00	1.00
☐	94	Bobby Rousseau	7.00	3.50	.70
☐	95	Claude Provost	7.00	3.50	.70
☐	96	Marc Reaume	7.00	3.50	.70

			NRMT	VG-E	GOOD
☐	97	Dave Balon	7.00	3.50	.70
☐	98	Gump Worsley	17.00	8.50	1.70
☐	99	Cesare Maniago	21.00	5.00	1.00

1990-91 Pro Set I

The first series of 1990-91 Pro Set contains 405 cards measuring the standard size (2½" by 3½"). The fronts feature a color action photo, banded above and below in the team's colors. The horizontally oriented backs have a head shot of each player and player information sandwiched between color stripes in the team's colors. Included in this set are 337 player cards, 40 NHL All-Star cards, 12 HOF player cards, and 17 NHL Trophy Collectibles. The set is numbered below alphabetically according to team names as follows: Boston Bruins (1-16), Buffalo Sabres (17-32), Calgary Flames (33-48), Chicago Blackhawks (49-64), Detroit Red Wings (65-80), Edmonton Oilers (81-97), Hartford Whalers (98-113), Los Angeles Kings (114-129), Minnesota North Stars (130-145), Montreal Canadiens (146-61), New Jersey Devils (162-177), New York Islanders (178-194), New York Rangers (195-210), Philadelphia Flyers (211-226), Pittsburgh Penguins (227-242), Quebec Nordiques (243-258), St. Louis Blues (259-274), Toronto Maple Leafs (275-290), Vancouver Canucks (291-306), Washington Capitals (307-322), and Winnipeg Jets (323-336). Also, the players' names are alphabetized within their teams. The set is further subdivided as follows: Campbell Conference (337-356), Wales Conference (357-376), Trophy Collectibles (377-393), and Statistical Leaders (394-405). Pro Set consistently misspelled Massachusetts and Connecticut as Massachussetts and Conneticut for players born in those states; those errors were never corrected.

Le jeu Pro Set 1990-91 contient 405 cartes de format standard (2½" x 3½"). La face représente une photo d'action en couleurs, et une bande en les couleurs de l'équipe souligne le haut et le bas. Le dos, orienté horizontalement, comporte un portrait du joueur, et présente des données sur le joueur, placées entre des rayures en les couleurs de l'équipe. Le jeu inclut 337 cartes de joueurs, 40 cartes All-Star de la NHL, 12 cartes de joueurs HOF, et 17 de trophées NHL à collectionner. Le jeu est numéroté suivant les

noms des équipes, rangés par ordre alphabétique, comme suit: Boston Bruins (1-16), Buffalo Sabres (17-32), Calgary Flames (33-48), Chicago Blackhawks (49-64), Detroit Red Wings (65-80), Edmonton Oilers (81-97), Hartford Whalers (98-113), Los Angeles Kings (114-129), Minnesota North Stars (130-145), Montréal Canadiens (146-61), New Jersey Devils (162-177), New York Islanders (178-194), New York Rangers (195- 210), Philadelphia Flyers (211-226), Pittsburgh Penguins (227- 242), Québec Nordiques (243-258), St. Louis Blues (259-274), Toronto Maple Leafs (275-290), Vancouver Canucks (291-306), Washington Capitals (307-322), et Winnipeg Jets (323-336). Les noms des joueurs sont également rangés par ordre alphabétique sous chaque équipe. Le jeu est, en plus, subdivisé comme suit: Conférence Campbell (337-356), Conférence Wales (357-376), trophées à collectionner (377-393), et meneurs statistiques (394- 405). Pro Set a immanquablement écrit les mots Massachusetts et Connecticut, Massachussetts et Conneticut, en mentionnant les joueurs nés dans ces états. Ces erreurs n'ont jamais été corrigées.

			MINT	EXC	G-VG
		COMPLETE SET (405)	16.00	8.00	1.60
		COMMON PLAYER (1-405)	.03	.01	.00
☐	1A	Brett Hull Promo	4.50	2.25	.45
		(Born 9/9/64, 85 games in '87-'88, height 6-0, TM under Pro Set logos)			
☐	1B	Ray Bourque ERR	1.00	.50	.10
		(Misspelled Borque on card front)			
☐	1C	Ray Bourque COR	.35	.17	.03
☐	2	Randy Burridge	.03	.01	.00
☐	3	Lyndon Byers	.10	.05	.01
☐	4	Bob Carpenter UER	.06	.03	.00
		(Front LW, back C)			
☐	5	John Carter	.10	.05	.01
☐	6	Dave Christian UER	.06	.03	.00
		(28 games with Washington, 50 with Boston)			
☐	7A	Garry Galley ERR	.25	.12	.02
		(Misspelled Gary on card back)			
☐	7B	Garry Galley COR	.12	.06	.01
☐	8	Craig Janney	.30	.15	.03
☐	9	Reggie Lemelin UER	.06	.03	.00
		(Wrong headings, not for goalie; '89-'90 stats are Andy Moog's)			
☐	10	Andy Moog UER	.15	.07	.01
		('89-'90 stats are Reggie Lemelin's; he was 3rd, not 2nd in Vezina voting)			
☐	11	Cam Neely UER	.25	.12	.02
		(Bruins not capitalized in text)			
☐	12	Allen Pedersen	.03	.01	.00
☐	13	Dave Poulin UER	.06	.03	.00
		(Flyers' stats missing from '89-'90)			
☐	14	Brian Propp UER	.08	.04	.01
		(No Flyer stats, only Boston)			
☐	15	Bob Sweeney	.03	.01	.00

			MINT	EXC	G-VG
☐	16	Glen Wesley	.06	.03	.00
☐	17A	Dave Andreychuk ERR	.15	.07	.01
		(Photo actually Scott Arniel on back)			
☐	17B	Dave Andreychuk COR	.06	.03	.00
☐	18A	Scott Arniel ERR	.15	.07	.01
		(Photo actually Dave Andreychuk on back)			
☐	18B	Scott Arniel COR	.06	.03	.00
☐	19	Doug Bodger	.03	.01	.00
☐	20	Mike Foligno	.03	.01	.00
☐	21A	Phil Housley	.20	.10	.02
		(No traded stripe)			
☐	21B	Phil Housley	.08	.04	.01
		(Traded stripe on card front)			
☐	22	Dean Kennedy UER	.10	.05	.01
		(Born Redvers, not Redver)			
☐	23	Uwe Krupp	.03	.01	.00
☐	24	Grant Ledyard	.12	.06	.01
☐	25	Clint Malarchuk UER	.06	.03	.00
		(Back in action 11 days after hurt, not 2 as said on card)			
☐	26	Alexander Mogilny	.50	.25	.05
☐	27	Daren Puppa UER	.12	.06	.01
		(Born 3/23/65, not 3/23/63)			
☐	28	Mike Ramsey	.03	.01	.00
☐	29	Christian Ruuttu UER	.03	.01	.00
		(Misspelled Ruutu)			
☐	30	Dave Snuggerud	.12	.06	.01
☐	31	Pierre Turgeon	.40	.20	.04
☐	32	Rick Vaive UER	.06	.03	.00
		(Sweater 22, not 12)			
☐	33	Theoren Fleury	.75	.35	.07
☐	34	Doug Gilmour	.06	.03	.00
☐	35	Al MacInnis UER	.15	.07	.01
		(Misspelled Allan on card back)			
☐	36	Brian MacLellan	.03	.01	.00
☐	37	Jamie Macoun UER	.06	.03	.00
		(Born 8/17/61, not 8/7/61)			
☐	38	Sergei Makarov	.40	.20	.04
☐	39A	Brad McCrimmon...................	.15	.07	.01
		(No traded stripe, 39 on front)			
☐	39B	Brad McCrimmon	.06	.03	.00
		(Traded stripe, 4 on front)			
☐	40A	Joe Mullen	.15	.07	.01
		(No traded stripe)			
☐	40B	Joe Mullen	.15	.07	.01
		(Traded stripe on card front)			
☐	41	Dana Murzyn	.03	.01	.00
☐	42A	Joe Nieuwendyk ERR	4.00	2.00	.40
		(Misspelled Niewendyk on card front)			
☐	42B	Joe Nieuwendyk COR...............	.40	.20	.04
☐	43	Joel Otto	.03	.01	.00
☐	44	Paul Ranheim UER	.25	.12	.02
		(Front LW, Back C)			

			MINT	EXC	G-VG
☐	45	Gary Roberts	.06	.03	.00
☐	46	Gary Suter UER	.10	.05	.01
		(No space between sentences)			
☐	47	Mike Vernon	.15	.07	.01
☐	48	Rick Wamsley	.06	.03	.00
☐	49	Keith Brown	.03	.01	.00
☐	50	Adam Creighton	.08	.04	.01
☐	51	Dirk Graham UER	.03	.01	.00
		(Sparking, should be sparkling; season was '88-'89, not '89-'90)			
☐	52	Steve Konroyd UER	.03	.01	.00
		(Front D, back LW)			
☐	53A	Steve Larmer ERR	.20	.10	.02
		(Position and sweater number in white, should be black)			
☐	53B	Steve Larmer COR	.10	.05	.01
☐	54A	Dave Manson ERR	.15	.07	.01
		(Both photos actually Steve Konroyd)			
☐	54B	Dave Manson COR	.06	.03	.00
☐	55A	Bob McGill ERR	.15	.07	.01
		(No PIM totals on back)			
☐	55B	Bob McGill COR	.06	.03	.00
☐	56	Greg Millen	.06	.03	.00
☐	57A	Troy Murray	.15	.07	.01
		(Position and sweater number are white)			
☐	57B	Troy Murray	.06	.03	.00
		(Position and sweater number are black)			
☐	58	Jeremy Roenick	1.50	.75	.15
☐	59A	Denis Savard	.30	.15	.03
		(No traded stripe; played 70 games in '86-'87)			
☐	59B	Denis Savard	.15	.07	.01
		(Traded stripe; played 70 games in '86-'87)			
☐	60A	Al Secord	.15	.07	.01
		(Called Alan on back)			
☐	60B	Al Secord	.06	.03	.00
		(Called Al on back)			
☐	61A	Duane Sutter	.15	.07	.01
		(No retired stripe)			
☐	61B	Duane Sutter	.06	.03	.00
		(Retired stripe on front)			
☐	62	Steve Thomas	.06	.03	.00
☐	63A	Doug Wilson	.25	.12	.02
		(Position and sweater number are white)			
☐	63B	Doug Wilson	.12	.06	.01
		(Position and sweater number are black)			
☐	64	Trent Yawney	.08	.04	.01
☐	65	David Barr	.03	.01	.00
☐	66	Shawn Burr	.03	.01	.00
☐	67	Jimmy Carson	.15	.07	.01
☐	68	John Chabot	.03	.01	.00
☐	69	Steve Chiasson	.06	.03	.00

			MINT	EXC	G-VG
☐	70	**Bernie Federko UER**	.06	.03	.00
		(Says only player from Foam Lake, but Elynuik was too)			
☐	71	**Gerald Gallant**	.10	.05	.01
☐	72	**Glen Hanlon**	.06	.03	.00
☐	73	**Joey Kocur**	.15	.07	.01
☐	74	**Lea Norwood**	.03	.01	.00
☐	75	**Mike O'Connell**	.03	.01	.00
		(No retired stripe)			
☐	76	**Bob Probert**	.15	.07	.01
☐	77	**Torrie Robertson**	.03	.01	.00
☐	78	**Daniel Shank**	.12	.06	.01
☐	79	**Steve Yzerman**	.30	.15	.03
☐	80	**Rick Zombo**	.12	.06	.01
☐	81	**Glenn Anderson**	.08	.04	.01
☐	82	**Grant Fuhr**	.15	.07	.01
☐	83	**Martin Gelinas UER**	.35	.17	.03
		(Back photo actually Joe Murphy)			
☐	84	**Adam Graves UER**	.25	.12	.02
		(Stats missing '89-'90 Detroit info)			
☐	85	**Charlie Huddy**	.06	.03	.00
		(No accent in 1st e in Defenseur)			
☐	86	**Petr Klima UER**	.10	.05	.01
		(Born Chomulov, should be Chaomutov)			
☐	87A	**Jari Kurri**	.40	.20	.04
		(No signed stripe)			
☐	87B	**Jari Kurri**	.20	.10	.02
		(Signed with Milan)			
☐	88	**Mark Lamb**	.15	.07	.01
☐	89	**Kevin Lowe**	.08	.04	.01
		(No accent in 1st e in Defenseur)			
☐	90	**Craig MacTavish**	.03	.01	.00
☐	91	**Mark Messier**	.35	.17	.03
☐	92	**Craig Muni**	.03	.01	.00
☐	93	**Joe Murphy**	.25	.12	.02
☐	94	**Bill Ranford**	.15	.07	.01
☐	95	**Craig Simpson**	.08	.04	.01
		(Should be LW, not C)			
☐	96	**Steve Smith**	.10	.05	.01
		(No accent in 1st e in Defenseur)			
☐	97	**Esa Tikkanen**	.12	.06	.01
☐	98	**Mikael Andersson**	.08	.04	.01
☐	99	**Dave Babych**	.06	.03	.00
		(Extra space included after Forum)			
☐	100	**Yvon Corriveau**	.08	.04	.01
		(Washington and Hartford games not separate)			
☐	101	**Randy Cunneyworth UER**	.03	.01	.00
		(Front LW, back C)			
☐	102	**Kevin Dineen**	.06	.03	.00
☐	103	**Dean Evason**	.03	.01	.00
☐	104	**Ray Ferraro**	.03	.01	.00
☐	105	**Ron Francis**	.10	.05	.01

		MINT	EXC	G-VG
☐ 106	**Grant Jennings**	.12	.06	.01
☐ 107	**Todd Krygier**	.12	.06	.01
☐ 108	**Randy Ladouceur**	.03	.01	.00
☐ 109	**Ulf Samuelsson**	.06	.03	.00
☐ 110	**Brad Shaw**	.12	.06	.01
☐ 111	**Dave Tippett UER**	.03	.01	.00
	(Front LW, back C)			
☐ 112	**Pat Verbeek**	.08	.04	.01
☐ 113	**Scott Young**	.08	.04	.01
☐ 114	**Brian Benning**	.03	.01	.00
	(St. Louis and Los Angeles stats not separate)			
☐ 115	**Steve Duchesne**	.06	.03	.00
	(Kings, should be Kings')			
☐ 116	**Todd Elik**	.20	.10	.02
☐ 117	**Tony Granato**	.20	.10	.02
	(Plays RW, not C)			
☐ 118	**Wayne Gretzky**	1.25	.60	.12
☐ 119	**Kelly Hrudey**	.08	.04	.01
☐ 120	**Steve Kasper**	.06	.03	.00
☐ 121A	**Mike Kushelnyski ERR**	.20	.10	.02
	(No position and number on card front)			
☐ 121B	**Mike Kushelnyski COR**	.10	.05	.01
☐ 122	**Bob Kudelski**	.15	.07	.01
	(Born Springfield, not Feeding Hills)			
☐ 123	**Tom Laidlaw**	.03	.01	.00
☐ 124	**Marty McSorley**	.08	.04	.01
☐ 125	**Larry Robinson**	.10	.05	.01
☐ 126	**Luc Robitaille**	.25	.12	.02
	(Kings, should be Kings')			
☐ 127	**Tomas Sandstrom UER**	.10	.05	.01
	('89-'90 Rangers stats not printed)			
☐ 128	**Dave Taylor**	.06	.03	.00
☐ 129	**John Tonelli UER**	.06	.03	.00
	(Misspelled Tonnelli on card front)			
☐ 130	**Brian Bellows UER**	.12	.06	.01
	(Back photo actually Dave Gagner; front LW, back RW)			
☐ 131	**Aaron Broten**	.03	.01	.00
	(New Jersey and Minnesota stats not separate)			
☐ 132	**Neal Broten**	.06	.03	.00
☐ 133	**Jon Casey UER**	.15	.07	.01
	(GAA 3.22, not 3122)			
☐ 134	**Shawn Chambers UER**	.06	.03	.00
	(Back photo reversed)			
☐ 135	**Shane Churla**	.15	.07	.01
☐ 136	**Ulf Dahlen**	.06	.03	.00
	(Rangers and Minnesota stats not separate)			
☐ 137	**Gaetan Duchesne**	.06	.03	.00
☐ 138	**Dave Gagner**	.12	.06	.01

			MINT	EXC	G-VG
☐ 139	Stewart Gavin		.06	.03	.00
☐ 140	Curt Giles		.03	.01	.00
☐ 141	Basil McRae		.10	.05	.01
☐ 142	Mike Modano		1.00	.50	.10
☐ 143	Larry Murphy		.03	.01	.00
☐ 144	Ville Siren		.08	.04	.01
☐ 145	Mark Tinordi		.35	.17	.03
☐ 146	Guy Carbonneau		.06	.03	.00
☐ 147A	Chris Chelios		2.00	1.00	.20
	(No traded stripe)				
☐ 147B	Chris Chelios		.10	.05	.01
	(Traded stripe)				
☐ 148	Shayne Corson		.12	.06	.01
☐ 149	Russ Courtnall UER		.06	.03	.00
	(Front RW, back C)				
☐ 150	Brian Hayward		.06	.03	.00
☐ 151	Mike Keane		.10	.05	.01
☐ 152	Stephan Lebeau		.40	.20	.04
☐ 153	Claude Lemieux		.10	.05	.01
	(Reason is misspelled as reson)				
☐ 154	Craig Ludwig		.03	.01	.00
☐ 155	Mike McPhee		.06	.03	.00
☐ 156	Stephane Richer		.12	.06	.01
☐ 157	Patrick Roy		.25	.12	.02
☐ 158	Mathieu Schneider		.20	.10	.02
☐ 159	Brian Skrudland		.06	.03	.00
☐ 160	Bobby Smith		.10	.05	.01
	(No mention of trade from Montreal to Minnesota)				
☐ 161	Petr Svoboda		.03	.01	.00
☐ 162	Tommy Albelin		.03	.01	.00
☐ 163	Doug Brown		.03	.01	.00
	(Born 6/12/64, not 7/12/64)				
☐ 164	Sean Burke		.08	.04	.01
☐ 165	Ken Daneyko		.08	.04	.01
☐ 166	Bruce Driver		.03	.01	.00
☐ 167A	Viacheslav Fetisov		.40	.20	.04
	ERR (Misspelled Vlacheslav on front)				
☐ 167B	Viacheslav Fetisov		.20	.10	.02
	COR				
☐ 168	Mark Johnson		.03	.01	.00
☐ 169	Alexei Kasatonov		.20	.10	.02
	(Stats should indicate either Soviet or NHL)				
☐ 170	John MacLean		.08	.04	.01
	(Should have apostrophe after Devils)				
☐ 171A	David Maley		.25	.12	.02
	(Front LW, back C)				
☐ 171B	David Maley		.12	.06	.01
	(LW on both sides)				
☐ 172	Kirk Muller		.08	.04	.01
☐ 173	Janne Ojanen		.08	.04	.01
☐ 174	Brendan Shanahan		.08	.04	.01

		MINT	EXC	G-VG
☐ 175A	Peter Stastny ERR	.30	.15	.03
	(Front photo actually Patrik Sundstrom)			
☐ 175B	Peter Stastny COR	.15	.07	.01
☐ 176A	Patrik Sundstrom ERR	.15	.07	.01
	(Front photo actually Peter Stastny)			
☐ 176B	Patrik Sundstrom COR	.06	.03	.00
☐ 177	Sylvain Turgeon	.03	.01	.00
☐ 178	Ken Baumgartner	.12	.06	.01
☐ 179	Doug Crossman	.03	.01	.00
	(Born 6/30/60, not 5/30/60)			
☐ 180	Gerald Diduck	.03	.01	.00
☐ 181	Mark Fitzpatrick	.10	.05	.00
☐ 182	Pat Flatley	.03	.01	.00
	(Front C, back RW)			
☐ 183	Glen Healy	.12	.06	.01
	(Misspelled Glenn on card back)			
☐ 184	Alan Kerr	.03	.01	.00
☐ 185	Derek King	.03	.01	.00
☐ 186	Pat LaFontaine	.20	.10	.02
☐ 187	Don Maloney	.03	.01	.00
☐ 188	Hubie McDonough	.08	.04	.01
	(Kings and Islanders stats not separate)			
☐ 189	Jeff Norton	.03	.01	.00
	(Born Cambridge, Mass., not Acton)			
☐ 190	Gary Nylund	.03	.01	.00
☐ 191	Brent Sutter	.06	.03	.00
☐ 192	Bryan Trottier	.15	.07	.01
	(Finish the season, not finished)			
☐ 193	David Volek	.06	.03	.00
	(Front LW, back RW)			
☐ 194	Randy Wood	.03	.01	.00
☐ 195	Jan Erixon	.03	.01	.00
☐ 196	Mike Gartner	.10	.05	.01
	(Minnesota and Rangers stats not separate)			
☐ 197	Ron Greschner	.06	.03	.00
☐ 198A	Miloslav Horava ERR	.25	.12	.02
	(Misspelled Miroslav)			
☐ 198B	Miloslav Horava COR	.12	.06	.01
☐ 199	Mark Janssens	.08	.04	.01
☐ 200	Kelly Kisio	.03	.01	.00
☐ 201	Brian Leetch	.50	.25	.05
☐ 202	Randy Moller	.03	.01	.00
☐ 203	Brian Mullen	.06	.03	.00
☐ 204	Bernie Nicholls	.15	.07	.01
	(Kings and Rangers stats not separate)			
☐ 205A	Chris Nilan	.15	.07	.01
	(No traded stripe)			
☐ 205B	Chris Nilan	.06	.03	.00
	(Traded stripe on front)			
☐ 206	John Ogrodnick	.06	.03	.00

		MINT	EXC	G-VG
☐ 207	James Patrick	.03	.01	.00
☐ 208	Darren Turcotte	.80	.40	.08
☐ 209	John Vanbiesbrouck	.10	.05	.01
	(Front C, back G)			
☐ 210	Carey Wilson	.03	.01	.00
☐ 211	Mike Bullard	.03	.01	.00
☐ 212	Terry Carkner	.03	.01	.00
☐ 213	Jeff Chychrun	.10	.05	.01
☐ 214	Murray Craven	.06	.03	.00
☐ 215	Pelle Eklund	.06	.03	.00
	(Centre and previous, not Center and previously)			
☐ 216	Ron Hextall	.15	.07	.01
	(Born 5/3/64, not 3/3/64)			
☐ 217	Mark Howe	.08	.04	.01
☐ 218	Tim Kerr	.08	.04	.01
☐ 219	Ken Linseman	.03	.01	.00
	(Bruins and Flyers stats not separate)			
☐ 220	Scott Mellanby	.06	.03	.00
☐ 221	Gordon Murphy	.15	.07	.01
☐ 222	Kjell Samuelsson	.03	.01	.00
	(Born 10/18/58, not 10/18/56)			
☐ 223	Ilka Sinisalo	.03	.01	.00
☐ 224	Ron Sutter	.06	.03	.00
☐ 225	Rick Tocchet	.15	.07	.01
☐ 226	Ken Wregget	.10	.05	.01
☐ 227	Tom Barrasso	.08	.04	.01
☐ 228A	Phil Bourque ERR	.15	.07	.01
	(Misspelled Borque on both sides)			
☐ 228B	Phil Bourque COR	.06	.03	.00
☐ 229	Rob Brown	.15	.07	.01
	(Front RW, back C)			
☐ 230	Alain Chevrier	.06	.03	.00
	(Chicago and Pittsburgh stats not separate)			
☐ 231	Paul Coffey	.25	.12	.02
☐ 232	John Cullen	.30	.15	.03
☐ 233	Gord Dineen	.10	.05	.01
	(Born Toronto, not Quebec City)			
☐ 234	Bob Errey	.03	.01	.00
☐ 235	Jim Johnson	.03	.01	.00
	(Born Minnesota, not Michigan)			
☐ 236	Mario Lemieux	1.00	.50	.10
	(Missed 21 games, not 11)			
☐ 237	Troy Loney	.12	.06	.01
☐ 238	Barry Pederson	.03	.01	.00
	(No Vancouver stats included)			
☐ 239	Mark Recchi	1.50	.75	.15
☐ 240	Kevin Stevens	1.00	.50	.10
	(Front LW, back C)			
☐ 241	Tony Tanti	.06	.03	.00
	(No Vancouver stats included)			

		MINT	EXC	G-VG
☐ 242	**Zarley Zalapski**	.10	.05	.01
	(Pittsburgh misspelled as Pittsburg)			
☐ 243	**Joe Cirella**	.03	.01	.00
☐ 244	**Lucien Deblois**	.03	.01	.00
	(Front C, back RW)			
☐ 245	**Marc Fortier**	.15	.07	.01
	(Misspelled Mark on both sides)			
☐ 246	**Paul Gillis**	.06	.03	.00
☐ 247	**Mike Hough**	.08	.04	.01
☐ 248	**Tony Hrkac**	.03	.01	.00
	(Blues and Nordiques stats not separate)			
☐ 249	**Jeff Johnson**	.03	.01	.00
☐ 250	**Guy Lafleur**	.15	.07	.01
☐ 251	**Curtis Leschyshyn**	.10	.05	.01
☐ 252	**Claude Loiselle**	.12	.06	.01
☐ 253	**Mario Marois**	.03	.01	.00
☐ 254	**Tony McKegney**	.03	.01	.00
	(Red Wings and Nordiques stats not separate)			
☐ 255	**Ken McRae**	.10	.05	.01
☐ 256A	**Michel Petit ERR**	.15	.07	.01
	(Front 21, back 24)			
☐ 256B	**Michel Petit COR**	.06	.03	.00
☐ 257	**Joe Sakic**	.75	.35	.07
	(Front 88, back 19)			
☐ 258	**Ron Tugnutt**	.10	.05	.01
☐ 259	**Rod Brind'Amour**	.40	.20	.04
	(Misspelled Rob on card back)			
☐ 260	**Jeff Brown**	.06	.03	.00
	(Nordiques and Blues stats not separate)			
☐ 261	**Gino Cavallini**	.06	.03	.00
	(On back Meagher is misspelled as Meager)			
☐ 262	**Paul Cavallini**	.06	.03	.00
☐ 263	**Brett Hull**	1.25	.60	.12
☐ 264	**Mike Lalor**	.10	.05	.01
	(No mention of trade to Washington)			
☐ 265	**Dave Lowry**	.10	.05	.01
☐ 266	**Paul MacLean**	.06	.03	.00
☐ 267	**Rick Meagher**	.03	.01	.00
☐ 268	**Sergio Momesso**	.15	.07	.01
	(Text has 55 pts. in '89-'90, stats 56)			
☐ 269	**Adam Oates**	.25	.12	.02
☐ 270	**Vincent Riendeau**	.30	.15	.03
☐ 271	**Gordie Roberts**	.03	.01	.00
☐ 272	**Rich Sutter**	.06	.03	.00
	(Canucks and Blues stats not separate)			
☐ 273	**Steve Tuttle**	.03	.01	.00

		MINT	EXC	G-VG
☐ 274	Peter Zezel	.06	.03	.00
	(No traded stripe)			
☐ 275A	Allan Bester ERR	.15	.07	.01
	(Misspelled Alan on card front)			
☐ 275B	Allan Bester COR	.06	.03	.00
☐ 276	Wendel Clark	.06	.03	.00
☐ 277	Brian Curran	.03	.01	.00
	(Plays, not played)			
☐ 278	Vincent Damphousse	.10	.05	.01
	(Name not listed on one line)			
☐ 279A	Tom Fergus ERR	.15	.07	.01
	(Fourth line in bio has TI, should be that)			
☐ 279B	Tom Fergus COR	.06	.03	.00
☐ 280	Lou Franceschetti	.10	.05	.01
☐ 281	Al Iafrate	.06	.03	.00
☐ 282	Tom Kurvers	.03	.01	.00
	(Played for Toronto in 71, not 70)			
☐ 283	Gary Leeman	.06	.03	.00
☐ 284	Daniel Marois	.10	.05	.01
☐ 285	Brad Marsh	.03	.01	.00
☐ 286	Ed Olczyk	.08	.04	.01
	(Front C, back RW)			
☐ 287	Mark Osborne	.03	.01	.00
☐ 288	Rob Ramage	.06	.03	.00
☐ 289	Luke Richardson	.03	.01	.00
☐ 290	Gilles Thibaudeau	.08	.04	.01
	(Islanders and Leafs stats not separate)			
☐ 291	Greg Adams	.03	.01	.00
	(Front LW, back C)			
☐ 292	Jim Benning	.03	.01	.00
☐ 293	Steve Bozek	.03	.01	.00
☐ 294	Brian Bradley	.03	.01	.00
☐ 295	Garth Butcher	.06	.03	.00
☐ 296	Vladimir Krutov	.15	.07	.01
☐ 297	Igo Larionov	.20	.10	.02
	(Stats should indicate either Soviet or NHL)			
☐ 298	Doug Lidster	.03	.01	.00
☐ 299	Trevor Linden	.25	.12	.02
☐ 300	Jyrki Lumme	.12	.06	.01
	('89-'90 Canadiens and Canucks stats not separate)			
☐ 301A	Andrew McBain ERR	.50	.25	.05
	(Back photo actually Jim Sandlak)			
☐ 301B	Andrew McBain COR	.10	.05	.01
☐ 302	Kirk McLean	.08	.04	.01
	(Career GAA should be 3.46, not 6.50)			
☐ 303	Dan Quinn	.06	.03	.00
	(Penguins and Canucks stats not separate)			

		MINT	EXC	G-VG
☐ 304	Paul Reinhart	.06	.03	.00
	(Born 1/8/60, not 1/6/60)			
☐ 305	Jim Sandlak	.03	.01	.00
☐ 306	Petri Skriko	.03	.01	.00
☐ 307	Don Beaupre	.06	.03	.00
☐ 308	Dino Ciccarelli	.10	.05	.01
☐ 309	Geoff Courtnall	.12	.06	.01
☐ 310	John Druce	.25	.12	.02
☐ 311	Kevin Hatcher	.08	.04	.01
☐ 312	Dale Hunter	.03	.01	.00
	(Text has rougish, should be roguish)			
☐ 313	Calle Johansson	.03	.01	.00
	(No accent in first e in Defenseur)			
☐ 314	Rod Langway	.08	.04	.01
☐ 315	Stephen Leach	.03	.01	.00
☐ 316	Mike Liut	.06	.03	.00
	(Capitals and Whalers stats not separate)			
☐ 317	Alan May	.10	.05	.01
☐ 318	Kelly Miller	.06	.03	.00
	(Front LW, back C)			
☐ 319	Michal Pivonka	.15	.07	.01
☐ 320A	Mike Ridley ERR	.15	.07	.01
	(Errant text reads points.s)			
☐ 320B	Mike Ridley COR	.06	.03	.00
☐ 321	Scott Stevens	.08	.04	.01
	(No accent in first e in Defenseur)			
☐ 322	John Tucker	.03	.01	.00
☐ 323	Brent Ashton	.03	.01	.00
☐ 324	Laurie Boschman	.03	.01	.00
☐ 325	Randy Carlyle	.03	.01	.00
☐ 326	David Ellett	.03	.01	.00
☐ 327	Pat Elynuik	.10	.05	.01
☐ 328	Bob Essensa	.25	.12	.02
☐ 329	Paul Fenton	.06	.03	.00
	(Front LW, back C)			
☐ 330A	Dale Hawerchuk	.30	.15	.03
	(No traded stripe)			
☐ 330B	Dale Hawerchuk	.15	.07	.01
	(Traded stripe on front)			
☐ 331	Paul MacDermid	.03	.01	.00
☐ 332	Moe Mantha	.03	.01	.00
☐ 333	Dave McLlwain	.03	.01	.00
	(Born 1/9/67, not 6/9/67)			
☐ 334	Teppo Numminen	.10	.05	.01
☐ 335A	Fredrik Olausson ERR	.15	.07	.01
	(Misspelled Frederik on both sides)			
☐ 335B	Fredrik Olausson COR	.06	.03	.00
☐ 336	Greg Paslawski	.03	.01	.00
	(TM after Jets is larger than other TM symbols)			
☐ 337	Al MacInnis AS	.10	.05	.01
☐ 338	Mike Vernon AS	.08	.04	.01

		MINT	EXC	G-VG
☐ 339	Kevin Lowe AS	.06	.03	.00
☐ 340	Wayne Gretzky AS	.50	.25	.05
☐ 341	Luc Robitaille AS	.15	.07	.01
	(Fewest shots by Eastern AS's, not Boston)			
☐ 342	Brett Hull AS	.45	.22	.04
☐ 343	Joe Mullen AS	.08	.04	.01
☐ 344	Joe Nieuwendyk AS	.15	.07	.01
	(Front 26, should be 25)			
☐ 345	Steve Larmer AS	.08	.04	.01
☐ 346	Doug Wilson AS	.08	.04	.01
	(Premier is spelled premiere)			
☐ 347	Steve Yzerman AS	.25	.12	.02
☐ 348A	Jari Kurri AS	.30	.15	.03
	(No signed stripe)			
☐ 348B	Jari Kurri AS	.15	.07	.01
	(Signed stripe on front)			
☐ 349	Mark Messier AS	.15	.07	.01
☐ 350	Steve Duchesne AS	.06	.03	.00
	(Shot record held by Boston, not East)			
☐ 351	Mike Gartner AS	.08	.04	.01
	(Front 12, should be 11)			
☐ 352	Bernie Nicholls AS	.10	.05	.01
☐ 353	Paul Cavallini AS	.06	.03	.00
☐ 354	Al Iafrate AS	.06	.03	.00
☐ 355	Kirk McLean AS	.06	.03	.00
☐ 356	Thomas Steen AS	.06	.03	.00
	(Should be Doug Smail)			
☐ 357	Ray Bourque AS	.15	.07	.01
☐ 358	Cam Neely AS	.20	.10	.02
☐ 359	Patrick Roy AS	.15	.07	.01
☐ 360	Brian Propp AS	.06	.03	.00
	(Games misspelled as gamies)			
☐ 361	Paul Coffey AS	.15	.07	.01
	(Front 7, should be 77)			
☐ 362	Mario Lemieux AS	.40	.20	.04
☐ 363	Dave Andreychuk AS	.06	.03	.00
☐ 364	Phil Housley AS	.06	.03	.00
☐ 365	Daren Puppa AS	.10	.05	.01
☐ 366	Pierre Turgeon AS	.15	.07	.01
☐ 367	Ron Francis AS	.08	.04	.01
☐ 368	Chris Chelios AS	.08	.04	.01
☐ 369A	Shayne Corson AS ERR	.25	.12	.02
	(Misspelled Shane)			
☐ 369B	Shayne Corson AS COR	.12	.06	.01
☐ 370	Stephane Richer AS	.10	.05	.01
☐ 371	Kirk Muller AS	.06	.03	.00
☐ 372	Pat LaFontaine AS	.12	.06	.01
☐ 373	Brian Leetch AS	.15	.07	.01
☐ 374	Rick Tocchet AS	.08	.04	.01
☐ 375	Joe Sakic AS	.20	.10	.02
☐ 376	Kevin Hatcher AS	.06	.03	.00

		MINT	EXC	G-VG
☐ 377	Bob Murdoch Adams	.03	.01	.00
☐ 378	Brett Hull Byng (Should be Lady Byng Memorial Trophy)	.40	.20	.04
☐ 379	Sergei Makarov Calder	.15	.07	.01
☐ 380	Kevin Lowe Clancy	.06	.03	.00
☐ 381	Mark Messier Hart	.15	.07	.01
☐ 382	Moog/Lemelin Jennings	.06	.03	.00
☐ 383	Gord Kluzak Mast (Should be Bill Masterton Memorial Trophy)	.03	.01	.00
☐ 384	Ray Bourque Norris	.15	.07	.01
☐ 385A	Len Ceglarski Patrick ERR (No number on back)	.75	.35	.07
☐ 385B	Len Ceglarski Patrick COR	.08	.04	.01
☐ 386	Mark Messier Pearson	.15	.07	.01
☐ 387	Boston Bruins	.06	.03	.00
☐ 388	Wayne Gretzky Ross (Gretzky has won eight Art Ross Trophies)	.45	.22	.04
☐ 389	Rick Meagher Selke	.03	.01	.00
☐ 390	Bill Ranford Smythe	.08	.04	.01
☐ 391	Patrick Roy Vezina	.15	.07	.01
☐ 392	Edmonton Oilers (Should be Clarence S. Campbell Bowl)	.06	.03	.00
☐ 393	Boston Bruins	.06	.03	.00
☐ 394	Wayne Gretzky LL	.40	.20	.04
☐ 395	Brett Hull LL (Born 8/9/64, not 9/9/64)	.40	.20	.04
☐ 396	Sergei Makarov ROY	.15	.07	.01
☐ 397	Mark Messier MVP	.15	.07	.01
☐ 398	Mike Richter RLL (Plays, not lays)	.20	.10	.02
☐ 399	Patrick Roy LL	.15	.07	.01
☐ 400	Darren Turcotte RLL (Front RW, back C)	.25	.12	.02
☐ 401	Owen Nolan FDP	.80	.40	.08
☐ 402	Petr Nedved FDP	1.00	.50	.10
☐ 403	Phil Esposito HOF	.15	.07	.01
☐ 404	Darryl Sittler HOF (Career: 15 seasons, not stats)	.10	.05	.01
☐ 405	Stan Mikita HOF	.15	.07	.01
☐ xxx	Stanley Cup Hologram	250.00	125.00	25.00

1990-91 Pro Set II

The Pro Set (Series II) hockey set contains 300 cards measuring the standard size (2¹/₂" by 3¹/₂"). The fronts feature a color action photo, banded above and below in the team's colors. The horizontally oriented backs have a head shot of each player and player information sandwiched between color stripes in the team's colors. The set is numbered below alphabetically according to team names as follows: Boston Bruins (406-413), Buffalo Sabres (414-420), Calgary Flames (421-426), Chicago Blackhawks (427-434), Detroit Red Wings (435-438), Edmonton Oilers (439-446), Hartford Whalers (447-453), Los Angeles Kings (454-458), Minnesota North Stars (459-465), Montreal Canadiens (466-475), New Jersey Devils (476-481), New York Islanders (482-488), New York Rangers (489-496), Philadelphia Flyers (497-503), Pittsburgh Penguins (504-512), Quebec Nordiques (513-519), St. Louis Blues (520-529), Toronto Maple Leafs (530-542), Vancouver Canucks (543-549), Washington Capitals (550-556), and Winnipeg Jets (557-565). Also, the players' names are alphabetized within their teams. The set is further subdivided as follows: teams (566-586), rookies (587-649), career point leaders (650-656), Hall of Fame (657-660), coaches (661-680), and referees (681-702). This second series of Pro Set was released in February 1991, about six months after Pro Set's first release.

Le jeu Pro Set (série II) contient 300 cartes de format standard (2¹/₂" x 3¹/₂"). La face représente une photo d'action en couleurs, avec une bande dans les couleurs de l'équipe bordant le haut et le bas de la face. Le dos, orienté horizontalement, comporte un portrait du joueur, et présente des données sur le joueur entre des rayures en les couleurs de l'équipe. Le jeu est numéroté suivant les noms des équipes, rangés par ordre alphabétique, comme suit: Boston Bruins (406-413), Buffalo Sabres (414-420), Calgary Flames (421-426), Chicago Blackhawks (427-434), Detroit Red Wings (435-438), Edmonton Oilers (439-446), Hartford Whalers (447-453), Los Angeles Kings (454-458) Minnesota North Stars (459-465), Montréal Canadiens (466-475), New Jersey Devils (476-481), New York Islanders (482-488), New York Rangers (489-496), Philadelphia Flyers (497-503), Pittsburgh Penguins (504-512), Québec Nordiques (513-519), St. Louis Blues (520-529), Toronto Maple Leafs (530-542), Vancouver Canucks

(543-549), *Washington Capitals* (550-556), et *Winnipeg Jets* (557-565). *Les noms des joueurs sont également rangés par ordre alphabétique sous chaque équipe. Le jeu est, en plus, subdivisé comme suit: équipes* (566-586), *débutants* (587-659), *meneurs en nombre de points* (650-656), *Hall of Fame* (657-660), *entraîneurs* (661-680), *et arbitres* (681-702). *Cette deuxième série de Pro Set fut distribuée en février 1991, à peu près six mois suivant la première distribution Pro Set.*

			MINT	EXC	G-VG
	COMPLETE SET (300)		16.00	8.00	1.60
	COMMON PLAYER (406-705)		.03	.01	.00
☐ 406	Andy Brickley		.03	.01	.00
	(Front LW, back C/LW)				
☐ 407	Peter Douris		.08	.04	.01
☐ 408	Nevin Markwart		.03	.01	.00
☐ 409	Chris Nilan		.03	.01	.00
☐ 410	Stephane Quintal		.08	.04	.01
☐ 411	Bruce Shoebottom		.08	.04	.01
☐ 412	Don Sweeney		.08	.04	.01
☐ 413	Jim Wiemer		.08	.04	.01
☐ 414	Mike Hartman		.08	.04	.01
☐ 415	Dale Hawerchuk		.15	.07	.01
☐ 416	Benoit Hogue		.08	.04	.01
☐ 417	Bill Houlder		.08	.04	.01
☐ 418	Mikko Makela		.03	.01	.00
☐ 419	Robert Ray		.10	.05	.01
☐ 420	John Tucker		.03	.01	.00
☐ 421	Jiri Hrdina		.10	.05	.01
	(Calgary logo on front, should be Pittsburgh)				
☐ 422	Mark Hunter		.03	.01	.00
☐ 423	Tim Hunter		.10	.05	.01
☐ 424	Roger Johansson		.08	.04	.01
☐ 425	Frantisek Musil		.03	.01	.00
☐ 426	Ric Nattress		.03	.01	.00
☐ 427	Chris Chelios		.10	.05	.01
☐ 428	Jacques Cloutier		.12	.06	.01
	(White position and number on front, not black)				
☐ 429	Greg Gilbert		.03	.01	.00
☐ 430	Michel Goulet		.10	.05	.01
	(White position and number on front, not black)				
☐ 431	Mike Hudson		.15	.07	.01
☐ 432	Jocelyn Lemieux		.10	.05	.01
☐ 433	Brian Noonan		.03	.01	.00
☐ 434	Wayne Presley		.03	.01	.00
☐ 435	Brent Fedyk		.25	.12	.02
☐ 436	Rick Green		.03	.01	.00
☐ 437	Marc Habsheid		.03	.01	.00
☐ 438	Brad McCrimmon		.03	.01	.00
☐ 439	Jeff Beukeboom		.10	.05	.01
☐ 440	Dave Brown		.10	.05	.01

		MINT	EXC	G-VG
☐ 441	Kelly Buchberger	.10	.05	.01
☐ 442	Greg Hawgood	.03	.01	.00
☐ 443	Chris Joseph	.10	.05	.01
☐ 444	Ken Linseman	.03	.01	.00
☐ 445	Eldon Reddick	.15	.07	.01
	(G on back in smaller type)			
☐ 446	Geoff Smith	.10	.05	.01
☐ 447	Adam Burt	.10	.05	.01
☐ 448	Sylvain Cote	.03	.01	.00
☐ 449	Paul Cyr	.03	.01	.00
☐ 450	Ed Kastelic	.08	.04	.01
☐ 451	Peter Sidorkiewicz	.08	.04	.01
☐ 452	Mike Tomlak	.10	.05	.01
☐ 453	Carey Wilson	.03	.01	.00
☐ 454	Dan Berthiaume	.08	.04	.01
☐ 455	Scott Bjugstad	.03	.01	.00
☐ 456	Rod Buskas	.10	.05	.01
☐ 457	John McIntyre	.12	.06	.01
☐ 458	Tim Watters	.03	.01	.00
☐ 459	Perry Berezan	.08	.04	.01
☐ 460	Brian Propp	.08	.04	.01
☐ 461	Ilkka Sinisalo	.03	.01	.00
☐ 462	Doug Smail	.06	.03	.00
☐ 463	Bobby Smith	.10	.05	.01
☐ 464	Chris Dahlquist	.10	.05	.01
☐ 465	Neil Wilkinson	.10	.05	.01
☐ 466	J.J. Daigneault	.10	.05	.01
	(Front Jean Jacques, back J.J.)			
☐ 467	Eric Desjardins	.12	.06	.01
☐ 468	Gerald Diduck	.03	.01	.00
☐ 469	Donald Dufresne	.10	.05	.01
☐ 470	Todd Ewen	.10	.05	.01
☐ 471	Brent Gilchrist	.10	.05	.01
☐ 472	Sylvain Lefebvre	.12	.06	.01
☐ 473	Denis Savard	.15	.07	.01
☐ 474	Sylvain Turgeon	.03	.01	.00
☐ 475	Ryan Walter	.06	.03	.00
	(Front C, back C/LW)			
☐ 476	Laurie Boschman	.03	.01	.00
☐ 477	Pat Conacher	.10	.05	.01
☐ 478	Claude Lemieux	.10	.05	.01
☐ 479	Walt Poddubny	.03	.01	.00
☐ 480	Alan Stewart	.10	.05	.01
☐ 481	Chris Terreri	.35	.17	.03
☐ 482	Brad Dalgarno	.03	.01	.00
☐ 483	David Chyzowski	.10	.05	.01
☐ 484	Craig Ludwig	.03	.01	.00
☐ 485	Wayne McBean	.10	.05	.01
☐ 486	Richard Pilon	.08	.04	.01
☐ 487	Joe Reekie	.08	.04	.01
☐ 488	Mick Vukota	.08	.04	.01
☐ 489	Mark Hardy	.03	.01	.00
☐ 490	Jody Hull	.10	.05	.01

		MINT	EXC	G-VG
☐ 491	Kris King	.10	.05	.01
☐ 492	Troy Mallette	.12	.06	.01
☐ 493	Kevin Miller	.35	.17	.03
☐ 494	Normand Rochefort	.03	.01	.00
☐ 495	David Shaw	.03	.01	.00
☐ 496	Ray Sheppard	.03	.01	.00
☐ 497	Keith Acton	.03	.01	.00
☐ 498	Craig Berube	.15	.07	.01
☐ 499	Tony Horacek	.15	.07	.01
☐ 500	Normand Lacombe	.08	.04	.01
☐ 501	Jiri Latal	.15	.07	.01
☐ 502	Pete Peeters	.08	.04	.01
☐ 503	Derrick Smith	.08	.04	.01
☐ 504	Jay Caulfield	.08	.04	.01
☐ 505	Peter Taglianetti	.03	.01	.00
	(Front Pete, back Peter)			
☐ 506	Randy Gilhen	.10	.05	.01
☐ 507	Randy Hillier	.03	.01	.00
☐ 508	Joe Mullen	.08	.04	.01
☐ 509	Frank Pietrangelo	.15	.07	.01
☐ 510	Gordie Roberts	.03	.01	.00
☐ 511	Bryan Trottier	.15	.07	.01
☐ 512	Wendell Young	.15	.07	.01
☐ 513	Shawn Anderson	.10	.05	.01
☐ 514	Steven Finn	.10	.05	.01
☐ 515	Bryan Fogarty	.25	.12	.02
☐ 516	Mike Hough	.03	.01	.00
	(Front RW, back LW)			
☐ 517	Darin Kimble	.12	.06	.01
☐ 518	Randy Velischek	.03	.01	.00
☐ 519	Craig Wolanin	.10	.05	.01
☐ 520	Bob Bassen	.10	.05	.01
☐ 521	Geoff Courtnall	.10	.05	.01
☐ 522	Robert Dirk	.10	.05	.01
☐ 523	Glen Featherstone	.10	.05	.01
☐ 524	Mario Marois	.03	.01	.00
☐ 525	Herb Raglan	.10	.05	.01
☐ 526	Cliff Ronning	.10	.05	.01
☐ 527	Harold Snepsts	.06	.03	.00
☐ 528	Scott Stevens	.08	.04	.01
☐ 529	Ron Wilson	.03	.01	.00
☐ 530	Aaron Broten	.03	.01	.00
☐ 531	Lucien DeBlois	.03	.01	.00
☐ 532	Dave Ellett	.03	.01	.00
☐ 533A	Paul Fenton ERR	.15	.07	.01
	(Trademark on front next to name)			
☐ 533B	Paul Fenton COR	.06	.03	.00
☐ 534	Todd Gill	.10	.05	.01
☐ 535	Dave Hannan	.03	.01	.00
☐ 536	John Kordic	.12	.06	.01
☐ 537	Mike Krushelnyski	.06	.03	.00
☐ 538	Kevin Maguire	.10	.05	.01
☐ 539	Michel Petit	.06	.03	.00

			MINT	EXC	G-VG
☐ 540	Jeff Reese		.15	.07	.01
☐ 541	Dave Reid		.15	.07	.01
☐ 542	Doug Shedden		.03	.01	.01
☐ 543	Dave Capuano		.12	.06	.01
☐ 544	Craig Coxe		.10	.05	.01
☐ 545	Kevan Guy		.10	.05	.01
☐ 546	Rob Murphy		.10	.05	.01
☐ 547	Robert Nordmark		.08	.04	.01
☐ 548	Stan Smyl		.06	.03	.00
☐ 549	Ronnie Stern		.08	.04	.01
☐ 550	Tim Bergland		.08	.04	.01
☐ 551	Nick Kypreos		.08	.04	.01
☐ 552	Mike Lalor		.03	.01	.00
☐ 553	Rob Murray		.12	.06	.01
☐ 554	Bob Rouse		.03	.01	.00
☐ 555	Dave Tippett		.03	.01	.00
☐ 556	Peter Zezel		.06	.03	.00
	(Card says he's 25, sweater shows 9)				
☐ 557	Scott Arniel		.03	.01	.00
☐ 558	Don Barber		.10	.05	.01
☐ 559	Shawn Cronin		.10	.05	.01
☐ 560	Gord Donnelly		.10	.05	.01
☐ 561	Doug Evans		.10	.05	.01
☐ 562	Phil Housley		.08	.04	.01
☐ 563	Ed Olczyk		.08	.04	.01
☐ 564	Mark Osborne		.03	.01	.00
☐ 565	Thomas Steen		.06	.03	.00
☐ 566	Boston Bruins Logo		.03	.01	.00
☐ 567	Buffalo Sabres Logo		.03	.01	.00
☐ 568	Calgary Flames Logo		.03	.01	.00
☐ 569	Chicago Blackhawks Logo		.03	.01	.00
☐ 570	Detroit Red Wings Logo		.03	.01	.00
☐ 571	Edmonton Oilers Logo		.03	.01	.00
☐ 572	Hartford Whalers Logo		.03	.01	.00
☐ 573	Los Angeles Kings Logo		.03	.01	.00
☐ 574	Minn. North Stars Logo		.03	.01	.00
☐ 575	Montreal Canadiens Logo		.03	.01	.00
☐ 576	New Jersey Devils Logo		.03	.01	.00
☐ 577	New York Islanders Logo		.03	.01	.00
☐ 578	New York Rangers Logo		.03	.01	.00
☐ 579	Philadelphia Flyers Logo		.03	.01	.00
☐ 580	Pittsburgh Penguins Logo		.03	.01	.00
☐ 581	Quebec Nordiques Logo		.03	.01	.00

		MINT	EXC	G-VG
☐ 582	St. Louis Blues Logo	.03	.01	.00
☐ 583	Toronto Maple Leafs Logo	.03	.01	.00
☐ 584	Vancouver Canucks Logo	.03	.01	.00
☐ 585	Washington Capitals Logo	.03	.01	.00
☐ 586	Winnipeg Jets Logo	.03	.01	.00
☐ 587	Ken Hodge Jr.	1.50	.75	.15
☐ 588	Vladimir Ruzicka	.30	.15	.03
☐ 589	Wes Walz	.25	.12	.02
☐ 590	Greg Brown	.12	.06	.01
☐ 591	Brad Miller	.08	.04	.01
☐ 592	Darrin Shannon	.12	.06	.01
☐ 593	Stephane Matteau (Front RW, back LW)	.25	.12	.02
☐ 594	Sergei Priakin	.12	.06	.01
☐ 595	Robert Reichel	.50	.25	.05
☐ 596	Ken Sabourin (Front LW, back D)	.10	.05	.01
☐ 597	Tim Sweeney	.10	.05	.01
☐ 598	Ed Belfour (Born Carmen, should be Carman)	3.00	1.50	.30
☐ 599	Frantisek Kucera	.12	.06	.01
☐ 600	Mike McNeil UER (Front C, back LW)	.12	.06	.01
☐ 601	Mike Peluso	.12	.06	.01
☐ 602	Tim Cheveldae	.30	.15	.03
☐ 603	Per Djoos	.10	.05	.01
☐ 604	Sergei Fedorov	5.00	2.50	.50
☐ 605	Johan Garpenlov	.50	.25	.05
☐ 606	Keith Primeau	.50	.25	.05
☐ 607	Paul Ysebaert	.25	.12	.02
☐ 608	Anatoli Semenov	.30	.15	.03
☐ 609	Robert Holik	.75	.35	.07
☐ 610	Kay Whitmore	.15	.07	.01
☐ 611	Rob Blake	.75	.35	.07
☐ 612	Francois Breault	.15	.07	.01
☐ 613	Mike Craig (Wearing 50, card says 20)	.40	.20	.04
☐ 614	J.C. Bergeron (Front J.C., back Jean Claude)	.15	.07	.01
☐ 615	Andrew Cassels	.20	.10	.02
☐ 616	Tom Chorske	.10	.05	.01
☐ 617	Lyle Odelein	.10	.05	.01
☐ 618	Mark Pederson	.15	.07	.01
☐ 619	Zdeno Ciger	.15	.07	.01
☐ 620	Troy Crowder	.15	.07	.01
☐ 621	Jon Morris	.10	.05	.01
☐ 622	Eric Weinrich	.30	.15	.03

			MINT	EXC	G-VG
☐ 623	Dave Marcinyshyn		.10	.05	.01
	(Card number smaller than other cards in set)				
☐ 624	Jeff Hackett		.20	.10	.02
☐ 625	Rob DiMaio		.10	.05	.01
☐ 626	Steven Rice		.50	.25	.05
☐ 627	Mike Richter		.50	.25	.05
☐ 628	Dennis Vial		.10	.05	.01
☐ 629	Martin Hostak		.10	.05	.01
☐ 630	Pat Murray		.10	.05	.01
☐ 631	Mike Ricci		1.25	.60	.12
	(Born October, not November)				
☐ 632	Jaromir Jagr		2.50	1.25	.25
☐ 633	Paul Stanton		.10	.05	.01
☐ 634	Scott Gordon		.10	.05	.01
☐ 635	Owen Nolan		.65	.30	.06
☐ 636	Mats Sundin		1.25	.60	.12
☐ 637	John Tanner		.20	.10	.02
☐ 638	Curtis Joseph		.30	.15	.03
☐ 639	Peter Ing		.30	.15	.03
☐ 640	Scott Thornton		.20	.10	.02
☐ 641	Troy Gamble		.45	.22	.04
☐ 642	Robert Kron		.25	.12	.02
☐ 643	Petr Nedved		.75	.35	.07
☐ 644	Adrien Plavsic		.10	.05	.01
☐ 645	Peter Bondra		.50	.25	.05
☐ 646	Jim Hrivnak		.10	.05	.01
☐ 647	Mikhail Tatarinov		.45	.22	.04
☐ 648	Stephane Beauregard		.20	.10	.02
☐ 649	Rick Tabaracci		.10	.05	.01
☐ 650	Mike Bossy CPL		.15	.07	.01
☐ 651	Bobby Clarke CPL		.12	.06	.01
☐ 652	Alex Delvecchio CPL		.12	.06	.01
☐ 653	Marcel Dionne CPL		.12	.06	.01
☐ 654	Gordie Howe CPL		.25	.12	.02
☐ 655	Stan Mikita CPL		.12	.06	.01
☐ 656	Denis Potvin CPL		.12	.06	.01
☐ 657	Bobby Clarke HOF		.12	.06	.01
☐ 658	Alex Delvecchio HOF		.12	.06	.01
☐ 659	Tony Esposito HOF		.12	.06	.01
☐ 660	Gordie Howe HOF		.25	.12	.02
☐ 661	Mike Milbury CO		.03	.01	.00
☐ 662	Rick Dudley CO		.03	.01	.00
☐ 663	Doug Risebrough CO		.03	.01	.00
☐ 664	Bryan Murray CO		.06	.03	.00
☐ 665	John Muckler CO		.06	.03	.00
☐ 666	Rick Ley CO		.03	.01	.00
☐ 667	Tom Webster CO		.03	.01	.00
☐ 668	Bob Gainey CO UER		.06	.03	.00
	(Stats and bio are Bob McCammon's)				
☐ 669	Pat Burns CO		.06	.03	.00
☐ 670	John Cunniff CO		.06	.03	.00

		MINT	EXC	G-VG
☐ 671	Al Arbour CO	.03	.01	.00
☐ 672	Roger Neilson CO	.06	.03	.00
☐ 673	Paul Holmgren CO	.03	.01	.00
☐ 674	Bob Johnson CO	.06	.03	.00
☐ 675	Dave Chambers CO	.06	.03	.00
☐ 676	Brian Sutter CO	.03	.01	.00
☐ 677	Tom Watt CO	.06	.03	.00
☐ 678	Bob McCammon CO UER	.06	.03	.00
	(Stats and bio are			
	Bob Gainey's)			
☐ 679	Terry Murray CO	.03	.01	.00
☐ 680	Bob Murdoch CO	.03	.01	.00
☐ 681	Ron Asselstine REF	.03	.01	.00
☐ 682	Wayne Bonney REF	.03	.01	.00
☐ 683	Kevin Collins REF	.03	.01	.00
☐ 684	Pat Dapuzzo REF	.03	.01	.00
☐ 685	Ron Finn REF	.03	.01	.00
☐ 686	Kerry Fraser REF	.03	.01	.00
☐ 687	Gerard Gauthier REF	.03	.01	.00
☐ 688	Terry Gregson REF	.03	.01	.00
☐ 689	Bob Hodges REF	.03	.01	.00
☐ 690	Ron Hoggarth REF	.03	.01	.00
☐ 691	Don Koharski REF	.03	.01	.00
☐ 692	Dan Marouelli REF	.03	.01	.00
☐ 693	Danny McCourt REF	.03	.01	.00
	(Front Dan, back Danny)			
☐ 694	Bill McCreary REF	.03	.01	.00
☐ 695	Denis Morel REF	.03	.01	.00
☐ 696	Jerry Pateman REF	.03	.01	.00
☐ 697	Ray Scapinello REF	.03	.01	.00
☐ 698	Rob Shick REF	.03	.01	.00
☐ 699	Paul Stewart REF	.03	.01	.00
☐ 700	Leon Stickle REF	.03	.01	.00
☐ 701	Andy van Hellemond REF	.03	.01	.00
☐ 702	Mark Vines REF	.03	.01	.00
☐ 703	Wayne Gretzky 2000th	1.00	.50	.10
	(2.33 goals per game,			
	should be points)			
☐ 704	Stanley Cup Champs	.20	.10	.02
☐ 705	The Puck-La Rondelle	.25	.12	.02

1990-91 Score

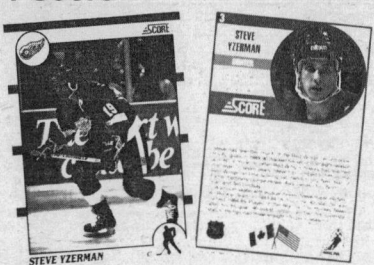

STEVE YZERMAN

The 1990-91 Score hockey set contains 440 cards, each measuring the standard size, 2¹/₂" by 3¹/₂". The fronts feature a color action photo, superimposed over blue and red stripes on a white background. The team logo appears in the upper left hand corner, while an image of a hockey player (in various colors) appears in the lower right hand corner. The backs are outlined in a blue border and show a head shot of the player on the upper half. The career statistics and highlights on the lower half are printed on a pale yellow background. The complete set price does not include the five Eric Lindros bonus cards (441-445) that were only available in factory sets sold to hobby dealers. The few card numbers that are different in the Canadian and U.S. versions are labeled with an A (American) or C (Canadian) suffix after the card number.

Le jeu Score 1990-91 contient 440 cartes de format standard, 2¹/₂" x 3¹/₂". La face représente une photo d'action en couleurs, superposée à des rayures bleues et rouges sur fond blanc. L'emblème de l'équipe apparaît au coin supérieur gauche, alors que l'image d'un joueur de hockey (en différentes couleurs) se trouve au coin inférieur droit. Le dos est bordé de bleu, et comporte un portrait du joueur à la moitié supérieure. La moitié inférieure présente, sur un fond jaune pale, les statistiques et moments marquants de la carrière. Le prix du jeu complet n'inclut pas les cinq cartes-prime Eric Lindros (441-445), uniquement disponibles dans les jeux venant de l'usine et vendus aux négociants.

			MINT	EXC	G-VG
	COMPLETE SET (440)		27.00	13.50	2.70
	COMMON PLAYER (1-440)		.03	.01	.00
☐	1	Wayne Gretzky	1.25	.60	.12
☐	2	Mario Lemieux	.90	.45	.09
☐	3	Steve Yzerman	.30	.15	.03
☐	4	Cam Neely	.30	.15	.03
☐	5	Al MacInnis	.15	.07	.01
☐	6	Paul Coffey	.25	.12	.02
☐	7	Brian Bellows	.12	.06	.01
☐	8	Joe Sakic	.75	.35	.07
☐	9	Bernie Nicholls	.12	.06	.01

			MINT	EXC	G-VG
☐	10	Patrick Roy	.25	.12	.02
☐	11	Doug Houda	.08	.04	.01
☐	12	David Volek	.06	.03	.00
☐	13	Esa Tikkanen	.12	.06	.01
☐	14	Thomas Steen	.06	.03	.00
☐	15	Chris Chelios	.10	.05	.01
☐	16	Bob Carpenter	.06	.03	.00
☐	17	Dirk Graham	.03	.01	.00
☐	18	Garth Butcher	.06	.03	.00
☐	19	Patrik Sundstrom	.06	.03	.00
☐	20	Rod Langway	.08	.04	.01
☐	21	Scott Young	.08	.04	.01
☐	22	Ulf Dahlen	.06	.03	.00
☐	23	Mike Ramsey	.03	.01	.00
☐	24	Peter Zezel	.06	.03	.00
☐	25	Ron Hextall	.12	.06	.01
☐	26	Steve Duchesne	.06	.03	.00
☐	27	Allan Bester	.06	.03	.00
☐	28	Everett Sanipass	.12	.06	.01
☐	29	Steve Konroyd	.03	.01	.00
☐	30A	Joe Nieuwendyk ERR (Text says, now I fell, should say feel)	.40	.20	.04
☐	30B	Joe Nieuwendyk COR	.40	.20	.04
☐	31A	Brent Ashton ERR	.20	.10	.02
☐	31B	Brent Ashton COR	.08	.04	.01
☐	32	Trevor Linden	.30	.15	.03
☐	33	Mike Ridley	.03	.01	.00
☐	34	Sean Burke	.08	.04	.01
☐	35	Pat Verbeek	.06	.03	.00
☐	36	Rob Ramage	.06	.03	.00
☐	37	Kelly Kisio	.03	.01	.00
☐	38A	Craig Muni ERR (Back photo actually Craig Simpson)	.20	.10	.02
☐	38B	Craig Muni COR	.08	.04	.01
☐	39	Brent Sutter	.06	.03	.00
☐	40	Gary Leeman	.06	.03	.00
☐	41	Jeff Brown	.06	.03	.00
☐	42	Greg Millen	.06	.03	.00
☐	43	Alexander Mogilny	.50	.25	.05
☐	44	Dale Hunter	.03	.01	.00
☐	45	Randy Moller	.03	.01	.00
☐	46	Peter Sidorkiewicz	.08	.04	.01
☐	47	Terry Carkner	.03	.01	.00
☐	48	Tony Granato	.20	.10	.02
☐	49	Shawn Burr	.03	.01	.00
☐	50	Dale Hawerchuk	.15	.07	.01
☐	51A	Don Sweeney ERR	.25	.12	.02
☐	51B	Don Sweeney ERR	.12	.06	.01
☐	52	Mike Vernon (Text says won WHL MVP twice, should be once)	.15	.07	.01
☐	53	**Kevin Stevens**	**1.25**	**.60**	**.12**

			MINT	EXC	G-VG
☐	54	Bryan Fogarty	.25	.12	.02
☐	55	Dan Quinn	.06	.03	.00
☐	56	Murray Craven	.06	.03	.00
☐	57	Shawn Chambers	.06	.03	.00
☐	58	Craig Simpson	.10	.05	.01
☐	59	Doug Crossman	.03	.01	.00
☐	60	Daren Puppa	.12	.06	.01
☐	61	Bobby Smith	.10	.05	.01
☐	62	Viacheslav Fetisov	.25	.12	.02
☐	63	Gino Cavallini	.06	.03	.00
☐	64	Jimmy Carson	.12	.06	.01
☐	65	Dave Ellett	.03	.01	.00
☐	66	Steve Thomas	.06	.03	.00
☐	67	Mike Lalor	.10	.05	.01
☐	68	Mike Liut	.08	.04	.01
☐	69	Tom Laidlaw	.03	.01	.00
☐	70	Ron Francis	.12	.06	.01
☐	71	Sergei Makarov	.50	.25	.05
☐	72	Randy Burridge	.03	.01	.00
☐	73	Doug Lidster	.03	.01	.00
☐	74	Mike Richter	.50	.25	.05
☐	75	Stephane Richer	.12	.06	.01
☐	76	Randy Hillier	.03	.01	.00
☐	77	Christian Ruuttu	.03	.01	.00
☐	78	Marc Fortier	.08	.04	.01
☐	79	Bill Ranford	.15	.07	.01
☐	80	Rick Tocchet	.15	.07	.01
☐	81	Fredrik Olausson	.03	.01	.00
☐	82	Adam Creighton	.08	.04	.01
☐	83	Sylvain Cote	.03	.01	.00
☐	84	Brian Mullen	.06	.03	.00
☐	85	Adam Oates	.25	.12	.02
☐	86	Gary Nylund	.03	.01	.00
☐	87	Tim Cheveldae	.30	.15	.03
☐	88	Gary Suter	.10	.05	.01
☐	89	John Tonelli	.06	.03	.00
☐	90	Kevin Hatcher	.08	.04	.01
☐	91	Guy Carbonneau	.06	.03	.00
☐	92	Curtis Leschyshyn	.10	.05	.01
☐	93	Kirk McLean	.08	.04	.01
☐	94	Curt Giles	.03	.01	.00
☐	95	Vincent Damphousse	.10	.05	.01
☐	96	Peter Stastny	.15	.07	.01
☐	97	Glen Wesley	.06	.03	.00
☐	98	David Shaw	.03	.01	.00
☐	99	Brad Shaw	.12	.06	.01
☐	100	Mark Messier	.30	.15	.03
☐	101	Rick Zombo	.12	.06	.01
☐	102A	Mark Fitzpatrick (Catches right)	.25	.12	.02
☐	102B	Mark Fitzpatrick (Catches left)	.12	.06	.01
☐	103	Rick Vaive	.06	.03	.00
☐	104	Mark Osborne	.03	.01	.00
☐	105	Rob Brown	.15	.07	.01

			MINT	EXC	G-VG
☐ 106	Gary Roberts		.03	.01	.00
☐ 107	Vince Riendeau		.30	.15	.03
☐ 108	Dave Gagner		.12	.06	.01
☐ 109	Bruce Driver		.03	.01	.00
☐ 110	Pierre Turgeon		.35	.17	.03
☐ 111	Claude Lemieux		.10	.05	.01
☐ 112	Bob Essensa		.25	.12	.02
☐ 113	John Ogrodnick		.06	.03	.00
☐ 114	Glenn Anderson		.08	.04	.01
☐ 115	Kelly Hrudey		.08	.04	.01
☐ 116	Sylvain Turgeon		.03	.01	.00
☐ 117	Gord Murphy		.15	.07	.01
☐ 118	Craig Janney		.30	.15	.03
☐ 119	Randy Wood		.03	.01	.00
☐ 120	Mike Modano		1.25	.60	.12
☐ 121	Tom Barrasso		.08	.04	.01
☐ 122	Daniel Marois		.10	.05	.01
☐ 123	Igor Larionov		.20	.10	.02
☐ 124	Geoff Courtnall		.12	.06	.01
☐ 125	Denis Savard		.15	.07	.01
☐ 126	Ron Tugnutt		.12	.06	.01
☐ 127	Mathieu Schneider		.25	.12	.02
☐ 128	Joel Otto		.03	.01	.00
☐ 129	Steve Smith		.10	.05	.01
☐ 130	Mike Gartner		.10	.05	.01
☐ 131	Rod Brind'Amour		.50	.25	.05
☐ 132	Jyrki Lumme		.12	.06	.01
☐ 133	Mike Foligno		.03	.01	.00
☐ 134	Ray Ferraro		.03	.01	.00
☐ 135	Steve Larmer		.12	.06	.01
☐ 136	Randy Carlyle		.06	.03	.00
☐ 137	Tony Tanti		.06	.03	.00
☐ 138	Jeff Chychrun		.10	.05	.01
☐ 139	Gerald Diduck		.03	.01	.00
☐ 140	Andy Moog		.15	.07	.01
☐ 141	Paul Gillis		.03	.01	.00
☐ 142	Tom Kurvers		.03	.01	.00
☐ 143	Bob Probert		.15	.07	.01
☐ 144	Neal Broten		.06	.03	.00
☐ 145	Phil Housley		.08	.04	.01
☐ 146	Brendan Shanahan		.08	.04	.01
☐ 147	Bob Rouse		.03	.01	.00
☐ 148	Russ Courtnall		.06	.03	.00
☐ 149	Normand Rochefort		.03	.01	.00
☐ 150	Luc Robitaille		.25	.12	.02
☐ 151	Curtis Joseph		.25	.12	.02
☐ 152	Ulf Samuelsson		.06	.03	.00
☐ 153	Ron Sutter		.06	.03	.00
☐ 154	Petri Skriko		.03	.01	.00
☐ 155	Doug Gilmour		.08	.04	.01
☐ 156	Paul Fenton		.06	.03	.00
☐ 157	Jeff Norton		.03	.01	.00
☐ 158	Jari Kurri		.20	.10	.02
☐ 159	Reggie Lemelin		.06	.03	.00
☐ 160	Kirk Muller		.08	.04	.01

		MINT	EXC	G-VG
☐ 161	Keith Brown	.03	.01	.00
☐ 162	Aaron Broten UER	.03	.01	.00
	(Photo actually Dave Archibald)			
☐ 163	Adam Graves	.20	.10	.02
☐ 164	John Cullen	.35	.17	.03
☐ 165	Craig Ludwig	.03	.01	.00
☐ 166	Dave Taylor	.06	.03	.00
☐ 167	Craig Wolanin	.10	.05	.01
☐ 168	Kelly Miller	.06	.03	.00
☐ 169	Uwe Krupp	.03	.01	.00
☐ 170	Kevin Lowe	.08	.04	.01
☐ 171	Wendel Clark	.06	.03	.00
☐ 172	Dave Babych	.06	.03	.00
☐ 173	Paul Reinhart	.06	.03	.00
☐ 174	Patrick Flatley	.03	.01	.00
☐ 175	John Vanbiesbrouck	.10	.05	.01
☐ 176	Teppo Numminen	.10	.05	.01
☐ 177	Tim Kerr	.08	.04	.01
☐ 178	Ken Daneyko	.08	.04	.01
☐ 179	Jeremy Roenick	2.00	1.00	.20
☐ 180	Gerard Gallant	.10	.05	.01
☐ 181	Allen Pederson	.03	.01	.00
☐ 182	Jon Casey	.15	.07	.01
☐ 183	Tomas Sandstrom	.10	.05	.01
☐ 184	Brad McCrimmon	.03	.01	.00
☐ 185	Paul Cavallini	.08	.04	.01
☐ 186	Mark Recchi	2.25	1.10	.22
☐ 187	Michel Petit	.03	.01	.00
☐ 188	Scott Stevens	.08	.04	.01
☐ 189	Dave Andreychuk	.06	.03	.00
☐ 190	John MacLean	.08	.04	.01
☐ 191	Petr Svoboda	.03	.01	.00
☐ 192	Dave Tippett	.03	.01	.00
☐ 193	Dave Manson	.03	.01	.00
☐ 194	James Patrick	.03	.01	.00
☐ 195	Al Iafrate	.06	.03	.00
☐ 196	Doug Smail	.06	.03	.00
☐ 197	Kjell Samuelsson	.03	.01	.00
☐ 198	Brian Bradley	.03	.01	.00
☐ 199	Charlie Huddy	.06	.03	.00
☐ 200	Ray Bourque	.30	.15	.03
☐ 201	Joey Kocur	.15	.07	.01
☐ 202	Jim Johnson	.03	.01	.00
	(Born Michigan, not Minnesota)			
☐ 203	Paul MacLean	.06	.03	.00
☐ 204	Tim Watters	.03	.01	.00
☐ 205	Pat Elynuik	.10	.05	.01
☐ 206	Larry Murphy	.03	.01	.00
☐ 207	Claude Loiselle	.10	.05	.01
☐ 208	Joe Mullen	.08	.04	.01
☐ 209	Alexei Kasatonov	.20	.10	.02
☐ 210	Ed Olczyk	.08	.04	.01
☐ 211	Doug Bodger	.03	.01	.00
☐ 212	Kevin Dineen	.06	.03	.00
☐ 213	Shayne Corson	.12	.06	.01

		MINT	EXC	G-VG
☐ 214	Steve Chiasson	.06	.03	.00
☐ 215	Don Beaupre	.06	.03	.00
☐ 216	Jamie Macoun	.06	.03	.00
☐ 217	Dave Poulin	.06	.03	.00
☐ 218	Zarley Zalapski	.08	.04	.01
☐ 219	Brad Marsh	.03	.01	.00
☐ 220	Mark Howe	.08	.04	.01
☐ 221	Michel Goulet	.10	.05	.01
☐ 222	Hubie McDonough	.10	.05	.01
☐ 223	Frantisek Musil	.08	.04	.01
☐ 224	Sergio Momesso	.15	.07	.01
☐ 225	Brian Leetch	.50	.25	.05
☐ 226	Theoren Fleury	.75	.35	.07
☐ 227	Mike Krushelnyski	.06	.03	.00
☐ 228	Glen Hanlon	.06	.03	.00
☐ 229	Mario Marois	.03	.01	.00
☐ 230	Dino Ciccarelli	.10	.05	.01
☐ 231A	Dave McLlwain (Shoots right)	.20	.10	.02
☐ 231B	Dave McLlwain (Shoots left)	.08	.04	.01
☐ 232	Petr Klima	.10	.05	.01
☐ 233	Grant Ledyard	.12	.06	.01
☐ 234	Phil Bourque	.03	.01	.00
☐ 235	Rob Sweeney	.03	.01	.00
☐ 236	Luke Richardson	.03	.01	.00
☐ 237	Todd Krygier	.12	.06	.01
☐ 238	Brian Skrudland	.06	.03	.00
☐ 239	Chris Terreri	.35	.17	.03
☐ 240	Greg Adams	.03	.01	.00
☐ 241	Darren Turcotte	.75	.35	.07
☐ 242	Scott Mellanby	.06	.03	.00
☐ 243	Troy Murray	.06	.03	.00
☐ 244	Stewart Gavin	.06	.03	.00
☐ 245	Gordie Roberts	.03	.01	.00
☐ 246	John Druce	.30	.15	.03
☐ 247	Steve Kasper	.06	.03	.00
☐ 248	Paul Ranheim	.25	.12	.02
☐ 249	Greg Paslawski	.03	.01	.00
☐ 250	Pat LaFontaine	.20	.10	.02
☐ 251	Scott Arniel	.03	.01	.00
☐ 252	Bernie Federko	.06	.03	.00
☐ 253	Garry Galley	.12	.06	.01
☐ 254	Carey Wilson	.03	.01	.00
☐ 255	Bob Errey	.03	.01	.00
☐ 256	Tony Hrkac	.03	.01	.00
☐ 257	Andrew McBain	.03	.01	.00
☐ 258	Craig MacTavish	.03	.01	.00
☐ 259A	Dean Evason ERR (Reversed negative)	.20	.10	.02
☐ 259B	Dean Evason COR	.08	.04	.01
☐ 260	Larry Robinson	.10	.05	.01
☐ 261	Basil McRae	.10	.05	.01
☐ 262	Stephan Lebeau	.50	.25	.05
☐ 263	Ken Wregget	.10	.05	.01

		MINT	EXC	G-VG
☐ 264	Greg Gilbert	.03	.01	.00
☐ 265	Ken Baumgartner	.12	.06	.01
☐ 266	Lou Franceschetti	.10	.05	.01
☐ 267	Rick Meagher	.03	.01	.00
☐ 268	Michal Pivonka	.15	.07	.01
☐ 269	Brian Propp	.08	.04	.01
☐ 270	Bryan Trottier	.15	.07	.01
☐ 271	Marty McSorley	.08	.04	.01
☐ 272	Jan Erixon	.03	.01	.00
☐ 273	Vladimir Krutov	.15	.07	.01
☐ 274	Dana Murzyn	.03	.01	.00
☐ 275	Grant Fuhr	.15	.07	.01
☐ 276	Randy Cunneyworth	.03	.01	.00
☐ 277	John Chabot	.03	.01	.00
☐ 278	Walt Poddubny	.03	.01	.00
☐ 279	Steve Leach	.03	.01	.00
☐ 280	Doug Wilson	.10	.05	.01
☐ 281	Rich Sutter	.06	.03	.00
☐ 282	Stephane Beauregard (Played at Ft. Worth, should be Ft. Wayne)	.20	.10	.02
☐ 283	John Carter	.10	.05	.01
☐ 284	Don Barber	.10	.05	.01
☐ 285	Tom Fergus	.03	.01	.00
☐ 286	Ilkka Sinisalo	.03	.01	.00
☐ 287	Kevin McClelland (Back has shoots, but no side indicated)	.03	.01	.00
☐ 288	Troy Mallette	.12	.06	.01
☐ 289	Clint Malarchuk UER (Photo actually Tom Barrasso)	.06	.03	.00
☐ 290	Guy Lafleur	.15	.07	.01
☐ 291	Bob Joyce	.06	.03	.00
☐ 292	Trent Yawney	.08	.04	.01
☐ 293	Joe Murphy	.25	.12	.02
☐ 294	Glenn Healy	.12	.06	.01
☐ 295	Dave Christian	.06	.03	.00
☐ 296	Paul MacDermid	.03	.01	.00
☐ 297	Todd Elik	.20	.10	.02
☐ 298	Wendell Young	.12	.06	.01
☐ 299	Dean Kennedy	.10	.05	.01
☐ 300	Brett Hull	1.00	.50	.10
☐ 301A	Keith Acton	.03	.01	.00
☐ 301C	Martin Gelinas	.60	.30	.06
☐ 302A	Yvon Corriveau	.10	.05	.01
☐ 302C	Ric Nattress	.03	.01	.00
☐ 303A	Don Maloney	.03	.01	.00
☐ 303C	Jim Sandlak	.03	.01	.00
☐ 304C	Brian Hayward	.06	.03	.00
☐ 304A	Mark Tinordi	.50	.25	.05
☐ 305C	Joe Cirella	.06	.03	.00
☐ 305A	Bob Kudelski	.20	.10	.02
☐ 306A	Brian Benning	.03	.01	.00
☐ 306C	Randy Gregg	.08	.04	.01
☐ 307A	Alan Kerr	.03	.01	.00

		MINT	EXC	G-VG
☐ 307C	Sylvain Lefebvre	.15	.07	.01
☐ 308A	Pelle Eklund	.06	.03	.00
☐ 308C	Mark Lamb	.30	.15	.03
☐ 309A	Calle Johansson	.03	.01	.00
☐ 309C	Rick Wamsley	.06	.03	.00
☐ 310C	Moe Mantha	.03	.01	.00
☐ 310A	David Maley	.15	.07	.01
☐ 311A	Chris Nilan	.06	.03	.00
☐ 311C	Tony McKegney	.03	.01	.00
☐ 312	Patrick Roy AS1	.15	.07	.01
☐ 313	Ray Bourque AS1	.15	.07	.01
☐ 314	Al MacInnis AS1	.10	.05	.01
☐ 315	Mark Messier AS1	.15	.07	.01
☐ 316	Luc Robitaille AS1	.15	.07	.01
☐ 317	Brett Hull AS1	.40	.20	.04
☐ 318	Daren Puppa AS2	.10	.05	.01
☐ 319	Paul Coffey AS2	.15	.07	.01
☐ 320	Doug Wilson AS2	.08	.04	.01
☐ 321	Wayne Gretzky AS2	.45	.22	.04
☐ 322	Brian Bellows AS2	.08	.04	.01
☐ 323	Cam Neely AS2	.15	.07	.01
☐ 324	Bob Essensa ART	.12	.06	.01
☐ 325	Brad Shaw ART	.08	.04	.01
☐ 326	Geoff Smith ART	.08	.04	.01
☐ 327	Mike Modano ART	.25	.12	.02
☐ 328	Rod Brind'Amour ART	.20	.10	.02
☐ 329	Sergei Makarov ART	.20	.10	.02
☐ 330A	Kip Miller Hobey ERR (No Score logo on card front)	1.00	.50	.10
☐ 330B	Kip Miller Hobey COR	.50	.25	.05
☐ 330C	Memorial Cup	3.00	1.50	.30
☐ 331	Edmonton Oilers Champs	.06	.03	.00
☐ 332	Paul Coffey Speed	.15	.07	.01
☐ 333	Mike Gartner Speed	.08	.04	.01
☐ 334	Al Iafrate Blaster	.06	.03	.00
☐ 335	Al MacInnis Blaster	.10	.05	.01
☐ 336	Wayne Gretzky Sniper	.45	.22	.04
☐ 337	Mario Lemieux Sniper	.30	.15	.03
☐ 338	Wayne Gretzky Magic	.45	.22	.04
☐ 339	Steve Yzerman Magic	.20	.10	.02
☐ 340	Cam Neely Banger	.20	.10	.02
☐ 341	Scott Stevens Banger	.06	.03	.00
☐ 342	Esa Tikkanen Shadow	.08	.04	.01
☐ 343	Jan Erixon Shadow	.03	.01	.00
☐ 344	Patrick Roy Stopper	.15	.07	.01
☐ 345	Bill Ranford Stopper	.08	.04	.01
☐ 346	Brett Hull RB	.35	.17	.03
☐ 347	Wayne Gretzky RB	.45	.22	.04
☐ 348	Jari Kurri LL	.15	.07	.01
☐ 349	Paul Cavallini LL	.03	.01	.00
☐ 350	Sergei Makarov RLL	.15	.07	.01
☐ 351	Brett Hull LL	.35	.17	.03
☐ 352	Wayne Gretzky LL	.45	.22	.04

			MINT	EXC	G-VG
☐ 353	Wayne Gretzky LL		.45	.22	.04
☐ 354	P. Roy/Liut LL		.12	.06	.01
☐ 355	Gilbert Perreault HOF		.10	.05	.01
☐ 356	Bill Barber HOF		.08	.04	.01
☐ 357	Fern Flaman HOF		.06	.03	.00
☐ 358	Bill Ranford Smythe		.08	.04	.01
☐ 359	Rick Meagher Selke		.03	.01	.00
☐ 360	Mark Messier Hart		.15	.07	.01
☐ 361	Wayne Gretzky Ross		.45	.22	.04
☐ 362	Sergei Makarov Calder		.15	.07	.01
☐ 363	Ray Bourque Norris		.15	.07	.01
☐ 364	Patrick Roy Vezina		.15	.07	.01
☐ 365	Moog/Lemelin Jennings		.06	.03	.00
☐ 366	Brett Hull Byng		.35	.17	.03
☐ 367	Gord Kluzak Mast		.03	.01	.00
☐ 368	Boston/Washington (Line 11, Janney misspelled as Janny)		.06	.03	.00
☐ 369	Edmonton/Chicago		.06	.03	.00
☐ 370	Adam Burt		.10	.05	.01
☐ 371	Troy Loney		.10	.05	.01
☐ 372	Dave Chyzowski		.10	.05	.01
☐ 373	Geoff Smith		.12	.06	.01
☐ 374	Stan Smyl		.06	.03	.00
☐ 375	Gaetan Duchesne		.06	.03	.00
☐ 376	Bob Murray		.03	.01	.00
☐ 377	Daniel Shank		.12	.06	.01
☐ 378	Tommy Albelin		.03	.01	.00
☐ 379	Perry Berezan		.10	.05	.01
☐ 380	Ken Linseman		.03	.01	.00
☐ 381	Stephane Matteau		.25	.12	.02
☐ 382	Mario Thyer		.10	.05	.01
☐ 383	Nelson Emerson		.25	.12	.02
☐ 384	Kory Kocur		.12	.06	.01
☐ 385	Bob Beers		.10	.05	.01
☐ 386	Jim Hrivnak		.10	.05	.01
☐ 387	Mark Pederson		.15	.07	.01
☐ 388	Jeff Hackett		.20	.10	.02
☐ 389	Eic Weinrich		.30	.15	.03
☐ 390	Steven Rice		.50	.25	.05
☐ 391	Stu Barnes		.10	.05	.01
☐ 392	Olaf Kolzig		.20	.10	.02
☐ 393	Francois Leroux		.10	.05	.01
☐ 394	Adrien Plavsic		.08	.04	.01
☐ 395	Michel Mongeau		.12	.06	.01
☐ 396	Rick Corriveau		.12	.06	.01
☐ 397	Wayne Doucet		.08	.04	.01
☐ 398	Mats Sundin		1.25	.60	.12
☐ 399	Murray Baron		.10	.05	.01
☐ 400	Rick Bennett		.12	.06	.01
☐ 401	Jon Morris		.10	.05	.01
☐ 402	Kay Whitmore		.15	.07	.01
☐ 403	Peter Lappin		.10	.05	.01
☐ 404	Kris Draper		.15	.07	.01
☐ 405	Shayne Stevenson		.25	.12	.02

			MINT	EXC	G-VG
☐ 406	**Paul Ysebaert**		.25	.12	.02
☐ 407A	**Jimmy Waite**		.35	.17	.03
	(Catches right)				
☐ 407B	**Jimmy Waite**		.15	.07	.01
	(Catches left)				
☐ 408	**Cam Russell**		.12	.06	.01
☐ 409	**Kim Issel**		.10	.05	.01
	(Photo shoots left, text has right)				
☐ 410	**Darrin Shannon**		.12	.06	.01
☐ 411	**Link Gaetz**		.15	.07	.01
☐ 412	**Craig Fisher**		.20	.10	.02
☐ 413	**Bruce Hoffort**		.15	.07	.01
☐ 414	**Peter Ing**		.35	.17	.03
☐ 415	**Stephane Fiset**		.15	.07	.01
☐ 416	**Dominic Lavoie**		.10	.05	.01
☐ 417	**Steve Maltais**		.12	.06	.01
☐ 418	**Wes Walz**		.35	.17	.03
☐ 419	**Terry Yake**		.10	.05	.01
☐ 420	**Jamie Leach**		.20	.10	.02
☐ 421	**Rob Blake**		.65	.30	.06
☐ 422	**Andrew Cassels**		.25	.12	.02
☐ 423	**Marc Bureau**		.25	.12	.02
☐ 424	**Scott Allison**		.10	.05	.01
☐ 425	**Darryl Sydor**		.20	.10	.02
☐ 426	**Turner Stevenson**		.15	.07	.01
☐ 427	**Brad May**		.15	.07	.01
☐ 428	**Jaromir Jagr**		3.00	1.50	.30
☐ 429	**Shawn Antoski**		.15	.07	.01
☐ 430	**Derian Hatcher**		.15	.07	.01
☐ 431	**Mark Greig UER**		.25	.12	.02
	(No indication of how he shoots on card back)				
☐ 432	**Scott Scissons**		.15	.07	.01
☐ 433	**Mike Ricci**		1.25	.60	.12
☐ 434	**Drake Berehowsky**		.30	.15	.03
☐ 435	**Owen Nolan**		.65	.30	.06
☐ 436	**Keith Primeau**		.50	.25	.05
☐ 437	**Karl Dykhuis**		.20	.10	.02
☐ 438	**Trevor Kidd**		.40	.20	.04
☐ 439	**Martin Brodeur**		.20	.10	.02
☐ 440	**Eric Lindros**		12.00	6.00	1.20
☐ 441	**Eric Lindros**		2.50	1.25	.25
	Junior B Team				
☐ 442	**Eric Lindros**		2.50	1.25	.25
	Regular Junior OHL				
☐ 443	**Eric Lindros**		2.50	1.25	.25
	OHL All-Star				
☐ 444	**Eric Lindros**		2.50	1.25	.25
	Oshawa Generals (Non-action pose; head shot with his gloves over his mouth)				

		MINT	EXC	G-VG
☐ 445	**Eric Lindros**	2.50	1.25	.25
	Oshawa Generals			
	(Non-action pose;			
	shot from waist up,			
	arms draped over hockey			
	stick across his back)			

1990-91 Score Traded

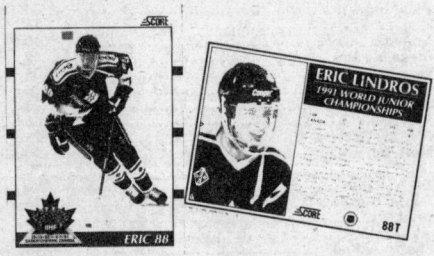

The 1990-91 Score Rookie and Traded hockey set contains 110 cards measuring the standard size, 2¹/₂" by 3¹/₂". The fronts feature a color action photo, superimposed over blue and red stripes on a white background. The team logo appears in the upper left hand corner, while an image of a hockey player (in various colors) appears in the lower right hand corner. Yellow stripes appear at the top and bottom of the card front. The backs are outlined in a yellow border and show a head shot of the player on the upper half. The career statistics and highlights on the lower half are printed on a pale blue background.

Le jeu Score Rookie et Traded de 1990-91 contient 110 cartes de format standard, 2¹/₂" x 3¹/₂". La face comporte une photo d'action en couleurs, superposée à des rayures bleues et rouges sur fond blanc. L'emblème de l'équipe apparaît au coin supérieur gauche, alors qu'une image d'un joueur de hockey (en différentes couleurs) se trouve au coin inférieur droit. Le haut et le bas de la face sont bordés de bandes jaunes. Le dos est entouré d'un bord jaune, et comporte un portrait du joueur à la moitié supérieure. Les statistiques et moments marquants de la carrière sont imprimés sur la moitié inférieure, sur fond bleu pâle.

	MINT	EXC	G-VG
COMPLETE SET (110)	27.00	13.50	2.70
COMMON PLAYER (1-110)	.05	.02	.00

		MINT	EXC	G-VG
☐ 1T	Denis Savard	.15	.07	.01
☐ 2T	Dale Hawerchuk	.15	.07	.01
☐ 3T	Phil Housley	.08	.04	.01
☐ 4T	Chris Chelios	.10	.05	.01
☐ 5T	Geoff Courtnall	.10	.05	.01
☐ 6T	Peter Zezel	.08	.04	.01
☐ 7T	Joe Mullen	.08	.04	.01
☐ 8T	Craig Ludwig	.05	.02	.00
☐ 9T	Claude Lemieux	.08	.04	.01
☐ 10T	Bobby Holik	1.00	.50	.10
☐ 11T	Peter Ing	.20	.10	.02
☐ 12T	Rod Buskas	.10	.05	.01
☐ 13T	Tim Sweeney	.10	.05	.01
☐ 14T	Don Barber	.05	.02	.00
☐ 15T	Ray Ferraro	.05	.02	.00
☐ 16T	Peter Taglianetti	.05	.02	.00
☐ 17T	Johan Garpenlov	.50	.25	.05
☐ 18T	Kevin Miller	.50	.25	.05
☐ 19T	Frantisek Musil	.05	.02	.00
☐ 20T	Sergei Fedorov	7.50	3.75	.75
☐ 21T	Aaron Broten	.05	.02	.00
☐ 22T	Chris Nilan	.05	.02	.00
☐ 23T	Gerald Diduck	.05	.02	.00
☐ 24T	Marc Habscheid	.05	.02	.00
☐ 25T	Glen Featherstone	.10	.05	.01
☐ 26T	Mikko Makela	.05	.02	.00
☐ 27T	Paul Stanton	.10	.05	.01
☐ 28T	Mark Osborne	.05	.02	.00
☐ 29T	Dave Tippett	.05	.02	.00
☐ 30T	Robert Reichel	.60	.30	.06
☐ 31T	Grant Jennings	.15	.07	.01
☐ 32T	Troy Gamble	.50	.25	.05
☐ 33T	Mark Janssens	.08	.04	.01
☐ 34T	Brian Propp	.08	.04	.01
☐ 35T	Donald Dufresne	.10	.05	.01
☐ 36T	Martin Hostak	.10	.05	.01
☐ 37T	Brad McCrimmon	.05	.02	.00
☐ 38T	Dave Lowry	.15	.07	.01
☐ 39T	Anatoli Semenov	.50	.25	.05
☐ 40T	Scott Stevens	.08	.04	.01
☐ 41T	Paul Broten	.10	.05	.01
☐ 42T	Carey Wilson	.05	.02	.00
☐ 43T	Troy Crowder	.20	.10	.02
☐ 44T	Vladimir Ruzicka	.35	.17	.03
☐ 45T	Richard Pilon	.10	.05	.01
☐ 46T	John McIntyre	.15	.07	.01
☐ 47T	Mike Krushelnyski	.05	.02	.00
☐ 48T	Dave Snuggerud	.12	.06	.01
☐ 49T	Bob McGill	.05	.02	.00
☐ 50T	Petr Nedved	1.25	.60	.12
☐ 51T	Ed Olczyk	.08	.04	.01
☐ 52T	Doug Crossman	.05	.02	.00
☐ 53T	Mikhail Tatarinov	.60	.30	.06

			MINT	EXC	G-VG
☐ 54T	Michel Petit		.05	.02	.00
☐ 55T	Frank Pietrangelo		.30	.15	.03
☐ 56T	Brian MacLellan		.05	.02	.00
☐ 57T	Paul Fenton		.05	.02	.00
☐ 58T	Eric Desjardins		.15	.07	.01
☐ 59T	Mike Craig		.50	.25	.05
☐ 60T	Mike Ricci		1.00	.50	.10
☐ 61T	Harold Snepsts		.05	.02	.00
☐ 62T	John Byce		.10	.05	.01
☐ 63T	Laurie Boschman		.05	.02	.00
☐ 64T	Randy Velischek		.05	.02	.00
☐ 65T	Robert Kron		.30	.15	.03
☐ 66T	Jocelyn Lemieux		.10	.05	.01
☐ 67T	Dave Ellett		.05	.02	.00
☐ 68T	Scott Arniel		.05	.02	.00
☐ 69T	Doug Smail		.05	.02	.00
☐ 70T	Jaromir Jagr		3.00	1.50	.30
☐ 71T	Peter Bondra		.50	.25	.05
☐ 72T	Paul Cyr		.05	.02	.00
☐ 73T	Daniel Berthiaume		.08	.04	.01
☐ 73T	Donald Audette		.05	.02	.00
☐ 74T	Lee Norwood		.05	.02	.00
☐ 75T	Bobby Smith		.10	.05	.01
☐ 76T	Kris King		.12	.06	.01
☐ 77T	Mark Hunter		.05	.02	.00
☐ 78T	Brian Hayward		.08	.04	.01
☐ 79T	Greg Hawgood		.05	.02	.00
☐ 80T	Owen Nolan		.65	.30	.06
☐ 81T	Cliff Ronning		.15	.07	.01
☐ 82T	Zdeno Ciger		.15	.07	.01
☐ 83T	Gordie Roberts		.05	.02	.00
☐ 84T	Rick Green		.05	.02	.00
☐ 85T	Ken Hodge Jr.		2.00	1.00	.20
☐ 86T	Derek King		.05	.02	.00
☐ 87T	Brent Gilchrist		.15	.07	.01
☐ 88T	Eric Lindros		7.50	3.75	.75
☐ 89T	Steve Bozek		.05	.02	.00
☐ 90T	Keith Primeau		.50	.25	.05
☐ 91T	Roger Johansson		.10	.05	.01
☐ 92T	Wayne Presley		.05	.02	.00
☐ 93T	Ilkka Sinisalo		.05	.02	.00
☐ 94T	Mario Marois		.05	.02	.00
☐ 95T	Ken Linseman		.05	.02	.00
☐ 96T	Greg Brown		.12	.06	.01
☐ 97T	Ray Sheppard		.05	.02	.00
☐ 98T	Mike Lalor		.05	.02	.00
☐ 99T	Norman Lacombe		.12	.06	.01
☐100T	Mats Sundin		1.00	.50	.10
☐101T	Jergus Baca		.12	.06	.01
☐102T	Mike Keane		.15	.07	.01
☐103T	Ed Belfour		4.00	2.00	.40
☐104T	Mark Hardy		.05	.02	.00
☐105T	Dave Capuano		.15	.07	.01

		MINT	EXC	G-VG
☐106T	Bryan Trottier	.15	.07	.01
☐107T	Per Djoos	.10	.05	.01
☐108T	Sylvain Turgeon	.05	.02	.00
☐109T	Dave Reid	.15	.07	.01
☐110T	Gretzky's 2000th	1.25	.60	.12

1954-55 Topps

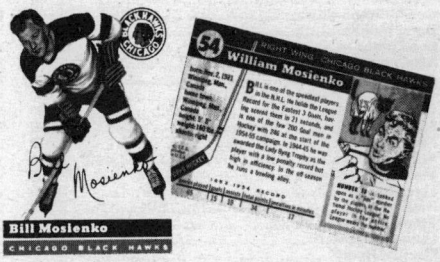

The 1954-55 set marks Topps' first hockey set and includes 60 cards of players on the four American teams. Cards measure 2⁵/₈" by 3³/₄". The cards, in color, have facsimile autographs on the fronts, and the backs, printed in red and blue, contain player biographies, player vital statistics, 1953-54 records, and a hockey fact section. The cards were printed in the USA. Numbers appear on the backs of the cards. The best rookie card in this set is Doug Mohns.

Le jeu de 1954-55 représente le premier jeu de hockey de Topps' et inclut 60 cartes de joueurs des quatre équipes américaines. Les cartes, en couleurs, mesurent 2⁵/₈" x 3³/₄". Elles comportent une copie de l'autographe sur la face, et le dos, imprimé en rouge et bleu, présente la biographie et les données personnelles du joueur, les statistiques pour 1953-54, et une section de faits notables de hockey. Les cartes ont été imprimées aux USA. Les numéros se trouvent au dos de la carte. Doug Mohns est le débutant prometteur de ce jeu.

		NRMT	VG-E	GOOD
	COMPLETE SET (60)	2700.00	1250.00	275.00
	COMMON PLAYER (1-60)	20.00	10.00	2.00
☐ 1	Dick Gamble	40.00	12.00	2.50
☐ 2	Bob Chrystal	20.00	10.00	2.00
☐ 3	Harry Howell	40.00	20.00	4.00
☐ 4	Johnny Wilson	20.00	10.00	2.00

			NRMT	VG-E	GOOD
☐	5	Red Kelly	50.00	25.00	5.00
☐	6	Real Chevrefils	20.00	10.00	2.00
☐	7	Bob Armstrong	20.00	10.00	2.00
☐	8	Gordie Howe	1100.00	450.00	100.00
☐	9	Benny Woit	20.00	10.00	2.00
☐	10	Gump Worsley	80.00	40.00	8.00
☐	11	Andy Bathgate	45.00	22.50	4.50
☐	12	Bucky Hollingworth	20.00	10.00	2.00
☐	13	Ray Timgren	20.00	10.00	2.00
☐	14	Jack Evans	20.00	10.00	2.00
☐	15	Paul Ronty	20.00	10.00	2.00
☐	16	Glen Skov	20.00	10.00	2.00
☐	17	Gus Mortson	20.00	10.00	2.00
☐	18	Doug Mohns	35.00	17.50	3.50
☐	19	Leo Labine	20.00	10.00	2.00
☐	20	Bill Gadsby	35.00	17.50	3.50
☐	21	Jerry Toppazzini	20.00	10.00	2.00
☐	22	Wally Hergesheimer	20.00	10.00	2.00
☐	23	Danny Lewicki	20.00	10.00	2.00
☐	24	Metro Prystai	20.00	10.00	2.00
☐	25	Fern Flaman	35.00	17.50	3.50
☐	26	Al Rollins	22.00	11.00	2.20
☐	27	Marcel Pronovost	35.00	17.50	3.50
☐	28	Lou Jankowski	20.00	10.00	2.00
☐	29	Nick Mickoski	20.00	10.00	2.00
☐	30	Frank Martin	20.00	10.00	2.00
☐	31	Lorne Ferguson	20.00	10.00	2.00
☐	32	Camille Henry	25.00	12.50	2.50
☐	33	Pete Conacher	20.00	10.00	2.00
☐	34	Marty Pavelich	20.00	10.00	2.00
☐	35	Don McKenney	20.00	10.00	2.00
☐	36	Fleming Mackell	20.00	10.00	2.00
☐	37	Jim Henry	22.00	11.00	2.20
☐	38	Hal Laycoe	20.00	10.00	2.00
☐	39	Alex Delvecchio	50.00	25.00	5.00
☐	40	Larry Wilson	20.00	10.00	2.00
☐	41	Allan Stanley	35.00	17.50	3.50
☐	42	George Sullivan	20.00	10.00	2.00
☐	43	Jack McIntyre	20.00	10.00	2.00
☐	44	Ivan Irwin	20.00	10.00	2.00
☐	45	Tony Leswick	20.00	10.00	2.00
☐	46	Bob Goldham	20.00	10.00	2.00
☐	47	Cal Gardner	20.00	10.00	2.00
☐	48	Ed Sandford	20.00	10.00	2.00
☐	49	Bill Quackenbush	35.00	17.50	3.50
☐	50	Warren Godfrey	20.00	10.00	2.00
☐	51	Ted Lindsay	50.00	25.00	5.00
☐	52	Earl Reibel	20.00	10.00	2.00
☐	53	Don Raleigh	20.00	10.00	2.00
☐	54	Bill Mosienko	35.00	17.50	3.50
☐	55	Larry Popein	20.00	10.00	2.00
☐	56	Edgar Laprade	20.00	10.00	2.00
☐	57	Bill Dineen	22.00	11.00	2.20

			NRMT	VG-E	GOOD
☐	58	Terry Sawchuk	175.00	85.00	18.00
☐	59	Marcel Bonin	20.00	10.00	2.00
☐	60	Milt Schmidt	100.00	25.00	5.00

1957-58 Topps

Red Kelly · defense
DETROIT RED WINGS

The 1957-58 Topps set contains 66 color cards of the four American teams. For some reason there were no Topps hockey sets for 1955-56 or 1956-57. Cards in the set measure 2½" by 3½". The backs, in both English and French, feature 1956-57 records, the card number, player vital statistics, a short player biography, and a cartoon question and answer section. The cards were printed in the USA. The key rookie cards in this set are Johnny Bucyk, Glenn Hall, Pierre Pilote, and Norm Ullman.

Le jeu Topps 1957-58 contient 66 cartes en couleurs, comprenant quatre équipes américaines. Pour une raison inconnue, il n'existe pas de jeux de cartes de hockey Topps pour les années 1955-56 et 1956-57. Les cartes mesurent 2½" x 3½". Le dos, imprimé en anglais et en français, présente les statistiques pour 1956-57, le numéro de carte, les données personnelles du joueur, une biographie concise, et une section question/réponse illustrée d'une caricature. Les cartes ont été imprimées aux USA. Les débutants importants de ce jeu sont Johnny Bucyk, Glenn Hall, Pierre Pilote et Norm Ullman.

			NRMT	VG-E	GOOD
		COMPLETE SET (66)	1400.00	200.00	40.00
		COMMON PLAYER (1-66)	10.00	5.00	1.00
☐	1	Real Chevrefils	18.00	6.00	1.20
☐	2	Jack Bionda	10.00	5.00	1.00
☐	3	Bob Armstrong	10.00	5.00	1.00
☐	4	Fern Flaman	14.00	7.00	1.40
☐	5	Jerry Toppazzini	10.00	5.00	1.00

			NRMT	VG-E	GOOD
☐	6	Larry Regan	10.00	5.00	1.00
☐	7	Bronco Horvath	10.00	5.00	1.00
☐	8	Jack Caffery	10.00	5.00	1.00
☐	9	Leo Labine	10.00	5.00	1.00
☐	10	Johnny Bucyk	135.00	65.00	13.50
☐	11	Vic Stasiuk	10.00	5.00	1.00
☐	12	Doug Mohns	12.00	6.00	1.20
☐	13	Don McKenney	10.00	5.00	1.00
☐	14	Don Simmons	10.00	5.00	1.00
☐	15	Allan Stanley	14.00	7.00	1.40
☐	16	Fleming Mackell	10.00	5.00	1.00
☐	17	Larry Hillman	10.00	5.00	1.00
☐	18	Leo Boivin	14.00	7.00	1.40
☐	19	Bob Bailey	10.00	5.00	1.00
☐	20	Glenn Hall	135.00	65.00	13.50
☐	21	Ted Lindsay	18.00	9.00	1.80
☐	22	Pierre Pilote	55.00	27.50	5.50
☐	23	Jim Thomson	10.00	5.00	1.00
☐	24	Eric Nesterenko	12.00	6.00	1.20
☐	25	Gus Mortson	10.00	5.00	1.00
☐	26	Ed Litzenberger	10.00	5.00	1.00
☐	27	Elmer Vasko	14.00	7.00	1.40
☐	28	Jack McIntyre	10.00	5.00	1.00
☐	29	Ron Murphy	10.00	5.00	1.00
☐	30	Glen Skov	10.00	5.00	1.00
☐	31	Hec Lalonde	10.00	5.00	1.00
☐	32	Nick Mickoski	10.00	5.00	1.00
☐	33	Wally Hergesheimer	10.00	5.00	1.00
☐	34	Alex Delvecchio	18.00	9.00	1.80
☐	35	Terry Sawchuk UER	75.00	37.50	7.50
		(Misspelled Sawchuck on card front)			
☐	36	Guyle Fielder	10.00	5.00	1.00
☐	37	Tom McCarthy	10.00	5.00	1.00
☐	38	Al Arbour	14.00	7.00	1.40
☐	39	Billy Dea	10.00	5.00	1.00
☐	40	Lorne Ferguson	10.00	5.00	1.00
☐	41	Warren Godfrey	10.00	5.00	1.00
☐	42	Gordie Howe	350.00	175.00	35.00
☐	43	Marcel Pronovost	14.00	7.00	1.40
☐	44	Bill McNeil	10.00	5.00	1.00
☐	45	Earl Reibel	10.00	5.00	1.00
☐	46	Norm Ullman	65.00	32.50	6.50
☐	47	Johnny Wilson	10.00	5.00	1.00
☐	48	Red Kelly	18.00	9.00	1.80
☐	49	Bill Dineen	10.00	5.00	1.00
☐	50	Forbes Kennedy	10.00	5.00	1.00
☐	51	Harry Howell	14.00	7.00	1.40
☐	52	Guy Gendron	10.00	5.00	1.00
☐	53	Gump Worsley	25.00	12.50	2.50
☐	54	Larry Popein	10.00	5.00	1.00
☐	55	Jack Evans	10.00	5.00	1.00
☐	56	George Sullivan	10.00	5.00	1.00

			NRMT	VG-E	GOOD
☐	57	Gerry Foley	10.00	5.00	1.00
☐	58	Andy Hebenton	10.00	5.00	1.00
☐	59	Larry Cahan	10.00	5.00	1.00
☐	60	Andy Bathgate	14.00	7.00	1.40
☐	61	Danny Lewicki	10.00	5.00	1.00
☐	62	Dean Prentice	14.00	7.00	1.40
☐	63	Camille Henry	10.00	5.00	1.00
☐	64	Lou Fontinato	10.00	5.00	1.00
☐	65	Bill Gadsby	14.00	7.00	1.40
☐	66	Dave Creighton	18.00	6.00	1.20

1958-59 Topps

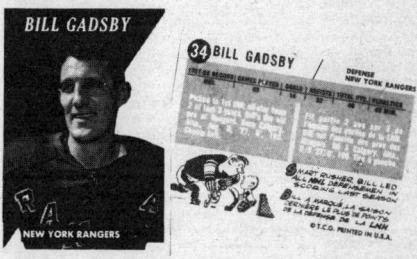

The 1958-59 Topps set contains 66 cards in full color of the four American teams. Cards measure 2½" by 3½". The backs, in both English and French, feature the card number, 1957-58 records, player biographies, and a cartoon information section on the player. The cards were printed in the USA. The set features the first hockey card of Bobby Hull. Other notable rookie cards include Eddie Shack and Ken Wharram.

Le jeu Topps 1958-59 contient 66 cartes en couleurs des quatre équipes américaines. es cartes mesurent 2½" x 3½". Le dos, imprimé en anglais et en français, comprend le numéro de carte, les statistiques pour 1957-58, la biographie du joueur, et une section fournissant des données sur le joueur sous forme de caricature. Les cartes ont été imprimées aux USA. Le jeu comprend la première carte de hockey de Bobby Hull. D'autres cartes notables de débutants importants incluent Eddie Shack et Ken Wharram.

	NRMT	VG-E	GOOD
COMPLETE SET (66)	2250.00	1000.00	225.00
COMMON PLAYER (1-66)	9.00	4.50	.90

			NRMT	VG-E	GOOD
☐	1	Bob Armstrong	15.00	5.00	1.00
☐	2	Terry Sawchuk	75.00	37.50	7.50
☐	3	Glen Skov	9.00	4.50	.90
☐	4	Leo Labine	9.00	4.50	.90
☐	5	Dollard St. Laurent	9.00	4.50	.90
☐	6	Danny Lewicki	9.00	4.50	.90
☐	7	John Hanna	9.00	4.50	.90
☐	8	Gordie Howe	300.00	150.00	30.00
☐	9	Vic Stasiuk	9.00	4.50	.90
☐	10	Larry Regan	9.00	4.50	.90
☐	11	Forbes Kennedy	9.00	4.50	.90
☐	12	Elmer Vasko	9.00	4.50	.90
☐	13	Glenn Hall	45.00	22.50	4.50
☐	14	Ken Wharram	15.00	7.50	1.50
☐	15	Len Lunde	9.00	4.50	.90
☐	16	Ed Litzenberger	9.00	4.50	.90
☐	17	Norm Johnson	9.00	4.50	.90
☐	18	Earl Ingarfield	9.00	4.50	.90
☐	19	Les Colwill	9.00	4.50	.90
☐	20	Leo Boivin	14.00	7.00	1.40
☐	21	Andy Bathgate	14.00	7.00	1.40
☐	22	Johnny Wilson	9.00	4.50	.90
☐	23	Larry Cahan	9.00	4.50	.90
☐	24	Marcel Pronovost	14.00	7.00	1.40
☐	25	Larry Hillman	9.00	4.50	.90
☐	26	Jim Bartlett	9.00	4.50	.90
☐	27	Nick Mickoski	9.00	4.50	.90
☐	28	Larry Popein	9.00	4.50	.90
☐	29	Fleming Mackell	9.00	4.50	.90
☐	30	Eddie Shack	22.00	11.00	2.20
☐	31	Jack Evans	9.00	4.50	.90
☐	32	Dean Prentice	12.50	6.25	1.25
☐	33	Claude LaForge	9.00	4.50	.90
☐	34	Bill Gadsby	14.00	7.00	1.40
☐	35	Bronco Horvath	9.00	4.50	.90
☐	36	Pierre Pilote	20.00	10.00	2.00
☐	37	Earl Balfour	9.00	4.50	.90
☐	38	Gus Mortson	9.00	4.50	.90
☐	39	Gump Worsley	22.00	11.00	2.20
☐	40	Johnny Bucyk	45.00	22.50	4.50
☐	41	Lou Fontinato	9.00	4.50	.90
☐	42	Tod Sloan	9.00	4.50	.90
☐	43	Charlie Burns	9.00	4.50	.90
☐	44	Don Simmons	9.00	4.50	.90
☐	45	Jerry Toppazzini	9.00	4.50	.90
☐	46	Andy Hebenton	9.00	4.50	.90
☐	47	Pete Goegan	9.00	4.50	.90
☐	48	George Sullivan	9.00	4.50	.90
☐	49	Hank Ciesla	9.00	4.50	.90
☐	50	Doug Mohns	11.00	5.50	1.10
☐	51	Guy Gendron	9.00	4.50	.90
☐	52	Alex Delvecchio	17.00	8.50	1.70
☐	53	Eric Nesterenko	11.00	5.50	1.10

			NRMT	VG-E	GOOD
☐	54	Camille Henry	9.00	4.50	.90
☐	55	Lorne Ferguson	9.00	4.50	.90
☐	56	Fern Flaman	14.00	7.00	1.40
☐	57	Earl Reibel	9.00	4.50	.90
☐	58	Warren Godfrey	9.00	4.50	.90
☐	59	Ron Murphy	9.00	4.50	.90
☐	60	Harry Howell	14.00	7.00	1.40
☐	61	Red Kelly	17.00	8.50	1.70
☐	62	Don McKenney	9.00	4.50	.90
☐	63	Ted Lindsay	17.00	8.50	1.70
☐	64	Al Arbour	14.00	7.00	1.40
☐	65	Norm Ullman	25.00	12.50	2.50
☐	66	Bobby Hull	1500.00	600.00	125.00

1959-60 Topps

The 1959-60 Topps set contains 66 color cards of the four American teams. Cards measure 2½" by 3½". The backs, in both English and French, feature the card number, 1958-59 records, a short biography, and a cartoon question section. The backs, in red-orange and black ink, state the cards were printed in the USA. The best rookie card in this set is Murray Balfour.

Le jeu Topps 1959-60 contient 66 cartes en couleurs des quatre équipes américaines. Les cartes mesurent 2½" x 3½". Le dos, imprimé en français et en anglais, comprend le numéro de carte, les statistiques pour 1958-59, une biographie concise, et une section de questions, illustrée d'une caricature. Le dos, imprimé en encre rouge-orange et noire, indique que les cartes furent imprimées aux USA. La carte du débutant prometteur représente Murray Balfour.

			NRMT	VG-E	GOOD
		COMPLETE SET (66)	1250.00	600.00	125.00
		COMMON PLAYER (1-66)	7.50	3.75	.75
☐	1	Eric Nesterenko	16.00	5.00	1.00
☐	2	Pierre Pilote	12.50	6.25	1.25
☐	3	Elmer Vasko	7.50	3.75	.75
☐	4	Peter Goegan	7.50	3.75	.75
☐	5	Lou Fontinato	7.50	3.75	.75
☐	6	Ted Lindsay	15.00	7.50	1.50
☐	7	Leo Labine	7.50	3.75	.75
☐	8	Alex Delvecchio	15.00	7.50	1.50
☐	9	Don McKenney	7.50	3.75	.75
☐	10	Earl Ingarfield	7.50	3.75	.75
☐	11	Don Simmons	7.50	3.75	.75
☐	12	Glen Skov	7.50	3.75	.75
☐	13	Tod Sloan	7.50	3.75	.75
☐	14	Vic Stasiuk	7.50	3.75	.75
☐	15	Gump Worsley	20.00	10.00	2.00
☐	16	Andy Hebenton	7.50	3.75	.75
☐	17	Dean Prentice	11.00	5.50	1.10
☐	18	Action picture	9.00	4.50	.90
☐	19	Fleming Mackell	7.50	3.75	.75
☐	20	Harry Howell	12.50	6.25	1.25
☐	21	Larry Popein	7.50	3.75	.75
☐	22	Len Lunde	7.50	3.75	.75
☐	23	Johnny Bucyk	28.00	14.00	2.80
☐	24	Guy Gendron	7.50	3.75	.75
☐	25	Barry Cullen	7.50	3.75	.75
☐	26	Leo Boivin	12.50	6.25	1.25
☐	27	Warren Godfrey	7.50	3.75	.75
☐	28	Action picture (Glenn Hall and Camille Henry)	11.00	5.50	1.10
☐	29	Fern Flaman	12.50	6.25	1.25
☐	30	Jack Evans	7.50	3.75	.75
☐	31	John Hanna	7.50	3.75	.75
☐	32	Glenn Hall	28.00	14.00	2.80
☐	33	Murray Balfour	12.50	6.25	1.25
☐	34	Andy Bathgate	12.50	6.25	1.25
☐	35	Al Arbour	12.50	6.25	1.25
☐	36	Jim Morrison	7.50	3.75	.75
☐	37	Nick Mickoski	7.50	3.75	.75
☐	38	Jerry Toppazzini	7.50	3.75	.75
☐	39	Bob Armstrong	7.50	3.75	.75
☐	40	Charlie Burns	7.50	3.75	.75
☐	41	Bill McNeil	7.50	3.75	.75
☐	42	Terry Sawchuk	55.00	27.50	5.50
☐	43	Dollard St. Laurent	7.50	3.75	.75
☐	44	Marcel Pronovost	12.50	6.25	1.25
☐	45	Norm Ullman	17.00	8.50	1.70
☐	46	Camille Henry	7.50	3.75	.75
☐	47	Bobby Hull	350.00	175.00	35.00

			NRMT	VG-E	GOOD
☐	48	Action picture (Gordie Howe and Jack Evans)	60.00	30.00	6.00
☐	49	Lou Marcon	7.50	3.75	.75
☐	50	Earl Balfour	7.50	3.75	.75
☐	51	Jim Bartlett	7.50	3.75	.75
☐	52	Forbes Kennedy	7.50	3.75	.75
☐	53	Action picture (Nick Mickoski and Johnny Hanna)	7.50	3.75	.75
☐	54	Action picture (Norm Johnson, Gump Worsley, and Harry Howell)	10.00	5.00	1.00
☐	55	Brian Cullen	7.50	3.75	.75
☐	56	Bronco Horvath	7.50	3.75	.75
☐	57	Eddie Shack	11.00	5.50	1.10
☐	58	Doug Mohns	9.00	4.50	.90
☐	59	George Sullivan	7.50	3.75	.75
☐	60	Action picture (Pierre Pilote and Flem Mackell)	9.00	4.50	.90
☐	61	Ed Litzenberger	7.50	3.75	.75
☐	62	Bill Gadsby	12.50	6.25	1.25
☐	63	Gordie Howe	250.00	125.00	25.00
☐	64	Claude LaForge	7.50	3.75	.75
☐	65	Red Kelly	15.00	7.50	1.50
☐	66	Ron Murphy	15.00	5.00	1.00

1960-61 Topps

The 1960-61 Topps set contains 66 color cards featuring players from the Boston, Chicago, and New York teams. Cards measure the standard 2½" by 3½". Some All-time Great players are included. The All-time Great players included in the set are numbers 1-5, 8, 10, 15-17, 19, 20, 26, 27, 29, 32, 34, 35, 38, 44, 46-48, 55, 59, 60, and 63. The backs feature the card number, 1959-60 records, and a cartoon trivia question section, the answer for which can be found by placing a piece of red cellophane over the backs. The backs are in French and English, and the cards were printed in the USA. The key rookie card in this set is Stan Mikita.

Le jeu Topps 1960-61 contient 66 cartes en couleurs, représentant des joueurs des équipes de Boston, Chicago, et New York. Les cartes mesurent 2½" x 3½". Quelques étoiles All-Time sont inclues, portant les numéros 1-5, 8, 10, 15-17, 19, 20, 26, 27, 29, 32, 34, 35, 38, 44, 46-48, 55, 59, 60, et 63. Le dos comporte le numéro de carte, les statistiques pour 1959-60, et une section de questions peuvent être résolues en plaçant un morceau de cellophane rouge au-dessus du dos, accompagné d'une caricature. Le dos est imprimé en français et en anglais, et les cartes ont été imprimées aux USA. Le débutant important de ce jeu est Stan Mikita.

			NRMT	VG-E	GOOD
	COMPLETE SET (66)		1250.00	600.00	125.00
	COMMON PLAYER (1-66)		7.00	3.50	.70
☐	1	Lester Patrick	30.00	8.00	1.60
☐	2	Paddy Moran	10.00	5.00	1.00
☐	3	Joe Malone	9.00	4.50	.90
☐	4	Earnie Johnson	9.00	4.50	.90
☐	5	Nels Stewart	9.00	4.50	.90
☐	6	Bill Hay	11.00	5.50	1.10
☐	7	Eddie Shack	10.00	5.00	1.00
☐	8	Cy Denneny	9.00	4.50	.90

			NRMT	VG-E	GOOD
☐	9	Jim Morrison	7.00	3.50	.70
☐	10	Bill Cook	9.00	4.50	.90
☐	11	Johnny Bucyk	21.00	10.50	2.10
☐	12	Murray Balfour	7.00	3.50	.70
☐	13	Leo Labine	7.00	3.50	.70
☐	14	Stan Mikita	425.00	200.00	42.00
☐	15	George Hay	7.00	3.50	.70
☐	16	Mervyn Dutton	10.00	5.00	1.00
☐	17	Dickie Boon	10.00	5.00	1.00
☐	18	George Sullivan	7.00	3.50	.70
☐	19	Georges Vezina	25.00	12.50	2.50
☐	20	Eddie Shore	25.00	12.50	2.50
☐	21	Ed Litzenberger	7.00	3.50	.70
☐	22	Bill Gadsby	11.00	5.50	1.10
☐	23	Elmer Vasko	7.00	3.50	.70
☐	24	Charlie Burns	7.00	3.50	.70
☐	25	Glenn Hall	22.00	11.00	2.20
☐	26	Dit Clapper	12.50	6.25	1.25
☐	27	Art Ross	12.50	6.25	1.25
☐	28	Jerry Toppazzini	7.00	3.50	.70
☐	29	Frank Boucher	9.00	4.50	.90
☐	30	Jack Evans	7.00	3.50	.70
☐	31	Guy Gendron	7.00	3.50	.70
☐	32	Chuck Gardiner	12.50	6.25	1.25
☐	33	Ab McDonald	7.00	3.50	.70
☐	34	Frank Frederickson	9.00	4.50	.90
☐	35	Frank Nighbor	9.00	4.50	.90
☐	36	Gump Worsley	20.00	10.00	2.00
☐	37	Dean Prentice	10.00	5.00	1.00
☐	38	Hugh Lehman	7.00	3.50	.70
☐	39	Jack McCartan	7.00	3.50	.70
☐	40	Don McKenney	7.00	3.50	.70
☐	41	Ron Murphy	7.00	3.50	.70
☐	42	Andy Hebenton	7.00	3.50	.70
☐	43	Don Simmons	7.00	3.50	.70
☐	44	Herb Gardiner	10.00	5.00	1.00
☐	45	Andy Bathgate	12.50	6.25	1.25
☐	46	Cyclone Taylor	10.00	5.00	1.00
☐	47	King Clancy	20.00	10.00	2.00
☐	48	Newsy Lalonde	14.00	7.00	1.40
☐	49	Harry Howell	11.00	5.50	1.10
☐	50	Ken Schinkel	7.00	3.50	.70
☐	51	Tod Sloan	7.00	3.50	.70
☐	52	Doug Mohns	8.00	4.00	.80
☐	53	Camille Henry	7.00	3.50	.70
☐	54	Bronco Horvath	7.00	3.50	.70
☐	55	Tiny Thompson	11.00	5.50	1.10
☐	56	Bob Armstrong	7.00	3.50	.70
☐	57	Fern Flaman	11.00	5.50	1.10
☐	58	Bobby Hull	225.00	110.00	22.00
☐	59	Howie Morenz	35.00	17.50	3.50
☐	60	Dick Irvin	7.00	3.50	.70
☐	61	Lou Fontinato	7.00	3.50	.70

			NRMT	VG-E	GOOD
☐	62	Leo Boivin	11.00	5.50	1.10
☐	63	Moose Goheen	7.00	3.50	.70
☐	64	Al Arbour	11.00	5.50	1.10
☐	65	Pierre Pilote	11.00	5.50	1.10
☐	66	Vic Stasiuk	15.00	4.50	.90

1961-62 Topps

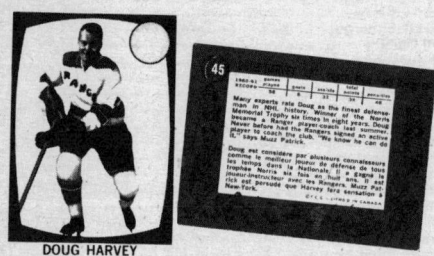

DOUG HARVEY

The 1961-62 Topps set contains 66 color cards featuring players from Boston, Chicago, and New York. The card numbering in this set is basically by team order, e.g., Boston Bruins (1-22), Chicago Blackhawks (23-44), and New York Rangers (45-65). Cards in the set measure 2½" by 3½". The backs, in both French and English, contain the card number, 1960-61 records, and a brief resume of the player's career. The cards were printed in Canada. The key rookie cards in this set are Rod Gilbert and Jean Ratelle.

Le jeu Topps 1961-62 contient 66 cartes en couleurs, représentant des joueurs de Boston, Chicago, et New York. Les cartes sont numérotées essentiellement par équipe, c.à.d., Boston Bruins (1-22), Chicago Blackhawks (23-44), et New York Rangers (45-65). Les cartes mesurent 2½" x 3½". Le dos, imprimé en français et en anglais, comprend le numéro de carte, les statistiques pour 1960-61, et un résumé de la carrière du joueur. les cartes ont été imprimées au Canada. Les débutants importants de ce jeu sont Rod Gilbert et Jean Ratelle.

			NRMT	VG-E	GOOD
	COMPLETE SET (66)		1100.00	550.00	125.00
	COMMON PLAYER (1-66)		6.00	3.00	.60
☐	1	Phil Watson	12.50	4.00	.80
☐	2	Ted Green	15.00	7.50	1.50
☐	3	Earl Balfour	6.00	3.00	.60

			NRMT	VG-E	GOOD
☐	4	Dallas Smith	15.00	7.50	1.50
☐	5	Andre Pronovost	6.00	3.00	.60
☐	6	Dick Meissner	6.00	3.00	.60
☐	7	Leo Boivin	9.00	4.50	.90
☐	8	Johnny Bucyk	20.00	10.00	2.00
☐	9	Jerry Toppazzini	6.00	3.00	.60
☐	10	Doug Mohns	7.00	3.50	.70
☐	11	Charlie Burns	6.00	3.00	.60
☐	12	Don McKenney	6.00	3.00	.60
☐	13	Bob Armstrong	6.00	3.00	.60
☐	14	Murray Oliver	6.00	3.00	.60
☐	15	Orland Kurtenbach	10.00	5.00	1.00
☐	16	Terry Gray	6.00	3.00	.60
☐	17	Don Head	6.00	3.00	.60
☐	18	Pat Stapleton	14.00	7.00	1.40
☐	19	Cliff Pennington	6.00	3.00	.60
☐	20	Team Picture Boston Bruins	16.00	8.00	1.60
☐	21	Action Picture (Earl Balfour and Fern Flaman)	7.00	3.50	.70
☐	22	Action Picture (Andy Bathgate and Glenn Hall)	9.00	4.50	.90
☐	23	Rudy Pilous	10.00	5.00	1.00
☐	24	Pierre Pilote	9.00	4.50	.90
☐	25	Elmer Vasko	6.00	3.00	.60
☐	26	Reg Fleming	8.00	4.00	.80
☐	27	Ab McDonald	6.00	3.00	.60
☐	28	Eric Nesterenko	7.00	3.50	.70
☐	29	Bobby Hull	160.00	80.00	16.00
☐	30	Ken Wharram	7.00	3.50	.70
☐	31	Dollard St. Laurent	6.00	3.00	.60
☐	32	Glenn Hall	20.00	10.00	2.00
☐	33	Murray Balfour	6.00	3.00	.60
☐	34	Ron Murphy	6.00	3.00	.60
☐	35	Bill Hay	6.00	3.00	.60
☐	36	Stan Mikita	100.00	50.00	10.00
☐	37	Denis DeJordy	14.00	7.00	1.40
☐	38	Wayne Hillman	6.00	3.00	.60
☐	39	Rino Robazzo	6.00	3.00	.60
☐	40	Bronco Horvath	6.00	3.00	.60
☐	41	Bob Turner	6.00	3.00	.60
☐	42	Blackhawks Team	16.00	8.00	1.60
☐	43	Action Picture Ken Wharram IA	7.00	3.50	.70
☐	44	Action Picture Dollard St. Laurent helps Glenn Hall	7.00	3.50	.70
☐	45	Doug Harvey	21.00	10.50	2.10
☐	46	Junior Langlois	6.00	3.00	.60
☐	47	Irv Spencer	6.00	3.00	.60
☐	48	George Sullivan	6.00	3.00	.60

			NRMT	VG-E	GOOD
☐	49	**Earl Ingarfield**	6.00	3.00	.60
☐	50	**Gump Worsley**	18.00	9.00	1.80
☐	51	**Harry Howell**	9.00	4.50	.90
☐	52	**Larry Cahan**	6.00	3.00	.60
☐	53	**Andy Bathgate**	10.00	5.00	1.00
☐	54	**Dean Prentice**	8.00	4.00	.80
☐	55	**Andy Hebenton**	6.00	3.00	.60
☐	56	**Camille Henry**	6.00	3.00	.60
☐	57	**Guy Gendron**	6.00	3.00	.60
☐	58	**Pat Hannigan**	6.00	3.00	.60
☐	59	**Ted Hampson**	6.00	3.00	.60
☐	60	**Jean Ratelle**	125.00	60.00	12.50
☐	61	**Al Lebrun**	6.00	3.00	.60
☐	62	**Rod Gilbert**	125.00	60.00	12.50
☐	63	**Team Picture** New York Rangers	16.00	8.00	1.60
☐	64	**Action Picture** (Dick Meissner and Gump Worsley)	8.00	4.00	.80
☐	65	**Action Picture** (Gump Worsley IA)	11.00	5.50	1.10
☐	66	**Checklist Card**	150.00	25.00	5.00

1962-63 Topps

The 1962-63 Topps set contains 66 color cards featuring players from Boston, Chicago, and New York. The card numbering in this set is basically by team order, e.g., Boston Bruins (1-22), Chicago Blackhawks (23-44), and New York Rangers (45-65). Cards measure 2½" by 3½". The backs, in both French and English, feature 1961-62 records, the card number, and a short resume of the player's career. The cards were printed in Canada. The notable rookie cards in this set include Vic Hadfield and Chico Maki.

Le jeu Topps 1962-63 contient 66 cartes en couleurs, représentant des joueurs de Boston, Chicago, et New York. Les cartes sont numérotées essentiellement par équipe, c.à.d., Boston Bruins (1-22), Chicago Blackhawks (23-44), et New York Rangers (45-65). Les cartes mesurent 2¹/₂" x 3¹/₂". Le dos, imprimé en français et en anglais, comprend le numéro de carte, les statistiques pour 1961-62, et un résumé de la carrière du joueur. les cartes ont été imprimées au Canada. Les débutants importants de ce jeu sont Vic Hadfield et Chico Maki.

			NRMT	VG-E	GOOD
		COMPLETE SET (66)	850.00	425.00	85.00
		COMMON PLAYER (1-66)	6.00	3.00	.60
☐	1	Phil Watson	12.00	4.00	.80
☐	2	Bob Perreault	6.00	3.00	.60
☐	3	Bruce Gamble	6.00	3.00	.60
☐	4	Warren Godfrey	6.00	3.00	.60
☐	5	Leo Boivin	9.00	4.50	.90
☐	6	Doug Mohns	7.00	3.50	.70
☐	7	Ted Green	7.00	3.50	.70
☐	8	Pat Stapleton	7.00	3.50	.70
☐	9	Dallas Smith	7.00	3.50	.70
☐	10	Don McKenney	6.00	3.00	.60
☐	11	Johnny Bucyk	16.00	8.00	1.60
☐	12	Murray Oliver	6.00	3.00	.60
☐	13	Jerry Toppazzini	6.00	3.00	.60
☐	14	Cliff Pennington	6.00	3.00	.60
☐	15	Charlie Burns	6.00	3.00	.60
☐	16	Guy Gendron	6.00	3.00	.60
☐	17	Irv Spencer	6.00	3.00	.60
☐	18	Wayne Connelly	6.00	3.00	.60
☐	19	Andre Pronovost	6.00	3.00	.60
☐	20	Terry Gray	6.00	3.00	.60
☐	21	Tom Williams	6.00	3.00	.60
☐	22	Bruins Team	15.00	7.50	1.50
☐	23	Rudy Pilous	8.00	4.00	.80
☐	24	Glenn Hall	16.00	8.00	1.60
☐	25	Denis DeJordy	7.00	3.50	.70
☐	26	Jack Evans	6.00	3.00	.60
☐	27	Elmer Vasko	6.00	3.00	.60
☐	28	Pierre Pilote	9.00	4.50	.90
☐	29	Bob Turner	6.00	3.00	.60
☐	30	Dollard St. Laurent	6.00	3.00	.60
☐	31	Wayne Hillman	6.00	3.00	.60
☐	32	Al McNeil	6.00	3.00	.60
☐	33	Bobby Hull	150.00	75.00	15.00
☐	34	Stan Mikita	75.00	37.50	7.50
☐	35	Bill Hay	6.00	3.00	.60
☐	36	Murray Balfour	6.00	3.00	.60
☐	37	Chico Maki	12.50	6.25	1.25
☐	38	Ab McDonald	6.00	3.00	.60
☐	39	Ken Wharram	7.00	3.50	.70
☐	40	Ron Murphy	6.00	3.00	.60
☐	41	Eric Nesterenko	7.00	3.50	.70

			NRMT	VG-E	GOOD
☐	42	Reg Fleming	6.00	3.00	.60
☐	43	Murray Hall	6.00	3.00	.60
☐	44	Blackhawks Team	15.00	7.50	1.50
☐	45	Gump Worsley	16.00	8.00	1.60
☐	46	Harry Howell	9.00	4.50	.90
☐	47	Albert Langlois	6.00	3.00	.60
☐	48	Larry Cahan	6.00	3.00	.60
☐	49	Jim Neilson	9.00	4.50	.90
☐	50	Al Lebrun	6.00	3.00	.60
☐	51	Earl Ingarfield	6.00	3.00	.60
☐	52	Andy Bathgate	10.00	5.00	1.00
☐	53	Dean Prentice	8.00	4.00	.80
☐	54	Andy Hebenton	6.00	3.00	.60
☐	55	Ted Hampson	6.00	3.00	.60
☐	56	Dave Balon	6.00	3.00	.60
☐	57	Bert Olmstead	9.00	4.50	.90
☐	58	Jean Ratelle	35.00	17.50	3.50
☐	59	Rod Gilbert	35.00	17.50	3.50
☐	60	Vic Hadfield	20.00	10.00	2.00
☐	61	Frank Paice	6.00	3.00	.60
☐	62	Camille Henry	6.00	3.00	.60
☐	63	Bronco Horvath	6.00	3.00	.60
☐	64	Pat Hannigan	6.00	3.00	.60
☐	65	Rangers Team	15.00	7.50	1.50
☐	66	Checklist Card	100.00	20.00	4.00

1963-64 Topps

The 1963-64 Topps set contains 66 color cards featuring players from Boston, Chicago, and New York. Cards in the set measure 2½" by 3½". The backs, in both French and English, contain the card number, 1962-63 records, a short player biogra-

phy, and a question section, the answer for which could be obtained by rubbing the edge of a coin over a blank space under the question. The cards were printed in Canada. The notable rookie cards in this set are Ed Johnston, Gilles Villemure, and Ed Westfall.

Le jeu Topps 1963-64 contient 66 cartes en couleurs, représentant des joueurs de Boston, Chicago, et New York. Les cartes mesurent 2¹/₂" x 3¹/₂"". Le dos, imprimé en français et en anglais, comprend le numéro de carte, les statistiques pour 1962-63, une biographie concise du joueur, et une section de questions dont les réponses peuvent être obtenues en grattant l'endroit approprié sous la question avec une pièce de monnaie. Les cartes ont été imprimées au Canada. Les cartes notables de débutants importants de ce jeu représentent Ed Johnston, Gilles Villemure, et Ed Westfall.

			NRMT	VG-E	GOOD
		COMPLETE SET (66)	800.00	400.00	80.00
		COMMON PLAYER (1-66)	6.00	3.00	.60
☐	1	Milt Schmidt	16.00	5.00	1.00
☐	2	Ed Johnston	17.00	8.50	1.70
☐	3	Doug Mohns	7.00	3.50	.70
☐	4	Tom Johnson	9.00	4.50	.90
☐	5	Leo Boivin	9.00	4.50	.90
☐	6	Bob McCord	6.00	3.00	.60
☐	7	Ted Green	7.00	3.50	.70
☐	8	Ed Westfall	12.00	6.00	1.20
☐	9	Charlie Burns	6.00	3.00	.60
☐	10	Murray Oliver	6.00	3.00	.60
☐	11	Johnny Bucyk	14.00	7.00	1.40
☐	12	Tom Williams	6.00	3.00	.60
☐	13	Dean Prentice	8.00	4.00	.80
☐	14	Bob Leiter	6.00	3.00	.60
☐	15	Andy Hebenton	6.00	3.00	.60
☐	16	Guy Gendron	6.00	3.00	.60
☐	17	Wayne Rivers	6.00	3.00	.60
☐	18	Jerry Toppazzini	6.00	3.00	.60
☐	19	Forbes Kennedy	6.00	3.00	.60
☐	20	Orland Kurtenbach	7.00	3.50	.70
☐	21	Bruins Team	15.00	7.50	1.50
☐	22	Billy Reay CO	6.00	3.00	.60
☐	23	Glenn Hall	15.00	7.50	1.50
☐	24	Denis DeJordy	7.00	3.50	.70
☐	25	Pierre Pilote	9.00	4.50	.90
☐	26	Elmer Vasko	6.00	3.00	.60
☐	27	Wayne Hillman	6.00	3.00	.60
☐	28	Al McNeil	6.00	3.00	.60
☐	29	Howie Young	6.00	3.00	.60
☐	30	Ed Van Impe	6.00	3.00	.60
☐	31	Reg Fleming	6.00	3.00	.60
☐	32	Bob Turner	6.00	3.00	.60
☐	33	Bobby Hull	135.00	65.00	13.50
☐	34	Bill Hay	6.00	3.00	.60
☐	35	Murray Balfour	6.00	3.00	.60
☐	36	Stan Mikita	55.00	27.50	5.50

			NRMT	VG-E	GOOD
☐	37	Ab McDonald	6.00	3.00	.60
☐	38	Ken Wharram	6.00	3.00	.60
☐	39	Eric Nesterenko	7.00	3.50	.70
☐	40	Ron Murphy	6.00	3.00	.60
☐	41	Chico Maki	6.00	3.00	.60
☐	42	John McKenzie	6.00	3.00	.60
☐	43	Blackhawks Team	15.00	7.50	1.50
☐	44	George Sullivan	6.00	3.00	.60
☐	45	Jacques Plante	50.00	25.00	5.00
☐	46	Gilles Villemure	17.00	8.50	1.70
☐	47	Doug Harvey	18.00	9.00	1.80
☐	48	Harry Howell	9.00	4.50	.90
☐	49	Albert Langlois	6.00	3.00	.60
☐	50	Jim Neilson	6.00	3.00	.60
☐	51	Larry Cahan	6.00	3.00	.60
☐	52	Andy Bathgate	9.00	4.50	.90
☐	53	Don McKenney	6.00	3.00	.60
☐	54	Vic Hadfield	9.00	4.50	.90
☐	55	Earl Ingarfield	6.00	3.00	.60
☐	56	Camille Henry	6.00	3.00	.60
☐	57	Rod Gilbert	18.00	9.00	1.80
☐	58	Phil Goyette	6.00	3.00	.60
☐	59	Don Marshall	6.00	3.00	.60
☐	60	Dick Meissner	6.00	3.00	.60
☐	61	Val Fonteyne	6.00	3.00	.60
☐	62	Ken Schinkel	6.00	3.00	.60
☐	63	Jean Ratelle	18.00	9.00	1.80
☐	64	Don Johns	6.00	3.00	.60
☐	65	Rangers Team	15.00	7.50	1.50
☐	66	Checklist Card	100.00	20.00	4.00

1964-65 Topps

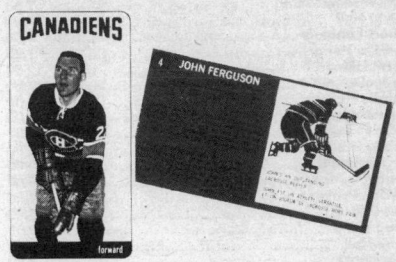

The 1964-65 Topps hockey set features 110 color cards of players of both Canadian and American teams (all six NHL teams are represented). The size of the card is larger than in previous years, à la the 1965 Topps football card set. These tall cards measure 2¹/₂" by 4¹¹/₁₆". The backs, in both French and English, contain the card number, 1963-64 records, a brief player career resume, and a cartoon section featuring a fact about the player portrayed on the card. The cards were printed in Canada. Eleven of the numbers in the last series appear to have been short printed. The key rookies in this set are single prints of Gary Dornhoefer and Marcel Paille found in the last series.

Le jeu Topps 1964-65 contient 110 cartes en couleurs de joueurs d'équipes canadiennes et américaines (les six équipes NHL sont représentés). La carte est plus grande que les années précédentes, ressemblant au jeu de cartes de football Topps de 1965. Ces cartes assez longues mesurent 2¹/₂ x 4¹¹/₁₆". Le dos, imprimé en français et en anglais, contient le numéro de carte, les statistiques pour 1963-64, un sommaire de la carrière du joueur, et un fait notable concernant le joueur, illustré d'une caricature. Les cartes ont été imprimées au Canada. Il semble que onze des numéros de la dernière série n'ont pas été imprimés. Les débutants importants de ce jeu sont Gary Dornhoefer et Marcel Paille, en cartes simples dans la dernière série.

		NRMT	VG-E	GOOD
	COMPLETE SET (110)	4000.00	2000.00	400.00
	COMMON PLAYER (1-55)	7.50	3.75	.75
	COMMON PLAYER (56-110)	22.50	11.00	2.00
☐ 1	Pit Martin	25.00	7.50	1.50
☐ 2	Gilles Tremblay	7.50	3.75	.75
☐ 3	Terry Harper	7.50	3.75	.75
☐ 4	John Ferguson	10.00	5.00	1.00
☐ 5	Elmer Vasko	7.50	3.75	.75
☐ 6	Terry Sawchuk	45.00	22.50	4.50

			NRMT	VG-E	GOOD
☐	7	Bill Hay	7.50	3.75	.75
☐	8	Gary Bergman	7.50	3.75	.75
☐	9	Doug Barkley	7.50	3.75	.75
☐	10	Bob McCord	7.50	3.75	.75
☐	11	Parker MacDonald	7.50	3.75	.75
☐	12	Glenn Hall	18.00	9.00	1.80
☐	13	Albert Langlois	7.50	3.75	.75
☐	14	Camille Henry	7.50	3.75	.75
☐	15	Norm Ullman	12.50	6.25	1.25
☐	16	Ab McDonald	7.50	3.75	.75
☐	17	Charlie Hodge	9.00	4.50	.90
☐	18	Orland Kurtenbach	9.00	4.50	.90
☐	19	Dean Prentice	10.00	5.00	1.00
☐	20	Bobby Hull	165.00	75.00	15.00
☐	21	Ed Johnston	10.00	5.00	1.00
☐	22	Denis DeJordy	9.00	4.50	.90
☐	23	Claude Provost	7.50	3.75	.75
☐	24	Rod Gilbert	16.00	8.00	1.60
☐	25	Doug Mohns	9.00	4.50	.90
☐	26	Al McNeil	7.50	3.75	.75
☐	27	Billy Harris	7.50	3.75	.75
☐	28	Ken Wharram	7.50	3.75	.75
☐	29	George Sullivan	7.50	3.75	.75
☐	30	John McKenzie	7.50	3.75	.75
☐	31	Stan Mikita	60.00	30.00	6.00
☐	32	Ted Green	9.00	4.50	.90
☐	33	Jean Beliveau	40.00	20.00	4.00
☐	34	Arnie Brown	7.50	3.75	.75
☐	35	Reg Fleming	7.50	3.75	.75
☐	36	Jim Mikol	7.50	3.75	.75
☐	37	Dave Balon	7.50	3.75	.75
☐	38	Billy Reay CO	7.50	3.75	.75
☐	39	Marcel Pronovost	12.00	6.00	1.20
☐	40	Johnny Bower	14.00	7.00	1.40
☐	41	Wayne Hillman	7.50	3.75	.75
☐	42	Floyd Smith	7.50	3.75	.75
☐	43	Toe Blake	10.00	5.00	1.00
☐	44	Red Kelly	14.00	7.00	1.40
☐	45	George Imlach	9.00	4.50	.90
☐	46	Dick Duff	7.50	3.75	.75
☐	47	Roger Crozier	10.00	5.00	1.00
☐	48	Henri Richard	22.00	11.00	2.20
☐	49	Larry Jeffrey	7.50	3.75	.75
☐	50	Leo Boivin	12.00	6.00	1.20
☐	51	Ed Westfall	10.00	5.00	1.00
☐	52	Jean Guy Talbot	7.50	3.75	.75
☐	53	Jacques Laperriere	12.00	6.00	1.20
☐	54	1st Checklist	100.00	20.00	4.00
☐	55	2nd Checklist	100.00	20.00	4.00
☐	56	Ron Murphy	22.50	11.00	2.00
☐	57	Bob Baun	22.50	11.00	2.00
☐	58	Tom Williams SP	100.00	50.00	10.00
☐	59	Pierre Pilote SP	175.00	85.00	18.00

			NRMT	VG-E	GOOD
☐	60	Bob Pulford	35.00	17.50	3.50
☐	61	Red Berenson	27.00	13.50	2.70
☐	62	Vic Hadfield	25.00	12.50	2.50
☐	63	Bob Leiter	22.50	11.00	2.00
☐	64	Jim Pappin	27.00	13.50	2.70
☐	65	Earl Ingarfield	22.50	11.00	2.00
☐	66	Lou Angotti	27.00	13.50	2.70
☐	67	Rod Seiling	22.50	11.00	2.00
☐	68	Jacques Plante	75.00	37.50	7.50
☐	69	George Armstrong	35.00	17.50	3.50
☐	70	Milt Schmidt	35.00	17.50	3.50
☐	71	Eddie Shack	25.00	12.50	2.50
☐	72	Gary Dornhoefer SP	150.00	75.00	15.00
☐	73	Chico Maki SP	100.00	50.00	10.00
☐	74	Gilles Villemure SP	125.00	60.00	12.50
☐	75	Carl Brewer	22.50	11.00	2.00
☐	76	Bruce MacGregor	22.50	11.00	2.00
☐	77	Bob Nevin	22.50	11.00	2.00
☐	78	Ralph Backstrom	22.50	11.00	2.00
☐	79	Murray Oliver	22.50	11.00	2.00
☐	80	Bobby Rousseau SP	125.00	60.00	12.50
☐	81	Don McKenney	22.50	11.00	2.00
☐	82	Ted Lindsay	42.00	20.00	4.00
☐	83	Harry Howell	35.00	17.50	3.50
☐	84	Doug Robinson	22.50	11.00	2.00
☐	85	Frank Mahovlich	65.00	32.50	6.50
☐	86	Andy Bathgate	40.00	20.00	4.00
☐	87	Phil Goyette	22.50	11.00	2.00
☐	88	J.C. Tremblay	22.50	11.00	2.00
☐	89	Gordie Howe	300.00	150.00	30.00
☐	90	Murray Balfour	22.50	11.00	2.00
☐	91	Eric Nesterenko SP	125.00	60.00	12.50
☐	92	Marcel Paille SP	250.00	125.00	25.00
☐	93	Sid Abel	30.00	15.00	3.00
☐	94	Dave Keon	42.00	21.00	4.00
☐	95	Alex Delvecchio	42.00	21.00	4.00
☐	96	Bill Gadsby	35.00	17.50	3.50
☐	97	Don Marshall	22.50	11.00	2.00
☐	98	Bill Hicke	22.50	11.00	2.00
☐	99	Ron Stewart SP	100.00	50.00	10.00
☐	100	Johnny Bucyk	55.00	27.50	5.50
☐	101	Tom Johnson	35.00	17.50	3.50
☐	102	Tim Horton	45.00	22.50	4.50
☐	103	Jim Neilson	22.50	11.00	2.00
☐	104	Allan Stanley	35.00	17.50	3.50
☐	105	Tim Horton AS SP	150.00	75.00	15.00
☐	106	Stan Mikita AS SP	150.00	75.00	15.00
☐	107	Bobby Hull AS	125.00	60.00	12.50
☐	108	Ken Wharram AS	22.50	11.00	2.00
☐	109	Pierre Pilote AS	35.00	17.50	3.50
☐	110	Glenn Hall AS	65.00	20.00	4.00

1965-66 Topps

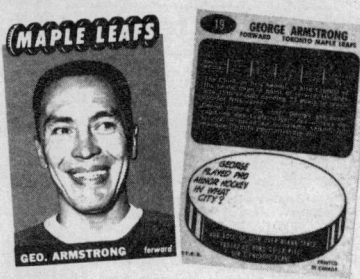

The 1965-66 Topps set contains 128 color cards featuring all teams in the NHL. Cards measure the standard 2½" by 3½". The backs, printed in both English and French, contain the card number, 1964-65 records, a short biography, and a scratch-off question section. The cards were printed in Canada. Cards 122-128 seem to be harder to find; they are not even included on the checklist card 121. The key rookies in this set are Gerry Cheevers, Yvan Cournoyer, Phil Esposito, Ed Giacomin, Ken Hodge, and Dennis Hull.

Le jeu Topps 1965-66 contient 128 cartes en couleurs, représentant toutes les équipes de la NHL. Les cartes ont le format standard, 2½" x 3½". Le dos, imprimé en français et en anglais, contient le numéro de carte, les statistiques pour 1964-65, une biographie concise, et une section de questions, dont les réponses apparaissent en grattant l'endroit approprié avec une pièce de monnaie. Les cartes ont été imprimées au Canada. Les numéros 122-128 semblent être plus difficiles à trouver; elles ne sont même pas inclues sur la carte de contrôle numéro 121. Les débutants importants de ce jeu sont Gerry Cheevers, Yvan Cournoyer, Phil Esposito, Ed Giacomin, Ken Hodge, et Dennis Hull.

			NRMT	VG-E	GOOD
	COMPLETE SET (128)		2250.00	1100.00	250.00
	COMMON PLAYER (1-128)		6.00	3.00	.60
☐	1	Toe Blake	14.00	5.00	1.00
☐	2	Gump Worsley	15.00	7.50	1.50
☐	3	Jacques Laperriere	9.00	4.50	.90
☐	4	Jean Guy Talbot	6.00	3.00	.60
☐	5	Ted Harris	7.00	3.50	.70
☐	6	Jean Beliveau	27.00	13.50	2.70

			NRMT	VG-E	GOOD
☐	7	Dick Duff	6.00	3.00	.60
☐	8	Claude Provost	6.00	3.00	.60
☐	9	Red Berenson	7.00	3.50	.70
☐	10	John Ferguson	7.00	3.50	.70
☐	11	George Imlach	7.00	3.50	.70
☐	12	Terry Sawchuk	30.00	15.00	3.00
☐	13	Bob Baun	6.00	3.00	.60
☐	14	Kent Douglas	6.00	3.00	.60
☐	15	Red Kelly	11.00	5.50	1.10
☐	16	Jim Pappin	6.00	3.00	.60
☐	17	Dave Keon	10.00	5.00	1.00
☐	18	Bob Pulford	9.00	4.50	.90
☐	19	George Armstrong	9.00	4.50	.90
☐	20	Orland Kurtenbach	7.00	3.50	.70
☐	21	Ed Giacomin	75.00	37.50	7.50
☐	22	Harry Howell	9.00	4.50	.90
☐	23	Rod Seiling	6.00	3.00	.60
☐	24	Mike McMahon	6.00	3.00	.60
☐	25	Jean Ratelle	12.00	6.00	1.20
☐	26	Doug Robinson	6.00	3.00	.60
☐	27	Vic Hadfield	7.00	3.50	.70
☐	28	Garry Peters	6.00	3.00	.60
☐	29	Don Marshall	6.00	3.00	.60
☐	30	Bill Hicke	6.00	3.00	.60
☐	31	Gerry Cheevers	80.00	40.00	8.00
☐	32	Leo Boivin	9.00	4.50	.90
☐	33	Albert Langlois	6.00	3.00	.60
☐	34	Murray Oliver	6.00	3.00	.60
☐	35	Tom Williams	6.00	3.00	.60
☐	36	Ron Schock	6.00	3.00	.60
☐	37	Ed Westfall	7.00	3.50	.70
☐	38	Gary Dornhoefer	7.00	3.50	.70
☐	39	Bob Dillabough	6.00	3.00	.60
☐	40	Poul Popiel	6.00	3.00	.60
☐	41	Sid Abel	7.00	3.50	.70
☐	42	Roger Crozier	7.00	3.50	.70
☐	43	Doug Barkley	6.00	3.00	.60
☐	44	Bill Gadsby	9.00	4.50	.90
☐	45	Bryan Watson	6.00	3.00	.60
☐	46	Bob McCord	6.00	3.00	.60
☐	47	Alex Delvecchio	11.00	5.50	1.10
☐	48	Andy Bathgate	10.00	5.00	1.00
☐	49	Norm Ullman	10.00	5.00	1.00
☐	50	Ab McDonald	6.00	3.00	.60
☐	51	Paul Henderson	12.00	6.00	1.20
☐	52	Pit Martin	6.00	3.00	.60
☐	53	Billy Harris	6.00	3.00	.60
☐	54	Billy Reay CO	6.00	3.00	.60
☐	55	Glenn Hall	15.00	7.50	1.50
☐	56	Pierre Pilote	9.00	4.50	.90
☐	57	Al McNeil	6.00	3.00	.60
☐	58	Camille Henry	6.00	3.00	.60
☐	59	Bobby Hull	115.00	50.00	10.00

			NRMT	VG-E	GOOD
☐	60	Stan Mikita	30.00	15.00	3.00
☐	61	Ken Wharram	6.00	3.00	.60
☐	62	Bill Hay	6.00	3.00	.60
☐	63	Fred Stanfield	9.00	4.50	.90
☐	64	Dennis Hull	20.00	10.00	2.00
☐	65	Ken Hodge	20.00	10.00	2.00
☐	66	Checklist Card	85.00	10.00	2.00
☐	67	Charlie Hodge	7.00	3.50	.70
☐	68	Terry Harper	7.00	3.50	.70
☐	69	J.C. Tremblay	7.00	3.50	.70
☐	70	Bobby Rousseau	6.00	3.00	.60
☐	71	Henri Richard	12.50	6.25	1.25
☐	72	Dave Balon	6.00	3.00	.60
☐	73	Ralph Backstrom	6.00	3.00	.60
☐	74	Jim Roberts	6.00	3.00	.60
☐	75	Claude Larose	6.00	3.00	.60
☐	76	Yvan Cournoyer UER	75.00	37.50	7.50
☐	77	Johnny Bower	12.00	6.00	1.20
☐	78	Carl Brewer	6.00	3.00	.60
☐	79	Tim Horton	15.00	7.50	1.50
☐	80	Marcel Pronovost	9.00	4.50	.90
☐	81	Frank Mahovlich	22.00	11.00	2.20
☐	82	Ron Ellis	6.00	3.00	.60
☐	83	Larry Jeffrey	6.00	3.00	.60
☐	84	Pete Stemkowski	6.00	3.00	.60
☐	85	Eddie Joyal	6.00	3.00	.60
☐	86	Mike Walton	8.00	4.00	.80
☐	87	George Sullivan	6.00	3.00	.60
☐	88	Don Simmons	6.00	3.00	.60
☐	89	Jim Neilson	6.00	3.00	.60
☐	90	Arnie Brown	6.00	3.00	.60
☐	91	Rod Gilbert	12.00	6.00	1.20
☐	92	Phil Goyette	6.00	3.00	.60
☐	93	Bob Nevin	6.00	3.00	.60
☐	94	John McKenzie	6.00	3.00	.60
☐	95	Ted Taylor	6.00	3.00	.60
☐	96	Milt Schmidt	9.00	4.50	.90
☐	97	Ed Johnston	8.00	4.00	.80
☐	98	Ted Green	7.00	3.50	.70
☐	99	Don Awrey	6.00	3.00	.60
☐	100	Bob Woytowich	6.00	3.00	.60
☐	101	Johnny Bucyk	15.00	7.50	1.50
☐	102	Dean Prentice	8.00	4.00	.80
☐	103	Ron Stewart	6.00	3.00	.60
☐	104	Reg Fleming	6.00	3.00	.60
☐	105	Parker MacDonald	6.00	3.00	.60
☐	106	Hank Bassen	6.00	3.00	.60
☐	107	Gary Bergman	6.00	3.00	.60
☐	108	Gordie Howe	125.00	60.00	12.50
☐	109	Floyd Smith	6.00	3.00	.60
☐	110	Bruce MacGregor	6.00	3.00	.60
☐	111	Ron Murphy	6.00	3.00	.60
☐	112	Don McKenney	6.00	3.00	.60

		NRMT	VG-E	GOOD
☐ 113	Denis DeJordy	7.00	3.50	.70
☐ 114	Elmer Vasko	6.00	3.00	.60
☐ 115	Matt Ravlich	6.00	3.00	.60
☐ 116	Phil Esposito	500.00	250.00	50.00
☐ 117	Chico Maki	6.00	3.00	.60
☐ 118	Doug Mohns	7.00	3.50	.70
☐ 119	Eric Nesterenko	7.00	3.50	.70
☐ 120	Pat Stapleton	7.00	3.50	.70
☐ 121	Checklist Card	85.00	10.00	2.00
☐ 122	Gordie Howe SP	175.00	85.00	18.00
	(600 Goals)			
☐ 123	Toronto Maple Leafs	36.00	18.00	3.60
	Team Card SP			
☐ 124	Chicago Blackhawks	36.00	18.00	3.60
	Team Card SP			
☐ 125	Detroit Red Wings	36.00	18.00	3.60
	Team Card SP			
☐ 126	Montreal Canadiens	36.00	18.00	3.60
	Team Card SP			
☐ 127	New York Rangers	36.00	18.00	3.60
	Team Card SP			
☐ 128	Boston Bruins	90.00	20.00	4.00
	Team Card SP			

1966-67 Topps

The 1966-67 Topps set features 132 cards in full color of all teams in the NHL. The cards in the set measure 2½" by 3½". The front features a distinctive wood grain border with a television screen look. The backs, printed in both French and English, feature the card number, a short biography, and the player's complete NHL record. The cards were printed in Canada. The key card in the set is Bobby Orr's first card.

Le jeu Topps 1966-67 contient 132 cartes en couleurs de toutes les équipes de la NHL. Les cartes de ce jeu mesurent 2¹/₂" x 3¹/₂". Le bord entourant la face, imitant le bois, encadre une surface ressemblant à un écran de télévision. Le dos, imprimé en français et en anglais, comporte le numéro de carte, une biographie concise, et la fiche NHL complète du joueur. Les cartes ont été imprimées au Canada. La première carte de Bobby Orr est la carte importante de ce jeu.

			NRMT	VG-E	GOOD
		COMPLETE SET (132)	2700.00	1250.00	350.00
		COMMON PLAYER (1-132)	5.00	2.50	.50
☐	1	Toe Blake	14.00	4.00	.80
☐	2	Gump Worsley	15.00	7.50	1.50
☐	3	Jean Guy Talbot	5.00	2.50	.50
☐	4	Gilles Tremblay	5.00	2.50	.50
☐	5	J.C. Tremblay	6.00	3.00	.60
☐	6	Jim Roberts	5.00	2.50	.50
☐	7	Bobby Rousseau	5.00	2.50	.50
☐	8	Henri Richard	13.50	6.50	1.25
☐	9	Claude Provost	5.00	2.50	.50
☐	10	Claude Larose	5.00	2.50	.50
☐	11	George Imlach	6.00	3.00	.60
☐	12	Johnny Bower	12.00	6.00	1.20
☐	13	Terry Sawchuk	30.00	15.00	3.00
☐	14	Mike Walton	6.00	3.00	.60
☐	15	Pete Stemkowski	5.00	2.50	.50
☐	16	Allan Stanley	7.50	3.75	.75
☐	17	Eddie Shack	6.00	3.00	.60
☐	18	Brit Selby	5.00	2.50	.50
☐	19	Bob Pulford	7.50	3.75	.75
☐	20	Marcel Pronovost	7.50	3.75	.75
☐	21	Emile Francis	10.00	5.00	1.00
☐	22	Rod Seiling	5.00	2.50	.50
☐	23	Ed Giacomin	18.00	9.00	1.80
☐	24	Don Marshall	5.00	2.50	.50
☐	25	Orland Kurtenbach	6.00	3.00	.60
☐	26	Rod Gilbert	11.00	5.50	1.10
☐	27	Bob Nevin	5.00	2.50	.50
☐	28	Phil Goyette	5.00	2.50	.50
☐	29	Jean Ratelle	11.00	5.50	1.10
☐	30	Earl Ingarfield	5.00	2.50	.50
☐	31	Harry Sinden	11.00	5.50	1.10
☐	32	Ed Westfall	6.00	3.00	.60
☐	33	Joe Watson	6.00	3.00	.60
☐	34	Bob Woytowich	5.00	2.50	.50
☐	35	Bobby Orr	1500.00	750.00	150.00
☐	36	Gilles Marotte	7.50	3.75	.75
☐	37	Ted Green	6.00	3.00	.60
☐	38	Tom Williams	5.00	2.50	.50
☐	39	Johnny Bucyk	13.50	6.50	1.20
☐	40	Wayne Connelly	5.00	2.50	.50
☐	41	Pit Martin	5.00	2.50	.50
☐	42	Sid Abel	6.00	3.00	.60

			NRMT	VG-E	GOOD
☐	43	Roger Crozier	6.00	3.00	.60
●	44	Andy Bathgate	7.50	3.75	.75
☐	45	Dean Prentice	6.00	3.00	.60
☐	46	Paul Henderson	6.00	3.00	.60
☐	47	Gary Bergman	5.00	2.50	.50
☐	48	Bryan Watson	5.00	2.50	.50
☐	49	Bob Wall	5.00	2.50	.50
☐	50	Leo Boivin	7.50	3.75	.75
☐	51	Bert Marshall	5.00	2.50	.50
☐	52	Norm Ullman	8.50	4.25	.85
☐	53	Billy Reay CO	5.00	2.50	.50
●	54	Glenn Hall	13.50	6.50	1.20
☐	55	Wally Boyer	5.00	2.50	.50
☐	56	Fred Stanfield	5.00	2.50	.50
☐	57	Pat Stapleton	6.00	3.00	.60
☐	58	Matt Ravlich	5.00	2.50	.50
☐	59	Pierre Pilote	7.50	3.75	.75
☐	60	Eric Nesterenko	6.00	3.00	.60
☐	61	Doug Mohns	6.00	3.00	.60
●	62	Stan Mikita	27.00	13.50	2.70
●	63	Phil Esposito	150.00	75.00	15.00
●	64	Leading Scorer	40.00	20.00	4.00
		(Bobby Hull)			
☐	65	Vezina Trophy	8.50	4.25	.85
		(Charlie Hodge/			
		Gump Worsley)			
☐	66	Checklist Card	85.00	10.00	2.00
☐	67	Jacques Laperriere	7.50	3.75	.75
☐	68	Terry Harper	6.00	3.00	.60
☐	69	Ted Harris	6.00	3.00	.60
☐	70	John Ferguson	6.00	3.00	.60
☐	71	Dick Duff	5.00	2.50	.50
●	72	Yvan Cournoyer	20.00	10.00	2.00
☐	73	Jean Beliveau	21.00	10.50	2.10
☐	74	Dave Balon	5.00	2.50	.50
☐	75	Ralph Backstrom	5.00	2.50	.50
☐	76	Jim Pappin	5.00	2.50	.50
☐	77	Frank Mahovlich	18.00	9.00	1.80
☐	78	Dave Keon	10.00	5.00	1.00
☐	79	Red Kelly	10.00	5.00	1.00
☐	80	Tim Horton	12.00	6.00	1.20
☐	81	Ron Ellis	5.00	2.50	.50
☐	82	Kent Douglas	5.00	2.50	.50
☐	83	Bob Baun	5.00	2.50	.50
☐	84	George Armstrong	7.50	3.75	.75
●	85	Boom Boom Geoffrion	18.00	9.00	1.80
☐	86	Vic Hadfield	6.00	3.00	.60
☐	87	Wayne Hillman	5.00	2.50	.50
☐	88	Jim Neilson	5.00	2.50	.50
☐	89	Al McNeil	5.00	2.50	.50
☐	90	Arnie Brown	5.00	2.50	.50
☐	91	Harry Howell	7.50	3.75	.75
☐	92	Red Berenson	6.00	3.00	.60

		NRMT	VG-E	GOOD
☐ 93	Reg Fleming	5.00	2.50	.50
☐ 94	Ron Stewart	5.00	2.50	.50
☐ 95	Murray Oliver	5.00	2.50	.50
☐ 96	Ron Murphy	5.00	2.50	.50
☐ 97	John McKenzie	5.00	2.50	.50
☐ 98	Bob Dillabough	5.00	2.50	.50
☐ 99	Ed Johnston	6.00	3.00	.60
☐ 100	Ron Schock	5.00	2.50	.50
☐ 101	Dallas Smith	6.00	3.00	.60
☐ 102	Alex Delvecchio	10.00	5.00	1.00
☐ 103	Peter Mahovlich	10.00	5.00	1.00
☐ 104	Bruce MacGregor	5.00	2.50	.50
☐ 105	Murray Hall	5.00	2.50	.50
☐ 106	Floyd Smith	5.00	2.50	.50
☐ 107	Hank Bassen	5.00	2.50	.50
☐ 108	Val Fonteyne	5.00	2.50	.50
☐ 109	Gordie Howe	125.00	60.00	12.50
☐ 110	Chico Maki	5.00	2.50	.50
☐ 111	Doug Jarrett	5.00	2.50	.50
☐ 112	Bobby Hull	100.00	50.00	10.00
☐ 113	Dennis Hull	9.00	4.50	.90
☐ 114	Ken Hodge	9.00	4.50	.90
☐ 115	Denis DeJordy	6.00	3.00	.60
☐ 116	Lou Angotti	5.00	2.50	.50
☐ 117	Ken Wharram	5.00	2.50	.50
☐ 118	Montreal Canadiens Team Card	13.50	6.50	1.20
☐ 119	Detroit Red Wings Team Card	13.50	6.50	1.20
☐ 120	Checklist Card	85.00	10.00	2.00
☐ 121	Gordie Howe AS	70.00	35.00	7.00
☐ 122	Jacques Laperriere AS	6.50	3.25	.65
☐ 123	Pierre Pilote AS	6.50	3.25	.65
☐ 124	Stan Mikita AS	18.00	9.00	1.80
☐ 125	Bobby Hull AS	55.00	27.50	5.50
☐ 126	Glenn Hall AS	10.00	5.00	1.00
☐ 127	Jean Beliveau AS	15.00	7.50	1.50
☐ 128	Allan Stanley AS	6.50	3.25	.65
☐ 129	Pat Stapleton AS	6.00	3.00	.60
☐ 130	Gump Worsley AS	10.00	5.00	1.00
☐ 131	Frank Mahovlich AS	13.50	6.50	1.20
☐ 132	Bobby Rousseau AS	12.00	3.50	.70

1967-68 Topps

The 1967-68 Topps set features 132 color cards portraying players from the six original NHL teams. Players on the six expansion teams (Los Angeles, Minnesota, Oakland, Philadelphia, Pittsburgh, and St. Louis) were not included in this set. Cards are 2½" by 3½". The backs, in both French and English, feature the card number, a short biography, and complete NHL records. The backs are identical in format to the 1966-67 cards. The cards were printed in Canada. The key rookie cards in this set are Jacques Lemaire, Derek Sanderson, Glen Sather, and Rogatien Vachon.

Le jeu Topps 1967-68 contient 132 cartes en couleurs. représentant des joueurs des six équipes originales de la NHL. Les joueurs des six équipes d'expansion (Los Angeles, Minnesota, Oakland, Philadelphia, Pittsburgh, et St. Louis) n'ont pas été inclus dans ce jeu. Les cartes mesurent 2½" x 3½". Le dos, imprimé en français et en anglais, comporte le numéro de carte, une biographie concise, et les statistiques NHL complets. Le format du dos est identique àcelui des cartes de 1966-67. Les cartes ont été imprimées au Canada. Les débutants importants de ce jeu sont Jacques Lemaire, Derek Sanderson, Glen Sather, et Rogatien Vachon.

			NRMT	VG-E	GOOD
		COMPLETE SET (132)	1800.00	900.00	200.00
		COMMON PLAYER (1-132)	5.00	2.50	.50
☐	1	Gump Worsley	20.00	6.50	1.30
☐	2	Dick Duff	5.00	2.50	.50
☐	3	Jacques Lemaire	28.00	14.00	2.80
☐	4	Claude Larose	5.00	2.50	.50
☐	5	Gilles Tremblay	5.00	2.50	.50
☐	6	Terry Harper	6.00	3.00	.60
☐	7	Jacques Laperriere	7.50	3.75	.75
☐	8	Garry Monahan	5.00	2.50	.50
☐	9	Carol Vadnais	7.50	3.75	.75

			NRMT	VG-E	GOOD
☐	10	Ted Harris	5.00	2.50	.50
☐	11	Dave Keon	8.50	4.25	.85
☐	12	Pete Stemkowski	5.00	2.50	.50
☐	13	Allan Stanley	7.50	3.75	.75
☐	14	Ron Ellis	5.00	2.50	.50
☐	15	Mike Walton	6.00	3.00	.60
☐	16	Tim Horton	12.00	6.00	1.20
☐	17	Brian Conacher	5.00	2.50	.50
☐	18	Bruce Gamble	5.00	2.50	.50
☐	19	Bob Pulford	7.50	3.75	.75
☐	20	Duane Rupp	5.00	2.50	.50
☐	21	Larry Jeffrey	5.00	2.50	.50
☐	22	Wayne Hillman	5.00	2.50	.50
☐	23	Don Marshall	5.00	2.50	.50
☐	24	Red Berenson	6.00	3.00	.60
☐	25	Phil Goyette	5.00	2.50	.50
☐	26	Camille Henry	5.00	2.50	.50
☐	27	Rod Seiling	5.00	2.50	.50
☐	28	Bob Nevin	5.00	2.50	.50
☐	29	Boom Boom Geoffrion	15.00	7.50	1.50
☐	30	Reg Fleming	5.00	2.50	.50
☐	31	Jean Ratelle	9.00	4.50	.90
☐	32	Phil Esposito	75.00	37.50	7.50
☐	33	Derek Sanderson	12.00	6.00	1.20
☐	34	Eddie Shack	6.00	3.00	.60
☐	35	Ross Lonsberry	7.00	3.50	.70
☐	36	Fred Stanfield	5.00	2.50	.50
☐	37	Don Awrey UER (Photo actually Skip Krake)	5.00	2.50	.50
☐	38	Glen Sather	15.00	7.50	1.50
☐	39	John McKenzie	5.00	2.50	.50
☐	40	Tom Williams	5.00	2.50	.50
☐	41	Dallas Smith	5.00	2.50	.50
☐	42	Johnny Bucyk	11.00	5.50	1.10
☐	43	Gordie Howe	100.00	50.00	10.00
☐	44	Gary Jarrett	5.00	2.50	.50
☐	45	Dean Prentice	6.00	3.00	.60
☐	46	Bert Marshall	5.00	2.50	.50
☐	47	Gary Bergman	5.00	2.50	.50
☐	48	Roger Crozier	6.00	3.00	.60
☐	49	Howie Young	5.00	2.50	.50
☐	50	Doug Roberts	5.00	2.50	.50
☐	51	Alex Delvecchio	10.00	5.00	1.00
☐	52	Floyd Smith	5.00	2.50	.50
☐	53	Doug Shelton	5.00	2.50	.50
☐	54	Gerry Goyer	5.00	2.50	.50
☐	55	Wayne Maki	5.00	2.50	.50
☐	56	Dennis Hull	6.00	3.00	.60
☐	57	Dave Dryden	8.50	4.25	.85
☐	58	Paul Terbenche	5.00	2.50	.50
☐	59	Gilles Marotte	6.00	3.00	.60
☐	60	Eric Nesterenko	6.00	3.00	.60

			NRMT	VG-E	GOOD
☐	61	Pat Stapleton	6.00	3.00	.60
☐	62	Pierre Pilote	7.50	3.75	.75
☐	63	Doug Mohns	6.00	3.00	.60
☐	64	Triple Winner (Stan Mikita)	16.00	8.00	1.60
☐	65	Vezina Trophy (Glenn Hall/ Denis DeJordy)	8.00	4.00	.80
☐	66	Checklist Card	85.00	10.00	2.00
☐	67	Ralph Backstrom	5.00	2.50	.50
☐	68	Bobby Rousseau	5.00	2.50	.50
☐	69	John Ferguson	6.00	3.00	.60
☐	70	Yvan Cournoyer	15.00	7.50	1.50
☐	71	Claude Provost	5.00	2.50	.50
☐	72	Henri Richard	10.00	5.00	1.00
☐	73	J.C. Tremblay	6.00	3.00	.60
☐	74	Jean Beliveau	20.00	10.00	2.00
☐	75	Rogatien Vachon	28.00	14.00	2.80
☐	76	Johnny Bower	11.00	5.50	1.10
☐	77	Wayne Carleton	5.00	2.50	.50
☐	78	Jim Pappin	5.00	2.50	.50
☐	79	Frank Mahovlich	18.00	9.00	1.80
☐	80	Larry Hillman	5.00	2.50	.50
☐	81	Marcel Pronovost	7.50	3.75	.75
☐	82	Murray Oliver	5.00	2.50	.50
☐	83	George Armstrong	7.50	3.75	.75
☐	84	Harry Howell	7.50	3.75	.75
☐	85	Ed Giacomin	12.00	6.00	1.20
☐	86	Gilles Villemure	6.00	3.00	.60
☐	87	Orland Kurtenbach	6.00	3.00	.60
☐	88	Vic Hadfield	6.00	3.00	.60
☐	89	Arnie Brown	5.00	2.50	.50
☐	90	Rod Gilbert	9.00	4.50	.90
☐	91	Jim Neilson	5.00	2.50	.50
☐	92	Bobby Orr	375.00	175.00	37.00
☐	93	Skip Krake	5.00	2.50	.50
☐	94	Ted Green	6.00	3.00	.60
☐	95	Ed Westfall	6.00	3.00	.60
☐	96	Ed Johnston	6.00	3.00	.60
☐	97	Gary Doak	7.00	3.50	.70
☐	98	Ken Hodge	6.00	3.00	.60
☐	99	Gerry Cheevers	16.00	8.00	1.60
☐	100	Ron Murphy	5.00	2.50	.50
☐	101	Norm Ullman	7.50	3.75	.75
☐	102	Bruce MacGregor	5.00	2.50	.50
☐	103	Paul Henderson	6.00	3.00	.60
☐	104	Jean Guy Talbot	5.00	2.50	.50
☐	105	Bart Crashley	5.00	2.50	.50
☐	106	Roy Edwards	5.00	2.50	.50
☐	107	Jim Watson	5.00	2.50	.50
☐	108	Ted Hampson	5.00	2.50	.50
☐	109	Bill Orban	5.00	2.50	.50
☐	110	Geoffrey Powis	5.00	2.50	.50

		NRMT	VG-E	GOOD
☐ 111	**Chico Maki**	5.00	2.50	.50
☐ 112	**Doug Jarrett**	5.00	2.50	.50
☐ 113	**Bobby Hull** *$125*	75.00	37.50	7.50
☐ 114	**Stan Mikita**	25.00	12.50	2.50
☐ 115	**Denis DeJordy**	6.00	3.00	.60
☐ 116	**Pit Martin**	5.00	2.50	.50
☐ 117	**Ken Wharram**	5.00	2.50	.50
☐ 118	**Calder Trophy**	165.00	75.00	15.00
	(Bobby Orr) *$275*			
☐ 119	**Norris Trophy**	6.50	3.25	.65
	(Harry Howell)			
☐ 120	**Checklist Card**	85.00	10.00	2.00
☐ 121	**Harry Howell AS**	6.50	3.25	.65
☐ 122	**Pierre Pilote AS**	6.50	3.25	.65
☐ 123	**Ed Giacomin AS**	7.50	3.75	.75
☐ 124	**Bobby Hull AS** *65.00*	40.00	20.00	4.00
☐ 125	**Ken Wharram AS**	6.00	3.00	.60
☐ 126	**Stan Mikita AS** *18.00*	15.00	7.50	1.50
☐ 127	**Tim Horton AS**	7.50	3.75	.75
☐ 128	**Bobby Orr AS** *$275*	165.00	75.00	15.00
☐ 129	**Glenn Hall AS**	9.00	4.50	.90
☐ 130	**Don Marshall AS**	6.00	3.00	.60
☐ 131	**Gordie Howe AS**	60.00	30.00	6.00
☐ 132	**Norm Ullman AS**	14.00	5.00	1.00

1968-69 Topps

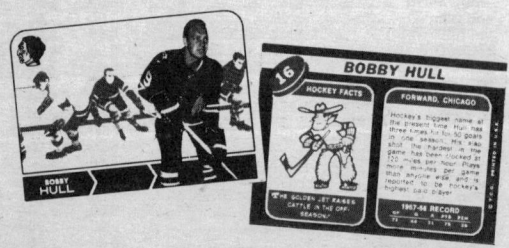

The 1968-69 Topps set consists of 132 color cards featuring players on each of the twelve NHL teams. Cards are 2½" by 3½". The front features a horizontal format with the player in the foreground and a washed-out hockey scene in the background. The backs, in English only, feature the card number, a short biography of the player, his

1967-68 record, and a hockey facts cartoon section. The cards were printed in the USA. The key rookie card in this set is Bernie Parent.

Le jeu Topps 1968-69 contient 132 cartes en couleurs, représentant des joueurs de chacune des douze équipes de la NHL. Les cartes mesurent 2¹/₂" x 3¹/₂". La face est orientée horizontalement, avec le joueur à l'avant-plan, et une scène de hockey en flou à l'arrière-plan. Le dos, imprimé en anglais seulement, comporte le numéro de carte, une biographie concise du joueur, sa fiche pour 1967-68, et une section illustrant un fait notable. Les cartes ont été imprimées aux Etats-Unis. Bernie Parent est le débutant important de ce jeu.

			NRMT	VG-E	GOOD
		COMPLETE SET (132)	500.00	250.00	50.00
		COMMON PLAYER (1-132)	1.25	.60	.12
☐	1	Gerry Cheevers	15.00	5.00	1.00
☐	2	Bobby Orr	135.00	65.00	13.50
☐	3	Don Awrey UER	1.25	.60	.12
		(Photo actually Skip Krake)			
☐	4	Ted Green	2.00	1.00	.20
☐	5	Johnny Bucyk	7.00	3.50	.70
☐	6	Derek Sanderson	2.50	1.25	.25
☐	7	Phil Esposito	35.00	17.50	3.50
☐	8	Ken Hodge	2.50	1.25	.25
☐	9	John McKenzie	1.25	.60	.12
☐	10	Fred Stanfield	1.25	.60	.12
☐	11	Tom Williams	1.25	.60	.12
☐	12	Denis DeJordy	2.00	1.00	.20
☐	13	Doug Jarrett	1.25	.60	.12
☐	14	Gilles Marotte	2.00	1.00	.20
☐	15	Pat Stapleton	2.00	1.00	.20
☐	16	Bobby Hull	50.00	25.00	5.00
☐	17	Chico Maki	1.25	.60	.12
☐	18	Pit Martin	1.25	.60	.12
☐	19	Doug Mohns	2.00	1.00	.20
☐	20	Stan Mikita	12.50	6.25	1.25
☐	21	Jim Pappin	1.25	.60	.12
☐	22	Ken Wharram	1.25	.60	.12
☐	23	Roger Crozier	2.00	1.00	.20
☐	24	Bob Baun	1.25	.60	.12
☐	25	Gary Bergman	1.25	.60	.12
☐	26	Kent Douglas	1.25	.60	.12
☐	27	Ron Harris	1.25	.60	.12
☐	28	Alex Delvecchio	7.00	3.50	.70
☐	29	Gordie Howe	55.00	27.50	5.50
☐	30	Bruce MacGregor	1.25	.60	.12
☐	31	Frank Mahovlich	12.00	6.00	1.20
☐	32	Dean Prentice	2.50	1.25	.25
☐	33	Pete Stemkowski	1.25	.60	.12
☐	34	Terry Sawchuk	20.00	10.00	2.00
☐	35	Larry Cahan	1.25	.60	.12
☐	36	Real Lemieux	1.25	.60	.12
☐	37	Bill White	3.00	1.50	.30

		NRMT	VG-E	GOOD
☐ 38	Gord Labossiere	1.25	.60	.12
☐ 39	Ted Irvine	1.25	.60	.12
☐ 40	Eddie Joyal	1.25	.60	.12
☐ 41	Dale Rolfe	1.25	.60	.12
☐ 42	Lowell MacDonald	2.00	1.00	.20
☐ 43	Skip Krake UER	1.25	.60	.12
	(Photo actually Don Awrey)			
☐ 44	Terry Gray	1.25	.60	.12
☐ 45	Cesare Maniago	2.00	1.00	.20
☐ 46	Mike McMahon	1.25	.60	.12
☐ 47	Wayne Hillman	1.25	.60	.12
☐ 48	Larry Hillman	1.25	.60	.12
☐ 49	Bob Woytowich	1.25	.60	.12
☐ 50	Wayne Connelly	1.25	.60	.12
☐ 51	Claude Larose	1.25	.60	.12
☐ 52	Danny Grant	2.00	1.00	.20
☐ 53	Andre Boudrias	1.25	.60	.12
☐ 54	Ray Cullen	1.25	.60	.12
☐ 55	Parker MacDonald	1.25	.60	.12
☐ 56	Gump Worsley	6.50	3.25	.65
☐ 57	Terry Harper	2.00	1.00	.20
☐ 58	Jacques Laperriere	3.00	1.50	.30
☐ 59	J.C. Tremblay	2.00	1.00	.20
☐ 60	Ralph Backstrom	1.25	.60	.12
☐ 61	Jean Beliveau	12.00	6.00	1.20
☐ 62	Yvan Cournoyer	6.00	3.00	.60
☐ 63	Jacques Lemaire	6.00	3.00	.60
☐ 64	Henri Richard	6.50	3.25	.65
☐ 65	Bobby Rousseau	1.25	.60	.12
☐ 66	Gilles Tremblay	1.25	.60	.12
☐ 67	Ed Giacomin	5.50	2.75	.55
☐ 68	Arnie Brown	1.25	.60	.12
☐ 69	Harry Howell	4.00	2.00	.40
☐ 70	Jim Neilson	1.25	.60	.12
☐ 71	Rod Seiling	1.25	.60	.12
☐ 72	Rod Gilbert	6.50	3.25	.65
☐ 73	Phil Goyette	1.25	.60	.12
☐ 74	Vic Hadfield	2.00	1.00	.20
☐ 75	Don Marshall	1.25	.60	.12
☐ 76	Bob Nevin	1.25	.60	.12
☐ 77	Jean Ratelle	6.50	3.25	.65
☐ 78	Charlie Hodge	2.00	1.00	.20
☐ 79	Bert Marshall	1.25	.60	.12
☐ 80	Billy Harris	1.25	.60	.12
☐ 81	Carol Vadnais	1.25	.60	.12
☐ 82	Howie Young	1.25	.60	.12
☐ 83	John Brenneman	1.25	.60	.12
☐ 84	Gerry Ehman	1.25	.60	.12
☐ 85	Ted Hampson	1.25	.60	.12
☐ 86	Bill Hicke	1.25	.60	.12
☐ 87	Gary Jarrett	1.25	.60	.12
☐ 88	Doug Roberts	1.25	.60	.12
☐ 89	Bernie Parent	70.00	35.00	7.00

		NRMT	VG-E	GOOD
☐ 90	Joe Watson	1.25	.60	.12
☐ 91	Ed Van Impe	1.25	.60	.12
☐ 92	Larry Zeidel	1.25	.60	.12
☐ 93	John Miszuk	1.25	.60	.12
☐ 94	Gary Dornhoefer	2.00	1.00	.20
☐ 95	Leon Rochefort	1.25	.60	.12
☐ 96	Brit Selby	1.25	.60	.12
☐ 97	Forbes Kennedy	1.25	.60	.12
☐ 98	Ed Hoekstra	1.25	.60	.12
☐ 99	Garry Peters	1.25	.60	.12
☐ 100	Les Binkley	3.00	1.50	.30
☐ 101	Leo Boivin	3.25	1.60	.32
☐ 102	Earl Ingarfield	1.25	.60	.12
☐ 103	Lou Angotti	1.25	.60	.12
☐ 104	Andy Bathgate	3.50	1.75	.35
☐ 105	Wally Boyer	1.25	.60	.12
☐ 106	Ken Schinkel	1.25	.60	.12
☐ 107	Ab McDonald	1.25	.60	.12
☐ 108	Charlie Burns	1.25	.60	.12
☐ 109	Val Fonteyne	1.25	.60	.12
☐ 110	Noel Price	1.25	.60	.12
☐ 111	Glenn Hall	7.00	3.50	.70
☐ 112	Bob Plager	2.50	1.25	.25
☐ 113	Jim Roberts	1.25	.60	.12
☐ 114	Red Berenson	2.00	1.00	.20
☐ 115	Larry Keenan	1.25	.60	.12
☐ 116	Camille Henry	1.25	.60	.12
☐ 117	Gary Sabourin	1.25	.60	.12
☐ 118	Ron Schock	1.25	.60	.12
☐ 119	Gary Veneruzzo	1.25	.60	.12
☐ 120	Gerry Melnyk	1.25	.60	.12
☐ 121	Checklist Card	30.00	3.00	.60
☐ 122	Johnny Bower	6.00	3.00	.60
☐ 123	Tim Horton	6.50	3.25	.65
☐ 124	Pierre Pilote	3.00	1.50	.30
☐ 125	Marcel Pronovost	3.00	1.50	.30
☐ 126	Ron Ellis	1.25	.60	.12
☐ 127	Paul Henderson	2.00	1.00	.20
☐ 128	Dave Keon	4.50	2.25	.45
☐ 129	Bob Pulford	3.00	1.50	.30
☐ 130	Floyd Smith	1.25	.60	.12
☐ 131	Norm Ullman	4.50	2.25	.45
☐ 132	Mike Walton	5.00	1.00	.20

1969-70 Topps

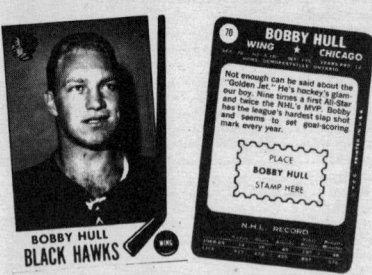

The 1969-70 Topps set consists of 132 color cards. Cards are 2½" by 3½". The backs, in English only, contain the card number, the player's NHL record, a short biography, and a cartoon-illustrated fact about the player. The cards were printed in the USA. Those players in this set who were also included in the insert of stamps have a place on the card back for placing that player's stamp; this is not recommended. The only notable rookie card in the set is Serge Savard.

Le jeu Topps 1969-70 contient 132 cartes en couleurs, mesurant 2½" x 3½". Le dos, imprimé uniquement en anglais, comporte le numéro de carte, la fiche NHL du joueur, une biographie concise, et une caricature d'un fait notable concernant le joueur. Les cartes ont été imprimées aux Etats-Unis. Les cartes des joueurs, dont le nom fut inclus dans le supplément de timbres, ont un endroit au dos pour y placer le timbre; ceci n'est pas recommandé. Le seul débutant important de ce jeu est Serge Savard.

			NRMT	VG-E	GOOD
	COMPLETE SET (132)		400.00	200.00	40.00
	COMMON PLAYER (1-132)		1.00	.50	.10
☐	1	Gump Worsley	13.50	5.00	1.00
☐	2	Ted Harris	1.00	.50	.10
☐	3	Jacques Laperriere	3.00	1.50	.30
☐	4	Serge Savard	25.00	12.50	2.50
☐	5	J.C. Tremblay	1.50	.75	.15
☐	6	Yvan Cournoyer	5.00	2.50	.50
☐	7	John Ferguson	1.50	.75	.15
☐	8	Jacques Lemaire	4.00	2.00	.40
☐	9	Bobby Rousseau	1.00	.50	.10
☐	10	Jean Beliveau	10.00	5.00	1.00
☐	11	Henri Richard	5.50	2.75	.55
☐	12	Glenn Hall	6.00	3.00	.60

			NRMT	VG-E	GOOD
☐	13	Bob Plager	1.50	.75	.15
☐	14	Jim Roberts	1.00	.50	.10
☐	15	Jean Guy Talbot	1.00	.50	.10
☐	16	Andre Boudrias	1.00	.50	.10
☐	17	Camille Henry	1.00	.50	.10
☐	18	Ab McDonald	1.00	.50	.10
☐	19	Gary Sabourin	1.00	.50	.10
☐	20	Red Berenson	1.50	.75	.15
☐	21	Phil Goyette	1.00	.50	.10
☐	22	Gerry Cheevers	5.00	2.50	.50
☐	23	Ted Green	1.50	.75	.15
☐	24	Bobby Orr	75.00	37.50	7.50
☐	25	Dallas Smith	1.50	.75	.15
☐	26	Johnny Bucyk	6.00	3.00	.60
☐	27	Ken Hodge	2.00	1.00	.20
☐	28	John McKenzie	1.00	.50	.10
☐	29	Ed Westfall	1.50	.75	.15
☐	30	Phil Esposito	21.00	10.50	2.10
☐	31	Derek Sanderson	1.50	.75	.15
☐	32	Fred Stanfield	1.00	.50	.10
☐	33	Ed Giacomin	4.25	2.10	.42
☐	34	Arnie Brown	1.00	.50	.10
☐	35	Jim Neilson	1.00	.50	.10
☐	36	Rod Seiling	1.00	.50	.10
☐	37	Rod Gilbert	5.00	2.50	.50
☐	38	Vic Hadfield	1.50	.75	.15
☐	39	Don Marshall	1.00	.50	.10
☐	40	Bob Nevin	1.00	.50	.10
☐	41	Ron Stewart	1.00	.50	.10
☐	42	Jean Ratelle	4.50	2.25	.45
☐	43	Walt Tkaczuk	5.00	2.50	.50
☐	44	Bruce Gamble	1.00	.50	.10
☐	45	Tim Horton	4.50	2.25	.45
☐	46	Ron Ellis	1.00	.50	.10
☐	47	Paul Henderson	1.50	.75	.15
☐	48	Brit Selby	1.00	.50	.10
☐	49	Floyd Smith	1.00	.50	.10
☐	50	Mike Walton	1.50	.75	.15
☐	51	Dave Keon	3.75	1.85	.37
☐	52	Murray Oliver	1.00	.50	.10
☐	53	Bob Pulford	2.75	1.35	.27
☐	54	Norm Ullman	4.00	2.00	.40
☐	55	Roger Crozier	1.50	.75	.15
☐	56	Roy Edwards	1.00	.50	.10
☐	57	Bob Baun	1.00	.50	.10
☐	58	Gary Bergman	1.00	.50	.10
☐	59	Carl Brewer	1.00	.50	.10
☐	60	Wayne Connelly	1.00	.50	.10
☐	61	Gordie Howe	50.00	25.00	5.00
☐	62	Frank Mahovlich	8.50	4.25	.85
☐	63	Bruce MacGregor	1.00	.50	.10
☐	64	Alex Delvecchio	5.50	2.75	.55
☐	65	Pete Stemkowski	1.00	.50	.10

			NRMT	VG-E	GOOD
☐	66	Denis DeJordy	1.50	.75	.15
☐	67	Doug Jarrett	1.00	.50	.10
☐	68	Gilles Marotte	1.50	.75	.15
☐	69	Pat Stapleton	1.50	.75	.15
☐	70	Bobby Hull	33.00	15.00	3.00
☐	71	Dennis Hull	2.00	1.00	.20
☐	72	Doug Mohns	1.00	.50	.10
☐	73	Jim Pappin	1.00	.50	.10
☐	74	Ken Wharram	1.00	.50	.10
☐	75	Pit Martin	1.00	.50	.10
☐	76	Stan Mikita	11.00	5.50	1.10
☐	77	Charlie Hodge	1.50	.75	.15
☐	78	Gary Smith	1.00	.50	.10
☐	79	Harry Howell	3.00	1.50	.30
☐	80	Bert Marshall	1.00	.50	.10
☐	81	Doug Roberts	1.00	.50	.10
☐	82	Carol Vadnais	1.00	.50	.10
☐	83	Gerry Ehman	1.00	.50	.10
☐	84	Bill Hicke	1.00	.50	.10
☐	85	Gary Jarrett	1.00	.50	.10
☐	86	Ted Hampson	1.00	.50	.10
☐	87	Earl Ingarfield	1.00	.50	.10
☐	88	Doug Favell	2.50	1.25	.25
☐	89	Bernie Parent	13.50	6.50	1.20
☐	90	Larry Hillman	1.00	.50	.10
☐	91	Wayne Hillman	.00	.50	.10
☐	92	Ed Van Impe	1.00	.50	.10
☐	93	Joe Watson	1.00	.50	.10
☐	94	Gary Dornhoefer	1.50	.75	.15
☐	95	Reg Fleming	1.00	.50	.10
☐	96	Jean Guy Gendron	1.00	.50	.10
☐	97	Jim Johnson	1.00	.50	.10
☐	98	Andre Lacroix	1.00	.50	.10
☐	99	Gerry Desjardins	2.50	1.25	.25
☐	100	Dale Rolfe	1.00	.50	.10
☐	101	Bill White	1.00	.50	.10
☐	102	Bill Flett	1.00	.50	.10
☐	103	Ted Irvine	1.00	.50	.10
☐	104	Ross Lonsberry	1.00	.50	.10
☐	105	Leon Rochefort	1.00	.50	.10
☐	106	Eddie Shack	1.50	.75	.15
☐	107	Dennis Hextall	2.50	1.25	.25
☐	108	Eddie Joyal	1.00	.50	.10
☐	109	Gord Labossiere	1.00	.50	.10
☐	110	Les Binkley	1.50	.75	.15
☐	111	Tracy Pratt	1.00	.50	.10
☐	112	Bryan Watson	1.00	.50	.10
☐	113	Bob Woytowich	1.00	.50	.10
☐	114	Keith McCreary	1.00	.50	.10
☐	115	Dean Prentice	2.00	1.00	.20
☐	116	Glen Sather	2.50	1.25	.25
☐	117	Ken Schinkel	1.00	.50	.10
☐	118	Wally Boyer	1.00	.50	.10

		NRMT	VG-E	GOOD
☐ 119	Val Fonteyne	1.00	.50	.10
☐ 120	Ron Schock	1.00	.50	.10
☐ 121	Cesare Maniago	1.50	.75	.15
☐ 122	Leo Boivin	3.00	1.50	.30
☐ 123	Bob McCord	1.00	.50	.10
☐ 124	John Miszuk	1.00	.50	.10
☐ 125	Danny Grant	1.00	.50	.10
☐ 126	Claude Larose	1.00	.50	.10
☐ 127	Jean Paul Parise	1.00	.50	.10
☐ 128	Tom Williams	1.00	.50	.10
☐ 129	Charlie Burns	1.00	.50	.10
☐ 130	Ray Cullen	1.00	.50	.10
☐ 131	Danny O'Shea	1.00	.50	.10
☐ 132	Checklist Card	22.00	2.00	.40

1970-71 Topps

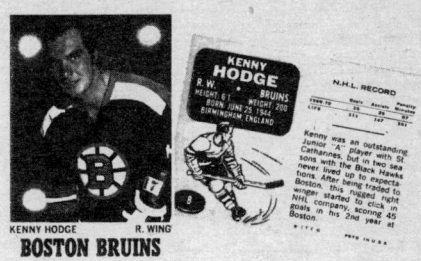

The 1970-71 Topps set consists of 132 color cards. Cards are 2¹/₂" by 3¹/₂". The backs, printed in English only with black and pea-green ink, feature the card number, the player's NHL record, and a short biography of the player. The cards were printed in the USA. All of the NHL teams have players included in the set, even the two new expansion franchises in Buffalo and Vancouver. The key rookie cards in this set are Brad Park and Gilbert Perreault.

Le set Topps 1970-71 contient 132 cartes en couleurs. Les cartes mesurent 2¹/₂" x 3 ¹/₂". Le dos, imprimé en noir et vert vif, et uniquement en anglais, comprend le numéro de carte, la fiche NHL et une biographie concise du joueur. Les cartes ont été imprimées aux Etats-Unis. Toutes les équipes de la NHL ont des joueurs dans ce jeu, même les deux nouvelles franchises d'expansion de Buffalo et de Vancouver. Les débutants importants de ce jeu sont Brad Park et Gilbert Perreault.

			NRMT	VG-E	GOOD
		COMPLETE SET (132)	350.00	175.00	35.00
		COMMON PLAYER (1-132)	.90	.45	.09
☐	1	Gerry Cheevers	12.00	4.00	.80
☐	2	Johnny Bucyk	4.50	2.25	.45
☐	3	Bobby Orr	55.00	27.50	5.50
☐	4	Don Awrey	.90	.45	.09
☐	5	Fred Stanfield	.90	.45	.09
☐	6	John McKenzie	.90	.45	.09
☐	7	Wayne Cashman	7.50	3.75	.75
☐	8	Ken Hodge	1.50	.75	.15
☐	9	Wayne Carleton	.90	.45	.09
☐	10	Garnet Bailey	.90	.45	.09
☐	11	Phil Esposito	15.00	7.50	1.50
☐	12	Lou Angotti	.90	.45	.09
☐	13	Jim Pappin	.90	.45	.09
☐	14	Dennis Hull	1.50	.75	.15
☐	15	Bobby Hull	22.00	11.00	2.20
☐	16	Doug Mohns	.90	.45	.09
☐	17	Pat Stapleton	1.25	.60	.12
☐	18	Pit Martin	.90	.45	.09
☐	19	Eric Nesterenko	1.25	.60	.12
☐	20	Stan Mikita	10.00	5.00	1.00
☐	21	Roy Edwards	.90	.45	.09
☐	22	Frank Mahovlich	8.00	4.00	.80
☐	23	Ron Harris	.90	.45	.09
☐	24	Bob Baun	.90	.45	.09
☐	25	Pete Stemkowski	.90	.45	.09
☐	26	Garry Unger	3.00	1.50	.30
☐	27	Bruce MacGregor	.90	.45	.09
☐	28	Larry Jeffrey	.90	.45	.09
☐	29	Gordie Howe	35.00	17.50	3.50
☐	30	Billy Dea	.90	.45	.09
☐	31	Denis DeJordy	1.25	.60	.12
☐	32	Matt Ravlich	.90	.45	.09
☐	33	Dave Amadio	.90	.45	.09
☐	34	Gilles Marotte	1.25	.60	.12
☐	35	Eddie Shack	1.25	.60	.12
☐	36	Bob Pulford	2.50	1.25	.25
☐	37	Ross Lonsberry	.90	.45	.09
☐	38	Gord Labossiere	.90	.45	.09
☐	39	Eddie Joyal	.90	.45	.09
☐	40	Gump Worsley	5.00	2.50	.50
☐	41	Bob McCord	.90	.45	.09
☐	42	Leo Boivin	2.50	1.25	.25
☐	43	Tom Reid	.90	.45	.09
☐	44	Charlie Burns	.90	.45	.09
☐	45	Bob Barlow	.90	.45	.09
☐	46	Bill Goldsworthy	1.25	.60	.12
☐	47	Danny Grant	.90	.45	.09
☐	48	Norm Beaudin	.90	.45	.09
☐	49	Rogatien Vachon	3.50	1.75	.35

			NRMT	VG-E	GOOD
☐	50	Yvan Cournoyer	4.00	2.00	.40
☐	51	Serge Savard	3.50	1.75	.35
☐	52	Jacques Laperriere	2.50	1.25	.25
☐	53	Terry Harper	1.25	.60	.12
☐	54	Ralph Backstrom	.90	.45	.09
☐	55	Jean Beliveau	9.00	4.50	.90
☐	56	Claude Larose	.90	.45	.09
☐	57	Jacques Lemaire	3.50	1.75	.35
☐	58	Peter Mahovlich	1.25	.60	.12
☐	59	Tim Horton	4.00	2.00	.40
☐	60	Bob Nevin	.90	.45	.09
☐	61	Dave Balon	.90	.45	.09
☐	62	Vic Hadfield	1.25	.60	.12
☐	63	Rod Gilbert	4.00	2.00	.40
☐	64	Ron Stewart	.90	.45	.09
☐	65	Ted Irvine	.90	.45	.09
☐	66	Arnie Brown	.90	.45	.09
☐	67	Brad Park	30.00	15.00	3.00
☐	68	Ed Giacomin	3.25	1.60	.32
☐	69	Gary Smith	.90	.45	.09
☐	70	Carol Vadnais	.90	.45	.09
☐	71	Doug Roberts	.90	.45	.09
☐	72	Harry Howell	2.50	1.25	.25
☐	73	Joe Szura	.90	.45	.09
☐	74	Mike Laughton	.90	.45	.09
☐	75	Gary Jarrett	.90	.45	.09
☐	76	Bill Hicke	.90	.45	.09
☐	77	Paul Andrea	.90	.45	.09
☐	78	Bernie Parent	10.00	5.00	1.00
☐	79	Joe Watson	.90	.45	.09
☐	80	Ed Van Impe	.90	.45	.09
☐	81	Larry Hillman	.90	.45	.09
☐	82	George Swarbrick	.90	.45	.09
☐	83	Bill Sutherland	.90	.45	.09
☐	84	Andre Lacroix	.90	.45	.09
☐	85	Gary Dornhoefer	1.25	.60	.12
☐	86	Jean Guy Gendron	.90	.45	.09
☐	87	Al Smith	.90	.45	.09
☐	88	Bob Woytowich	.90	.45	.09
☐	89	Duane Rupp	.90	.45	.09
☐	90	Jim Morrison	.90	.45	.09
☐	91	Ron Schock	.90	.45	.09
☐	92	Ken Schinkel	.90	.45	.09
☐	93	Keith McCreary	.90	.45	.09
☐	94	Bryan Hextall	.90	.45	.09
☐	95	Wayne Hicks	.90	.45	.09
☐	96	Gary Sabourin	.90	.45	.09
☐	97	Ernie Wakely	.90	.45	.09
☐	98	Bob Wall	.90	.45	.09
☐	99	Barclay Plager	1.50	.75	.15
☐	100	Jean Guy Talbot	.90	.45	.09
☐	101	Gary Veneruzzo	.90	.45	.09
☐	102	Tim Ecclestone	.90	.45	.09

		NRMT	VG-E	GOOD
☐ 103	Red Berenson	1.25	.60	.12
☐ 104	Larry Keenan	.90	.45	.09
☐ 105	Bruce Gamble	.90	.45	.09
☐ 106	Jim Dorey	.90	.45	.09
☐ 107	Mike Pelyk	.90	.45	.09
☐ 108	Rick Ley	1.50	.75	.15
☐ 109	Mike Walton	1.25	.60	.12
☐ 110	Norm Ullman	3.50	1.75	.35
☐ 111	Brit Selby	.90	.45	.09
☐ 112	Garry Monahan	.90	.45	.09
☐ 113	George Armstrong	2.50	1.25	.25
☐ 114	Gary Doak	.90	.45	.09
☐ 115	Darryl Sly	.90	.45	.09
☐ 116	Wayne Maki	.90	.45	.09
☐ 117	Orland Kurtenbach	1.25	.60	.12
☐ 118	Murray Hall	.90	.45	.09
☐ 119	Marc Reaume	.90	.45	.09
☐ 120	Pat Quinn	1.50	.75	.15
☐ 121	Andre Boudrias	.90	.45	.09
☐ 122	Poul Popiel	.90	.45	.09
☐ 123	Paul Terbenche	.90	.45	.09
☐ 124	Howie Menard	.90	.45	.09
☐ 125	Gerry Meehan	2.50	1.25	.25
☐ 126	Skip Krake	.90	.45	.09
☐ 127	Phil Goyette	.90	.45	.09
☐ 128	Reg Fleming	.90	.45	.09
☐ 129	Don Marshall	.90	.45	.09
☐ 130	Bill Inglis	.90	.45	.09
☐ 131	Gilbert Perreault	50.00	25.00	5.00
☐ 132	Checklist Card	18.00	1.50	.30

1971-72 Topps

ED
GIACOMIN
GOALIE

The 1971-72 Topps set consists of 132 color cards. Cards measure 2½" by 3½". The backs, printed in English only with green and yellow ink, feature the player's NHL year-by-year career record, the card number, a short biography of the player, and a cartoon-illustrated fact about the player. The cards were printed in the USA. Cards 1-6 (League Leaders) were only available in the Topps set; there were no League Leader cards available in the O-Pee-Chee set. The key rookie card in this set is Ken Dryden.

Le jeu Topps 1971-72 contient 132 cartes en couleurs. Les cartes mesurent 2½" x 3½". Le dos, imprimé en jaune et vert, et uniquement en anglais, comporte la fiche par année de carrière NHL du joueur, le numéro de carte, une biographie concise, et une caricature d'un fait notable concernant le joueur. Les cartes ont été imprimées aux Etats-Unis. Les cartes 1-6 (Champions) sont seulement disponibles dans le jeu Topps; le jeu O-Pee-Chee ne contenait pas de cartes de Champions. Le débutant important de ce jeu est Ken Dryden.

			NRMT	VG-E	GOOD
		COMPLETE SET (132)	325.00	160.00	32.00
		COMMON PLAYER (1-132)	.75	.35	.07
☐	1	**Goal Leaders**	12.00	4.00	.80
		Phil Esposito			
		Johnny Bucyk			
		Bobby Hull			
☐	2	**Assists Leaders**	12.00	6.00	1.20
		Bobby Orr			
		Phil Esposito			
		Johnny Bucyk			

			NRMT	VG-E	GOOD
☐	3	**Scoring Leaders** .... Phil Esposito Bobby Orr Johnny Bucyk	12.00	6.00	1.20
☐	4	**Goalies Win Leaders** .... Tony Esposito Ed Johnston Gerry Cheevers Ed Giacomin	3.00	1.50	.30
☐	5	**Shutouts Leaders**.......................... Ed Giacomin Tony Esposito Cesare Maniago	3.00	1.50	.30
☐	6	**Goals Against** .... **Average Leaders** Jacques Plante Ed Giacomin Tony Esposito	4.50	2.25	.45
☐	7	**Fred Stanfield**	.75	.35	.07
☐	8	**Mike Robitaille**	.75	.35	.07
☐	9	**Vic Hadfield**	1.00	.50	.10
☐	10	**Jacques Plante**	8.00	4.00	.80
☐	11	**Bill White**....................................	1.00	.50	.10
☐	12	**Andre Boudrias**	.75	.35	.07
☐	13	**Jim Lorentz**	.75	.35	.07
☐	14	**Arnie Brown**	.75	.35	.07
☐	15	**Yvan Cournoyer**	3.50	1.75	.35
☐	16	**Bryan Hextall**	.75	.35	.07
☐	17	**Gary Croteau**	.75	.35	.07
☐	18	**Gilles Villemure**	1.00	.50	.10
☐	19	**Serge Bernier**	.75	.35	.07
☐	20	**Phil Esposito**	12.00	6.00	1.20
☐	21	**Charlie Burns**...............................	.75	.35	.07
☐	22	**Doug Barrie**	.75	.35	.07
☐	23	**Eddie Joyal**..................................	.75	.35	.07
☐	24	**Rosaire Paiement**..........................	.75	.35	.07
☐	25	**Pat Stapleton**...............................	1.00	.50	.10
☐	26	**Garry Unger**	1.00	.50	.10
☐	27	**Al Smith**	.75	.35	.07
☐	28	**Bob Woytowich**.............................	.75	.35	.07
☐	29	**Marc Tardif**	1.00	.50	.10
☐	30	**Norm Ullman**................................	3.00	1.50	.30
☐	31	**Tom Williams**...............................	.75	.35	.07
☐	32	**Ted Harris**	.75	.35	.07
☐	33	**Andre Lacroix**	.75	.35	.07
☐	34	**Mike Byers**	.75	.35	.07
☐	35	**Johnny Bucyk**	3.50	1.75	.35
☐	36	**Roger Crozier**	1.00	.50	.10
☐	37	**Alex Delvecchio**	4.00	2.00	.40
☐	38	**Frank St. Marseille**	.75	.35	.07
☐	39	**Pit Martin**	.75	.35	.07
☐	40	**Brad Park**	6.00	3.00	.60
☐	41	**Greg Polis**	.75	.35	.07

			NRMT	VG-E	GOOD
☐	42	Orland Kurtenbach	.75	.35	.07
☐	43	Jim McKenny	.75	.35	.07
☐	44	Bob Nevin	.75	.35	.07
☐	45	Ken Dryden	80.00	40.00	8.00
☐	46	Carol Vadnais	.75	.35	.07
☐	47	Bill Flett	.75	.35	.07
☐	48	Jim Johnson	.75	.35	.07
☐	49	Allan Hamilton	.75	.35	.07
☐	50	Bobby Hull	22.00	11.00	2.20
☐	51	Chris Bordeleau	1.25	.60	.12
☐	52	Tim Ecclestone	.75	.35	.07
☐	53	Rod Seiling	.75	.35	.07
☐	54	Gerry Cheevers	4.50	2.25	.45
☐	55	Bill Goldsworthy	1.00	.50	.10
☐	56	Ron Schock	.75	.35	.07
☐	57	Jim Dorey	.75	.35	.07
☐	58	Wayne Maki	.75	.35	.07
☐	59	Terry Harper	.75	.35	.07
☐	60	Gilbert Perreault	14.00	7.00	1.40
☐	61	Ernie Hicke	.75	.35	.07
☐	62	Wayne Hillman	.75	.35	.07
☐	63	Denis DeJordy	1.00	.50	.10
☐	64	Ken Schinkel	.75	.35	.07
☐	65	Derek Sanderson	1.00	.50	.10
☐	66	Barclay Plager	1.00	.50	.10
☐	67	Paul Henderson	1.00	.50	.10
☐	68	Jude Drouin	.75	.35	.07
☐	69	Keith Magnuson	1.25	.60	.12
☐	70	Gordie Howe	36.00	18.00	3.60
☐	71	Jacques Lemaire	3.00	1.50	.30
☐	72	Doug Favell	1.00	.50	.10
☐	73	Bert Marshall	.75	.35	.07
☐	74	Gerry Meehan	1.00	.50	.10
☐	75	Walt Tkaczuk	1.00	.50	.10
☐	76	Bob Berry	1.25	.60	.12
☐	77	Syl Apps	.75	.35	.07
☐	78	Tom Webster	2.00	1.00	.20
☐	79	Danny Grant	.75	.35	.07
☐	80	Dave Keon	3.00	1.50	.30
☐	81	Ernie Wakely	.75	.35	.07
☐	82	John McKenzie	.75	.35	.07
☐	83	Doug Roberts	.75	.35	.07
☐	84	Peter Mahovlich	1.00	.50	.10
☐	85	Dennis Hull	1.25	.60	.12
☐	86	Juha Widing	.75	.35	.07
☐	87	Gary Doak	.75	.35	.07
☐	88	Phil Goyette	.75	.35	.07
☐	89	Gary Dornhoefer	1.00	.50	.10
☐	90	Ed Giacomin	2.50	1.25	.25
☐	91	Red Berenson	1.00	.50	.10
☐	92	Mike Pelyk	.75	.35	.07
☐	93	Gary Jarrett	.75	.35	.07
☐	94	Bob Pulford	2.00	1.00	.20

		NRMT	VG-E	GOOD
☐ 95	Dale Tallon	1.00	.50	.10
☐ 96	Eddie Shack	1.25	.60	.12
☐ 97	Jean Ratelle	3.50	1.75	.35
☐ 98	Jim Pappin	.75	.35	.07
☐ 99	Roy Edwards	.75	.35	.07
☐ 100	Bobby Orr	36.00	18.00	3.60
☐ 101	Ted Hampson	.75	.35	.07
☐ 102	Mickey Redmond	2.00	1.00	.20
☐ 103	Bob Plager	1.00	.50	.10
☐ 104	Bruce Gamble	.75	.35	.07
☐ 105	Frank Mahovlich	7.00	3.50	.70
☐ 106	Tony Featherstone	.75	.35	.07
☐ 107	Tracy Pratt	.75	.35	.07
☐ 108	Ralph Backstrom	.75	.35	.07
☐ 109	Murray Hall	.75	.35	.07
☐ 110	Tony Esposito	15.00	7.50	1.50
☐ 111	Checklist Card	12.00	1.00	.20
☐ 112	Jim Neilson	.75	.35	.07
☐ 113	Ron Ellis	.75	.35	.07
☐ 114	Bobby Clarke	30.00	15.00	3.00
☐ 115	Ken Hodge	1.25	.60	.12
☐ 116	Jim Roberts	.75	.35	.07
☐ 117	Cesare Maniago	1.00	.50	.10
☐ 118	Jean Pronovost	2.00	1.00	.20
☐ 119	Gary Bergman	.75	.35	.07
☐ 120	Henri Richard	3.50	1.75	.35
☐ 121	Ross Lonsberry	.75	.35	.07
☐ 122	Pat Quinn	1.00	.50	.10
☐ 123	Rod Gilbert	3.50	1.75	.35
☐ 124	Gary Smith	.75	.35	.07
☐ 125	Stan Mikita	8.00	4.00	.80
☐ 126	Ed Van Impe	.75	.35	.07
☐ 127	Wayne Connelly	.75	.35	.07
☐ 128	Dennis Hextall	1.00	.50	.10
☐ 129	Wayne Cashman	1.00	.50	.10
☐ 130	J.C. Tremblay	1.00	.50	.10
☐ 131	Bernie Parent	5.50	2.75	.55
☐ 132	Dunc McCallum	2.00	.75	.15

1972-73 Topps

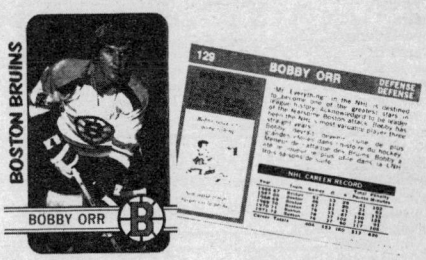

The 1972-73 Topps set consists of 176 color cards with the team name in the left hand border on the front. Cards are 2½" by 3½". The back, in English only, is printed in black and orange ink. The back contains the year-by-year NHL career record of the player, the card number, a short biography of the player, and a cartoon-illustrated fact about the player. The cards were printed in the USA. All of the NHL teams have players included in the set, even the two new expansion franchises in Atlanta and New York (Islanders). The key cards in the set are not rookie cards but are the first Topps cards of Marcel Dionne and Guy Lafleur as well as the card of superstar defenseman Bobby Orr. The set was printed on two sheets of 132 cards each necessitating 88 single-printed cards and 88 double-printed cards. The double prints are noted in the checklist below by DP.

Le jeu Topps 1972-73 contient 176 cartes en couleurs, portant le nom de l'équipe le long du bord gauche de la face. Les cartes mesurent 2½" x 3½". Le dos, en anglais seulement, est imprimé en encre noire et orange. Il comporte la fiche NHL par année du joueur, le numéro de carte, une biographie concise et un fait notable concernant le joueur, accompagné d'une caricature. Les cartes ont été imprimées aux Etats-Unis. Toutes les équipes de la NHL ont des joueurs représentés dans ce jeu, même les deux nouvelles franchises d'expansion d'Atlanta et de New York (Islanders). Les cartes importantes de ce jeu ne représentent pas de débutants notables, mais sont les premières cartes Topps de Marcel Dionne et Guy Lafleur, ainsi que la carte de Bobby Orr, superstar de la défense. Le jeu a été imprimé sur deux feuilles de 132 cartes chacune, nécessitant l'impression unique de 88 cartes, et l'impression en double de 88 cartes. Les cartes imprimées en double sont indiquées par les lettres "DP" dans la liste de contrôle ci-dessous.

	NRMT	VG-E	GOOD
COMPLETE SET (176)	300.00	150.00	30.00
COMMON PLAYER (1-176)	.60	.30	.06
COMMON PLAYER DP(1-176)	.50	.25	.05

			NRMT	VG-E	GOOD
☐	1	**World Champions DP**	4.00	1.00	.20
		Boston Bruins Team			
☐	2	**Playoff Game 1**	1.00	.50	.10
☐	3	**Playoff Game 2**	1.00	.50	.10
		Bruins 2			
		Rangers 1			
☐	4	**Playoff Game 3**	1.00	.50	.10
		Rangers 5			
		Bruins 2			
☐	5	**Playoff Game 4 DP**	.75	.35	.07
		Bruins 3			
		Rangers 2			
☐	6	**Playoff Game 5 DP**	.75	.35	.07
		Rangers 3			
		Bruins 2			
☐	7	**Playoff Game 6 DP**	.75	.35	.07
		Bruins 3			
		Rangers 0			
☐	8	**Stanley Cup Trophy**	3.00	1.50	.30
☐	9	**Ed Van Impe DP**	.50	.25	.05
☐	10	**Yvan Cournoyer DP**	2.75	1.35	.27
☐	11	**Syl Apps DP**	.50	.25	.05
☐	12	**Bill Plager**	1.00	.50	.10
☐	13	**Ed Johnston DP**	.75	.35	.07
☐	14	**Walt Tkaczuk**	.75	.35	.07
☐	15	**Dale Tallon DP**	.50	.25	.05
☐	16	**Gerry Meehan**	.75	.35	.07
☐	17	**Reg Leach**	1.75	.85	.17
☐	18	**Marcel Dionne DP**	30.00	15.00	3.00
☐	19	**Andre Dupont**	1.25	.60	.12
☐	20	**Tony Esposito**	5.00	2.50	.50
☐	21	**Bob Berry DP**	.75	.35	.07
☐	22	**Craig Cameron**	.60	.30	.06
☐	23	**Ted Harris**	.60	.30	.06
☐	24	**Jacques Plante**	6.50	3.25	.65
☐	25	**Jacques Lemaire DP**	2.50	1.25	.25
☐	26	**Simon Nolet DP**	.50	.25	.05
☐	27	**Keith McCreary DP**	.50	.25	.05
☐	28	**Duane Rupp**	.60	.30	.06
☐	29	**Wayne Cashman**	1.00	.50	.10
☐	30	**Brad Park**	3.25	1.60	.32
☐	31	**Roger Crozier**	.75	.35	.07
☐	32	**Wayne Maki**	.60	.30	.06
☐	33	**Tim Ecclestone**	.60	.30	.06
☐	34	**Rick Smith**	.60	.30	.06
☐	35	**Garry Unger DP**	1.00	.50	.10
☐	36	**Serge Bernier DP**	.50	.25	.05
☐	37	**Brian Glennie**	.60	.30	.06
☐	38	**Gerry Desjardins DP**	.75	.35	.07
☐	39	**Danny Grant**	.60	.30	.06
☐	40	**Bill White DP**	.75	.35	.07
☐	41	**Gary Dornhoefer DP**	.75	.35	.07
☐	42	**Peter Mahovlich**	.75	.35	.07

			NRMT	VG-E	GOOD
☐	43	Greg Polis DP	.50	.25	.05
☐	44	Larry Hale DP	.50	.25	.05
☐	45	Dallas Smith	.75	.35	.07
☐	46	Orland Kurtenbach DP	.50	.25	.05
☐	47	Steve Atkinson	.60	.30	.06
☐	48	Joey Johnston DP	.50	.25	.05
☐	49	Gary Bergman	.60	.30	.06
☐	50	Jean Ratelle	3.00	1.50	.30
☐	51	Rogatien Vachon DP	2.25	1.10	.22
☐	52	Phil Roberto DP	.50	.25	.05
☐	53	Brian Spencer DP	.50	.25	.05
☐	54	Jim McKenny DP	.50	.25	.05
☐	55	Gump Worsley	4.00	2.00	.40
☐	56	Stan Mikita DP	6.00	3.00	.60
☐	57	Guy Lapointe	1.50	.75	.15
☐	58	Lew Morrison DP	.50	.25	.05
☐	59	Ron Schock DP	.50	.25	.05
☐	60	Johnny Bucyk	3.00	1.50	.30
☐	61	Goals Leaders Phil Esposito Vic Hadfield Bobby Hull	5.00	2.50	.50
☐	62	Assists Leaders DP Bobby Orr Phil Esposito Jean Ratelle	10.00	5.00	1.00
☐	63	Scoring Leaders DP Phil Esposito Bobby Orr Jean Ratelle	10.00	5.00	1.00
☐	64	Goals Against Average Leaders Tony Esposito Gilles Villemure Gump Worsley	2.50	1.25	.25
☐	65	Penalty Minutes Leaders DP Bryan Watson Keith Magnuson Gary Dornhoefer	.75	.35	.07
☐	66	Jim Neilson	.60	.30	.06
☐	67	Nick Libett DP	.50	.25	.05
☐	68	Jim Lorentz	.60	.30	.06
☐	69	Gilles Meloche	1.25	.60	.12
☐	70	Pat Stapleton	.75	.35	.07
☐	71	Frank St. Marseille DP	.50	.25	.05
☐	72	Butch Goring	2.00	1.00	.20
☐	73	Paul Henderson DP	.75	.35	.07
☐	74	Doug Favell	.75	.35	.07
☐	75	Jocelyn Guevremont DP	.50	.25	.05
☐	76	Tom Miller	.60	.30	.06
☐	77	Bill MacMillan	.60	.30	.06
☐	78	Doug Mohns	.60	.30	.06

			NRMT	VG-E	GOOD
☐	79	Guy Lafleur DP	30.00	15.00	3.00
☐	80	Rod Gilbert DP	2.75	1.35	.27
☐	81	Gary Doak	.60	.30	.06
☐	82	Dave Burrows DP	.50	.25	.05
☐	83	Gary Croteau	.60	.30	.06
☐	84	Tracy Pratt DP	.50	.25	.05
☐	85	Carol Vadnais DP	.50	.25	.05
☐	86	Jacques Caron DP	.50	.25	.05
☐	87	Keith Magnuson	.75	.35	.07
☐	88	Dave Keon	2.50	1.25	.25
☐	89	Mike Corrigan	.60	.30	.06
☐	90	Bobby Clarke	11.00	5.50	1.10
☐	91	Dunc Wilson DP	.50	.25	.05
☐	92	Gerry Hart	1.00	.50	.10
☐	93	Lou Nanne	.75	.35	.07
☐	94	Checklist 1-176 DP	10.00	.75	.15
☐	95	Red Berenson DP	.75	.35	.07
☐	96	Bob Plager	.75	.35	.07
☐	97	Jim Rutherford	.75	.35	.07
☐	98	Rick Foley DP	.50	.25	.05
☐	99	Pit Martin DP	.50	.25	.05
☐	100	Bobby Orr DP	35.00	17.50	3.50
☐	101	Stan Gilbertson	.60	.30	.06
☐	102	Barry Wilkins	.60	.30	.06
☐	103	Terry Crisp DP	1.25	.60	.12
☐	104	Cesare Maniago DP	.75	.35	.07
☐	105	Marc Tardif	.75	.35	.07
☐	106	Don Luce DP	.50	.25	.05
☐	107	Mike Pelyk	.60	.30	.06
☐	108	Juha Widing DP	.50	.25	.05
☐	109	Phil Myre DP	1.25	.60	.12
☐	110	Vic Hadfield DP	.75	.35	.07
☐	111	Arnie Brown DP	.50	.25	.05
☐	112	Ross Lonsberry DP	.50	.25	.05
☐	113	Dick Redmond	.60	.30	.06
☐	114	Gary Smith	.50	.25	.05
☐	115	Bill Goldsworthy	.75	.35	.07
☐	116	Bryan Watson	.60	.30	.06
☐	117	Dave Balon DP	.50	.25	.05
☐	118	Bill Mikkelson DP	.50	.25	.05
☐	119	Terry Harper DP	.50	.25	.05
☐	120	Gilbert Perreault DP	6.00	3.00	.60
☐	121	Tony Esposito AS1	3.50	1.75	.35
☐	122	Bobby Orr AS1	15.00	7.50	1.50
☐	123	Brad Park AS1	2.25	1.10	.22
☐	124	Phil Esposito AS1 (Brother Tony pictured in background)	6.50	3.25	.65
☐	125	Rod Gilbert AS1	2.50	1.25	.25
☐	126	Bobby Hull AS1	12.00	6.00	1.20
☐	127	Ken Dryden AS2 DP	12.00	6.00	1.20
☐	128	Bill White AS2 DP	.75	.35	.07
☐	129	Pat Stapleton AS2 DP	.75	.35	.07
☐	130	Jean Ratelle AS2 DP	2.00	1.00	.20

			NRMT	VG-E	GOOD
☐ 131	Yvan Cournoyer AS2 DP		2.00	1.00	.20
☐ 132	Vic Hadfield AS2 DP		.75	.35	.07
☐ 133	Ralph Backstrom DP		.50	.25	.05
☐ 134	Bob Baun DP		.50	.25	.05
☐ 135	Fred Stanfield DP		.50	.25	.05
☐ 136	Barclay Plager DP		.75	.35	.07
☐ 137	Gilles Villemure		.75	.35	.07
☐ 138	Ron Harris DP		.50	.25	.05
☐ 139	Bill Flett DP		.50	.25	.05
☐ 140	Frank Mahovlich		5.00	2.50	.50
☐ 141	Alex Delvecchio DP		4.00	2.00	.40
☐ 142	Poul Popiel		.60	.30	.06
☐ 143	Jean Pronovost DP		.75	.35	.07
☐ 144	Denis DeJordy DP		.75	.35	.07
☐ 145	Rick Martin DP		1.75	.85	.17
☐ 146	Ivan Boldirev		1.50	.75	.15
☐ 147	Jack Egers		.60	.30	.06
☐ 148	Jim Pappin		.60	.30	.06
☐ 149	Rod Seiling		.60	.30	.06
☐ 150	Phil Esposito		10.00	5.00	1.00
☐ 151	Gary Edwards		.60	.30	.06
☐ 152	Ron Ellis DP		.50	.25	.05
☐ 153	Jude Drouin		.60	.30	.06
☐ 154	Ernie Hicke DP		.50	.25	.05
☐ 155	Mickey Redmond		.75	.35	.07
☐ 156	Joe Watson DP		.50	.25	.05
☐ 157	Bryan Hextall		.60	.30	.06
☐ 158	Andre Boudrias		.60	.30	.06
☐ 159	Ed Westfall		1.00	.50	.10
☐ 160	Ken Dryden		33.00	15.00	3.00
☐ 161	Rene Robert DP		1.50	.75	.15
☐ 162	Bert Marshall DP		.50	.25	.05
☐ 163	Gary Sabourin		.60	.30	.06
☐ 164	Dennis Hull		1.00	.50	.10
☐ 165	Ed Giacomin DP		2.50	1.25	.25
☐ 166	Ken Hodge		1.00	.50	.10
☐ 167	Gilles Marotte DP		.75	.35	.07
☐ 168	Norm Ullman DP		2.00	1.00	.20
☐ 169	Barry Gibbs		.60	.30	.06
☐ 170	Art Ross Trophy		1.50	.75	.15
☐ 171	Hart Memorial Trophy		1.50	.75	.15
☐ 172	James Norris Trophy		1.50	.75	.15
☐ 173	Vezina Trophy DP		1.25	.60	.12
☐ 174	Calder Trophy DP		1.25	.60	.12
☐ 175	Lady Byng Trophy DP		1.25	.60	.12
☐ 176	Conn Smythe Trophy DP		3.50	.75	.15

1973-74 Topps

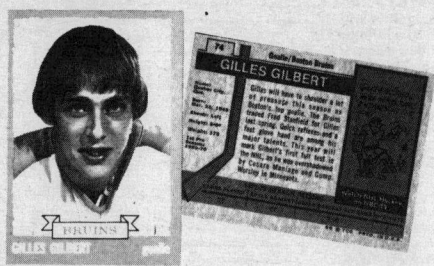

The 1973-74 Topps set consists of 198 cards of NHL players. Cards are 2½" by 3½". The fronts of the cards have a distinct bluish tint. The backs, printed in dark brown and yellow-orange ink, are in English only. The player's 1972-73 season record, the card number, a short biography of the player, and a cartoon-illustrated fact about the player are contained on the back. Team cards (92-107) give team and player records on the back. The cards were printed in the USA. Since the set was printed on two 132-card sheets, there are 66 double-printed (DP) cards in the set that are easier to obtain than the other cards in the set. The key rookie cards in this set are Bill Barber and Billy Smith.

Le jeu Topps 1973-74 contient 198 cartes de joueurs de la NHL. Les cartes mesurent 2½" x 3½". La face a une teinte bleuâtre assez marquée. Le dos, brun foncé et jaune-orange, est imprimé uniquement en anglais. Il comporte la fiche du joueur pour la saison 1972-73, le numéro de carte, une biographie concise, et un fait notable concernant le joueur, accompagné d'une caricature. Les cartes d'équipe (92-107) fournissent, au dos, les statistiques pour l'équipe et pour le joueur. Les cartes ont été imprimées aux Etats- Unis. Parce que le jeu a été imprimé sur deux feuilles de 132 cartes chacune, il contient 66 cartes imprimées en double (DP), plus faciles à obtenir que les autres cartes du jeu. Les débutants importants de ce jeu sont Bill Barber et Billy Smith.

		NRMT	VG-E	GOOD
	COMPLETE SET (198)	190.00	90.00	20.00
	COMMON PLAYER (1-198)	.45	.22	.04
	COMMON PLAYER DP(1-198)	.35	.17	.03
☐ 1	Goal Leaders	5.00	1.50	.30
	Phil Esposito			
	Rick MacLeish			

			NRMT	VG-E	GOOD
☐	2	**Assists Leaders**	3.50	1.75	.35
		Phil Esposito			
		Bobby Clarke			
☐	3	**Scoring Leaders**	3.50	1.75	.35
		Phil Esposito			
		Bobby Clarke			
☐	4	**Goals Against**	3.00	1.50	.30
		Average Leaders			
		Ken Dryden			
		Tony Esposito			
☐	5	**Penalty Min. Leaders**	.75	.35	.07
		Jim Schoenfeld			
		Dave Schultz			
☐	6	**Power Play Goals**	2.25	1.10	.22
		Leaders			
		Rick MacLeish			
☐	7	**Paul Henderson DP**	.45	.22	.04
☐	8	**Gregg Sheppard DP**	.35	.17	.03
☐	9	**Rod Seiling DP**	.35	.17	.03
☐	10	**Ken Dryden**	20.00	10.00	2.00
☐	11	**Jean Pronovost DP**	.45	.22	.04
☐	12	**Dick Redmond**	.45	.22	.04
☐	13	**Keith McCreary DP**	.35	.17	.03
☐	14	**Ted Harris DP**	.35	.17	.03
☐	15	**Garry Unger**	.75	.35	.07
☐	16	**Neil Komadoski**	.45	.22	.04
☐	17	**Marcel Dionne**	11.00	5.50	1.10
☐	18	**Ernie Hicke DP**	.35	.17	.03
☐	19	**Andre Boudrias**	.45	.22	.04
☐	20	**Bill Flett**	.45	.22	.04
☐	21	**Marshall Johnston**	.45	.22	.04
☐	22	**Gerry Meehan**	.75	.35	.07
☐	23	**Ed Johnston DP**	.75	.35	.07
☐	24	**Serge Savard**	1.75	.85	.17
☐	25	**Walt Tkaczuk**	.75	.35	.07
☐	26	**Johnny Bucyk**	2.25	1.10	.22
☐	27	**Dave Burrows**	.45	.22	.04
☐	28	**Cliff Koroll**	.45	.22	.04
☐	29	**Rey Comeau DP**	.35	.17	.03
☐	30	**Barry Gibbs**	.45	.22	.04
☐	31	**Wayne Stephenson**	1.00	.50	.10
☐	32	**Dan Maloney DP**	.75	.35	.07
☐	33	**Henry Boucha DP**	.35	.17	.03
☐	34	**Gerry Hart**	.45	.22	.04
☐	35	**Bobby Schmautz**	.45	.22	.04
☐	36	**Ross Lonsberry DP**	.35	.17	.03
☐	37	**Ted McAneeley**	.45	.22	.04
☐	38	**Don Luce DP**	.35	.17	.03
☐	39	**Jim McKenny DP**	.35	.17	.03
☐	40	**Frank Mahovlich**	4.00	2.00	.40
☐	41	**Bill Fairbairn**	.45	.22	.04
☐	42	**Dallas Smith**	.60	.30	.06

			NRMT	VG-E	GOOD
☐	43	Bryan Hextall	.45	.22	.04
☐	44	Keith Magnuson	.75	.35	.07
☐	45	Dan Bouchard	.60	.30	.06
☐	46	Jean Paul Parise DP	.35	.17	.03
☐	47	Barclay Plager	.75	.35	.07
☐	48	Mike Corrigan	.45	.22	.04
☐	49	Nick Libett DP	.35	.17	.03
☐	50	Bobby Clarke	7.50	3.75	.75
☐	51	Bert Marshall DP	.35	.17	.03
☐	52	Craig Patrick	.75	.35	.07
☐	53	Richard Lemieux	.45	.22	.04
☐	54	Tracy Pratt DP	.35	.17	.03
☐	55	Ron Ellis DP	.35	.17	.03
☐	56	Jacques Lemaire	1.75	.85	.17
☐	57	Steve Vickers DP	.35	.17	.03
☐	58	Carol Vadnais	.45	.22	.04
☐	59	Jim Rutherford DP	.60	.30	.06
☐	60	Dennis Hull	.75	.35	.07
☐	61	Pat Quinn DP	.60	.30	.06
☐	62	Bill Goldsworthy DP	.60	.30	.06
☐	63	Fran Huck	.45	.22	.04
☐	64	Rogatien Vachon DP	1.50	.75	.15
☐	65	Gary Bergman DP	.35	.17	.03
☐	66	Bernie Parent	3.50	1.75	.35
☐	67	Ed Westfall	.75	.35	.07
☐	68	Ivan Boldirev	.60	.30	.06
☐	69	Don Tannahill DP	.35	.17	.03
☐	70	Gilbert Perreault DP	3.50	1.75	.35
☐	71	Mike Pelyk DP	.35	.17	.03
☐	72	Guy Lafleur DP	10.00	5.00	1.00
☐	73	Jean Ratelle	2.00	1.00	.20
☐	74	Gilles Gilbert DP	1.50	.75	.15
☐	75	Greg Polis	.45	.22	.04
☐	76	Doug Jarrett DP	.35	.17	.03
☐	77	Phil Myre DP	.60	.30	.06
☐	78	Fred Harvey DP	.35	.17	.03
☐	79	Jack Egers	.45	.22	.04
☐	80	Terry Harper	.45	.22	.04
☐	81	Bill Barber	15.00	7.50	1.50
☐	82	Roy Edwards DP	.35	.17	.03
☐	83	Brian Spencer	.45	.22	.04
☐	84	Reg Leach DP	.75	.35	.07
☐	85	Dave Keon	2.00	1.00	.20
☐	86	Jim Schoenfeld	1.25	.60	.12
☐	87	Henri Richard DP	2.75	1.35	.27
☐	88	Rod Gilbert DP	1.75	.85	.17
☐	89	Don Marcotte DP	.35	.17	.03
☐	90	Tony Esposito	4.00	2.00	.40
☐	91	Joe Watson	.45	.22	.04
☐	92	Flames Team	.90	.45	.09
☐	93	Bruins Team	.90	.45	.09
☐	94	Sabres Team DP	.75	.35	.07
☐	95	Golden Seals Team DP	.75	.35	.07

			NRMT	VG-E	GOOD
☐	96	Blackhawks Team	.90	.45	.09
☐	97	Red Wings Team DP	.75	.35	.07
☐	98	Kings Team DP	.75	.35	.07
☐	99	North Stars Team	.90	.45	.09
☐	100	Canadiens Team	.90	.45	.09
☐	101	Islanders Team	.90	.45	.09
☐	102	Rangers Team DP	.75	.35	.07
☐	103	Flyers Team DP	.75	.35	.07
☐	104	Penguins Team	.90	.45	.09
☐	105	Blues Team	.90	.45	.09
☐	106	Maple Leafs Team	.90	.45	.09
☐	107	Canucks Team	.90	.45	.09
☐	108	Roger Crozier DP	.60	.30	.06
☐	109	Tom Reid	.45	.22	.04
☐	110	Hilliard Graves	.45	.22	.04
☐	111	Don Lever	.45	.22	.04
☐	112	Jim Pappin	.45	.22	.04
☐	113	Ron Schock DP	.35	.17	.03
☐	114	Gerry Desjardins	.75	.35	.07
☐	115	Yvan Cournoyer DP	2.25	1.10	.22
☐	116	Checklist Card	7.50	.50	.10
☐	117	Bob Leiter	.45	.22	.04
☐	118	Ab Demarco	.45	.22	.04
☐	119	Doug Favell	.75	.35	.07
☐	120	Phil Esposito	9.00	4.50	.90
☐	121	Mike Robitaille	.45	.22	.04
☐	122	Real Lemieux	.45	.22	.04
☐	123	Jim Neilson	.45	.22	.04
☐	124	Tim Ecclestone DP	.35	.17	.03
☐	125	Jude Drouin	.45	.22	.04
☐	126	Gary Smith DP	.35	.17	.03
☐	127	Walt McKechnie	.45	.22	.04
☐	128	Lowell MacDonald	.75	.35	.07
☐	129	Dale Tallon DP	.35	.17	.03
☐	130	Billy Harris	.45	.22	.04
☐	131	Randy Manery DP	.35	.17	.03
☐	132	Darryl Sittler DP	3.50	1.75	.35
☐	133	Ken Hodge	.75	.35	.07
☐	134	Bob Plager	.75	.35	.07
☐	135	Rick MacLeish	2.00	1.00	.20
☐	136	Dennis Hextall	.75	.35	.07
☐	137	Jacques Laperriere DP	1.50	.75	.15
☐	138	Butch Goring	1.00	.50	.10
☐	139	Rene Robert	.75	.35	.07
☐	140	Ed Giacomin	2.00	1.00	.20
☐	141	Alex Delvecchio DP	2.50	1.25	.25
☐	142	Jocelyn Guevremont	.45	.22	.04
☐	143	Joey Johnston	.45	.22	.04
☐	144	Bryan Watson DP	.35	.17	.03
☐	145	Stan Mikita	5.00	2.50	.50
☐	146	Cesare Maniago	.60	.30	.06
☐	147	Craig Cameron	.45	.22	.04
☐	148	Norm Ullman DP	1.50	.75	.15

		NRMT	VG-E	GOOD
☐ 149	Dave Schultz	2.00	1.00	.20
☐ 150	Bobby Orr	24.00	12.00	2.40
☐ 151	Phil Roberto	.45	.22	.04
☐ 152	Curt Bennett	.45	.22	.04
☐ 153	Gilles Villemure DP	.60	.30	.06
☐ 154	Chuck Lefley	.45	.22	.04
☐ 155	Richard Martin	1.00	.50	.10
☐ 156	Juha Widing	.45	.22	.04
☐ 157	Orland Kurtenbach	.60	.30	.06
☐ 158	Bill Collins DP	.35	.17	.03
☐ 159	Bob Stewart	.45	.22	.04
☐ 160	Syl Apps	.45	.22	.04
☐ 161	Danny Grant	.45	.22	.04
☐ 162	Billy Smith	22.00	11.00	2.20
☐ 163	Brian Glennie	.45	.22	.04
☐ 164	Pit Martin DP	.45	.22	.04
☐ 165	Brad Park	2.00	1.00	.20
☐ 166	Wayne Cashman DP	.60	.30	.06
☐ 167	Gary Dornhoefer	.60	.30	.06
☐ 168	Steve Durbano	.60	.30	.06
☐ 169	Jacques Richard	.45	.22	.04
☐ 170	Guy Lapointe	1.00	.50	.10
☐ 171	Jim Lorentz	.45	.22	.04
☐ 172	Bob Berry DP	.60	.30	.06
☐ 173	Dennis Kearns	.45	.22	.04
☐ 174	Red Berenson	.75	.35	.07
☐ 175	Gilles Meloche DP	.60	.30	.06
☐ 176	Al McDonough	.45	.22	.04
☐ 177	Dennis O'Brien	.45	.22	.04
☐ 178	Germain Gagnon DP	.35	.17	.03
☐ 179	Rick Kehoe DP	.60	.30	.06
☐ 180	Bill White	.60	.30	.06
☐ 181	Vic Hadfield DP	.60	.30	.06
☐ 182	Derek Sanderson	.75	.35	.07
☐ 183	Andre Dupont DP	.35	.17	.03
☐ 184	Gary Sabourin	.45	.22	.04
☐ 185	Larry Romanchych	.45	.22	.04
☐ 186	Peter Mahovlich	.75	.35	.07
☐ 187	Dave Dryden	.75	.35	.07
☐ 188	Gilles Marotte	.75	.35	.07
☐ 189	Bobby Lalonde	.45	.22	.04
☐ 190	Mickey Redmond	.75	.35	.07
☐ 191	Series A Canadiens 4 Sabres 2	.90	.45	.09
☐ 192	Series B Flyers 4 North Stars 2	.90	.45	.09
☐ 193	Series C Blackhawks 4 Blues 1	.90	.45	.09
☐ 194	Series D Rangers 4 Bruins	.90	.45	.09

	NRMT	VG-E	GOOD
☐ **195 Series E**	.90	.45	.09
Canadiens 4			
Flyers 1			
☐ **196 Series F**	.90	.45	.09
Blackhawks 4			
Rangers 1			
☐ **197 Series G**	.90	.45	.09
Canadiens 4			
Blackhawks 2			
☐ **198 Stanley Cup Champs**	2.00	.50	.10
Montreal Canadiens			

1974-75 Topps NHL

The 1974-75 Topps set consists of 264 color cards. Cards are 2½" by 3½". The fronts of the O-Pee-Chee cards of this set are identical through card number 264; however, the O-Pee-Chee set contains an additional 132 cards. The backs, in English only, feature the card number, the player's NHL record, a short biography, and a cartoon-illustrated fact about the player. The cards were printed in the USA. All of the NHL teams have players included in the set, even the two new expansion franchises in Kansas City and Washington. The key rookie cards in this set are Lanny McDonald and Denis Potvin.

Le jeu Topps 1974-75 contient 264 cartes en couleurs. Les cartes mesurent 2½" x 3½". Les faces des cartes O-Pee-Chee de ce jeu sont identiques jusqu'au numéro 264 inclus. Le jeu O-Pee-Chee contient, cependant, 132 cartes additionnelles. Le dos, imprimé uniquement en anglais, comporte le numéro de carte, la fiche NHL du joueur, une biographie concise, et un fait notable concernant le joueur, accompagné d'une caricature. Les cartes ont été imprimées aux Etats-Unis. Ce jeu représente des joueurs de toutes les équipes de la NHL, même des deux nouvelles franchises d'expansion de

Kansas City et de Washington. Les cartes des débutants importants représentent Lanny McDonald et Denis Potvin.

			NRMT	VG-E	GOOD
		COMPLETE SET (264)	190.00	90.00	20.00
		COMMON PLAYER (1-264)	.30	.15	.03
☐	1	Goal Leaders	2.00	.75	.15
		Phil Esposito			
		Bill Goldsworthy			
☐	2	Assists Leaders	3.50	1.75	.35
		Bobby Orr			
		Dennis Hextall			
☐	3	Scoring Leaders	3.00	1.50	.30
		Phil Esposito			
		Bobby Clarke			
☐	4	Goals Against Average Leaders	.90	.45	.09
		Doug Favell			
		Bernie Parent			
☐	5	Penalty Min. Leaders	.50	.25	.05
		Bryan Watson			
		Dave Schultz			
☐	6	Power Play Goal Leaders	.50	.25	.05
		Mickey Redmond			
		Rick MacLeish			
☐	7	Gary Bromley	.30	.15	.03
☐	8	Bill Barber	3.00	1.50	.30
☐	9	Emile Francis CO	.60	.30	.06
☐	10	Gilles Gilbert	.50	.25	.05
☐	11	John Davidson	.90	.45	.09
☐	12	Ron Ellis	.30	.15	.03
☐	13	Syl Apps	.30	.15	.03
☐	14	Flames Leaders	.50	.25	.05
		Jacques Richard			
		Tom Lysiak			
		Tom Lysiak			
		Keith McCreary			
☐	15	Dan Bouchard	.50	.25	.05
☐	16	Ivan Boldirev	.50	.25	.05
☐	17	Gary Coalter	.30	.15	.03
☐	18	Bob Berry	.50	.25	.05
☐	19	Red Berenson	.50	.25	.05
☐	20	Stan Mikita	4.25	2.10	.42
☐	21	Fred Shero CO	1.25	.60	.12
☐	22	Gary Smith	.30	.15	.03
☐	23	Bill Mikkelson	.30	.15	.03
☐	24	Jacques Lemaire UER	1.75	.85	.17
		(Shown in Sabres sweater)			
☐	25	Gilbert Perreault	3.00	1.50	.30
☐	26	Cesare Maniago	.50	.25	.05
☐	27	Bobby Schmautz	.30	.15	.03

			NRMT	VG-E	GOOD
☐	28	Bruins Leaders	7.00	3.50	.70
		Phil Esposito			
		Bobby Orr			
		Phil Esposito			
		Johnny Bucyk			
☐	29	Steve Vickers...........................	.30	.15	.03
☐	30	Lowell MacDonald	.50	.25	.05
☐	31	Fred Stanfield	.30	.15	.03
☐	32	Ed Westfall.............................	.50	.25	.05
☐	33	Curt Bennett	.30	.15	.03
☐	34	Bep Guidolin CO	.30	.15	.03
☐	35	Cliff Koroll	.30	.15	.03
☐	36	Gary Croteau	.30	.15	.03
☐	37	Mike Corrigan	.30	.15	.03
☐	38	Henry Boucha	.30	.15	.03
☐	39	Ron Low	.50	.25	.05
☐	40	Darryl Sittler	1.75	.85	.17
☐	41	Tracy Pratt	.30	.15	.03
☐	42	Sabres Leaders.........................	.50	.25	.05
		Richard Martin			
		Rene Robert			
		Richard Martin			
		Richard Martin			
☐	43	Larry Carriere	.30	.15	.03
☐	44	Gary Dornhoefer	.50	.25	.05
☐	45	Denis Herron	.90	.45	.09
☐	46	Doug Favell	.50	.25	.05
☐	47	Dave Gardner	.30	.15	.03
☐	48	Morris Mott	.30	.15	.03
☐	49	Marc Boileau CO	.30	.15	.03
☐	50	Brad Park	1.75	.85	.17
☐	51	Bob Leiter	.30	.15	.03
☐	52	Tom Reid	.30	.15	.03
☐	53	Serge Savard...........................	1.50	.75	.15
☐	54	Checklist 1-132	5.00	.35	.07
☐	55	Terry Harper	.30	.15	.03
☐	56	Golden Seals............................	.50	.25	.05
		Leaders			
		Joey Johnston			
		Joey Johnston			
		Walt McKechnie			
☐	57	Guy Charron	.30	.15	.03
☐	58	Pit Martin	.30	.15	.03
☐	59	Chris Evans	.30	.15	.03
☐	60	Bernie Parent	2.50	1.25	.25
☐	61	Jim Lorentz	.30	.15	.03
☐	62	Dave Kryskow	.30	.15	.03
☐	63	Lou Angotti CO	.30	.15	.03
☐	64	Bill Flett	.30	.15	.03
☐	65	Vic Hadfield	.50	.25	.05
☐	66	Wayne Merrick	.30	.15	.03
☐	67	Andre Dupont	.30	.15	.03

		NRMT	VG-E	GOOD
☐ 68	Tom Lysiak	.75	.35	.07
☐ 69	Blackhawks Leaders	.90	.45	.09
	Jim Pappin			
	Stan Mikita			
	J.P. Bordeleau			
☐ 70	Guy Lapointe	.75	.35	.07
☐ 71	Gerry O'Flaherty	.30	.15	.03
☐ 72	Marcel Dionne	9.00	4.50	.90
☐ 73	Brent Hughes	.30	.15	.03
☐ 74	Butch Goring	.60	.30	.06
☐ 75	Keith Magnuson	.50	.25	.05
☐ 76	Red Kelly CO	1.25	.60	.12
☐ 77	Pete Stemkowski	.30	.15	.03
☐ 78	Jim Roberts	.30	.15	.03
	Montreal Canadiens			
☐ 79	Don Luce	.30	.15	.03
☐ 80	Don Awrey	.30	.15	.03
☐ 81	Rick Kehoe	.50	.25	.05
☐ 82	Billy Smith	3.00	1.50	.30
☐ 83	Jean Paul Parise	.30	.15	.03
☐ 84	Red Wings Leaders	1.00	.50	.10
	Mickey Redmond			
	Marcel Dionne			
	Marcel Dionne			
	Bill Hogaboam			
☐ 85	Ed Van Impe	.30	.15	.03
☐ 86	Randy Manery	.30	.15	.03
☐ 87	Barclay Plager	.50	.25	.05
☐ 88	Inge Hammarstrom	.30	.15	.03
☐ 89	Ab Demarco	.30	.15	.03
☐ 90	Bill White	.50	.25	.05
☐ 91	Al Arbour CO	1.25	.60	.12
☐ 92	Bob Stewart	.30	.15	.03
☐ 93	Jack Egers	.30	.15	.03
☐ 94	Don Lever	.30	.15	.03
☐ 95	Reg Leach	.60	.30	.06
☐ 96	Dennis O'Brien	.30	.15	.03
☐ 97	Peter Mahovlich	.50	.25	.05
☐ 98	Kings Leaders	.50	.25	.05
	Butch Goring			
	Frank St. Marseille			
	Butch Goring			
	Don Kozak			
☐ 99	Gerry Meehan	.60	.30	.06
☐ 100	Bobby Orr	20.00	10.00	2.00
☐ 101	Jean Potvin	.75	.35	.07
☐ 102	Rod Seiling	.30	.15	.03
☐ 103	Keith McCreary	.30	.15	.03
☐ 104	Phil Maloney CO	.30	.15	.03
☐ 105	Denis Dupere	.30	.15	.03
☐ 106	Steve Durbano	.30	.15	.03
☐ 107	Bob Plager UER	.50	.25	.05
	(Photo actually Barclay Plager)			

		NRMT	VG-E	GOOD
□ 108	Chris Oddleifson	.30	.15	.03
□ 109	Jim Neilson	.30	.15	.03
□ 110	Jean Pronovost	.50	.25	.05
□ 111	Don Kozak	.30	.15	.03
□ 112	North Stars	.50	.25	.05
	Leaders			
	Bill Goldsworthy			
	Dennis Hextall			
	Dennis Hextall			
	Danny Grant			
□ 113	Jim Pappin	.30	.15	.03
□ 114	Richard Lemieux	.30	.15	.03
□ 115	Dennis Hextall	.50	.25	.05
□ 116	Bill Hogaboam	.30	.15	.03
□ 117	Canucks Leaders	.50	.25	.05
	Dennis Ververgaert			
	Bob Schmautz			
	Andre Boudrias			
	Andre Boudrias			
	Don Tannahill			
□ 118	Jimmy Anderson CO	.30	.15	.03
□ 119	Walt Tkaczuk	.50	.25	.05
□ 120	Mickey Redmond	.50	.25	.05
□ 121	Jim Schoenfeld	.60	.30	.06
□ 122	Jocelyn Guevremont	.30	.15	.03
□ 123	Bob Nystrom	1.00	.50	.10
□ 124	Canadiens Leaders	2.00	1.00	.20
	Yvan Cournoyer			
	Frank Mahovlich			
	Frank Mahovlich			
	Claude Larose			
□ 125	Lew Morrison	.30	.15	.03
□ 126	Terry Murray	1.00	.50	.10
□ 127	Richard Martin AS	.50	.25	.05
□ 128	Ken Hodge AS	.50	.25	.05
□ 129	Phil Esposito AS	4.00	2.00	.40
□ 130	Bobby Orr AS	12.00	6.00	1.20
□ 131	Brad Park AS	1.00	.50	.10
□ 132	Gilles Gilbert AS	.50	.25	.05
□ 133	Lowell MacDonald AS	.50	.25	.05
□ 134	Bill Goldsworthy AS	.50	.25	.05
□ 135	Bobby Clarke AS	3.50	1.75	.35
□ 136	Bill White AS	.50	.25	.05
□ 137	Dave Burrows AS	.50	.25	.05
□ 138	Bernie Parent AS	1.75	.85	.17
□ 139	Jacques Richard	.30	.15	.03
□ 140	Yvan Cournoyer	2.00	1.00	.20
□ 141	Rangers Leaders	1.75	.85	.17
	Rod Gilbert			
	Brad Park			
	Brad Park			
	Rod Gilbert			
□ 142	Rene Robert	.50	.25	.05

		NRMT	VG-E	GOOD
☐ 143	J. Bob Kelly	.30	.15	.03
☐ 144	Ross Lonsberry	.30	.15	.03
☐ 145	Jean Ratelle	1.75	.85	.17
☐ 146	Dallas Smith	.50	.25	.05
☐ 147	Boom Boom Geoffrion CO	1.25	.60	.12
☐ 148	Ted McAneeley	.30	.15	.03
☐ 149	Pierre Plante	.30	.15	.03
☐ 150	Dennis Hull	.60	.30	.06
☐ 151	Dave Keon	1.50	.75	.15
☐ 152	Dave Dunn	.30	.15	.03
☐ 153	Michel Belhumeur	.50	.25	.05
☐ 154	Flyers Leaders	1.75	.85	.17
	Bobby Clarke			
	Bobby Clarke			
	Bobby Clarke			
	Dave Schultz			
☐ 155	Ken Dryden	10.00	5.00	1.00
☐ 156	John Wright	.30	.15	.03
☐ 157	Larry Romanchych	.30	.15	.03
☐ 158	Ralph Stewart	.30	.15	.03
☐ 159	Mike Robitaille	.30	.15	.03
☐ 160	Ed Giacomin	1.50	.75	.15
☐ 161	Don Cherry CO	3.25	1.60	.32
☐ 162	Checklist 133-264	5.00	.35	.07
☐ 163	Rick MacLeish	1.00	.50	.10
☐ 164	Greg Polis	.30	.15	.03
☑ 165	Carol Vadnais	.30	.15	.03
☐ 166	Pete Laframboise	.30	.15	.03
☐ 167	Ron Schock	.30	.15	.03
☐ 168	Lanny McDonald	27.00	13.50	2.70
☐ 169	Scouts Emblem	.60	.30	.06
	Draft Selections on back			
☐ 170	Tony Esposito	3.50	1.75	.35
☐ 171	Pierre Jarry	.30	.15	.03
☐ 172	Dan Maloney	.50	.25	.05
☐ 173	Peter McDuffe	.30	.15	.03
☐ 174	Danny Grant	.30	.15	.03
☐ 175	John Stewart	.30	.15	.03
☐ 176	Floyd Smith CO	.30	.15	.03
☐ 177	Bert Marshall	.30	.15	.03
☐ 178	Chuck Lefley	.30	.15	.03
	(Photo actually Pierre Bouchard)			
☐ 179	Gilles Villemure	.50	.25	.05
☐ 180	Borje Salming	6.00	3.00	.60
☐ 181	Doug Mohns	.30	.15	.03
☐ 182	Barry Wilkins	.30	.15	.03
☐ 183	Penguins Leaders	.50	.25	.05
	Lowell MacDonald			
	Syl Apps			
	Syl Apps			
	Lowell MacDonald			
☐ 184	Gregg Sheppard	.30	.15	.03
☐ 185	Joey Johnston	.30	.15	.03

			NRMT	VG-E	GOOD
☐ 186	Dick Redmond		.30	.15	.03
☐ 187	Simon Nolet		.30	.15	.03
☐ 188	Ron Stackhouse		.30	.15	.03
☐ 189	Marshall Johnston		.30	.15	.03
☐ 190	Rick Martin		.60	.30	.06
☐ 191	Andre Boudrias		.30	.15	.03
☐ 192	Steve Atkinson		.30	.15	.03
☐ 193	Nick Libett		.30	.15	.03
☐ 194	Bob Murdoch		.50	.25	.05
	Los Angeles Kings				
☐ 195	Denis Potvin		36.00	18.00	3.60
☐ 196	Dave Schultz		.50	.25	.05
☐ 197	Blues Leaders		.50	.25	.05
	Garry Unger				
	Garry Unger				
	Garry Unger				
	Pierre Plante				
☐ 198	Jim McKenny		.30	.15	.03
☐ 199	Gerry Hart		.30	.15	.03
☐ 200	Phil Esposito		6.50	3.25	.65
☐ 201	Rod Gilbert		1.75	.85	.17
☐ 202	Jacques Laperriere		1.00	.50	.10
☐ 203	Barry Gibbs		.30	.15	.03
☐ 204	Billy Reay CO		.30	.15	.03
☐ 205	Gilles Meloche		.50	.25	.05
☐ 206	Wayne Cashman		.50	.25	.05
☐ 207	Dennis Ververgaert		.30	.15	.03
☐ 208	Phil Roberto		.30	.15	.03
☐ 209	Quarter Finals		.60	.30	.06
	Flyers sweep Flames				
☐ 210	Quarter Finals		.60	.30	.06
	Rangers over Canadiens				
☐ 211	Quarter Finals		.60	.30	.06
	Bruins sweep Maple Leafs				
☐ 212	Quarter Finals		.60	.30	.06
	Blackhawks over L.A. Kings				
☐ 213	Semi-Finals		.60	.30	.06
	Flyers over Rangers				
☐ 214	Semi-Finals		.60	.30	.06
	Bruins over Blackhawks				
☐ 215	1973-74 Finals		.60	.30	.06
	Flyers over Bruins				
☐ 216	Cup Champions		.90	.45	.09
	Philadelphia Flyers				
☐ 217	Joe Watson		.30	.15	.03
☐ 218	Wayne Stephenson		.50	.25	.05
☐ 219	Maple Leaf Leaders		.90	.45	.09
	Darryl Sittler				
	Norm Ullman				
	Darryl Sittler				
	Paul Henderson				
	Denis Dupere				
☐ 220	Bill Goldsworthy		.50	.25	.05

		NRMT	VG-E	GOOD
☐ 221	Don Marcotte	.30	.15	.03
☐ 222	Alex Delvecchio CO	1.25	.60	.12
☐ 223	Stan Gilbertson	.30	.15	.03
☐ 224	Mike Murphy	.30	.15	.03
☐ 225	Jim Rutherford	.50	.25	.05
☐ 226	Phil Russell	.30	.15	.03
☐ 227	Lynn Powis	.30	.15	.03
☐ 228	Billy Harris	.30	.15	.03
☐ 229	Bob Pulford CO	1.00	.50	.10
☐ 230	Ken Hodge	.60	.30	.06
☐ 231	Bill Fairbairn	.30	.15	.03
☐ 232	Guy Lafleur	10.00	5.00	1.00
☐ 233	Islanders Leaders	1.25	.60	.12
	Bill Harris			
	Ralph Stewart			
	Denis Potvin			
	Denis Potvin			
	Ralph Stewart			
☐ 234	Fred Barrett	.30	.15	.03
☐ 235	Rogatien Vachon	1.25	.60	.12
☐ 236	Norm Ullman	1.50	.75	.15
☐ 237	Garry Unger	.60	.30	.06
☐ 238	Jack Gordon CO	.30	.15	.03
☐ 239	Johnny Bucyk	1.50	.75	.15
☐ 240	Bob Dailey	.30	.15	.03
☐ 241	Dave Burrows	.50	.25	.05
☐ 242	Len Frig	.30	.15	.03
☐ 243	Masterson Trophy	1.50	.75	.15
	Henri Richard			
☐ 244	Hart Trophy	3.50	1.75	.35
	Phil Esposito			
☐ 245	Byng Trophy	1.00	.50	.10
	Johnny Bucyk			
☐ 246	Ross Trophy	3.50	1.75	.35
	Phil Esposito			
☐ 247	Prince of Wales Trophy	.60	.30	.06
	Boston Bruins			
☐ 248	Norris Trophy	10.00	5.00	1.00
	Bobby Orr			
☐ 249	Vezina Trophy	1.25	.60	.12
	Bernie Parent			
☐ 250	Stanley Cup	.75	.35	.07
	Philadelphia Flyers			
☐ 251	Smythe Trophy	1.25	.60	.12
	Bernie Parent			
☐ 252	Calder Trophy	6.50	3.25	.65
	Denis Potvin			
☐ 253	Campbell Trophy	.60	.30	.06
	Philadelphia Flyers			
☐ 254	Pierre Bouchard	.30	.15	.03
☐ 255	Jude Drouin	.30	.15	.03

		NRMT	VG-E	GOOD
☐ 256	Capitals Emblem	.60	.30	.06
	(Draft Selections on back)			
☐ 257	Michel Plasse	.50	.25	.05
☐ 258	Juha Widing	.30	.15	.03
☐ 259	Bryan Watson	.30	.15	.03
☐ 260	Bobby Clarke	6.50	3.25	.65
☐ 261	Scotty Bowman CO	1.50	.75	.15
☐ 262	Craig Patrick	.50	.25	.05
☐ 263	Craig Cameron	.30	.15	.03
☐ 264	Ted Irvine	.50	.25	.05

1975-76 Topps NHL

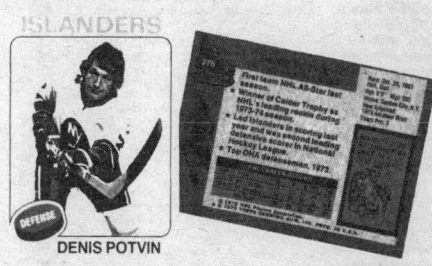

DENIS POTVIN

The 1975-76 Topps set consists of 330 color cards, which have the same fronts as the first 330 cards of the 1975-76 O-Pee-Chee set of 396. Cards are the standard 2¹/₂" by 3¹/₂". The backs, printed in black and orange and in English only, feature the player's year-by-year NHL career record, the card number, a short biography, and a cartoon-illustrated hockey fact or referee's signal. Team cards (81-98) have a team checklist (of that team's players in the set) on the back. Both the NHL Players Association's and Topps' copyright are featured on these USA-printed cards. The best rookie cards in this set are Clark Gillies and Pierre Larouche.

Le jeu Topps 1975-76 contient 330 cartes en couleurs, dont la face est identique à celle des 330 premières cartes du jeu O-Pee-Chee de 396 cartes pour 1975-76. Les cartes mesurent 2¹/₂" x 3¹/₂". Le dos, imprimé en noir et en orange et uniquement en anglais, comporte la fiche par année de carrière NHL du joueur, le numéro de carte, une biographie concise, et un fait notable de hockey ou un signal d'arbitre, accompagné d'une caricature. Les cartes d'équipe (81-98) ont, au dos, une liste de contrôle d'équipe (des joueurs de l'équipe de ce jeu). Le droit d'auteur de l'Association des Joueurs de la NHL, ainsi que celui de Topps, apparaissent sur ces cartes imprimées aux Etats-Unis.

Topps 75-6: Les cartes des débutants importants de ce jeu représentent Clark Gillies et Pierre Larouche.

			NRMT	VG-E	GOOD
		COMPLETE SET (330)	165.00	75.00	15.00
		COMMON PLAYER (1-330)	.20	.10	.02
☐	1	Stanley Cup Finals	2.25	.50	.10
		Philadelphia 4			
		Buffalo 2			
☐	2	Semi-Finals	.60	.30	.06
		Philadelphia 4			
		N.Y. Islanders 3			
☐	3	Semi-Finals	.60	.30	.06
		Buffalo 4			
		Montreal			
☐	4	Quarter Finals	.60	.30	.06
		N.Y. Islanders 4			
		Pittsburgh 2			
☐	5	Quarter Finals	.60	.30	.06
		Montreal 4			
		Vancouver 1			
☐	6	Quarter Finals	.60	.30	.06
		Buffalo 4			
		Chicago 1			
☐	7	Quarter Finals	.60	.30	.06
		Philadelphia 4			
		Toronto 0			
☐	8	Curt Bennett	.20	.10	.02
☐	9	Johnny Bucyk	1.25	.60	.12
☐	10	Gilbert Perreault	2.50	1.25	.25
☐	11	Darryl Edestrand	.20	.10	.02
☐	12	Ivan Boldirev	.20	.10	.02
☐	13	Nick Libett	.20	.10	.02
☐	14	Jim McElmury	.20	.10	.02
☐	15	Frank St. Marseille	.20	.10	.02
☐	16	Blake Dunlop	.20	.10	.02
☐	17	Yvon Lambert	.20	.10	.02
☐	18	Gerry Hart	.20	.10	.02
☐	19	Steve Vickers	.20	.10	.02
☐	20	Rick MacLeish	.60	.30	.06
☐	21	Bob Paradise	.20	.10	.02
☐	22	Red Berenson	.35	.17	.03
☐	23	Lanny McDonald	3.00	1.50	.30
☐	24	Mike Robitaille	.20	.10	.02
☐	25	Ron Low	.35	.17	.03
☐	26	Bryan Hextall	.35	.17	.03
☐	27	Carol Vadnais	.20	.10	.02
☐	28	Jim Lorentz	.20	.10	.02
☐	29	Gary Simmons	.35	.17	.03
☐	30	Stan Mikita	3.50	1.75	.35
☐	31	Bryan Watson	.20	.10	.02
☐	32	Guy Charron	.20	.10	.02

			NRMT	VG-E	GOOD
☐	33	Bob Murdoch	.20	.10	.02
		Los Angeles Kings			
☐	34	Norm Gratton	.20	.10	.02
☐	35	Ken Dryden	8.00	4.00	.80
☐	36	Jean Potvin	.20	.10	.02
☐	37	Rick Middleton	2.00	1.00	.20
☐	38	Ed Van Impe	.20	.10	.02
☐	39	Rick Kehoe	.35	.17	.03
☐	40	Garry Unger	.50	.25	.05
☐	41	Ian Turnbull	.20	.10	.02
☐	42	Dennis Ververgaert	.20	.10	.02
☐	43	Mike Marson	.20	.10	.02
☐	44	Randy Manery	.20	.10	.02
☐	45	Gilles Gilbert	.35	.17	.03
☐	46	Rene Robert	.35	.17	.03
☐	47	Bob Stewart	.20	.10	.02
☐	48	Pit Martin	.20	.10	.02
☐	49	Danny Grant	.20	.10	.02
☐	50	Peter Mahovlich	.35	.17	.03
☐	51	Dennis Patterson	.20	.10	.02
☐	52	Mike Murphy	.20	.10	.02
☐	53	Dennis O'Brien	.20	.10	.02
☐	54	Garry Howatt	.20	.10	.02
☐	55	Ed Giacomin	1.50	.75	.15
☐	56	Andre Dupont	.20	.10	.02
☐	57	Chuck Arnason	.20	.10	.02
☐	58	Bob Gassoff	.20	.10	.02
☐	59	Ron Ellis	.20	.10	.02
☐	60	Andre Boudrias	.20	.10	.02
☐	61	Yvon Labre	.20	.10	.02
☐	62	Hilliard Graves	.20	.10	.02
☐	63	Wayne Cashman	.35	.17	.03
☐	64	Danny Gare	.90	.45	.09
☐	65	Rick Hampton	.20	.10	.02
☐	66	Darcy Rota	.20	.10	.02
☐	67	Bill Hogaboam	.20	.10	.02
☐	68	Denis Herron	.35	.17	.03
☐	69	Sheldon Kannegiesser	.20	.10	.02
☐	70	Yvan Cournoyer UER	2.00	1.00	.20
		(Misspelled Yvon on card front)			
☐	71	Ernie Hicke	.20	.10	.02
☐	72	Bert Marshall	.20	.10	.02
☐	73	Derek Sanderson	.35	.17	.03
☐	74	Tom Bladon	.20	.10	.02
☐	75	Ron Schock	.20	.10	.02
☐	76	Larry Sacharuk	.20	.10	.02
☐	77	George Ferguson	.20	.10	.02
☐	78	Ab Demarco	.20	.10	.02
☐	79	Tom Williams	.20	.10	.02
☐	80	Phil Roberto	.20	.10	.02
☐	81	Bruins Team	.75	.35	.07
		(checklist back)			

			NRMT	VG-E	GOOD
☐	82	Seals Team .... (checklist back)	.75	.35	.07
☐	83	Sabres Team .... (checklist back)	.75	.35	.07
☐	84	Blackhawks Team .... (checklist back)	.75	.35	.07
☐	85	Flames Team .... (checklist back)	.75	.35	.07
☐	86	Kings Team .... (checklist back)	.75	.35	.07
☐	87	Red Wings Team .... (checklist back)	.75	.35	.07
☐	88	Scouts Team .... (checklist back)	.75	.35	.07
☐	89	North Stars Team .... (checklist back)	.75	.35	.07
☐	90	Canadiens Team .... (checklist back)	.75	.35	.07
☐	91	Maple Leafs Team .... (checklist back)	.75	.35	.07
☐	92	Islanders Team .... (checklist back)	.75	.35	.07
☐	93	Penguins Team .... (checklist back)	.75	.35	.07
☐	94	Rangers Team .... (checklist back)	.75	.35	.07
☐	95	Flyers Team .... (checklist back)	.75	.35	.07
☐	96	Blues Team .... (checklist back)	.75	.35	.07
☐	97	Canucks Team .... (checklist back)	.75	.35	.07
☐	98	Capitals Team .... (checklist back)	.75	.35	.07
☐	99	Checklist 1-110........................	3.50	.25	.05
☐	100	Bobby Orr	16.00	8.00	1.60
☐	101	Germain Gagnon	.20	.10	.02
☐	102	Phil Russell	.20	.10	.02
☐	103	Billy Lochead.........................	.20	.10	.02
☐	104	Robin Burns	.20	.10	.02
☐	105	Gary Edwards	.20	.10	.02
☐	106	Dwight Bialowas	.20	.10	.02
☐	107	Doug Risebrough	1.50	.75	.15
☐	108	Dave Lewis............................	.20	.10	.02
☐	109	Bill Fairbairn	.20	.10	.02
☐	110	Ross Lonsberry.......................	.20	.10	.02
☐	111	Ron Stackhouse	.20	.10	.02
☐	112	Claude Larose	.20	.10	.02
☐	113	Don Luce	.20	.10	.02
☐	114	Errol Thompson	.20	.10	.02
☐	115	Gary Smith............................	.20	.10	.02
☐	116	Jack Lynch	.20	.10	.02
☐	117	Jacques Richard	.20	.10	.02

		NRMT	VG-E	GOOD
☐ 118	Dallas Smith	.20	.10	.02
☐ 119	Dave Gardner	.20	.10	.02
☐ 120	Mickey Redmond	.35	.17	.03
☐ 121	John Marks	.20	.10	.02
☐ 122	Dave Hudson	.20	.10	.02
☐ 123	Bob Nevin	.35	.17	.03
☐ 124	Fred Barrett	.20	.10	.02
☐ 125	Gerry Desjardins	.50	.25	.05
☐ 126	Guy Lafleur UER	8.00	4.00	.80
	(Listed as Defense on card front)			
☐ 127	Jean Paul Parise	.20	.10	.02
☐ 128	Walt Tkaczuk	.35	.17	.03
☐ 129	Gary Dornhoefer	.35	.17	.03
☐ 130	Syl Apps	.20	.10	.02
☐ 131	Bob Plager	.35	.17	.03
☐ 132	Stan Weir	.20	.10	.02
☐ 133	Tracy Pratt	.20	.10	.02
☐ 134	Jack Egers	.20	.10	.02
☐ 135	Eric Vail	.50	.25	.05
☐ 136	Al Sims	.20	.10	.02
☐ 137	Larry Patey	.20	.10	.02
☐ 138	Jim Schoenfeld	.50	.25	.05
☐ 139	Cliff Koroll	.20	.10	.02
☐ 140	Marcel Dionne	7.50	3.75	.75
☐ 141	Jean Guy Lagace	.20	.10	.02
☐ 142	Juha Widing	.20	.10	.02
☐ 143	Lou Nanne	.20	.10	.02
☐ 144	Serge Savard	1.25	.60	.12
☐ 145	Glenn Resch	1.75	.85	.17
☐ 146	Ron Greschner	1.50	.75	.15
☐ 147	Dave Schultz	.35	.17	.03
☐ 148	Barry Wilkins	.20	.10	.02
☐ 149	Floyd Thomson	.20	.10	.02
☐ 150	Darryl Sittler	1.25	.60	.12
☐ 151	Paulin Bordeleau	.20	.10	.02
☐ 152	Ron Lalonde	.20	.10	.02
☐ 153	Larry Romanchych	.20	.10	.02
☐ 154	Larry Carriere	.20	.10	.02
☐ 155	Andre Savard	.20	.10	.02
☐ 156	Dave Hrechkosy	.20	.10	.02
☐ 157	Bill White	.35	.17	.03
☐ 158	Dave Kryshow	.20	.10	.02
☐ 159	Denis Dupere	.20	.10	.02
☐ 160	Rogatien Vachon	1.00	.50	.10
☐ 161	Doug Rombough	.20	.10	.02
☐ 162	Murray Wilson	.20	.10	.02
☐ 163	Bob Bourne	1.25	.60	.12
☐ 164	Gilles Marotte	.35	.17	.03
☐ 165	Vic Hadfield	.35	.17	.03
☐ 166	Reg Leach	.50	.25	.05
☐ 167	Jerry Butler	.20	.10	.02
☐ 168	Inge Hammarstrom	.20	.10	.02
☐ 169	Chris Oddleifson	.20	.10	.02

			NRMT	VG-E	GOOD
☐ 170	Greg Joly		.20	.10	.02
☐ 171	Checklist 111-220		3.50	.25	.05
☐ 172	Pat Quinn		.35	.17	.03
☐ 173	Dave Forbes		.20	.10	.02
☐ 174	Len Frig		.20	.10	.02
☐ 175	Rick Martin		.50	.25	.05
☐ 176	Keith Magnuson		.35	.17	.03
☐ 177	Dan Maloney		.35	.17	.03
☐ 178	Craig Patrick		.35	.17	.03
☐ 179	Tom Williams		.20	.10	.02
☐ 180	Bill Goldsworthy		.35	.17	.03
☐ 181	Steve Shutt		2.00	1.00	.20
☐ 182	Ralph Stewart		.20	.10	.02
☐ 183	John Davidson		.35	.17	.03
☐ 184	Bob Kelly		.20	.10	.02
☐ 185	Ed Johnston		.35	.17	.03
☐ 186	Dave Burrows		.35	.17	.03
☐ 187	Dave Dunn		.20	.10	.02
☐ 188	Dennis Kearns		.20	.10	.02
☐ 189	Bill Clement		.75	.35	.07
☐ 190	Gilles Meloche		.35	.17	.03
☐ 191	Bob Leiter		.20	.10	.02
☐ 192	Jerry Korab		.20	.10	.02
☐ 193	Joey Johnston		.20	.10	.02
☐ 194	Walt McKechnie		.20	.10	.02
☐ 195	Wilf Paiement		.75	.35	.07
☐ 196	Bob Berry		.35	.17	.03
☐ 197	Dean Talafous		.20	.10	.02
☐ 198	Guy Lapointe		.60	.30	.06
☐ 199	Clark Gillies		2.25	1.10	.22
☐ 200	Phil Esposito		5.00	2.50	.50
☐ 201	Greg Polis		.20	.10	.02
☐ 202	Jim Watson		.20	.10	.02
☐ 203	Gord McRae		.20	.10	.02
☐ 204	Lowell MacDonald		.35	.17	.03
☐ 205	Barclay Plager		.35	.17	.03
☐ 206	Don Lever		.20	.10	.02
☐ 207	Bill Mikkelson		.20	.10	.02
☐ 208	Goals Leaders		2.00	1.00	.20
	Phil Esposito				
	Guy Lafleur				
	Rick Martin				
☐ 209	Assists Leaders		2.50	1.25	.25
	Bobby Clarke				
	Bobby Orr				
	Pete Mahovlich				
☐ 210	Scoring Leaders		5.00	2.50	.50
	Bobby Orr				
	Phil Esposito				
	Marcel Dionne				

		NRMT	VG-E	GOOD
☐ 211	Penalty Min. Leaders	.35	.17	.03
	Dave Schultz			
	Andre Dupont			
	Phil Russell			
☐ 212	Power Play	.75	.35	.07
	Goal Leaders			
	Phil Esposito			
	Rick Martin			
	Danny Grant			
☐ 213	Goals Against	2.50	1.25	.25
	Average Leaders			
	Bernie Parent			
	Rogatien Vachon			
	Ken Dryden			
☐ 214	Barry Gibbs	.20	.10	.02
☐ 215	Ken Hodge	.50	.25	.05
☐ 216	Jocelyn Guevremont	.20	.10	.02
☐ 217	Warren Williams	.20	.10	.02
☐ 218	Dick Redmond	.20	.10	.02
☐ 219	Jim Rutherford	.35	.17	.03
☐ 220	Simon Nolet	.20	.10	.02
☐ 221	Butch Goring	.35	.17	.03
☐ 222	Glen Sather	.60	.30	.06
☐ 223	Mario Tremblay	.90	.45	.09
☐ 224	Jude Drouin	.20	.10	.02
☐ 225	Rod Gilbert	1.50	.75	.15
☐ 226	Bill Barber	1.50	.75	.15
☐ 227	Gary Inness	.20	.10	.02
☐ 228	Wayne Merrick	.20	.10	.02
☐ 229	Rod Seiling	.20	.10	.02
☐ 230	Tom Lysiak	.35	.17	.03
☐ 231	Bob Dailey	.20	.10	.02
☐ 232	Michel Belhumeur	.35	.17	.03
☐ 233	Bill Hajt	.20	.10	.02
☐ 234	Jim Pappin	.20	.10	.02
☐ 235	Gregg Sheppard	.20	.10	.02
☐ 236	Gary Bergman	.20	.10	.02
☐ 237	Randy Rota	.20	.10	.02
☐ 238	Neil Komadoski	.20	.10	.02
☐ 239	Craig Cameron	.20	.10	.02
☐ 240	Tony Esposito	2.50	1.25	.25
☐ 241	Larry Robinson	6.00	3.00	.60
☐ 242	Billy Harris	.20	.10	.02
☐ 243	Jean Ratelle	1.50	.75	.15
☐ 244	Ted Irvine	.20	.10	.02
	(Photo actually Ted Harris)			
☐ 245	Bob Kelly	.20	.10	.02
☐ 246	Bobby Lalonde	.20	.10	.02
☐ 247	Ron Jones	.20	.10	.02
☐ 248	Rey Comeau	.20	.10	.02
☐ 249	Michel Plasse	.35	.17	.03
☐ 250	Bobby Clarke	4.00	2.00	.40
☐ 251	Bobby Schmautz	.20	.10	.02

			NRMT	VG-E	GOOD
☐ 252	Peter McNab		.50	.25	.05
☐ 253	Al MacAdam		.50	.25	.05
☐ 254	Dennis Hull		.50	.25	.05
☐ 255	Terry Harper		.20	.10	.02
☐ 256	Peter McDuffe		.20	.10	.02
☐ 257	Jean Hamel		.20	.10	.02
☐ 258	Jacques Lemaire		1.25	.60	.12
☐ 259	Bob Nystrom		.35	.17	.03
☐ 260	Brad Park		1.25	.60	.12
☐ 261	Cesare Maniago		.35	.17	.03
☐ 262	Don Saleski		.20	.10	.02
☐ 263	J. Bob Kelly		.20	.10	.02
☐ 264	Bob Hess		.20	.10	.02
☐ 265	Blaine Stoughton		.35	.17	.03
☐ 266	John Gould		.20	.10	.02
☐ 267	Checklist 221-330		3.50	.25	.05
☐ 268	Dan Bouchard		.35	.17	.03
☐ 269	Don Marcotte		.20	.10	.02
☐ 270	Jim Neilson		.20	.10	.02
☐ 271	Craig Ramsay		.20	.10	.02
☐ 272	Grant Mulvey		.65	.30	.06
☐ 273	Larry Giroux		.20	.10	.02
☐ 274	Real Lemieux		.20	.10	.02
☐ 275	Denis Potvin		10.00	5.00	1.00
☐ 276	Don Kozak		.20	.10	.02
☐ 277	Tom Reid		.20	.10	.02
☐ 278	Bob Gainey		2.50	1.25	.25
☐ 279	Nick Beverley		.20	.10	.02
☐ 280	Jean Pronovost		.35	.17	.03
☐ 281	Joe Watson		.20	.10	.02
☐ 282	Chuck Lefley		.20	.10	.02
☐ 283	Borje Salming		1.25	.60	.12
☐ 284	Garnet Bailey		.20	.10	.02
☐ 285	Gregg Boddy		.20	.10	.02
☐ 286	Bobby Clarke AS1		2.00	1.00	.20
☐ 287	Denis Potvin AS1		2.50	1.25	.25
☐ 288	Bobby Orr AS1		10.00	5.00	1.00
☐ 289	Rick Martin AS1		.35	.17	.03
☐ 290	Guy Lafleur AS1		3.00	1.50	.30
☐ 291	Bernie Parent AS1		1.50	.75	.15
☐ 292	Phil Esposito AS2		2.00	1.00	.20
☐ 293	Guy Lapointe AS2		.50	.25	.05
☐ 294	Borje Salming AS2		.50	.25	.05
☐ 295	Steve Vickers AS2		.35	.17	.03
☐ 296	Rene Robert AS2		.35	.17	.03
☐ 297	Rogatien Vachon AS2		.60	.30	.06
☐ 298	Buster Harvey		.20	.10	.02
☐ 299	Gary Sabourin		.20	.10	.02
☐ 300	Bernie Parent		2.00	1.00	.20
☐ 301	Terry O'Reilly		.90	.45	.09
☐ 302	Ed Westfall		.35	.17	.03
☐ 303	Pete Stemkowski		.20	.10	.02
☐ 304	Pierre Bouchard		.35	.17	.03

		NRMT	VG-E	GOOD
☐ 305	**Pierre Larouche**	**2.50**	**1.25**	**.25**
☐ 306	**Lee Fogolin**	.20	.10	.02
☐ 307	**Gerry O'Flaherty**	.20	.10	.02
☐ 308	**Phil Myre**............................	.35	.17	.03
☐ 309	**Pierre Plante**	.20	.10	.02
☐ 310	**Dennis Hextall**	.35	.17	.03
☐ 311	**Jim McKenny**............................	.20	.10	.02
☐ 312	**Vic Venasky**	.20	.10	.02
☐ 313	**Flames Leaders**	.35	.17	.03
	Eric Vail			
	Tom Lysiak			
	Tom Lysiak			
	Tom Lysiak			
☐ 314	**Bruins Leaders**	**6.00**	**3.00**	**.60**
	Phil Esposito			
	Bobby Orr			
	Phil Esposito			
	Johnny Bucyk			
☐ 315	**Sabres Leaders**............................	.35	.17	.03
	Rick Martin			
	Rene Robert			
	Rene Robert			
	Rick Martin			
☐ 316	**Seals Leaders**	.35	.17	.03
	Dave Hrechkosy			
	Larry Patey			
	Stan Weir			
	Stan Weir			
	Larry Patey			
	Dave Hrechkosy			
☐ 317	**Blackhawks Leaders**	**1.00**	**.50**	**.10**
	Stan Mikita			
	Jim Pappin			
	Stan Mikita			
	Stan Mikita			
	Stan Mikita			
☐ 318	**Red Wings Leaders**	.75	.35	.07
	Danny Grant			
	Marcel Dionne			
	Marcel Dionne			
	Danny Grant			
☐ 319	**Scouts Leaders**............................	.35	.17	.03
	Simon Nolet			
	Wilf Paiement			
	Simon Nolet			
	Guy Charron			
	Simon Nolet			

		NRMT	VG-E	GOOD
☐ 320	**Kings Leaders**	.35	.17	.03
	Bob Nevin			
	Bob Nevin			
	Bob Nevin			
	Bob Nevin			
	Juha Widing			
	Bob Berry			
☐ 321	**North Stars Leaders**	.35	.17	.03
	Bill Goldsworthy			
	Dennis Hextall			
	Dennis Hextall			
	Bill Goldsworthy			
☐ 322	**Canadiens Leaders**	1.25	.60	.12
	Guy Lafleur			
	Pete Mahovlich			
	Guy Lafleur			
	Guy Lafleur			
☐ 323	**Islanders Leaders**	.75	.35	.07
	Bob Nystrom			
	Denis Potvin			
	Denis Potvin			
	Clark Gillies			
☐ 324	**Rangers Leaders**	.75	.35	.07
	Steve Vickers			
	Steve Vickers			
	Rod Gilbert			
	Rod Gilbert			
	Jean Ratelle			
☐ 325	**Flyers Leaders**	.75	.35	.07
	Reggie Leach			
	Bobby Clarke			
	Bobby Clarke			
	Reggie Leach			
☐ 326	**Penguins Leaders**	.35	.17	.03
	Jean Pronovost			
	Ron Schock			
	Ron Schock			
	Jean Pronovost			
☐ 327	**Blues Leaders**	.35	.17	.03
	Garry Unger			
	Garry Unger			
	Garry Unger			
	Garry Unger			
	Larry Sacharuk			
☐ 328	**Maple Leafs Leaders**	1.25	.60	.12
	Darryl Sittler			
	Darryl Sittler			
	Darryl Sittler			
	Darryl Sittler			
☐ 329	**Canucks Leaders**	.35	.17	.03
	Don Lever			
	Don Lever			
	Andre Boudrias			
	Andre Boudrias			

	NRMT	VG-E	GOOD
☐ 330 **Capitals Leaders**	.50	.25	.05

Tommy Williams
Garnet Bailey
Tommy Williams
Garnet Bailey
Tommy Williams

1976-77 Topps NHL

BOB GAINEY • L.WING

The 1976-77 Topps set features 264 color cards which are nearly identical to the first 264 cards of this year's O-Pee-Chee NHL set of 396. The only different (player) cards are 102, 159, 183, and 243. Cards are 2½" by 3½". Several Record Breaker (RB) cards feature achievements from the previous season. Team cards (132-149) have a team checklist on the back. The backs, printed in black, dark blue, and green, in English only, feature the player's NHL record, the card number, a short biography, and a cartoon-illustrated fact. The cards, printed in the USA, have the Topps' and the NHL Players Association's copyright on them. The key rookie card in this set is Bryan Trottier.

Le jeu Topps 1976-77 contient 264 cartes en couleurs, presque identiques aux premières 264 cartes d'un jeu de 396 cartes NHL d'O-Pee-Chee de cette année. Les seules cartes (de joueur) différentes sont les cartes numéros 102, 159, 183, et 243. Les cartes mesurent 2½" x 3½". Plusieurs cartes Record Breaker (RB) représentent des exploits de la saison précédente. Les cartes d'équipe (132- 149) ont une liste de contrôle d'équipe au dos. Le dos, imprimé en noir, bleu foncé et vert, et uniquement en anglais, comporte la fiche NHL du joueur, le numéro de carte, une biographie concise, et un fait notable, accompagné d'une caricature. Les cartes, imprimées aux Etats-Unis, portent le droit d'auteur de Topps et de l'Association des Joueurs de la NHL. La carte du débutant important représente Bryan Trottier.

			NRMT	VG-E	GOOD
		COMPLETE SET (264)	110.00	55.00	11.00
		COMMON PLAYER (1-264)	.15	.07	.01
☐	1	Goals Leaders	1.25	.35	.07
		Reggie Leach			
		Guy Lafleur			
		Pierre Larouche			
☐	2	Assists Leaders	1.50	.75	.15
		Bobby Clarke			
		Peter Mahovlich			
		Guy Lafleur			
		Gilbert Perrault			
		Jean Ratelle			
☐	3	Scoring Leaders	1.50	.75	.15
		Guy Lafleur			
		Bobby Clarke			
		Gilbert Perreault			
☐	4	Penalty Min. Leaders	.25	.12	.02
		Steve Durbano			
		Bryan Watson			
		Dave Schultz			
☐	5	Power Play Goals................................	1.50	.75	.15
		Leaders			
		Phil Esposito			
		Guy Lafleur			
		Rick Martin			
		Pierre Larouche			
		Denis Potvin			
☐	6	Goals Against	.90	.45	.09
		Average Leaders			
		Ken Dryden			
		Glenn Resch			
		Michel Larocque			
☐	7	Gary Doak	.15	.07	.01
☐	8	Jacques Richard	.15	.07	.01
☐	9	Wayne Dillon	.15	.07	.01
☐	10	Bernie Parent	2.00	1.00	.20
☐	11	Ed Westfall	.25	.12	.02
☐	12	Dick Redmond	.15	.07	.01
☐	13	Bryan Hextall	.25	.12	.02
☐	14	Jean Pronovost....................................	.25	.12	.02
☐	15	Peter Mahovlich	.25	.12	.02
☐	16	Danny Grant	.15	.07	.01
☐	17	Phil Myre	.25	.12	.02
☐	18	Wayne Merrick	.15	.07	.01
☐	19	Steve Durbano	.15	.07	.01
☐	20	Derek Sanderson	.25	.12	.02
☐	21	Mike Murphy	.15	.07	.01
☐	22	Borje Salming	.50	.25	.05
☐	23	Mike Walton	.25	.12	.02
☐	24	Randy Manery	.15	.07	.01
☐	25	Ken Hodge	.35	.17	.03

			NRMT	VG-E	GOOD
☐	26	Mel Bridgman	.50	.25	.05
☐	27	Jerry Korab	.15	.07	.01
☐	28	Gilles Gratton	.25	.12	.02
☐	29	Andre St. Laurent	.15	.07	.01
☐	30	Yvan Cournoyer	1.50	.75	.15
☐	31	Phil Russell	.15	.07	.01
☐	32	Dennis Hextall	.25	.12	.02
☐	33	Lowell MacDonald	.25	.12	.02
☐	34	Dennis O'Brien	.15	.07	.01
☐	35	Gerry Meehan	.25	.12	.02
☐	36	Gilles Meloche	.25	.12	.02
☐	37	Wilf Paiement	.25	.12	.02
☐	38	Bob MacMillan	.25	.12	.02
☐	39	Ian Turnbull	.15	.07	.01
☐	40	Rogatien Vachon	1.00	.50	.10
☐	41	Nick Beverley	.15	.07	.01
☐	42	Rene Robert	.25	.12	.02
☐	43	Andre Savard	.15	.07	.01
☐	44	Bob Gainey	1.00	.50	.10
☐	45	Joe Watson	.15	.07	.01
☐	46	Billy Smith	1.00	.50	.10
☐	47	Darcy Rota	.15	.07	.01
☐	48	Rick Lapointe	.35	.17	.03
☐	49	Pierre Jarry	.15	.07	.01
☐	50	Syl Apps	.15	.07	.01
☐	51	Eric Vail	.25	.12	.02
☐	52	Greg Joly	.15	.07	.01
☐	53	Don Lever	.15	.07	.01
☐	54	Bob Murdoch	.15	.07	.01
		Seals Right Wing			
☐	55	Denis Herron	.25	.12	.02
☐	56	Mike Bloom	.15	.07	.01
☐	57	Bill Fairbairn	.15	.07	.01
☐	58	Fred Stanfield	.15	.07	.01
☐	59	Steve Shutt	1.00	.50	.10
☐	60	Brad Park	1.25	.60	.12
☐	61	Gilles Villemure	.25	.12	.02
☐	62	Bert Marshall	.15	.07	.01
☐	63	Chuck Lefley	.15	.07	.01
☐	64	Simon Nolet	.15	.07	.01
☐	65	Reggie Leach RB	.25	.12	.02
		Most Goals, Playoffs			
☐	66	Darryl Sittler RB	.75	.35	.07
		Most Points, Game			
☐	67	Bryan Trottier RB	3.50	1.75	.35
		Most Points, Season, Rookie			
☐	68	Garry Unger RB	.25	.12	.02
		Most Consecutive Games, Lifetime			
☐	69	Ron Low	.25	.12	.02
☐	70	Bobby Clarke	2.50	1.25	.25
☐	71	Michel Bergeron	.90	.45	.09
☐	72	Ron Stackhouse	.15	.07	.01
☐	73	Bill Hogaboam	.15	.07	.01

		NRMT	VG-E	GOOD
☐ 74	Bob Murdoch	.15	.07	.01
	Kings Defenseman			
☐ 75	Steve Vickers	.15	.07	.01
☐ 76	Pit Martin	.15	.07	.01
☐ 77	Gerry Hart	.15	.07	.01
☐ 78	Craig Ramsay	.15	.07	.01
☐ 79	Michel Larocque	.25	.12	.02
☐ 80	Jean Ratelle	1.50	.75	.15
☐ 81	Don Saleski	.15	.07	.01
☐ 82	Bill Clement	.25	.12	.02
☐ 83	Dave Burrows	.25	.12	.02
☐ 84	Wayne Thomas	.35	.17	.03
☐ 85	John Gould	.15	.07	.01
☐ 86	Dennis Maruk	1.75	.85	.17
☐ 87	Ernie Hicke	.15	.07	.01
☐ 88	Jim Rutherford	.25	.12	.02
☐ 89	Dale Tallon	.15	.07	.01
☐ 90	Rod Gilbert	1.50	.75	.15
☐ 91	Marcel Dionne	6.00	3.00	.60
☐ 92	Chuck Arnason	.15	.07	.01
☐ 93	Jean Potvin	.15	.07	.01
☐ 94	Don Luce	.15	.07	.01
☐ 95	Johnny Bucyk	1.50	.75	.15
☐ 96	Larry Goodenough	.15	.07	.01
☐ 97	Mario Tremblay	.25	.12	.02
☐ 98	Nelson Pyatt	.15	.07	.01
☐ 99	Brian Glennie	.15	.07	.01
☐ 100	Tony Esposito	2.00	1.00	.20
☐ 101	Dan Maloney	.25	.12	.02
☐ 102	Barry Wilkins	.15	.07	.01
☐ 103	Dean Talafous	.15	.07	.01
☐ 104	Ed Staniowski	.50	.25	.05
☐ 105	Dallas Smith	.15	.07	.01
☐ 106	Jude Drouin	.15	.07	.01
☐ 107	Pat Hickey	.15	.07	.01
☐ 108	Jocelyn Guevremont	.15	.07	.01
☐ 109	Doug Risebrough	.25	.12	.02
☐ 110	Reggie Leach	.35	.17	.03
☐ 111	Dan Bouchard	.25	.12	.02
☐ 112	Chris Oddleifson	.15	.07	.01
☐ 113	Rick Hampton	.15	.07	.01
☐ 114	John Marks	.15	.07	.01
☐ 115	Bryan Trottier	36.00	18.00	3.60
☐ 116	Checklist 1-132	2.50	.20	.04
☐ 117	Greg Polis	.15	.07	.01
☐ 118	Peter McNab	.15	.07	.01
☐ 119	Jim Roberts	.15	.07	.01
	Montreal Canadiens			
☐ 120	Gerry Cheevers	1.75	.85	.17
☐ 121	Rick MacLeish	.35	.17	.03
☐ 122	Billy Lochead	.15	.07	.01
☐ 123	Tom Reid	.15	.07	.01
☐ 124	Rick Kehoe	.25	.12	.02

			NRMT	VG-E	GOOD
☐ 125	Keith Magnuson		.25	.12	.02
☐ 126	Clark Gillies		.50	.25	.05
☐ 127	Rick Middleton		1.00	.50	.10
☐ 128	Bill Hajt		.15	.07	.01
☐ 129	Jacques Lemaire		1.00	.50	.10
☐ 130	Terry O'Reilly		.50	.25	.05
☐ 131	Andre Dupont		.15	.07	.01
☐ 132	Flames Team (checklist back)		.55	.27	.05
☐ 133	Bruins Team (checklist back)		.55	.27	.05
☐ 134	Sabres Team (checklist back)		.55	.27	.05
☐ 135	Seals Team (checklist back)		.55	.27	.05
☐ 136	Blackhawks Team (checklist back)		.55	.27	.05
☐ 137	Red Wings Team (checklist back)		.55	.27	.05
☐ 138	Scouts Team (checklist back)		.55	.27	.05
☐ 139	Kings Team (checklist back)		.55	.27	.05
☐ 140	North Stars Team (checklist back)		.55	.27	.05
☐ 141	Canadiens Team (checklist back)		.55	.27	.05
☐ 142	Islanders Team (checklist back)		.55	.27	.05
☐ 143	Rangers Team (checklist back)		.55	.27	.05
☐ 144	Flyers Team (checklist back)		.55	.27	.05
☐ 145	Penguins Team (checklist back)		.55	.27	.05
☐ 146	Blues Team (checklist back)		.55	.27	.05
☐ 147	Maple Leafs Team (checklist back)		.55	.27	.05
☐ 148	Canucks Team (checklist back)		.55	.27	.05
☐ 149	Capitals Team (checklist back)		.55	.27	.05
☐ 150	Dave Schultz		.25	.12	.02
☐ 151	Larry Robinson		1.75	.85	.17
☐ 152	Al Smith		.15	.07	.01
☐ 153	Bob Nystrom		.25	.12	.02
☐ 154	Ron Greschner		.35	.17	.03
☐ 155	Gregg Sheppard		.15	.07	.01
☐ 156	Alain Daigle		.15	.07	.01
☐ 157	Ed Van Impe		.15	.07	.01
☐ 158	Tim Young		.15	.07	.01
☐ 159	Gary Bergman		.15	.07	.01

			NRMT	VG-E	GOOD
☐ 160	Ed Giacomin		1.00	.50	.10
☐ 161	Yvon Labre		.15	.07	.01
☐ 162	Jim Lorentz		.15	.07	.01
☐ 163	Guy Lafleur		6.00	3.00	.60
☐ 164	Tom Bladon		.15	.07	.01
☐ 165	Wayne Cashman		.25	.12	.02
☐ 166	Pete Stemkowski		.15	.07	.01
☐ 167	Grant Mulvey		.25	.12	.02
☐ 168	Yves Belanger		.25	.12	.02
☐ 169	Bill Goldsworthy		.25	.12	.02
☐ 170	Denis Potvin		3.50	1.75	.35
☐ 171	Nick Libett		.15	.07	.01
☐ 172	Michel Plasse		.25	.12	.02
☐ 173	Lou Nanne		.15	.07	.01
☐ 174	Tom Lysiak		.25	.12	.02
☐ 175	Dennis Ververgaert		.15	.07	.01
☐ 176	Gary Simmons		.25	.12	.02
☐ 177	Pierre Bouchard		.25	.12	.02
☐ 178	Bill Barber		1.00	.50	.10
☐ 179	Darryl Edestrand		.15	.07	.01
☐ 180	Gilbert Perreault		1.75	.85	.17
☐ 181	Dave Maloney		.50	.25	.05
☐ 182	Jean Paul Parise		.15	.07	.01
☐ 183	Bobby Sheehan		.15	.07	.01
☐ 184	Pete Lopresti		.15	.07	.01
☐ 185	Don Kozak		.15	.07	.01
☐ 186	Guy Charron		.15	.07	.01
☐ 187	Stan Gilbertson		.15	.07	.01
☐ 188	Bill Nyrop		.35	.17	.03
☐ 189	Bobby Schmautz		.15	.07	.01
☐ 190	Wayne Stephenson		.25	.12	.02
☐ 191	Brian Spencer		.15	.07	.01
☐ 192	Gilles Marotte		.25	.12	.02
☐ 193	Lorne Henning		.15	.07	.01
☐ 194	Bob Neely		.15	.07	.01
☐ 195	Dennis Hull		.35	.17	.03
☐ 196	Walt McKechnie		.15	.07	.01
☐ 197	Curt Ridley		.15	.07	.01
☐ 198	Dwight Bialowas		.15	.07	.01
☐ 199	Pierre Larouche		.50	.25	.05
☐ 200	Ken Dryden		6.00	3.00	.60
☐ 201	Ross Lonsberry		.15	.07	.01
☐ 202	Curt Bennett		.15	.07	.01
☐ 203	Hartland Monahan		.15	.07	.01
☐ 204	John Davidson		.25	.12	.02
☐ 205	Serge Savard		.90	.45	.09
☐ 206	Garry Howatt		.15	.07	.01
☐ 207	Darryl Sittler		1.00	.50	.10
☐ 208	J.P. Bordeleau		.15	.07	.01
☐ 209	Henry Boucha		.15	.07	.01
☐ 210	Rick Martin		.35	.17	.03
☐ 211	Vic Venasky		.15	.07	.01
☐ 212	Buster Harvey		.15	.07	.01

		NRMT	VG-E	GOOD
☐ 213	**Bobby Orr**	15.00	7.50	1.50
☐ 214	**French Connection**	.90	.45	.09
	Rick Martin			
	Gilbert Perreault			
	Rene Robert			
☐ 215	**LCB Line**	1.25	.60	.12
	Bill Barber			
	Bobby Clarke			
	Reggie Leach			
☐ 216	**Long Island Lightning**	1.25	.60	.12
	Clark Gillies			
	Bryan Trottier			
	Billy Harris			
☐ 217	**Checking Line**	.50	.25	.05
	Bob Gainey			
	Doug Jarvis			
	Jim Roberts			
☐ 218	**Bicentennial Line**	.35	.17	.03
	Lowell MacDonald			
	Syl Apps			
	Jean Pronovost			
☐ 219	**Bob Kelly**	.15	.07	.01
☐ 220	**Walt Tkaczuk**	.25	.12	.02
☐ 221	**Dave Lewis**	.15	.07	.01
☐ 222	**Danny Gare**	.25	.12	.02
☐ 223	**Guy Lapointe**	.50	.25	.05
☐ 224	**Hank Nowak**	.15	.07	.01
☐ 225	**Stan Mikita**	3.00	1.50	.30
☐ 226	**Vic Hadfield**	.25	.12	.02
☐ 227	**Bernie Wolfe**	.15	.07	.01
☐ 228	**Bryan Watson**	.15	.07	.01
☐ 229	**Ralph Stewart**	.15	.07	.01
☐ 230	**Gerry Desjardins**	.25	.12	.02
☐ 231	**John Bednarski**	.15	.07	.01
☐ 232	**Yvon Lambert**	.15	.07	.01
☐ 233	**Orest Kindrachuk**	.15	.07	.01
☐ 234	**Don Marcotte**	.15	.07	.01
☐ 235	**Bill White**	.25	.12	.02
☐ 236	**Red Berenson**	.25	.12	.02
☐ 237	**Al MacAdam**	.25	.12	.02
☐ 238	**Rick Blight**	.15	.07	.01
☐ 239	**Butoh Goring**	.25	.12	.02
☐ 240	**Cesare Maniago**	.25	.12	.02
☐ 241	**Jim Schoenfeld**	.25	.12	.02
☐ 242	**Cliff Koroll**	.15	.07	.01
☐ 243	**Mickey Redmond**	.25	.12	.02
☐ 244	**Rick Chartraw**	.15	.07	.01
☐ 245	**Phil Esposito**	4.50	2.25	.45
☐ 246	**Dave Forbes**	.15	.07	.01
☐ 247	**Joe Watson**	.15	.07	.01
☐ 248	**Ron Schock**	.15	.07	.01
☐ 249	**Fred Barrett**	.15	.07	.01
☐ 250	**Glenn Resch**	1.00	.50	.10

			NRMT	VG-E	GOOD
☐ 251	Ivan Boldirev		.15	.07	.01
☐ 252	Billy Harris		.15	.07	.01
☐ 253	Lee Fogolin		.15	.07	.01
☐ 254	Murray Wilson		.15	.07	.01
☐ 255	Gilles Gilbert		.25	.12	.02
☐ 256	Gary Dornhoefer		.25	.12	.02
☐ 257	Carol Vadnais		.15	.07	.01
☐ 258	Checklist 133-264		2.50	.20	.04
☐ 259	Errol Thompson		.15	.07	.01
☐ 260	Garry Unger		.35	.17	.03
☐ 261	J. Bob Kelly		.15	.07	.01
☐ 262	Terry Harper		.15	.07	.01
☐ 263	Blake Dunlop		.15	.07	.01
☐ 264	Stanley Cup Champs		1.00	.25	.05
	Montreal Canadiens				

1977-78 Topps NHL

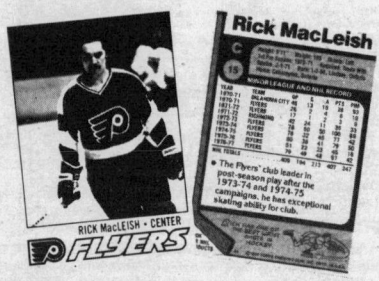

The 1977-78 Topps set consists of 264 color cards which are nearly the same as the 264 cards of the NHL O-Pee-Chee set of this year. Cards 203 and 255 are the only card numbers showing different players in the O-Pee-Chee set compared to the Topps hockey set this year. Cards are the standard 2½" by 3½". The backs, printed in English only, feature the card number, the player's minor league and NHL year-by-year record, a short biography, and a cartoon-illustrated fact about the player. The cards were printed in the USA. There are no key rookie cards in this set.

Le jeu Topps 1977-78 contient 264 cartes en couleurs, presque identiques aux 264 cartes du jeu NHL d'O-Pee-Chee de cette année. Les cartes 203 et 255 du jeu O-Pee-Chee sont les seules à représenter des joueurs différents du jeu Topps de cette année. Les cartes mesurent 2½" x 3½". Le dos, imprimé uniquement en anglais, comporte le numéro de carte, les statistiques par année de deuxième division et de carrière NHL du

joueur, une biographie concise, et un fait notable concernant le joueur, illustré d'une caricature. Les cartes ont été imprimées aux Etats-Unis. Ce jeu ne contient pas de cartes de débutants importants.

			NRMT	VG-E	GOOD
		COMPLETE SET (264)	90.00	45.00	9.00
		COMMON PLAYER (1-264)	.12	.06	.01
☐	1	**Goals Leaders** .... Steve Shutt Guy Lafleur Marcel Dionne	1.50	.40	.08
☐	2	**Assists Leaders** .... Guy Lafleur Marcel Dionne Larry Robinson Borje Salming Tim Young	1.25	.60	.12
☐	3	**Scoring Leaders** .... Guy Lafleur Marcel Dionne Steve Shutt	1.25	.60	.12
☐	4	**Penalty Min. Leaders** .... Dave Williams Dennis Polonich Bob Gassoff	.20	.10	.02
☐	5	**Power Play Goals Leaders** Lanny McDonald Phil Esposito Tom Williams	.75	.35	.07
☐	6	**Goals Against Average Leaders** Michel Larocque Ken Dryden Glenn Resch	.90	.45	.09
☐	7	**Game Winning Goals Leaders** Gilbert Perreault Steve Shutt Guy Lafleur Rick MacLeish Peter McNab	1.25	.60	.12
☐	8	**Shutouts Leaders** .... Ken Dryden Rogatien Vachon Bernie Parent Dunc Wilson	.90	.45	.09
☐	9	**Brian Spencer**	.12	.06	.01
☐	10	**Denis Potvin AS2**	2.00	1.00	.20
☐	11	**Nick Fotiu**	.12	.06	.01
☐	12	**Bob Murray**	.12	.06	.01
☐	13	**Pete Lopresti**	.12	.06	.01

			NRMT	VG-E	GOOD
☐	14	J. Bob Kelly	.12	.06	.01
☐	15	Rick MacLeish	.40	.20	.04
☐	16	Terry Harper	.12	.06	.01
☐	17	Willi Plett	.12	.06	.01
☐	18	Peter McNab	.12	.06	.01
☐	19	Wayne Thomas	.20	.10	.02
☐	20	Pierre Bouchard	.12	.06	.01
☐	21	Dennis Maruk	.40	.20	.04
☐	22	Mike Murphy	.12	.06	.01
☐	23	Cesare Maniago	.20	.10	.02
☐	24	Paul Gardner	.30	.15	.03
☐	25	Rod Gilbert	1.25	.60	.12
☐	26	Orest Kindrachuk	.12	.06	.01
☐	27	Bill Hajt	.12	.06	.01
☐	28	John Davidson	.20	.10	.02
☐	29	Jean Paul Parise	.12	.06	.01
☐	30	Larry Robinson AS1	1.25	.60	.12
☐	31	Yvon Labre	.12	.06	.01
☐	32	Walt McKechnie	.12	.06	.01
☐	33	Rick Kehoe	.20	.10	.02
☐	34	Randy Holt	.12	.06	.01
☐	35	Garry Unger	.30	.15	.03
☐	36	Lou Nanne	.12	.06	.01
☐	37	Dan Bouchard	.20	.10	.02
☐	38	Darryl Sittler	.90	.45	.09
☐	39	Bob Murdoch	.12	.06	.01
☐	40	Jean Ratelle	1.10	.55	.11
☐	41	Dave Maloney	.20	.10	.02
☐	42	Danny Gare	.20	.10	.02
☐	43	Jim Watson	.12	.06	.01
☐	44	Tom Williams	.12	.06	.01
☐	45	Serge Savard	.90	.45	.09
☐	46	Derek Sanderson	.20	.10	.02
☐	47	John Marks	.12	.06	.01
☐	48	Al Cameron	.12	.06	.01
☐	49	Dean Talafous	.12	.06	.01
☐	50	Glenn Resch	.80	.40	.08
☐	51	Ron Schock	.12	.06	.01
☐	52	Gary Croteau	.12	.06	.01
☐	53	Gerry Meehan	.20	.10	.02
☐	54	Ed Staniowski	.20	.10	.02
☐	55	Phil Esposito	3.00	1.50	.30
☐	56	Dennis Ververgaert	.12	.06	.01
☐	57	Rick Wilson	.12	.06	.01
☐	58	Jim Lorentz	.12	.06	.01
☐	59	Bobby Schmautz	.12	.06	.01
☐	60	Guy Lapointe AS2	.30	.15	.03
☐	61	Ivan Boldirev	.12	.06	.01
☐	62	Bob Nystrom	.20	.10	.02
☐	63	Rick Hampton	.12	.06	.01
☐	64	Jack Valiquette	.12	.06	.01
☐	65	Bernie Parent	1.50	.75	.15
☐	66	Dave Burrows	.12	.06	.01

			NRMT	VG-E	GOOD
☐	67	Butch Goring	.30	.15	.03
☐	68	Checklist 1-132	1.50	.15	.03
☐	69	Murray Wilson	.12	.06	.01
☐	70	Ed Giacomin	.90	.45	.09
☐	71	Flames Team	.40	.20	.04
☐	72	Bruins Team	.40	.20	.04
☐	73	Sabres Team	.40	.20	.04
☐	74	Blackhawks Team	.40	.20	.04
☐	75	Barons Team	.40	.20	.04
☐	76	Rockies Team	.40	.20	.04
☐	77	Red Wings Team	.40	.20	.04
☐	78	Kings Team	.40	.20	.04
☐	79	North Stars Team	.40	.20	.04
☐	80	Canadiens Team	.40	.20	.04
☐	81	Islanders Team	.40	.20	.04
☐	82	Rangers Team	.40	.20	.04
☐	83	Flyers Team	.40	.20	.04
☐	84	Penguins Team	.40	.20	.04
☐	85	Blues Team	.40	.20	.04
☐	86	Maple Leafs Team	.40	.20	.04
☐	87	Canucks Team	.40	.20	.04
☐	88	Capitals Team	.40	.20	.04
☐	89	Keith Magnuson	.12	.06	.01
☐	90	Walt Tkaczuk	.20	.10	.02
☐	91	Bill Nyrop	.20	.10	.02
☐	92	Michel Plasse	.20	.10	.02
☐	93	Bob Bourne	.20	.10	.02
☐	94	Lee Fogolin	.12	.06	.01
☐	95	Gregg Sheppard	.12	.06	.01
☐	96	Hartland Monahan	.12	.06	.01
☐	97	Curt Bennett	.12	.06	.01
☐	98	Bob Dailey	.12	.06	.01
☐	99	Bill Goldsworthy	.20	.10	.02
☐	100	Ken Dryden AS1	5.00	2.50	.50
☐	101	Grant Mulvey	.20	.10	.02
☐	102	Pierre Larouche	.30	.15	.03
☐	103	Nick Libett	.12	.06	.01
☐	104	Rick Smith	.12	.06	.01
☐	105	Bryan Trottier	8.00	4.00	.80
☐	106	Pierre Jarry	.12	.06	.01
☐	107	Red Berenson	.20	.10	.02
☐	108	Jim Schoenfeld	.20	.10	.02
☐	109	Gilles Meloche	.20	.10	.02
☐	110	Lanny McDonald AS2	1.00	.50	.10
☐	111	Don Lever	.12	.06	.01
☐	112	Greg Polis	.12	.06	.01
☐	113	Gary Sargent	.40	.20	.04
☐	114	Earl Anderson	.12	.06	.01
☐	115	Bobby Clarke	2.00	1.00	.20
☐	116	Dave Lewis	.12	.06	.01
☐	117	Darcy Rota	.12	.06	.01
☐	118	Andre Savard	.12	.06	.01
☐	119	Denis Herron	.20	.10	.02

		NRMT	VG-E	GOOD
☐ 120	Steve Shutt AS1	.80	.40	.08
☐ 121	Mel Bridgman	.20	.10	.02
☐ 122	Buster Harvey	.12	.06	.01
☐ 123	Roland Eriksson	.12	.06	.01
☐ 124	Dale Tallon	.12	.06	.01
☐ 125	Gilles Gilbert	.20	.10	.02
☐ 126	Billy Harris	.12	.06	.01
☐ 127	Tom Lysiak	.20	.10	.02
☐ 128	Jerry Korab	.12	.06	.01
☐ 129	Bob Gainey	.80	.40	.08
☐ 130	Wilf Paiement	.20	.10	.02
☐ 131A	Tom Bladon (Standing)	.20	.10	.02
☐ 131B	Tom Bladon (Crouched for face off)	.20	.10	.02
☐ 132	Ernie Hicke	.12	.06	.01
☐ 133	J.P. Leblanc	.12	.06	.01
☐ 134	Mike Milbury	1.00	.50	.10
☐ 135	Pit Martin	.12	.06	.01
☐ 136	Steve Vickers	.12	.06	.01
☐ 137	Don Awrey	.12	.06	.01
☐ 138A	Bernie Wolfe ERR (Photo actually Al MacAdam looking straight ahead)	2.00	1.00	.20
☐ 138B	Bernie Wolfe COR	.40	.20	.04
☐ 139	Doug Jarvis	.40	.20	.04
☐ 140	Borje Salming AS1	.40	.20	.04
☐ 141	Bob MacMillan	.20	.10	.02
☐ 142	Wayne Stephenson	.20	.10	.02
☐ 143	Dave Forbes	.12	.06	.01
☐ 144	Jean Potvin	.12	.06	.01
☐ 145	Guy Charron	.12	.06	.01
☐ 146	Cliff Koroll	.12	.06	.01
☐ 147	Danny Grant	.12	.06	.01
☐ 148	Bill Hogaboam	.12	.06	.01
☐ 149A	Al MacAdam ERR (Photo actually Bernie Wolfe looking left)	2.00	1.00	.20
☐ 149B	Al MacAdam COR	.40	.20	.04
☐ 150	Gerry Desjardins	.20	.10	.02
☐ 151	Yvon Lambert	.12	.06	.01
☐ 152A	Rick Lapointe (shooting, facing right, without mustache)	10.00	5.00	1.00
☐ 152B	Rick Lapointe (with mustache)	.40	.20	.04
☐ 153	Ed Westfall	.20	.10	.02
☐ 154	Carol Vadnais	.12	.06	.01
☐ 155	Johnny Bucyk	1.00	.50	.10
☐ 156	J.P. Bordeleau	.12	.06	.01
☐ 157	Ron Stackhouse	.12	.06	.01
☐ 158	Glen Sharpley	.12	.06	.01
☐ 159	Michel Bergeron	.30	.15	.03

		NRMT	VG-E	GOOD
☐ 160	Rogatien Vachon AS2	.80	.40	.08
☐ 161	Fred Stanfield	.12	.06	.01
☐ 162	Gerry Hart	.12	.06	.01
☐ 163	Mario Tremblay	.20	.10	.02
☐ 164	Andre Dupont	.12	.06	.01
☐ 165	Don Marcotte	.12	.06	.01
☐ 166	Wayne Dillon	.12	.06	.01
☐ 167	Claude Larose	.12	.06	.01
☐ 168	Eric Vail	.20	.10	.02
☐ 169	Tom Edur	.12	.06	.01
☐ 170	Tony Esposito	1.50	.75	.15
☐ 171	Andre St. Laurent	.12	.06	.01
☐ 172	Dan Maloney	.20	.10	.02
☐ 173	Dennis O'Brien	.12	.06	.01
☐ 174	Blair Chapman	.12	.06	.01
☐ 175	Dennis Kearns	.12	.06	.01
☐ 176	Wayne Merrick	.12	.06	.01
☐ 177	Michel Larocque	.30	.15	.03
☐ 178	Bob Kelly	.12	.06	.01
☐ 179	Dave Farrish	.12	.06	.01
☐ 180	Rick Martin AS2	.30	.15	.03
☐ 181	Gary Doak	.12	.06	.01
☐ 182	Jude Drouin	.12	.06	.01
☐ 183	Barry Dean	.12	.06	.01
☐ 184	Gary Smith	.20	.10	.02
☐ 185	Reggie Leach	.30	.15	.03
☐ 186	Ian Turnbull	.12	.06	.01
☐ 187	Vic Venasky	.12	.06	.01
☐ 188	Wayne Bianchin	.12	.06	.01
☐ 189	Doug Risebrough	.20	.10	.02
☐ 190	Brad Park	.90	.45	.09
☐ 191	Craig Ramsay	.12	.06	.01
☐ 192	Ken Hodge	.30	.15	.03
☐ 193	Phil Myre	.20	.10	.02
☐ 194	Garry Howatt	.12	.06	.01
☐ 195	Stan Mikita	2.00	1.00	.20
☐ 196	Garnet Bailey	.12	.06	.01
☐ 197	Dennis Hextall	.20	.10	.02
☐ 198	Nick Beverley	.12	.06	.01
☐ 199	Larry Patey	.12	.06	.01
☐ 200	Guy Lafleur AS1	5.00	2.50	.50
☐ 201	Don Edwards	.80	.40	.08
☐ 202	Gary Dornhoefer	.20	.10	.02
☐ 203	Stan Gilbertson	.20	.10	.02
☐ 204	Alex Pirus	.12	.06	.01
☐ 205	Peter Mahovlich	.20	.10	.02
☐ 206	Bert Marshall	.12	.06	.01
☐ 207	Gilles Gratton	.20	.10	.02
☐ 208	Alain Daigle	.12	.06	.01
☐ 209	Chris Oddleifson	.12	.06	.01
☐ 210	Gilbert Perreault AS2	1.25	.60	.12
☐ 211	Mike Palmateer	.80	.40	.08
☐ 212	Billy Lochead	.12	.06	.01

			NRMT	VG-E	GOOD
☐ 213	Dick Redmond		.12	.06	.01
☐ 214	Guy Lafleur RB Most Points, RW, Season		1.50	.75	.15
☐ 215	Ian Turnbull RB Most Goals, Defenseman, Game		.20	.10	.02
☐ 216	Guy Lafleur RB Longest Point Scoring Streak		1.50	.75	.15
☐ 217	Steve Shutt RB Most Goals, LW, Season		.30	.15	.03
☐ 218	Guy Lafleur RB Most Assists, RW, Season		1.50	.75	.15
☐ 219	Lorne Henning		.12	.06	.01
☐ 220	Terry O'Reilly		.40	.20	.04
☐ 221	Pat Hickey		.12	.06	.01
☐ 222	Rene Robert		.20	.10	.02
☐ 223	Tim Young		.12	.06	.01
☐ 224	Dunc Wilson		.20	.10	.02
☐ 225	Dennis Hull		.30	.15	.03
☐ 226	Rod Seiling		.12	.06	.01
☐ 227	Bill Barber		.75	.35	.07
☐ 228	Dennis Polonich		.12	.06	.01
☐ 229	Billy Smith		.75	.35	.07
☐ 230	Yvan Cournoyer		1.00	.50	.10
☐ 231	Don Luce		.12	.06	.01
☐ 232	Mike McEwen		.30	.15	.03
☐ 233	Don Saleski		.12	.06	.01
☐ 234	Wayne Cashman		.20	.10	.02
☐ 235	Phil Russell		.12	.06	.01
☐ 236	Mike Corrigan		.12	.06	.01
☐ 237	Guy Chouinard		.20	.10	.02
☐ 238	Steve Jensen		.12	.06	.01
☐ 239	Jim Rutherford		.20	.10	.02
☐ 240	Marcel Dionne AS1		4.00	2.00	.40
☐ 241	Rejean Houle		.20	.10	.02
☐ 242	Jocelyn Guevremont		.12	.06	.01
☐ 243	Jim Harrison		.12	.06	.01
☐ 244	Don Murdoch		.12	.06	.01
☐ 245	Rick Green		.75	.35	.07
☐ 246	Rick Middleton		.80	.40	.08
☐ 247	Joe Watson		.12	.06	.01
☐ 248	Syl Apps		.12	.06	.01
☐ 249	Checklist 133-264		1.50	.15	.03
☐ 250	Clark Gillies		.30	.15	.03
☐ 251	Bobby Orr		15.00	7.50	1.50
☐ 252	Nelson Pyatt		.12	.06	.01
☐ 253	Gary McAdam		.20	.10	.02
☐ 254	Jacques Lemaire		.90	.45	.09
☐ 255	Bill Fairbairn		.12	.06	.01

		NRMT	VG-E	GOOD
☐ 256	Ron Greschner	.30	.15	.03
☐ 257	Ross Lonsberry	.12	.06	.01
☐ 258	Dave Gardner	.12	.06	.01
☐ 259	Rick Blight	.12	.06	.01
☐ 260	Gerry Cheevers	1.25	.60	.12
☐ 261	Jean Pronovost	.20	.10	.02
☐ 262	Semi-Finals .... Canadiens Skate Past Islanders	.40	.20	.04
☐ 263	Semi-Finals .... Bruins Advance to Finals	.40	.20	.04
☐ 264	Finals .... Canadiens Win 20th Stanley Cup	1.00	.25	.05

1978-79 Topps

The 1978-79 Topps set consists of 264 color cards which are the same as the first 264 cards of the NHL O-Pee-Chee set of 396 this year. Cards are 2½" by 3½". The backs, in English only, are printed with green and orange ink. The card number, a short biography, the player's NHL record, and a facsimile autograph are included on the back. The cards were printed in the USA. The key rookie cards in this set are Mike Bossy, Bernie Federko, and Doug Wilson.

Le jeu Topps 1978-79 contient 264 cartes en couleurs, identiques aux premières 264 cartes du jeu NHL de 396 cartes d'O-Pee-Chee de cette année. Les cartes mesurent 2½" x 3½". Le dos, vert et orange, est imprimé uniquement en anglais. Il comporte le numéro de carte, une biographie concise, la fiche NHL du joueur et une copie de son autographe. Les cartes ont été imprimées aux Etats-Unis. Les cartes des débutants importants de ce jeu représentent Mike Bossy, Bernie Federko, et Doug Wilson.

			NRMT	VG-E	GOOD
		COMPLETE SET (264)	90.00	45.00	9.00
		COMMON PLAYER (1-264)	.11	.05	.01
☐	1	Mike Bossy HL .... Goals by Rookie	7.50	1.50	.30
☐	2	Phil Esposito HL .... 29th Hat Trick	1.00	.50	.10
☐	3	Guy Lafleur HL .... Scores Against Every Team	1.25	.60	.12
☐	4	Darryl Sittler HL .... Goals in Nine Straight Games	.35	.17	.03
☐	5	Garry Unger HL .... 803 Consec. Games	.20	.10	.02
☐	6	Gary Edwards	.20	.10	.02
☐	7	Rick Blight	.11	.05	.01
☐	8	Larry Patey	.11	.05	.01
☐	9	Craig Ramsay	.11	.05	.01
☐	10	Bryan Trottier AS1	3.50	1.75	.35
☐	11	Don Murdoch	.11	.05	.01
☐	12	Phil Russell	.11	.05	.01
☐	13	Doug Jarvis	.20	.10	.02
☐	14	Gene Carr	.11	.05	.01
☐	15	Bernie Parent	1.25	.60	.12
☐	16	Perry Miller	.11	.05	.01
☐	17	Kent-Erik Andersson	.11	.05	.01
☐	18	Gregg Sheppard	.11	.05	.01
☐	19	Dennis Owchar	.11	.05	.01
☐	20	Rogatien Vachon	.75	.35	.07
☐	21	Dan Maloney	.20	.10	.02
☐	22	Guy Charron	.11	.05	.01
☐	23	Dick Redmond	.11	.05	.01
☐	24	Checklist 1-132	1.25	.10	.02
☐	25	Anders Hedberg	.20	.10	.02
☐	26	Mel Bridgman	.11	.05	.01
☐	27	Lee Fogolin	.11	.05	.01
☐	28	Gilles Meloche	.20	.10	.02
☐	29	Garry Howatt	.11	.05	.01
☐	30	Darryl Sittler AS2	.75	.35	.07
☐	31	Curt Bennett	.11	.05	.01
☐	32	Andre St. Laurent	.11	.05	.01
☐	33	Blair Chapman	.11	.05	.01
☐	34	Keith Magnuson	.11	.05	.01
☐	35	Pierre Larouche	.25	.12	.02
☐	36	Michel Plasse	.20	.10	.02
☐	37	Gary Sargent	.20	.10	.02
☐	38	Mike Walton	.20	.10	.02
☐	39	Robert Picard	.11	.05	.01
☐	40	Terry O'Reilly AS2	.25	.12	.02
☐	41	Dave Farrish	.11	.05	.01
☐	42	Gary McAdam	.20	.10	.02
☐	43	Joe Watson	.11	.05	.01

			NRMT	VG-E	GOOD
☐	44	Yves Belanger	.20	.10	.02
☐	45	Steve Jensen	.11	.05	.01
☐	46	Bob Stewart	.11	.05	.01
☐	47	Darcy Rota	.11	.05	.01
☐	48	Dennis Hextall	.20	.10	.02
☐	49	Bert Marshall	.11	.05	.01
☐	50	Ken Dryden AS1	4.00	2.00	.40
☐	51	Peter Mahovlich	.20	.10	.02
☐	52	Dennis Ververgaert	.11	.05	.01
☐	53	Inge Hammarstrom	.11	.05	.01
☐	54	Doug Favell	.20	.10	.02
☐	55	Steve Vickers	.11	.05	.01
☐	56	Syl Apps	.11	.05	.01
☐	57	Errol Thompson	.11	.05	.01
☐	58	Don Luce	.11	.05	.01
☐	59	Mike Milbury	.25	.12	.02
☐	60	Yvan Cournoyer	1.00	.50	.10
☐	61	Kirk Bowman	.11	.05	.01
☐	62	Billy Smith	.70	.35	.07
☐	63	Goal Leaders Guy Lafleur Mike Bossy Steve Shutt	1.25	.60	.12
☐	64	Assist Leaders Bryan Trottier Guy Lafleur Darryl Sittler	1.25	.60	.12
☐	65	Scoring Leaders Guy Lafleur Bryan Trottier Darryl Sittler	1.25	.60	.12
☐	66	Penalty Minutes Leaders Dave Schultz Dave Williams Dennis Polonich	.20	.10	.02
☐	67	Power Play Goal Leaders Mike Bossy Phil Esposito Steve Shutt	1.25	.60	.12
☐	68	Goals Against Average Leaders Ken Dryden Bernie Parent Gilles Gilbert	.80	.40	.08
☐	69	Game Winning Goal Leaders Guy Lafleur Bill Barber Darryl Sittler Bob Bourne	1.25	.60	.12

			NRMT	VG-E	GOOD
☐	70	Shutout Leaders	1.00	.50	.10
		Bernie Parent			
		Ken Dryden			
		Don Edwards			
		Tony Esposito			
		Mike Palmateer			
☐	71	Bob Kelly	.11	.05	.01
☐	72	Ron Stackhouse	.11	.05	.01
☐	73	Wayne Dillon	.11	.05	.01
☐	74	Jim Rutherford	.20	.10	.02
☐	75	Stan Mikita	1.75	.85	.17
☐	76	Bob Gainey	.70	.35	.07
☐	77	Gerry Hart	.11	.05	.01
☐	78	Lanny McDonald	.75	.35	.07
☐	79	Brad Park	.80	.40	.08
☐	80	Rick Martin	.25	.12	.02
☐	81	Bernie Wolfe	.11	.05	.01
☐	82	Bob MacMillan	.20	.10	.02
☐	83	Brad Maxwell	.11	.05	.01
☐	84	Mike Fidler	.11	.05	.01
☐	85	Carol Vadnais	.11	.05	.01
☐	86	Don Lever	.11	.05	.01
☐	87	Phil Myre	.20	.10	.02
☐	88	Paul Gardner	.20	.10	.02
☐	89	Bob Murray	.11	.05	.01
☐	90	Guy Lafleur AS1	4.00	2.00	.40
☐	91	Bob Murdoch	.11	.05	.01
☐	92	Ron Ellis	.11	.05	.01
☐	93	Jude Drouin	.11	.05	.01
☐	94	Jocelyn Guevremont	.11	.05	.01
☐	95	Gilles Gilbert	.20	.10	.02
☐	96	Bob Sirois	.11	.05	.01
☐	97	Tom Lysiak	.20	.10	.02
☐	98	Andre Dupont	.11	.05	.01
☐	99	Per-Olov Brasar	.11	.05	.01
☐	100	Phil Esposito	2.50	1.25	.25
☐	101	J.P. Bordeleau	.11	.05	.01
☐	102	Pierre Mondou	.45	.22	.04
☐	103	Wayne Bianchin	.11	.05	.01
☐	104	Dennis O'Brien	.11	.05	.01
☐	105	Glenn Resch	.60	.30	.06
☐	106	Dennis Polonich	.11	.05	.01
☐	107	Kris Manery	.11	.05	.01
☐	108	Bill Hajt	.11	.05	.01
☐	109	Jere Gillis	.11	.05	.01
☐	110	Garry Unger	.25	.12	.02
☐	111	Nick Beverley	.11	.05	.01
☐	112	Pat Hickey	.11	.05	.01
☐	113	Rick Middleton	.60	.30	.06
☐	114	Orest Kindrachuk	.11	.05	.01
☐	115	Mike Bossy	36.00	18.00	3.60
☐	116	Pierre Bouchard	.11	.05	.01
☐	117	Alain Daigle	.11	.05	.01

			NRMT	VG-E	GOOD
☐	118	Terry Martin	.11	.05	.01
☐	119	Tom Edur	.11	.05	.01
☐	120	Marcel Dionne	3.50	1.75	.35
☐	121	Barry Beck	1.00	.50	.10
☐	122	Billy Lochead	.11	.05	.01
☐	123	Paul Harrison	.11	.05	.01
☐	124	Wayne Cashman	.20	.10	.02
☐	125	Rick MacLeish	.25	.12	.02
☐	126	Bob Bourne	.20	.10	.02
☐	127	Ian Turnbull	.11	.05	.01
☒	128	Gerry Meehan	.20	.10	.02
☐	129	Eric Vail	.20	.10	.02
☐	130	Gilbert Perreault	1.00	.50	.10
☐	131	Bob Dailey	.11	.05	.01
☐	132	Dale McCourt	.25	.12	.02
☐	133	John Wensink	.11	.05	.01
☐	134	Bill Nyrop	.20	.10	.02
☐	135	Ivan Boldirev	.11	.05	.01
☐	136	Lucien Deblois	.20	.10	.02
☐	137	Brian Spencer	.11	.05	.01
☐	138	Tim Young	.11	.05	.01
☐	139	Ron Sedlbauer	.11	.05	.01
☐	140	Gerry Cheevers	1.00	.50	.10
☐	141	Dennis Maruk	.20	.10	.02
☐	142	Barry Dean	.11	.05	.01
☐	143	Bernie Federko	5.00	2.50	.50
☐	144	Stefan Persson	.35	.17	.03
☐	145	Wilf Paiement	.20	.10	.02
☐	146	Dale Tallon	.11	.05	.01
☐	147	Yvon Lambert	.11	.05	.01
☐	148	Greg Joly	.11	.05	.01
☐	149	Dean Talafous	.11	.05	.01
☐	150	Don Edwards AS2	.20	.10	.02
☐	151	Butch Goring	.25	.12	.02
☐	152	Tom Bladon	.11	.05	.01
☐	153	Bob Nystrom	.20	.10	.02
☐	154	Ron Greschner	.20	.10	.02
☐	155	Jean Ratelle	.80	.40	.08
☐	156	Russ Anderson	.11	.05	.01
☐	157	John Marks	.11	.05	.01
☐	158	Michel Larocque	.20	.10	.02
☐	159	Paul Woods	.11	.05	.01
☐	160	Mike Palmateer	.20	.10	.02
☐	161	Jim Lorentz	.11	.05	.01
☐	162	Dave Lewis	.11	.05	.01
☐	163	Harvey Bennett	.11	.05	.01
☐	164	Rick Smith	.11	.05	.01
☐	165	Reggie Leach	.25	.12	.02
☐	166	Wayne Thomas	.20	.10	.02
☐	167	Dave Forbes	.11	.05	.01
☐	168	Doug Wilson	13.50	6.00	1.20
☐	169	Dan Bouchard	.20	.10	.02
☐	170	Steve Shutt AS2	.60	.30	.06

		NRMT	VG-E	GOOD
☐ 171	Mike Kaszycki	.11	.05	.01
☐ 172	Denis Herron	.20	.10	.02
☐ 173	Rick Bowness	.20	.10	.02
☐ 174	Rick Hampton	.11	.05	.01
☐ 175	Glen Sharpley	.11	.05	.01
☐ 176	Bill Barber	.75	.35	.07
☐ 177	Ron Duguay	1.00	.50	.10
☐ 178	Jim Schoenfeld	.20	.10	.02
☐ 179	Pierre Plante	.11	.05	.01
☐ 180	Jacques Lemaire	.75	.35	.07
☐ 181	Stan Jonathan	.11	.05	.01
☐ 182	Billy Harris	.11	.05	.01
☐ 183	Chris Oddleifson	.11	.05	.01
☐ 184	Jean Pronovost	.20	.10	.02
☐ 185	Fred Barrett	.11	.05	.01
☐ 186	Ross Lonsberry	.11	.05	.01
☐ 187	Mike McEwen	.20	.10	.02
☐ 188	Rene Robert	.20	.10	.02
☐ 189	J. Bob Kelly	.11	.05	.01
☐ 190	Serge Savard AS2	.75	.35	.07
☐ 191	Dennis Kearns	.11	.05	.01
☐ 192	Flames Team	.35	.17	.03
☐ 193	Bruins Team	.35	.17	.03
☐ 194	Sabres Team	.35	.17	.03
☐ 195	Blackhawks Team	.35	.17	.03
☐ 196	Rockies Team	.35	.17	.03
☐ 197	Red Wings Team	.35	.17	.03
☐ 198	Kings Team	.35	.17	.03
☐ 199	North Stars Team	.35	.17	.03
☐ 200	Canadiens Team	.35	.17	.03
☐ 201	Islanders Team	.35	.17	.03
☐ 202	Rangers Team	.35	.17	.03
☐ 203	Flyers Team	.35	.17	.03
☐ 204	Penguins Team	.35	.17	.03
☐ 205	Blues Team	.35	.17	.03
☐ 206	Maple Leafs Team	.35	.17	.03
☐ 207	Canucks Team	.35	.17	.03
☐ 208	Capitals Team	.35	.17	.03
☐ 209	Danny Gare	.20	.10	.02
☐ 210	Larry Robinson AS1	1.00	.50	.10
☐ 211	John Davidson	.20	.10	.02
☐ 212	Peter McNab	.11	.05	.01
☐ 213	Rick Kehoe	.20	.10	.02
☐ 214	Terry Harper	.11	.05	.01
☐ 215	Bobby Clarke	1.75	.85	.17
☐ 216	Bryan Maxwell UER (Photo actually Brad Maxwell)	.11	.05	.01
☐ 217	Ted Bulley	.11	.05	.01
☐ 218	Red Berenson	.20	.10	.02
☐ 219	Ron Grahame	.20	.10	.02
☐ 220	Clark Gillies AS1	.25	.12	.02
☐ 221	Dave Maloney	.20	.10	.02
☐ 222	Derek Smith	.25	.12	.02

		NRMT	VG-E	GOOD
☐ 223	Wayne Stephenson	.20	.10	.02
☐ 224	John Van Boxmeer	.11	.05	.01
☐ 225	Dave Schultz	.25	.12	.02
☐ 226	Reed Larson	.35	.17	.03
☐ 227	Rejean Houle	.20	.10	.02
☐ 228	Doug Hicks	.11	.05	.01
☐ 229	Mike Murphy	.11	.05	.01
☐ 230	Pete Lopresti	.11	.05	.01
☐ 231	Jerry Korab	.11	.05	.01
☐ 232	Ed Westfall	.20	.10	.02
☐ 233	Greg Malone	.11	.05	.01
☐ 234	Paul Holmgren	.50	.25	.05
☐ 235	Walt Tkaczuk	.20	.10	.02
☐ 236	Don Marcotte	.11	.05	.01
☐ 237	Ron Low	.20	.10	.02
☐ 238	Rick Chartraw	.11	.05	.01
☐ 239	Cliff Koroll	.11	.05	.01
☐ 240	Borje Salming AS1	.35	.17	.03
☐ 241	Roland Eriksson	.11	.05	.01
☐ 242	Ric Seiling	.11	.05	.01
☐ 243	Jim Bedard	.20	.10	.02
☐ 244	Peter Lee	.11	.05	.01
☐ 245	Denis Potvin AS2	1.75	.85	.17
☐ 246	Greg Polis	.11	.05	.01
☐ 247	Jim Watson	.11	.05	.01
☐ 248	Bobby Schmautz	.11	.05	.01
☐ 249	Doug Risebrough	.11	.05	.01
☐ 250	Tony Esposito	1.25	.60	.12
☐ 251	Nick Libett	.11	.05	.01
☐ 252	Ron Zanussi	.11	.05	.01
☐ 253	Andre Savard	.11	.05	.01
☐ 254	Dave Burrows	.11	.05	.01
☐ 255	Ulf Nilsson	.20	.10	.02
☐ 256	Richard Mulhern	.11	.05	.01
☐ 257	Don Saleski	.11	.05	.01
☐ 258	Wayne Merrick	.11	.05	.01
☐ 259	Checklist 133-264	1.25	.10	.02
☐ 260	Guy Lapointe	.25	.12	.02
☐ 261	Grant Mulvey	.20	.10	.02
☐ 262	Stanley Cup: Semis	.30	.15	.03
	Canadiens sweep Maple Leafs			
☐ 263	Stanley Cup: Semis	.30	.15	.03
	Bruins skate past Flyers			
☐ 264	Stanley Cup: Finals	.75	.20	.04
	Canadiens win 3rd Straight Cup			

1979-80 Topps

The 1979-80 Topps set consists of 264 color cards which are the same as the first 264 cards of the NHL O-Pee-Chee set of 396 this year. Cards are 2½" by 3½". The fronts contain a distinctive blue border. The backs, in English only, are printed in dark brown and light blue ink. The card number, the player's 1978-79 and lifetime playing record, a very short biography, and a cartoon-illustrated fact about the player appear on the back. The cards were printed in the USA. Cards in the set include players from all of the NHL teams, even including the former WHA franchises in Edmonton, Hartford, Quebec, and Winnipeg. The set features the first hockey card of Wayne Gretzky and the last active card appearance for Bobby Hull and Gordie Howe.

Le jeu Topps 1979-80 contient 264 cartes en couleurs, identiques aux premières 264 cartes du jeu NHL de 396 cartes d'O-Pee-Chee de cette année. Les cartes mesurent 2½" x 3½". La face est entourée d'un bord bleu distinctif. Le dos, brun foncé et bleu clair, est imprimé uniquement en anglais. Il comporte le numéro de carte, la fiche pour 1978-79 et pour la carrière du joueur, une biographie très concise, et un fait notable concernant le joueur, accompagné d'une caricature. Les cartes ont été imprimées aux Etats-Unis. Elles incluent des joueurs de toutes les équipes de la NHL, même des franchises précédentes de la WHA àEdmonton, Hartford, Québec, et Winnipeg. Le jeu inclut la première carte de hockey de Wayne Gretzky et les dernières cartes de Bobby Hull et Gordie Howe.

			MINT	EXC	G-VG
	COMPLETE SET (264)	....	525.00	250.00	50.00
	COMMON PLAYER (1-264)	....	.10	.05	.01
☐	1	Goal Leaders	1.50	.40	.08
		Mike Bossy			
		Marcel Dionne			
		Guy Lafleur			

			MINT	EXC	G-VG
☐	2	**Assist Leaders**	1.00	.50	.10
		Bryan Trottier			
		Guy Lafleur			
		Marcel Dionne			
		Bob MacMillan			
☐	3	**Scoring Leaders**	1.00	.50	.10
		Bryan Trottier			
		Marcel Dionne			
		Guy Lafleur			
☐	4	**Penalty Minutes**	.17	.08	.01
		Leaders			
		Dave Williams			
		Randy Holt			
		Dave Schultz			
☐	5	**Power Play**	.60	.30	.06
		Goal Leaders			
		Mike Bossy			
		Marcel Dionne			
		Paul Gardner			
		Lanny McDonald			
☐	6	**Goals Against**	1.00	.50	.10
		Average Leaders			
		Ken Dryden			
		Glenn Resch			
		Bernie Parent			
☐	7	**Game Winning**	1.00	.50	.10
		Goals Leaders			
		Guy Lafleur			
		Mike Bossy			
		Bryan Trottier			
		Jean Pronovost			
		Ted Bulley			
☐	8A	**Shutout Leaders ERR**	6.00	3.00	.60
		Ken Dryden			
		Tony Esposito			
		Mario Lessard			
		Mike Palmateer			
		Bernie Parent			
		(Palmateer and Lessard			
		photos switched)			
☐	8B	**Shutout Leaders COR**	1.00	.50	.10
		Ken Dryden			
		Tony Esposito			
		Mario Lessard			
		Mike Palmateer			
		Bernie Parent			
☐	9	**Greg Malone**	.10	.05	.01
☐	10	**Rick Middleton**	.50	.25	.05
☐	11	**Greg Smith**	.10	.05	.01
☐	12	**Rene Robert**	.17	.08	.01
☐	13	**Doug Risebrough**	.10	.05	.01
☐	14	**Bob Kelly**	.10	.05	.01
☐	15	**Walt Tkaczuk**	.17	.08	.01

			MINT	EXC	G-VG
☐	16	John Marks	.10	.05	.01
☐	17	Willie Huber	.10	.05	.01
☐	18	Wayne Gretzky	375.00	175.00	37.00
☐	19	Ron Sedlbauer	.10	.05	.01
☐	20	Glenn Resch AS2	.50	.25	.05
☐	21	Blair Chapman	.10	.05	.01
☐	22	Ron Zanussi	.10	.05	.01
☐	23	Brad Park	.60	.30	.06
☐	24	Yvon Lambert	.10	.05	.01
☐	25	Andre Savard	.10	.05	.01
☐	26	Jim Watson	.10	.05	.01
☐	27	Hal Philipoff	.10	.05	.01
☐	28	Dan Bouchard	.17	.08	.01
☐	29	Bob Sirois	.10	.05	.01
☐	30	Ulf Nilsson	.17	.08	.01
☐	31	Mike Murphy	.10	.05	.01
☐	32	Stefan Persson	.17	.08	.01
☐	33	Garry Unger	.25	.12	.02
☐	34	Rejean Houle	.10	.05	.01
☐	35	Barry Beck	.25	.12	.02
☐	36	Tim Young	.10	.05	.01
☐	37	Rick Dudley	.17	.08	.01
☐	38	Wayne Stephenson	.17	.08	.01
☐	39	Peter McNab	.10	.05	.01
☐	40	Borje Salming AS2	.25	.12	.02
☐	41	Tom Lysiak	.17	.08	.01
☐	42	Don Maloney	1.00	.50	.10
☐	43	Mike Rogers	.17	.08	.01
☐	44	Dave Lewis	.10	.05	.01
☐	45	Peter Lee	.10	.05	.01
☐	46	Marty Howe	.25	.12	.02
☐	47	Serge Bernier	.10	.05	.01
☐	48	Paul Woods	.10	.05	.01
☐	49	Bob Sauve	.25	.12	.02
☐	50	Larry Robinson AS1	.80	.40	.08
☐	51	Tom Gorence	.10	.05	.01
☐	52	Gary Sargent	.10	.05	.01
☐	53	Thomas Gradin	.40	.20	.04
☐	54	Dean Talafous	.10	.05	.01
☐	55	Bob Murray	.10	.05	.01
☐	56	Bob Bourne	.17	.08	.01
☐	57	Larry Patey	.10	.05	.01
☐	58	Ross Lonsberry	.10	.05	.01
☐	59	Rick Smith	.10	.05	.01
☐	60	Guy Chouinard	.17	.08	.01
☐	61	Danny Gare	.17	.08	.01
☐	62	Jim Bedard	.17	.08	.01
☐	63	Dale McCourt	.17	.08	.01
☐	64	Steve Payne	.30	.15	.03
☐	65	Pat Hughes	.10	.05	.01
☐	66	Mike McEwen	.17	.08	.01
☐	67	Reg Kerr	.25	.12	.02
☐	68	Walt McKechnie	.10	.05	.01

			MINT	EXC	G-VG
☐	69	Michel Plasse	.17	.08	.01
☐	70	Denis Potvin AS1	1.50	.75	.15
☐	71	Dave Dryden	.17	.08	.01
☐	72	Gary McAdam	.10	.05	.01
☐	73	Andre St. Laurent	.10	.05	.01
☐	74	Jerry Korab	.10	.05	.01
☐	75	Rick MacLeish	.25	.12	.02
☐	76	Dennis Kearns	.10	.05	.01
☐	77	Jean Pronovost	.17	.08	.01
☐	78	Ron Greschner	.17	.08	.01
☐	79	Wayne Cashman	.17	.08	.01
☐	80	Tony Esposito	1.00	.50	.10
☐	81	Cup Semi-Finals	.30	.15	.03
		Canadiens squeak			
		past Bruins			
☐	82	Cup Semi-Finals	.30	.15	.03
		Rangers upset			
		Islanders in Six			
☐	83	Stanley Cup Finals	.35	.17	.03
		Canadiens Make It			
		Four Straight Cups			
☐	84	Brian Sutter	.50	.25	.05
☐	85	Gerry Cheevers	1.00	.50	.10
☐	86	Pat Hickey	.10	.05	.01
☐	87	Mike Kaszycki	.10	.05	.01
☐	88	Grant Mulvey	.17	.08	.01
☐	89	Derek Smith	.10	.05	.01
☐	90	Steve Shutt	.50	.25	.05
☐	91	Robert Picard	.17	.08	.01
☐	92	Dan Labraaten	.10	.05	.01
☐	93	Glen Sharpley	.10	.05	.01
☐	94	Denis Herron	.17	.08	.01
☐	95	Reggie Leach	.25	.12	.02
☐	96	John Van Boxmeer	.10	.05	.01
☐	97	Dave Williams	.25	.12	.02
☐	98	Butch Goring	.17	.08	.01
☐	99	Don Marcotte	.10	.05	.01
☐	100	Bryan Trottier AS1	2.00	1.00	.20
☐	101	Serge Savard AS2	.60	.30	.06
☐	102	Cliff Koroll	.10	.05	.01
☐	103	Gary Smith	.17	.08	.01
☐	104	Al MacAdam	.17	.08	.01
☐	105	Don Edwards	.17	.08	.01
☐	106	Errol Thompson	.10	.05	.01
☐	107	Andre Lacroix	.17	.08	.01
☐	108	Marc Tardif	.17	.08	.01
☐	109	Rick Kehoe	.17	.08	.01
☐	110	John Davidson	.17	.08	.01
☐	111	Behn Wilson	.25	.12	.02
☐	112	Doug Jarvis	.17	.08	.01
☐	113	Tom Rowe	.10	.05	.01
☐	114	Mike Milbury	.17	.08	.01
☐	115	Billy Harris	.10	.05	.01

			MINT	EXC	G-VG
☐ 116	Greg Fox		.10	.05	.01
☐ 117	Curt Fraser		.10	.05	.01
☐ 118	Jean Paul Parise		.10	.05	.01
☐ 119	Ric Seiling		.10	.05	.01
☐ 120	Darryl Sittler		.60	.30	.06
☐ 121	Rick Lapointe		.17	.08	.01
☐ 122	Jim Rutherford		.17	.08	.01
☐ 123	Mario Tremblay		.17	.08	.01
☐ 124	Randy Carlyle		.40	.20	.04
☐ 125	Bobby Clarke		1.50	.75	.15
☐ 126	Wayne Thomas		.17	.08	.01
☐ 127	Ivan Boldirev		.10	.05	.01
☐ 128	Ted Bulley		.10	.05	.01
☐ 129	Dick Redmond		.10	.05	.01
☐ 130	Clark Gillies AS1		.25	.12	.02
☐ 131	Checklist 1-132		1.25	.10	.02
☐ 132	Vaclav Nedomansky		.10	.05	.01
☐ 133	Richard Mulhern		.10	.05	.01
☐ 134	Dave Schultz		.17	.08	.01
☐ 135	Guy Lapointe		.25	.12	.02
☐ 136	Gilles Meloche		.17	.08	.01
☐ 137	Randy Pierce UER		.10	.05	.01
	(Photo actually Ron Delorme)				
☐ 138	Cam Connor		.10	.05	.01
☐ 139	George Ferguson		.10	.05	.01
☐ 140	Bill Barber		.60	.30	.06
☐ 141	Mike Walton		.17	.08	.01
☐ 142	Wayne Babych		.25	.12	.02
☐ 143	Phil Russell		.10	.05	.01
☐ 144	Bobby Schmautz		.10	.05	.01
☐ 145	Carol Vadnais		.10	.05	.01
☐ 146	John Tonelli		3.00	1.50	.30
☐ 147	Peter Marsh		.25	.12	.02
☐ 148	Thommie Bergman		.10	.05	.01
☐ 149	Rick Martin		.25	.12	.02
☐ 150	Ken Dryden AS1		3.50	1.75	.35
☐ 151	Kris Manery		.10	.05	.01
☐ 152	Guy Charron		.10	.05	.01
☐ 153	Lanny McDonald		.60	.30	.06
☐ 154	Ron Stackhouse		.10	.05	.01
☐ 155	Stan Mikita		1.25	.60	.12
☐ 156	Paul Holmgren		.17	.08	.01
☐ 157	Perry Miller		.10	.05	.01
☐ 158	Gary Croteau		.10	.05	.01
☐ 159	Dave Maloney		.17	.08	.01
☐ 160	Marcel Dionne AS2		3.00	1.50	.30
☐ 161	Mike Bossy RB		1.50	.75	.15
	Most Goals, RW Season				
☐ 162	Don Maloney RB		.17	.08	.01
	Rookie Most Points,				
	Playoff Series				
☐ 163	Ulf Nilsson RB		.17	.08	.01
	Highest Scoring				
	Percentage, Season				

		MINT	EXC	G-VG
☐ 164	**Brad Park RB**	.30	.15	.03
	Most Career Playoff			
	Goals, Defenseman			
☐ 165	**Bryan Trottier RB**	.60	.30	.06
	Most Points, Period			
☐ 166	**Al Hill**	.10	.05	.01
☐ 167	**Gary Bromley**	.17	.08	.01
☐ 168	**Don Murdoch**	.10	.05	.01
☐ 169	**Wayne Merrick**	.10	.05	.01
☐ 170	**Bob Gainey**	.50	.25	.05
☐ 171	**Jim Schoenfeld**	.17	.08	.01
☐ 172	**Gregg Sheppard**	.10	.05	.01
☐ 173	**Dan Bolduc**	.10	.05	.01
☐ 174	**Blake Dunlop**	.10	.05	.01
☐ 175	**Gordie Howe**	22.50	10.00	2.00
☐ 176	**Richard Brodeur**	.75	.35	.07
☐ 177	**Tom Younghans**	.10	.05	.01
☐ 178	**Andre Dupont**	.10	.05	.01
☐ 179	**Ed Johnstone**	.10	.05	.01
☐ 180	**Gilbert Perreault**	.75	.35	.07
☐ 181	**Bob Lorimer**	.10	.05	.01
☐ 182	**John Wensink**	.10	.05	.01
☐ 183	**Lee Fogolin**	.10	.05	.01
☐ 184	**Greg Carroll**	.10	.05	.01
☐ 185	**Bobby Hull**	20.00	10.00	2.00
☐ 186	**Harold Snepsts**	.60	.30	.06
☐ 187	**Peter Mahovlich**	.17	.08	.01
☐ 188	**Eric Vail**	.17	.08	.01
☐ 189	**Phil Myre**	.17	.08	.01
☐ 190	**Wilf Paiement**	.17	.08	.01
☐ 191	**Charlie Simmer**	2.00	1.00	.20
☐ 192	**Per-Olov Brasar**	.10	.05	.01
☐ 193	**Lorne Henning**	.10	.05	.01
☐ 194	**Don Luce**	.10	.05	.01
☐ 195	**Steve Vickers**	.10	.05	.01
☐ 196	**Bob Miller**	.10	.05	.01
☐ 197	**Mike Palmateer**	.25	.12	.02
☐ 198	**Nick Libett**	.10	.05	.01
☐ 199	**Pat Ribble**	.10	.05	.01
☐ 200	**Guy Lafleur AS1**	3.50	1.75	.35
☐ 201	**Mel Bridgman**	.10	.05	.01
☐ 202	**Morris Lukowich**	.40	.20	.04
☐ 203	**Don Lever**	.10	.05	.01
☐ 204	**Tom Bladon**	.10	.05	.01
☐ 205	**Garry Howatt**	.10	.05	.01
☐ 206	**Bobby Smith**	6.00	3.00	.60
☐ 207	**Craig Ramsay**	.10	.05	.01
☐ 208	**Ron Duguay**	.17	.08	.01
☐ 209	**Gilles Gilbert**	.17	.08	.01
☐ 210	**Bob MacMillan**	.17	.08	.01
☐ 211	**Pierre Mondou**	.17	.08	.01
☐ 212	**J.P. Bordeleau**	.10	.05	.01
☐ 213	**Reed Larson**	.17	.08	.01

			MINT	EXC	G-VG
☐ 214	Dennis Ververgaert		.10	.05	.01
☐ 215	Bernie Federko		.75	.35	.07
☐ 216	Mark Howe		1.00	.50	.10
☐ 217	Bob Nystrom		.17	.08	.01
☐ 218	Orest Kindrachuk		.10	.05	.01
☐ 219	Mike Fidler		.10	.05	.01
☐ 220	Phil Esposito		1.75	.85	.17
☐ 221	Bill Hajt		.10	.05	.01
☐ 222	Mark Napier		.25	.12	.02
☐ 223	Dennis Maruk		.17	.08	.01
☐ 224	Dennis Polonich		.10	.05	.01
☐ 225	Jean Ratelle		.60	.30	.06
☐ 226	Bob Dailey		.10	.05	.01
☐ 227	Alain Daigle		.10	.05	.01
☐ 228	Ian Turnbull		.10	.05	.01
☐ 229	Jack Valiquette		.10	.05	.01
☐ 230	Mike Bossy AS2		13.50	6.00	1.20
☐ 231	Brad Maxwell		.10	.05	.01
☐ 232	Dave Taylor		2.50	1.25	.25
☐ 233	Pierre Larouche		.17	.08	.01
☐ 234	Rod Schutt		.10	.05	.01
☐ 235	Rogatien Vachon		.50	.25	.05
☐ 236	Ryan Walter		.75	.35	.07
☐ 237	Checklist 133-264		1.25	.10	.02
☐ 238	Terry O'Reilly		.25	.12	.02
☐ 239	Real Cloutier		.17	.08	.01
☐ 240	Anders Hedberg		.17	.08	.01
☐ 241	Ken Linseman		1.75	.85	.17
☐ 242	Billy Smith		.60	.30	.06
☐ 243	Rick Chartraw		.10	.05	.01
☐ 244	Flames Team		.35	.17	.03
☐ 245	Bruins Team		.35	.17	.03
☐ 246	Sabres Team		.35	.17	.03
☐ 247	Blackhawks Team		.35	.17	.03
☐ 248	Rockies Team		.35	.17	.03
☐ 249	Red Wings Team		.35	.17	.03
☐ 250	Kings Team		.35	.17	.03
☐ 251	North Stars Team		.35	.17	.03
☐ 252	Canadiens Team		.35	.17	.03
☐ 253	Islanders Team		.35	.17	.03
☐ 254	Rangers Team		.35	.17	.03
☐ 255	Flyers Team		.35	.17	.03
☐ 256	Penguins Team		.35	.17	.03
☐ 257	Blues Team		.35	.17	.03
☐ 258	Maple Leafs Team		.35	.17	.03
☐ 259	Canucks Team		.35	.17	.03
☐ 260	Capitals Team		.35	.17	.03
☐ 261	New NHL Entries		2.00	1.00	.20
	Edmonton Oilers				
	Hartford Whalers				
	Quebec Nordiques				
	Winnipeg Jets				
☐ 262	Jean Hamel		.10	.05	.01

		MINT	EXC	G-VG
☐ 263	Stan Jonathan	.10	.05	.01
☐ 264	Russ Anderson	.25	.12	.02

1980-81 Topps

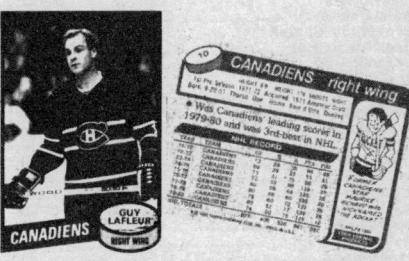

The 1980-81 Topps set features 264 cards which are the same as the first 264 cards of the 396 O-Pee-Chee set of the same year. Cards are the standard 2½" by 3½". The fronts contain a black scratch-off section at the bottom which reveals the player's name. The backs, in English only, are printed in light green and dark green ink. The card number, the player's career record, a short biography, and a cartoon-illustrated hockey fact are included on the back. The cards were printed in the USA. Members of the U.S. Olympic team are designated by USO. The first five cards (1-5) in the set feature Record-Breaking (RB) achievements which occurred during the previous season. The key rookie cards in this set are Ray Bourque, Mike Gartner, Michel Goulet, Mike Liut, and Brian Propp.

Le jeu Topps 1980-81 contient 264 cartes identiques aux 264 premières cartes du jeu de 396 cartes d'O-Pee-Chee de la même année. Les cartes ont les dimensions standards 2½" x 3½". La partie inférieure de la face contient une section de couleur noire, pouvant être grattée pour révéler le nom du joueur. Le dos, vert clair et vert foncé, est imprimé uniquement en anglais. Il comporte le numéro de carte, la fiche de carrière du joueur, une biographie concise et un fait notable concernant le joueur, accompagné d'une caricature. Les cartes ont été imprimées aux Etats-Unis. Les membres de l'équipe olympique des USA sont indiqués par USO. Les premières cinq cartes (1-5) de ce jeu représentent des exploits battant des records (RB) durant la saison précédente. Les cartes des débutants importants représentent Ray Bourque, Mike Gartner, Michel Goulet, Mike Liut, et Brian Propp.

	MINT	EXC	G-VG
COMPLETE SET (264)	250.00	125.00	25.00
COMMON PLAYER (1-264)	.08	.04	.01

			MINT	EXC	G-VG
☐	1	**Phila. Flyers RB**	.40	.10	.02
		35 Game Streak,			
		Longest in Sports History			
☐	2	**Ray Bourque RB**	6.50	3.25	.65
		65 Pts.; Record for			
		Rookie Defenseman			
☐	3	**Wayne Gretzky RB**	24.00	12.00	2.40
		Youngest Ever,			
		50-goal Scorer			
☐	4	**Charlie Simmer RB**	.14	.07	.01
		Scores in 13th Straight			
		Game, NHL Record			
☐	5	**Billy Smith RB**	.25	.12	.02
		First Goalie to			
		Score a Goal			
☐	6	**Jean Ratelle**	.50	.25	.05
☐	7	**Dave Maloney**	.14	.07	.01
☐	8	**Phil Myre**	.14	.07	.01
☐	9	**Ken Morrow USO**	.50	.25	.05
☐	10	**Guy Lafleur**	2.00	1.00	.20
☐	11	**Bill Derlago**	.14	.07	.01
☐	12	**Doug Wilson**	1.00	.50	.10
☐	13	**Craig Ramsay**	.08	.04	.01
☐	14	**Pat Boutette**	.08	.04	.01
☐	15	**Eric Vail**	.14	.07	.01
☐	16	**Red Wings Leaders**	.14	.07	.01
		Mike Foligno			
☐	17	**Bobby Smith**	.60	.30	.06
☐	18	**Rick Kehoe**	.14	.07	.01
☐	19	**Joel Quenneville**	.08	.04	.01
☐	20	**Marcel Dionne**	1.75	.85	.17
☐	21	**Kevin McCarthy**	.08	.04	.01
☐	22	**Jim Craig USO**	.60	.30	.06
☐	23	**Steve Vickers**	.08	.04	.01
☐	24	**Ken Linseman**	.25	.12	.02
☐	25	**Mike Bossy**	5.00	2.50	.50
☐	26	**Serge Savard**	.50	.25	.05
☐	27	**Blackhawks Leaders**	.14	.07	.01
		Grant Mulvey			
☐	28	**Pat Hickey**	.08	.04	.01
☐	29	**Peter Sullivan**	.08	.04	.01
☐	30	**Blaine Stoughton**	.14	.07	.01
☐	31	**Mike Liut**	3.00	1.50	.30
☐	32	**Blair MacDonald**	.08	.04	.01
☐	33	**Rick Green**	.14	.07	.01
☐	34	**Al MacAdam**	.14	.07	.01
☐	35	**Robbie Ftorek**	.20	.10	.02
☐	36	**Dick Redmond**	.08	.04	.01
☐	37	**Ron Duguay**	.14	.07	.01
☐	38	**Sabres Leaders**	.14	.07	.01
		Danny Gare			
☐	39	**Brian Propp**	5.00	2.50	.50
☐	40	**Bryan Trottier**	1.50	.75	.15

			MINT	EXC	G-VG
☐	41	Rich Preston	.08	.04	.01
☐	42	Pierre Mondou	.08	.04	.01
☐	43	Reed Larson	.08	.04	.01
☐	44	George Ferguson	.08	.04	.01
☐	45	Guy Chouinard	.14	.07	.01
☐	46	Billy Harris	.08	.04	.01
☐	47	Gilles Meloche	.14	.07	.01
☐	48	Blair Chapman	.08	.04	.01
☐	49	Capitals Leaders	.60	.30	.06
		Mike Gartner			
☐	50	Darryl Sittler	.50	.25	.05
☐	51	Rick Martin	.14	.07	.01
☐	52	Ivan Boldirev	.08	.04	.01
☐	53	Craig Norwich	.08	.04	.01
☐	54	Dennis Polonich	.08	.04	.01
☐	55	Bobby Clarke	1.25	.60	.12
☐	56	Terry O'Reilly	.20	.10	.02
☐	57	Carol Vadnais	.08	.04	.01
☐	58	Bob Gainey	.40	.20	.04
☐	59	Whalers Leaders	.14	.07	.01
		Blaine Stoughton			
☐	60	Billy Smith	.50	.25	.05
☐	61	Mike O'Connell	.20	.10	.02
☐	62	Lanny McDonald	.50	.25	.05
☐	63	Lee Fogolin	.08	.04	.01
☐	64	Rocky Saganiuk	.08	.04	.01
☐	65	Rolf Edberg	.08	.04	.01
☐	66	Paul Shmyr	.08	.04	.01
☐	67	Michel Goulet	8.00	4.00	.80
☐	68	Dan Bouchard	.14	.07	.01
☐	69	Mark Johnson USO	.50	.25	.05
☐	70	Reggie Leach	.20	.10	.02
☐	71	Blues Leaders	.20	.10	.02
		Bernie Federko			
☐	72	Peter Mahovlich	.14	.07	.01
☐	73	Anders Hedberg	.14	.07	.01
☐	74	Brad Park	.50	.25	.05
☐	75	Clark Gillies	.20	.10	.02
☐	76	Doug Jarvis	.14	.07	.01
☐	77	John Garrett	.14	.07	.01
☐	78	Dave Hutchinson	.08	.04	.01
☐	79	John Anderson	.08	.04	.01
☐	80	Gilbert Perreault	.75	.35	.07
☐	81	Marcel Dionne AS1	.90	.45	.09
☐	82	Guy Lafleur AS1	1.25	.60	.12
☐	83	Charlie Simmer AS1	.14	.07	.01
☐	84	Larry Robinson AS1	.40	.20	.04
☐	85	Borje Salming AS1	.20	.10	.02
☐	86	Tony Esposito AS1	.50	.25	.05
☐	87	Wayne Gretzky AS2	35.00	17.50	3.50
☐	88	Danny Gare AS2	.14	.07	.01
☐	89	Steve Shutt AS2	.20	.10	.02
☐	90	Barry Beck AS2	.14	.07	.01

			MINT	EXC	G-VG
☐	91	Mark Howe AS2	.20	.10	.02
☐	92	Don Edwards AS2	.14	.07	.01
☐	93	Tom McCarthy	.14	.07	.01
☐	94	Bruins Leaders	.14	.07	.01
		Peter McNab			
		Rick Middleton			
☐	95	Mike Palmateer	.14	.07	.01
☐	96	Jim Schoenfeld	.14	.07	.01
☐	97	Jordy Douglas	.08	.04	.01
☐	98	Keith Brown	.08	.04	.01
☐	99	Dennis Ververgaert	.08	.04	.01
☐	100	Phil Esposito	1.50	.75	.15
☐	101	Jack Brownschidle	.08	.04	.01
☐	102	Bob Nystrom	.14	.07	.01
☐	103	Steve Christoff USO	.14	.07	.01
☐	104	Rob Palmer	.08	.04	.01
☐	105	Dave Williams	.14	.07	.01
☐	106	Flames Leaders	.14	.07	.01
		Kent Nilsson			
☐	107	Morris Lukowich	.14	.07	.01
☐	108	Jack Valiquette	.08	.04	.01
☐	109	Richie Dunn	.08	.04	.01
☐	110	Rogatien Vachon	.40	.20	.04
☐	111	Mark Napier	.14	.07	.01
☐	112	Gordie Roberts	.08	.04	.01
☐	113	Stan Jonathan	.08	.04	.01
☐	114	Brett Callighen	.08	.04	.01
☐	115	Rick MacLeish	.20	.10	.02
☐	116	Ulf Nilsson	.14	.07	.01
☐	117	Penguins Leaders	.14	.07	.01
		Rick Kehoe			
☐	118	Dan Maloney	.14	.07	.01
☐	119	Terry Ruskowski	.14	.07	.01
☐	120	Denis Potvin	1.25	.60	.12
☐	121	Wayne Stephenson	.14	.07	.01
☐	122	Rich Leduc	.08	.04	.01
☐	123	Checklist 1-132	1.00	.08	.01
☐	124	Don Lever	.08	.04	.01
☐	125	Jim Rutherford	.14	.07	.01
☐	126	Ray Allison	.08	.04	.01
☐	127	Mike Ramsey USO	.35	.17	.03
☐	128	Canucks Leaders	.14	.07	.01
		Stan Smyl			
☐	129	Al Secord	1.00	.50	.10
☐	130	Denis Herron	.14	.07	.01
☐	131	Bob Dailey	.08	.04	.01
☐	132	Dean Talafous	.08	.04	.01
☐	133	Ian Turnbull	.08	.04	.01
☐	134	Ron Sedlbauer	.08	.04	.01
☐	135	Tom Bladon	.08	.04	.01
☐	136	Bernie Federko	.20	.10	.02
☐	137	Dave Taylor	.60	.30	.06
☐	138	Bob Lorimer	.08	.04	.01

		MINT	EXC	G-VG
☐ 139	**North Stars Leaders**	.14	.07	.01
	Al MacAdam			
	Steve Payne			
☐ 140	**Ray Bourque**	75.00	37.50	7.50
☐ 141	**Glen Hanlon**	.35	.17	.03
☐ 142	**Willy Lindstrom**	.08	.04	.01
☐ 143	**Mike Rogers**	.14	.07	.01
☐ 144	**Tony McKegney**	.35	.17	.03
☐ 145	**Behn Wilson**	.08	.04	.01
☐ 146	**Lucien Deblois**	.08	.04	.01
☐ 147	**Dave Burrows**	.08	.04	.01
☐ 148	**Paul Woods**	.08	.04	.01
☐ 149	**Rangers Leaders**	.60	.30	.06
	Phil Esposito			
☐ 150	**Tony Esposito**	1.00	.50	.10
☐ 151	**Pierre Larouche**	.14	.07	.01
☐ 152	**Brad Maxwell**	.08	.04	.01
☐ 153	**Stan Weir**	.08	.04	.01
☐ 154	**Ryan Walter**	.14	.07	.01
☐ 155	**Dale Hoganson**	.08	.04	.01
☐ 156	**Anders Kallur**	.20	.10	.02
☐ 157	**Paul Reinhart**	.90	.45	.09
☐ 158	**Greg Millen**	.35	.17	.03
☐ 159	**Ric Seiling**	.08	.04	.01
☐ 160	**Mark Howe**	.35	.17	.03
☐ 161	**Goals Leaders**	.14	.07	.01
	Danny Gare (1)			
	Charlie Simmer (1)			
	Blaine Stoughton (1)			
☐ 162	**Assists Leaders**	7.50	3.75	.75
	Wayne Gretzky (1)			
	Marcel Dionne (2)			
	Guy Lafleur (3)			
☐ 163	**Scoring Leaders**	7.50	3.75	.75
	Marcel Dionne (1)			
	Wayne Gretzky (1)			
	Guy Lafleur (3)			
☐ 164	**Penalty Minutes**	.14	.07	.01
	Leaders			
	Jimmy Mann (1)			
	Dave Williams (2)			
	Paul Holmgren (3)			
☐ 165	**Power Play Goals**	.20	.10	.02
	Leaders			
	Charlie Simmer (1)			
	Marcel Dionne (2)			
	Danny Gare (2)			
	Steve Shutt (2)			
	Darryl Sittler (2)			

		MINT	EXC	G-VG
☐ 166	**Goals Against Average** Leaders Bob Sauve (1) Denis Herron (2) Don Edwards (3)	.14	.07	.01
☐ 167	**Game-Winning Goals** Leaders Danny Gare (1) Peter McNab (2) Blaine Stoughton (2)	.14	.07	.01
☐ 168	**Shutout Leaders** Tony Esposito (1) Gerry Cheevers (2) Bob Sauve (2) Rogatien Vachon (2)	.35	.17	.03
☐ 169	**Perry Turnbull**	.25	.12	.02
☐ 170	**Barry Beck**	.14	.07	.01
☐ 171	**Kings Leaders** Charlie Simmer	.14	.07	.01
☐ 172	**Paul Holmgren**	.14	.07	.01
☐ 173	**Willie Huber**	.08	.04	.01
☐ 174	**Tim Young**	.08	.04	.01
☐ 175	**Gilles Gilbert**	.14	.07	.01
☐ 176	**Dave Christian** USO	.60	.30	.06
☐ 177	**Lars Lindgren**	.08	.04	.01
☐ 178	**Real Cloutier**	.08	.04	.01
☐ 179	**Laurie Boschman**	.35	.17	.03
☐ 180	**Steve Shutt**	.45	.22	.04
☐ 181	**Bob Murray**	.08	.04	.01
☐ 182	**Oilers Leaders** Wayne Gretzky	15.00	7.50	1.50
☐ 183	**John Van Boxmeer**	.08	.04	.01
☐ 184	**Nick Fotiu**	.08	.04	.01
☐ 185	**Mike McEwen**	.14	.07	.01
☐ 186	**Greg Malone**	.08	.04	.01
☐ 187	**Mike Foligno**	.75	.35	.07
☐ 188	**Dave Langevin**	.14	.07	.01
☐ 189	**Mel Bridgman**	.08	.04	.01
☐ 190	**John Davidson**	.14	.07	.01
☐ 191	**Mike Milbury**	.14	.07	.01
☐ 192	**Ron Zanussi**	.08	.04	.01
☐ 193	**Maple Leafs Leaders** Darryl Sittler	.25	.12	.02
☐ 194	**John Marks**	.08	.04	.01
☐ 195	**Mike Gartner**	8.00	4.00	.80
☐ 196	**Dave Lewis**	.08	.04	.01
☐ 197	**Kent Nilsson**	1.25	.60	.12
☐ 198	**Rick Ley**	.14	.07	.01
☐ 199	**Derek Smith**	.08	.04	.01
☐ 200	**Bill Barber**	.50	.25	.05
☐ 201	**Guy Lapointe**	.14	.07	.01
☐ 202	**Vaclav Nedomansky**	.08	.04	.01
☐ 203	**Don Murdoch**	.08	.04	.01

			MINT	EXC	G-VG
☐ 204	Islanders Leaders		.90	.45	.09
	Mike Bossy				
☐ 205	Pierre Hamel		.08	.04	.01
☐ 206	Mike Eaves		.08	.04	.01
☐ 207	Doug Halward		.08	.04	.01
☐ 208	Stan Smyl		.35	.17	.03
☐ 209	Mike Zuke		.08	.04	.01
☐ 210	Borje Salming		.20	.10	.02
☐ 211	Walt Tkaczuk		.14	.07	.01
☐ 212	Grant Mulvey		.14	.07	.01
☐ 213	Rob Ramage		1.50	.75	.15
☐ 214	Tom Rowe		.08	.04	.01
☐ 215	Don Edwards		.14	.07	.01
☐ 216	Canadiens Leaders		.40	.20	.04
	Guy Lafleur				
	Pierre Larouche				
☐ 217	Dan Labraaten		.08	.04	.01
☐ 218	Glen Sharpley		.08	.04	.01
☐ 219	Stefan Persson		.14	.07	.01
☐ 220	Peter McNab		.08	.04	.01
☐ 221	Doug Hicks		.08	.04	.01
☐ 222	Bengt Gustafsson		.30	.15	.03
☐ 223	Michel Dion		.14	.07	.01
☐ 224	Jim Watson		.08	.04	.01
☐ 225	Wilf Paiement		.08	.04	.01
☐ 226	Phil Russell		.08	.04	.01
☐ 227	Jets Leaders		.14	.07	.01
	Morris Lukowich				
☐ 228	Ron Stackhouse		.08	.04	.01
☐ 229	Ted Bulley		.08	.04	.01
☐ 230	Larry Robinson		.60	.30	.06
☐ 231	Don Maloney		.14	.07	.01
☐ 232	Rob McClanahan USO		.25	.12	.02
☐ 233	Al Sims		.08	.04	.01
☐ 234	Errol Thompson		.08	.04	.01
☐ 235	Glenn Resch		.40	.20	.04
☐ 236	Bob Miller		.08	.04	.01
☐ 237	Gary Sargent		.08	.04	.01
☐ 238	Nordiques Leaders		.14	.07	.01
	Real Cloutier				
☐ 239	Rene Robert		.14	.07	.01
☐ 240	Charlie Simmer		.25	.12	.02
☐ 241	Thomas Gradin		.14	.07	.01
☐ 242	Rick Vaive		3.00	1.50	.30
☐ 243	Ron Wilson		.08	.04	.01
☐ 244	Brian Sutter		.25	.12	.02
☐ 245	Dale McCourt		.08	.04	.01
☐ 246	Yvon Lambert		.08	.04	.01
☐ 247	Tom Lysiak		.14	.07	.01
☐ 248	Ron Greschner		.14	.07	.01
☐ 249	Flyers Leaders		.14	.07	.01
	Reggie Leach				
☐ 250	Wayne Gretzky		125.00	60.00	12.50

		MINT	EXC	G-VG
☐ 251	Rick Middleton	.35	.17	.03
☐ 252	Al Smith	.08	.04	.01
☐ 253	Fred Barrett	.08	.04	.01
☐ 254	Butch Goring	.14	.07	.01
☐ 255	Robert Picard	.14	.07	.01
☐ 256	Marc Tardif	.14	.07	.01
☐ 257	Checklist 133-264	1.00	.08	.01
☐ 258	Barry Long	.08	.04	.01
☐ 259	Rockies Leaders	.14	.07	.01
	Rene Robert			
☐ 260	Danny Gare	.14	.07	.01
☐ 261	Rejean Houle	.08	.04	.01
☐ 262	Stanley Cup Semi's	.20	.10	.02
	Islanders-Sabres			
☐ 263	Stanley Cup Semi's	.20	.10	.02
	Flyers-North Stars			
☐ 264	Stanley Cup Finals	.50	.12	.02
	Islanders win 1st			

1981-82 Topps

RIGHT WING

This set is very different in concept from the O-Pee-Chee set of this year. Cards are 2½" by 3½". While the first 66 cards of the set were distributed nationwide, two regional subsets, numbered 67 East through 132 East and 67 West through 132 West, were distributed regionally. The appearance of the cards was quite similar to the O-Pee-Chee cards of this year with the Topps logo and team logo appearing within the frame line on the front and the team name in large letters appearing inside the frame line on the front. The backs, printed in black and blue ink, feature player biographies, statistics, and a 1981 Topps copyright date on a gray card stock. The card numbering is according to teams, for example, Boston Bruins (E67-E74), Buffalo Sabres (E75-

E80), Pittsburgh Penguins (E81, E112-E114, E116), Hartford Whalers (E82-E86, E108, E115), New York Islanders (E87-E93), New York Rangers (E94-E102), Philadelphia Flyers (E103-E110, E109-E110), Washington Capitals (E117-E122), Chicago Blackhawks (W67-W72), Winnipeg Jets (W79), Colorado Rockies (W80-W85), Detroit Red Wings (W87-W95), Los Angeles Kings (W96-W98, W100-W101), Toronto Maple Leafs (W99), Minnesota North Stars (W102-113), and St. Louis Blues (W114-W119, W121-W124). The key rookie cards in this set are Don Beaupre, Dino Ciccarelli, Jari Kurri, Denis Savard, and Peter Stastny.

Ce jeu est très différent du jeu O-Pee-Chee de cette année. Les cartes mesurent 2¹/₂" x 3¹/₂". Alors que les 66 premières cartes du jeu furent distribuées dans le pays entier, deux jeux publiés régionalement, et numérotés 67 est à 132 est inclus, et 67 ouest à 132 ouest inclus, ne furent distribués que localement. Les cartes ressemblent aux cartes O-Pee-Chee de cette année, avec l'emblème Topps et l'emblème de l'équipe encadrés dans la ligne encadrant la face, et le nom de l'équipe en grandes lettres à l'intérieur du cadre de la face. Le dos, imprimé en noir et bleu sur une pâte grise, présente les biographies des joueurs, les statistiques, et l'annnée 1981 comme date de droit d'auteur de Topps. Les cartes sont numérotées suivant les équipes, par exemple, Boston Bruins (E67-E74), Buffalo Sabres (E75- E80), Pittsburgh Penguins (E81, E112-E114, E116), Hartford Whalers (E82-E86, E108, E115), New York Islanders (E87-E93), New York Rangers (E94-E102), Philadelphia Flyers (E103-E110, E109-E110), Washington Capitals (E117-E122), Chicago Black Hawks (W67-W72), Winnipeg Jets (W79), Colorado Rockies (W80- W85), Detroit Red Wings (W87-W95), Los Angeles Kings (W96- W98, W100-W101), Toronto Maple Leafs (W99), Minnesota North Stars (W102-113), et St. Louis Blues (W114-W119, W121-W124). Les cartes des débutants importants représentent Don Beaupré, Dino Ciccarelli, Jari Kurri, Denis Savard, et Peter Stastny.

			MINT	EXC	G-VG
		COMPLETE SET (198)	90.00	45.00	9.00
		COMMON CARD (1-66)	.05	.02	.00
		COMMON CARD (E67-E132)	.10	.05	.01
		COMMON CARD (W67-W132)	.15	.07	.01
☐	1	Dave Babych	.40	.10	.02
☐	2	Bill Barber	.40	.20	.04
☐	3	Barry Beck	.10	.05	.01
☐	4	Mike Bossy	1.75	.85	.17
☐	5	Ray Bourque	4.50	2.25	.45
☐	6	Guy Chouinard	.05	.02	.00
☐	7	Dave Christian	.10	.05	.01
☐	8	Bill Derlago	.05	.02	.00
☐	9	Marcel Dionne	.90	.45	.09
☐	10	Brian Engblom	.05	.02	.00
☐	11	Tony Esposito	.65	.30	.06
☐	12	Bernie Federko	.15	.07	.01
☐	13	Bob Gainey	.25	.12	.02
☐	14	Danny Gare	.05	.02	.00
☐	15	Thomas Gradin	.05	.02	.00
☐	16	Wayne Gretzky	15.00	7.50	1.50
☐	17	Rick Kehoe	.05	.02	.00
☐	18	Jari Kurri	9.00	4.50	.90
☐	19	Guy Lafleur	1.00	.50	.10
☐	20	Mike Liut	.30	.15	.03

			MINT	EXC	G-VG
☐	21	Dale McCourt	.05	.02	.00
☐	22	Rick Middleton	.25	.12	.02
☐	23	Mark Napier	.05	.02	.00
☐	24	Kent Nilsson	.10	.05	.01
☐	25	Wilf Paiement	.05	.02	.00
☐	26	Willi Plett	.05	.02	.00
☐	27	Denis Potvin	.75	.35	.07
☐	28	Paul Reinhart	.15	.07	.01
☐	29	Jacques Richard	.05	.02	.00
☐	30	Pat Riggin	.35	.17	.03
☐	31	Larry Robinson	.40	.20	.04
☐	32	Mike Rogers	.10	.05	.01
☐	33	Borje Salming	.20	.10	.02
☐	34	Steve Shutt	.25	.12	.02
☐	35	Charlie Simmer	.15	.07	.01
☐	36	Darryl Sittler	.35	.17	.03
☐	37	Bobby Smith	.20	.10	.02
☐	38	Stan Smyl	.05	.02	.00
☐	39	Peter Stastny	5.50	2.75	.55
☐	40	Dave Taylor	.35	.17	.03
☐	41	Bryan Trottier	1.25	.60	.12
☐	42	Ian Turnbull	.05	.02	.00
☐	43	Eric Vail	.05	.02	.00
☐	44	Rick Vaive	.20	.10	.02
☐	45	Behn Wilson	.05	.02	.00
☐	46	Boston Scoring: Rick Middleton	.15	.07	.01
☐	47	Buffalo Scoring: Danny Gare	.10	.05	.01
☐	48	Calgary Flames Scoring Leaders Kent Nilsson	.10	.05	.01
☐	49	Chicago Blackhawks Scoring Leaders Tom Lysiak	.10	.05	.01
☐	50	Colorado Rockies Scoring Leaders Lanny McDonald	.15	.07	.01
☐	51	Red Wings Scoring: Dale McCourt	.10	.05	.01
☐	52	Edmonton Scoring: Wayne Gretzky	3.50	1.75	.35
☐	53	Hartford Whalers Scoring Leaders Mike Rogers	.10	.05	.01
☐	54	L.A. Kings Scoring: Marcel Dionne	.35	.17	.03
☐	55	Minnesota North Stars Scoring Leaders Bobby Smith	.10	.05	.01
☐	56	Montreal Scoring: Steve Shutt	.20	.10	.02

			MINT	EXC	G-VG
☐	57	**Islanders Scoring:**	.45	.22	.04
		Mike Bossy			
☐	58	**Rangers Scoring:**	.10	.05	.01
		Anders Hedberg			
☐	59	**Flyers Scoring:**	.20	.10	.02
		Bill Barber			
☐	60	**Penguins Scoring:**	.10	.05	.01
		Rick Kehoe			
☐	61	**Quebec Nordiques**	.50	.25	.05
		Scoring Leaders			
		Peter Stastny			
☐	62	**Blues Scoring:**	.10	.05	.01
		Bernie Federko			
☐	63	**Toronto Scoring:**	.10	.05	.01
		Wilf Paiement			
☐	64	**Vancouver Canucks**	.10	.05	.01
		Scoring Leaders			
		Thomas Gradin			
☐	65	**Washington Capitals**	.10	.05	.01
		Scoring Leaders			
		Dennis Maruk			
☐	66	**Winnipeg Jets**	.10	.05	.01
		Scoring Leaders			
		Dave Christian			
☐	E67	**Dwight Foster**	.10	.05	.01
☐	E68	**Steve Kasper**	.60	.30	.06
☐	E69	**Peter McNab**	.10	.05	.01
☐	E70	**Mike O'Connell**	.15	.07	.01
☐	E71	**Terry O'Reilly**	.20	.10	.02
☐	E72	**Brad Park**	.40	.20	.04
☐	E73	**Dick Redmond**	.10	.05	.01
☐	E74	**Rogatien Vachon**	.35	.17	.03
☐	E75	**Don Edwards**	.15	.07	.01
☐	E76	**Tony McKegney**	.10	.05	.01
☐	E77	**Bob Sauve**	.15	.07	.01
☐	E78	**Andre Savard**	.10	.05	.01
☐	E79	**Derek Smith**	.10	.05	.01
☐	E80	**John Van Boxmeer**	.10	.05	.01
☐	E81	**Pat Boutette**	.10	.05	.01
☐	E82	**Mark Howe**	.25	.12	.02
☐	E83	**Dave Keon**	.40	.20	.04
☐	E84	**Warren Miller**	.10	.05	.01
☐	E85	**Al Sims**	.10	.05	.01
☐	E86	**Blaine Stoughton**	.15	.07	.01
☐	E87	**Bob Bourne**	.15	.07	.01
☐	E88	**Clark Gillies**	.20	.10	.02
☐	E89	**Butch Goring**	.15	.07	.01
☐	E90	**Anders Kallur**	.10	.05	.01
☐	E91	**Ken Morrow**	.15	.07	.01
☐	E92	**Stefan Persson**	.15	.07	.01
☐	E93	**Billy Smith**	.40	.20	.04
☐	E94	**Mike Allison**	.15	.07	.01
☐	E95	**John Davidson**	.10	.05	.01

		MINT	EXC	G-VG
☐ E96	Ron Duguay	.15	.07	.01
☐ E97	Ron Greschner	.15	.07	.01
☐ E98	Anders Hedberg	.15	.07	.01
☐ E99	Ed Johnstone	.10	.05	.01
☐ E100	Dave Maloney	.15	.07	.01
☐ E101	Don Maloney	.15	.07	.01
☐ E102	Ulf Nilsson	.15	.07	.01
☐ E103	Bobby Clarke	.75	.35	.07
☐ E104	Bob Dailey	.10	.05	.01
☐ E105	Paul Holmgren	.15	.07	.01
☐ E106	Reggie Leach	.15	.07	.01
☐ E107	Ken Linseman	.15	.07	.01
☐ E108	Rick MacLeish	.20	.10	.02
☐ E109	Pete Peeters	.50	.25	.05
☐ E110	Brian Propp	.65	.30	.06
☐ E111	Checklist: 1-132	.50	.05	.01
☐ E112	Randy Carlyle	.15	.07	.01
☐ E113	Paul Gardner	.10	.05	.01
☐ E114	Peter Lee	.10	.05	.01
☐ E115	Greg Millen	.15	.07	.01
☐ E116	Rod Schutt	.10	.05	.01
☐ E117	Mike Gartner	1.25	.60	.12
☐ E118	Rick Green	.15	.07	.01
☐ E119	Bob Kelly	.10	.05	.01
☐ E120	Dennis Maruk	.15	.07	.01
☐ E121	Mike Palmateer	.15	.07	.01
☐ E122	Ryan Walter	.15	.07	.01
☐ E123	Bill Barber SA	.20	.10	.02
☐ E124	Barry Beck SA	.15	.07	.01
☐ E125	Mike Bossy SA	1.25	.60	.12
☐ E126	Ray Bourque SA	2.00	1.00	.20
☐ E127	Danny Gare SA	.10	.05	.01
☐ E128	Rick Kehoe SA	.10	.05	.01
☐ E129	Rick Middleton SA	.20	.10	.02
☐ E130	Denis Potvin SA	.50	.25	.05
☐ E131	Mike Rogers SA	.10	.05	.01
☐ E132	Bryan Trottier SA	.75	.35	.07
☐ W67	Keith Brown	.15	.07	.01
☐ W68	Ted Bulley	.15	.07	.01
☐ W69	Tim Higgins	.15	.07	.01
☐ W70	Reg Kerr	.15	.07	.01
☐ W71	Tom Lysiak	.20	.10	.02
☐ W72	Grant Mulvey	.20	.10	.02
☐ W73	Bob Murray	.15	.07	.01
☐ W74	Terry Ruskowski	.20	.10	.02
☐ W75	Denis Savard	10.00	5.00	1.00
☐ W76	Glen Sharpley	.15	.07	.01
☐ W77	Darryl Sutter	.45	.22	.04
☐ W78	Doug Wilson	.65	.30	.06
☐ W79	Lucien Deblois	.15	.07	.01
☐ W80	Paul Gagne	.15	.07	.01
☐ W81	Merlin Malinowski	.15	.07	.01
☐ W82	Lanny McDonald	.35	.17	.03

		MINT	EXC	G-VG
☐ W83	Joel Quenneville	.15	.07	.01
☐ W84	Rob Ramage	.25	.12	.02
☐ W85	Glenn Resch	.35	.17	.03
☐ W86	Steve Tambellini	.15	.07	.01
☐ W87	Mike Foligno	.15	.07	.01
☐ W88	Gilles Gilbert	.20	.10	.02
☐ W89	Willie Huber	.15	.07	.01
☐ W90	Mark Kirton	.15	.07	.01
☐ W91	Jim Korn	.15	.07	.01
☐ W92	Reed Larson	.15	.07	.01
☐ W93	Gary McAdam	.15	.07	.01
☐ W94	Vaclav Nedomansky	.15	.07	.01
☐ W95	John Ogrodnick	.75	.35	.07
☐ W96	Billy Harris	.15	.07	.01
☐ W97	Jerry Korab	.15	.07	.01
☐ W98	Mario Lessard	.35	.17	.03
☐ W99	Don Luce	.15	.07	.01
☐ W100	Larry Murphy	1.00	.50	.10
☐ W101	Mike Murphy	.15	.07	.01
☐ W102	Kent-Erik Andersson	.15	.07	.01
☐ W103	Don Beaupre	2.00	1.00	.20
☐ W104	Steve Christoff	.15	.07	.01
☐ W105	Dino Ciccarelli	6.00	3.00	.60
☐ W106	Craig Hartsburg	.15	.07	.01
☐ W107	Al MacAdam	.15	.07	.01
☐ W108	Tom McCarthy	.15	.07	.01
☐ W109	Gilles Meloche	.20	.10	.02
☐ W110	Steve Payne	.15	.07	.01
☐ W111	Gordie Roberts	.15	.07	.01
☐ W112	Greg Smith	.15	.07	.01
☐ W113	Tim Young	.15	.07	.01
☐ W114	Wayne Babych	.15	.07	.01
☐ W115	Blair Chapman	.15	.07	.01
☐ W116	Tony Currie	.15	.07	.01
☐ W117	Blake Dunlop	.15	.07	.01
☐ W118	Ed Kea	.15	.07	.01
☐ W119	Rick Lapointe	.15	.07	.01
☐ W120	Checklist 1-132	.50	.05	.01
☐ W121	Jorgen Pettersson	.30	.15	.03
☐ W122	Brian Sutter	.25	.12	.02
☐ W123	Perry Turnbull	.20	.10	.02
☐ W124	Mike Zuke	.15	.07	.01
☐ W125	Marcel Dionne SA	.65	.30	.06
☐ W126	Tony Esposito SA	.50	.25	.05
☐ W127	Bernie Federko SA	.20	.10	.02
☐ W128	Mike Liut SA	.25	.12	.02
☐ W129	Dale McCourt SA	.15	.07	.01
☐ W130	Charlie Simmer SA	.20	.10	.02
☐ W131	Bobby Smith SA	.25	.12	.02
☐ W132	Dave Taylor SA	.60	.30	.06

1984-85 Topps

This set of 165 cards measuring 2¹/₂" by 3¹/₂" marks the resumption of hockey cards by Topps. There were no Topps hockey sets produced in 1982-83 or 1983-84, although O-Pee-Chee still produced sets. The set contains 66 single prints and 99 double prints; the single prints are noted in the checklist by SP. The NHL All-Star selections are indicated on cards 153-164. Teams from the United States have a greater player representation than the Canadian teams. Card backs are printed with red and blue ink on gray card stock. Card backs contain NHL (and WHA) statistics. The style of the obverse is very similar to the design used in 1983 and 1984 on the Topps baseball card issues. The key rookie cards in this set are Pat Lafontaine and Steve Yzerman.

Ce jeu de 165 cartes, mesurant 2¹/₂" x 3¹/₂", est le premier jeu émis à nouveau par Topps après la période 1982-1984, quoique O-Pee-Chee continua à produire des jeux. Le jeu contient 66 cartes simples et 99 cartes doubles. Les cartes simples sont indiquées dans la liste de contrôle par "SP". Les sélections All-Star de la NHL sont indiquées sur les cartes 153-164. Les joueurs des équipes des Etats-Unis sont mieux représentés que les joueurs des équipes canadiennes. Le dos est imprimé en rouge et bleu sur une pâte de papier grise. Il présente des statistiques NHL (et WHA). Le style de la face ressemble beaucoup à celui employé en 1983 et 1984 pour les cartes de baseball Topps. Les cartes des débutants importants représentent Pat Lafontaine et Steve Yzerman.

			MINT	EXC	G-VG
	COMPLETE SET (165)		48.00	22.00	4.00
	COMMON PLAYER (1-165)		.05	.02	.00
	COMMON PLAYER SP		.10	.05	.01
☐	1	Ray Bourque	2.00	.50	.10
☐	2	Keith Crowder SP	.10	.05	.01
☐	3	Tom Fergus	.05	.02	.00
☐	4	Doug Keans	.20	.10	.02

			MINT	EXC	G-VG
☐	5	Gord Kluzak SP	.15	.07	.01
☐	6	Mike Krushelnyski SP	.30	.15	.03
☐	7	Nevin Markwart	.05	.02	.00
☐	8	Rick Middleton	.20	.10	.02
☐	9	Mike O'Connell	.05	.02	.00
☐	10	Terry O'Reilly SP	.25	.12	.02
☐	11	Barry Pederson	.15	.07	.01
☐	12	Pete Peeters	.15	.07	.01
☐	13	Dave Andreychuk SP	1.50	.75	.15
☐	14	Tom Barrasso	1.50	.75	.15
☐	15	Real Cloutier SP	.10	.05	.01
☐	16	Mike Foligno	.05	.02	.00
☐	17	Bill Hajt SP	.10	.05	.01
☐	18	Phil Housley SP	1.00	.50	.10
☐	19	Gilbert Perreault	.40	.20	.04
☐	20	Larry Playfair SP	.15	.07	.01
☐	21	Craig Ramsay SP	.10	.05	.01
☐	22	Mike Ramsey	.05	.02	.00
☐	23	Lindy Ruff SP	.15	.07	.01
☐	24	Ed Beers	.15	.07	.01
☐	25	Rejean Lemelin SP	.35	.17	.03
☐	26	Lanny McDonald	.25	.12	.02
☐	27	Murray Bannerman	.15	.07	.01
☐	28	Keith Brown SP	.10	.05	.01
☐	29	Curt Fraser	.05	.02	.00
☐	30	Steve Larmer	.75	.35	.07
☐	31	Tom Lysiak	.10	.05	.01
☐	32	Bob Murray	.05	.02	.00
☐	33	Jack O'Callahan SP	.15	.07	.01
☐	34	Rich Preston	.05	.02	.00
☐	35	Denis Savard	.75	.35	.07
☐	36	Darryl Sutter	.10	.05	.01
☐	37	Doug Wilson	.30	.15	.03
☐	38	Ivan Boldirev	.05	.02	.00
☐	39	Colin Campbell SP	.10	.05	.01
☐	40	Ron Duguay SP	.15	.07	.01
☐	41	Dwight Foster SP	.10	.05	.01
☐	42	Danny Gare SP	.15	.07	.01
☐	43	Ed Johnstone	.05	.02	.00
☐	44	Reed Larson SP	.10	.05	.01
☐	45	Eddie Mio SP	.30	.15	.03
☐	46	John Ogrodnick	.10	.05	.01
☐	47	Brad Park	.25	.12	.02
☐	48	Greg Stefan SP	.40	.20	.04
☐	49	Steve Yzerman	12.00	6.00	1.20
☐	50	Paul Coffey	2.50	1.25	.25
☐	51	Wayne Gretzky	10.00	5.00	1.00
☐	52	Jari Kurri	.75	.35	.07
☐	53	Bob Crawford	.15	.07	.01
☐	54	Ron Francis	.75	.35	.07
☐	55	Marty Howe	.10	.05	.01
☐	56	Mark Johnson SP	.15	.07	.01
☐	57	Greg Malone SP	.10	.05	.01

		MINT	EXC	G-VG
☐ 58	Greg Millen SP	.15	.07	.01
☐ 59	Ray Neufeld	.05	.02	.00
☐ 60	Joel Quenneville SP	.10	.05	.01
☐ 61	Risto Siltanen	.05	.02	.00
☐ 62	Sylvain Turgeon	.45	.22	.04
☐ 63	Mike Zuke SP	.10	.05	.01
☐ 64	Marcel Dionne	.65	.30	.06
☐ 65	Brian Engblom SP	.10	.05	.01
☐ 66	Jim Fox SP	.10	.05	.01
☐ 67	Bernie Nicholls	2.00	1.00	.20
☐ 68	Terry Ruskowski SP	.10	.05	.01
☐ 69	Charlie Simmer	.10	.05	.01
☐ 70	Don Beaupre	.15	.07	.01
☐ 71	Brian Bellows	1.00	.50	.10
☐ 72	Neal Broten SP	.50	.25	.05
☐ 73	Dino Ciccarelli	.25	.12	.02
☐ 74	Paul Holmgren SP	.15	.07	.01
☐ 75	Al MacAdam SP	.15	.07	.01
☐ 76	Dennis Maruk	.10	.05	.01
☐ 77	Brad Maxwell SP	.10	.05	.01
☐ 78	Tom McCarthy SP	.10	.05	.01
☐ 79	Gilles Meloche SP	.15	.07	.01
☐ 80	Steve Payne	.05	.02	.00
☐ 81	Guy Lafleur	1.00	.50	.10
☐ 82	Larry Robinson	.25	.12	.02
☐ 83	Bobby Smith	.20	.10	.02
☐ 84	Mel Bridgman	.05	.02	.00
☐ 85	Joe Cirella	.15	.07	.01
☐ 86	Don Lever	.05	.02	.00
☐ 87	Dave Lewis	.05	.02	.00
☐ 88	Jan Ludvig	.05	.02	.00
☐ 89	Glenn Resch	.20	.10	.02
☐ 90	Pat Verbeek	1.75	.85	.17
☐ 91	Mike Bossy	1.00	.50	.10
☐ 92	Bob Bourne	.05	.02	.00
☐ 93	Greg Gilbert	.30	.15	.03
☐ 94	Clark Gillies SP	.20	.10	.02
☐ 95	Butch Goring SP	.15	.07	.01
☐ 96	Pat LaFontaine SP	10.00	5.00	1.00
☐ 97	Ken Morrow	.10	.05	.01
☐ 98	Bob Nystrom SP	.15	.07	.01
☐ 99	Stefan Persson SP	.15	.07	.01
☐ 100	Denis Potvin	.50	.25	.05
☐ 101	Billy Smith SP	.30	.15	.03
☐ 102	Brent Sutter SP	.30	.15	.03
☐ 103	John Tonelli	.10	.05	.01
☐ 104	Bryan Trottier	.50	.25	.05
☐ 105	Barry Beck	.10	.05	.01
☐ 106	Glen Hanlon SP	.15	.07	.01
☐ 107	Anders Hedberg SP	.15	.07	.01
☐ 108	Pierre Larouche SP	.15	.07	.01
☐ 109	Don Maloney SP	.15	.07	.01
☐ 110	Mark Osborne SP	.20	.10	.02

			MINT	EXC	G-VG
☐	111	**Larry Patey**	.05	.02	.00
☐	112	**James Patrick**	.50	.25	.05
☐	113	**Mark Pavelich SP**	.25	.12	.02
☐	114	**Mike Rogers SP**	.15	.07	.01
☐	115	**Reijo Ruotsalainen SP**	.35	.17	.03
☐	116	**Peter Sundstrom SP**	.40	.20	.04
☐	117	**Bob Froese**	.30	.15	.03
☐	118	**Mark Howe**	.25	.12	.02
☐	119	**Tim Kerr SP**	.45	.22	.04
☐	120	**Dave Poulin**	.60	.30	.06
☐	121	**Darryl Sittler SP**	.45	.22	.04
☐	122	**Ron Sutter**	.35	.17	.03
☐	123	**Mike Bullard SP**	.35	.17	.03
☐	124	**Ron Flockhart SP**	.10	.05	.01
☐	125	**Rick Kehoe**	.10	.05	.01
☐	126	**Kevin McCarthy SP**	.10	.05	.01
☐	127	**Mark Taylor**	.05	.02	.00
☐	128	**Dan Bouchard SP**	.10	.05	.01
☐	129	**Michel Goulet**	.25	.12	.02
☐	130	**Peter Stastny SP**	.90	.45	.09
☐	131	**Bernie Federko**	.15	.07	.01
☐	132	**Mike Liut**	.20	.10	.02
☐	133	**Joey Mullen SP**	.60	.30	.06
☐	134	**Rob Ramage**	.10	.05	.01
☐	135	**Brian Sutter**	.10	.05	.01
☐	136	**John Anderson SP**	.10	.05	.01
☐	137	**Dan Daoust**	.05	.02	.00
☐	138	**Rick Vaive**	.10	.05	.01
☐	139	**Darcy Rota SP**	.10	.05	.01
☐	140	**Stan Smyl SP**	.15	.07	.01
☐	141	**Tony Tanti**	.25	.12	.02
☐	142	**Dave Christian SP**	.15	.07	.01
☐	143	**Mike Gartner SP**	.40	.20	.04
☐	144	**Bengt Gustafsson SP**	.10	.05	.01
☐	145	**Doug Jarvis**	.10	.05	.01
☐	146	**Al Jensen**	.15	.07	.01
☐	147	**Rod Langway**	.25	.12	.02
☐	148	**Pat Riggin**	.10	.05	.01
☐	149	**Scott Stevens SP**	.90	.45	.09
☐	150	**Dave Babych**	.10	.05	.01
☐	151	**Laurie Boschman**	.05	.02	.00
☐	152	**Dale Hawerchuk**	.75	.35	.07
☐	153	**Michel Goulet AS**	.25	.12	.02
☐	154	**Wayne Gretzky AS**	4.00	2.00	.40
☐	155	**Mike Bossy AS**	.75	.35	.07
☐	156	**Rod Langway AS**	.15	.07	.01
☐	157	**Ray Bourque AS**	.65	.30	.06
☐	158	**Tom Barrasso AS**	.30	.15	.03
☐	159	**Mark Messier AS**	1.50	.75	.15
☐	160	**Bryan Trottier AS**	.35	.17	.03
☐	161	**Jari Kurri AS**	.60	.30	.06
☐	162	**Denis Potvin AS**	.40	.20	.04
☐	163	**Paul Coffey AS**	.90	.45	.09

		MINT	EXC	G-VG
☐ 164	Pat Riggin AS	.10	.05	.01
☐ 165	Checklist 1-165 SP	.75	.06	.01

1985-86 Topps

This set of 165 cards measuring 2¹/₂" by 3¹/₂" is very similar to Topps' hockey set of the previous season. There are 66 single prints and 99 double prints; the single prints are noted in the checklist by SP. Card backs are printed with red and blue ink on gray card stock. Card backs contain NHL (and WHA) statistics. The wax boxes had cards printed on the bottom with four players per box; these wax box cards are "lettered" A-P rather than numbered. The set is considered complete without these wax box cards. The key rookie in this set is Mario Lemieux. Other notable rookie cards include Kevin Dineen, Kelly Hrudey, Kirk Muller, Ed Olczyk, Tomas Sandstrom, and Peter Zezel.

Ce jeu de 165 cartes, mesurant 2¹/₂" x 3¹/₂", ressemble beaucoup au jeu de hockey Topps de la saison précédente. Il y a 66 cartes simples et 99 cartes doubles; les cartes simples sont indiquées par "SP" dans la liste de contrôle. Le dos est imprimé en rouge et bleu sur la pâte grise. Il présente les statistiques NHL (et WHA). Les boîtes paraffinées avaient des cartes imprimées sur le fond, avec quatre joueurs par boîte. Ces cartes portent les lettres A- P au lieu d'être numérotées. Le jeu est considéré comme complet sans ces cartes. Le débutant important de ce jeu est Mario Lemieux. D'autres cartes notables de débutants importants incluent Kevin Dineen, Kelly Hrudey, Kirk Muller, Ed Olczyk, Tomas Sandstrom et Peter Zezel.

	MINT	EXC	G-VG
COMPLETE SET (165)	180.00	90.00	18.00
COMMON PLAYER (1-165)	.06	.03	.00
COMMON PLAYER SP	.12	.06	.01

			MINT	EXC	G-VG
☐	1	Lanny McDonald	.40	.08	.01
☐	2	Mike O'Connell SP	.12	.06	.01

			MINT	EXC	G-VG
☐	3	Curt Fraser SP	.12	.06	.01
☐	4	Steve Penney	.12	.06	.01
☐	5	Brian Engblom	.06	.03	.00
☐	6	Ron Sutter	.12	.06	.01
☐	7	Joe Mullen	.25	.12	.02
☐	8	Rod Langway	.15	.07	.01
☐	9	Mario Lemieux	120.00	60.00	12.00
☐	10	Dave Babych	.12	.06	.01
☐	11	Bob Nystrom	.06	.03	.00
☐	12	Andy Moog SP	1.00	.50	.10
☐	13	Dino Ciccarelli	.25	.12	.02
☐	14	Dwight Foster SP	.12	.06	.01
☐	15	James Patrick SP	.20	.10	.02
☐	16	Thomas Gradin SP	.15	.07	.01
☐	17	Mike Foligno	.06	.03	.00
☐	18	Mario Gosselin	.60	.30	.06
☐	19	Mike Zuke SP	.12	.06	.01
☐	20	John Anderson SP	.12	.06	.01
☐	21	Dave Pichette	.06	.03	.00
☐	22	Nick Fotiu SP	.12	.06	.01
☐	23	Tom Lysiak	.12	.06	.01
☐	24	Peter Zezel	1.75	.85	.17
☐	25	Denis Potvin	.35	.17	.03
☐	26	Bob Carpenter	.20	.10	.02
☐	27	Murray Bannerman SP	.15	.07	.01
☐	28	Gordie Roberts SP	.12	.06	.01
☐	29	Steve Yzerman	10.00	5.00	1.00
☐	30	Phil Russell	.06	.03	.00
☐	31	Peter Stastny	.60	.30	.06
☐	32	Craig Ramsay SP	.12	.06	.01
☐	33	Terry Ruskowski SP	.12	.06	.01
☐	34	Kevin Dineen SP	2.50	1.25	.25
☐	35	Mark Howe	.20	.10	.02
☐	36	Glenn Resch	.20	.10	.02
☐	37	Danny Gare SP	.15	.07	.01
☐	38	Doug Bodger	.40	.20	.04
☐	39	Mike Rogers	.12	.06	.01
☐	40	Ray Bourque	2.00	1.00	.20
☐	41	John Tonelli	.15	.07	.01
☐	42	Mel Bridgman	.06	.03	.00
☐	43	Sylvain Turgeon SP	.15	.07	.01
☐	44	Mark Johnson	.12	.06	.01
☐	45	Doug Wilson	.25	.12	.02
☐	46	Mike Gartner	.25	.12	.02
☐	47	Brent Peterson	.06	.03	.00
☐	48	Paul Reinhart SP	.15	.07	.01
☐	49	Mike Krushelnyski	.12	.06	.01
☐	50	Brian Bellows	.50	.25	.05
☐	51	Chris Chelios	2.00	1.00	.20
☐	52	Barry Pederson SP	.15	.07	.01
☐	53	Murray Craven SP	.35	.17	.03
☐	54	Pierre Larouche SP	.15	.07	.01
☐	55	Reed Larson	.06	.03	.00

			MINT	EXC	G-VG
☐ 56	Pat Verbeek SP		.50	.25	.05
☐ 57	Randy Carlyle		.12	.06	.01
☐ 58	Ray Neufeld SP		.12	.06	.01
☐ 59	Keith Brown SP		.12	.06	.01
☐ 60	Bryan Trottier		.45	.22	.04
☐ 61	Jim Fox SP		.12	.06	.01
☐ 62	Scott Stevens		.35	.17	.03
☐ 63	Phil Housley		.20	.10	.02
☐ 64	Rick Middleton		.20	.10	.02
☐ 65	Steve Payne		.06	.03	.00
☐ 66	Dave Lewis		.06	.03	.00
☐ 67	Mike Bullard		.12	.06	.01
☐ 68	Stan Smyl SP		.15	.07	.01
☐ 69	Mark Pavelich SP		.15	.07	.01
☐ 70	John Ogrodnick		.12	.06	.01
☐ 71	Bill Derlago SP		.12	.06	.01
☐ 72	Brad Marsh SP		.12	.06	.01
☐ 73	Denis Savard		.75	.35	.07
☐ 74	Mark Fusco		.06	.03	.00
☐ 75	Pete Peeters		.12	.06	.01
☐ 76	Doug Gilmour		.35	.17	.03
☐ 77	Mike Ramsey		.06	.03	.00
☐ 78	Anton Stastny SP		.15	.07	.01
☐ 79	Steve Kasper SP		.15	.07	.01
☐ 80	Bryan Erickson SP		.20	.10	.02
☐ 81	Clark Gillies		.15	.07	.01
☐ 82	Keith Acton		.06	.03	.00
☐ 83	Pat Flatley		.12	.06	.01
☐ 84	Kirk Muller		3.00	1.50	.30
☐ 85	Paul Coffey		1.50	.75	.15
☐ 86	Ed Olczyk		3.00	1.50	.30
☐ 87	Charlie Simmer SP		.15	.07	.01
☐ 88	Mike Liut		.15	.07	.01
☐ 89	Dave Maloney		.12	.06	.01
☐ 90	Marcel Dionne		.50	.25	.05
☐ 91	Tim Kerr		.20	.10	.02
☐ 92	Ivan Boldirev SP		.12	.06	.01
☐ 93	Ken Morrow SP		.15	.07	.01
☐ 94	Don Maloney SP		.15	.07	.01
☐ 95	Rejean Lemelin		.15	.07	.01
☐ 96	Curt Giles		.06	.03	.00
☐ 97	Bob Bourne		.06	.03	.00
☐ 98	Joe Cirella		.12	.06	.01
☐ 99	Dave Christian SP		.15	.07	.01
☐ 100	Darryl Sutter		.12	.06	.01
☐ 101	Kelly Kisio		.30	.15	.03
☐ 102	Mats Naslund		.30	.15	.03
☐ 103	Joel Quenneville SP		.12	.06	.01
☐ 104	Bernie Federko		.15	.07	.01
☐ 105	Tom Barrasso		.25	.12	.02
☐ 106	Rick Vaive		.12	.06	.01
☐ 107	Brent Sutter		.12	.06	.01
☐ 108	Wayne Babych		.06	.03	.00

		MINT	EXC	G-VG
☐ 109	Dale Hawerchuk	.50	.25	.05
☐ 110	Pelle Lindbergh SP	7.00	3.50	.70
☐ 111	Dennis Maruk SP	.15	.07	.01
☐ 112	Reijo Ruotsalainen SP	.15	.07	.01
☐ 113	Tom Fergus SP	.12	.06	.01
☐ 114	Bob Murray SP	.12	.06	.01
☐ 115	Patrik Sundstrom	.12	.06	.01
☐ 116	Ron Duguay SP	.15	.07	.01
☐ 117	Alan Haworth SP	.12	.06	.01
☐ 118	Greg Malone	.06	.03	.00
☐ 119	Bill Hajt	.06	.03	.00
☐ 120	Wayne Gretzky	13.50	6.00	1.25
☐ 121	Craig Redmond	.06	.03	.00
☐ 122	Kelly Hrudey	4.00	2.00	.40
☐ 123	Tomas Sandstrom	8.00	4.00	.80
☐ 124	Neal Broten	.15	.07	.01
☐ 125	Moe Mantha SP	.25	.12	.02
☐ 126	Greg Gilbert SP	.15	.07	.01
☐ 127	Bruce Driver SP	.45	.22	.04
☐ 128	Dave Poulin	.15	.07	.01
☐ 129	Morris Lukowich SP	.12	.06	.01
☐ 130	Mike Bossy	.75	.35	.07
☐ 131	Larry Playfair SP	.12	.06	.01
☐ 132	Steve Larmer	.90	.45	.09
☐ 133	Doug Keans SP	.15	.07	.01
☐ 134	Bob Manno	.06	.03	.00
☐ 135	Brian Sutter	.12	.06	.01
☐ 136	Pat Riggin	.12	.06	.01
☐ 137	Pat LaFontaine	3.00	1.50	.30
☐ 138	Barry Beck SP	.15	.07	.01
☐ 139	Rich Preston SP	.12	.06	.01
☐ 140	Ron Francis	.50	.25	.05
☐ 141	Brian Propp SP	.35	.17	.03
☐ 142	Don Beaupre	.15	.07	.01
☐ 143	Dave Andreychuk SP	.25	.12	.02
☐ 144	Ed Beers	.06	.03	.00
☐ 145	Paul MacLean	.15	.07	.01
☐ 146	Troy Murray SP	.35	.17	.03
☐ 147	Larry Robinson	.25	.12	.02
☐ 148	Bernie Nicholls	1.25	.60	.12
☐ 149	Glen Hanlon SP	.15	.07	.01
☐ 150	Michel Goulet	.25	.12	.02
☐ 151	Doug Jarvis SP	.15	.07	.01
☐ 152	Warren Young	.25	.12	.02
☐ 153	Tony Tanti	.12	.06	.01
☐ 154	Tomas Jonsson SP	.15	.07	.01
☐ 155	Jari Kurri	.80	.40	.08
☐ 156	Tony McKegney	.06	.03	.00
☐ 157	Greg Stefan SP	.15	.07	.01
☐ 158	Brad McCrimmon SP	.25	.12	.02
☐ 159	Keith Crowder SP	.12	.06	.01
☐ 160	Gilbert Perreault	.35	.17	.03
☐ 161	Tim Bothwell SP	.15	.07	.01

			MINT	EXC	G-VG
☐ 162	Bob Crawford SP	....	.12	.06	.01
☐ 163	Paul Gagne SP	....	.12	.06	.01
☐ 164	Dan Daoust SP	....	.12	.06	.01
☐ 165	Checklist 1-165 SP	....	.50	.05	.01

1986-87 Topps

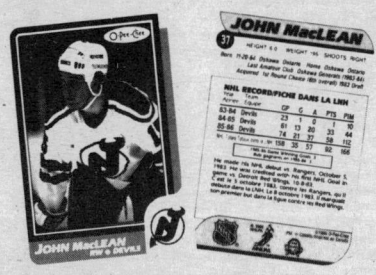

This set of 198 cards measuring 2½" by 3½" is again very similar to Topps' hockey set of the previous seasons. There are 66 double prints and 132 single prints; the double prints are noted in the checklist by DP. Card backs are printed with black and blue ink on gray card stock. Card backs contain NHL (and WHA) statistics. There were also 16 cards printed on the bottom of the wax pack boxes, four to a box. These cards were "lettered" rather than numbered and are not considered part of the complete set; they are listed and priced at the end of the checklist below. The key rookie in this set is Patrick Roy. Other notable rookie cards include Russ Courtnall, Petr Klima, John MacLean, Gary Suter, and John Vanbiesbrouck.

Ce jeu de 198 cartes, mesurant 2½" x 3½", ressemble également beaucoup au jeu de hockey Topps des saisons précédentes. Il y a 66 cartes doubles et 132 cartes simples; les cartes doubles sont indiquées par "DP" dans la liste de contrôle. Le dos est imprimé en noir et bleu sur une pâte grise. Il présente les statistiques NHL (et WHA). Seize cartes furent également imprimées sur le fond de boîtes paraffinées, quatre cartes par boîte. Ces cartes se distinguent par des lettres au lieu d'être numérotées, et ne sont pas considérées comme faisant partie du jeu. Elles sont indiquées et évaluées à la fin de la liste ci-dessous. Le débutant prometteur de ce jeu est Patrick Roy. D'autres cartes notables de débutants importants incluent Russ Courtnall, Petr Klima, John MacLean, Gary Suter, et John Vanbiesbrouck.

	MINT	EXC	G-VG
COMPLETE SET (198)	110.00	55.00	11.00
COMMON PLAYER (1-198)	.07	.03	.01
COMMON PLAYER DP	.04	.02	.00

			MINT	EXC	G-VG
☐	1	Ray Bourque	1.75	.40	.08
☐	2	Pat LaFontaine DP	1.00	.50	.10
☐	3	Wayne Gretzky	11.00	5.50	1.10
☐	4	Lindy Ruff	.07	.03	.01
☐	5	Brad McCrimmon	.07	.03	.01
☐	6	Dave Williams	.12	.06	.01
☐	7	Denis Savard DP	.40	.20	.04
☐	8	Lanny McDonald	.25	.12	.02
☐	9	John Vanbiesbrouck DP	1.25	.60	.12
☐	10	Greg Adams	.50	.25	.05
		New Jersey Devils			
☐	11	Steve Yzerman	7.00	3.50	.70
☐	12	Craig Hartsburg	.07	.03	.01
☐	13	John Anderson DP	.04	.02	.00
☐	14	Bob Bourne DP	.04	.02	.00
☐	15	Kjell Dahlin	.35	.17	.03
☐	16	Dave Andreychuk	.12	.06	.01
☐	17	Rob Ramage DP	.07	.03	.01
☐	18	Ron Greschner DP	.07	.03	.01
☐	19	Bruce Driver	.12	.06	.01
☐	20	Peter Stastny	.50	.25	.05
☐	21	Dave Christian	.12	.06	.01
☐	22	Doug Keans	.12	.06	.01
☐	23	Scott Bjugstad	.07	.03	.01
☐	24	Doug Bodger DP	.07	.03	.01
☐	25	Troy Murray DP	.07	.03	.01
☐	26	Al Iafrate	.50	.25	.05
☐	27	Kelly Hrudey	.50	.25	.05
☐	28	Doug Jarvis	.12	.06	.01
☐	29	Rich Sutter	.12	.06	.01
☐	30	Marcel Dionne	.40	.20	.04
☐	31	Curt Fraser	.07	.03	.01
☐	32	Doug Lidster	.12	.06	.01
☐	33	Brian MacLellan	.07	.03	.01
☐	34	Barry Pederson	.12	.06	.01
☐	35	Craig Laughlin	.07	.03	.01
☐	36	Ilkka Sinisalo DP	.07	.03	.01
☐	37	John MacLean	5.00	2.50	.50
☐	38	Brian Mullen	.25	.12	.02
☐	39	Duane Sutter DP	.07	.03	.01
☐	40	Brian Engblom	.07	.03	.01
☐	41	Chris Cichocki	.07	.03	.01
☐	42	Gordie Roberts	.07	.03	.01
☐	43	Ron Francis	.45	.22	.04
☐	44	Joe Mullen	.20	.10	.02
☐	45	Moe Mantha DP	.04	.02	.00
☐	46	Pat Verbeek	.20	.10	.02
☐	47	Clint Malarchuk	.50	.25	.05
☐	48	Bob Brooke DP	.04	.02	.00
☐	49	Darryl Sutter DP	.07	.03	.01
☐	50	Stan Smyl DP	.07	.03	.01

			MINT	EXC	G-VG
☐	51	Greg Stefan	.12	.06	.01
☐	52	Bill Hajt DP	.04	.02	.00
☐	53	Patrick Roy	30.00	15.00	3.00
☐	54	Gord Kluzak	.12	.06	.01
☐	55	Bob Froese DP	.07	.03	.01
☐	56	Grant Fuhr	1.25	.60	.12
☐	57	Mark Hunter DP	.07	.03	.01
☐	58	Dana Murzyn	.15	.07	.01
☐	59	Mike Gartner	.20	.10	.02
☐	60	Dennis Maruk	.12	.06	.01
☐	61	Rich Preston	.07	.03	.01
☐	62	Larry Robinson DP	.20	.10	.02
☐	63	Dave Taylor DP	.12	.06	.01
☐	64	Bob Murray DP	.04	.02	.00
☐	65	Ken Morrow	.12	.06	.01
☐	66	Mike Ridley	.75	.35	.07
☐	67	John Tucker	.25	.12	.02
☐	68	Miroslav Frycer	.07	.03	.01
☐	69	Danny Gare	.12	.06	.01
☐	70	Randy Burridge	.20	.10	.02
☐	71	Dave Poulin	.15	.07	.01
☐	72	Brian Sutter	.12	.06	.01
☐	73	Dave Babych	.12	.06	.01
☐	74	Dale Hawerchuk DP	.35	.17	.03
☐	75	Brian Bellows	.35	.17	.03
☐	76	Dave Pasin DP	.04	.02	.00
☐	77	Pete Peeters DP	.07	.03	.01
☐	78	Tomas Jonsson DP	.04	.02	.00
☐	79	Gilbert Perreault DP	.25	.12	.02
☐	80	Glenn Anderson DP	.25	.12	.02
☐	81	Don Maloney	.12	.06	.01
☐	82	Ed Olczyk DP	.25	.12	.02
☐	83	Mike Bullard DP	.07	.03	.01
☐	84	Tom Fergus	.07	.03	.01
☐	85	Dave Lewis	.07	.03	.01
☐	86	Brian Propp	.20	.10	.02
☐	87	John Ogrodnick	.12	.06	.01
☐	88	Kevin Dineen DP	.20	.10	.02
☐	89	Don Beaupre	.15	.07	.01
☐	90	Mike Bossy DP	.60	.30	.06
☐	91	Tom Barrasso DP	.20	.10	.02
☐	92	Michel Goulet DP	.20	.10	.02
☐	93	Doug Gilmour	.20	.10	.02
☐	94	Kirk Muller	.35	.17	.03
☐	95	Larry Melnyk DP	.04	.02	.00
☐	96	Bob Gainey DP	.15	.07	.01
☐	97	Steve Kasper	.12	.06	.01
☐	98	Petr Klima	4.50	2.25	.45
☐	99	Neal Broten DP	.07	.03	.01
☐	100	Al Secord DP	.07	.03	.01
☐	101	Bryan Erickson DP	.04	.02	.00
☐	102	Rejean Lemelin	.15	.07	.01
☐	103	Sylvain Turgeon	.12	.06	.01

		MINT	EXC	G-VG
☐ 104	Bob Nystrom	.07	.03	.01
☐ 105	Bernie Federko	.15	.07	.01
☐ 106	Doug Wilson DP	.20	.10	.02
☐ 107	Alan Haworth	.07	.03	.01
☐ 108	Jari Kurri	.65	.30	.06
☐ 109	Ron Sutter	.12	.06	.01
☐ 110	Reed Larson DP	.04	.02	.00
☐ 111	Terry Ruskowski DP	.04	.02	.00
☐ 112	Mark Johnson DP	.07	.03	.01
☐ 113	James Patrick	.12	.06	.01
☐ 114	Paul MacLean	.12	.06	.01
☐ 115	Mike Ramsey DP	.04	.02	.00
☐ 116	Kelly Kisio DP	.07	.03	.01
☐ 117	Brent Sutter	.12	.06	.01
☐ 118	Joel Quenneville	.07	.03	.01
☐ 119	Curt Giles DP	.04	.02	.00
☐ 120	Tony Tanti DP	.07	.03	.01
☐ 121	Doug Sulliman DP	.04	.02	.00
☐ 122	Mario Lemieux	40.00	20.00	4.00
☐ 123	Mark Howe DP	.15	.07	.01
☐ 124	Bob Sauve	.07	.03	.01
☐ 125	Anton Stastny	.12	.06	.01
☐ 126	Scott Stevens DP	.15	.07	.01
☐ 127	Mike Foligno	.07	.03	.01
☐ 128	Reijo Ruotsalainen DP	.04	.02	.00
☐ 129	Denis Potvin	.35	.17	.03
☐ 130	Keith Crowder	.07	.03	.01
☐ 131	Bob Janecyk DP	.07	.03	.01
☐ 132	John Tonelli	.15	.07	.01
☐ 133	Mike Liut DP	.15	.07	.01
☐ 134	Tim Kerr DP	.15	.07	.01
☐ 135	Al Jensen	.12	.06	.01
☐ 136	Mel Bridgman	.07	.03	.01
☐ 137	Paul Coffey DP	.75	.35	.07
☐ 138	Dino Ciccarelli DP	.20	.10	.02
☐ 139	Steve Larmer	.50	.25	.05
☐ 140	Mike O'Connell	.07	.03	.01
☐ 141	Clark Gillies	.15	.07	.01
☐ 142	Phil Russell DP	.04	.02	.00
☐ 143	Dirk Graham DP	.15	.07	.01
☐ 144	Randy Carlyle	.12	.06	.01
☐ 145	Charlie Simmer	.15	.07	.01
☐ 146	Ron Flockhart DP	.04	.02	.00
☐ 147	Tom Laidlaw	.07	.03	.01
☐ 148	Dave Tippett	.25	.12	.02
☐ 149	Wendel Clark DP	1.25	.60	.12
☐ 150	Bob Carpenter DP	.12	.06	.01
☐ 151	Bill Watson	.07	.03	.01
☐ 152	Roberto Romano DP	.07	.03	.01
☐ 153	Doug Shedden	.12	.06	.01
☐ 154	Phil Housley	.20	.10	.02
☐ 155	Bryan Trottier	.40	.20	.04
☐ 156	Patrik Sundstrom DP	.07	.03	.01

			MINT	EXC	G-VG
☐	157	Rick Middleton DP	.15	.07	.01
☐	158	Glenn Resch	.20	.10	.02
☐	159	Bernie Nicholls DP	.45	.22	.04
☐	160	Ray Ferraro	.35	.17	.03
☐	161	Mats Naslund DP	.15	.07	.01
☐	162	Pat Flatley DP	.07	.03	.01
☐	163	Joe Cirella	.12	.06	.01
☐	164	Rod Langway DP	.12	.06	.01
☐	165	Checklist 1-99	.20	.02	.00
☐	166	Carey Wilson	.25	.12	.02
☐	167	Murray Craven	.12	.06	.01
☐	168	Paul Gillis	.07	.03	.01
☐	169	Borje Salming	.20	.10	.02
☐	170	Perry Turnbull	.12	.06	.01
☐	171	Chris Chelios	.65	.30	.06
☐	172	Keith Acton	.07	.03	.01
☐	173	Al MacInnis	9.00	4.50	.90
☐	174	Russ Courtnall	4.50	2.25	.45
☐	175	Brad Marsh	.07	.03	.01
☐	176	Guy Carbonneau	.25	.12	.02
☐	177	Ray Neufeld	.07	.03	.01
☐	178	Craig MacTavish	.40	.20	.04
☐	179	Rick Lanz	.07	.03	.01
☐	180	Murray Bannerman	.12	.06	.01
☐	181	Brent Ashton	.07	.03	.01
☐	182	Jim Peplinski	.07	.03	.01
☐	183	Mark Napier	.12	.06	.01
☐	184	Laurie Boschman	.07	.03	.01
☐	185	Larry Murphy	.12	.06	.01
☐	186	Mark Messier	1.75	.85	.17
☐	187	Risto Siltanen	.12	.06	.01
☐	188	Bobby Smith	.20	.10	.02
☐	189	Gary Suter	2.00	1.00	.20
☐	190	Peter Zezel	.25	.12	.02
☐	191	Rick Vaive	.12	.06	.01
☐	192	Dale Hunter	.12	.06	.01
☐	193	Mike Krushelnyski	.12	.06	.01
☐	194	Scott Arniel	.07	.03	.01
☐	195	Larry Playfair	.07	.03	.01
☐	196	Doug Risebrough	.12	.06	.01
☐	197	Kevin Lowe	.50	.25	.05
☐	198	Checklist 100-198	.20	.02	.00

1987-88 Topps

The 1987-88 Topps hockey set contains 198 standard size (2¹/₂" by 3¹/₂") cards. The fronts feature color photos with white borders. The card backs show career statistics and highlights. There were cards printed on the bottoms of the wax boxes; these cards are similar to the regular issue cards but are "lettered" A-P rather than numbered. These wax box cards are not considered part of the complete set price below, as they are usually offered separately or as an extra. The key rookies in this set are Jimmy Carson, Kevin Hatcher, Ron Hextall, Adam Oates, Luc Robitaille, Craig Simpson, Esa Tikkanen, and Rick Tocchet.

Le jeu de hockey Topps 1987-88 contient 198 cartes de format standard (2¹/₂" x 3¹/₂"). La face comporte une photo en couleurs bordée de blanc. Le dos indique les statistiques et moments importants de la carrière. Certaines cartes furent imprimées sur le fond de boîtes paraffinées; elles ressemblent aux cartes régulières, mais se distinguent par les lettres A-P au lieu d'être numérotées. Elles ne sont pas considérées comme faisant partie du jeu complet, puisqu'elle sont, en général, offertes séparément ou en prime. Les débutants importants de ce jeu incluent Jimmy Carson, Kevin Hatcher, Ron Hextall, Adam Oates, Luc Robitaille, Craig Simpson, Esa Tikkanen et Rick Tocchet.

			MINT	EXC	G-VG
	COMPLETE SET (198)		110.00	55.00	11.00
	COMMON PLAYER (1-198)		.06	.03	.00
	COMMON PLAYER DP		.04	.02	.00
☐	1	Denis Potvin DP	.30	.10	.02
☐	2	Rick Tocchet	12.00	6.00	1.20
☐	3	Dave Andreychuk	.12	.06	.01
☐	4	Stan Smyl	.10	.05	.01
☐	5	Dave Babych DP	.06	.03	.00
☐	6	Pat Verbeek	.20	.10	.02
☐	7	Esa Tikkanen	6.00	3.00	.60

			MINT	EXC	G-VG
☐	8	Mike Ridley	.12	.06	.01
☐	9	Randy Carlyle	.10	.05	.01
☐	10	Greg Paslawski	.12	.06	.01
☐	11	Neal Broten	.12	.06	.01
☐	12	Wendel Clark DP	.12	.06	.01
☐	13	Bill Ranford DP	1.50	.75	.15
☐	14	Doug Wilson	.20	.10	.02
☐	15	Mario Lemieux	15.00	7.50	1.50
☐	16	Mats Naslund	.15	.07	.01
☐	17	Mel Bridgman	.06	.03	.00
☐	18	James Patrick DP	.06	.03	.00
☐	19	Rollie Melanson	.20	.10	.02
☐	20	Lanny McDonald	.20	.10	.02
☐	21	Peter Stastny	.45	.22	.04
☐	22	Murray Craven	.10	.05	.01
☐	23	Ulf Samuelsson DP	.50	.25	.05
☐	24	Mike Thelvin DP	.06	.03	.00
☐	25	Scott Stevens	.20	.10	.02
☐	26	Petr Klima	.85	.40	.08
☐	27	Brent Sutter DP	.06	.03	.00
☐	28	Tomas Sandstrom	.70	.35	.07
☐	29	Tim Bothwell	.06	.03	.00
☐	30	Bob Carpenter DP	.06	.03	.00
☐	31	Brian MacLellan DP	.04	.02	.00
☐	32	John Chabot	.06	.03	.00
☐	33	Phil Housley DP	.15	.07	.01
☐	34	Patrik Sundstrom DP	.06	.03	.00
☐	35	Dave Ellett	.25	.12	.02
☐	36	John Vanbiesbrouck	.35	.17	.03
☐	37	Dave Lewis	.06	.03	.00
☐	38	Tom McCarthy DP	.04	.02	.00
☐	39	Dave Poulin	.10	.05	.01
☐	40	Mike Foligno	.06	.03	.00
☐	41	Gordie Roberts	.06	.03	.00
☐	42	Luc Robitaille	25.00	12.50	2.50
☐	43	Duane Sutter	.10	.05	.01
☐	44	Pete Peeters	.10	.05	.01
☐	45	John Anderson	.06	.03	.00
☐	46	Aaron Broten	.06	.03	.00
☐	47	Keith Brown	.06	.03	.00
☐	48	Bobby Smith	.15	.07	.01
☐	49	Don Maloney	.10	.05	.01
☐	50	Mark Hunter	.10	.05	.01
☐	51	Moe Mantha	.06	.03	.00
☐	52	Charlie Simmer	.10	.05	.01
☐	53	Wayne Gretzky	10.00	5.00	1.00
☐	54	Mark Howe	.15	.07	.01
☐	55	Bob Gould	.06	.03	.00
☐	56	Steve Yzerman DP	3.00	1.50	.30
☐	57	Larry Playfair	.06	.03	.00
☐	58	Alain Chevrier	.25	.12	.02
☐	59	Steve Larmer	.35	.17	.03
☐	60	Bryan Trottier	.35	.17	.03

		MINT	EXC	G-VG
☐ 61	Stewart Gavin DP	.06	.03	.00
☐ 62	Russ Courtnall DP	.40	.20	.04
☐ 63	Mike Ramsey DP	.04	.02	.00
☐ 64	Bob Brooke	.06	.03	.00
☐ 65	Rick Wamsley DP	.10	.05	.01
☐ 66	Ken Morrow DP	.06	.03	.00
☐ 67	Gerard Gallant	1.50	.75	.15
☐ 68	Kevin Hatcher	2.00	1.00	.20
☐ 69	Cam Neely	3.25	1.60	.32
☐ 70	Sylvain Turgeon DP	.06	.03	.00
☐ 71	Peter Zezel	.12	.06	.01
☐ 72	Al MacInnis	2.75	1.35	.27
☐ 73	Terry Ruskowski DP	.04	.02	.00
☐ 74	Troy Murray	.10	.05	.01
☐ 75	Jim Fox DP	.04	.02	.00
☐ 76	Kelly Kisio	.10	.05	.01
☐ 77	Michel Goulet DP	.12	.06	.01
☐ 78	Tom Barrasso DP	.12	.06	.01
☐ 79	Bruce Driver DP	.06	.03	.00
☐ 80	Craig Simpson DP	1.50	.75	.15
☐ 81	Dino Ciccarelli	.20	.10	.02
☐ 82	Gary Nylund DP	.04	.02	.00
☐ 83	Bernie Federko	.12	.06	.01
☐ 84	John Tonelli DP	.06	.03	.00
☐ 85	Brad McCrimmon DP	.04	.02	.00
☐ 86	Dave Tippett DP	.04	.02	.00
☐ 87	Ray Bourque DP	1.00	.50	.10
☐ 88	Dave Christian	.06	.03	.00
☐ 89	Glen Hanlon	.10	.05	.01
☐ 90	Brian Curran	.10	.05	.01
☐ 91	Paul MacLean	.10	.05	.01
☐ 92	Jimmy Carson	2.25	1.10	.22
☐ 93	Willie Huber	.06	.03	.00
☐ 94	Brian Bellows	.30	.15	.03
☐ 95	Doug Jarvis DP	.06	.03	.00
☐ 96	Clark Gillies	.10	.05	.01
☐ 97	Tony Tanti	.10	.05	.01
☐ 98	Pelle Eklund DP	.60	.30	.06
☐ 99	Paul Coffey	1.00	.50	.10
☐ 100	Brent Ashton DP	.04	.02	.00
☐ 101	Mark Johnson	.06	.03	.00
☐ 102	Greg Johnston	.06	.03	.00
☐ 103	Ron Flockhart	.06	.03	.00
☐ 104	Ed Olczyk	.20	.10	.02
☐ 105	Mike Bossy	.65	.30	.06
☐ 106	Chris Chelios	.30	.15	.03
☐ 107	Gilles Meloche	.10	.05	.01
☐ 108	Rod Langway	.12	.06	.01
☐ 109	Ray Ferraro DP	.06	.03	.00
☐ 110	Ron Duguay DP	.06	.03	.00
☐ 111	Al Secord DP	.06	.03	.00
☐ 112	Mark Messier	1.25	.60	.12
☐ 113	Ron Sutter	.10	.05	.01

		MINT	EXC	G-VG
☐ 114	Darren Veitch	.10	.05	.01
☐ 115	Rick Middleton DP	.10	.05	.01
☐ 116	Doug Sulliman	.06	.03	.00
☐ 117	Dennis Maruk DP	.06	.03	.00
☐ 118	Dave Taylor	.15	.07	.01
☐ 119	Kelly Hrudey	.25	.12	.02
☐ 120	Tom Fergus	.06	.03	.00
☐ 121	Christian Ruuttu	.35	.17	.03
☐ 122	Brian Benning	.20	.10	.02
☐ 123	Adam Oates	25.00	12.50	2.50
☐ 124	Kevin Dineen	.20	.10	.02
☐ 125	Doug Bodger DP	.06	.03	.00
☐ 126	Joe Mullen	.20	.10	.02
☐ 127	Denis Savard	.50	.25	.05
☐ 128	Brad Marsh	.06	.03	.00
☐ 129	Marcel Dionne DP	.25	.12	.02
☐ 130	Bryan Erickson	.06	.03	.00
☐ 131	Reed Larson DP	.04	.02	.00
☐ 132	Don Beaupre	.12	.06	.01
☐ 133	Larry Murphy DP	.06	.03	.00
☐ 134	John Ogrodnick DP	.06	.03	.00
☐ 135	Greg Adams DP	.12	.06	.01
	New Jersey Devils			
☐ 136	Pat Flatley	.10	.05	.01
☐ 137	Scott Arniel DP	.04	.02	.00
☐ 138	Dana Murzyn	.06	.03	.00
☐ 139	Greg C. Adams	.06	.03	.00
	Washington Capitals			
☐ 140	Bob Sauve	.10	.05	.01
☐ 141	Mike O'Connell	.06	.03	.00
☐ 142	Walt Poddubny DP	.12	.06	.01
☐ 143	Paul Reinhart	.10	.05	.01
☐ 144	Tim Kerr DP	.12	.06	.01
☐ 145	Brian Lawton	.15	.07	.01
☐ 146	Gino Cavallini	.30	.15	.03
☐ 147	Doug Keans DP	.06	.03	.00
☐ 148	Jari Kurri	.60	.30	.06
☐ 149	Dale Hawerchuk	.45	.22	.04
☐ 150	Randy Cunneyworth	.25	.12	.02
☐ 151	Jay Wells	.06	.03	.00
☐ 152	Mike Liut DP	.15	.07	.01
☐ 153	Steve Konroyd	.06	.03	.00
☐ 154	John Tucker	.06	.03	.00
☐ 155	Rick Vaive DP	.06	.03	.00
☐ 156	Bob Murray	.06	.03	.00
☐ 157	Kirk Muller DP	.12	.06	.01
☐ 158	Brian Propp	.20	.10	.02
☐ 159	Ron Greschner	.10	.05	.01
☐ 160	Rob Ramage	.10	.05	.01
☐ 161	Craig Laughlin	.06	.03	.00
☐ 162	Steve Kasper DP	.06	.03	.00
☐ 163	Patrick Roy	5.00	2.50	.50
☐ 164	Shawn Burr DP	.15	.07	.01

		MINT	EXC	G-VG
☐ 165	Craig Hartsburg DP	.04	.02	.00
☐ 166	Dean Evason	.20	.10	.02
☐ 167	Bob Bourne	.06	.03	.00
☐ 168	Mike Gartner	.20	.10	.02
☐ 169	Ron Hextall	3.00	1.50	.30
☐ 170	Joe Cirella	.10	.05	.01
☐ 171	Dan Quinn DP	.06	.03	.00
☐ 172	Tony McKegney	.06	.03	.00
☐ 173	Pat LaFontaine DP	.45	.22	.04
☐ 174	Allen Pedersen DP	.04	.02	.00
☐ 175	Doug Gilmour	.12	.06	.01
☐ 176	Gary Suter DP	.20	.10	.02
☐ 177	Barry Pederson DP	.06	.03	.00
☐ 178	Grant Fuhr DP	.50	.25	.05
☐ 179	Wayne Presley	.30	.15	.03
☐ 180	Wilf Paiement	.06	.03	.00
☐ 181	Doug Smail	.15	.07	.01
☐ 182	Doug Crossman DP	.06	.03	.00
☐ 183	Bernie Nichols	.45	.22	.04
☐ 184	Dirk Graham	.10	.05	.01
☐ 185	Anton Stastny	.10	.05	.01
☐ 186	Greg Stefan	.10	.05	.01
☐ 187	Ron Francis	.40	.20	.04
☐ 188	Steve Thomas DP	.12	.06	.01
☐ 189	Kelly Miller	.40	.20	.04
☐ 190	Tomas Jonsson	.06	.03	.00
☐ 191	John MacLean	.85	.40	.08
☐ 192	Larry Robinson DP	.15	.07	.01
☐ 193	Doug Wickenheiser DP	.04	.02	.00
☐ 194	Keith Crowder DP	.04	.02	.00
☐ 195	Bob Froese	.10	.05	.01
☐ 196	Jim Johnson	.06	.03	.00
☐ 197	Checklist 1-99	.15	.01	.00
☐ 198	Checklist 100-198	.15	.01	.00

1988-89 Topps

The 1988-89 Topps hockey set contains 198 standard size (2½" by 3½") cards. The fronts feature color photos with various colored borders and each player's team logo. The backs show career statistics and highlights. There were cards printed on the bottoms of the wax boxes; these cards are similar to the regular issue cards but are "lettered" A-P rather than numbered. These wax box cards are not considered part of the complete set price below, as they are usually offered separately or as an extra. The key rookies in this set are Rob Brown, Brett Hull, Joe Nieuwendyk, Bob Probert, and Pierre Turgeon.

Le jeu Topps 1988-89 contient 198 cartes de format standard (2½" x 3½"). La face comporte une photo en couleurs entourée d'un bord de couleur variable, et l'emblème de l'équipe de chaque joueur. Le dos indique les statistiques et moments marquants de la carrière du joueur. Certaines cartes furent imprimées sur le fond de boîtes paraffinées; elles ressemblent aux cartes régulières, mais se distinguent par les lettres A-P au lieu de numéros. Elles ne sont pas considérées comme faisant partie du jeu complet, puisqu'elle sont, en général, offertes séparément ou en prime. Les débutants importants du jeu incluent Rob Brown, Brett Hull, Joe Nieuwendyk, Bob Probert, et Pierre Turgeon.

			MINT	EXC	G-VG
	COMPLETE SET (198)		130.00	65.00	13.00
	COMMON PLAYER (1-198)		.05	.02	.00
	COMMON PLAYER DP		.03	.01	.00
☐	1	Mario Lemieux DP	7.50	1.50	.30
☐	2	Bob Joyce DP	.25	.12	.02
☐	3	Joel Quenneville DP	.03	.01	.00
☐	4	Tony McKegney	.05	.02	.00
☐	5	Stephane Richer DP	.60	.30	.06
☐	6	Mark Howe DP	.10	.05	.01

			MINT	EXC	G-VG
☐	7	Brent Sutter DP	.05	.02	.00
☐	8	Gilles Meloche DP	.05	.02	.00
☐	9	Jimmy Carson DP	.25	.12	.02
☐	10	John MacLean	.45	.22	.04
☐	11	Gary Leeman	.15	.07	.01
☐	12	Gerard Gallant DP	.20	.10	.02
☐	13	Marcel Dionne	.30	.15	.03
☐	14	Dave Christian DP	.03	.01	.00
☐	15	Gary Nylund	.05	.02	.00
☐	16	Joe Nieuwendyk	11.00	5.50	1.10
☐	17	Billy Smith DP	.12	.06	.01
☐	18	Christian Ruutu	.10	.05	.01
☐	19	Randy Cunneyworth	.05	.02	.00
☐	20	Brian Lawton	.05	.02	.00
☐	21	Scott Mellanby DP	.20	.10	.02
☐	22	Peter Stastny DP	.25	.12	.02
☐	23	Gord Kluzak	.05	.02	.00
☐	24	Sylvain Turgeon	.05	.02	.00
☐	25	Clint Malarchuk	.15	.07	.01
☐	26	Denis Savard	.40	.20	.04
☐	27	Craig Simpson	.30	.15	.03
☐	28	Petr Klima	.40	.20	.04
☐	29	Pat Verbeek	.15	.07	.01
☐	30	Moe Mantha	.05	.02	.00
☐	31	Chris Nilan	.05	.02	.00
☐	32	Barry Pederson	.05	.02	.00
☐	33	Randy Burridge	.05	.02	.00
☐	34	Ron Hextall	.60	.30	.06
☐	35	Gaston Gingras	.05	.02	.00
☐	36	Kevin Dineen DP	.10	.05	.01
☐	37	Tom Laidlaw	.05	.02	.00
☐	38	Paul MacLean DP	.05	.02	.00
☐	39	John Chabot DP	.03	.01	.00
☐	40	Lindy Ruff	.05	.02	.00
☐	41	Dan Quinn DP	.05	.02	.00
☐	42	Don Beaupre	.10	.05	.01
☐	43	Gary Suter	.20	.10	.02
☐	44	Mikko Makela DP	.12	.06	.01
☐	45	Mark Johnson DP	.03	.01	.00
☐	46	Dave Taylor	.12	.06	.01
☐	47	Ulf Dahlen DP	.15	.07	.01
☐	48	Jeff Sharples	.15	.07	.01
☐	49	Chris Chelios	.25	.12	.02
☐	50	Mike Gartner DP	.12	.06	.01
☐	51	Darren Pang DP	.20	.10	.02
☐	52	Ron Francis	.35	.17	.03
☐	53	Ken Morrow	.05	.02	.00
☐	54	Michel Goulet	.20	.10	.02
☐	55	Ray Sheppard	.75	.35	.07
☐	56	Doug Gilmour	.12	.06	.01
☐	57	David Shaw DP	.03	.01	.00
☐	58	Cam Neely DP	1.00	.50	.10
☐	59	Grant Fuhr DP	.40	.20	.04

			MINT	EXC	G-VG
☐	60	Scott Stevens	.15	.07	.01
☐	61	Bob Brooke	.05	.02	.00
☐	62	Dave Hunter	.05	.02	.00
☐	63	Alan Kerr	.05	.02	.00
☐	64	Brad Marsh	.05	.02	.00
☐	65	Dale Hawerchuk DP	.35	.17	.03
☐	66	Brett Hull DP	60.00	30.00	6.00
☐	67	Patrik Sundstrom DP	.05	.02	.00
☐	68	Greg Stefan	.10	.05	.01
☐	69	James Patrick	.10	.05	.01
☐	70	Dale Hunter DP	.03	.01	.00
☐	71	Al Iafrate	.12	.06	.01
☐	72	Bob Carpenter	.10	.05	.01
☐	73	Ray Bourque DP	.60	.30	.06
☐	74	John Tucker DP	.03	.01	.00
☐	75	Carey Wilson	.05	.02	.00
☐	76	Joe Mullen	.15	.07	.01
☐	77	Rick Vaive	.10	.05	.01
☐	78	Shawn Burr DP	.03	.01	.00
☐	79	Murray Craven DP	.05	.02	.00
☐	80	Clark Gillies	.10	.05	.01
☐	81	Bernie Federko	.10	.05	.01
☐	82	Tony Tanti	.10	.05	.01
☐	83	Greg Gilbert	.10	.05	.01
☐	84	Kirk Muller	.15	.07	.01
☐	85	Dave Tippett	.05	.02	.00
☐	86	Kevin Hatcher DP	.30	.15	.03
☐	87	Rick Middleton DP	.10	.05	.01
☐	88	Bobby Smith	.15	.07	.01
☐	89	Doug Wilson DP	.15	.07	.01
☐	90	Scott Arniel	.05	.02	.00
☐	91	Brian Mullen	.10	.05	.01
☐	92	Mike O'Connell DP	.03	.01	.00
☐	93	Mark Messier DP	.65	.30	.06
☐	94	Sean Burke	.75	.35	.07
☐	95	Brian Bellows DP	.20	.10	.02
☐	96	Doug Bodger	.05	.02	.00
☐	97	Bryan Trottier	.25	.12	.02
☐	98	Anton Stastny	.10	.05	.01
☐	99	Checklist Card	.15	.01	.00
☐	100	Dave Poulin DP	.06	.03	.00
☐	101	Bob Bourne DP	.03	.01	.00
☐	102	John Vanbiesbrouck	.15	.07	.01
☐	103	Allen Pedersen	.05	.02	.00
☐	104	Mike Ridley	.10	.05	.01
☐	105	Andrew McBain	.05	.02	.00
☐	106	Troy Murray DP	.05	.02	.00
☐	107	Tom Barrasso	.15	.07	.01
☐	108	Tomas Jonsson	.05	.02	.00
☐	109	Rob Brown	3.50	1.75	.35
☐	110	Hakan Loob DP	.15	.07	.01
☐	111	Ilkka Sinisalo DP	.05	.02	.00
☐	112	Dave Archibald	.20	.10	.02

		MINT	EXC	G-VG
☐ 113	Doug Halward	.05	.02	.00
☐ 114	Ray Ferraro	.10	.05	.01
☐ 115	Doug Brown	.12	.06	.01
☐ 116	Patrick Roy DP	1.00	.50	.10
☐ 117	Greg Millen	.10	.05	.01
☐ 118	Ken Linseman	.10	.05	.01
☐ 119	Phil Housley DP	.12	.06	.01
☐ 120	Wayne Gretzky	20.00	10.00	2.00
	(Holding up Kings sweater)			
☐ 121	Tomas Sandstrom	.25	.12	.02
☐ 122	Brendan Shanahan	1.50	.75	.15
☐ 123	Pat LaFontaine	.45	.22	.04
☐ 124	Luc Robitaille DP	2.50	1.25	.25
☐ 125	Ed Olczyk DP	.12	.06	.01
☐ 126	Ron Sutter	.10	.05	.01
☐ 127	Mike Liut	.12	.06	.01
☐ 128	Brent Ashton DP	.03	.01	.00
☐ 129	Tony Hrkac	.35	.17	.03
☐ 130	Kelly Miller	.10	.05	.01
☐ 131	Alan Haworth	.05	.02	.00
☐ 132	Dave McIlwain	.20	.10	.02
☐ 133	Mike Ramsey	.05	.02	.00
☐ 134	Bob Sweeney	.20	.10	.02
☐ 135	Dirk Graham DP	.03	.01	.00
☐ 136	Ulf Samuelsson	.15	.07	.01
☐ 137	Petri Skriko	.10	.05	.01
☐ 138	Aaron Broten DP	.03	.01	.00
☐ 139	Jim Fox	.05	.02	.00
☐ 140	Randy Wood DP	.10	.05	.01
☐ 141	Larry Murphy	.10	.05	.01
☐ 142	Daniel Berthiaume DP	.25	.12	.02
☐ 143	Kelly Kisio	.10	.05	.01
☐ 144	Neal Broten	.10	.05	.01
☐ 145	Reed Larson	.05	.02	.00
☐ 146	Peter Zezel DP	.05	.02	.00
☐ 147	Jari Kurri	.45	.22	.04
☐ 148	Jim Johnson	.05	.02	.00
☐ 149	Gino Cavallini DP	.05	.02	.00
☐ 150	Glen Hanlon DP	.05	.02	.00
☐ 151	Bengt Gustafsson	.05	.02	.00
☐ 152	Mike Bullard DP	.05	.02	.00
☐ 153	John Ogrodnick	.10	.05	.01
☐ 154	Steve Larmer	.25	.12	.02
☐ 155	Kelly Hrudey	.15	.07	.01
☐ 156	Mats Naslund	.15	.07	.01
☐ 157	Bruce Driver	.10	.05	.01
☐ 158	Randy Hillier	.05	.02	.00
☐ 159	Craig Hartsburg	.05	.02	.00
☐ 160	Rollie Melanson	.10	.05	.01
☐ 161	Adam Oates DP	2.50	1.25	.25
☐ 162	Greg Adams DP	.05	.02	.00
	Vancouver Canucks			
☐ 163	Dave Andreychuk DP	.05	.02	.00

		MINT	EXC	G-VG
☐ 164	Dave Babych	.10	.05	.01
☐ 165	Brian Noonan	.10	.05	.01
☐ 166	Glen Wesley	.75	.35	.07
☐ 167	Dave Ellett	.10	.05	.01
☐ 168	Brian Propp	.15	.07	.01
☐ 169	Bernie Nicholls	.35	.17	.03
☐ 170	Walt Poddubny	.10	.05	.01
☐ 171	Steve Konroyd	.05	.02	.00
☐ 172	Doug Sulliman DP	.03	.01	.00
☐ 173	Mario Gosselin	.15	.07	.01
☐ 174	Brian Benning	.05	.02	.00
☐ 175	Dino Ciccarelli	.15	.07	.01
☐ 176	Steve Kasper	.10	.05	.01
☐ 177	Rick Tocchet	2.25	1.10	.22
☐ 178	Brad McCrimmon	.05	.02	.00
☐ 179	Paul Coffey	.75	.35	.07
☐ 180	Pete Peeters	.10	.05	.01
☐ 181	Bob Probert DP	2.50	1.25	.25
☐ 182	Steve Duchesne DP	1.25	.60	.12
☐ 183	Russ Courtnall	.20	.10	.02
☐ 184	Mike Foligno DP	.03	.01	.00
☐ 185	Wayne Presley DP	.03	.01	.00
☐ 186	Rejean Lemelin	.15	.07	.01
☐ 187	Mark Hunter	.05	.02	.00
☐ 188	Joe Cirella	.05	.02	.00
☐ 189	Glenn Anderson DP	.15	.07	.01
☐ 190	John Anderson	.05	.02	.00
☐ 191	Pat Flatley	.05	.02	.00
☐ 192	Rod Langway	.12	.06	.01
☐ 193	Brian MacLellan	.05	.02	.00
☐ 194	Pierre Turgeon	8.00	4.00	.80
☐ 195	Brian Hayward	.15	.07	.01
☐ 196	Steve Yzerman DP	1.00	.50	.10
☐ 197	Doug Crossman	.10	.05	.01
☐ 198	Checklist Card	.15	.01	.00

1989-90 Topps

The 1989-90 Topps hockey set contains 198 cards measuring the standard size (2½" by 3½"). The cards were sold in packs of 13 cards (with a sticker and gum) for 50 cents. The fronts feature color action photos with various color borders and each player's team logo at the lower right hand corner. Aqua-blue stripes appear at the top and bottom on the card face, with marble gray background along the sides. The backs are tinted red with black lettering on gray card stock, and provide career statistics and highlights. Topps printed this set in two sheets of 132, necessitating 66 double-printed cards which are marked as DP in the checklist below.

Le jeu Topps 1989-90 contient 198 cartes de format standard (2½" x 3½"). Les cartes se vendaient en paquet de 13 cartes (avec autocollant et chewing-gum) pour 50 cents. La face comporte une photo d'action en couleurs, entourée d'un bord de différentes couleurs, et montrant l'emblème de l'équipe de chaque joueur au coin inférieur droit. Des bandes bleues-vertes soulignent le haut et le bas de la face, avec un fond gris marbré longeant les côtés. Le dos, d'une teinte rougeâtre avec des lettres noires sur une pâte grise, présente les statistiques et moments marquants de la carrière. Topps a imprimé ce jeu sur deux feuilles de 132 cartes, nécessitant l'impression en double de 66 cartes. Ces cartes imprimées en double sont désignées par les lettres "DP" dans la liste de contrôle ci-dessous.

			MINT	EXC	G-VG
		COMPLETE SET (198)	40.00	20.00	4.00
		COMMON PLAYER (1-198)	.05	.02	.00
		COMMON PLAYER DP	.03	.01	.00
☐	1	Mario Lemieux	2.50	.50	.10
☐	2	Ulf Dahlen	.05	.02	.00
☐	3	Terry Carkner	.10	.05	.01
☐	4	Tony McKegney	.05	.02	.00
☐	5	Dennis Savard	.25	.12	.02

			MINT	EXC	G-VG
☐	6	Derek King DP	.08	.04	.01
☐	7	Lanny McDonald	.12	.06	.01
☐	8	John Tonelli	.08	.04	.01
☐	9	Tom Kurvers DP	.03	.01	.00
☐	10	David Archibald	.05	.02	.00
☐	11	Peter Sidorkiewicz	.45	.22	.04
☐	12	Esa Tikkanen	.35	.17	.03
☐	13	Dave Barr	.05	.02	.00
☐	14	Brent Sutter	.08	.04	.01
☐	15	Cam Neely	.50	.25	.05
☐	16	Calle Johansson	.10	.05	.01
☐	17	Patrick Roy DP	.40	.20	.04
☐	18	Dale DeGray DP	.08	.04	.01
☐	19	Phil Bourque	.30	.15	.03
☐	20	Kevin Dineen	.10	.05	.01
☐	21	Mike Bullard DP	.03	.01	.00
☐	22	Gary Leeman	.10	.05	.01
☐	23	Greg Stefan DP	.06	.03	.00
☐	24	Brian Mullen	.08	.04	.01
☐	25	Pierre Turgeon DP	.65	.30	.06
☐	26	Bob Rouse DP	.08	.04	.01
☐	27	Peter Zezel	.08	.04	.01
☐	28	Jeff Brown DP	.20	.10	.02
☐	29	Andy Brickley DP	.08	.04	.01
☐	30	Mike Gartner	.10	.05	.01
☐	31	Darren Pang	.08	.04	.01
☐	32	Pat Verbeek	.10	.05	.01
☐	33	Petri Skriko DP	.03	.01	.00
☐	34	Tom Laidlaw	.05	.02	.00
☐	35	Randy Wood	.05	.02	.00
☐	36	Tom Barrasso DP	.08	.04	.01
☐	37	John Tucker DP	.03	.01	.00
☐	38	Andrew McBain	.05	.02	.00
☐	39	David Shaw DP	.03	.01	.00
☐	40	Rejean Lemelin	.08	.04	.01
☐	41	Dino Ciccarelli DP	.10	.05	.01
☐	42	Jeff Sharples	.05	.02	.00
☐	43	Jari Kurri	.30	.15	.03
☐	44	Murray Craven DP	.05	.02	.00
☐	45	Cliff Ronning DP	.50	.25	.05
☐	46	Dave Babych	.05	.02	.00
☐	47	Bernie Nicholls DP	.20	.10	.02
☐	48	Jon Casey	2.00	1.00	.20
☐	49	Al MacInnis	.30	.15	.03
☐	50	Bob Errey DP	.08	.04	.01
☐	51	Glen Wesley	.08	.04	.01
☐	52	Dirk Graham	.05	.02	.00
☐	53	Guy Carbonneau DP	.05	.02	.00
☐	54	Tomas Sandstrom	.12	.06	.01
☐	55	Rod Langway DP	.08	.04	.01
☐	56	Patrik Sundstrom	.08	.04	.01
☐	57	Michel Goulet	.10	.05	.01
☐	58	Dave Taylor	.08	.04	.01

			MINT	EXC	G-VG
☐	59	Phil Housley	.08	.04	.01
☐	60	Pat LaFontaine DP	.25	.12	.02
☐	61	Kirk McLean DP	.40	.20	.04
☐	62	Ken Linseman	.05	.02	.00
☐	63	Randy Cunneyworth	.05	.02	.00
☐	64	Tony Hrkac DP	.03	.01	.00
☐	65	Mark Messier DP	.40	.20	.04
☐	66	Carey Wilson DP	.03	.01	.00
☐	67	Stephen Leach	.25	.12	.02
☐	68	Christian Ruuttu	.05	.02	.00
☐	69	Dave Ellett	.05	.02	.00
☐	70	Ray Ferraro	.05	.02	.00
☐	71	Colin Patterson	.10	.05	.01
☐	72	Tim Kerr	.08	.04	.01
☐	73	Bob Joyce	.08	.04	.01
☐	74	Doug Gilmour DP	.08	.04	.01
☐	75	Lee Norwood DP	.03	.01	.00
☐	76	Dale Hunter	.05	.02	.00
☐	77	Jim Johnson DP	.03	.01	.00
☐	78	Mike Foligno DP	.03	.01	.00
☐	79	Al Iafrate DP	.05	.02	.00
☐	80	Rick Tocchet DP	.30	.15	.03
☐	81	Greg Hawgood DP	.15	.07	.01
☐	82	Steve Thomas	.08	.04	.01
☐	83	Steve Yzerman DP	.40	.20	.04
☐	84	Mike McPhee	.08	.04	.01
☐	85	Dave Volek DP	.30	.15	.03
☐	86	Brian Benning	.05	.02	.00
☐	87	Neal Broten	.08	.04	.01
☐	88	Luc Robitaille	.90	.45	.09
☐	89	Trevor Linden	2.50	1.25	.25
☐	90	James Patrick DP	.05	.02	.00
☐	91	Brian Lawton	.05	.02	.00
☐	92	Sean Burke DP	.12	.06	.01
☐	93	Scott Stevens	.12	.06	.01
☐	94	Pat Elynuik DP	.50	.25	.05
☐	95	Paul Coffey	.50	.25	.05
☐	96	Jan Erixon DP	.03	.01	.00
☐	97	Mike Liut	.08	.04	.01
☐	98	Wayne Presley	.05	.02	.00
☐	99	Craig Simpson	.20	.10	.02
☐	100	Kjell Samuelsson	.15	.07	.01
☐	101	Shawn Burr DP	.03	.01	.00
☐	102	John MacLean	.12	.06	.01
☐	103	Tom Fergus	.05	.02	.00
☐	104	Mike Krushelnyski	.05	.02	.00
☐	105	Gary Nylund	.05	.02	.00
☐	106	Dave Andreychuk	.08	.04	.01
☐	107	Bernie Federko	.08	.04	.01
☐	108	Gary Suter	.12	.06	.01
☐	109	Dave Gagner DP	.40	.20	.04
☐	110	Ray Bourque	.50	.25	.05
☐	111	Geoff Courtnall	1.50	.75	.15

		MINT	EXC	G-VG
☐ 112	Doug Wilson	.12	.06	.01
☐ 113	Joe Sakic	11.00	5.50	1.10
☐ 114	John Vanbiesbrouck	.12	.06	.01
☐ 115	Dave Poulin	.08	.04	.01
☐ 116	Rick Meagher	.05	.02	.00
☐ 117	Kirk Muller DP	.08	.04	.01
☐ 118	Mats Naslund	.08	.04	.01
☐ 119	Ray Sheppard	.05	.02	.00
☐ 120	Jeff Norton	.15	.07	.01
☐ 121	Randy Burridge DP	.03	.01	.00
☐ 122	Dale Hawerchuk DP	.15	.07	.01
☐ 123	Steve Duchesne	.25	.12	.02
☐ 124	John Anderson	.05	.02	.00
☐ 125	Rick Vaive DP	.05	.02	.00
☐ 126	Randy Hillier	.05	.02	.00
☐ 127	Jimmy Carson	.25	.12	.02
☐ 128	Larry Murphy	.08	.04	.01
☐ 129	Paul MacLean DP	.05	.02	.00
☐ 130	Joe Cirella	.08	.04	.01
☐ 131	Kelly Miller DP	.08	.04	.01
☐ 132	Alain Chevrier DP	.05	.02	.00
☐ 133	Ed Olczyk	.08	.04	.01
☐ 134	Dave Tippett	.05	.02	.00
☐ 135	Bob Sweeney	.05	.02	.00
☐ 136	Brian Leetch	4.00	2.00	.40
☐ 137	Greg Millen	.08	.04	.01
☐ 138	Joe Nieuwendyk	1.25	.60	.12
☐ 139	Brian Propp	.10	.05	.01
☐ 140	Mike Ramsey	.05	.02	.00
☐ 141	Mike Allison	.05	.02	.00
☐ 142	Shawn Chambers	.15	.07	.01
☐ 143	Peter Stastny DP	.15	.07	.01
☐ 144	Glen Hanlon	.08	.04	.01
☐ 145	John Cullen	2.50	1.25	.25
☐ 146	Kevin Hatcher	.20	.10	.02
☐ 147	Brendan Shanahan	.25	.12	.02
☐ 148	Paul Reinhart	.08	.04	.01
☐ 149	Bryan Trottier	.20	.10	.02
☐ 150	Dave Manson	.30	.15	.03
☐ 151	Marc Habscheid DP	.10	.05	.01
☐ 152	Dan Quinn	.08	.04	.01
☐ 153	Stephane Richer DP	.20	.10	.02
☐ 154	Doug Bodger DP	.03	.01	.00
☐ 155	Ron Hextall	.30	.15	.03
☐ 156	Wayne Gretzky	3.50	1.75	.35
☐ 157	Steve Tuttle DP	.08	.04	.01
☐ 158	Charlie Huddy DP	.05	.02	.00
☐ 159	Dave Christian DP	.03	.01	.00
☐ 160	Andy Moog	.15	.07	.01
☐ 161	Tony Granato	1.00	.50	.10
☐ 162	Sylvain Cote	.10	.05	.01
☐ 163	Mike Vernon	.35	.17	.03
☐ 164	Steve Chiasson	.30	.15	.03

		MINT	EXC	G-VG
☐ 165	Mike Ridley	.08	.04	.01
☐ 166	Kelly Hrudey	.10	.05	.01
☐ 167	Bobby Carpenter DP	.05	.02	.00
☐ 168	Zarley Zalapski	.75	.35	.07
☐ 169	Derek Laxdal	.10	.05	.01
☐ 170	Clint Malarchuk DP	.05	.02	.00
☐ 171	Kelly Kisio	.05	.02	.00
☐ 172	Gerard Gallant	.15	.07	.01
☐ 173	Ron Sutter	.08	.04	.01
☐ 174	Chris Chelios	.15	.07	.01
☐ 175	Ron Francis	.15	.07	.01
☐ 176	Gino Cavallini	.05	.02	.00
☐ 177	Brian Bellows DP	.15	.07	.01
☐ 178	Greg C. Adams DP	.05	.02	.00
	Vancouver Canucks			
☐ 179	Steve Larmer	.25	.12	.02
☐ 180	Aaron Broten	.05	.02	.00
☐ 181	Brent Ashton DP	.03	.01	.00
☐ 182	Gerald Diduck DP	.08	.04	.01
☐ 183	Paul MacDermid	.10	.05	.01
☐ 184	Walt Poddubny DP	.05	.02	.00
☐ 185	Adam Oates	.90	.45	.09
☐ 186	Brett Hull	11.00	5.50	1.10
☐ 187	Scott Arniel	.05	.02	.00
☐ 188	Bobby Smith	.10	.05	.01
☐ 189	Guy Lafleur	.35	.17	.03
☐ 190	Craig Janney	2.75	1.35	.27
☐ 191	Mark Howe	.08	.04	.01
☐ 192	Grant Fuhr DP	.20	.10	.02
☐ 193	Rob Brown	.45	.22	.04
☐ 194	Steve Kasper DP	.05	.02	.00
☐ 195	Pete Peeters	.10	.05	.01
☐ 196	Joe Mullen	.10	.05	.01
☐ 197	Checklist 1-99	.08	.01	.00
☐ 198	Checklist 100-198 DP	.08	.01	.00

1990-91 Topps

The 1990-91 Topps hockey set contains 396 cards measuring the standard size, 2¹/₂" by 3¹/₂". The fronts feature color action photos with borders in two different colors per card. A hockey stick is superimposed over the picture at the top border. The backs have blue lettering on a pale green background, and have biographical information and career statistics. The cards were sold in 50-cent packs of 14 cards each, with one glossy insert and one piece of gum. Included in the 396 cards are a three-card tribute to Wayne Gretzky, three 1989-90 highlights cards, 21 Pro Prospect cards, 21 team cards, and 12 All-Star cards. The team cards are actually unidentified and uncaptioned action scenes with the team's previous season standings and power play stats on the card back. The set was also produced in a high-gloss Tiffany version with supposedly only 3000 sets produced; the values for the Tiffany version are approximately five times the values listed below.

Le jeu Topps 1990-91 contient 396 cartes de format standard, 2¹/₂" x 3¹/₂". La face comporte une photo d'action en couleurs, entourée d'un bord bicolore, différent pour chaque carte. Un stick de hockey est superposé à la photo au bord supérieur. Le dos comporte des lettres bleues sur fond vert pale, et présente des données biographiques et statistiques. Les cartes se vendaient en paquet de 14 cartes pour 50 cents par paquet, avec une carte additionnelle luisante et un morceau de chewing-gum. Les 396 cartes comprennent trois cartes honorant Wayne Gretzky, trois cartes des moments marquants de 1989-90, 21 cartes Pro Prospect, 21 cartes d'équipe, et 12 cartes All-Star. Le jeu existe également en une version Tiffany très luisante, mais apparemment, seulement 3000 jeux de cette version ont été produits. Les versions Tiffany valent à peu près quatre fois les prix indiqués ci-dessous.

			MINT	EXC	G-VG
	COMPLETE SET (396)		15.00	7.50	1.50
	COMMON PLAYER (1-396)		.03	.01	.00
☐ 1	Gretzky Tribute		.50	.15	.03
	Indianapolis Racers				

			MINT	EXC	G-VG
☐	2	Gretzky Tribute	.30	.15	.03
		Edmonton Oilers			
☐	3	Gretzky Tribute	.30	.15	.03
		Los Angeles Kings			
☐	4	Brett Hull HL	.25	.12	.02
☐	5	Jari Kurri HL	.08	.04	.01
		(Jari, not Jarri)			
☐	6	Bryan Trottier HL	.08	.04	.01
☐	7	Jeremy Roenick	1.50	.75	.15
☐	8	Brian Propp	.08	.04	.01
☐	9	Jim Hrivnak	.10	.05	.01
☐	10	Mick Vukota	.08	.04	.01
☐	11	Tom Kurvers	.03	.01	.00
☐	12	Ulf Dahlen	.06	.03	.00
☐	13	Bernie Nicholls	.15	.07	.01
☐	14	Peter Sidorkiewicz	.08	.04	.01
☐	15	Peter Zezel	.06	.03	.00
☐	16	Mike Hartman	.10	.05	.01
☐	17	Kings Team	.06	.03	.00
☐	18	Jim Sandlak	.03	.01	.00
☐	19	Rob Brown	.15	.07	.01
☐	20	Paul Ranheim	.25	.12	.02
☐	21	Rick Zombo	.12	.06	.01
☐	22	Paul Gillis	.03	.01	.00
☐	23	Brian Hayward	.06	.03	.00
☐	24	Brent Ashton	.03	.01	.00
☐	25	Mark Lamb	.15	.07	.01
☐	26	Rick Tocchet	.15	.07	.01
☐	27	Viacheslav Fetisov	.20	.10	.02
☐	28	Denis Savard	.15	.07	.01
☐	29	Chris Chelios	.10	.05	.01
☐	30	Janne Ojanen	.08	.04	.01
☐	31	Don Maloney	.03	.01	.00
☐	32	Allan Bester	.06	.03	.00
☐	33	Geoff Smith	.10	.05	.01
☐	34	Daniel Shank	.12	.06	.01
☐	35	Mikael Andersson	.08	.04	.01
☐	36	Gino Cavallini	.06	.03	.00
☐	37	Rob Murphy	.10	.05	.01
☐	38	Flames Team	.06	.03	.00
☐	39	Laurie Boschman	.03	.01	.00
☐	40	Craig Wolanin	.12	.06	.01
☐	41	Phil Bourque	.03	.01	.00
☐	42	Alexander Mogilny	.50	.25	.05
☐	43	Ray Bourque	.30	.15	.03
☐	44	Mike Liut	.06	.03	.00
☐	45	Ron Sutter	.06	.03	.00
☐	46	Bob Kudelski	.15	.07	.01
☐	47	Larry Murphy	.03	.01	.00
☐	48	Darren Turcotte	.75	.35	.07
☐	49	Paul Ysebaert	.25	.12	.02
☐	50	Alan Kerr	.03	.01	.00

			MINT	EXC	G-VG
☐	51	Randy Carlyle	.03	.01	.00
☐	52	Iiro Jarvi	.08	.04	.01
☐	53	Don Barber	.10	.05	.01
☐	54	Carey Wilson UER	.03	.01	.00
		(Misspelled Cary on both sides)			
☐	55	Joey Kocur	.12	.06	.01
☐	56	Steve Larmer	.12	.06	.01
☐	57	Paul Cavallini	.06	.03	.00
☐	58	Shayne Corson	.12	.06	.01
☐	59	Canucks Team	.06	.03	.00
☐	60	Sergei Makarov	.40	.20	.04
☐	61	Kjell Samuelsson	.03	.01	.00
☐	62	Tony Granato	.20	.10	.02
☐	63	Tom Fergus	.03	.01	.00
☐	64	Martin Gelinas	.30	.15	.03
☐	65	Tom Barrasso	.08	.04	.01
☐	66	Pierre Turgeon	.40	.20	.04
☐	67	Randy Cunneyworth	.03	.01	.00
☐	68	Michael Pivonka	.15	.07	.01
☐	69	Cam Neely	.30	.15	.03
☐	70	Brian Bellows	.12	.06	.01
☐	71	Pat Elynuik	.10	.05	.01
☐	72	Doug Crossman	.03	.01	.00
☐	73	Sylvain Turgeon	.03	.01	.00
☐	74	Shawn Burr	.03	.01	.00
☐	75	John Vanbiesbrouck	.10	.05	.01
☐	76	Steve Bozek	.03	.01	.00
☐	77	Brett Hull	1.00	.50	.10
☐	78	Zarley Zalapski	.08	.04	.01
☐	79	Wendel Clark	.06	.03	.00
☐	80	Flyers Team	.06	.03	.00
☐	81	Kelly Miller	.06	.03	.00
☐	82	Mark Pederson	.15	.07	.01
☐	83	Adam Creighton	.08	.04	.01
☐	84	Scott Young	.08	.04	.01
☐	85	Petr Klima	.10	.05	.01
☐	86	Steve Duchesne	.06	.03	.00
☐	87	Joe Nieuwendyk	.35	.17	.03
☐	88	Andy Brickley	.03	.01	.00
☐	89	Phil Housley	.08	.04	.01
☐	90	Neal Broten	.06	.03	.00
☐	91	Al Iafrate	.06	.03	.00
☐	92	Steve Thomas	.06	.03	.00
☐	93	Guy Carbonneau	.06	.03	.00
☐	94	Steve Chisson	.06	.03	.00
☐	95	Mike Tomlak	.10	.05	.01
☐	96	Roger Johansson	.08	.04	.01
☐	97	Randy Wood	.03	.01	.00
☐	98	Jim Johnson	.03	.01	.00
☐	99	Bob Sweeney	.03	.01	.00
☐	100	Dino Ciccarelli	.10	.05	.01
☐	101	Rangers Team	.06	.03	.00
☐	102	Mike Ramsey	.03	.01	.00

		MINT	EXC	G-VG
☐ 103	Kelly Hrudey	.08	.04	.01
☐ 104	Dave Ellett	.03	.01	.00
☐ 105	Bob Brooke	.03	.01	.00
☐ 106	Greg Adams	.03	.01	.00
	Vancouver Canucks			
☐ 107	Joe Cirella	.03	.01	.00
☐ 108	Jari Kurri	.20	.10	.02
☐ 109	Pete Peeters	.08	.04	.01
☐ 110	Paul MacLean	.06	.03	.00
☐ 111	Doug Wilson	.10	.05	.01
☐ 112	Pat Verbeek	.08	.04	.01
☐ 113	Bob Beers	.10	.05	.01
☐ 114	Mike O'Connell	.03	.01	.00
☐ 115	Brian Bradley	.03	.01	.00
☐ 116	Paul Coffey	.25	.12	.02
☐ 117	Doug Brown	.03	.01	.00
☐ 118	Aaron Broten	.03	.01	.00
☐ 119	Bob Essensa	.25	.12	.02
☐ 120	Wayne Gretzky UER	1.00	.50	.10
	(1302 career assists, not 13102)			
☐ 121	Vincent Damphousse	.12	.06	.01
☐ 122	Nordiques Team	.06	.03	.00
☐ 123	Mike Foligno	.03	.01	.00
☐ 124	Russ Courtnall	.06	.03	.00
☐ 125	Rick Meagher	.03	.01	.00
☐ 126	Craig Fisher	.20	.10	.02
☐ 127	Al MacInnis	.15	.07	.01
☐ 128	Derek King	.03	.01	.00
☐ 129	Dale Hunter	.03	.01	.00
☐ 130	Mark Messier UER	.30	.15	.03
	(Shown as LW, should be C)			
☐ 131	James Patrick	.03	.01	.00
	(Orange border, should be blue)			
☐ 132	Checklist Card UER	.06	.01	.00
	(54 Cary Wilson, should be Carey)			
☐ 133	Red Wings Team	.06	.03	.00
☐ 134	Barry Pederson	.03	.01	.00
☐ 135	Gary Leeman	.06	.03	.00
☐ 136	Doug Gilmour	.06	.03	.00
☐ 137	Mike McPhee	.06	.03	.00
☐ 138	Bob Murray	.03	.01	.00
☐ 139	Bob Carpenter	.06	.03	.00
☐ 140	Sean Burke	.08	.04	.01
☐ 141	Dale Hawerchuk	.15	.07	.01
☐ 142	Guy Lafleur	.20	.10	.02
☐ 143	Lindy Ruff	.03	.01	.00
☐ 144	Whalers Team	.06	.03	.00
☐ 145	Glenn Anderson	.08	.04	.01
☐ 146	Dave Chyzowski	.10	.05	.01

			MINT	EXC	G-VG
☐ 147	Kevin Hatcher		.08	.04	.01
☐ 148	Rick Vaive		.06	.03	.00
☐ 149	Adam Oates		.25	.12	.02
☐ 150	Garth Butcher		.08	.04	.01
☐ 151	Basil McRae		.10	.05	.01
☐ 152	Ilkka Sinisalo		.03	.01	.00
☐ 153	Steve Kasper		.06	.03	.00
☐ 154	Greg Paslawski		.03	.01	.00
☐ 155	Brad Marsh		.03	.01	.00
☐ 156	Esa Tikkanen		.12	.06	.01
☐ 157	Tony Tanti		.06	.03	.00
☐ 158	Mario Marois		.03	.01	.00
☐ 159	Sylvain Lefebvre		.12	.06	.01
☐ 160	Troy Murray		.06	.03	.00
☐ 161	Gary Roberts		.06	.03	.00
☐ 162	Randy Ladouceur		.03	.01	.00
☐ 163	John Chabot		.03	.01	.00
☐ 164	Calle Johansson		.03	.01	.00
☐ 165	Bruins Team		.06	.03	.00
☐ 166	Jeff Norton		.03	.01	.00
☐ 167	Mike Krushelnyski		.03	.01	.00
☐ 168	Dave Gagner		.12	.06	.01
☐ 169	Dave Andreychuk		.06	.03	.00
☐ 170	Dave Capuano		.12	.06	.01
☐ 171	Curtis Joseph		.25	.12	.02
☐ 172	Bruce Driver		.03	.01	.00
☐ 173	Scott Mellanby		.06	.03	.00
☐ 174	John Ogrodnick		.06	.03	.00
☐ 175	Mario Lemieux		.90	.45	.09
☐ 176	Marc Fortier		.06	.03	.00
☐ 177	Vincent Riendeau		.30	.15	.03
☐ 178	Mark Johnson		.03	.01	.00
☐ 179	Dirk Graham		.03	.01	.00
☐ 180	Jets Team		.06	.03	.00
☐ 181	Robb Stauber		.20	.10	.02
☐ 182	Christian Ruuttu		.03	.01	.00
☐ 183	Dave Tippett		.03	.01	.00
☐ 184	Pat LaFontaine		.20	.10	.02
☐ 185	Mark Howe		.06	.03	.00
☐ 186	Stephane Richer		.12	.06	.01
☐ 187	Jan Erixon		.03	.01	.00
☐ 188	Neil Sheehy		.03	.01	.00
☐ 189	Craig MacTavish		.03	.01	.00
☐ 190	Randy Burridge		.03	.01	.00
☐ 191	Bernie Federko		.06	.03	.00
☐ 192	Shawn Chambers		.06	.03	.00
☐ 193	Mark Messier AS1		.15	.07	.01
☐ 194	Luc Robitaille AS1		.15	.07	.01
☐ 195	Brett Hull AS1		.45	.22	.04
☐ 196	Ray Bourque AS1		.15	.07	.01
☐ 197	Al Macinnis AS1		.10	.05	.01
☐ 198	Patrick Roy AS1		.15	.07	.01
☐ 199	Wayne Gretzky AS2		.50	.25	.05

		MINT	EXC	G-VG
☐ 200	Brian Bellows AS2	.10	.05	.01
☐ 201	Cam Neely AS2	.15	.07	.01
☐ 202	Paul Coffey AS2	.15	.07	.01
☐ 203	Doug Wilson AS2	.08	.04	.01
☐ 204	Daren Puppa AS2 UER	.10	.05	.01
	(Misspelled Darren on front and back)			
☐ 205	Gary Suter	.10	.05	.01
☐ 206	Ed Olczyk	.08	.04	.01
☐ 207	Doug Lidster	.03	.01	.00
☐ 208	John Cullen	.25	.12	.02
☐ 209	Luc Robitaille	.25	.12	.02
☐ 210	Tim Kerr	.08	.04	.01
☐ 211	Scott Stevens	.08	.04	.01
☐ 212	Craig Janney	.25	.12	.02
☐ 213	Kevin Dineen	.06	.03	.01
☐ 214	Jim Waite	.12	.06	.01
☐ 215	Benoit Hogue	.10	.05	.01
☐ 216	Curtis Leschyshyn	.10	.05	.01
☐ 217	Brad Lauer	.03	.01	.00
☐ 218	Joe Mullen	.08	.04	.01
☐ 219	Patrick Roy	.20	.10	.02
☐ 220	Blues Team	.06	.03	.00
☐ 221	Brian Leetch	.50	.25	.05
☐ 222	Steve Yzerman	.30	.15	.03
☐ 223	Steph Beauregard	.20	.10	.02
☐ 224	John MacLean	.08	.04	.01
☐ 225	Trevor Linden	.25	.12	.02
☐ 226	Bill Ranford	.15	.07	.01
☐ 227	Mark Osborne	.03	.01	.00
☐ 228	Curt Giles	.03	.01	.00
☐ 229	Mikko Makela	.03	.01	.00
☐ 230	Bob Errey	.03	.01	.00
☐ 231	Jimmy Carson	.15	.07	.01
☐ 232	Kay Whitmore	.15	.07	.01
☐ 233	Gary Nylund	.03	.01	.00
☐ 234	Jiri Hrdina	.10	.05	.01
☐ 235	Stephan Leach	.03	.01	.00
☐ 236	Greg Hawgood UER	.03	.01	.00
	(Photo actually Don Sweeney)			
☐ 237	Jocelyn Lemieux	.10	.05	.01
☐ 238	Daren Puppa	.12	.06	.01
☐ 239	Kelly Kisio	.03	.01	.00
☐ 240	Craig Simpson	.10	.05	.01
☐ 241	Maple Leafs Team	.06	.03	.00
☐ 242	Frederik Olausson	.03	.01	.00
☐ 243	Ron Hextall	.12	.06	.01
☐ 244	Sergio Momesso	.15	.07	.01
☐ 245	Kirk Muller	.08	.04	.01
☐ 246	Petr Svoboda	.03	.01	.00
☐ 247	Daniel Berthiaume	.08	.04	.01
☐ 248	Andrew McBain	.03	.01	.00

			MINT	EXC	G-VG
☐ 249	Jeff Jackson (Game total for '89-'90 is 65, not 0)		.03	.01	.00
☐ 250	Randy Gilhen		.10	.05	.01
☐ 251	Oilers Team		.06	.03	.00
☐ 252	Rick Bennett		.10	.05	.01
☐ 253	Don Beaupre		.06	.03	.00
☐ 254	Pelle Eklund		.06	.03	.00
☐ 255	Greg Gilbert		.03	.01	.00
☐ 256	Gordie Roberts		.03	.01	.00
☐ 257	Kirk McLean		.08	.04	.01
☐ 258	Brent Sutter		.06	.03	.00
☐ 259	Brendan Shanahan		.08	.04	.01
☐ 260	Todd Krygier		.12	.06	.01
☐ 261	Larry Robinson UER (No '80-'81 stats on card, totals wrong)		.10	.05	.01
☐ 262	Sabres Team		.06	.03	.00
☐ 263	Dave Christian		.06	.03	.00
☐ 264	Checklist Card		.06	.01	.00
☐ 265	Jamie Macoun		.06	.03	.00
☐ 266	Glen Hanlon		.06	.03	.00
☐ 267	Daniel Marois		.10	.05	.01
☐ 268	Doug Smail		.06	.03	.00
☐ 269	Jon Casey		.15	.07	.01
☐ 270	Brian Skrudland		.06	.03	.00
☐ 271	Michel Petit		.03	.01	.00
☐ 272	Dan Quinn		.06	.03	.00
☐ 273	Geoff Courtnall		.10	.05	.01
☐ 274	Mike Bullard		.03	.01	.00
☐ 275	Randy Gregg		.10	.05	.01
☐ 276	Keith Brown		.03	.01	.00
☐ 277	Troy Mallette		.12	.06	.01
☐ 278	Steve Tuttle		.03	.01	.00
☐ 279	Brad Shaw		.12	.06	.01
☐ 280	Mark Recchi		1.50	.75	.15
☐ 281	John Tonelli		.06	.03	.00
☐ 282	Doug Bodger		.03	.01	.00
☐ 283	Thomas Steen		.06	.03	.00
☐ 284	Devils Team		.06	.03	.00
☐ 285	Lee Norwood		.03	.01	.00
☐ 286	Brian MacLellan		.03	.01	.00
☐ 287	Bobby Smith		.10	.05	.01
☐ 288	Robert Cimetta		.15	.07	.01
☐ 289	Rob Zettler		.10	.05	.01
☐ 290	David Reid		.15	.07	.01
☐ 291	Bryan Trottier		.15	.07	.01
☐ 292	Brian Mullen		.06	.03	.00
☐ 293	Paul Reinhart		.06	.03	.00
☐ 294	Andy Moog		.15	.07	.01
☐ 295	Jeff Brown		.06	.03	.00
☐ 296	Ryan Walter		.06	.03	.00
☐ 297	Trent Yawney		.10	.05	.01

			MINT	EXC	G-VG
☐ 298	John Druce		.25	.12	.02
☐ 299	Dave McLlwain		.03	.01	.00
	(Card says shoots right, should be left)				
☐ 300	David Volek		.06	.03	.00
☐ 301	Tomas Sandstrom		.10	.05	.01
☐ 302	Gord Murphy		.15	.07	.01
☐ 303	Lou Franceschetti		.10	.05	.01
☐ 304	Dana Murzyn		.03	.01	.00
☐ 305	North Stars Team		.06	.03	.00
☐ 306	Patrik Sundstrom		.06	.03	.00
☐ 307	Kevin Lowe		.08	.04	.01
☐ 308	Dave Barr		.03	.01	.00
☐ 309	Wendell Young		.12	.06	.01
☐ 310	Darrin Shannon		.12	.06	.01
☐ 311	Ron Francis		.12	.06	.01
☐ 312	Stephane Fiset		.15	.07	.01
☐ 313	Paul Fenton		.06	.03	.00
☐ 314	Dave Taylor		.08	.04	.01
☐ 315	Islanders Team		.06	.03	.00
☐ 316	Petri Skriko		.03	.01	.00
☐ 317	Rob Ramage		.06	.03	.00
☐ 318	Murray Craven		.06	.03	.00
☐ 319	Gaetan Duchesne		.06	.03	.00
☐ 320	Brad McCrimmon		.03	.01	.00
☐ 321	Grant Fuhr		.15	.07	.01
☐ 322	Gerard Gallant		.10	.05	.01
☐ 323	Tommy Albelin		.03	.01	.00
☐ 324	Scott Arniel		.03	.01	.00
☐ 325	Mike Keane		.10	.05	.01
☐ 326	Penguins Team		.06	.03	.00
☐ 327	Mike Ridley		.03	.01	.00
☐ 328	Dave Babych		.06	.03	.00
☐ 329	Michel Goulet		.10	.05	.01
☐ 330	Mike Richter		.50	.25	.05
☐ 331	Garry Galley		.12	.06	.01
☐ 332	Rod Brind'Amour		.40	.20	.04
☐ 333	Tony McKegney		.03	.01	.00
☐ 334	Peter Stastny		.15	.07	.01
☐ 335	Greg Millen		.06	.03	.00
☐ 336	Ray Ferraro		.03	.01	.00
☐ 337	Miloslav Horava		.10	.05	.01
☐ 338	Paul MacDermid		.03	.01	.00
☐ 339	Craig Coxe		.08	.04	.01
☐ 340	Dave Snuggerud		.12	.06	.01
☐ 341	Mike Lalor		.10	.05	.01
☐ 342	Marc Habscheid		.03	.01	.00
☐ 343	Rejean Lemelin		.06	.03	.00
☐ 344	Charlie Huddy		.06	.03	.00
☐ 345	Ken Linseman		.03	.01	.00
☐ 346	Canadiens Team		.06	.03	.00
☐ 347	Troy Loney		.10	.05	.01
☐ 348	Mike Modano		1.00	.50	.10

		MINT	EXC	G-VG
☐ 349	Jeff Reese	.15	.07	.01
☐ 350	Patrick Flatley	.03	.01	.00
☐ 351	Mike Vernon	.15	.07	.01
☐ 352	Todd Elik	.20	.10	.02
☐ 353	Rod Langway	.06	.03	.00
☐ 354	Moe Mantha	.03	.01	.00
☐ 355	Keith Acton	.03	.01	.00
☐ 356	Scott Pearson	.20	.10	.02
☐ 357	Perry Berezan	.08	.04	.01
☐ 358	Alexel Kasatonov	.15	.07	.01
☐ 359	Igor Larionov	.15	.07	.01
☐ 360	Kevin Stevens	1.00	.50	.10
☐ 361	Yves Racine	.12	.06	.01
☐ 362	Dave Poulin	.06	.03	.00
☐ 363	Blackhawks Team	.06	.03	.00
☐ 364	Yvon Corriveau	.08	.04	.01
☐ 365	Brian Benning	.03	.01	.00
☐ 366	Hubie McDonough	.08	.04	.01
☐ 367	Ron Tugnutt	.10	.05	.01
☐ 368	Steve Smith	.10	.05	.01
☐ 369	Joel Otto	.03	.01	.00
☐ 370	Dave Lowry	.10	.05	.01
☐ 371	Clint Malarchuk	.06	.03	.00
☐ 372	Mathieu Schneider	.20	.10	.02
☐ 373	Mike Gartner	.10	.05	.01
☐ 374	John Tucker	.03	.01	.00
☐ 375	Chris Terreri	.35	.17	.03
☐ 376	Dean Evason	.03	.01	.00
☐ 377	Jamie Leach	.20	.10	.02
☐ 378	Jacques Cloutier	.12	.06	.01
☐ 379	Glen Wesley	.06	.03	.00
☐ 380	Vladimir Krutov	.15	.07	.01
☐ 381	Terry Carkner	.03	.01	.00
☐ 382	John Mcintyre	.12	.06	.01
☐ 383	Ville Siren	.08	.04	.01
☐ 384	Joe Sakic	.75	.35	.07
☐ 385	Teppo Numminen	.10	.05	.01
☐ 386	Theo Fleury	.75	.35	.07
☐ 387	Glen Featherstone	.10	.05	.01
☐ 388	Stephan Lebeau	.40	.20	.04
☐ 389	Kevin McClelland	.03	.01	.00
☐ 390	Uwe Krupp	.03	.01	.00
☐ 391	Mark Janssens	.08	.04	.01
☐ 392	Marty McSorley	.10	.05	.01
☐ 393	Vladimir Ruzicka	.35	.17	.03
☐ 394	Capitals Team	.06	.03	.00
☐ 395	Mark Fitzpatrick	.10	.05	.01
☐ 396	Checklist Card	.06	.01	.00

1990-91 Upper Deck

The 1990-91 Upper Deck hockey set contains 400 cards, each measuring the standard size, 2¹/₂" by 3¹/₂". The fronts feature color action photos, bordered on the right and bottom in the team's colors with the team logo in the lower right hand corner. The player's name and position in black lettering appear in a pale blue bar at the top of the card front. Two-thirds of the back shows another color action photo, while the remaining third presents biographical information and career statistics in a pale blue box running the length of the card. The French version of this Upper Deck series is relatively scarce compared to the English version; the French values are approximately three times the values listed below.

Le jeu Upper Deck 1990-91 contient 400 cartes de format standard, 2¹/₂" x 3¹/₂". La face comporte une photo d'action en couleurs, bordée à droite et en bas des couleurs de l'équipe, avec l'emblème de l'équipe au coin inférieur droit. Le nom et la position du joueur apparaissent en lettres noires dans une bande bleue pâle au haut de la face. Une autre photo d'action en couleurs occupe les deux tiers du dos, et le tiers restant présente des données biographiques et des statistiques de carrière dans une boîte bleue pale occupant la largeur de la carte.

			MINT	EXC	G-VG
	COMPLETE SET (400)		55.00	27.50	5.50
	COMMON PLAYER (1-400)		.05	.02	.00
☐	1	David Volek	.10	.02	.00
☐	2	Brian Propp	.10	.05	.01
☐	3	Wendel Clark	.08	.04	.01
☐	4	Adam Creighton	.10	.05	.01
☐	5	Mark Osborne	.05	.02	.00
☐	6	Murray Craven	.08	.04	.01
☐	7	Doug Crossman	.05	.02	.00
☐	8	Mario Marois	.05	.02	.00

			MINT	EXC	G-VG
☐	9	Curt Giles	.05	.02	.00
☐	10	Rick Wamsley	.08	.04	.01
☐	11	Troy Mallette	.15	.07	.01
☐	12	John Cullen	.50	.25	.05
☐	13	Miloslav Horava	.12	.06	.01
☐	14	Kevin Stevens	3.00	1.50	.30
☐	15	David Shaw	.05	.02	.00
☐	16	Randy Wood	.05	.02	.00
☐	17	Peter Zezel	.08	.04	.01
☐	18	Glenn Healy	.15	.07	.01
☐	19	Sergio Momesso	.20	.10	.02
☐	20	Don Maloney	.05	.02	.00
☐	21	Craig Muni	.05	.02	.00
☐	22	Phil Housley	.10	.05	.01
☐	23	Martin Gelinas	.60	.30	.06
☐	24	Alexander Mogilny	1.00	.50	.10
☐	25	John Byce	.12	.06	.01
☐	26	Joe Niewendyk	.60	.30	.06
☐	27	Ron Tugnutt	.15	.07	.01
☐	28	Don Barber	.12	.06	.01
☐	29	Gary Roberts	.05	.02	.00
☐	30	Basil McRae	.12	.06	.01
☐	31	Phil Bourque	.05	.02	.00
☐	32	Mike Richter	1.25	.60	.12
☐	33	Zarley Zalapski	.12	.06	.01
☐	34	Bernie Nicholls	.15	.07	.01
☐	35	Bob Corkum	.12	.06	.01
☐	36	Rod Brind'Amour	.90	.45	.09
☐	37	Mark Fitzpatrick (Back says catches right, not left)	.12	.06	.01
☐	38	Gino Cavellini	.08	.04	.01
☐	39	Mick Vukota	.12	.06	.01
☐	40	Mike Lalor	.12	.06	.01
☐	41	Dave Andreychuk	.08	.04	.01
☐	42	Bill Ranford	.15	.07	.01
☐	43	Pierre Turgeon	.60	.30	.06
☐	44	Mark Messier	.50	.25	.05
☐	45	Rob Blake	1.25	.60	.12
☐	46	Mike Modano	3.00	1.50	.30
☐	47	Theoren Fleury	1.50	.75	.15
☐	48	Neal Broten	.08	.04	.01
☐	49	Paul Gillis	.05	.02	.00
☐	50	Doug Bodger	.05	.02	.00
☐	51	Stephan Lebeau	.90	.45	.09
☐	52	Larry Robinson	.12	.06	.01
☐	53	Dale Hawerchuk	.20	.10	.02
☐	54	Wayne Gretzky (Feet and inches reversed in stat table)	3.00	1.50	.30
☐	55	Ed Belfour (Turned pro with Gears, should be Generals)	7.50	3.75	.75

			MINT	EXC	G-VG
☐	56	Steve Yzerman	.50	.25	.05
☐	57	Rod Langway	.10	.05	.01
☐	58	Bernie Federko	.08	.04	.01
☐	59	Lemieux's Scoring Streak	.60	.30	.06
☐	60	Doug Lidster	.05	.02	.00
☐	61	Dave Christian	.08	.04	.01
☐	62	Rob Ramage	.08	.04	.01
☐	63	Jeremy Roenick	5.00	2.50	.50
☐	64	Ray Bourque	.45	.22	.04
☐	65	Jon Morris	.15	.07	.01
☐	66	Sean Burke	.10	.05	.01
☐	67	Ron Francis	.15	.07	.01
☐	68	Ron Sutter	.08	.04	.01
☐	69	Peter Sidorkiewicz	.10	.05	.01
☐	70	Sylvain Turgeon	.05	.02	.00
☐	71	Dave Ellett	.05	.02	.00
☐	72	Bobby Smith	.12	.06	.01
☐	73	Luc Robitaille	.30	.15	.03
☐	74	Pat Elynuik	.12	.06	.01
☐	75	Jason Soules	.12	.06	.01
☐	76	Dino Ciccarelli	.10	.05	.01
☐	77	Vladimir Krutov	.15	.07	.01
☐	78	Lee Norwood	.05	.02	.00
☐	79	Brian Bradley	.05	.02	.00
☐	80	Michal Pivonka	.20	.10	.02
☐	81	Mark LaForest	.15	.07	.01
☐	82	Trent Yawney	.10	.05	.01
☐	83	Tom Fergus	.05	.02	.00
☐	84	Andy Brickley	.05	.02	.00
☐	85	Dave Manson	.05	.02	.00
☐	86	Gord Murphy	.15	.07	.01
☐	87	Scott Young	.10	.05	.01
☐	88	Tommy Albelin	.05	.02	.00
☐	89	Ken Wregget	.12	.06	.01
☐	90	Brad Shaw	.15	.07	.01
☐	91	Mario Gosselin	.08	.04	.01
☐	92	Paul Fenton	.08	.04	.01
☐	93	Brian Skrudland	.08	.04	.01
☐	94	Thomas Steen	.08	.04	.01
☐	95	John Tonelli	.08	.04	.01
☐	96	Steve Chiasson UER (Back photo actually Yves Racine)	.08	.04	.01
☐	97	Mike Ridley	.05	.02	.00
☐	98	Garth Butcher	.10	.05	.01
☐	99	Daniel Shank	.15	.07	.01
☐	100	Checklist 1-100	.08	.01	.00
☐	101	Jamie Macoun	.08	.04	.01
☐	102	Wendell Young	.15	.07	.01
☐	103	Laurie Boschman	.05	.02	.00
☐	104	Paul Ranheim	.35	.17	.03
☐	105	Doug Smail	.08	.04	.01

		MINT	EXC	G-VG
☐ 106	Shawn Chambers	.08	.04	.01
☐ 107	Steve Weeks	.08	.04	.01
☐ 108	Gaetan Duchesne	.08	.04	.01
☐ 109	Kevin Hatcher	.10	.05	.01
☐ 110	Paul Reinhart	.08	.04	.01
☐ 111	Shawn Burr	.05	.02	.00
☐ 112	Troy Murray	.08	.04	.01
☐ 113	John Chabot	.05	.02	.00
☐ 114	Jacques Cloutier	.15	.07	.01
☐ 115	Rick Zombo	.15	.07	.01
☐ 116	Kjell Samuelsson	.05	.02	.00
☐ 117	Tim Watters	.05	.02	.00
☐ 118	Patrick Flatley	.05	.02	.00
☐ 119	Tom Laidlaw	.05	.02	.00
☐ 120	Ilkka Sinisalo	.05	.02	.00
☐ 121	Tom Barrasso	.10	.05	.01
☐ 122	Bob Essensa	.35	.17	.03
☐ 123	Sergei Makarov	.75	.35	.07
☐ 124	Paul Coffey	.40	.20	.04
☐ 125	Bob Beers	.20	.10	.02
☐ 126	Brian Bellows	.15	.07	.01
☐ 127	Mike Liut	.10	.05	.01
☐ 128	Igor Larionov	.35	.17	.03
☐ 129	Craig Simpson	.15	.07	.01
☐ 130	Kelly Miller	.10	.05	.01
☐ 131	Dirk Graham	.05	.02	.00
☐ 132	Jimmy Carson	.20	.10	.02
☐ 133	Michel Goulet	.12	.06	.01
☐ 134	Gerard Gallant	.12	.06	.01
☐ 135	Bruce Hoffort	.15	.07	.01
☐ 136	Steve Duchesne	.08	.04	.01
☐ 137	Bryan Trottier	.20	.10	.02
☐ 138	Pelle Eklund	.08	.04	.01
☐ 139	Gary Nylund	.05	.02	.00
☐ 140	Steve Kasper	.08	.04	.01
☐ 141	Joel Otto	.05	.02	.00
☐ 142	Rob Brown	.20	.10	.02
☐ 143	Al MacInnis	.25	.12	.02
☐ 144	Mario Lemieux	1.50	.75	.15
☐ 145	Peter Eriksson UER	.15	.07	.01
	(Photo actually Tommy Lehmann)			
☐ 146	Jari Kurri	.30	.15	.03
☐ 147	Petri Skriko	.05	.02	.00
☐ 148	Steve Smith	.12	.06	.01
☐ 149	Calle Johansson	.05	.02	.00
☐ 150	Stewart Gavin	.08	.04	.01
☐ 151	Randy Ladouceur	.05	.02	.00
☐ 152	Vincent Riendeau	.75	.35	.07
☐ 153	Patrick Roy	.35	.17	.03
	(Feet and inches reversed in stat table)			
☐ 154	Brett Hull	3.00	1.50	.30

		MINT	EXC	G-VG
☐ 155	Craig Fisher UER	.35	.17	.03
	(Photo actually Jay Wells)			
☐ 156	Cam Neely	.45	.22	.04
☐ 157	Al Iafrate	.08	.04	.01
☐ 158	Bob Carpenter	.08	.04	.01
☐ 159	Doug Brown	.05	.02	.00
☐ 160	Tom Kurvers	.05	.02	.00
☐ 161	John MacLean	.10	.05	.01
☐ 162	Guy Lafleur	.30	.15	.03
☐ 163	Peter Stastny	.20	.10	.02
☐ 164	Joe Sakic	1.50	.75	.15
☐ 165	Robb Stauber	.30	.15	.03
☐ 166	Daren Puppa	.15	.07	.01
☐ 167	Esa Tikkanen	.15	.07	.01
☐ 168	Mike Ramsey	.05	.02	.00
☐ 169	Craig MacTavish	.05	.02	.00
☐ 170	Christian Ruuttu	.05	.02	.00
☐ 171	Brian Hayward	.08	.04	.01
☐ 172	Pat Verbeek	.10	.05	.01
☐ 173	Adam Oates	.30	.15	.03
☐ 174	Chris Chelios	.15	.07	.01
☐ 175	Curtis Joseph	.50	.25	.05
☐ 176	Viacheslav Fetisov	.40	.20	.04
☐ 177	Dave Poulin	.08	.04	.01
☐ 178	Mark Recchi	5.00	2.50	.50
☐ 179	Daniel Marois	.15	.07	.01
☐ 180	Mark Johnson	.05	.02	.00
☐ 181	Michel Petit	.05	.02	.00
☐ 182	Brian Mullen	.08	.04	.01
☐ 183	Chris Terreri	.60	.30	.06
☐ 184	Tony Hrkac	.05	.02	.00
☐ 185	James Patrick	.05	.02	.00
☐ 186	Craig Ludwig	.05	.02	.00
☐ 187	Uwe Krupp	.05	.02	.00
☐ 188	Guy Carbonneau	.08	.04	.01
☐ 189	Dave Snuggerud	.15	.07	.01
☐ 190	Joe Murphy	.45	.22	.04
☐ 191	Jeff Brown	.08	.04	.01
☐ 192	Dean Evason	.05	.02	.00
☐ 193	Petr Svoboda	.05	.02	.00
☐ 194	Dave Babych	.08	.04	.01
☐ 195	Steve Tuttle	.05	.02	.00
☐ 196	Randy Burridge	.05	.02	.00
☐ 197	Tony Tanti	.08	.04	.01
☐ 198	Bob Sweeney	.05	.02	.00
☐ 199	Brad Marsh	.05	.02	.00
☐ 200	Checklist 101-200	.08	.01	.00
☐ 201	Bill Ranford	.12	.06	.01
	Conn Smythe			
	Trophy Winner			
☐ 202	Calder Trophy	.25	.12	.02
	Sergei Makarov			

			MINT	EXC	G-VG
☐ 203	**Lady Byng Trophy**		.60	.30	.06
	Brett Hull				
☐ 204	**Norris Trophy**		.25	.12	.02
	Ray Bourque				
☐ 205	**Art Ross Trophy**		.60	.30	.06
	Wayne Gretzky				
☐ 206	**Hart Trophy**		.25	.12	.02
	Mark Messier				
☐ 207	**Vezina Trophy**		.15	.07	.01
	Patrick Roy				
☐ 208	**Frank Selke Trophy**		.05	.02	.00
	Rick Meagher				
☐ 209	**William Jennings Trophy**		.08	.04	.01
	Andy Moog and Reggie Lemelin				
☐ 210	**Aaron Broten**		.05	.02	.00
☐ 211	**John Carter**		.15	.07	.01
☐ 212	**Marty McSorley**		.15	.07	.01
☐ 213	**Greg Millen**		.08	.04	.01
☐ 214	**Dave Taylor**		.10	.05	.01
☐ 215	**Rejean Lemelin**		.08	.04	.01
☐ 216	**Dave McLlwain**		.05	.02	.00
☐ 217	**Don Beaupre**		.08	.04	.01
☐ 218	**Paul MacDermid**		.05	.02	.00
☐ 219	**Dale Hunter**		.05	.02	.00
☐ 220	**Brent Ashton**		.05	.02	.00
☐ 221	**Steve Thomas**		.08	.04	.01
☐ 222	**Ed Olczyk**		.10	.05	.01
☐ 223	**Doug Wilson**		.10	.05	.01
☐ 224	**Vincent Damphousse**		.12	.06	.01
☐ 225	**Rob DiMaio**		.12	.06	.01
☐ 226	**Hubie McDonough**		.12	.06	.01
☐ 227	**Ron Hextall**		.15	.07	.01
☐ 228	**Dave Chyzowski**		.15	.07	.01
☐ 229	**Larry Murphy**		.05	.02	.00
☐ 230	**Mike Bullard**		.05	.02	.00
☐ 231	**Kelly Hrudey**		.10	.05	.01
☐ 232	**Andy Moog**		.20	.10	.02
☐ 233	**Todd Elik**		.50	.25	.05
☐ 234	**Craig Janney**		.45	.22	.04
☐ 235	**Peter Lappin**		.15	.07	.01
☐ 236	**Scott Stevens**		.10	.05	.01
☐ 237	**Fredrik Olausson**		.05	.02	.00
☐ 238	**Geoff Courtnall**		.15	.07	.01
☐ 239	**Greg Paslawski**		.05	.02	.00
☐ 240	**Alan May**		.15	.07	.01
☐ 241	**Allan Bester**		.08	.04	.01
☐ 242	**Steve Larmer**		.15	.07	.01
☐ 243	**Gary Leeman**		.08	.04	.01
☐ 244	**Denis Savard**		.20	.10	.02
☐ 245	**Eric Weinrich**		.50	.25	.05
☐ 246	**Pat LaFontaine**		.25	.12	.02

			MINT	EXC	G-VG
☐	247	Tim Kerr	.10	.05	.01
☐	248	Dave Gagner	.20	.10	.02
☐	249	Brent Sutter	.08	.04	.01
☐	250	Claude Vilgrain	.12	.06	.01
☐	251	Tomas Sandstrom	.15	.07	.01
☐	252	Joey Mullen	.10	.05	.01
☐	253	Brian Leetch	.75	.35	.07
☐	254	Mike Vernon	.20	.10	.02
☐	255	Daniel Dore	.12	.06	.01
☐	256	Trevor Linden	.50	.25	.05
☐	257	Dave Barr	.05	.02	.00
☐	258	John Ogrodnick	.08	.04	.01
☐	259	Russ Courtnall	.08	.04	.01
☐	260	Dan Quinn	.08	.04	.01
☐	261	Mark Howe	.10	.05	.01
☐	262	Kevin Lowe	.10	.05	.01
☐	263	Rick Tocchet	.20	.10	.02
☐	264	Grant Fuhr	.20	.10	.02
☐	265	Andrew Cassels	.40	.20	.04
☐	266	Kevin Dineen	.08	.04	.01
☐	267	Kirk Muller	.12	.06	.01
☐	268	Randy Cunneyworth	.05	.02	.00
☐	269	Brendan Shanahan	.10	.05	.01
☐	270	Dave Tippett	.05	.02	.00
☐	271	Doug Gilmour	.10	.05	.01
☐	272	Tony Granato	.30	.15	.03
☐	273	Gary Suter	.12	.06	.01
☐	274	Darren Turcotte	1.75	.85	.17
☐	275	Murray Baron	.12	.06	.01
☐	276	Stephane Richer	.15	.07	.01
☐	277	Mike Gartner	.12	.06	.01
☐	278	Kirk McLean	.10	.05	.01
☐	279	John Vanbiesbrouck	.12	.06	.01
☐	280	Shayne Carson	.15	.07	.01
☐	281	Paul Cavallini	.10	.05	.01
☐	282	Petr Klima	.15	.07	.01
☐	283	Ulf Dahlen	.08	.04	.01
☐	284	Glenn Anderson	.10	.05	.01
☐	285	Rick Meagher	.05	.02	.00
☐	286	Alexei Kasatonov	.30	.15	.03
☐	287	Ulf Samuelsson	.08	.04	.01
☐	288	Patrik Sundstrom	.08	.04	.01
☐	289	Ray Ferraro	.05	.02	.00
☐	290	Janne Ojanen	.12	.06	.01
☐	291	Jeff Jackson	.05	.02	.00
☐	292	Jiri Hrdina	.12	.06	.01
☐	293	Joe Cirella	.05	.02	.00
☐	294	Brad McCrimmon	.05	.02	.00
☐	295	Curtis Leschyshyn	.15	.07	.01
☐	296	Kelly Kisio	.05	.02	.00
☐	297	Jyrki Lumme	.25	.12	.02
☐	298	Mark Janssens	.12	.06	.01
☐	299	Stan Smyl	.08	.04	.01

		MINT	EXC	G-VG
☐ 300	Checklist 201-300..........................	.08	.01	.00
☐ 301	Quebec Nordiques TC	.60	.30	.06
	Joe Sakic			
☐ 302	Vancouver Canucks TC	.05	.02	.00
	Petri Skriko			
☐ 303	Detroit Red Wings TC	.30	.15	.03
	Steve Yzerman			
☐ 304	Phila. Flyers TC.............................	.08	.04	.01
	Tim Kerr			
☐ 305	Pitts. Penguins TC	.45	.22	.04
	Mario Lemieux			
☐ 306	N.Y. Islanders TC	.15	.07	.01
	Pat LaFontaine			
☐ 307	L.A. Kings TC.................................	.60	.30	.06
	Wayne Gretzky			
☐ 308	Minn. North Stars TC	.10	.05	.01
	Brian Bellows			
☐ 309	Wash. Capitals TC	.08	.04	.01
	Rod Langway			
☐ 310	Tor. Maple Leafs TC	.08	.04	.01
	Gary Leeman			
☐ 311	N.J. Devils TC	.08	.04	.01
	Kirk Muller			
☐ 312	St. Louis Blues TC	.60	.30	.06
	Brett Hull			
☐ 313	Winnipeg Jets TC..........................	.08	.04	.01
	Thomas Steen			
☐ 314	Hartford Whalers TC	.10	.05	.01
	Ron Francis			
☐ 315	N.Y. Rangers TC	.25	.12	.02
	Brian Leetch			
☐ 316	Chic. Blackhawks TC	.60	.30	.06
	Jeremy Roenick			
☐ 317	Mont. Canadiens TC	.20	.10	.02
	Patrick Roy			
☐ 318	Buffalo Sabres TC	.20	.10	.02
	Pierre Turgeon			
☐ 319	Calgary Flames TC	.15	.07	.01
	Al MacInnis			
☐ 320	Boston Bruins TC...........................	.20	.10	.02
	Ray Bourque			
☐ 321	Edmonton Oilers TC	.20	.10	.02
	Mark Messier			
☐ 322	Jody Hull.....................................	.15	.07	.01
☐ 323	Chris Joseph	.15	.07	.01
☐ 324	Adam Burt	.12	.06	.01
☐ 325	Jason Herter	.50	.25	.05
☐ 326	Geoff Smith	.15	.07	.01
☐ 327	Brad Shaw	.10	.05	.01
☐ 328	Rich Sutter	.08	.04	.01
☐ 329	Barry Pederson.............................	.05	.02	.00
☐ 330	Paul MacLean	.08	.04	.01
☐ 331	Randy Carlyle	.08	.04	.01

		MINT	EXC	G-VG
☐ 332	Donald Dufresne	.15	.07	.01
☐ 333	Brent Hughes	.15	.07	.01
☐ 334	Mathieu Schneider	.50	.25	.05
☐ 335	Jason Miller	.40	.20	.04
☐ 336	Sergei Makarov	.25	.12	.02
☐ 337	Bob Essensa	.15	.07	.01
☐ 338	Claude Loiselle	.12	.06	.01
☐ 339	Wayne Presley	.05	.02	.00
☐ 340	Tony McKegney	.05	.02	.00
☐ 341	Charlie Huddy	.08	.04	.01
☐ 342	Greg Adams	.08	.04	.01
	(Front photo actually Igor Larionov)			
☐ 343	Mike Tomlak	.12	.06	.01
☐ 344	Adam Graves	.45	.22	.04
☐ 345	Michel Mongeau	.20	.10	.02
☐ 346	Mike Modano	.35	.17	.03
☐ 347	Rod Brind'Amour	.25	.12	.02
☐ 348	Dana Murzyn	.05	.02	.00
☐ 349	Dave Lowry	.25	.12	.02
☐ 350	Star Rookie CL	.08	.01	.00
☐ 351	First Four Picks	1.00	.50	.10
	Owen Nolan			
	Keith Primeau			
	Petr Nedved			
	Mike Ricci			
	Top Ten Draft Pick CL			
☐ 352	Owen Nolan FDP	.90	.45	.09
☐ 353	Petr Nedved	2.00	1.00	.20
☐ 354	Keith Primeau	.80	.40	.08
☐ 355	Mike Ricci	3.00	1.50	.30
	(Born October, not November 27)			
☐ 356	Jaromir Jagr	7.00	3.50	.70
☐ 357	Scott Scissons	.35	.17	.03
☐ 358	Daryl Sydor	.60	.30	.06
☐ 359	Derian Hatcher	.35	.17	.03
☐ 360	John Slaney	.75	.35	.07
☐ 361	Drake Berehowsky	.60	.30	.06
☐ 362	Luke Richardson	.05	.02	.00
☐ 363	Lucien Deblois	.05	.02	.00
☐ 364	Dave Reid	.20	.10	.02
☐ 365	Mats Sundin	3.00	1.50	.30
☐ 366	Jan Erixon	.05	.02	.00
☐ 367	Troy Loney	.12	.06	.01
☐ 368	Chris Nilan	.08	.04	.01
☐ 369	Gord Dineen	.10	.05	.01
☐ 370	Jeff Bloemberg	.12	.06	.01
☐ 371	John Druce	.45	.22	.04
☐ 372	Brian MacLellan	.05	.02	.00
☐ 373	Bruce Driver	.05	.02	.00
☐ 374	Marc Habscheid	.08	.04	.01
☐ 375	Paul Ysebaert	.50	.25	.05
☐ 376	Rick Vaive	.08	.04	.01

			MINT	EXC	G-VG
☐ 377	Glen Wesley		.08	.04	.01
☐ 378	Mike Foligno		.05	.02	.00
☐ 379	Garry Galley		.15	.07	.01
☐ 380	Dean Kennedy		.12	.06	.01
☐ 381	Daniel Berthiaume		.10	.05	.01
☐ 382	Mike Keane		.25	.12	.02
☐ 383	Frantisek Musil		.10	.05	.01
☐ 384	Mike McPhee		.10	.05	.01
☐ 385	Jon Casey		.30	.15	.03
☐ 386	Jeff Norton		.05	.02	.00
☐ 387	John Tucker		.05	.02	.00
☐ 388	Alan Kerr		.05	.02	.00
☐ 389	Bob Rouse		.05	.02	.00
☐ 390	Gerald Diduck		.05	.02	.00
☐ 391	Greg Hawgood		.05	.02	.00
☐ 392	Randy Velischek		.05	.02	.00
☐ 393	Tim Cheveldae		.65	.30	.06
☐ 394	Mike Krushelnyski		.08	.04	.01
☐ 395	Glen Hanlon		.08	.04	.01
☐ 396	Lou Franceschetti		.15	.07	.01
☐ 397	Scott Arniel		.05	.02	.00
☐ 398	Terry Carkner		.05	.02	.00
☐ 399	Clint Malarchuk		.08	.04	.01
☐ 400	Checklist 301-400		.08	.01	.00

1990-91 Upper Deck Extended

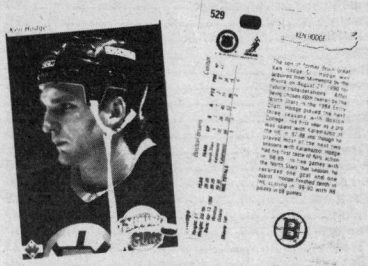

The 1990-91 Upper Deck Extended (or High Numbers Series) hockey set contains 150 cards and includes newest rookies, traded players, All Stars, Heroes of the NHL, and members of the Canadian National Junior Team. The fronts are in the same design as the regular issue: color action photos bordered on the right and bottom in the team's colors with the team logo in the lower right hand corner. The player's name and position in black lettering appear in a pale blue bar at the top of the card front. Two-thirds of the back shows another color action photo, while the remaining third presents biographical information and career statistics in a pale blue box running the length of the card. The French version of this Upper Deck series is relatively scarce compared to the English version; the French values are approximately six times the values listed below.

Le jeu Upper Deck Extended (ou série à numéros élevés) 1990-91 contient 150 cartes, et inclut les derniers débutants, les joueurs acquis, les All Stars, les héros de la NHL, et les membres de l'équipe junior nationale canadienne. Le style de la face est identique aux cartes régulières: une photo d'action en couleurs, bordée à droite et en bas des couleurs de l'équipe, avec l'emblème de l'équipe au coin inférieur droit. Le nom et la position du joueur apparaissent en lettres noires dans une bande bleue pale en haut de la face. Une autre photo d'action en couleurs occupe les deux tiers du dos, et le tiers restant présente des données biographiques et des statistiques de carrière dans une boîte bleue pale occupant la largeur de la carte.

		MINT	EXC	G-VG
	COMPLETE SET (150)	45.00	22.50	4.50
	COMMON PLAYER (401-550)	.07	.03	.01
☐ 401	Mikhail Tatarinov	1.00	.50	.10
☐ 402	Benoit Hogue.....................................	.25	.12	.02
☐ 403	Frank Pietrangelo...............................	.40	.20	.04
☐ 404	Paul Stanton	.20	.10	.02
☐ 405	Anatoli Semenov	.75	.35	.07

		MINT	EXC	G-VG
☐ 406	Bobby Smith	.15	.07	.01
☐ 407	Derek King	.07	.03	.01
☐ 408	J.C. Bergeron	.30	.15	.03
☐ 409	Brian Propp	.15	.07	.01
☐ 410	Jiri Latal	.20	.10	.02
☐ 411	Joey Kocur	.25	.12	.02
☐ 412	Daniel Berthiaume	.12	.06	.01
☐ 413	Dave Ellett	.07	.03	.01
☐ 414	Jay Miller	.25	.12	.02
☐ 415	Stephane Beauregard	.25	.12	.02
☐ 416	Mark Hardy	.10	.05	.01
☐ 417	Todd Krygier	.20	.10	.02
☐ 418	Randy Moller	.10	.05	.01
☐ 419	Doug Crossman	.07	.03	.01
☐ 420	Ray Sheppard	.10	.05	.01
☐ 421	Sylvain Lefebvre	.20	.10	.02
☐ 422	Chris Chelios	.15	.07	.01
☐ 423	Joe Mullen	.15	.07	.01
☐ 424	Pete Peeters	.10	.05	.01
☐ 425	Bryan Trottier	.25	.12	.02
☐ 426	Denis Savard	.20	.10	.02
☐ 427	Ken Daneyko	.12	.06	.01
☐ 428	Eric Desjardins	.30	.15	.03
☐ 429	Zdena Ciger	.20	.10	.02
☐ 430	Brad McCrimmon	.07	.03	.01
☐ 431	Ed Olczyk	.12	.06	.01
☐ 432	Peter Ing	.60	.30	.06
☐ 433	Bob Kudelski	.35	.17	.03
☐ 434	Troy Gamble	.80	.40	.08
☐ 435	Phil Housley	.15	.07	.01
☐ 436	Scott Stevens	.15	.07	.01
☐ 437	Normand Rochefort	.10	.05	.01
☐ 438	Geoff Courtnall	.15	.07	.01
☐ 439	Ken Baumgartner	.15	.07	.01
☐ 440	Kris King	.30	.15	.03
☐ 441	Troy Crowder	.25	.12	.02
☐ 442	Chris Nilan	.10	.05	.01
☐ 443	Dale Hawerchuk	.25	.12	.02
☐ 444	Kevin Miller	.75	.35	.07
☐ 445	Keith Acton	.07	.03	.01
☐ 446	Jeff Chychrun	.20	.10	.02
☐ 447	Claude Lemieux	.15	.07	.01
☐ 448	Bob Probert	.90	.45	.09
☐ 449	Brian Hayward	.10	.05	.01
☐ 450	Craig Berube	.20	.10	.02
☐ 451	Team Canada	1.00	.50	.10
	Canadian National Junior Team Photo			
☐ 452	Mike Sillinger	1.00	.50	.10
☐ 453	Jason Marshall	.50	.25	.05
☐ 454	Patrice Brisebois	.50	.25	.05
☐ 455	Brad May	.50	.25	.05
☐ 456	Pierre Sevigny	.30	.15	.03

		MINT	EXC	G-VG
☐ 457	John Slaney	.75	.35	.07
☐ 458	Felix Potvin	.75	.35	.07
☐ 459	Scott Thornton	.50	.25	.05
☐ 460	Greg Johnson	.60	.30	.06
☐ 461	Scott Niedermayer	4.00	2.00	.40
☐ 462	Steven Rice	1.75	.85	.17
☐ 463	Trevor Kidd	1.50	.75	.15
☐ 464	Dale Craigwell	.30	.15	.03
☐ 465	Kent Manderville	.50	.25	.05
☐ 466	Kris Draper	.50	.25	.05
☐ 467	Martin Lapointe	2.50	1.25	.25
☐ 468	Chris Snell	.50	.25	.05
☐ 469	Pat Falloon	4.50	2.25	.45
☐ 470	David Harlock	.30	.15	.03
☐ 471	Karl Dykhuis	.40	.20	.04
☐ 472	Mike Craig	1.00	.50	.10
☐ 473	Canada's Captains	12.50	6.25	1.25
	Kris Draper			
	Steven Rice			
	Eric Lindros			
☐ 474	Brett Hull AS	1.00	.50	.10
☐ 475	Darren Turcotte AS	.60	.30	.06
☐ 476	Wayne Gretzky AS	1.00	.50	.10
☐ 477	Steve Yzerman AS	.35	.17	.03
☐ 478	Theoren Fleury AS	.60	.30	.06
☐ 479	Pat LaFontaine AS	.15	.07	.01
☐ 480	Trevor Linden AS	.20	.10	.02
☐ 481	Jeremy Roenick AS	1.00	.50	.10
☐ 482	Scott Stevens AS	.10	.05	.01
☐ 483	Adam Oates AS	.25	.12	.02
☐ 484	Vin Damphousse AS	.12	.06	.01
☐ 485	Brian Leetch AS	.30	.15	.03
☐ 486	Kevin Hatcher AS	.10	.05	.01
☐ 487	Mark Recchi AS	1.00	.50	.10
☐ 488	Rick Tocchet AS	.12	.06	.01
☐ 489	Ray Bourque AS	.25	.12	.02
☐ 490	Joe Sakic AS	.60	.30	.06
☐ 491	Chris Chelios AS	.12	.06	.01
☐ 492	John Cullen AS	.30	.15	.03
☐ 493	Cam Neely AS	.30	.15	.03
☐ 494	Mark Messier AS	.25	.12	.02
☐ 495	Mike Vernon AS	.12	.06	.01
☐ 496	Patrick Roy AS	.20	.10	.02
☐ 497	Al MacInnis AS	.12	.06	.01
☐ 498	Paul Coffey AS	.20	.10	.02
☐ 499	Steve Larmer AS	.12	.06	.01
☐ 500	Checklist Card	.10	.01	.00
☐ 501	Heroes Checklist	.10	.01	.00
☐ 502	Red Kelly HERO	.10	.05	.01
☐ 503	Eric Nesterenko HERO	.07	.03	.01
☐ 504	Darryl Sittler HERO	.10	.05	.01
☐ 505	Jim Schoenfeld HERO	.07	.03	.01
☐ 506	Serge Savard HERO	.10	.05	.01

		MINT	EXC	G-VG
☐ 507	Glenn Resch HERO	.10	.05	.01
☐ 508	Lanny McDonald HERO	.10	.05	.01
☐ 509	Bobby Clarke HERO	.15	.07	.01
☐ 510	Phil Esposito HERO	.25	.12	.02
☐ 511	Harry Howell HERO	.10	.05	.01
☐ 512	Rod Gilbert HERO	.10	.05	.01
☐ 513	Pit Martin HERO	.07	.03	.01
☐ 514	Jimmy Watson HERO	.07	.03	.01
☐ 515	Denis Potvin HERO	.15	.07	.01
☐ 516	Rob Ray	.15	.07	.01
☐ 517	Danton Cole	.15	.07	.01
☐ 518	Gino Odjick	.25	.12	.02
☐ 519	Donald Audette	.20	.10	.02
☐ 520	Rick Tabaracci	.15	.07	.01
☐ 521	Young Guns Checklist	4.00	2.00	.40
	Sergei Federov			
	Johan Garpenlov			
☐ 522	Kip Miller YG	1.00	.50	.10
☐ 523	Johan Garpenlov YG	.90	.45	.09
☐ 524	Stephane Morin YG	1.50	.75	.15
☐ 525	Sergei Fedorov YG	20.00	10.00	2.00
☐ 526	Pavel Bure YG	4.00	2.00	.40
☐ 527	Wes Walz	.60	.30	.06
☐ 528	Robert Kron YG	.50	.25	.05
☐ 529	Ken Hodge YG	4.00	2.00	.40
☐ 530	Gary Valk YG	.40	.20	.04
☐ 531	Tim Sweeney YG	.15	.07	.01
☐ 532	Mark Pederson YG	.30	.15	.03
☐ 533	Robert Reichel YG	1.00	.50	.10
☐ 534	Bobby Holik YG	2.00	1.00	.20
☐ 535	Stephane Matteau YG	.50	.25	.05
☐ 536	Peter Bondra YG	1.00	.50	.10
☐ 537	Dimitri Khristich	.80	.40	.08
☐ 538	Vladimir Ruzicka	.75	.35	.07
☐ 539	Al Iafrate	.10	.05	.01
☐ 540	Rick Bennett	.20	.10	.02
☐ 541	Daryl Reaugh	.40	.20	.04
☐ 542	Martin Hostak	.15	.07	.01
☐ 543	Kari Takko	.20	.10	.02
☐ 544	Jocelyn Lemieux	.15	.07	.01
☐ 545	Gretzky's 2000th Point	2.50	1.25	.25
☐ 546	Hull's 50 goals	2.50	1.25	.25
☐ 547	Neil Wilkinson	.30	.15	.03
☐ 548	Bryan Fogarty	.75	.35	.07
☐ 549	Zamboni Machine	.35	.17	.03
☐ 550	Checklist Card	.10	.01	.00

ABOUT THE AUTHOR

Jim Beckett, the leading authority on sport card values in the United States, maintains a wide range of activities in the world of sports. He possesses one of the finest collections of sports cards and autographs in the world, has made numerous appearances on radio and television, and has been frequently cited and quoted in many national publications. He was awarded the first "Special Achievement Award" for Contributions to the Hobby by the National Sports Collectors Convention in 1980, the "Jock-Jasperson Award" for Hobby Dedication in 1983, and the "Buck Barker, Spirit of the Hobby" award in 1991.

Dr. Beckett is the author of *The Sport Americana Baseball Card Price Guide, The Official Price Guide to Baseball Cards, The Sport Americana Price Guide to Baseball Collectibles, The Sport Americana Baseball Memorabilia and Autograph Price Guide, The Sport Americana Football, Hockey, Basketball and Boxing Price Guide, The Official Price Guide to Football Cards, The Official Price Guide to Hockey and Basketball Cards,* and *The Sport Americana Alphabetical Baseball Card Checklist.* In addition, he is the publisher and editor of *Beckett Baseball Card Monthly, Beckett Football Card Monthly, Beckett Basketball Monthly, Beckett Hockey Monthly,* and *Focus on Future Stars,* publications dedicated to advancing the card collecting hobby.

Jim Beckett received his Ph.D. in Statistics from Southern Methodist University in 1975. He resides in Dallas with his wife, Patti, and their daughters, Christina, Rebecca, and Melissa.

A PROPOS DE L'AUTEUR

Jim Beckett, l'autorité incontestée aux Etats-Unis concernant l'évaluation des cartes sur les sports, maintient une variété étendue d'activités dans le monde sportif. Il possède l'une des plus fameuses collections de cartes et d'autographes du monde; il est passé de nombreuses fois à la radio et à la télévision et a été fréquemment mentionné et cité dans des publications à l'échelon national. Il reçut la première récompense "Special Achievement Award" pour sa contribution à ce passe-temps au cours de l'assemblée nationale de 1980 des collectionneurs de cartes sportives; puis en 1983 il reçut la récompense "Jock-Jasperson Award" pour sa consécration à ce passe-temps, enfin en 1991 le "Buck Barker, Spirit of the Hobby."

Le Dr. Beckett est l'auteur du recueil des prix des cartes de base-ball américain (*The Sport Americana Baseball Card Price Guide*), du guide officiel des prix des cartes de base-ball (*The Official Price Guide to Baseball Cards*), du guide des prix des objets de collection relatifs au base-ball en Amérique (*The Sport Americana Price Guide to Baseball Collectibles*), du mémoire du base-ball américain et de la valeur des autographes (*The Sport Americana Baseball Memorabilia and Autograph Price Guide*), du guide des prix pour le foot-ball américain, le hockey, le basket-ball et la boxe (*The Sport Americana Football, Hockey, Basketball and Boxing Price Guide*), du recueil officiel des prix des cartes de foot-ball (*The Official Price Guide to Football Cards*), du recueil officiel des prix des cartes de hockey, de basket-ball et de foot-ball (*The Official Price Guide to Hockey and Basketball Cards*), et du relevé alphabétique des cartes de base-ball américain (*The Sport Americana Alphabetical Baseball Card Checklist*). En outre, il est l'éditeur et l'auteur du mensuel sur les cartes de base-ball *Beckett Baseball Card Monthly*, du mensuel sur les cartes de foot-ball *Beckett Football Card Monthly*, du mensuel sur le basket-ball *Beckett Basketball Monthly*, du mensuel sur le hockey *Beckett Hockey Monthly* et de la revue consacrée aux futures vedettes sportives *Focus on Future Stars*, publications dédiées à l'évolution de la collection des cartes.

Jim Beckett a obtenu un doctorat en statistiques en 1975 à l'université "Southern Methodist University." Il habite Dallas avec sa femme Patti et leurs filles Christina, Rébecca et Mélissa.

TIME OUT!

 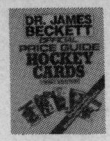 

What do football, hockey, and basketball have in common?—DR. JAMES BECKETT, the leading authority on sport card values!

All three price guides contain:

- All of the major series, including Topps

- Current market values

- Valuable tips on buying, selling, and finding cards

- Helpful three-price grading system

THESE BOOKS CAN'T BE BEAT!

TEMDEE
Wholesale & Retail

We Carry A Full Line Of:

- **Complete Sets**
  Football, Baseball, Hockey, Basketball, and Non-Sports cards.
- **Manufacturers**
  Topps, Fleer, Donruss, Score, Bowman, Leaf, Star, O-P-C, Upper Deck, Kelloggs, Pro Set Football, Hoops, Sportflics & others.
- **Supplies**
  Card Pages (all sizes), Binders (2" & 3"), Boxes (100, 400, 500, 600 & 800), Single Card Sleeves, Lucite Holders, Ball & Bat Holders, Plastic Cases and much more!
- **Pennants**
  All sports and major colleges plus specials.
- **Autographed Baseballs**
- **Photographs**
- **Porcelain Figurines & Plates**
  Sports Impressions & Gartlans.
- **Unopened Boxes & Packs**
- **Yearbooks & Price Guides**
- **Souvenirs**
  Hats, Scarfs, Bobble Dolls, Buttons & more.
- **Starting Line Ups**
  For '88 & '89 in Baseball, Football & Basketball.
- **Minor League Sets**
  Pro Cards, Star Co. & Grand Slam.
- **Want Lists**
  Filled for all sports. Send for specific wants or needs with an S.A.S.E.

WE BUY AND SELL

TEMDEE

1201 Black Horse Pike
Turnersville, N.J. 08012
(609) 228-8645

Store open Mon.- Fri. Noon - 8 p.m.
Sat. 10 a.m. - 5 p.m. Sun. Noon - 5 p.m.
Let us know what your interests are. To get our FREE catalog, send 55 cents
or large 45-cent self-addressed stamped envelope.

BECKETT
FOOTBALL CARD MONTHLY

SUBSCRIBE TODAY!

Check the appropriate box:

		Reg. Price	Your Price
	1 year (12 issues)	$30.00	**$19.95**
	2 years (24 issues)	$60.00	**$35.95**

Please Print Clearly

Name _____ Age _____

Address _____

City _____ State _____ Zip _____

Daytime Phone Number: (_____)_____

Payment enclosed via: ☐ Check or Money Order   ☐ VISA or MasterCard

Card # ☐☐☐☐☐ – ☐☐☐☐☐ – ☐☐☐☐☐ – ☐☐☐☐☐

Signature _____ Exp. _____

Satisfaction Guaranteed!   Please do not send cash.

All foreign addresses add $12 per year for postage (includes G.S.T.). All payments
payable in U.S.funds. Please allow 6 to 8 weeks for delivery of your first copy.

Mail to:
Beckett Subscriptions, Beckett Football Card Monthly,
P.O. Box 1915, Marion, OH 43305-1915   DHH92

BECKETT

BASEBALL CARD MONTHLY

SUBSCRIBE TODAY!

Check the appropriate box:

		Reg. Price	Your Price
	1 year (12 issues)	$30.00	**$19.95**
	2 years (24 issues)	$60.00	**$35.95**

Please Print Clearly

Name _____ Age_____

Address _____

City _____ State _____ Zip _____

Daytime Phone Number: (_____)_____

Payment enclosed via: ☐ Check or Money Order   ☐ VISA or MasterCard

Card # ☐☐☐☐ – ☐☐☐☐ – ☐☐☐☐ – ☐☐☐☐

Signature _____ Exp. _____

Satisfaction Guaranteed!   Please do not send cash.

All foreign addresses add $12 per year for postage (includes G.S.T.). All payments payable in U.S.funds. Please allow 6 to 8 weeks for delivery of your first copy.

Mail to:
Beckett Subscriptions, Beckett Baseball Card Monthly,
P.O. Box 1915, Marion, OH 43305-1915

DHH92

BECKETT

BASKETBALL MONTHLY

SUBSCRIBE TODAY!

Check the appropriate box:		Reg. Price	Your Price
☐	1 year (12 issues)	$30.00	**$19.95**
☐	2 years (24 issues)	$60.00	**$35.95**

Please Print Clearly

Name _____ Age_____

Address _____

City _____ State _____ Zip _____

Daytime Phone Number: (_____)_____

Payment enclosed via: ☐ Check or Money Order   ☐ VISA or MasterCard

Card # ☐☐☐☐ – ☐☐☐☐ – ☐☐☐☐ – ☐☐☐☐

Signature _____ Exp. _____

Satisfaction Guaranteed!   Please do not send cash.

All foreign addresses add $12 per year for postage (includes G.S.T.). All payments payable in U.S.funds. Please allow 6 to 8 weeks for delivery of your first copy.

Mail to:
Beckett Subscriptions, Beckett Basketball Monthly,
P.O. Box 1915, Marion, OH 43305-1915

DHH92

SUBSCRIBE TODAY!

Check the appropriate box:	Reg. Price	Your Price
1 year (12 issues)	$30.00	**$19.95**
2 years (24 issues)	$60.00	**$35.95**

Please Print Clearly

Name _____ Age _____

Address _____

City _____ State _____ Zip _____

Daytime Phone Number: (_____)_____

Payment enclosed via: ☐ Check or Money Order ☐ VISA or MasterCard

Card # ☐☐☐☐ - ☐☐☐☐ - ☐☐☐☐ - ☐☐☐☐

Signature _____ Exp. _____

Satisfaction Guaranteed!   Please do not send cash.

All foreign addresses add $12 per year for postage (includes G.S.T.). All payments payable in U.S.funds. Please allow 6 to 8 weeks for delivery of your first copy.

Mail to:
Beckett Subscriptions, Beckett Focus On Future Stars,
P.O. Box 1915, Marion, OH 43305-1915

DHH92

BECKETT

HOCKEY MONTHLY

SUBSCRIBE TODAY!

Check the appropriate box:	Reg. Price	Your Price
1 year (12 issues)	$30.00	**$19.95**
2 years (24 issues)	$60.00	**$35.95**

Please Print Clearly

Name _____ Age_____

Address _____

City _____ State _____ Zip _____

Daytime Phone Number: (_____)_____

Payment enclosed via: ☐ Check or Money Order   ☐ VISA or MasterCard

Card # ☐☐☐☐ - ☐☐☐☐ - ☐☐☐☐ - ☐☐☐☐

Signature _____ Exp. _____

Satisfaction Guaranteed!   Please do not send cash.

All foreign addresses add $12 per year for postage (includes G.S.T.). All payments payable in U.S.funds. Please allow 6 to 8 weeks for delivery of your first copy.

Mail to:
Beckett Subscriptions, Beckett Hockey Monthly,
P.O. Box 1915, Marion, OH 43305-1915   DHH92